DATE DUE

23 MAR 16 D

DATE DUE

THE PREHISTORY OF NUBIA

THE PREHISTORY OF

Combined Prehistoric Expedition to Egyptian and Sudanese Nubia

Papers Assembled and Edited by

FRED WENDORF

VOLUME ONE

**FORT BURGWIN RESEARCH CENTER and
SOUTHERN METHODIST UNIVERSITY PRESS**

The Prehistory of Nubia, in two volumes, contains the final reports on research conducted by the Combined Prehistoric Expedition to Nubia jointly sponsored by Columbia University, the Museum of New Mexico, and Southern Methodist University and with the joint participation of the Fort Burgwin Research Center, Inc., Taos, New Mexico; the Geological and Mineral Research Department, Cairo, Egypt, U.A.R.; the Fonds National de la Recherche Scientifique, Brussels, Belgium; the Geologisch Instituit, Universiteit te Gent, Belgium; the Centre National de la Recherche Scientifique, Paris, France; the Laboratoire de Prehistoire, University of Bordeaux, Bordeaux, France; and the Institute of History of Material Culture, Polish Academy of Science, Warsaw, Poland.

This research project has been supported by National Science Foundation Grants G 17942, GS-4, GS-275, GS-427, and GS-539, by United States State Department Grant SCC-29658, and by Smithsonian Institution Grant SFCP-21.

PUBLICATION NUMBER 5 OF THE FORT BURGWIN RESEARCH CENTER, INC.

SOUTHERN METHODIST UNIVERSITY CONTRIBUTIONS IN ANTHROPOLOGY, NO. 2

LIBRARY OF CONGRESS CATALOG CARD NUMBER 68-18382

Distributed by Southern Methodist University Press, Dallas, Texas 75222, U.S.A.

PRINTED IN THE UNITED STATES OF AMERICA
BY THE SOUTHERN METHODIST UNIVERSITY PRINTING DEPARTMENT
AT DALLAS, TEXAS

Dedicated to

JOHN OTIS BREW

distinguished archaeologist and inspiring teacher

PREFACE

ON APRIL 7, 1961, President Kennedy in a message to Congress made known the decision by the United States government to participate in the international effort to preserve the archaeological treasures of Nubia which were to be destroyed by the construction of the New High Dam at Aswan in Southern Egypt. The reservoir which was to be impounded behind the new dam was to inundate the valley of the Nile for nearly three hundred miles, thus covering almost all of the habitable area in which occurred some of the most significant developments in the history of man. Since the beginning of written records, and doubtless before that, the Nile River has been a major thoroughfare connecting tropical Africa with the Mediterranean and the Near East, and it was along the Nile that one of the earliest and most important civilizations developed.

My own interest in Nubia began with the initial appeal issued by UNESCO in 1960 on behalf of the United Arab Republic and the Republic of Sudan, requesting that international action be taken to preserve the treasures of Nubia. Largely through the influence of Professor J. O. Brew, who is Chairman of the Committee for the Recovery of Archaeological Remains, and Jesse L. Nusbaum, then Staff Archaeologist of the U. S. Department of Interior, I became aware of the problems of preserving our historical and archaeological heritage from the onslaught of building and construction inherent in modern life. Much of my professional career has been devoted to the salvage of archaeological materials threatened by the construction of highways, pipelines, and reservoirs in the United States, and therefore my interest in the Nubian campaign is understandable. Here was to be the largest archaeological salvage effort ever undertaken, and it was to be done in an area of critical importance to the history of civilization.

Throughout the world, scholars and specialists of Ancient Egyptian life planned numerous expeditions to salvage the majestic temples and other remains of the Pharaonic and the later Christian eras in Nubia. There was comparatively little interest, however, in those much less impressive remains of the Paleolithic, that long period of man's cultural development prior to the advent of written records. Part of this lack of interest was due to the fact that very little was known about the Paleolithic of Nubia, and only a few sites were recorded anywhere along the Nile. But Paleolithic sites were undoubtedly present, and it seemed a tragedy that the information concerning and antecedents of one of the world's great civilizations would shortly be destroyed. I decided, therefore, to concentrate my efforts on the Paleolithic in Nubia. This decision was prompted not only because the post-Paleolithic remains were receiving most of the salvage efforts, but also because their study required specialized knowledge and background in Egyptology which I did not have.

As a prehistorian specializing in North American archaeology, I felt my background and training would be more compatible with the type of work needed at Paleolithic sites. In a broad sense this was true, and certainly the experience with large-scale archaeological salvage projects in North America was indispensable in organizing and managing the expedition in Nubia, but I found that the approach to Paleolithic archaeology was totally foreign. Not only are the types of tools markedly different, but the methods of analysis and basic concepts employed by most prehistorians in the Old World are significantly different from those used by North American archaeologists. A great deal of time was lost during the first season before the magnitude of these differences was realized and appropriate adjustments made in the techniques we used in both the field and the laboratory.

The project has experienced a somewhat complicated history of sponsorship. The preliminary outlines developed from an initial reconnaissance survey undertaken during the fall and winter of 1961-62 by Professors Ralph Solecki and Rhodes Fairbridge of Columbia University. At that time Solecki and Fairbridge were planning a long-range program of Paleolithic studies in the Sudanese section of the Reservoir. Preliminary plans were also under way at this time in Santa Fe at the Laboratory of Anthropology, where I was then Director, for a similar project in Egypt. Meanwhile, because of the pressure of other commitments, Solecki and Fairbridge reluctantly decided not to continue their Sudanese plans and invited me to undertake the direction of a combined project which would conduct salvage operations in both Egypt and Sudan. This invitation was gratefully accepted, and the project functioned under this arrangement for two seasons: the winters of 1962-63 and 1963-64. It was known as the Combined Prehistoric Expedition. In the spring of 1964 I moved to Southern Methodist University, and the sponsorship of the project was changed accordingly. Two additional seasons of work were completed under the new administration, and the final field season was closed in March, 1966.

Generous financial support for this work was received from a number of sources. The major funds were provided by several grants from the U.S. State Department, the National Science Foundation, the Fort Burgwin Research Center, Inc., and during the final season, the Smithsonian Institution. In particular I wish to acknowledge the encouragement and guidance which we received from Miss Annis Sandvos, of the Bureau of Educational and Cultural Affairs of the Department of State, and Drs. Albert C. Spaulding, Allan H. Smith, and Richard W. Lieban, successive Program Directors for Anthropology, National Science Foundation, during the existence of the project.

Significant support, either directly in the form of salaries and travel expenses or indirectly through research facilities, was also received from the "home" universities and organizations of several members of the staff. Grants-in-aid were also received from the Fonds National de la Recherche Scientifique, Belgium; the Centre National de la Recherche Scientifique, France;

and the Institute of Material Culture, Polish Academy of Science. The generosity of these organizations made it possible for the Expedition to be undertaken as a truly international effort. In Egypt we also had the benefit of working directly with a party of the Egyptian Geological Survey. This opportunity was made possible through the good offices of Dr. G. H. Awad, then Under Secretary of State for Mineral Wealth, United Arab Republic. Through this arrangement, the logistical and equipment requirements of the Expedition were greatly simplified and, therefore, our full attention could be given to the archaeological problems. Our sincere thanks are due Dr. Bahay Issawy and his superb staff, who were our hosts, for their patience and friendship under what often must have been trying circumstances.

The Department of Antiquities in Egypt awarded the Expedition a license to conduct prehistoric research along the west bank of the Nile from the New High Dam to the Sudan frontier, with the exception of a short distance between Korosko and Ineiba, which was awarded to the Yale University expedition. In Sudan the area of the license extended on the west bank from the Egyptian frontier to the head of the Reservoir and, on the east bank, the area south from near the Second Cataracts. The Sudanese concession overlapped with those awarded to several other expeditions concerned primarily with the salvage of Pharaonic or Christian remains. In almost all instances these expeditions graciously permitted our group to work in their areas and frequently assisted our efforts by providing labor, equipment, and shelter. In this connection I wish to express thanks to Dr. Walter B. Emery, Director, Egyptian Exploration Society Expedition at Buhen; Dr. Garcia Guinea, Director of the Spanish Expedition; Dr. Kazimierz Michalowski, Director of the Polish Expedition at Faras; Dr. P. L. Shinnie, Director of the University of Ghana Expedition; Dr. Torgny Save-Soderbergh, Director of the Scandinavian Joint Expedition, and Dr. Jean Vercoutter, Director of the Franco-Argentine Expedition at Mirgissa.

It was also our good fortune to have the effective support and guidance of Mr. Louis A. Christophe and Dr. William Y. Adams of the

UNESCO staff in Egypt and Sudan respectively. On numerous occasions their knowledge of the regulations and procedures which governed our work in these countries was a direct benefit to the Expedition.

Throughout the several seasons which were spent in Nubia, the Combined Prehistoric Expedition enjoyed the full support of the appropriate government agencies in our host countries of Egypt and Sudan. The friendly and generous reception which we received from these agencies and their staff not only facilitated our work, but made our stay a pleasurable experience. In the U.A.R., Dr. Gamal Mukhtar, Director General, Antiquities Service Department, and his predecessors in this office, the late Dr. Mohammed Mahdi Ibrahim and Dr. Anwar Shukry, all have been most helpful and co-operative throughout. Among the staff of the Antiquities Department, Mr. Gamal El-Din, the late Mr. Zaki Razkallah, Mr. Achmed Hindy, and Mr. Fathy Afifi all made many special efforts on our behalf.

In Sudan, we were most fortunate to work under the supervision of Commissioner T. H. Thabit and Inspector Nigm ed Din Mohammed Sherif of the Sudan Antiquities Service. Their interest and concern with the problems of archaeological salvage contributed in no small way to the successful conclusion of the Nubian campaign in Sudan.

I wish to acknowledge also my thanks and appreciation to my colleagues who worked with me in Nubia. Although the total staff of the expedition through the 1964 season has been listed elsewhere (Wendorf, 1965, p. v), it seems appropriate in this, the final report of the work of the Expedition, also to include a complete list of field personnel, whose joint efforts made this book possible:

Dr. Claude C. Albritton, Geologist, Southern Methodist University.[5]

Dr. Maria Chmielewska, Archaeologist, Polish Academy of Science.[3]

Dr. Waldemar Chmielewski, Archaeologist, Polish Academy of Science.[2-3-4]

Mrs. Kathryn Clisby, Pollen Analyst, Oberlin College.[2-3]

Dr. Richard B. Daugherty, Field Director, Washington State University.[2]

Mr. Frank Eddy, Archaeologist, Museum of New Mexico.[3]

Mr. Philip Evans, Assistant Archaeologist, Washington State University.[3]

Dr. Rhodes Fairbridge, Project Director, Columbia University.[1]

Dr. Jean Guichard, Archaeologist, University of Bordeaux.[1-2-3]

Mrs. Genevieve Guichard, Archaeologist, University of Bordeaux.[2-3]

Dr. Jean de Heinzelin, Geologist, University of Ghent.[1-2-3-4]

Dr. James J. Hester, Field Director, Egypt, Museum of New Mexico.[3]

Mrs. Audrey Hobler, Laboratory Supervisor, Museum of New Mexico.[3]

Mr. Philip Hobler, Assistant Archaeologist, Museum of New Mexico.[3]

Mr. William Hootkins, Princeton University.[5]

Dr. Bahay Issawy, Assistant Geologist, Egyptian Geological Survey.[2-3-4-5]

Dr. Anthony E. Marks, Archaeologist, Columbia University and Southern Methodist University.[1-3-4]

Miss Francine Martin, Biologist, University of Ghent.[3]

Mr. William McHugh, Archaeologist, University of Wisconsin.[3]

Mr. William Merrill, Draftsman, Museum of New Mexico.[3]

Miss Nadia Mostafa, Laboratory Assistant, Columbia University.[3]

Miss Jane Nettle, Laboratory Assistant, Museum of New Mexico.[3]

Miss Cathrine J. Newman, Secretary, Museum of New Mexico.[3]

Dr. Roland Paepe, Assistant Geologist, University of Ghent.[1-2-3]

Dr. Dexter Perkins, Paleontologist, Philadelphia Academy of Science.[1-2-3]

Mr. Harvey S. Rice, Assistant Archaeologist, Washington State University.[2]

Mr. Jay Ruby, Assistant Archaeologist, University of California, L.A.[2]

Dr. Rushdi Said, Geologist, University of Cairo.[2-3-4-5]

Dr. Romuald Schild, Archaeologist, Polish Academy of Science.[3-4]

Dr. Joel L. Shiner, Field Director, Sudan, Southern Methodist University.[3-4]

Mrs. Maxine Shiner, Bookkeeper and House Manager, Museum of New Mexico.[3]

Mr. Bob H. Slaughter, Paleontologist, Southern Methodist University.[5]

Dr. Robert Stigler, Jr., Archaeologist, Columbia University.[1]

Dr. Ralph Solecki, Project Director, Columbia University.[1]

Miss Mary B. Stokes, Laboratory Supervisor, Museum of New Mexico.[3]

Dr. John Waechter, Field Director, University of London.[2]

Dr. Fred Wendorf, Project Director, Southern Methodist University.[2-3-4-5]

Dr. Ronald K. Wetherington, Archaeologist, Southern Methodist University.[5]

Among this group I owe a special debt to Drs. Anthony E. Marks and Joel L. Shiner for their patience and generosity in helping me to learn at least the more elementary aspects of lithic typology in North Africa.

I also wish to record my special debt to Dr.

---

[1] 1961-1962 season.
[2] 1962-1963 season.
[3] 1963-1964 season.
[4] 1964-1965 season.
[5] 1965-1966 season.

Rushdi Said. It was planned that a contribution by Dr. Said on the geology of the Ballana area would be included in these reports; however, the recent events in the Near East made it impossible for the manuscript to be received prior to the publication deadline. It is to be hoped that it will appear elsewhere. In addition to being a most valuable member of the Expedition staff throughout the project, Dr. Said was instrumental in arranging for the participation of the Egyptian Geological Survey, and on many occasions facilitated the work of the Expedition in Egypt.

The line drawings in those papers by Marks, Shiner, and Wendorf are by Miss Mary Beth Stokes and Mrs. Lucile R. Addington, both of Southern Methodist University. In the other contributions the drawings are either the work of the author, or credit has been indicated in the text.

Mr. Edward J. Clement, the Associate Editor for these volumes, assumed most of the routine editorial task of preparing the several included manuscripts for the printer. Mr. Clement received only a nominal compensation for his efforts, and to a very large extent, his time to this endeavor must be regarded as a contribution for which I am most grateful. I also wish to thank Mrs. Margaret L. Hartley and Mrs. Frances Clifton of the staff of the S.M.U. Press for their most valuable assistance in editorial matters, and to express my appreciation to Mrs. Virginia B. Martin for her expert typing of the manuscripts.

Finally, it is most appropriate to express my thanks to Dr. J. O. Brew, who more than anyone else is responsible for my own concern for the preservation of our historical heritage, and who, despite considerable opinion to the contrary, continued to insist that significant prehistoric remains existed in the area to be flooded in Nubia and that these remains should be saved. To J. O. Brew, my friend and mentor, these volumes are gratefully dedicated.

FRED WENDORF

Southern Methodist University
September 15, 1967

CONTENTS: VOLUME I

THE PREHISTORY OF NUBIA

INTRODUCTION

Fred Wendorf

(SOUTHERN METHODIST UNIVERSITY)

FOR THOUSANDS of years the vast deserts which bound the Nile on both sides have forced man to live near the river, in the very area to be inundated by the reservoir of the New High Dam now under construction at Aswan in Egypt. When full, the reservoir behind this dam will be more than 350 miles in length, and in some places nearly 50 miles wide. It will extend from near the First Cataract in Egypt, southward over the Sudan-Egyptian frontier to the Third Cataract (fig. 1). It will cover virtually all of what is now known as Lower Nubia. Almost all of the remains of the entire period of human development along this long stretch of the river are to be lost forever beneath this tremendous man-made lake. The building of the New High Dam has posed a major challenge to the civilized world to take joint action to preserve these records of man's history, for this is one of the most important and richest archaeological and historical areas known. In response to this challenge, a group of scholars worked together from 1961 to 1966, in both Egyptian and Sudanese Nubia, to study the prehistoric remains within the reservoir. These two volumes present the results of this joint effort.

Nubia long has been known to be rich in archaeological materials dating from the time of the Pharaohs, including numerous spectacular temples, rich graveyards and large villages. Many of these remains were recorded during the archaeological salvage projects undertaken when the first Aswan dam was built in 1902 and enlarged in 1907 (Reisner, 1910; Firth, 1912, 1935), or when the dam was again raised in 1929 (Emery and Kirwan, 1935). These surveys were concerned primarily with the Pharaonic and later Christian remains, and little was known about the prehistoric occupations. A few prehistoric sites were known from the reservoir area. One of these was at Dibeira, just south of the Sudan-Egyptian frontier (Sandford and

Arkell, 1933, pp. 48-49), and another was at Abka, below Wadi Halfa near the Second Cataract (Myers, 1958, 1960). On the whole, however, there was considerable question as to whether extensive prehistoric remains existed in the area to be covered by the new reservoir. It was feared that most of the prehistoric sites were covered when the first reservoir was impounded, and indeed, many of the sites between Aswan and the Sudan-Egyptian frontier must have been destroyed at that time. A large section of the area to be inundated, in particular those sections south of Ineiba, however, were not seriously affected by the initial Aswan reservoir. This section, a distance along the river nearly 200 miles in length, was virtually unexplored for prehistoric remains.

When the international campaign to preserve the archaeological treasures of Nubia was first organized at the joint request of the United Arab Republic and the Republic of Sudan, and sponsored by UNESCO, studies of prehistoric sites were included in the overall program, in spite of the occasional doubts as to whether or not significant remains of this period would be present in any quantity. However, the majority of the expeditions which were organized for participation in the Nubian emergency salvage program were concerned primarily with the extensive and well-known materials of the Pharaonic and later periods. Only two major expeditions were organized primarily to study the prehistoric material in the New Aswan Reservoir: one jointly sponsored by the Peabody Museum of Yale University and the National Museum of Canada; and the other, the Combined Prehistoric Expedition, the results of which are the subject of these reports. Several of the other expeditions organized primarily for work at historic sites did some investigation of the prehistoric remains in their concession areas, among which were the Indian and Soviet Union parties in Egypt, and the Joint Scandinavian and University of

3

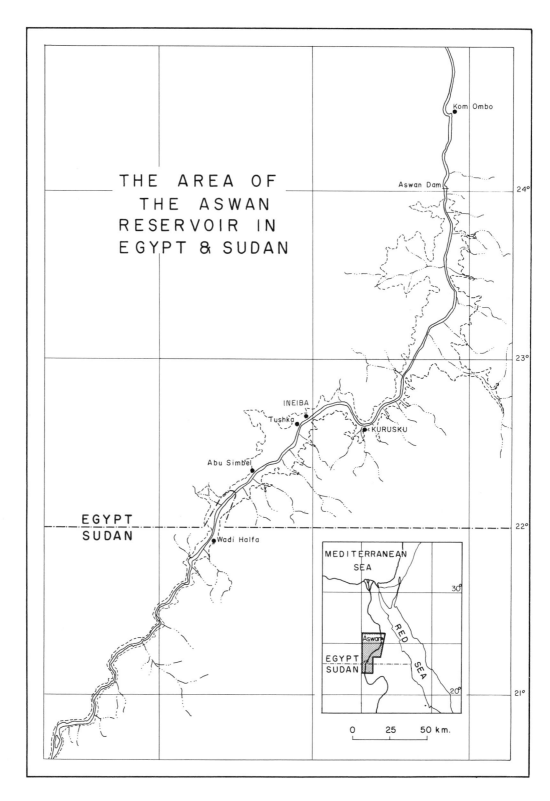

Fig. 1—Map of the New Dam Reservoir area, Egypt and Sudan.

Fig. 2—View of the Batn el-Hajar, looking toward the west bank, near Saras, south of the Second Cataract.

Colorado groups in Sudan. Even more attention probably would have been given the prehistoric sites by other expeditions except for the fact that significantly different methodology from that used on historic remains is required, including the participation of non-archaeological specialists, such as geologists and paleontologists, not normally needed at historic sites.

The emphasis on historic remains in part reflected the fact that sites of this period were known to be abundant and rich, and that few prehistoric sites had been reported. But also, this emphasis developed by default, because in recent years many prehistorians had accepted the view that Egypt and Sudan were outside of the mainstream of developments during much of the Paleolithic, and that few remains of any consequence would be found in the Reservoir area. Egypt and Nubia were believed to have been culturally conservative and almost unchanging from the Middle Paleolithic until just before the beginning of the Neolithic, and according to this view the area presumably did not participate in the developments of the Upper Paleolithic, in the beginnings of food production and urban civilization, all of which are problems which recently have absorbed much of the attention of those prehistorians working in Europe and the Near East, and who normally would have been intensely concerned with the inundation of such a vast stretch of one of the major waterways of

the world. Our research has shown that those assumptions were unfounded, for not only are there many parallels evident between the contemporary Nubian Late Paleolithic industries and the Upper Paleolithic of Europe and the Levant, but also evidence was recovered which suggests that the utilization of grain, one of the basic steps which eventually led to food production, may have occurred several thousands of years earlier along the Nile than elsewhere.

The Nile, which has its source in the high mountains of Tanganyika, Kenya, and Ethiopia, and is fed by the summer storms of the Tropical Rain Belt, becomes a mighty river at the coalescence of the Blue and the White Nile at Khartoum in central Sudan. From there the course of the Nile is generally northward to the junction with the Atbara, which heads in northern Ethiopia, but flows only during the summer months. Beyond the Atbara the Nile receives no other water through its entire course to the Mediterranean.

At Abu Hamed, about midway from Khartoum to the Sudanese-Egyptian frontier, the Nile turns abruptly southeast, and then north again to pass through the dome of Precambrian shales and granites, known as the Batn el-Hajar or Belly of Rocks (fig. 2). The Batn el-Hajar ends with the Second Cataract at Wadi Halfa, and northward from here to Kom Ombo, except for a short stretch of the First Cataract near Aswan, the

Nile is bounded by a desiccated Nubia Sandstone Plateau of Cretaceous age. It is this sandstone area, from the Batn el-Hajar to Kom Ombo, that is known as Lower Nubia.

The Nubian desert is one of the most desolate areas on earth. Even along the Nile there is no vegetation, except for a few discontinuous strips of arable land, where irrigation has made possible the growth of a narrow gallery of palm trees and small gardens. In a very few non-cultivated areas of dune sands immediately adjacent to the Nile there are clumps of tamarisk occasionally growing. Beyond these exceptions, however, on both sides of the river, from the edge of the water, or from the edge of the cultivation where this occurs, extends a seemingly unending expanse of bare sand and rock, broken here and there by steep-sided inselbergs or mesas. This is one of the dryest parts of the great belt of the Sahara Desert which extends across all of North Africa.

Since the time of Herodotus the Nile has been recognized as the divide between the Western or Libyan Desert and the Eastern or Arabian Desert. There are physiographic distinctions which set these two deserts apart. The Red Sea hills, a mass of igneous mountains which form a high backbone along the east side of Egypt roughly parallel to the coast of the Red Sea, are unique features of the Eastern Desert. Because of this high backbone, the sandstone plateau which flanks the Red Sea hills in southern Egypt is intensely and deeply dissected by ravines which, in Nubia, drain toward the Nile. The Red Sea hills, because of their higher elevation, receive more moisture than the Western Desert, or the adjacent dissected plateau of the Eastern Desert, and the floors of these ravines or wadis which head in the Red Sea hills often contain vegetation in their upper reaches.

The Western Desert is physiographically more mature. It is a vast plateau with broad expanses of rocky ground and, except near the Nile, with poorly marked internal drainage into numerous closed basins. Contrary to popular opinion, it is not an area of vast sand dunes. In a few limited areas, where the spectacular "sand seas" occur, there are impressive dunes, but for the most part where the terrain is not rocky and broken there are flat expanses of drifted sand, grading from one divide to the next. Trucks and other vehicles can move easily in these areas.

A limestone escarpment, known as Sinn el-Kaddab, roughly parallels the west side of the Nile, but from 60 to 100 km. distant, and forms a prominent landmark of the Western Desert in Lower Nubia. Internal drainage basins occur both on top of the limestone plateau and below the escarpment, between it and the drainage network of the Nile. These basins are now dry, although there is archaeological evidence that some of them contained water during at least part of the year as recent as the late Neolithic. At two places along this stretch the dissection of the escarpment has breached the artesian aquifer which underlies the limestone cap of the escarpment, and small wells have developed. These are at Dungul and at Kurkur, both of which were examined by parties of the Combined Prehistoric Expedition.

Within the area of the High Dam reservoir (fig. 1), the valley of the Nile may be divided into several physiographic provinces. Both the north and south ends of the reservoir are in areas of Precambrian rocks, mostly shales and granites, which erode into rounded domes with pockets of loose sand between the domes. The valley here is closely bounded on both sides by cliffs of these Basement rocks, and silt remnants are limited to narrow patches, mostly at the mouths of wadis.

Beginning just south of Wadi Halfa and extending almost to Aswan, the river passes through an area of horizontally bedded Nubia Sandstone rocks. Along this reach the sandstone has been eroded into a mesa or inselberg topography, and broad exposures of silts frequently are preserved between the inselbergs close to the Nile.

The topographic development of this area appears to be primarily controlled by structural features. A major line of faults parallels the river from the Second Cataract and Wadi Halfa at the mouth of the Batn el-Hajar to the Ballana area on the Egyptian-Sudanese frontier (de Heinzelin and Paepe, 1965, p. 54). East of this faultline are the dissected remnants of a sandstone plateau. It is an area of inselbergs or mesas, some of which are close to the river, while others

Fig. 3—Gebel el Sedd near Ineiba, Egypt. Typical inselberg typography of the dissected Abu Simbel Plateau on the west bank of the Nile.

are set back, leaving *rincons* into which Nile silts were deposited during intervals when the Nile was higher than it is today. West of the fault, including the entire west bank, is a subdued plain on which are extensive silt deposits. Low outcrops of sandstone occasionally occur here, but there are no prominent inselbergs, and back from the river the topography gradually grades to an old pedimentary surface.

Near the Sudan-Egyptian frontier another fault, running in a general east-west direction, separates the subdued plain of the Halfa-Ballana area from an elevated plateau through which the Nile had to cut a narrow canyon with vertical cliffs over 90 m. high (Said and Issawy, 1965, pp. 6-12). The river enters this canyon area through a gradually constricted funnel along the sides of which are remnants of old silts protected by the adjacent escarpments. Immediately north of Abu Simbel the valley on the west bank widens abruptly again, leaving remnants in the form of scattered inselbergs (fig. 3). There are several fairly extensive

exposures of old silts in this section, the more important of which are at Tushka and Ineiba. The east bank in this area presents a more youthful profile. The sandstone escarpment, although deeply dissected, fronts right against the river, and behind the escarpment are a series of platforms that rise toward the east into the fantastic badlands of the Kurusku Highlands.

North of Ineiba the Nile bends first eastward, then back south, and again to the north as it passes through the Kurusku water gap, where the river is bounded on both sides by vertical sandstone escarpments. South of Seiyala the sandstone escarpments again retreat abruptly back from both sides of the river at the emergence of the broad valleys of the Wadi Allaqi and Wadi Dakka. As do most other tributaries in this stretch, both of the wadis enter the river at right angles, along courses that appear to be structurally controlled.

Northward from Allaqi the Nile again flows through a deeply dissected plateau, with low, but continuous escarpments along both banks of the river. If old silts were present along this reach they were buried beneath the waters of the original Aswan reservoir. Near Kalabsha a finger of granite and schist intrudes across the river from beneath the sandstone caprock, then disappears, and reappears again south of Aswan, where it forms the First Cataract.

In the pioneer work of Sandford and Arkell (1933) on the geology and Pleistocene history of Nubia, the role of tectonic activity in the development of the Nile was believed to have been of minor importance. The Nile also was believed to have been essentially as we now know it as early as Pliocene times. The geologic studies by Said and Issawy (1965) and de Heinzelin and Paepe (1965), however, have challenged this interpretation. According to these recent studies, the Nile, as a stream extending from the Ethiopean highlands to the Mediterranean, is of comparatively recent origin, perhaps as recent as Late Pleistocene. The critical evidence for this is found in the absence of the distinctive heavy minerals of Ethiopean origin in the gravels and other fluvial deposits which are earlier than Late Pleistocene in age. There were sizable streams in the area, but these did not cross the Batn el-Hajar to tap what is now the headwaters of the Nile. Before the formation of the present Nile, presumably these Ethiopean headwaters fed Lake Sudd, which is believed to have existed in central and southern Sudan during the Early and Middle Pleistocene. The precise time when the Batn el-Hajar was breached has not been determined; it may have occurred during the time Late Acheulean industries were in vogue, but more likely it was considerably later, after the initial development of the Late Paleolithic.

Once the present course of the river was established, the distinctive Nile silts began to be deposited. These silts are essentially like those which are laid down by the Nile today. They are, however, divisible into several units on the basis of elevation, minor differences in associated fauna, and related archaeological materials. Each unit of silt aggradation probably represents a complex sequence of rising water levels, separated from each other by intervals when the water level was low. During these periods of low water level there was lateral erosion, and

eolian deposits accumulated over the surface of the exposed silts which had been deposited during the preceding phase of aggradation. Formational names are proposed for these units by de Heinzelin in the contribution which follows.

CLIMATE

The almost complete absence of rainfall is the most distinctive feature about the climate of Lower Nubia. Precipitation in Northeast Africa is derived from two sources. In northern Egypt, in a narrow strip along the Mediterranean coast, is a zone of winter rainfall, with an average of less than eight inches along the coast and decreasing rapidly inland to only one inch at Cairo. Southern and central Sudan, and as far north as Merowe, receive precipitation from the Tropical Rain Belt, with rainfall occurring mostly during the summer. Rainfall from this source is greatest in southern Sudan and decreases toward the north. Lower Nubia, which lies beyond the outer limits of both of these precipitation zones, receives virtually no rainfall, except for an occasional storm which may penetrate the area on the average of once every ten years. Even these limited rains occur at highly irregular intervals. This regional pattern of rainfall distribution is summarized in Table 1 below:

TABLE 1
SUMMARY OF CLIMATIC FEATURES IN EGYPT AND SUDAN (FROM KASSAS, 1955)

Station	Latitude	Mean Annual Temp. C.	Relative Humidity	Annual Rainfall, mm.
Alexandria 1901-1945	31°12′	20.2	71	184.0
Cairo (Giza) 1902-1945	30°02′	19.9	68	24.0
Aswan 1901-1945	24°02′	25.8	34	3.0
Wadi Halfa 1902-1940	21°55′	25.7	31	0.1
Karima 1905-1940	18°33′	29.3	23	25.0
Khartoum 1900-1940	15°37′	29.6	32	163.0

Temperatures on this same north-south traverse across Egypt and Sudan show a progressive increase toward the south. January is usually the coldest month, with high temperatures prevailing throughout Lower Nubia from May through September. Absolute maximum temperatures have been recorded as high as 52.5°C.

Fig. 4—The Khor Musa south of Wadi Halfa. Note vegetation in Wadi bottom.

(126.5°F.), and temperatures of 49°C. (120°F.) are not uncommon. From November to April the climate is delightful, with cool nights and clear, bright days. Freezing temperatures have been recorded, but only twice. Humidity is low, sometimes approaching almost zero, and clouds are rare, averaging less than 1 per cent throughout the year.

The prevailing wind direction is from the north or northwest, with only an occasional strong wind, usually accompanying the passage of a depression which moves from west to east along the Mediterranean coast. Calm conditions prevail between 25 per cent and 50 per cent of the time. Between March and June, perhaps two or three times a year, there will be strong easterly winds, accompanied by increased temperatures, and followed by dry, hot southerly winds. These storms may last for two or three days and will lift sand high in the air and occasionally develop into real sandstorms. Other sandstorms occur in the summer, mostly during June and July, when strong southern and southwestern winds develop along the edge of the summer storms. These may extend as far north as Wadi Halfa, and in their passage, these "haboobs" will raise a curtain of dust, often several thousand feet into the air, but they usually last only a few hours.

Vegetation and Fauna

Throughout Lower Nubia one is struck by the sharp contrast between the thin and discontinuous gallery of date palm trees which fringe the banks of the Nile wherever irrigation occurs, and the desolate deserts which bound the river on both sides. The initial impression of these deserts is that they are totally without plant or animal life. This is not entirely correct.

In both the Eastern and Western Deserts the sandy floors of the larger wadis[1] will occasionally support widely scattered patches of perennials such as Fagonietum (*F. parviflora*), grass (*Panicum turgidum, Desmostachya bipinnata, Sporobolus spicatus*), shrubs (*Salsola baryosma*), and rarely a solitary acacia (*A. nilotica* and *A. arabica*) (fig. 4). The acacia are limited to those areas where conditions are particularly favorable. This vegetation pattern has been referred to as "accidental" (Kassas, 1955, p. 56), since it occurs only in those limited areas where runoff is concentrated. The typical cycle is as follows: when a rain occurs within the drainage area of the wadi, the vegetation will flourish for a brief interval. The wadi then quickly dries up and the vegetation becomes desiccated. Years later, when there is another rain, there will be another brief resurgence. The areas of the desert between the wadis, and even the floors of those smaller wadis which drain a limited area, are devoid of vegetation. This zone of accidental vegetation extends from near Cairo in northern Egypt to just north of Atbara in Sudan. It is bounded on the north by the narrow fringes of coastal vegetation which roughly coincide with the area of winter rainfall, and on the south by the zone of Acacia Desert Shrubs of central Sudan that is supported by the tropical summer rains of that area.

Along the Nile the vegetation presents a very different aspect. On the lower floodplain, and elsewhere where irrigation was possible, date palms were grown, usually as a thin line immediately adjacent to the water, but occasionally in thin, jungle-like groves, together with acacia (*A. nilotica*) and Dom palm (*Hyphaene thebaica*). The irrigated areas were also used to grow clover, barley, wheat, and a wide variety of vegetables and melons. Weeds and Halfa grass grow along the ditches and other damp areas, and where deep sand has accumulated, especially along the west bank, are clumps of tamarisk (*T. nilotica*).[2]

---

[1] A wadi is a dried stream bed.

[2] The flora of Lower Nubia is described in detail in Boulos, 1966.

The geological and paleontological data indicate that a different vegetation pattern may have been present in Lower Nubia during part of the Late Pleistocene. It seems reasonable to infer that significant modifications in the vegetation could occur only if there were an increase in precipitation. A depression of summer temperatures might also be effective, but, nevertheless, a regular pattern of rainfall would be essential. In the simplest terms, if the increase in precipitation were to occur primarily in the winter months, the expected response would be the southward migration of the grasses and low shrubs now confined to the Mediterranean coast, particularly the inland plain. Conversely, were the increase to occur as summer rain, then there would probably be a northward shift of the acacia shrub community of central Sudan. In all probability, however, the Late Pleistocene climates and vegetation of this area involved more complex modifications than just precipitation. Temperatures, humidity, and wind direction may also have been affected.

The superficial impression of animal life in the Nubian Desert is similar to that of vegetation; that is, it appears to be almost absent. As in the case of vegetation, however, this is not entirely accurate. Along the Nile there are rabbits, gazelles, fox, wolves, and hyenas, as well as numerous birds, including kites, geese, crows, sparrows, and partridge. Even out in the desert several miles from the river an occasional partridge will be seen feeding on droppings along the main camel trails between Sudan and Egypt. In the more rocky areas there are scorpions, cobras, and horned vipers, and the river itself is rich in fish, some of which reach considerable size. There are a few crocodiles in the river also, but these have been heavily hunted in recent years and are rarely seen today.

It is not rich in fauna, and except for the fish, it would be difficult to sustain even a small population by hunting alone. There is abundant evidence, however, that the fauna was not always this restricted. There is historic evidence that the hippopotamus was present during the Dynastic periods, and there is archaeological evidence that hartebeest, large gazelle, and wild cattle were fairly abundant in Lower Nubia until around 8,000 B.C.

Previous Investigations in Lower Nubia

Although there are several references to the discovery of prehistoric materials in Egypt and Sudan during the early years of this Century (Schweinfurth, 1903, 1904, 1905, 1909; Currelly, 1913; Sterns, 1917), interest in this area really began shortly after World War I, and continued at a brisk pace until World War II when it abruptly ceased. The two decades of the 1920's and 1930's saw the first systematic surveys and limited excavations that resulted in the now classic studies by Sandford (1934), Sandford and Arkell (1929, 1933, 1939), Vignard (1921a, 1921b, 1923, 1928, 1934a, 1934b, 1935, 1955a, 1955b, 1955c, 1957), Caton-Thompson and Gardner (1934), and Caton-Thompson (1946a, 1952).

After World War II, however, this interest was not revived, in part because of political developments, but more directly because the concept of the prehistory which emerged from these pioneer studies of the preceeding two decades: that is, that the Nile Valley had been isolated and culturally conservative or even retarded from the Middle Paleolithic onward until the Pharaonic era (Movius, 1953, p. 175). Even the earlier sites were believed to be of limited interest, for while artifacts of late Early Paleolithic and Middle Paleolithic types were found in the Nile terraces, and on the deserts beyond, living sites were not reported at least in datable geologic contexts. With one possible exception (Abbasyyah Plain, Bovier-Lapierre, 1925, 1926), the still earlier pebble tool horizon was unknown, and this one site offered little promise when compared with those known in South and East Africa. The later prehistory of the Nile valley was interpreted as an internal development, sheltered from outside contacts, and thus contributing little to the evolution of the Upper Paleolithic in Europe and the Near East (Huzayyin, 1941, p. 269; Caton-Thompson, 1946a, p. 59). Even the beginnings of agriculture, long regarded as possibly occurring along the Nile (Childe, 1936), were shifted elsewhere when radiocarbon dates on the early Neolithic settlements of the Fayum showed these primitive communities were several thousand years later than the much more advanced remains in Palestine and Syria. Small wonder then, with so much to learn about the areas where these new developments of great significance for the history of mankind were believed to have occurred, that prehistorians had little interest in the events in the "stagnant" Nile valley.

The basis for the view that during later Paleolithic times the lower Nile valley was retarded may be traced to the initial work by Vignard (1923; 1928) at Kom Ombo, although the later studies by Caton-Thompson (1946a; 1952) at Kharga Oasis served to reinforce this interpretation. The Kom Ombo material was collected from the surface of a series of silt deposits preserved in what was once a broad embayment of the Nile. Some of the sites were obviously *in situ*, but the precise relationship to various silt units was not established. The assemblages were grouped into three stages within a presumably long developmental sequence. The earliest, named Sebilian I, occurred on the highest levels of silt. It was a flake industry with a high frequency of Levallois technology, and with a complex series of tools formed by steep retouch employed either as a backing or as distal or basal truncations, or in combinations of these. Preferred materials were a variety of tough diorite and other Precambrian rocks and indurated sandstone. Sebilian I was believed to have developed from, and to have immediately followed, the Middle Paleolithic in Egypt, and to be the local equivalent of the Upper Paleolithic in Europe and the Levant. Sebilian II also occurred on the highest silts, but more frequently on silts at a lower level. This stage was characterized by smaller sized flakes, by a decline in the frequency of Levallois, by the introduction of opposed platform cores and blades, by the use of chert and flint, and by the appearance of a few new tool types, such as the lunate. Sebilian III, which occurred on the lowest level of silts, was a true microlithic chert and flint industry which included truncations and evolved geometric forms made on both flakes and blades. Levallois flakes were still present but represented only a minor increment.

A number of features carried through the entire Sebilian sequence. In addition to the Levallois technology, some of these were the use of steep retouch and truncations to form tools and microburins. The indicated developmental sequence of microburin technology led Vignard (1923, pp. 75-76; 1928, pp. 219-220; 1934a, pp. 66-67 and 100-103; 1934b, p. 173; 1935) to suggest that the Sebilian was the source of those other microlithic industries of Africa and Europe where the microburin technique was employed. While this hypothesis was not generally accepted (Huzayyin, 1941, p. 254; Caton-Thompson, 1946a; p. 118), the sequence was seen to demonstrate" . . . as no other series collected on one spot had done to an equal degree, the stages by which a Levalloisian industry may gradually develop, mainly through the medium of steep marginal retouch, into one of a backed-blade, microlithic character." (Caton-Thompson, 1946a, p. 118).

In the years following Vignard's discovery at Kom Ombo, artifacts identified as Sebilian were reported from Northern Egypt at the Fayum (Sandford and Arkell, 1929, pp. 52-65), and to the south in Sudan near Wadi Halfa (Sandford and Arkell, 1933, pp. 48-52). These finds provided a basis for dating the Sebilian. The Sebilian-like artifacts in Lower Egypt were recovered from silts and beach deposits which were correlated with the Post Monastirian regression (Sandford and Arkell, 1939, p. 73), or with the Monastirian II regression (Ball, 1939) of the Mediterranean. These regressions were, in turn, correlated with either early Wurm I or Wurm II, and thus, on this basis, the Sebilian was believed to be fully contemporary with the beginning of the Upper Paleolithic in Europe.

The identification of the material from Lower Egypt as Sebilian was first challenged by Huzayyin (1941, pp. 257-260) who pointed out that there were significant differences between the Kom Ombo Sebilian and the long flake and blade industry identified as Sebilian from the Fayum and the Delta. He pointed out that while the few pieces recovered *in situ* from the Nile silts could not be conclusively eliminated from the Sebilian, the larger collections from surface sites in this area yielded numerous small Levallois cores and small flakes and blades, and lacked the distinctive abrupt retouch and truncations which are the hallmark of the Sebilian. He suggested that the Sebilian was restricted to Nubia, and that to the north along the Nile there developed a different industry which, to emphasize both the small size and the Levallois character of the technology, he named "Diminutive Levalloisian." The Diminutive Levalloisian was seen as a parallel regional development, contemporary with the Sebilian in Nubia. Caton-Thompson (1946a, pp. 100-118) further emphasized this distinction between the Late Paleolithic of northern and southern Egypt, but proposed that the northern industries be termed "Epi-Levalloisian," rather than Diminutive Levalloisian, since some of the flakes were of moderate size. She also divided the Epi-Levalloisian into three stages paralleling the Sebilian sequence and terminating in a microlithic stage.

It is significant that the correlation of the Sebilian as contemporary with the Epi-Levalloisian was based on typological parallels, not on geological evidence, for the major evidence that the Fayum beach (28 mm.) and lower Nile gravels containing the Epi-Levalloisian artifacts was contemporary with the "Lower Sebilian" silts in Nubia, was the prior identification of these artifacts as Sebilian. The typological identification was challenged, but the date for the Sebilian was not, evidently because the Middle Paleolithic-like features of the Sebilian suggested an antiquity commensurate with that indicated by the correlation with the Post-Monastirian Regression.

Vignard (1921 a and b, 1955a, 1955b, 1957) also reported an "Aurignacian" industry at two localities which contained burins, side, end, and strangled scrapers on blades and flakes, all with mostly semi-steep retouch, plus flaked axes with edges resharpened by transverse flakes. A close resemblance was seen to the Upper Paleolithic blade industries of the Palestine area. The Paleolithic age of this industry, however, was challenged by Huzayyin (1937, pp. 198-199; 1939, pp. 243-244; 1941, p. 237) who ascribed it to the pre-Dynastic. Recent work in central Egypt, however, has confirmed the Late Pleistocene age of blade industries very much like those reported by Vignard (Wendorf and Said, 1967).

While these developments were underway concerning the Sebilian and other Late Paleolithic industries in the Nile Valley and the Fayum, attention was also being given to the earlier industries, both in the Nile Valley and in the

desert areas beyond. In 1925 Caton-Thompson and Gardner (1926) began an examination of the paleolithic industries associated with the lake beaches in the Fayum, and in the same year Sandford (1926) and Arkell began a survey of the Pleistocene deposits in the Nile Valley. This was followed in 1930-1932 with work at Kharga Oasis in the desert west of the Nile, again by Caton-Thompson and Gardner (1932). The survey and excavations resulted in the discovery of Early and Middle Paleolithic implements (as well as later material) *in situ,* and in the definition of a complex geologic sequence built around the stratigraphic positions of the deposits and their associated artifacts. A different terminology which emphasized the dominant Levallois aspect of the "Mousterian" industries was proposed by Caton-Thompson (1946a). Under this scheme Early Mousterian was termed "Acheulio-Levalloisian," and typical Mousterian as "Lower Levalloisian," and Final Mousterian as "Upper Levalloisian." The series of classic reports which describe these studies (Caton-Thompson, 1952; Caton-Thompson and Gardner, 1934; Sandford, 1934; Sandford and Arkell, 1929, 1933, 1939) provided the geological and archaeological framework for Egyptian and Nubian prehistory as it was understood at the beginning of the Nubian Campaign.

Along the Nile the sequence was as follows (Caton-Thompson, 1946a, p. 68):

Nilotic Events	Cultures	Mediterranean Events
100 ft. Terrace	Chellean and Early Acheulean[3]	
50 ft. Terrace	Developed Acheulean	
30 ft. Terrace	Early Mousterian	Monastirian I
10-15 ft. Terrace in Upper Egypt; 25 ft. gravels of Middle Egypt; base of silts of Upper Egypt	Typical Mousterian	Monastirian II
Aggradation silts of Upper Egypt	Final Mousterian into Lower Sebilian in the top of the silts	
Degradation gravels of Upper and Middle Egypt	Sebilian II	Post-Monastirian

[3] Sandford and Arkell cultural terminology.

Nilotic Events	*Cultures*	*Mediterranean Events*
Further degradation	End of Paleolithic, Neolithic to Recent	

Various finds of Early and Middle Paleolithic artifacts were also reported from several localities in Sudan, some of which were in Lower Nubia (Arkell, 1949a). For the most part, however, these finds were limited to an occasional handaxe or flake, and except for Khor Abu Anga near Khartoum, they did not yield adequate samples for analysis. This problem points up the major weakness or deficiency in most of the studies during this period: the collections were not adequate to support the conclusions drawn from them. For example, in the "30 ft. terrace" in Egypt, there are only seven widely scattered artifacts reported *in situ*. There were no living floors or actual occupation horizons; thus all of the material was, in a sense, derived. Such samples today are not acceptable as sufficient either for definition of an industry or for dating the containing deposit. For this reason there has been widespread skepticism concerning the details of the classifications and the implied relationships with other industries around the Mediterranean.

A number of correlations of the Nile terraces with levels along the Mediterranean were attempted (summarized in Caton-Thompson, 1946a), but none were entirely satisfactory, and in view of the questions concerning the associated industries, they have played only a minor role in dating the Pleistocene fluctuations of the Mediterranean.

More satisfactory data were obtained from the oases in the Western Desert, especially Kharga Oasis (Caton-Thompson, 1952), where a classic study defined a sequence of complex geologic events and associated archaeological industries. Two major pluvial epochs were defined. Artifacts were associated only with the Second and latest of the two pluvials. This Second Pluvial was in turn, subdivided into six major periods of increased moisture. The earliest industries were represented by Upper Acheulean living floors enclosed within a fossil spring mound believed to have been active during the earliest of

the events within the Second Pluvial. This was followed by a sequence of three other industries, all of general Middle Paleolithic aspect, which were named Acheulio-Levalloisian, Lower Levalloisian, and Upper Levalloisian, and correlated with minor events within the Second Pluvial. The establishment of a sub-Recent drainage system at Kharga is correlated with a transitional Levallois-Khargan industry, followed by Khargan and Aterian. All of these were primarily flake industries with high frequency of Levallois technology.

The major deficiency in this sequence at Kharga was the same as that observed with assemblages from along the Nile, namely, the size of the collections. In spite of the fact that living floors were observed, the collections are rarely adequate for modern comparative purposes.

The Khargan was seen as a regional development paralleling—and thus presumably contemporary with—Sebilian I along the Nile (Caton-Thompson, 1946a, pp. 112-113). It was at this point in the sequence that the differentiation and specialization of the desert industries from those along the Nile became evident. This trend was further emphasized by the Aterian, for it was clearly a desert specialization which occurs widely through the Sahara and never penetrated the Nile (Caton-Thompson, 1946b, p. 89). As a result of the development of these regional variations, Egypt, at the beginning of the "Late Paleolithic," was seen as divided into three different areas: the Epi-Levalloisian of the northern Nile Valley and Delta, the Sebilian in Nubia, and the Khargan-Aterian of the desert. Each was seen as a regional variety which developed during the evolution of the Levalloisian, and persisted into Historic times.

Information on the later Paleolithic and early Neolithic industries of Egypt and Nubia was also acquired during this same period by excavations both in the desert at Fayum and Kharga, and along the Nile. The interval between the Late Pleistocene "Epi-Levalloisian III" and the initial Neolithic settlements in northern Egypt was represented by microlithic industries from two localities, Helwan and Wadi Angabyyah, both of which yielded triangles, lunates, backed pieces, and double backed pieces made on microblades and flakes. On the basis of similarities in the ridge-backed lunates and lateral notched points, a connection between the Helwan industry and the Natufian of Palestine has been suggested (Garrord, 1932).

The date of these Egyptian microlithic industries was unknown, although they were placed after the "Epi-Levalloisian III'" and separated from it by a considerable technological gap (Huzayyin, 1941, p. 260). They were believed to have survived long enough to have participated in the development of the full Neolithic, as seen at the settlements in the Fayum (especially "Fayum B") and Merinda (Caton-Thompson and Gardner, 1934; Huzayyin, 1941, p. 296), even though non-local features were evident or even dominant, so that an autochthonous emergence of these Neolithic cultures seemed unlikely. This was further supported by the fully modern character of the barley from the earliest Fayum settlements, which suggested that the grain had been under cultivation for a considerable interval in some other area prior to its appearance in the Fayum (Caton-Thompson and Gardner, 1934, p. 46-48).

The apparent break between the terminal Pleistocene and early Recent microlithic industries and the early Neolithic settlements, and the absence of a local developmental sequence leading into the earliest Egyptian food producing communities led many authorities to discount the role of Egypt in the emergence of plant and animal domestication in the Old World (Clark, 1962a, p. 213; Helbaek, 1959, p. 267; McBurney, 1960, p. 234; Braidwood, 1958). This view received added support when the comparatively simple Fayum settlements were dated by radiocarbon at 4,145 B.C. ± 250 years (C-457) and 4,441 B.C. ± 180 years (C-550, C-551). These late dates markedly contrasted with the much earlier ones, around 8,000 B.C., which were obtained from large, permanent communities such as Jerico and Beidha in Palestine. The presence of domestic grains (in some), plus the size and nature of these early permanent settlements in the Levant, strongly argued for an agricultural base, and, therefore, the origin of food production was assumed to have occurred in that area rather than in Egypt.

In southern Egypt and Nubia a significant cultural and chronological break also separated the microlithic industries of Sebilian III from the earliest Neolithic, known as the Tasian (Brunton, 1937), and the succeeding Badarian (Brunton and Caton-Thompson, 1928). Part of the chronological gap was filled with the excavation by Myers (1958, 1960) of a small rock shelter in the vicinity of the Second Cataract near Wadi Halfa. The evidence was far from adequate, but the sequence appeared to show a transition from microlithic industries dating around 6,300 B.C. into the local ceramic horizon.

The adjacent desert areas, such as Kharga Oasis (Caton-Thompson, 1952), also yielded late microlithic assemblages that were undoubtedly contemporary with the Fayum Neolithic, and perhaps even later. Some of the features of the "Bedouin Microlithic" were found in Fayum B, and strong Western Desert contacts, if not actual populations, were indicated (Arkell and Ucko, 1965, p. 147). The Bedouin Microlithic, however, could not be directly tied with earlier local industries, or with earlier material along the Nile, beyond a tenuous resemblance to Sebilian III. Instead, closer parallels were seen with the generalized Saharian microlithic industries which have been found westward from Kharga through much of North Africa.

Farther south, in central Sudan near Khartoum, a non-agricultural hunting and gathering, pottery using "Mesolithic" industry was reported by Arkell (1949b). The subsequent "Khartoum Neolithic" (Arkell, 1953) was dated around 3,300 B.C. (average of two dates) and was seen as a direct development of the earlier Khartoum "Mesolithic," thus providing a continuity, at least in one area, of a non-agricultural hunting and gathering economy into a food producing one. Subsequently, Arkell and Ucko (1965) have argued that much the same thing, that is, a transformance of local hunters and gatherers into agriculturalist through diffusion rather than invasion by outside groups, occurred throughout the Nile basin and the adjacent Sahara.

The above summary of concepts about the prehistory of Egypt and Nubia, which were held at the time the New High Dam archaeological salvage campaign began, points to several deficiencies in the data and the conclusions which have been drawn from them. Perhaps the most important shortcoming in these earlier studies was the inadequate collections on which most of the interpretations were based. The single exception to this generalization was the Sebilian at Kom Ombo, for which sizable collections were available. In this case, however, the stratigraphic position of this material was far from clear. Elsewhere, wide ranging correlations and comparisons were often made on the basis of a few scattered finds or a single artifact. While some justification is evident from the fact that these were the only collections available, nevertheless, the gross weakness of the structure thus erected is clearly evident. What was obviously required, if the prehistory of this area was to be adequately understood, was a concerted and integrated assault on the problem by a number of scholars. The opportunity for just this kind of an effort was provided by the emergency situation with the construction of the New High Dam. The data thus obtained have provided the basis for a revision of our concepts of the prehistory of Nubia and of North Africa as a whole.

The Area Investigated

The concession assigned to the Combined Prehistoric Expedition in Egypt was the entire reservoir area on the west bank from the New High Dam south to a point opposite Kurusku, and from Ineiba to the Sudan frontier. Permits were also awarded for work beyond the reservoir limits in the Western Desert near Dungul and Kurkur Oases. The east bank of the reservoir area, and the short stretch on the west bank between Ineiba and Kurusku, were the responsibility of the Peabody Museum, Yale University expedition.

The decision to do some work outside the reservoir at the adjacent desert oasis was based on the belief that these areas would provide comparative materials against which to view the developments along the Nile. It was felt that an unbroken sequence of occupation might be found there, while along the Nile there would undoubtedly be many breaks, especially during the intervals when the river was cutting its channel. In retrospect these views were naive, for the oases and deserts have always been marginal so far as human occupation is concerned,

and in times of stress there would necessarily be long periods when they were unoccupied. In addition, it is now evident that the lithic industries around the desert oases at Kurkur and Dungul are markedly different from those along the Nile, at least from Late Paleolithic time onward. This dichotomy of desert and riverine cultures still persists today. In part because the materials are so different, the results of the desert surveys and excavations will be published in a separate report.

In Sudan the Combined Prehistoric Expedition received a permit for the west bank of the reservoir, beginning at the southern end of the Egyptian concession, and extending from the Sudan-Egyptian frontier to the head of the reservoir near the Third Cataract. On the east bank it ran from approximately the Second Cataract to the Third Cataract. The area between the Egyptian border and the Second Cataract was awarded to the Joint Scandinavian Expedition, but almost all of the prehistoric materials previously collected by the Scandinavians from this area were made available to the Combined Expedition to study and to report.

The total area covered, in both Egypt and Sudan, was in excess of 300 miles along the Nile, at least half of it on both banks. The Sudanese concession, however, excluded all those sections which had been awarded to other expeditions. Most of these other concessions were assigned for a specific historic site or area. Through agreements with the expeditions concerned, all but one of these (University of Colorado) were eventually studied by the Combined Prehistoric Expedition.

Several surveys disclosed the area between the Second and Third Cataracts, the Batn el-Hajar, was most unfavorable for prehistoric sites. Similar unpromising results were obtained in Egypt in the section between the Dam and Kurusku, primarily because in this stretch most of the Nile silts were covered by the already existing Aswan reservoir. Although large workshops of Middle Paleolithic aspect occurred in both areas, these were either well above the limits of the reservoir, or no materials could be found *in situ*. As a result, it was decided to concentrate all efforts in Sudan on the section between the Egyptian frontier and the Second Cataract, on both the east and west banks, and in Egypt from the Sudan frontier north to Ineiba. These two adjoining areas combined are more than 60 miles (120 km.) in length. Numerous rich prehistoric sites occurred throughout, and many of them were in contexts which could be related to the regional geologic sequence.

RESEARCH METHODS

The fundamental goals of these studies may be stated simply. They were to preserve and to record the threatened archaeological data within and adjacent to the Reservoir area, and to begin the reconstruction of the Paleolithic culture history of Lower Nubia. The basic unit of study was the individual site or settlement. A collection of artifacts was obtained from each site, or, more correctly, from each occupation horizon or distinct area of occupation within the site. These individual site, horizon, or area collections are termed "assemblages." Each assemblage is believed to be a representative sample of the artifacts produced by a social group during the restricted interval of time when this group occupied that particular locality. These assemblages expectably reflect the specific economic and microenvironmental activities conducted at this locality, but they also record the historical background and lithic traditions of the group.

Most of the assemblages were grouped into several larger units which we have called "industries." Each industry is characterized by a specific series of technological and typological attributes, and is readily distinguished from all other industries defined for the area. The industries are an abstraction from the several different assemblages which may represent variations in time, space, and economic specialization. The industry is a convenient device for grouping together those assemblages which share similar features; but on a higher level of abstraction, they are also an attempt to convey the relationship which exists where a similar way of life is shared by several individual communities. This shared way of life may have considerable chronological depth, and thus have a traceable historic development, or it may exist on what is essentially a single time interval. For the later stages of the Paleolithic, at least, where there are complex stylistic and technological

variations, the industry might be viewed as the evident manifestation of a culture held by several social groups which shared a common historical background and development. The definition of these industries, the tracing of the historical changes evident within them, and the assessment of some of the factors responsible for these changes are viewed as the most significant results of our investigations in Lower Nubia.

A systematic program to recover the prehistoric remains from an area over 300 miles in length and up to 50 miles wide requires a very different approach from that normally used in prehistoric research where a single site or an adjacent group of sites are studied. The sheer magnitude of the area to be covered poses a number of problems rarely encountered in nonsalvage projects. In the instance of the Nubian program these problems were further compounded by the relative inaccessibility of much of the area. Except along the river there were no habitations, often food and water had to be brought from supply points a hundred or more miles distant, roads were virtually non-existent, and an international border divided what otherwise would have been a single project. When the project began so little was known of the area that there were even serious doubts if vehicles could be effectively operated in the deserts beyond the river.

These logistic problems paled, however, by comparison with the question of scientific methodology which had to be solved. In an area where virtually nothing was known of the prehistoric remains which would be encountered, the sites not only had to be identified, they had to be evaluated so that only those most significant would be selected for further study. The wealth of materials found in the reservoir precluded any attempt to dig all of the sites; there were neither sufficient funds nor time for this.

To a large extent these aspects of the problem which pertained to the emergency nature of the work were overriding. That is, the surveys and excavations were largely restricted to the pool area, and the schedule was planned so that those most important sites, at least, were dug first. Beyond these limitations, however, those considerations which consciously entered into the planning of the project were not unlike those which would have been faced had an emergency situation not existed. For example, sites were selected as important and worthy of further investigation when the presence of living floors could be documented and some of the material occurred *in situ* within a geologic unit. Surface sites were sometimes collected when there was no obvious later disturbance, and adequate samples of a particular cultural manifestation could not be obtained otherwise. Collections were avoided where the material had been reworked, or where the size of the sample was not adequate for statistical treatment.

Because so little was known about the area, the first priorities were given to the development of a regional stratigraphic sequence, to the definition of the industries to be found here, and to the relation of these industries to the geologic sequence. In some instances the concepts did not proceed beyond this elementary stage, but attention to the changes in settlement patterns and distributions were also encouraged because the cultural remains from a broad area were being studied through a long period of time. This has proved to be one of the major advantages of salvage projects of this nature, for it provides a breadth of data which otherwise would be accumulated only after many years, or even generations, of archaeological research conducted on a normal basis.

Emergency archaeology in research areas also imposes the advantage of close coordination with other specialists, particularly geologists, pollen analysts, and paleontologists. Of course, these non-archaeological specialists generally are participants on most modern archaeological projects, but rarely does their work closely coincide with the archaeology in a broad regional study. In the present instance, the results of the pollen studies were disappointing. Numerous samples were processed by Kathryn Clisby of Oberlin College, using the techniques which she has found to be successful in other arid zone deposits, but without success. Fortunately, most of the other special studies yielded useful results.

The basic field procedure among both the Egyptian and Sudanese parties was to make a systematic but rapid physical examination of a specifically assigned area, and then move from this area to another until the entire section was covered. Part of this survey was done by vehicle, moving slowly back and forth, looking for telltale clusters of broken rock or fossil bone which indicated a site. Particularly promising areas, as well as those sections which were too rough for the vehicles, were examined on foot.

When a site was found, it was given a field number, the position was located on the map, a descriptive form was completed, photographs taken, and, if the site was small, a surface collection was made. Larger sites were usually not disturbed at this point but were revisited at a later date when a large collection could be taken or a scatter pattern made. Unfortunately, in the first few months we failed to appreciate the need for large, statistically significant collections, and a number of sites were recorded from which adequate collections were not obtained. These sites are almost useless except in a very broad generalization. Many of these would never yield an adequate sample, and they probably did not warrant the time it took to record them.

Excavations were undertaken at almost all of the sites where material occurred *in situ*. The major emphasis at each was to ascertain the proper stratigraphic position of the assemblage and to recover a sample of both artifacts and associated fauna which would be adequate for descriptive purposes. Standard excavation procedures were employed, but the size of the area excavated and the type of horizontal and vertical control varied according to circumstance. These are discussed individually as part of the description of each site. The excavations were conducted by local labor and supervised by one or more archaeologists. The nature of the material sought, and the need to maintain close stratigraphic control both prevented the use of large labor crews. The most effective size crew ranged from three to five laborers for each supervisor.

The laboratory analyses were done in four widely separated areas: France, England, Poland, and the United States. This dispersion prevented as close coordination as would be desired, and the classifications used are obviously not identical. There was, however, fundamental agreement on typology, and throughout the study all of the classifications were based on the typological studies of F. Bordes (1961a) for the French Lower and Middle Paleolithic, de Sonneville Bordes and J. Perrot (1954, 1955, 1956a, 1956b) for the Upper Paleolithic, and J. de Heinzelin (1962), with special reference to his African materials. The recently issued typological classification for the North African Epi-Paleolithic by Tixier (1963) was not employed except in one instance where the lithic materials showed striking parallels with that area. For the most part, the Tixier classification is only marginally applicable to the Nubian assemblages. The Tixier type list does not include Levallois, and blade tools and flake tools are grouped together. These distinctions are significant in Nubia.

In the classifications used here, tools were sorted into defined types employing descriptive terminology wherever possible. In exceptional cases new types were defined and named. The types employed in these studies are morphological, and therefore, names such as "sidescraper," "borer," and the like do not necessarily connote function.

In addition to the typological analyses, detailed studies were made of the processes of stone working, the range of materials employed, and the internal relationships of various gross classes of artifacts at each site. From these data it has frequently been possible to arrive at a fuller understanding of the nature of the occupation at these sites, the work habits employed there, and the preferences in materials used — all of which must have cultural significance.

A project of this magnitude includes not only diverse specialists, but also many more archaeologists than are normally found on most excavation crews. While each of these archaeologists tended to specialize in the materials from one time horizon, there was also considerable overlap of effort. Because of the wide range in the training and approach represented in this group, different opinions and interpretations naturally occurred. Some of these could be resolved by reexamining the evidence in the field, but other differences, more philosophical in nature, could not. These are evident in the following reports. Some readers may prefer more consistency in the conclusions, and these differences may at times lead to some confusion, but the disadvantages are far outweighed by the opportunity to have the opposing points of view and the breadth of opinion they provide.

GEOLOGICAL HISTORY OF THE NILE VALLEY IN NUBIA

Jean de Heinzelin

(GEOLOGICAL INSTITUTE, UNIVERSITY OF GHENT)

INTRODUCTION

THE OBSERVATIONS presented in this report were made in the course of four field seasons: 1961-1962, 1962-1963, 1963-1964, and 1965.

The initial plan was to survey and investigate the whole area that will be flooded in Sudanese Nubia between Faras to the north and Akasha to the south, a stretch of about 150 km. as the crow flies. Most of this area lies in the Batn el-Hajar, the "belly of rocks," which proved to be exceptionally poor in prehistoric sites and Pleistocene formations. In contrast, the northern part— a stretch of about 60 km. between Faras and Abka—was exceedingly rich in stone artifacts associated with alluvial deposits or pediments. We had to limit ourselves to this area, for only there could some scientific results exceeding those of a more routine survey be attained.

The two first campaigns were restricted mainly to surveying and surface collecting. The last two campaigns brought the most valuable information, because of the number of archaeological excavations systematically undertaken.

The initial survey and the various researches were conducted by several parties, some operating independently; as a result, the indexing of sites is hybrid and somewhat complex.

The geological party followed a straight numbering system: 1-121; 200-356; 500-522. Some archaeologists followed a similar system: from 400 onwards and from 1,000 onwards. Other archaeological parties used a grid system based on the names of the sheets of the 1/25,000 maps of the Sudan Survey Department, 1960: for example, AN = Anquash sheet; WH = Wadi Halfa sheet; and D or DIW = Dibeira West sheet.

Not all observations were valid or valuable. A great many of them were no more than preliminary field notes. Some had to be emendated after checking. We had, thus, to make a careful choice between valid and invalid observation spots and to combine documents of various origins.

After considering these difficulties, we adopted the regional basis as the most appropriate way to describe the investigated territory. This one has been divided into "districts" separated by some "natural boundaries."

These districts are, in the order of their presentation (Atlas figs. 1A and 1B),[1] as follows:

1. Khor Musa district (east bank)
2. Mirgissa-Abu Sir district (west bank)
3. Airfield-Halfa Degheim district (east bank)
4. Abd el-Qadir—Buhen district (west bank)
5. Wadi Halfa-Jebel Shaitan district (east bank)
6. Dabarosa district (west bank)
7. Sahaba district (east bank)
8. Arkin district (west bank)
9. Dibeira East district (east bank)
10. Dibeira West district (west bank)
11. Sara-Faras East district (east bank)
12. Sara-Faras West district (west bank)
13. Ballana-Massmass district (west bank, Egypt)

The shortcomings of the maps made the determination of elevations difficult. We used several techniques, according to the local environments of the sites.

In some instances, we made transects with an Abney level and alidade (for example, at Localities 34, 81, 517-521). Usually, we made readings with a Thommen 3B1 altimeter between known points in accordance with the 1/25,000 map, interpolating an hourly correction. For sites of some importance, we made as many as three to six readings, taking the mean value after correction (for example, at Locality 343 and Locality 1017).

Scattered altimetric readings are strongly affected by an exceedingly high hourly and temperature correction (up to 40 m. between morning and noon).

---

[1] Figures marked Atlas in the text references will be found in a special section accompanying this volume.

We estimate that our corrected readings are valid within 1-2 m., in most instances.

GENERAL CROSS-SECTIONS

Seven general cross-sections have been traced. The contour lines of the 1/25,000 map were used. The tracings are located on the map (Atlas fig. 2). The tectonic interpretation relies partly on field observations of faulting and partly on geomorphological evidence. The tectonic pattern is a moderate block-faulting which has been active during a relatively long period of time, perhaps from Late Tertiary to Holocene. As a result, most scarps have now receded a long way from the fault lines, and these are no longer visible, being buried under pediment or alluvial deposits.

In a few cases, the dip, direction, and displacement of the fault plane were measurable. All are subvertical. Networks of small, discontinuous fractures filled with silicified breccia are often associated, which suggests that the faults are, in fact, complex and result from a number of small displacements and flexures.

The same pattern extends to the north in Egyptian Nubia, as shown by R. Said and B. Issawy.

The symbols used for the different formations are the following:

In black:	Nile channel
ALL.:	Modern floodplain
DUNE:	Recent dune
ARK.:	Arkin formation, third aggradation of the Nile
SAH.:	Sahaba formation, second aggradation of the Nile
D.J.:	Dibeira-Jer, first aggradation of the Nile
JER:	Jer facies, highest aggradation
VERT.:	Vertisol, black cracked clay
R.P.:	Reddish pediment
CALC.:	Hard calcified formation
DAB.:	Dabarosa formation
N.S.:	Nubia Sandstone
N.S. BASE:	Basal beds of N.S., rich in quartz gravel
P.C.:	Precambrian

The general cross-sections are as follows:

1. Across the Second Cataract southwest-northeast (Atlas fig. 3). An abnormal contact is visible at Locality 338. Western and eastern faulting in the Nubia Sandstone is inferred from the geomorphology.

2. Transverse section at Arkin west-east (Atlas fig. 4). The fault is inferred from the geomorphology. The Dabarosa formation extends along the west bank.

3. Transverse section at Faras northwest-southeast (Atlas fig. 5). Faults are inferred from the geomorphology. Remnants of the Dabarosa formation are on the east bank.

4. Section along the Desert Road, north of Wadi Halfa (Atlas fig. 6). The tops of the highest inselbergs are protected by caps of brown quartzite belonging to the Nubia Sandstone.

5. Longitudinal section east of Wadi Halfa, east bank (Atlas fig. 7). A marker bed of oolithic ironstone is included in the Nubia Sandstone. It is interrupted by the Jebel el-Sahaba fault.

6. West of Birbet el-Hamàn, west bank (Atlas fig. 8). The Dabarosa formation is displaced by faulting.

7. Northwest of Akasha, west bank (Atlas fig. 9). The landscape is protected by a group of closely associated layers of very hard brown quartzite, originally included in the Nubia Sandstone. These marker beds have shifted along a young fault scarp which is well expressed in the topography. The tectonic disturbances become very intricate more to the northeast but have not been studied in detail there.

The reader will have an overall picture of the landscape when comparing these cross-sections with the geomorphic mapping made from air photos by L. Daels.

LOCALITIES OF THE PROFILES

KHOR MUSA DISTRICT

1. Khor Musa is by far the most important wadi of the east bank. As the result of occasional rains, there is still some flow of water, as shown by small amounts of sedimentation and by recent erosional benches.

Its situation is quite peculiar, as it follows the northern margin of the Precambrian of the Batn el-Hajar. Outcrops of Precambrian are scarce on the north flank of the wadi, where all tributaries come from the dissected massif of Jebel Shaitan, composed of Nubia Sandstone.

FIG. 1—Locality 343, in the Khor Musa.

The elongated depression of Khor Musa probably follows a fault zone forming the boundary between the Precambrian and the Nubia Sandstone. This interpretation is based on two kinds of evidence: the geomorphology and the occurrence of abnormal contacts. From the air, the southern edge of Nubia Sandstone outcrops appears straight for a long distance, as a fault scarp would be expected to look. Abnormal contacts can be seen at Localities 337 and 338 along the lower branch of Khor Musa in the direction of N.125°E.

2. A first example of the complex Pleistocene fill of the depression occurs at Locality 343 (Atlas fig. 10), an almost west-east cut at the mouth of a side wadi south of the airfield (Text fig. 1). The main feature of this profile is a strongly developed vertisol (black tropical clay) of at least 3 m. depth (absolute elevation 146-149 m. and lower). Such soils develop in semi-lacustrine, temporarily and periodically flooded depressions, in equatorial to desert and Mediterranean climates. The vertisol rests partly on Precambrian rock, and partly on a sandy arkosic breccia with hardened petrocalcic horizons. These were formed before and during the vertisol development since huge slickensides curve and butt against them. Slickensides of 50 cm. are not rare. The vertisol development ended with a strong desiccation which opened deep cracks up to 2 m. in depth.

These cracks have been suddenly filled later on by a water flood bringing gravels of local origin, such as various Precambrian rocks from the Batn el-Hajar and quartz gravel from the Nubia Sandstone. Sands and gravels extend up to a maximum absolute elevation of 152 m. The fluviatile origin of the deposit and its relationship with the Nile basin is attested to by the presence of *Unio willcocksi* and *Corbicula vara,* the second being also found in the cracks.

The complex fill of vertisol and sandy gravel has been dissected down to at least 147 m. absolute elevation. A land surface with some kind of steppe vegetation established the place where a dense population of *Zootecus insularis* lived.

A second, more sandy aggradation followed up to an absolute elevation of 149 m.

3. The deep, cracked vertisol is a consistent marker bed in the whole area; it shows where appropriate cuts exist. Its thickness is over 3 m. at Locality 1024, 2 km. south of Locality 343 along the Khor Musa (Atlas fig. 11). An extensive prehistoric site was found there on the eroded surface of the vertisol, at an absolute elevation of 149 m.; it is a Sebilian flake industry made of brown quartzite characterized by an abundance of truncated tools. The concentration of artifacts is almost associated, *in situ,* with remnants of hearths. A few pebbles are the only traces of a thin veneer of sediments that once covered the site. Since it was undisturbed, and at the same level as the youngest fill of Locality 343, the industry postdates it or is, at the most, penecontemporaneous. Two datings on charcoal give consistent ages: 8,973 B.C. ± 140 years and 9,050 B.C. ± 120 years (WSU-188 and WSU-144).

In the neighboring area, remnants of sandy and gravelly formations equivalent to the highest fill of Locality 343 form elongated outcrops along the Khor Musa, at 151-154 m. absolute elevation. They contain *Corbicula vara.*

4. The stratigraphical position of the cracked vertisol is also well evidenced in the combined profile of Locality 443 and Locality 1018 at 1.5 km. north-northwest of Locality 343 (Atlas fig.

12). It is situated there at a lower elevation, 143 m., the slope being about 1.5 per cent between Localities 1024 and 443-1018. A first fluviatile deposit of fine sand and silt covers the desiccated vertisol, ending with the formation of a structured but poorly evolved paleosol. This subaerial episode came to an end with a thick deposit of coarse fluviatile sand and gravel culminating at about 152-153 m. absolute elevation in the long curved ridge to the north. This is the same elevation as at Locality 343 and nearby Locality 1024, about 30 m. above the modern floodplain. The fluviatile formation contains a few *Viviparus unicolor,* many *Cleopatra bulimoides,* some *Unio willcocksi,* and an abundance of *Corbicula vara,* at Localities 501 and 502 nearby.

The lithological composition of the gravels shows striking differences from those at Localities 343 and 1024. Many components of foreign, southern origin are present here: jasper and agate. They do not belong any more to the deposits of Khor Musa, which are of local origin only, but rather to the old channel of the Nile itself.

The 30 m. level alluviation suffered a strong dissection to less than 140 m. elevation, and the dissected landscape was partly filled with wadi sand and windblown sand. The formation of a second vertisol between 142 and 145 m. elevation marks a second phase of a semi-lacustrine, periodically flooded depression.

The Halfan prehistoric sites of Localities 443 and 1018 are situated at about 145-146 m. absolute elevation. They were established during or somewhat after the completion of the second, youngest vertisol, at the very edge of it and banked against the hill slope to the north. Calcareous crusts and concentrations developed into the basal parts of the cultural deposits when the water level was still high enough to provide salts and carbonates. The cementation is somewhat stronger and harder at Locality 1018 than it is at 443, which could indicate a slightly older occupation for 1018; but there was probably no real gap between both occupations which can be considered as penecontemporaneous. It is hard to tell if there has been any silt cover deposited on the sites; the former presence of some protective cover is, nevertheless, suggested by their state of preservation and their altimetric position.

Later on and until recently, side erosion has dissected the once continuous edge of the vertisol, leaving as remnants the more indurated parts of the prehistoric sites.

The living floor of Locality 443 has been dated on charcoal at 14,550 B.C. ± 500 years (WSU-201).

5. A similar site has been observed at Locality 1020, at about the same absolute elevation of 144 m., with the difference that the Halfan occupation occurred when the vertisol was still active, as cultural elements have been found deeply embedded in the clay. For this reason, the occupation of Locality 1020 can be dated as slightly older than that at 443-1018 (Atlas fig. 13).

6. North of Locality 1020, the prehistoric site of 1021 lies among outcrops of Precambrian at 151 m. absolute elevation (Atlas fig. 13). It consists of a surficial layer of mixed anthropic deposit resting on eroded remnants of fluviatile gravels. The stratigraphical evidence is poor, but it suggests a late date, which is in accordance with a radiocarbon dating of 5,100 B.C. ± 210 years (WSU-213). The industrial complex is some undefined microlithic assemblage with exceedingly small tools.

Locality 2014 is a later Halfan site situated on the other side of the wadi in front of Localities 443-1018 and 2.5 m. lower.

It has been dated 17,200 B.C. ± 375 years (WSU-332), which is seemingly too old according to the typology. The stratigraphic position is unknown. The views of the typologists and of the geologist about the chronological succession of the Sites 443-1018-1020-2014 are conflicting.

According to the typologists, the proper succession should be: Site 1020, similar to Site 1018; followed by Site 443, similar to Site 2014. They also admit that dating of 17,200 B.C. ± 375 years at Site 2014 is safer than that of 14,550 B.C. ± 500 years of Site 443. This would push back the date on Sites 1020 and 1018 to around 18,000 B.C.

For the geologist, the inferred succession would be: Site 2014 followed by Site 1020, followed by Site 1018, followed by Site 443, the three last being very near in time. This view relies on the following evidence: (*a*) altimetry; (*b*) relationship with vertisols, (*c*) consistency of radiocarbon dates, and (*d*) local paleogeography (see chapter 4 on Definitions of Formations). There is no reason to split Sites 443-1018-1020 over a considerable period of time.

In our scheme, occupations of Sites 278A and B (Sudan) and of Locality 8859 (Egypt) should slightly postdate Site 2014 and slightly antedate Sites 443-1018-1020.

Admittedly, Site 2014 may well be younger than Site 8859 as the real stratigraphical position is unknown and as the statistical errors of the radiocarbon dates overlap. If we take into account the sigma deviation (approximately a 65 per cent chance to have the right date in the span), the crucial datings compare as follows:

Site 443	15,050-14,050 B.C.
Site 2014	17,575-16,825 B.C.
Site 8859	17,200-16,100 B.C.

7. Locality 440 is about 1 km. to the east of 443-1018, and next to the end of the airfield strips. It was excavated, and a long trench was cut into the rather steep slope facing the wadi (Atlas figs. 14-15). Three sequences of deposits are clearly separated by disconformities.

The lower one is a thick accumulation of windblown sand in layers, or with calcic impregnations of roots. It contains an occupation level between 140-141 m. elevation (Industry 7), rich in fish remains. A second occupation level which occurs near the top (Industry 6) is associated with an incipient soil; it contains both fish and mammal remains. The industrial complexes seem very crude, but the typological analysis is biased by the fact that the artifacts made in brown quartzite have disintegrated by the dissolution of their matrix of silica. The datings on charcoal of Industry 6 give an average of 12,390 B.C. ± 500 years (WSU-290).

The soil of the occupation level has been progressively invaded by a silt aggradation starting somewhere below 139 m. absolute elevation. The silt can be followed inland under a rather thick cover of recent windblown sand. This is part of a third and younger sequence of deposits which is found also along the bottom of the present wadi.

The relationship of the silt aggradation with higher deposits is not clear (Atlas fig. 14, eastern section). A better insight is provided by Locality 1440, at a short distance to the west (Atlas figs.

14, 16). The dune sand there is very thin, resting on a strongly hardened silt. It is covered by an alluvial deposit which includes a vertisol, a sandy silt, and a gravel around 149 m. absolute elevation. This gravel is distinct from the highest aggradation deposits and has a different gravel count. At a short distance to the north, Locality 2440 shows the 149 m. gravel penetrating in and resting on a cracked vertisol (Atlas fig. 14).

Because there is too much conflicting evidence, one cannot arrive at a clear-cut picture of the succession of events and assess their dating. First of all, the crude typology of the industry does not seem to fit with the radiocarbon date.

One possible explanation is that the radiocarbon analysis was made on the remnants of the vegetation related to the soil zones H.Z. to C.S. and not on contemporary charcoal of Industry 6. There is in fact a strong discordancy (or discontinuity) between the dune sand D.S. which includes the occupation levels and the silts, at both Localities 440 and 1440.

The exact position of the silts is not obvious: basal part of highest aggradation or later. This has some bearing on the interpretation of the lowermost silt at Locality 1440.

8. The airfield area, built at the junction of the Nile and the Khor Musa, is the major and the most impressive extension of the highest and oldest aggradation. Its flat surface does not provide any clear-cut profile. A few outliers situated near the western corner are fossiliferous. Localities 280, 501, and 502 provide the customary assemblage of mollusks: *Corbicula vara*, *Cleopatra bulimoides*, *Unio willcocksi*, and *Viviparus unicolor*. Shells of 280 have been dated at 4,040 B.C. ± 100 years (WSU-108), which is unacceptable since it is much too young.

9. Extensive patches of the older fluviatile sequence with the same facies, and including the same characteristic impregnation of roots, are exposed west and south of 443-1018. Locality 1017, a very important site, is at an absolute elevation of 148-149 m. There the living floor of a hunters' camp has been excavated (Atlas fig. 17). The profile is not very deep and cuts only a few layers of the silty and sandy fluviatile aggradation. The prehistoric hunters chose to live on a small lens of sand laid down between two banks of silt. The living floor was preserved

at some places, with artifacts and burnt stones still *in situ*. It had been slightly disturbed elsewhere and redistributed at the base of the next layer. We can fairly estimate that the site was occupied a few days only; the industrial complex is consequently pure and devoid of contamination. It is distinguished by the simultaneous use of brown quartzite and pebbles of jasper and agate as raw material. Brown quartzite was used according to an evolved Levallois technique. The pebbles were used preferentially for the making of burins. This site is the type-locality of the Khormusan industrial complex.

The living floor of 1017 has been dated on charcoal at 20,750 B.C. ± 280 years (WSU-203). It is a consistent dating of the middle part of the Dibeira-Jer formation, oldest aggradation of the Nile under its typical sandy facies rich in calcic impregnation of roots.

The dating has been made on fragments of charcoal from a single lens. If a slight contamination is admitted, the dating is a minimum age.

10. Locality 448 is situated 1 km. west-northwest of 1017 (Atlas fig. 18). It is a surface site at 142 m. absolute elevation, a rather late occupation. The stratigraphical sequence shown by the cut was not directly related to the site and was similar to the oldest part of 443-1018. At the base is a strong paleosol of the vertisol type; then occurs a fluviatile aggradation of silty sand with calcic impregnation of roots; then, a subaerial episode with formation of a well structured but poorly evolved paleosol; and finally, a deposition of coarse fluviatile sand and gravel. This last deposit accumulated probably up to 152 m. absolute elevation but is now reduced to 143 m. absolute elevation.

11. Locality 278 is situated about 2.2 km. north of 448, near the Nile and along the old railway track which is now the road toward Abka-Akasha. The profile shows two different episodes of fluviatile aggradation, separated by subaerial deposits and soils (Atlas fig. 19).

The oldest sequence consists of compact fluviatile gravel and hardened silt, at 135 m. absolute elevation. It has been eroded; wadi sand and gravel were left in small channels, followed by dune sand accumulation, and, thereafter, by a small vertisol developed in a semi-lacustrine expansion. This small vertisol can be compared

with the second one of the Khor Musa sequence at 443-1018 (upper), 1020, and 440.

A prehistoric population lived at the top of the dune sand, leaving Industry A, when a faint podzolization developed; the latter can be compared to the calcic illuviated paleosol of 440 and to other paleosols described hereafter: Localities 27, 8863, and 8898.

A new phase of fluviatile action started with the erosion of part of the vertisol, so that part of Industry A has been distributed and rolled at the base of the next silt deposits. The second silt deposition was at first quite regular, well laminated; it contains a cultural horizon *in situ*, Industry B, accompanied by banks of caliche formation (both industrial complexes should be ancestral to Qadan). The silt deposition ended at 139 m. absolute elevation and was followed by coarse fluviatile sand and gravel containing many *Cleopatra bulimoides* and a few *Unio willcocksi*, *Etheria elliptica*, and *Corbicula vara*. This formation equates with the second sand aggradation of 343 and the last gravel of 1440.

Traces of an A-group site were found on the eroded surface of the sand.

12. The position of the sites of 277-1027 can be compared with that of 278. A large extension of coarse fluviatile sand and gravel at 137 m. absolute elevation contains many *Cleopatra bulimoides* and a few *Unio willcocksi*, *Etheria elliptica*, and *Corbicula vara*, which is the same assemblage as that at the top of 278.

Mesolithic and A-group artifacts are spread over the surface of the sand; thus they are younger than the fluviatile aggradation.

The present Nile floodplain is 16 m. lower among boulders, at about 123 m. absolute elevation.

13. Locality 412 is situated 1 km. southwest of 277-1027 (Atlas fig. 20). A large deflated exposure of artifacts had been first collected by the Scandinavian Expedition. Part of the site extends into the small hill at the east between two layers of silt at about 138 m. absolute elevation. Typology compares with that of Locality 278.

14. Locality 2004 is situated at Gemai, about 15 km. upstream (Atlas fig. 21). The industry is sealed into a silt and fine sand aggradation. It is a Later Khormusan assemblage. It compares with ANW-3 (treated later), is younger than

1017, and is possibly in the range of 16,050 B.C. to 15,050 B.C.

MIRGISSA-ABU SIR DISTRICT

1. The large branched wadi which drains towards the plain of Mirgissa is almost symmetrical to Khor Musa; its course is surprisingly toward the south, contrary to the main direction of the Nile. The Nile itself forces its way across the Second Cataract, where it is controlled by the structure of the Precambrian. The high scarp from the Mirgissa fortress to Gemai West, in a southwesterly direction, is certainly due to a fault, and the Abu Sir cliff and related channels are influenced by rock structure.

In this instance, it is hard to discriminate between the influence of an old Precambrian pattern and a possibly more recent, rejuvenated tectonic disturbance. Both must have occurred in the Second Cataract area as there are many other proofs of geologically recent block-faulting in the area up to Aswan. The block-faulted landscape of the Nubia Sandstone area to the north disappears into the rugged topography of the Precambrian area, the core of the Batn el-Hajar.

2. Two main groups of quite different sediments occur in the basin of the Mirgissa wadi.

The oldest is an extensive, thick and probably complex sheet of quartz gravel extending far inland to the west, at approximately 200 m. absolute elevation. We did not trace the western limit, which is perhaps as far away as Jebel Sula. The lithological composition and the situation of these gravels are quite different from those relating to the Nile. They are in no way related to it and seem to fill an old, very flat depression of the peneplain. They will be called Pre-Nile gravels in the course of the discussion.

In this area, the quartz gravels seem to have been essentially laid down as a residual pediment coming from the progressive recession of the Nubia Sandstone outcrop. This is not the case everywhere; more to the north, the cover of quartz gravel is of a more fluviatile, water-laid nature. It is thicker and stratified and occurs in elongated remnants, sometimes in inverted terrace relief. This water-laid facies will be defined later as a Dabarosa formation. Provisionally, and in the absence of a thorough investigation, other gravel facies situated at similar elevation can be accepted as correlative. All together they certainly cover a large time span and have a complex origin.

The branched Mirgissa wadi is deeply incised into the sheet of quartz gravels. The flat or rounded topography of the gravel outcrops contrasts with the scarps developed in the underlying Nubia Sandstone. Eventually, because of sheet erosion and wind deflation, the gravels roll down from their primitive position to lower surfaces, forming a mantle on the landscape together with dune sand.

3. Near its mouth, the Mirgissa wadi is restricted to Nile formations, characterized by silt, sand, and gravels with specific lithological content.

As in Khor Musa, two successive fluviatile aggradations can be detected. The oldest one reaches about 152 m. absolute elevation and is made of fine, sometimes hardened, silts with typical calcic impregnation of roots. This fill has been strongly dissected before the deposition, up to a minimum of 144 m. absolute elevation, of coarse, white, very fluid fluviatile sand which is at some places very rich in fossil shells. At Locality 515, there are very many *Cleopatra bulimoides;* somewhat fewer *Viviparus unicolor, Valvata nilotica,* and *Corbicula vara;* some *Ferrissia* sp.; and no *Unio willcocksi.*

Numerous prehistoric sites, mostly mixed, are distributed on the fluviatile sand and along its edge.

The modern floodplain is much higher here than it is below the Cataract, about 132 m. absolute elevation between boulders.

4. Coming back to the problem of the abnormal direction of flow of the Mirgissa wadi, we suggest two reasons for it: a slight tectonic tilt, or the disposition of the Pre-Nile gravel forming a sheet more resistant to erosion.

5. South of the Mirgissa fortress, the Precambrian contains several dykes or necks of a peculiar brown chert. Some outcrops have been extensively mined by prehistoric man; flaked material strewn all around indicates this. An example is at Locality 622, 5 km. southwest of Mirgissa (Atlas fig. 22).

AIRFIELD–HALFA DEGHEIM DISTRICT

1. North of Khor Musa, the airfield strips lie at

509 ft. absolute elevation, or 155.25 m. absolute elevation. The large flat surface is covered with quartz gravel containing some brown chert but no, or almost no, foreign elements. There, we are outside the Nile channel, on the gravelly fan spreading from the Nubia Sandstone massif of Jebel Shaitan. These gravel sheets of local origin connect somewhere to the west with true Nile gravels similar to those of Localities 501-502.

To the southeast, along the right bank of Khor Musa, and along the railway, extend similar sheets of gravel of local origin, which build a kind of "glacis" at the foot of Nubia Sandstone outcrops and scarps. There are still some low, smooth outcrops of Precambrian; their contact with the basal beds of Nubia Sandstone can be seen, for example, at 500, around 190 m. absolute elevation. Locality 256 is an outcrop of Precambrian, and 255 shows a mixture of Nubia Sandstone and Precambrian pebbles. Most of the quartz gravels are derived from the base of the Nubia Sandstone.

2. From the airfield to 4 km. northeast, the surface is almost flat. Locality 504 (Atlas fig. 23) is exactly at the farthermost edge of this large embayment. Several arcuate banks of stratified fossiliferous gravel form a subdued relief at the foot of the cliffs of Nubia Sandstone, around 157 m. absolute elevation. This is the highest observed elevation of Nile fauna remains. There we identified an abundance of *Corbicula vara* (many bivalve), some *Mutela* cf. *rostrata*, a few *Cleopatra bulimoides*, and three *Lanistes carinatus*. Although this fauna is typically fluviatile and Nilotic, the lithological content is not at all that of the Nile formations. It consists of fine quartz gravel, with rolled artifacts of several Paleolithic industries, devoid of foreign elements.

The quartz gravels rest on a reddish brown, unstratified pediment which can be followed higher up in the landscape along the wadis coming from Jebel Shaitan.

Locality 504 (Text fig. 2) shows a lateral, marshy facies of the highest Nile aggradation, built by sand and gravel bars in a convenient embayment. The highest water level of the Nile can properly have been very slightly lower.

The embayment of 504 was later dissected and deflated with the falling level of the Nile.

3. Farther to the north, the inselbergs and cliffs of Nubia Sandstone project nearer to the Nile and turn at a right angle in front of Halfa Degheim. This is part of the geometric pattern of the massifs of Nubia Sandstone along the right bank of the Nile; this pattern is highly suggestive of a block-faulted structure.

The scarps of Nubia Sandstone facing west are strongly dissected by small, deeply incised wadis which recede towards Jebel Shaitan.

At the foot of the scarps extend intricate remnants of Nile formations and wadi discharge with boulders and rubble. Remnants of the highest aggradation are scarce, around 152 m. absolute elevation; more extensive, and fossiliferous at some places, are the remnants of a second aggradation of coarse sand around 142 m. absolute elevation. At 506 we identified many *Cleopatra bulimoides* and a few *Viviparus unicolor, Unio willcocksi,* and *Corbicula vara.*

4. A third, somewhat lower aggradation of fluviatile deposits starts here and widens to the north. It consists of heavy gray silts almost devoid of calcareous concretions and of pedological structure. Their appearance is very uniform, so that they are easily identifiable. They stretch along the present channel of the Nile up to about 134 m. absolute elevation.

Abd el-Qadir–Buhen District

1. The left bank of the Nile is occupied here by a long and broad embayment filled with Nile aggradations and wadi rubble; it is bound by scarps of Nubia Sandstone capped with Pre-Nile gravels at about 2 km. from the river. These gravels extend farther inland in a flat topped landscape around 200 m. absolute elevation.

The fossil embayment is divided in two by a saddle extending from Abd el-Qadir (Abd el-Qadir tomb) and King Jer (Soliman tomb) hills. Abd el-Qadir hill is still capped with several meters of quartz gravel up to an absolute elevation of 184 m., showing that the Nile deeply entrenched a flat, peneplained landscape covered by a thick cover of Pre-Nile gravel.

2. The succession of Nile formations is similar in both parts of the embayment, north and south. The first, highest, and main fill is a complex succession of alluvial silt and sand interfingered with layers and lenses of windblown sand; an outstanding feature is the presence of a great

Fig. 2—Locality 504, near Wadi Halfa airfield.

many calcic impregnations of roots, including basal parts of standing stems, collapsed stems, and branches lying flat. This facies is so peculiar that it can be identified at once. The best examples are at Locality ANW-3, at an absolute elevation of 137.5 m. A surface site has been collected nearby. It was not in stratigraphical position (cfr. J. Waechter's report, Loc. 243).

Locality 1030 along the car track is situated at 139.5 m. absolute elevation. It is also a surface site but the discovery of a few flakes *in situ* seems to indicate that the industry was included in the deposit and was recently deflated and brought to the surface. The maximum elevation of sandy silts in the immediate vicinity is around 147 m.

absolute elevation, but it is more than 150 m. absolute elevation in the saddle west of King Jer hill.

3. The same complex interfingering of the alluvial silt and sand with windblown sand covers the northern part of the embayment. At 235, a complete succession was traced up to the very top of the deposits, at 157 m. absolute elevation (Atlas fig. 24).

The situation here is identical to that at 504 on the right bank. Here, too, several arcuate banks of finely stratified gravel form a subdued relief at the very edge of the highest Nile deposits; and the lithological components are mostly small quartz gravels, without admixture of foreign elements. Here, too, the molluscan association is Nilotic, with an abundance of *Corbicula vara* (many bivalve), many *Caelatura aegyptiaca,* some *Mutela* cf. *emini,* and a few *Mutela nilotica* and *Aspatharia caillaudi.*

The fossiliferous gravel does not rest on a pediment, as it does at Locality 504, but on a pure dune sand. In the lower portion of the slope, the dune sand interfingers with alluvial deposits, silt and sand containing characteristic calcic impregnation of roots, stems, and branches.

Patches of younger windblown sand or colluvial sands rest discordantly on the older aggradation, with *Zootecus insularis* at the contact.

Both 235 on the left, west bank, and 504 on the right, east bank, are similar in all aspects, symmetrically disposed, with the difference that wind action was more marked on the west bank than on the east bank, as it is today. Both deposits must be taken as strictly contemporaneous.

Shells of Locality 235 have been dated at 3,170 B.C. ± 100 years (WSU-110), which is unacceptable. They should be slightly younger than those of 1017, in the range of 18,050 B.C.

4. The main alluvial fill culminating at 157 m. absolute elevation has been dissected prior to the deposition of a second one, made of coarse white sand up to an absolute elevation of about 140-145 m. This deposit is much more restricted and belongs to the same aggradation as that at 515 below Mirgissa, or at Localities 278, 277-1027, and 506 on the right bank.

There is no definite remnant of a lower aggradation, but some gravel accumulations were observed at 4 to 5 m. above the present floodplain, as at 514 where a mixed surface site was collected.

The highest alluvial deposits disappear almost entirely near Buhen, where Nubia Sandstone scarps come close to the Nile. The coarse white sands of the middle aggradation lie around 140 m. absolute elevation there.

5. The relationship between Pre-Nile gravels and Nile aggradations is clearly exposed west of 235. The base of the Pre-Nile gravels there is at 166 m. absolute elevation, 9 m. higher than 235. The top of the Pre-Nile gravels is at 192 m. absolute elevation in the vicinity, 35 m. higher than at 235. The local thickness of the Pre-Nile gravels is presently 26 m. minimum.

Wadi Halfa–Jebel Shaitan District

1. The scope of the investigations was, in principle, limited to the maximum reservoir area, inside the 190 m. contour line. In order to present a more complete picture of the geology and of the position of the oldest cultural sequences, we needed observations outside this contour. The surroundings of Jebel Shaitan have been studied specially for this purpose.

To start with a broad, general picture, we can state that the desert, east of Wadi Halfa, is an extensive peneplained, tabular area bounded by complex and strongly dissected scarps disposed approximately at a right angle. One scarp faces southwest along the Khor Musa, and one scarp faces west-northwest along the right bank of the Nile.

At about 20 km. east of the Nile, the altitude of the peneplained landscape varies between 320 and 340 m. absolute elevation. A few inselbergs stand on this surface. Their general shape is smooth, rather rounded; but seen in detail, they are strongly eroded by wind action which developed caves, tunnels, and rock falls. The peneplained inselberg landscape has a characteristic outlook, not at all similar to that of the younger inselberg landscape situated closer to the Nile.

2. The cover of the peneplained landscape is quite variable: bare rocks of Nubia Sandstone, a thin cover of sand dunes, local gravel accumulations, reddish pediments, and paleosols. The reddish pediments are more extensive than usually suspected because they escape observation for two reasons: (*a*) natural cuts are exceptional, and (*b*) a thin mantle of sand in motion is present almost everywhere. At most places, any test pit reveals a rather thick reddish pediment below the thin blanket of mobile sand.

We noted the color of the reddish pediment at a few places, in order to show the range of variation. All localities fall outside the mapped area. The color is red to reddish yellow; near the end of the Cairo Road it is 2.5 YR dry 6/4; moist 4/6. Between Wadi Sara and Khor Adendan it is moist 5 YR 6/6.

3. The dissection of the scarps mentioned above develops an intricate and impressive landscape of inselbergs and mesas separated by braided wadis. This landscape begins at about 15 km.

from the Nile and from the Khor Musa. The highest point is Jebel Shaitan, at 1,075 ft. absolute elevation, or about 328 m. absolute elevation; most summits stand around 240-270 m. absolute elevation, which compares closely with the highest elevation on the west bank, around 230 m. absolute elevation.

As already stated, these inselbergs and the scarps of Nubia Sandstone differ totally in shape from the peneplained inselbergs; the slopes here are rather concave and steeper, giving the impression that one or several young cycles of erosion have been continuing. The channels of the braided wadis show usually three different sections on their length: (*a*) steep, irregular, chaotic heads, most of them above 200 m. absolute elevation; (*b*) broad, flat, braided channels filled with stratified sand and pediments, mostly between 150 and 200 m. absolute elevation, with the slope varying between 0.6 per cent to 1.5 per cent, being usually between 0.75 per cent and 0.9 per cent; and (*c*) the lowest part confines itself to the Nile terraces and is channeled by narrow incisions and gullies, which did not succeed in making a plain erosional surface (Atlas figs. 3 to 6).

Pediplanation, gullying, and lateral erosion are now almost inactive, because of a lack of rainfall, so that the landscape is fossilized as such except for the interference of wind action. We shall come back later to the dating of the erosional cycles, as we have to deal first with the factors of inselberg development.

4. The shape of the inselbergs and mesas depends directly on the composition of the underground, the beds of Nubia Sandstone. The general stratigraphy of this formation has not been worked out because of lack of time. The total thickness in the Jebel Shaitan area is of the order of 250 m.; the general dip is about 0.7 per cent to the north; and the beds are interrupted by minor faults, flexures, and shear zones.

The lower 10 or 20 m. are rich in quartz gravel, and the next 80 m. consist of thick banks of yellow sandstone with oblique stratification. A good marker bed of oolithic ironstone occurs at about 100 m. above the base; it is situated at 190 m. absolute elevation, southeast of Wadi Halfa, and it dips to 120 m. absolute elevation 10 km. north of El Sahaba, where it is

displaced by a fault. The oolithic ironstone marker bed is accompanied by sporadic development of mudstones, followed by a more sandy sedimentation. At about 150 m. above the base are interbedded several layers of very hard, brown quartzite. Other beds of brown quartzite were formed in later members of Nubia Sandstone, too, but with much less regular extension and shape. Silicified tree stems and plant impressions are abundant in the last 80 m. of Nubia Sandstone. The silicified stems are sometimes more than 10 m. in length and more than 50 cm. in diameter; they are associated with sandy deposits. Plant impressions are associated with purple shale and thin hematite beds. Locality 73, 6 km. southeast of Wadi Halfa and the southern shoulder of Jebel Shaitan, is rich in fossil plant impressions, mostly unidentifiable. The absolute elevation of this locality is about 270 m.

5. The hard layers of brown quartzite have been leading factors in the development of the erosion; they cap mesa-like hills and form structural platforms usually confined between 230 and 270 m. absolute elevation (Atlas figs. 25, 26, 27).

Prehistoric people found there a rich supply of good raw material, and some outcrops are littered with innumerable traces of quarrying, flaking, and debitage activities. As rich as they are, it is hard to believe that any of these sites was a true living site; most of them are certainly mixed. It is only by a careful mapping of concentrations that pure workshops and perhaps temporary occupations can be detected.

Among the inselberg localities reported are: 6, 36, 37, 38, 39, 40, 41, 42, 63, 70, 71, 77, 112, 113, 118, 119, 120, 121, and 401 and a number of sites collected by archaeologists, about which we have no information.

6. Many sites have been detected on the peneplain or at its edge, but in such a wind-worn condition that typological identification is hardly possible. It is, nevertheless, interesting to note the extension of prehistoric artifacts into the bare desert.

7. Reddish pediments and paleosols are sometimes preserved at the top of the inselbergs. The paleosols are reddish yellow, without definite horizons, hard, porous, and strongly structured. They compare best with ultisols, red Mediterranean soil. At Locality 63, the color is 5 YR dry

7/4 to 7/6; moist 5/4 (Atlas fig. 26). The paleosols seem to have developed into old colluvia and pediments resting on the weathered surface of the Nubia Sandstone. They are best preserved in a variety of elliptic sinkholes, probably as a result of differential weathering of bedrock under a vegetation cover. They secondarily suffered a strong desiccation, which led to hardening, shrinkage, and depression of the sinkholes. Shrinkage cracks are prominent and are filled with brown sand.

8. Small shells of *Zootecus insularis* are frequently found in the top of the reddish paleosols and around the cracks. Although they are certainly fossil or subfossil, they cannot be as old as the ultisol development for they show no trace of decalcification or weathering. They compare, in position, to the *Zootecus insularis* concentrations of Localities 343 (Khor Musa), 235 (Abu Sir-Buhen), 505, and 513 (discussed later).

9. We come now to the development of the platforms and of the wadis lower down. As we have already stated, the inselbergs capped with brown quartzite stand between 230 and 270 m. absolute elevation around Jebel Shaitan. Structural platforms extend at lower elevations, too, which still bear imprints of soil formations. In the neighborhood of Wadi Halfa, they are mainly developed between 180 and 200 m. absolute elevation. If we take altimetric relationship into account, the development of these surfaces can equate with the end of the deposition of the Pre-Nile gravels and related facies.

The development of the wadi system can best be understood if one imagines that it started with the incision of the 180-200 m. platforms near the Nile, climbing up with a general slope of about 0.75 per cent towards the edge of the peneplain.

10. Patches of pediments and alluvial sheets of several ages are preserved; they are scattered all along the wadi system, at the foot of the Nubia Sandstone scarps, in benches cut by more recent erosion, in spurs, and between branching wadis.

Unfortunately, too few excavations have been conducted in such areas to make possible a close stratigraphic interpretation; existing information shows that the erosion had gone very deep in Upper Acheulean times.

Localities 398, 399, and 400 afford the best observed profiles of the wadi pediments (Atlas figs. 27, 28, 29), in the neighborhood of quarries of brown quartzite which provided an abundance of raw material for several prehistoric populations.

The succession of events can be summarized as follows: (*a*) erosion of the landscape into deep, broad, concave valleys almost as extensive as the present wadis; (*b*) deposition of coarse reddish pediments at the edges and of fine reddish pediments in the middle of the valleys, the last stages of which include Acheulean artifacts; (*c*) dissection of the reddish pediments and deposition of yellowish pediments including derived Acheulean artifacts; (*d*) active erosion down to the bedrock of the Nubia Sandstone, along the slopes, rubble, and mining debitage accumulated at some places; and (*e*) flat channeling of the modern wadis.

11. The occurrence of the reddish pediments, called also Older Pediments, can easily be generalized by surface mapping, even on aerial photos. Their remnants stand now, in most instances, between 2 and 10 m. above the wadi floor. Having been subjected to deflation for a long time, the stones of brown quartzite have been concentrated at the surface and blackened with desert varnish. As a result, the individual patches are outstanding in the topography if not buried under sand. Here and there, they appear at the foot of the inselbergs or as elongated spurs between younger channels. They might contain slightly rolled, almost fresh Paleolithic artifacts such as Acheulean bifaces, Levallois nuclei, flakes, and tools (Locality 33, 220 m. absolute elevation). When tools are found at the surface after deflation, their edges are abraded by wind action. The Older Pediments once covered a whole system of valleys which were not too different in scope from the present ones. It is obvious that their deposition has not been a simple affair and that it may have taken a long time, over several climatic phases. In the absence of any extensive study of this topic, no closer stratigraphical analysis can be presented for the moment.

The occurrence of the yellowish pediments, called also Younger Pediments, is much less striking. They are thinner, and their pattern does not differ very much from that of the modern wadi system. No archaeological site has been found in them up to now, only scattered artifacts.

12. A major problem is the relationship between the Older and Younger Pediments and the Nile aggradations. In several instances, reddish and rather hardened wadi formations dip below the oldest and highest Nile aggradation, below 145 m. absolute elevation at least.

Erosional steps relating to lower water levels and branching from the Nile interrupt the downstream part of the main wadis. Various sheets of sediments spread on them are reddish to yellowish, poorly oxidized and poorly hardened. These relate to the Younger Pediments.

It can be admitted, as a whole, that the deposition of the Older Pediments ended with the highest Nile aggradation and that the deposition of the Younger Pediments ended with the last Nile aggradation.

13. A very striking succession was evidenced at Locality 513, between 140 and 141 m. absolute elevation, slightly north of the lower part of the Cairo Road and not too far from the Nile (Atlas fig. 30).

Remnants of a strongly developed vertisol rest on Nubia Sandstone or its weathering products. The vertisol ended with a general desiccation, evidenced by deep cracks which have been filled with a coarse sandy deposit while the top of the soil was eroded. A reddish zone of sandy and gravelly sediments may correspond to part of the Older Pediments. The color is reddish brown, 5 YR dry 6/3; moist 5/3. In the vicinity, the dissected and deflated top of the Older Pediments lies at 160 m. absolute elevation. After their erosion at 513 an upper zone of sandy gravelly sediments was laid down, which may equate with the Younger Pediments. The color is reddish yellow, 5 YR dry 7/4 to 7/6; moist 6/6. During the intermediate period there flourished a rich population of Zootecus insularis, the tests of which are now included in the base of the upper zone.

14. The localization of Zootecus insularis fauna in such a position, between two sandy fills, is not at all accidental as it is repeated at many places. We have already seen it at Localities 343, 235, and 513.

Another example occurred at 505, a locality

outside the map in a fully desertic environment several miles east of Jebel Shaitan and several miles north of the Sudan Railway track (Atlas fig. 31).

In a long wadi running to the south, at 270 m. absolute elevation, a small bench showed a yellowish sand resting on a reddish yellow sand with, at the contact area, an abundance of Zootecus insularis. A parallel can be tentatively traced between the two sand deposits and what have been called here the Older and Younger Pediments.

Around Jebel Shaitan, several localities show innumerable Zootecus insularis embedded in reddish sand deposits now in the course of erosion, but unfortunately without clear stratigraphical evidence.

It seems, therefore, that an outstanding development of a monospecific Zootecus insularis fauna took place between two aggradations of the Nile and between two pediment formations outside the Nile. To the same period belong probably the Zootecus insularis faunas occurring at the top of the inselbergs.

15. A third, lower aggradation of fluviatile deposits consisting mostly of heavy gray silt took place later. It extends from Halfa Degheim to Wadi Halfa and farther to the north, up to an absolute elevation of about 134 m., 13 m. above present floodplain. Its edge follows the foot of the cliffs of Jebel Halfa, as it does at 82. Older fluviatile formations were not recorded there.

No relevant formation can be traced in the wadis, where the influence of this third fluviatile episode seems to have been a limited gullying only.

R. Fairbridge published two dates on shells collected nearby 82 in 1961-1962. An Etheria shell coming from the base of the "10 m. aggradation" was dated at 9,250 B.C. ± 285 years (I-531), and Cleopatra shells coming from the top of the "10 m. aggradation" were dated at 7,375 B.C. ± 250 years (I-534). These dates are consistent with those of DIW 1 and DIW 50 (see later).

DABAROSA DISTRICT

1. This district includes the concession of the Colorado Expedition where we visited three sites without proper systematic investigation.

A large sheet of Pre-Nile gravels lies at a

slightly lower elevation than in the Mirgissa District; they are apparently not present above 190 m. absolute elevation. Some hills covered with these gravels are as low as 165 m. absolute elevation, as at nearby Locality 516.

This sheet of gravels, once continuous, caps both sides of the large straight wadi parallel to the Nile at 4.5 km. from it. This rectilinear depression directed N.40°E. follows with high probability a tectonic line, fault, or joint in the substratum of Nubia Sandstone. It is not an old channel of the Nile, nor is it a part of a subsequent wadi system parallel to the Nile.

The bottom of the depression is almost flat between 160 and 165 m. absolute elevation; it is covered with reddish sandy pediments. The origin and the dating of this depression are still conjectural, but we assume that it came into existence by differential erosion before the Nile aggradations.

2. The Nile aggradations themselves form a fringe of 1 to 2 km. along the river. The stratigraphical succession is simple, similar to that already seen in other districts, but it is sometimes difficult to picture it in detail in the absence of profiles.

A first, highest aggradation culminated at about 154 m. absolute elevation; after a strong dissection, a second middle aggradation was deposited up to above 142 m. absolute elevation at least. There is no trace of a lower aggradation which would correspond to that of Wadi Halfa.

3. At ANW-3, ex-Locality 228 (Atlas fig. 32), two fluviatile deposits situated between 137 and 140 m. absolute elevation are separated by a disconformity which corresponds probably to the erosional phase between the highest and middle aggradation. An industry (Later Khormusan) is included in a cross-bedded sand between both fluviatile deposits. It has been dated 15,850 B.C. ± 500 years (WSU-215).

4. Locality 516, or "South Colorado Site" 6G30, has been seen very briefly. A rich cultural horizon lies in a sandy formation at about 136 m. absolute elevation. Four meters higher, a fine fluviatile silt contains a molluscan assemblage of small forms including *Valvata nilotica, Anisus planorbis,* and *Gyraulus costulatus.* The top of the hill culminates at an elevation of 145 m.

We would personally suspect that the indus-

trial assemblage called Complex A by the excavators (Irwin) should be comparable to some Late Khormusan, in approximately the same stratigraphical position as ANW-3.

Several surface sites have been located on the sandy formations between 516 and the village of Dabarosa.

5. Locality 27 is the "First Colorado Site" 6B27. The profile described here was observed on January 14, 1963, before excavation. It is mentioned here for its geological implications and not for its prehistoric context (Atlas fig. 33) (Irwin and Wheat, 1965).

The lower part of the profile, at 139 m. absolute elevation and below, is a vertisol similar to that of Localities 343, 1024, 443-1018, and 513. A yellowish to pure white sand poorly stratified was deposited up to 142 m. absolute elevation, probably by a true fluviatile process. A well distinct soil development has been preserved with an almost complete sequence of horizons. It fits into the varieties of the non-calcic brown soils, part of the Ustalfs of the new soil nomenclature. Such soil needs a rather humid climate in order to develop with a warm or hot dry season of at least three months in the year; it is necessarily a soil of Mediterranean climate, without analogy with the soils that can develop today in the region.

An incipient gullying partly destroyed the soil, which was, thereafter, sealed under an alluvial cover of silts. These belong to the edge of the middle Nile aggradation, which is still preserved there up to 142 m. absolute elevation. A prehistoric occupation is included in the silt succession.

Three datings of the main layer of Site 6B27 gave, respectively: 4,200 B.C. ± 300 years (I-864); 7,325 B.C. ± 600 years (GX-0122); and 16,155 B.C. ± 1,200 years (I-863).

Site 6B29 nearby and on the same land surface has been dated 13,150 B.C. ± 750 years (GX-0120).

It seems probable that the dates of 4,200 B.C. and 7,325 B.C. are much too young as the water level was at that time much lower than the sites. The date of 13,150 B.C. ± 750 years would fit well in the stratigraphy.

6. Locality 28 is situated half a kilometer to the northeast of 27. The same silts as those at 27 lie discordantly on dissected hills of more struc-

tured silts, sands, and gravels which reach a somewhat higher elevation. These belong to a different, previous cycle of aggradation.

7. Starting from 27, we traced a transverse profile in a northwest to southeast direction. It shows a definite change in the composition of the gravels according to their elevation. Nowhere in the investigated area do foreign elements of southern origin occur above the level of the highest Nile aggradation, 35 m. above modern floodplain. The distinctive elements are various kinds of jasper and agate related to the Hudi chert and fresh fragments of Precambrian brought from the Batn el-Hajar.

SAHABA DISTRICT

1. A number of sites, many of which lack stratigraphical evidence, have been located and will serve only for the sake of the typology. This applies to Localities 115, 116, 118, 119, and 121.

2. Site 117 was discovered in 1962, but the actual existence of an old cemetery was not revealed prior to the 1965 season, and only after several test excavations (Atlas figs. 34-35).

The bodies lie at about 160 m. absolute elevation (Atlas fig. 35). They are included in a mixed and disturbed fill and were covered with slabs of Nubia Sandstone. The burial layer rests on a yellowish sandy sediment bearing traces of a truncated superficial soil. The top of the burial layer has been encrusted and hardened by calcium carbonate prior to the deposition of an upper sandy layer of hill wash. Qadan artifacts are associated with the bodies.

No clear-cut geological dating is possible. A postquam date is provided by the underlying sediment which belongs most probably to part of the Younger Pediments.

A possible antequam date is provided by the calcified crust above the burial layer which, to our knowledge, never occurs in relation with historical or Neolithic sites. A conservative estimate would be "more than 4,000 B.C."

3. The Nile deposits in front of 117 have been intensely prospected in the search of a possible living site. Many artifacts of Upper Paleolithic industrial complexes are scattered, but only two concentrations were found, neither directly related to the burials.

At a small distance from Locality 117, and lower on the slope, bare shells of *Corbicula* and *Unio* are scattered around 154 m. absolute elevation (Atlas fig. 34). One spur of fluviatile sand, connected to a dark soil zone still reaches 151 m. absolute elevation; its edge is connected to remnants of a dark gray paleosol. Around this spur, the Nile deposits are limited to 142-143 m. absolute elevation. Locality 2012 is a small Qadan site, on sand, and 2013 is a small but very rich concentration of Sebilian artifacts in brown quartzite.

On geological grounds, a relationship between the occupation at 2012 and the burial site at 117 is not excluded.

The gray silt of the lower aggradation reaches 113 m. absolute elevation.

4. South of 117, Locality 2001 is a surface Site on bare Nubia Sandstone at 149 m. absolute elevation.

The artifacts are made in both brown quartzite and chert pebbles; they include characteristic elements like semicircular scrapers and endscrapers. The industrial complex is not yet identified.

5. Localities 81 and 83 are situated a short distance from each other. They were studied in the same profile (Atlas figs. 36-37).

A lower deposit of strongly compacted and calcareous silt with sand and gravel intercalations belongs to the lower part of a first aggradation. It contains rolled artifacts and fossils in poor condition: *Cleopatra bulimoides, Unio willcocksi,* and *Corbicula vara.*

The first aggradation was truncated by erosion; the deposition of a younger fluviatile sediment followed thereafter. The surface of disconformity bears a faint soil development. The younger sand deposit ended with oblique gravel lenses at Locality 81, around 140-141 m. absolute elevation. Sand and gravel contain a rich molluscan assemblage: abundant *Cleopatra bulimoides;* many *Unio willcocksi* and *Corbicula vara;* fewer *Viviparus unicolor* and *Valvata nilotica;* and some *Bulinus truncatus* and *Gyraulus costulatus.*

The fluviatile gravel of 81 contains very many artifacts in both brown quartzite and chert: redeposited Qadan and Sebilian industrial complexes. The Qadan artifacts are absolutely fresh, and the Sebilian artifacts are slightly weathered.

At 83, a rich industry in brown quartzite and

very few cherts rested on the eroded surface of the lower silt; the upper formations were also eroded there. The problem of the relative dating of the various industrial complexes arose.

Investigating laterally the contact between the upper fluviatile sands and the lower silts, we found no artifacts. On the contrary, a few artifacts of brown quartzite were lying on the slope of the younger sand between 81 and 83, which seemingly made a link between both localities. We admit that pure concentrations of Sebilian artifacts originally rested on the top of, or were embedded in, the sandy formation. Recent wind action deflated the sandy area, leaving eventually the artifacts of 83 on the harder surface of the lower silt. The gravel benches, being more resistant, remained partly as residual reliefs in their original position.

6. Three kilometers north of 81-83, Jebel el-Sahaba ends abruptly on the Nile with cliffs of about 60 m. This is a very young feature in the landscape, the Nile actively cutting the nose of the Jebel. A fault is visible in the cliff, displacing the beds of Nubia Sandstone with a downthrow of the southern block and an uplift of the northern block (Atlas fig. 38).

The vertical displacement of the marker bed of oolithic ironstone is approximately 12 m. This bed was at 180 m. absolute elevation at Locality 69 near Jebel Shaitan; it is at 140 m. absolute elevation at 122 facing Arkin Island. It disappears below the modern floodplain a few meters south of the fault. North of the fault it is around 130 m. absolute elevation again. The general tectonic slope of the southern block is about 5 m/km.

Such a small tectonic movement can have little direct influence by itself on the landscape development, but it must be understood that it is part of a more general tectonic pattern of block-faulting which affected the whole region.

7. North of Jebel el-Sahaba, at Kashkush, Locality 17, the Scandinavian Expedition dug up A- and C-group cemeteries which afforded good profiles in the lower fluviatile aggradation (Atlas fig. 39). As in almost all Dynastic cemeteries, the A- and C-group tombs have been placed in the deep, gray, heavy silt of the third, lower Nile aggradation. The highest elevation of the eroded surface of the silts here is at about 129 m. abso-

lute elevation. The floor of one of the tombs rested on the substratum of the Nubia Sandstone and showed the basal, sandy, and gravelly layer of the silts which contained *Etheria elliptica* and a few rolled artifacts.

A sheet of gravel is spread between 130 and 132 m. absolute elevation; it is a remnant of the edge of the fluviatile formations. A somewhat higher sheet of gravel can be followed between 137 and 140 m. absolute elevation, which corresponds with the retreat of the middle aggradation and part of the Younger Pediments spread from the wadis. This sheet of gravel butts against the jebels.

8. Due east of Kashkush, at 2 km. inland, are situated the Localities 6, 35, and 36. Localities 6 and 36 are two inselbergs reaching 230-237 m. absolute elevation; their tops were exceedingly rich in debitage.

Sheets of mined and flaked raw material of brown quartzite are spread from quartzite outcrops and lie above thick remnants of reddish yellow paleosols exposed in a number of basin-shaped depressions. A hole dug at Locality 6 showed no trace of artifacts in its depth. The typology is Denticulate Mousterian at 36B and Nubian Mousterian with bifaces at 6.

Locality 35 is down from 36, below a scarp facing east. The absolute elevation was not measured, but according to the position, shape, and outlook of the gravel sheets, it is an outcrop of the Older Pediments. Quite a few Acheulean artifacts were found at the surface in abraded or rolled condition, together with fresher Levallois debitage.

ARKIN DISTRICT

1. This district has been surveyed by several parties and thoroughly explored and excavated by the Polish team. The numbering of sites is, therefore, heterogenous; to avoid confusion we are keeping the original numbering.

Between Nag Ambi and Nag el-Arab occur, a short distance apart, several sites with exceedingly rich and fascinating typology. They all belong to stages of the lower Nile aggradation (Atlas figs. 40 to 44).

2. Locality Dibeira West 1 (DIW 1 or D-1) was the first site to be explored (Atlas fig. 41). The profile was open between 131 and 135.5 m.

absolute elevation. The main industrial level of Arkinian typology is situated between two silt and sand deposits; it slips down toward the Nile, with the upper portion between 131 and 135.5 m. absolute elevation being almost *in situ*, and the lower portion being washed under fluviatile deposits at 131.5 m. absolute elevation.

A look at the details of the stratification seems to indicate that the prehistoric population lived on a sand bar at a slightly higher level in that portion of the site which is now barely denuded. Small modifications of the water channels may account for the partial washout. The site has been dated on charcoal at 7,410 B.C. ± 180 years (WSU-175).

There is almost no soil development below the industrial level. An upper industrial level is included in the top of the second sand and silt complex. There can be no big difference in the chronology of both industries.

3. Locality Dibeira West 51 (DIW 51 or D-51) is situated a couple of hundred meters south of DIW 1 and at a somewhat lower elevation—129 to 131 m. absolute elevation (Atlas fig. 42). The profile shows three oblique superposed complexes of silt and sand, the middle one containing many artifacts, burned stones, charcoal, and bones in disorder. It is also an Arkinian industrial complex as at DIW 1, lower level. It has been entirely redistributed and included in a sand bar deposit. The site has been dated on charcoal at 5,750 B.C. ± 120 years (WSU-176).

4. Locality Dibeira West 53 (DIW 53 or D-53) is situated 500 m. north of Locality DIW 1, at 127-128 m. absolute elevation (Atlas fig. 43). The profile, only 1 m. deep, shows a thin interlayer of gravel between silt and sand deposits. The Shamarkian industrial complex is more evolved than the Arkinian. The high content of artifacts seems to be the result of the riverine sheet wash of a cultural horizon. The position is thus similar to that of the derived DIW 51 industry, but one younger in age.

5. Locality Dibeira West 50 (DIW 50 or D-50), a couple of hundred meters to the north, lies between 126 and 127 m. absolute elevation (Atlas fig. 44). A Pre-dynastic settlement of Shamarki type was still partly embedded in the top of a lower silt deposit; a fireplace was still *in situ*. The site has been covered by a quiet sedimenta-

tion of finely stratified silt, without much disturbance. A date on charcoal gave 3,650 B.C. ± 200 years (WSU-174).

6. The Arkin-Shamarki sites form a comprehensive sequence of settlements related to the progressive lowering of the Nile high water between 7,550 B.C. and 3,550 B.C. People lived preferentially along the shores or on nearby sand and silt bars. These sites were partially washed away by high floods. The settlements moved down with the receding water level.

The chronological sequence of sites is fully demonstrated, from the highest to the lowest: D-1, D-51, D-53, and D-50.

7. Besides these important prehistoric sites, an interesting feature is the presence of a discontinuous gravel bench along the floodplain at about 5 m. above it, around 126-127 m. absolute elevation. It contains rolled artifacts and many gravel elements of foreign origin. It can be compared to 514 in the Abu Sir-Buhen district and also to the gravel accumulated at 522 which will be described later on (Dibeira East).

8. At about 2 km. northwest of Sites D-1 to D-50, W. Chmielewski excavated Arkin 8, a subsurface living floor containing an "Upper Acheulean of Khor Abu-Anga type" industrial complex in brown quartzite.

The site is situated at about 166 m. absolute elevation, in a very shallow wadi slightly lower than the subdued outcrops of the Dabarosa formation in the area. It is in direct association with a quartzose pediment in a 7.5 YR matrix (Atlas fig. 45).

9. Slightly lower in the same shallow wadi, around 163 m. absolute elevation and below, occur residual outcrops of gray "pseudo-travertine" with distinctive microrelief, strongly carved out by wind action (Atlas fig. 46).

They lie on a fill of coarse sand and gravel in a gray matrix which rests on eroded Nubia Sandstone; atypical artifacts of brown quartzite found near the base of the fill (Chmielewski) suggest that the Arkin 8 living floor is older than the pseudo-travertine.

The true nature of the latter remains doubtful, as the original structure has been destroyed by an intense development of calcic concretions. Has it been a travertine or unusual remnants of old fluviatile silts? They would be, in this case, the only occurrence of a "Proto-Nile" fluviatile formation at 42 m. above present floodplain.

10. Several profiles were dug by W. Chmielewski at Locality Arkin 14, between 146 and 152 m. absolute elevation (Atlas fig. 47).

A trial pit at 152 m. absolute elevation showed a thin residual cover of fluviatile silt, rich in *Corbicula vara*, resting on hardened pediment with 7.5 YR matrix. According to the position, this silt belongs to the highest Nile aggradation.

The trenches of Arkin 14 show a small lens of fluviatile silt at 147 m. absolute elevation, preserved between two sheets of pediments. The upper sheet of pediments interdigitates with the lens of silt and has much similarity with the Younger Pediments. The lower sheet, more hardened and reddish, is comparable to the Older Pediments.

A few scattered Paleolithic artifacts, including an almond shaped biface, have been recovered from the truncated paleosol horizon capping the lower sheet. This demonstrates that the Acheulean surface extended below 147 m. absolute elevation prior to the Nile aggradations.

DIBEIRA EAST DISTRICT

1. The transect profile between Qadrus to Nag Baba, Nag el-Ikhtiariya, and to a few kilometers inland is one of the most demonstrative. It will be described here from the highest to the lowest level.

At about 4 km. from the Nile stand several tabular inselbergs at elevations between 215 and 230 m. absolute. They are capped with hard banks of brown quartzite, of low quality as a raw material; the concentrations of artifacts and workshops are consequently small.

Nearer to the Nile, a conical inselberg stands east of El Ikhtiariya at 200 m. absolute elevation. Between it and the Nubia Sandstone outcrops of Nag Faqir Tibirki, 2 km. south, extends a large embayment once filled with fluviatile deposits up to more than 155 m. absolute elevation.

Most of this alluvial fill is now eroded or covered with wadi sand and rubble, but a complete profile is still preserved in the northern section, at the foot of the 200 m. conical inselberg we mentioned. Wadi erosion has been less active there, leaving a fringe of fluvial deposits.

2. The complete profile integrates several lo-cality numbers, given at various times by various surveyors and archaeologists: Localities 34, 96, 303, 1028, 3400, and 3401. Numbers 96 and 303 were ill-located and fell into disuse.

Five groups of sediments are separated by stratigraphical discontinuities and different associations of artifacts as follows: (*a*) unstratified pediments with no artifacts, 153 m. absolute elevation and higher; (*b*) thick cover of dune sand retained in a pre-existing valley, from below 140 to 148 m. absolute elevation, Industry A (Khormusan) being included in the top; (*c*) fluviatile aggradation post-Industry A (Khormusan) and pre-Industries C and 1028 (Qadan and Halfan), from below 137 to 155 m. absolute elevation; (*d*) fluviatile aggradation post-Industries C and 1028 (Qadan) from below 134 to 149 m. absolute elevation; and (*e*) fluviatile aggradation up to 135 m. absolute elevation.

The description of these groups and of their units follows.

3. Pediments are exposed below the highest silts of Locality 3401 (Atlas figs. 48, 49). A residual hill of fluviatile silt is preserved there. Corresponding beaches lie at 157 m. absolute elevation south of Wadi Halfa.

4. A thick cover of dune sand lies below the remnants of the first fluviatile aggradation (Atlas figs. 48, 50, 53 to 56).

In its very top are included one or two (Atlas fig. 55) layers of a Khormusan industrial complex in brown quartzite, characterized by a number of end-scrapers, burins, and strangled blades: Industry A and Industry D (in sq. 208, Atlas fig. 55).

Small patches of the original surface of the living site have been protected by a cover of later silt deposits. A relatively strong soil development penetrated the dune sand during and after the occupation.

The soil development has been complex. Calcic concretions, gypsum, traces of roots, and animal holes (termites?) have been first formed in a rather dry environment. Oxide staining (Fe, Mn) is secondary, formed in a more humid environment resulting probably from the rise of the water. A chemical patina corroded the surface of the artifacts in basic conditions; it is, thus, probably related to the carbonate and gypsum accumulations.

Fig. 3—Locality 34, pea gravel and silt resting on eolian sand.

Most of the Industry A concentration is now lying bare on the denuded surface of the dune sand. It is, in this position, very slightly eolized, but the chemical patina remains specific and valuable for identification.

5. The dune landscape has been covered by a thick alluvial aggradation, which started probably between 135 and 137 m. absolute elevation; we put it in correlation with the highest aggradation observed at Locality 3401. Dune sand and Industry A are frequently derived in the basal silty layers: SILT E, F, G of Locality 34 (Text fig. 3).

To this fluviatile aggradation are related the silty sands resting also on dune sand at a lower elevation: SILT B, C, D, together with D.S.R., D.S.B., D.S.C., D.S.R., D.S.T., and FL.S.A. These layers are obliquely cut by a later erosion surface, marked by the occupation of Industry 1028 and the oblique edge of Locality 3400. SILT E, F, G of 34 are similarly cut and dissected by an erosion surface at 34.

6. Later fluviatile deposits include sand, silt, slab gravels of local origin, and pebble gravel including elements of foreign origin such as chert, agate, jasper, and fresh Precambrian.

They include a new set of artifact types, the Qadan industrial complex. Shells of Nilotic mol-

lusks as well as fragments of bones are rather abundant.

Locality 3400 shows a clear cut contact between the coarse fluviatile sands of this sequence and the silts of a previous aggradation (Atlas fig. 50).

The sand contains a rich molluscan assemblage: many *Cleopatra bulimoides, Bulinus truncatus,* and *Unio willcocksi;* several *Gyraulus costulatus;* and a few *Viviparus unicolor* and *Corbicula vara.*

A piece of wood embedded in the underwater slumpings at 139 m. absolute elevation has been dated 10,600 B.C. ± 460 years (WSU-202). The actual elevation of the water at that time must have been several meters higher, as the fluviatile sand accumulated in a rather deep channel of the river.

R. Fairbridge published a date of 13,000 B.C. ± 300 years (I-533) made on *Unio willcocksi* shell collected in 1961-1962 at the approximate elevation of 20 m. above floodplain (141-142 m. absolute elevation ?), thus probably near Locality 3400. There is a discrepancy of about 2,500 years with the dating obtained on wood.

A little higher along the slope, 1028 is a deflated occupation site still partly *in situ* which has been buried under the fluviatile aggradation. The industrial complex is Halfan (Atlas figs. 50, 57).

The highest and probably latest deposits of the same fluviatile aggradation are the beach deposits of Locality 34, at 149 m. absolute elevation (Atlas figs. 48, 50 to 53).

The pebble gravel includes derived Industry A plus fresh and rolled elements of a Qadan industrial complex. Besides the artifacts, the gravel contains many calcic concretions derived from the highest silt of the former highest aggradation, bones, and an abundance of shells: a large quantity of *Unio willcocksi;* many *Corbicula vara;* several *Aspatharia hartmanni;* a few *Viviparus unicolor, Cleopatra bulimoides,* and *Mutela nilotica.* Two dates made on shells gave 9,250 B.C. ± 150 years (WSU-106) and 9,460 B.C. ± 270 years (WSU-189).

In squares 48-59, a similar gravel containing shells and Qadan artifacts lies below an upturned block of older weathered silt.

The lower part of the slope, under and below the houses, consists of heavy gray silt up to 135 m. absolute elevation. This is the third, lower fluviatile aggradation of the Nile. The surface sites investigated by the Scandinavian Expedition are possibly of that time.

7. Below Nag Baba and Nag el-Ikhtiariya extends a large and almost flat surface of approximately 2 km. width along the Nile. It can be divided into three parts. The central one, reaching 123 m. absolute elevation, is an old island, extending between Nag Batna and Hillet Kudal. The eastern part is an old channel of the Nile, now completely filled up, intensely irrigated and cultivated—a remnant of this channel is still open at 3 km. to the north, between Nag Mariya and Nag Fikrata. The western part is the modern alluvial floodplain at 121 m. absolute elevation.

8. The Scandinavian Expedition investigated a surface site on the northern spur of the island, at Locality 33. It is recorded as Neolithic, with crude pottery and atypical stone artifacts.

A very rich Pharaonic cemetery (Middle Kingdom) has been excavated at Qadrus, or Locality 522. The shafts have shown profiles into the old island (Atlas fig. 58).

The deposit is a coarse fluviatile sand mixed with gravel, in which many rolled artifacts of various industries are included, together with abundant elements of foreign origin, such as chert, jasper, and agate. The shiny patina is typically fluviatile; the gravels are more concentrated towards the top.

A fossil soil zone has developed to about a 40 cm. depth; a brown horizon was indicative of hydroxide and perhaps clay translocation. This soil developed in Neolithic to early Dynastic times.

The shafts of the Pharaonic cemetery were dug into the sand and gravel. The superstructures are missing, and a cover of 15-20 cm. of gravel enriched in carbonate is now spread over the graveyard. Owing to this neutral cover, the tombs entirely escaped robbery in later times.

The mode of deposition of this surface cover has been much debated. Archaeologists maintain that a very gentle flood covered the area, inducing the crumbling of the masonry and the homogenization of the whole cover. The flood should be only slightly younger than the tombs (Middle Kingdom high floods).

No evidence of fluviatile stratification could be detected in the surface cover which is quite homogenous. The carbonate does not seem to have been washed into the gravel. This suggests that the flood, if any, has been very gentle and of short duration.

The town to which the Pharaonic cemetery belonged had probably been destroyed later on as a result of the lateral shift of some modern channel of the Nile.

9. High fluviatile deposits are still visible north of Nag el-Ikhtiariya, for example, at Localities 301 at Hillet Ghâli, 298, 299, 300 at Nag el-Leithi, and 294 along Wadi Sara.

In this area between Dibeira and Wadi Sara, two important Paleolithic sites have been excavated successively by the Scandinavian Expedition and the Combined Nubian Campaign.

10. Locality 1033, formerly 508, is situated 1 km. southeast of Dibeira Station, on a residual hill at an absolute elevation of 163 m. according to the map or 166 m. according to our calculations (Atlas fig. 59). Anyway, it is 8 to 10 m. above the highest Nile aggradation observed at Locality 3401. Being on rather low wadi fills, this site is an intermediary between the "Inselberg" type and the "Older Pediments" type. Big residual boulders of brown quartzite have been

mined and flaked by Paleolithic man; the fragments were spread in two recognizable sheets; and they belong to a Nubian Mousterian without bifaces.

A first sheet of debris rests on lower pediments with red color 5.2 YR dry 5/4; moist 4/6. Its appearance compares closely with the oldest soils of the peneplain and of the top of the inselbergs. Another sheet of debris is embedded in brown to light brown pediments.

11. Locality 80, formerly 1034 (Scandinavian number 132), is situated 2 km. east on a large, flat surface around 200 m. absolute elevation, slightly below outcrops of Nubia Sandstone reaching 209 m. absolute elevation nearby (Atlas fig. 60).

The 200 m. absolute elevation surface is quite extensive in that area, and its remnants can be observed for over a kilometer. This important geomorphological feature links laterally with the Pre-Nile gravel of the west bank, which is only slightly lower near Dibeira West.

A rich Paleolithic site occupies an enormous surface, the dense concentration covering half a square kilometer.

We made only one test pit in the whole area. It showed three discontinuous layers of debris and artifacts, all in brown quartzite, at a depth of about 50 cm. The lower layer rests on a red soil matrix which compares with the lower layer of 1033 (ex-Locality 508) and with the oldest soils of the peneplain. The upper part of the profile is more brown, probably deoxidized. The surface layer of artifacts is strongly eolized and has evidently been concentrated by deflation from portions of the profile above.

All three layers are characterized by Levallois debitage, Nubian cores, Mousterian-like artifacts, and almost no tools; a few fragments of foliated bifaces were found at the surface. The artifacts belong to successive phases of a long occupation of the same site, which is actually no more than a huge workshop.

DIBEIRA WEST DISTRICT

1. A little south of Dibeira Island, at Locality 201 (ex-Locality Dibeira 8) elongated banks of fossil *Etheria* are protruding from below the silts (Atlas fig. 61). A close stratigraphical investigation showed that the *Etheria* beds are located on

FIG. 4—*Etheria* bed at Locality 201.

former underwater outcrops of Nubia Sandstone and that they are associated with, and covered by, the silts of the lower Nile aggradation (Text fig. 4). The highest level of *Etheria* cemented to rocks is at 132 m. absolute elevation. This affords a minimal figure for the low water level at that time. The high water level was several meters higher. In comparison with the present annual fluctuation, 135 m. absolute elevation, that is to say, 14 m. above modern floodplain, is a conservative estimate of the high water level. A similar elevation of the high water level of the lower aggradation was estimated at Wadi Halfa, Kashkush, Arkin, and Dibeira East.

A few *Cleopatra bulimoides* are located between the valves of *Etheria;* at 129 m. absolute elevation, a remnant of gravel capping the silts contains *Corbicula vara* and *Cleopatra bulimoides*. No concentration of artifacts was found in association with these deposits.

2. At about 1 to 2 km. to the north, flat outcrops of Nubia Sandstone occur at a somewhat

higher elevation and are covered by patches of gravel and sand. Locality Dibeira West 3 is situated at the northern tip, between 139 and 140 m. absolute elevation. Two profiles, a few meters apart, are described here (Atlas fig. 62). The lower parts of the profiles are cut into a compacted silt, hardened by calcareous concretions. This is a remnant of the truncated aggradation, now buried under more recent deposits; the situation is comparable to that of 278 in the Khor Musa district and 81 in the Sahaba district.

In the deeper cut, a sand dune rests on the eroded top of the lower silt. This subaerial deposit was followed by a new aggradation up to 140 m. absolute elevation minimum. This is the middle one, as at Localities 278, 1027, 515, 81-83, 34, and many other sites.

The gravel contains many rolled artifacts in chert and brown quartzite bearing a brilliant patina. Fluviatile sand is interstratified. The top of the deposit, now much deflated, was higher.

A rich Mesolithic industry including fragments of decorated ostrich eggshells has been collected at the surface. It belongs to the Shamarkian industrial complex.

3. North of Dibeira West 3 and closer to the Nile, Locality Dibeira West 4 is an extensive and very rich Neolithic site at low elevation. The main concentration is only a couple of meters above the floodplain, resting on the eroded heavy gray silt of the lower Nile aggradation. It belongs to a post-Shamarkian Neolithic, comparable to Dibeira West 50. A dating of 3,270 b.c. (WSU-103) has been cited by W. Chmielewski–R. Schild.

Nearer to the Nile, the concentration disappears in front of an old channel of the Nile filled with humid, salty clay. There are reasons to suspect that the living site extended lower than now, possibly below the modern floodplain, during a phase of low water level which might be called Neolithic recession.

4. Locality Dibeira West 6 is situated 200 m. north of the main concentration of Dibeira 4 (Atlas fig. 63).

A lower, sandy fluviatile formation was cut by an erosion surface on which rests a thin pinkish zone containing artifacts (not yet analyzed). A wedge of silt belonging to the lower Nile aggradation extends on the erosion surface up to about 130 m. absolute elevation. It was followed by

erosion again, hill wash mixed with windblown sand, then by an industrial level of perhaps Neolithic age.

All this complex has been covered by a thick calcareous travertine where traces of plants and algal incrustations are abundant. The travertine is grossly obliquely stratified, showing that it was laid along the slope by water seepage. It certainly has been more extensive than it now is because hardened remnants are still hanging against small cliffs a little south of and slightly higher than Dibeira West 6. This deposit has been used by the Christians to build the Birbet el-Hamâm monastery.

The travertine was caused by seepage of underground water stored under the peneplain during a humid period. Extensive seepage took place at this very point only, so that we are led to admit that a peculiar structure must exist into the bedrock in order to favor the flow towards the Birbet el-Hamâm wadi.

5. About 1 km. north of Birbet el-Hamâm, we traced a topographical profile in a northwesterly direction, starting from the Nile. The following localities are located along this profile: 323 (floodplain); 322 (135 m. absolute elevation); 321 (142 m. absolute elevation, fluviatile gravel); 320 (146 m. absolute elevation, Nubia Sandstone outcrop); 319 (152 m. absolute elevation, highest fluviatile aggradation with usual molluscan assemblage); 318 (157-158 m. absolute elevation, gravel count); 317 (160-161 m. absolute elevation, gravel count); 316 (165 m. absolute elevation, gravel count); 315 (185 m. absolute elevation, gravel count); and 314 (191 m. absolute elevation, gravel count).

Shells of 319 have been dated at 12,650 b.c. ± 100 years (WSU-107), which is probably too young.

The gravel counts were published in the preliminary report. They demonstrate, as at Dabarosa, that a sharp lithological boundary is located between 152 and 158 m. absolute elevation; true Nile aggradations with foreign elements of southern origin are restricted below this level.

The highest Nile aggradation covers a long stretch which is almost continuous between Localities 518-519 to the south (see later discussion) and the mountains south of Faras. The molluscan fauna included in its gravels has been closely investigated. At 319, we observed many *Corbicula vara* and a few *Cleopatra bulimoides* and *Unio willcocksi*.

At 509, 2 km. south, there are many *Corbicula vara* with a few *Cleopatra bulimoides*. Locality Dibeira West 5 is in the same position, 1 km. south.

6. The contact between the Pre-Nile or Dabarosa formation and Nile deposits has been closely investigated at Localities 517, 518, 519, and 520 (Atlas figs. 64-65).

A deep red soil developed in the substratum of Nubia Sandstone between 156 and 160 m. absolute elevation. It is comparable to the strongest soil development of the high peneplain east of Wadi Halfa and to that of Localities 80, lower, and 1033, lower. These soils can tentatively be classified as ultisols. At the moment, ultisols are best expressed on old stabilized geomorphic surfaces in a Mediterranean climate.

The top of the paleosol is strongly hardened by carbonate concretions, revealing an intervening dry period. It has been covered by 3 m. or more of coarse quartz pebble gravel in a red, sandy matrix. These gravels are correlated with the Pre-Nile gravels already described west of the Second Cataract, but they are less thick and less extensive here. The picture is that of a braided stream which gradually increased its transport capacity and eventually covered a large flat area with gravels of increasing size.

The flat surface that was once filled with quartz gravels has been strongly dissected previous to the Nile aggradation.

In the slope rubble of Locality 518, at 154 to 155 m. absolute elevation, abundant and rather crude artifacts in quartz have been collected. They include one biface and many choppers and chopping tools. They belong to several mixed industrial complexes according to W. Chmielewski.

The industrial level, which is not *in situ*, rests in a colluvial reddish brown soil zone; corresponding paleosols, would perhaps also rank in the category of ultisols, red Mediterranean soils, but here only are they faintly developed.

At somewhat lower elevation, Locality 517 locates the edge of the highest Nile aggradation, between 153 to 154 m. absolute elevation. The fine silts are banked against a dark gray paleosol

which is not a vertisol but is, nevertheless, strongly structured. It is an A-C inceptisol locally developed at the edge of the highest Nile aggradation. Fifty meters to the east, at 519, the silts are banked against a fluviatile gravel which contains characteristic foreign elements such as chert, agate, and jasper.

The two broken pieces of a very large subcircular nucleus in brown quartzite were found at the surface of the silts, at a distance of 15 m. from each other.

7. Somewhat to the south of 518, Locality D-52 lies in a similar position, exactly at the boundary between the highest Nile aggradation and the landscape above it.

A reddish soil similar to that of 518 here penetrates the substratum of Nubia Sandstone. Crude quartz artifacts rest on it and have been covered by a younger more leached horizon which rests also on the fluviatile silts. These contain some quartz artifacts washed from their original position on the strand.

A normal molluscan assemblage of *Corbicula vara* and *Cleopatra bulimoides* is associated with the silts.

8. Inland, west of Localities 518 and D-52, a straight profile cuts the ridge of Pre-Nile gravels. This ridge is rather low and narrow, up to 163-165 m. absolute elevation according to our measurements, 161-162 m. according to the map. Behind the ridge extends a depression which was probably cut prior to the Nile terrace aggradations as a result of differential erosion near the more resistant cap of quartz gravel.

A pit dug at 521 showed a redeposited quartz gravel resting on a calcic brown soil where the migration of clay and hydroxides is clearly visible (Atlas fig. 65). This calcic brown soil is possibly of the same age as that of the extensive vertisol development observed at a lower elevation. The bottom of the depression here is at 155 m. absolute elevation.

9. At about 2 km. west of the quartz gravel ridge, and at an absolute elevation of 174 m. is located the workshop of Locality Arkin 5 (Atlas fig. 66). The industrial complex is called "assemblages with foliated points" by W. Chmielewski.

In a very shallow cut, two layers are separated by a reddish soil formation, at some places mixed with it. This complex is covered by more yellow, less oxidized sand.

The reddish brown zone represents a genuine part of the anthropic soil development; it is interpreted as an incipient ultisol.

According to the position in the landscape, this paleosol and consequently the industry must be older than 521 and the main vertisol development.

10. At about 6 km. to the north of Arkin 5 is Locality 499 which shows an unusual elevation of the Dabarosa formation and evidence of its faulting (Atlas fig. 8).

The gravel count is characteristic: quartz, 62 per cent; Nubia Sandstone, 32 per cent; silicified wood, 1 per cent; rolled Precambrian, 4 per cent; and red chert, 1 per cent.

It is the same formation of Pre-Nile gravels which has been followed from Mirgissa to the north. It diminishes in thickness to the north and eventually stands in inverted relief along the Nile near Abu Simbel (see later discussion).

SARA-FARAS EAST DISTRICT

1. We have seen that the highest Nile aggradation follows consistently the foot of the jebels north of Dibeira up to 294 near Wadi Sara, where it is at 151-152 m. absolute elevation. It disappears north of Wadi Sara, where it is replaced by the middle Nile aggradation around 140 m. absolute elevation. So are the Localities 292, 293, 287, 288, 272, and 306. Locality 286 is perhaps the last remnant of the highest aggradation.

2. The paleontological content of 330 and of 503 close by has been carefully investigated. There are many *Cleopatra bulimoides*, somewhat fewer *Unio willcocksi*, and some *Viviparus unicolor*. The topography is even much deflated and undulating between 136 m. absolute elevation at Locality 330 and 138 m. absolute elevation at 503.

The Scandinavian Expedition collected a "microlithic" surface site in the neighborhood.

Shells of Locality 330 have been dated at 10,300 B.C. ± 200 years (WSU-109).

3. From Localities 330-503, we traced a straight profile inland up to an absolute elevation of 230 m. in direction N.145°E. (Atlas fig. 5).

There is no detectable remnant of the highest Nile aggradation. Formations referable to the

Younger Pediments are present as low as 143 m. absolute elevation; formations referable to the Older Pediments are present as low as 160 m. absolute elevation. Elevations of both sheets increase toward the heads of the wadis. The tops of the first inselbergs are at 230 m. absolute elevation. At their foot, situated at about 6 km. from the Nile, the Older Pediments lie between 190 and 195 m. absolute elevation.

Between 160 and 190 m. absolute elevation, the surface layer of gravels has a mixed lithological composition, intermediate between Older Pediments and Pre-Nile gravels composition: much quartz, less Nubia Sandstone, rolled Precambrian, and rare zonated agates, but no jasper and chert except Precambrian brown chert.

In this district, the cover of Pre-Nile gravels extends along the east bank and no longer to the west of the river.

SARA-FARAS WEST DISTRICT

1. North of the Dibeira West district, the landscape is cut by a very large wadi flowing from a northwest direction, almost at a right angle to the Nile. A dissected landscape rises north of it. The morphology shows a disrupted diagonal pattern which repeats itself behind Faras. The main trend of the wadis and scarps is N.45°W.-N.135°E. with a secondary trend at a right angle to it.

When we consider the geomorphology only, there are strong reasons to suspect a direct tectonic influence. To the southeast of the main tectonic scarp, hard banks of brown quartzite lie at about 175-185 m. absolute elevation; at Locality 325, above the main scarp, they stand obliquely at 265 m. absolute elevation, and lower. Very intricate faults were indeed evidenced in the front zone of the range, between Localities 325, 326, 327, 328, and 329. They are so intricate there that we were not able to map them in the short time of a first survey. As a whole, we have to deal with the fractured spur of a big faulted block, in front of the depressed area where the Nile flows. Rotational faulting can be inferred from the overall picture.

The same pattern repeats itself to a smaller extent, but more closely west and north of Faras. The landscape rises suddenly above 250 m. absolute elevation and is fully peneplained.

From the Second Cataract area to here, the landscape expresses consistently the major influence of block-faulting.

2. Remnants of the Pre-Nile gravels can be sparsely followed on the surfaces situated south of the faulted zone, around 180 m. absolute elevation. They then disappear entirely on the west bank, but they merge on the east bank south of Khor Adindan at a similar elevation.

The origin and the extension of the Pre-Nile gravels would be an important problem to solve, but it falls outside the present scope of investigations. As a working hypothesis, we suggest that the deposition of this gravel followed the main tectonic disturbances, filling a tectonic depression while the inselberg landscape was progressively carved out.

The Nile valley itself developed later, crossed the Pre-Nile gravels where it could, and contributed relatively little to the landscape development; it can be viewed as an occasional channel, where water happens to flow, not as a mature stream with its drainage pattern.

3. Turning now to that channel, we see a very slight development of the highest aggradation at 150-151 m. absolute elevation around Faras East. This deposit has been almost entirely replaced by a middle Nile aggradation, now undulating around 140 m. absolute elevation, then by a large extension of the heavy gray silts of the lower aggradation up to about 133 m. absolute elevation.

4. No important prehistoric sites were found in or on these formations. The attention must be focused on historical sites such as cemeteries, Aksha temple, and Faras Kom.

Cemeteries were put as a rule in the heavy gray silt of the lower aggradation, none of them in the alluvial floodplain.

5. At Aksha, the line of houses follows closely the edge of the floodplain. The substructures of the temple of Seti I-Ramses II and related formations of the floodplain were described in a previous publication (Loc. 18, Atlas fig. 68).

The location of the temple of Aksha shows that the surface of the modern floodplain was already in existence there more than three thousand years ago. The temple was out of reach of high floods.

The present floodplain was built to a large extent in Old Middle Kingdom times, after the Neolithic recession of the Nile. A decrease of the water level started in New Kingdom times. A rather long period of low water permitted the encroachment of dunes during Meroitic times; high floods resumed in Christian times, and a new encroachment of dunes is now in progress.

North of Aksha, the Nile followed in Pharaonic times the old meander left behind Faras, toward Adindan Island. The depression shows a peculiar morphology: large young dunes which are partly moving, partly dissected by wind, and partly fixed by tamarisk trees surrounding irregular depressions. The highest absolute elevation of some dunes is 133 m.; the lowest absolute elevation of some depressions is 115 m., thus below the high water level.

This topography is obviously very young, and sand dune accumulation is still very active behind Faras. The existence of a line of vegetation along the water is the primary factor for sand fixation. There has been a general migration of the dunes from west to east as they readjusted themselves along the water border where vegetation grows.

We suspect that the same general picture is valid for the historical interpretation of the Kom of Faras.

BALLANA-MASSMASS DISTRICT

1. The most important excavations and profiles are situated at Ballana, west bank (Atlas figs. 69 to 73).

Locality 8899 gives an overall picture of the succession of the main Nile deposits (Atlas figs. 69 to 71).

An extensive lower vertisol formation is largely exposed behind the village, up to slightly higher than 140 m. absolute elevation. An irregular but continuous network of deep and large cracks starts from the surface, going down to depths of several meters. Their pattern is evidenced by the quarrying activities of the villagers, who used the mixed clay of the fillings for improvements of their fields, leaving the hard compact black clay in relief.

A large dune formation covers the cracked surface of the lower vertisol. Its top includes two horizons with Sebilian artifacts in situ (Ballana formation).

This succession has been covered by an aggradation of the Nile, starting with a Low Humic Gley soil development in the sand dune, then following with a deposition of laminated silt with small gastropods, and ending with several meters of compact silt up to 145 m. absolute elevation. This upper silt also shows slickensides and cracks of the vertisol type.

Younger Pediments rest on the upper silt up to 149 m. absolute elevation. They can be followed inland along the nearby wadi, where they rest on a sheet of Older Pediments visible between 144-150 m. absolute elevation at the foot of the cliffs, climbing somewhat higher inland.

2. Locality 8859 is located in the same area, slightly to the east. A series of pits exposed an aggradational sequence of deposits resting on dune sand (Atlas fig. 72). This aggradation is comparable to the upper silt of 8899, but the facies of the deposits are different here: little silt, much redistributed dune sand, and pure fluviatile sand and gravel reaching an elevation of 142.5 m. Where the front of the dune sand joins the lowermost silt lenses (133.5 m. absolute elevation) a few Halfan artifacts were scattered. They are comparable to those of Locality 443 and 2014 in Sudan (dated respectively 14,550 B.C. ± 500 years and 17,200 B.C. ± 375 years). There is thus a broad consistency between these results. Associated charcoal has been dated 16,650 B.C. ± 550 years (WSU-318).

Locality 8896 is a site at ca. 142 m. absolute elevation; several cultures are mixed, resting on a high standing remnant of dune sand and under a thin veneer of silt. There is a radiocarbon date on charcoal of 12,050 B.C. ± 240 years (WSU-329).

Both dates pinpoint excellently a major oscillation of the Nile from regression to aggradation.

3. In the same area again, there are several outcrops of the top zone of the interstratified dune sand; this is due to the fact that calcic concretions hardened the soil profile in the early times of the next aggradation.

At Locality 8863 (Atlas fig. 73), two soil zones with definite leaching are superimposed. Calcified root casts developed later and were directly covered by the silt aggradation.

At 8898 (Atlas fig. 73), a well defined industrial horizon with Sebilian typology was included in the top zone of the dune sand, already mixed with fluviatile grains. It is associated with a leached soil zone.

4. Locality 8935 is situated at Ballana South (Atlas fig. 74). A complex of fluviatile silt and pediment gravel containing mixed artifacts rests on a remnant of dune sand, up to a maximum absolute elevation of 144.5 m. They are in the same position as the upper sequence of 8899.

5. In front of Abu Simbel, east bank, large flat surfaces extend at about 43-44 m. above present floodplain (Atlas fig. 75). They are covered with a rather thick deposit of coarse gravel; quarrying activities of the Abu Simbel Salvage operation exposed profiles into this gravel in a number of pits.

According to the lithology, the absence of foreign components, the very red matrix, the correlation holds good with the Pre-Nile gravels of the Dabarosa formation around Wadi Halfa-Dibeira (Atlas fig. 76).

The mode of deposition here is definitely fluviatile; the terrace gravels stand now in inverted relief as a result of their greater resistance to erosion. The wadi extending back towards Nubia Sandstone scarps dissected the gravel on a small scale only.

6. On the west bank again, the Tushka area is situated north of Abu Simbel.

The highest recorded elevation of fluviatile deposits is at Locality 78 (Atlas fig. 78), 144-145 m. absolute elevation. This record can be accepted as accurate, judging from the specific relationship existing there between the fossiliferous silts, the sheet of pediments, and the rockfalls at the foot of the cliffs of Nubia Sandstone.

7. Only one set of fluviatile deposits is detectable in the large embayment situated behind the elongated village of Tushka. There is the same succession as in the Ballana area: leached soils developed on top of a dune sand, then calcic concretions, followed by the drowning of the dune landscape and the deposition of silts, sand, and gravel.

At 8886 (Atlas figs. 77-78), a surface site was collected; the industry was probably originally included in a sandy fluviatile deposit which disappeared by deflation. Deflation is very active there, and it progressively lowers the natural surface, eroding the fluviatile formations away.

8. At Locality 8905, a small cluster of sites was partly preserved in their original position. The absolute elevation is around 140-142 m., not much below the highest elevation of silts recorded in the area.

On a general spread of dune sand comparable to the Ballana formation, occur here and there remnants of fluviatile deposits which correlate with the upper silt of Ballana.

The silt has been almost entirely eroded away here, owing to continuous deflation, leaving as witness fossil *Corbicula* and *Unio* shells, calcic concretions, and pebbles more or less eolized; some small areas stand in relief for they are more resistant to erosion. It seems that heaps of stones, concentrations of artifacts and hearths, or a denser concentration of calcic concretions had a protective effect.

Traces of occupation by man, burials, and artifacts were recovered from the mounds *in situ*. The occupation has possibly been multiple, both ante- and postdating the development of calcic concretions.[2]

A dating on charcoal included in silt gave 12,550 B.C. ± 490 years (WSU-315). This date appears to be correct, and would refer to an occupation prior to the Sahaba maximum.

9. Younger deposits are limited to narrow strips along the river and consist essentially of coarse highly polished gravels, rich in foreign elements and rolled artifacts of mixed origin (Atlas fig. 79). They reach 132-134 m. absolute elevation; their position is comparable to that of the last aggradation of the Nile (Arkin) in the Wadi Halfa-Dibeira area.

10. Molluscan assemblages are generally less abundant and diversified than they are in the Wadi Halfa area.

A great abundance of shells was found at Mass-mass in an elongated depression situated at about 20 m. above floodplain. We found very many *Cleopatra bulimoides*, fewer *Corbicula vara*, and some *Viviparus unicolor* and *Unio willcocksi*.

DEFINITIONS OF FORMATIONS

A major distinction must be made between

three groups of deposits having different lithological content and different soil associations.

The oldest fluviatile deposits contain only local gravel such as quartz, Nubia Sandstone, silicified wood, and brown chert; foreign elements such as jasper and variegated agate are absent. Strongly oxidized soils are associated with them (2.5 R to 2.5 YR). They will be referred to as the "Pre-Nile group."

Outside the narrow corridor of the valley, erosional processes of pedimentation gave rise to the system of lateral wadis in which the Older Pediments still subsist to some extent. Soils of 5 to 7.5 YR hue are associated with them. What happened in the river channel at that time is unknown, as no contemporary deposits have been authenticated (see dubious occurrence at Arkin 8). Their conjectural existence should be referred to as the Proto-Nile group.

Inside the channel of the valley, deposits related to the present Nile system never rise above 157 m. absolute elevation, 35 m. above the modern floodplain. They will be referred to as the Nile group.

Mention has been made in the foregoing descriptions of several bodies of sediments inside the Nile group; they can be considered as "formations," a formation consisting itself of several "units," layers, lenses, etc. The wording "terraces" which has been applied in a previous publication (de Heinzelin and Paepe, 1965, in Wendorf, 1965) is misleading in this instance because little or nothing usually remains of the morphological surfaces related originally to the "formations." We have to deal, in fact, with a number of deposits encased in each other, all of them being truncated by sheet erosion, gullying, and predominantly wind deflation. A constant deflation of long duration modeled the land surface in such a way that its appearance no longer resembles the classical terraced landscapes of intertropical and temperate areas. In order to put the accent on the "rock-units" concept of our analysis, we adopted the wording "aggradation" for labeling each consistent body of fluviatile formation, an abbreviated form of "Nile aggradation phase."

Each aggradation is the result of a rising water level which induced a broader and deeper sedimentation into the fluviatile channel.

---

[2] Excavations made by Wendorf and Albritton in 1966 provided a large amount of material, artifacts, and human and vertebrate remains. These will be described separately.

Two aggradations are separated by a "recession," an abbreviated form of "Nile recession phase," in which sedimentation was limited to a narrow channel so that erosion could proceed laterally.

There has been no essential opposition between the sedimentation processes in both aggradation and recession phases, but the fluctuating water level caused drastic changes in the pattern of sedimentation. This is why distinct bodies of sediments are still recognizable as rock-units despite the fact that the morphological units have now vanished.

A closer insight on the mechanism of sedimentation-erosion leads to the following reconstruction of events :

1. Mean Nile level increasing, positive aggradation: building up of silt-and-sand alluvial floodplain and islands in periods of high floods. The channel of the river is very deep; gravel and coarse fluviatile sands washed in channels with constant high water velocity.

2. Mean Nile level decreasing: high floods limited to deeper channels. The water table is still very high so that gullying can proceed very quickly in the soft sediments previously accumulated. Islands and levees are less subject to gullying due to faster depletion of the water table.

3. Mean Nile level oscillating: gullying almost stabilized, extension of vertisols in the embayments, cutting of benches; landscape subjected to deflation and accumulation of dune sands at the edge of the depressions.

4. Mean Nile level increasing: drowning of previous features, remodelling of channels, recession of the vertisols upstream in the embayments.

Pre-Nile Group

Although certainly complex in nature and in age, this group cannot be subdivided for the moment because of the lack of detailed mapping. It is accordingly taken as one complex formation, named Dabarosa. The type-locality is the gravel ridge situated at 4 km. from the Nile, west bank, above the name Dabarosa on the 1/25,000 map, at an absolute elevation of 180-185 m.

Similar gravels extend to the north, cross the Nile toward Faras East, and delimit large terraces in inverted relief in front of Abu Simbel. They presumably disappear in the gorges of the

Kurusku Highland. The following absolute elevations were noted:

Mirgissa: top above 200 m. (link with pediments and residual mantle from Nubia Sandstone outcrops).

Locality 235 (Buhen): 166 (base) to 192 m., 26 m. thick.

Locality Arkin 8 (Arkin): 165 (base) to 185 m., 20 m. thick.

Localities Arkin 5 and 520 (Dibeira West): 160 to 163 m. (or higher), over 3 m. thick.

Locality 499: 180 to 185 m. and from 217 to 222 m., 5 m. thick, evidence of faulting.

Faras East: 180 m., thin.

Abu Simbel East: 160 to 163 m., 3 m. thick.

This shows that the Dabarosa formation was accumulated by some Pre-Nile river system in a general direction south-southwest to north-northeast. In the area between Abu Simbel and Adindan, a depression was already in existence, bound by scarps of the major block-faulting episode.

Later on, a younger faulting episode displaced the gravels and caused fresh escarpments, particularly west of Dibeira and Faras.

Proto-Nile Group

What happened in the Nile valley between the Pre-Nile and the Nile group is entirely conjectural. The only deposit which could possibly be a witness is the pseudo-travertine near Locality Arkin 8.

Nile Group

This group of formations is characterized by its close relationship with the modern Nile in every respect: faunal assemblage facies, mode of deposition, mineral content of the sediments, and extension strictly limited to the narrow belt of the valley, usually less than 5 km. across.

The associated soils are poorly developed, never reddish. The Younger Pediments are the lateral facies of the wadi deposits. The successive formations are described hereafter.[3]

Ikhtiariya Formation

After a strong erosion of the Pre-Nile group

---

[3] Absolute elevations indicated hereafter are relative to the Wadi Halfa area. Elevations of corresponding levels are somewhat lower in Egyptian Nubia (Ballana-Tushka area).

and, if any, the Proto-Nile group, somewhat be-low 135 m. absolute elevation, a deep channel occupied the present course of the valley. Dunes extended across this valley, forming the Ikhtiariya formation. Locality 34, with a lower dune sand below a capping of silt, is the type locality.

Dibeira-Jer Formation

Incipient stages of Nile aggradations are found across 135 m. absolute elevation followed by regular and rapidly accumulating silt layers and sand bars similar to present Nile deposits.

The type-locality of the Khormusan industrial complex is a living site included in the aggrada-tion at 149 m. absolute elevation and dated 20,750 B.C. ± 280 years (possibly a little older if the carbon was slightly contaminated).

The very highest beaches are well expressed and very fossiliferous at 504 (east bank) and at 235 (west bank), both at 157 m. absolute elevation. Local observations show that the Nile floodplain itself was a little lower, around 156-157 m. absolute elevation. The usual elevation of the top of the aggradation is between 153 and 155 m. absolute elevation; its largest and most impressive extent is the Wadi Halfa airfield.

The last stages of the aggradation contain at some places characteristic accumulations of calci-fied roots and stems, remnants of a drowned vegetation, together with lenses of windblown sand. It is the Jer facies.

At the edge of the drowned basin, vertisols developed in alternating seasonal conditions (cracked clays or black tropical clays). They have left many traces in the Khor Musa-Wadi Halfa area, which can be correlated with the lower vertisol of Ballana in Egypt.

Ballana Formation

The water receded to about 133 m. absolute elevation, inducing a dissection of previous de-posits and local extensions of dune sand and wadi fans.

Windblown sand was spread from the west, the direction of the present dominant winds. At Ballana (Egypt), the dune sand of the Ballana formation is sandwiched between the Lower and the Upper Vertisol. In its top are included the oldest stages of the Sebilian. The Khormusan

tradition was not yet extinct, as evident at Site ANW-3 and at Gemai.

The type locality is 8899, which has dune sand with a Sebilian occupation in the top.

Sahaba Formation

The Nile rose again up to about 147 m. absolute elevation depositing side by side silts, fluviatile sands, and gravels. They contain frequently a great abundance of fluviatile and lacustrine shells, altogether the richest assemblage of fossil Nilotic mollusks.

The deposits underwent later truncation by deflation, and their top occurs in most instances between 141 and 144 m. absolute elevation. The Sahaba formation must seemingly be divided in two units according to observations at Localities 278 and 8859. Deposition started with a thin cover of silt and vertisols. After a short recession there was deposited the higher and thicker cover of fluviatile sands, silts, and gravels. At Ballana, a thick cover of cracked clays overlies the Ballana dune and its Sebilian level.

Three separate industrial complexes were in existence and are found in the silts or in the sand-and-gravel beaches: Sebilian, Halfan, and Qadan.

The type locality is 81, fluviatile sand and gravel above the lower silt. Qadan and Sebilian artifacts are included.

Birbet Formation

A short recession of the Nile is evidenced by small disconformities and encroachments of wind-blown sands; the river dropped to less than 130-129 m. around 9,000 B.C.

The youngest date of a Sebilian site is of that order: 9,050 B.C. ± 140 years at 1024. The Qadan industry lasted probably a little longer. Locality D-6, which is below a wedge of silt, is the type locality.

Arkin Formation

The Nile rose again up to 135 m. absolute elevation, depositing fresh silts and fine mica-ceous sand. This Arkin formation receded pro-gressively with the water level during approxi-mately 4,000 years.

On the west bank exclusively appeared a new industrial complex, the Arkinian which seems to have evolved *in situ.* Datings of sites at 135 m. and 131 m. absolute elevation are, respectively, 7,410 B.C. ± 180 years and 5,750 B.C. ± 120 years.

The Arkin formation still contains a Pleistocene mollusk assemblage including fossil forms such as *Unio willcocksi* and *Corbicula vara* which later disappeared.[4]

The type-locality is D-1, a silt bank with an Arkinian industrial complex dated 7,400 B.C. ± 180 years. Subsidiary type-localities are D-51, D-53, and D-50.

Qadrus Formation

The very last stages of the Arkin formation around 126 m. absolute elevation already contain a Neolithic industrial complex, dated at 3,650 B.C. ± 200 years. During later Neolithic and Predynastic times (around 3,350 B.C.) a sudden drop of the Nile exposed large surfaces of the river bed, and incipient soils could develop. At Qadrus, a gravel bank bears such a soil, which has been itself buried and covered by Middle Kingdom graves.

Locality 522, a gravel and soil formation cut by Pharaonic tombs, is the type-locality.

Early-Middle Kingdom Floodplain

The building of the modern floodplain started sometime during the A-Group and Early Kingdom periods. Most of the Predynastic occupation sites lie buried under later silt aggradation or have been destroyed by the meandering channels. This is why so little is known about this period when domestication occurred, whereas corresponding cemeteries situated at higher levels are still detectable.

Locality 18, below Aksha temple, is the type-locality.

Meroitic Recession

According to archaeological data, minor oscil-

lations occurred in historical times: high level during the Middle Kingdom; low level during the Meroitic period, and resuming of high floods during the Christian occupation.

The type-locality is 18, with ancient dunes below the Christian occupation.

THE NILE HIGH WATER CURVE

The method used in reconstructing the oscillations of the Nile High Water Curve has been described in a previous publication (de Heinzelin, 1965). The method takes into account over 20 radiocarbon datings and all possible evidence of former high water levels, excluding equivocal geomorphological evidences (fig. 5).

A comparison of the Curve with the successions of paleoclimatic events elsewhere leads to the following conclusions:

1. The Nile High Water Curve reflects a succession of paleoclimatic events which occurred in the higher basin of the White Nile, Blue Nile, and Atbara.

2. Peaks of High Water correspond to the colder phases of the Late Upper Pleistocene-Holocene (Stadials).

3. The general parallelism of the climatic fluctuations in the Northern Hemisphere, and in tropical and equatorial regions, is strengthened.

CLIMATIC FLUCTUATIONS IN NUBIA

Pre- and Proto-Nile Groups

The widespread distribution of red and reddish paleosols interpreted as ultisols and associated to these groups is indicative of the influence of Mediterranean climatic conditions as a whole. All these paleosols are now cracked by desiccation and covered with windblown sand. The older the soils, the redder they are, which seems indicative of a progressive maturation under a sequence of climatic impulses. The number and duration of these phases is unknown because systematic investigations along these lines were outside the scope of our program, and only occasional observations were possible. This subject is closely related to the dating of Lower and Middle Paleolithic sites, and it would have deserved the attention of a special project.

Nile Group

Local paleoclimatic evidence during the later

---

[4] The modern *Corbicula* is *C. consobrina*, distinct from *C. fluminalis* (Asia) and *C. vara* (fossil). As for *Unio willcocksi*, most authors agree on the use of this name for the Pleistocene shells; it is kept here for the sake of uniformity, but it is in fact a synonym of *U. abyssinicus*, living species now restricted to the Lake Tana area, where the water is colder than in the Nubian Nile.

Our interpretation is that the Nilotic faunal assemblages were primarily controlled by the fluctuations of water temperature and that the Upper Pleistocene Nile was colder than it is at present.

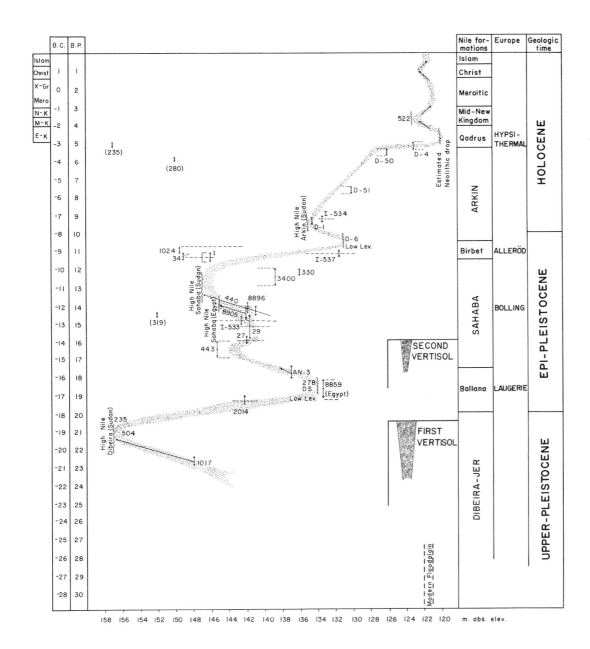

FIG. 5—Nile High Water Curve showing associated sites.

part of the Upper Pleistocene must be sought independently of the Nile High Water Curve.

The water of the river was certainly colder than now, as indicated by the presence of *Unio willcocksi* which has disappeared in the modern fauna except in the Lake Tana area. This name, *U. willcocksi*, used by most authors for the fossil specimens, must fall into synonymy with the name *U. abyssinicus* of the Lake Tana species. The replacement of *Corbicula vara* by the modern *C. consobrina* is supposedly a response to the same change of environment. The fish fauna is inconclusive.

Living conditions on land are reflected in some way by the associations of mammals and land snails. Khormusan, Halfan, and Qadan sites contain bones of *Bos primigenius, Equus, Hippopotamus,* and antelopes, in general a host of grazing animals which could not live there now. A land snail now restricted to less desertic conditions is commonly found in large accumulations inside the Younger Pediments, and traces of termite nests in sand suggest the presence of a vegetation cover, at least over the sands of the valley.

The complete dryness of the present climate of Nubia is a quite convenient point of comparison. In the absence of cultivation, the vegetation is now restricted to some grass and scrubs along the edge of the river and on islands, and in exceptional instances, in very loose patterns in the bottom of some large wadis.

Evidence from peculiar paleosols points also to a more humid climate in the Late Upper Pleistocene. Percolation of rain water was great enough to develop locally spodosols, the remnants of which are often related to the Sahaba formation and the land surfaces formed at that time. The vertisols, being mainly due to the rise and fall of the water in embayments, are no good as climatic evidence. At present, they have a distribution which ranges from desertic to Mediterranean climates.

The Younger Pediments are definitely more oxidized and chemically weathered than the modern wadi deposits. The large wadis, for example Khor Musa, had a rather good supply of water which was able to transport and stratify coarse gravel. At the same time, the climate of the aggradation phases was not altogether devoid of desertic influences, especially on the east bank as windblown sand interfingers at some places with alluvial formations.

During the recession phases, large dunes encroached on the Nile valley on both sides, and the climate was possibly somewhat drier.

The present extremely dry climate was probably already established in Neolithic times and has suffered little variation since then. Storage of fossil water diminished progressively, and ultimately the vegetation cover vanished as well.

LANDSCAPE DEVELOPMENT

A tentative synthesis of historical geology is offered in Table 1.

SUBSTRATUM

North of Wadi Halfa, the substratum consists of Nubia Sandstone, a continental deposit of Cretaceous age (Said, 1962). It once formed a continuous sheet over the Precambrian area which extends to the south, the Batn el-Hajar, where residual remnants of Nubia Sandstone still cap some mountains.

A long erosional cycle took place during the Tertiary, since the Paleocene or Eocene (at least 40 million years), already scraping the cover of Nubia Sandstone from the core of the Batn el-Hajar.

On the Nubia Sandstone plateau, a peneplained landscape was established at some unknown date; it was still dominated by low inselbergs with smooth outlines.

The nature and the main trend of the hydrographical system at that time are conjectural. There has probably been a direct link with Arabia in a general southwest-northeast direction; the large wadis of Darfur and Kordofan, Wadi Howar, and Wadi el-Melik are perhaps the latest witnesses of this hydrography.

In some shallow basins, lake beds were deposited and occasionally partly silicified. The same is true of the Hudi chert in the Shendi area.

NEOGENE AND LATER

Despite the many gaps in our information, it can be useful to sketch tentatively a somewhat reasonable account of the events.

This reconstruction must be taken as a sort of working hypothesis, to be tested in the future. It can be drafted into four comparative stages[5] (Atlas fig. 83).

Stage 1—Faulting

After the peneplanation was accomplished, a tectonic activity of the block-faulting type started. There is every reason to consider that it is a later offshoot of the main taphrogenesis of the Red Sea and Central African Rift Valleys.

The first rift movements started toward the end of the Oligocene (25-30 million years). If somewhat later, the block-faulting processes in Nubia started during the Neogene (5-25 million years). They have rejuvenated several times since

---

[5] No reference to "geological" stages as time-units.

TABLE 1

Fluviat. Deposits		Wadi Deposits	Paleosols	Fauna	Industrial Assemblages	Absolute Datings	Time Stratigraphy
Groups	Formations						
Nile	Recent dunes and Sand Veneer Islands Floodplain	Dunes Gullying Occasional Floods	Dessication and retractation Extensive deflation	cf. historical evidence	Islam Christian Meroitic New } Kingdom Middle } Early		Holocene
	Qadros	Younger Pediments	Incipient Brown Soil	[Domestication]	A-Group and Predynastic Neolithic	5,300	
	Arkin				↑ Shamarkian	5,500 See N H W C	
	Birbet			Corbicula vara and Unio abyssinicus U. willcocksi	Arkinian	9,500 11,500	
	Sahaba		Main Spodosols... Second... Vertisols	Main Zootecus insularis	Sebilian		Late
	Ballana			Bos primig. Equus Hippo Antelopes	↑ Qadan		Upper
	Dibeira-Jer		First Vertisols		↑ Halfan	~20,000	Pleistocene
	Ikhtiariya				Khormusan	>23,000	
Change of drainage		[Old Surface]			Mousterian and Lupembo-Sangoan		Upper and
Proto-Nile	[evasive]	Older Pediments	Ultisols	unknown	Upper and Middle Acheulean	not dated	Middle Pleistocene
Change of drainage		Unknown					
Pre-Nile	Dabarosa	General Pedimentation ~200 m. level	"Red Soils"	unknown	none	not dated	Unknown
		Long Period of Erosion					
Substratum							
Nubia Sandstone	Sandstone f. plants Mudstones Oolithic Ironstone Sandstone Quartz Gravel						Cretaceous
Batn-El-Hajar	Dykes Granites Metamorphics						Precambrian

then. As in the Rift area, the extrusion of volcanic bodies and dykes preceded or accompanied the main faulting (Western Desert).

Erosion progressively shaped the edges of the faulted blocks, and an incipient river or wadi system adjusted itself to the new geomorphic pattern.

Stage 2—Pre-Nile System

A large and thick body of quartz gravels was deposited in a southwest-northeast direction, from the Western Desert to the V-gap in the Abu Simbel plateau (Said and Issawy, 1964, map fig. 1; in Wendorf, 1965). This is the Dabarosa formation, which shows mixed characters of pedimentation and true fluviatile processes; it was undoubtedly of long duration.

The river system cannot be reconstructed as yet; it occupied locally the depression where the Nile now flows, but the lithological components of the gravels are quite different.

A major geomorphic surface developed sideways around 200 m. absolute elevation. Red soils are associated with this platform and the Dabarosa formation. They are comparable to the ultisols of the Mediterranean region, where they also usually cap the oldest geomorphic surfaces.

Stage 3—Older Pediments and ? Proto-Nile System

Renewed block-faulting followed, including the dissection of the 200 m. platform, further recession of the cliffs, and extension of gullies.

This has again been a period of long duration; very little stratigraphical evidence remains, apart from remnants of "Older Pediments" in the wadis. From their repartition, we know that the landscape ultimately reached a situation not very different from the present one. A main depression stabilized probably around 130-150 m. absolute elevation, approximately where the Nile now flows.

The dating relies entirely on the typological analysis of Paleolithic sites. The Middle Acheulean came in during the development of the Older Pediments, as artifacts of that type have been found deeply buried. The Upper Acheulean came in during the latest fills of Older Pediments, as artifacts of that type seem to be related to their surface. The sites of the Lupembo-Sangoan and Mousterian affinities are still more surficial (see archaeological reports).

If we compare dates with those obtained by J. D. Clark at Kalambo Falls, we can estimate that most of the deposition of the Older Pediments took place before 50,000 years ago, and that it stopped between 40,000 to 30,000 years ago.

No positive evidence of fluviatile deposits of that age has been found, and we are not able to decide if they ever existed, or if they were destroyed so much that they escaped detection.

Stage 4—Nile System

At some time around 25,000 years ago, a sudden outburst of Nile water discharged from the south around the edge of the Batn el-Hajar, bringing foreign gravels and minerals in abundance.

North of the Second Cataract, water formed ponds in preexisting depressions, and a first major aggradation of alluvial material reached 157 m. absolute elevation. According to the local en-

vironment, various events followed the drowning of the valley: the siltation covered pre-existing dunes, trees were buried, and vertisols developed in calm embayments.

A progressive change of the industrial complexes started—man was now using the foreign material of chert, agate, and jasper pebbles brought by the water.

After completion of the first major aggradation around 19,000 B.C. to 18,000 B.C., fluctuations of the water level induced a complex succession of erosional phases and renewed aggradation. The resulting complex body of sediments has been analyzed previously. The formation of the modern floodplain started after the deep recession of Neolithic times, around 3,000 B.C.

Wind erosion has probably always been active to some extent; it became extremely important in the last millennia, when present climatic conditions were established. Continuous deflation extensively shaped the exposed bodies of soft fluviatile sediments, destroying practically all traces of their original geomorphic features.

Sedimentary bodies in the wadis which correspond in age to the Nile group are the Younger Pediments. They rest in channels cut into the Older Pediments and are associated with moderately oxidized paleosols 5 YR to 7.5 YR hue. They include heavily rolled Acheulean artifacts and flake tools.

PHOTOGEOLOGY OF THE NILE VALLEY NORTH OF THE SECOND CATARACT, SUDAN

Luc Daels

(DEPARTMENT OF GEOGRAPHY, UNIVERSITY OF GHENT)

The area studied stretches along the Nile from the Second Cataract, somewhat south of Wadi Halfa, to Faras.

The scope of this photo interpretational study is to produce a map which shows the extension and mutual relationship of the main geological formations, including the quaternary deposits (Atlas fig. 83).

The elaboration of the interpretational key was based on the field observations related elsewhere by J. de Heinzelin.

PHOTOGRAPHIC AND CARTOGRAPHIC MATERIAL

With the exception of a few minor gaps, the

entire area is covered by ca. 200 airphotos of excellent quality. These were taken in 1956 on a scale of approximately 1/20,000, suitable for a general geological interpretation.

In our set, the photographs do not overlap for more than 5 per cent of their field along a flight line. Only a narrow strip in the lower area of each photograph could be viewed stereoscopically. This was a serious drawback for the interpretation, especially in the area with weak relief features.

The topographic maps on a scale of 1/25,000 are satisfactory; they were used as the base map.

METHOD OF INTERPRETATION

Representative areas were selected according to known data of age, lithology, and morphology of the formations; they were accordingly identified in terms of photographic characteristics: tone, texture, structure, pattern, and shadow. Associated features were taken into account when possible.

Eleven cartographic units were finally recognized and mapped:
1. Precambrian basement
2. Nubia Sandstone
3. Isolated hills and scarps of Nubia Sandstone
4. Dabarosa formation
5. Wadi deposits
6. Nile system, alias remnants of older floodplains
7. Modern floodplain
8. Older islands included in the modern floodplain
9. Old islands
10. Young islands and mud banks
11. Sand dunes.

INTERPRETATIONAL KEYS AND MAPPING

1. *Precambrian Basement*

a) Key—The tonality is dark gray with some spots nearly black. The texture is very fine to fine. The drainage pattern is a close dendritic system, often directly related to a system of joints. The joint pattern is, at some places, orthogonal; and a number of faults are detectable.

The wadis adapted themselves to the zone of weaknesses created by the joints and the faults; they appear as white, being filled with sandy material.

b) Cartographic distribution—The Precambrian basement occurs only in the southern part of the area. Its edge is dissected by the Second Cataract, which shows up between a great number of small islands.

c) Remarks—Some differences in tonality, texture, and pattern reflect lithological variations; however, they could not be mapped separately at the scale of our map.

2 and 3. *Nubia Sandstone*

This unit occurs under three different aspects: the peneplain on sandstone, the marl facies, and the isolated hills and scarps (3).

a) Key—The peneplain and the marl facies are characterized by a medium gray tonality. The isolated hills capped by a hard bank of brown quartzite are dark gray to black in tonality (3).

The texture of the peneplain and of the isolated hills is fine, and the marl facies shows a coarser texture. The drainage system of the sandstone peneplain is loose and lacks orientation. On the marl facies the network is denser, also without orientation.

The relief of all three subunits is almost flat; the stratification shows up along the scarps.

The tops of the isolated hills are flat when not too dissected; their slopes are strongly carved. Several linear structures occur on the west bank of the Nile; they remind one of dykes, but no definite interpretation can be proposed without new field observations.

b) Cartographic distribution—Large extension north of the Precambrian basement.

4. *Dabarosa formation*

a) Key—The pale grayish tonality reflects the high content of quartz pebbles. The texture is very fine. The drainage network forms a typical close dendritic pattern. The surface is flat or gently sloped.

b) Cartographic distribution—Large extension on the west bank in the southern half of the area. The strip crosses the Nile near Dibeira and occurs as smaller remnants on the east bank up to Faras.

5. *Wadi deposits*

a) Key—The tonality is pale grayish, spotted with darker outcrops corresponding to the Older

Pediments. The texture is very fine. The surface is flat, interrupted by the pattern of the wadi courses and by a very dense dendritic network of gullies.

b) Cartographic distribution—These deposits occur over the entire area studied. The side walls are more steeply and deeply entrenched in the Precambrian substratum than in the Nubia Sandstone. A possible interpretation is that a fossil weathering surface has been exhumed from below the Nubia Sandstone.

c) Remarks—Three different subunits were mapped together: Older Pediments, Younger Pediments, and modern wadis. It was impossible to map them separately, due to lack of stereovision.

6. *Nile System (alias remnants of older floodplains)*

a) Key—This unit is characterized by a heterogeneous tonality, medium gray in general, with darker and paler spots. Because of a continuous deflation, the surface shows a rough texture. It is crossed by the hydrographic system, the close dendritic or parallel network of the wadis and gullies.

b) Cartographic distribution—This unit forms almost continuous embankments on both sides of the Nile, varying slightly in width.

c) Remarks—The general appearance is highly variable because the nature of the subsoil is frequently reflected through the thin surface cover. The inhabitation is restricted to this formation and near the Nile.

7. *Modern Floodplain*

a) Key—The tonality is dark; the agricultural practice is important.

b) Cartographic distribution—Narrow strip at low level along the river.

c) Remarks—No inhabitation.

8. *Older Islands Included in the Modern Floodplain*

a) Key—The tonality is pale gray with white patches. The texture is often rough. The surface is flat, at a slightly higher elevation than the surrounding floodplain and the younger islands.

b) Cartographic distribution—They are included into the modern floodplain.

c) Remarks—The presence of both inhabitation and agricultural practice is typical.

9. *Old Islands*

a) Key—Same characteristics as for Number 8, but they lie inside the Nile channel.

b) Remarks—The presence of inhabitation and agricultural practice is typical.

10. *Young Islands and Mud Banks*

a) Key—The tonality varies from dark to white. A sedimentation pattern similar to ripple marks is often present on the mud banks.

b) Cartographic distribution—They occur generally in close association with the old islands, as a prolongation of them.

c) Remarks—No inhabitation, no agricultural practice.

11. *Sand Dunes*

a) Key—The tonality is white and the texture very fine. Forms of windblown accumulation are frequent. No hydrographic network is visible with the exception of a few large wadis which are only partially impeded.

b) Cartographic distribution—Principally on the west bank.

ATLAS OF MAPS, DRAWINGS, AND GEOLOGICAL PROFILES

Compiled by Jean de Heinzelin

In order to avoid a confusing dispersal of the descriptions, we have grouped the documents in a number of arbitrary "geological districts," in the same order as that adopted in the general discussion.

The order of their presentation is the following:

1. Khor Musa district (Sudan, east bank), including a few sites up to Gemai
2. Mirgissa-Abu Sir district (Sudan, west bank)
3. Airfield-Halfa Degheim district (Sudan, east bank)
4. Abd el-Qadir—Buhen district (Sudan, west bank)
5. Wadi Halfa-Jebel Shaitan district (Sudan, east bank)
6. Dabarosa district (Sudan, west bank)

7. Sahaba district (Sudan, east bank)
8. Arkin district (Sudan, west bank)
9. Dibeira East district (Sudan, east bank)
10. Dibeira West district (Sudan, west bank)
11. Sara-Faras East district (Sudan, east bank)
12. Sara-Faras West district (Sudan, west bank)
13. Ballana-Massmass district (Egypt, mostly west bank)

The map, Atlas Figure 1, shows the geographical location of the boundaries of the districts as adopted here and some of the most important sites.

The map, Atlas Figure 2, shows the transects of seven general profiles, exemplary of the geomorphological and tectonic interpretation of the area (Atlas figs. 3 to 9).

INDEXING OF SITES

As stated before, the indexing of sites is largely hybrid, because of the number of surveyors and independent parties which operated. We kept the original numbering. Some surveyors and excavators preferentially used "Locality" or "Locus"; others used "Site" as a general designation. Although this is a matter of convenience, we restrict the meaning of "Site" to a space of ground which has been excavated or which offers an abundance of prehistoric and paleontological material at the surface.

"Locality" has a less precise meaning, such as a survey observation or a purely geological feature.

ALTIMETRY

The determination of the accurate elevations of the profiles has been a major difficulty, owing to the shortcomings of the maps. Several techniques were used, according to the local environment of each site.

Barometric readings were usually made with a Thommen 3B1 altimeter, between known points of the 1/25,000 map, then interpolating an hourly correction. The level of the modern floodplain was determined in most instances from one or two known points. For sites of some importance,

we made as many as three to six readings, taking the median value after correction (for example at Localities 343 and 1017). Sites in close relationship were cross-checked for internal consistency.

It appeared that scattered readings, even affected by an hourly temperature correction, are of no value for close approximation, the corrections being exceedingly high, sometimes up to 40 m. between morning and afternoon.

In some instances, we made full transects with an alidade or an Abney level and a rod (for example, at Localities 34, 81, and 517-521). The results were always in close approximation with the corrected barometric readings.

We estimate that the corrected readings are valid within 1-2 m. at the most, very often less than one meter.

GRAVEL COUNTS

Abbreviations used mainly in gravel counts presented in the figure captions are listed below. The values given are in percentages.

Q:	Quartz
NS:	Nubia Sandstone
BC:	Brown chert
SW:	Silicified wood
RPC:	Rolled Precambrian
FPC:	Fresh Precambrian (includes sometimes G)
G:	Granite
JAC:	Jasper, agate, chert of foreign origin
SH:	Fossil shells
CONCR:	Calcic concretions, rootlike or durinodes
BONE:	Fragments of bones
ARTIF:	Artifacts

Identifications are made according to the authors of the paleontological and typological monographs.

As stated previously, the figures marked "Atlas" in the text references will be found in the special section accompanying this volume.

PLEISTOCENE MOLLUSKS FROM SUDANESE NUBIA

Francine Martin

(ASPIRANT AU FONDS NATIONAL DE LA RECHERCHE SCIENTIFIQUE DE BELGIQUE, BRUSSELS)

INTRODUCTION

THE MATERIAL studied here has been collected by the writer in the Sudanese Second Cataract area of the Nile valley and slightly to the north of it.

For comparison we used the collections of the Institut Royal des Sciences Naturelles de Belgique (IRSNB) and of the Musée Royal de l'Afrique Centrale-Tervuren (MRAC-Terv.).

We wish to express our grateful thanks to W. Adam, M. Glibert, and L. Vandepoel from the IRSNB and to P.L.G. Benoit from the MRAC-Terv. for the help received and for the frequent exchange of views from which we had all the benefit.

We thank especially E. Defrise (IRSNB) and A. Gautier (Geologisch Institut of the University of Ghent) for the kindness with which they helped us repeatedly in their respective fields of biometry and paleontology. We also thank M. Splingaer (IRSNB) for taking the photographs.

Our determinations of species and the correlative mentions of their distribution rest principally on the works of two authors: W. Adam (1957, 1959) and G. Mandahl-Barth (1954). An almost exhaustive synonymy is to be found in these works. We considered, therefore, that we might shorten our own lists of synonymy, keeping only the most usual references. The comments on the distribution of the fossil and modern shells are voluntarily shortened, too, and usually limited to the areas which surround the studied region.

The symbols and formulas used for biometry are stated in the Appendix at the end of this paper.

SHORT DESCRIPTION OF THE SITES

Most of the sites we were able to investigate are remnants of former Nile aggradations. Accordingly, the molluscan assemblages are mainly fluviatile.

Descriptions of the sites are summarized below. The order is the same as that in the distribution chart.

Modern fauna, right bank: Empty shells are found on sandy banks and in clefts of rocks at low Nile level, below Locality 278.

Modern fauna, left bank: Empty shells are also found on sandy banks at low Nile level, southwest of Abd el-Qadir, facing Ganassab Island.

Locality 201: Dibeira West district. *Etheria* beds are cemented to rocks and covered by silts of Arkin formation. The highest absolute elevation of *Etheria* is at 132 m. A few *Cleopatra bulimoides* are located between the valves of *Etheria*. At 129 m. absolute elevation a remnant of gravel contains *Corbicula vara* and *Cleopatra bulimoides*. This site should be similar to, or slightly older than, Locality DIW-1-A which has been dated 7,430 B.C. ± 180 years.

Locality 1027: Khor Musa district near the Nile. One kilometer southwest of Locality 278 lies this large extension of coarse fluviatile sand and gravel at 137-139 m. absolute elevation.

Locality 278: Khor Musa district, along the old railway track and near the Nile. An upper cover of fluviatile sand and gravel is at 139-142 m. absolute elevation.

Locality 515: Mirgissa district. This fluviatile fill, up to 144 m. absolute elevation, consists of coarse, white, very fluid fluviatile sand.

Locality 516: Dabarosa district. So-called South Colorado site. The fine fluviatile silt contains small forms of mollusks, 4 m. above a cultural horizon at 136 m. absolute elevation.

Locality 506: Airfield-Halfa Degheim district. Coarse fluviatile sand is present at 142 m. absolute elevation.

Locality 81 superior: Sahaba district. The oblique gravel deposits at the top of the profile contain many artifacts at absolute elevation of 141-142 m. The industries are mixed: Qadan plus Sebilian.

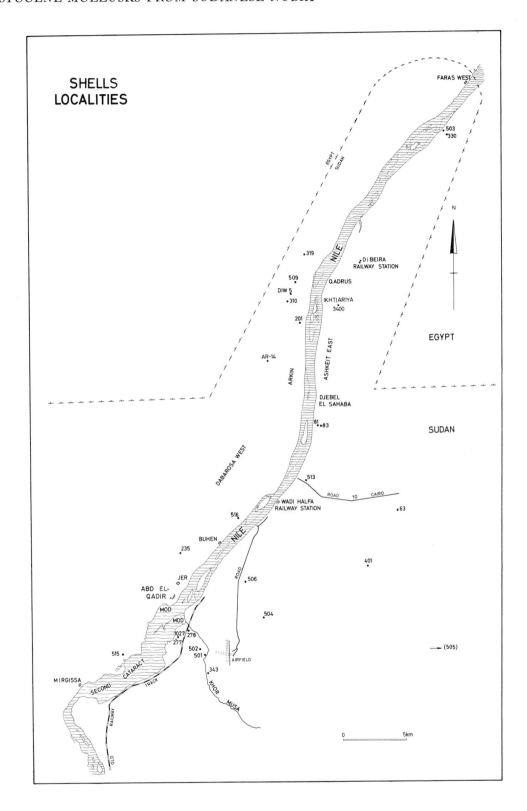

FIG. 1—Locations of the localities studied.

Locality 3400 (formerly indicated as Locality 34 inferior): Debeira East district—El Ikhtiariya site, lower part of the slope. The beach cut in the older fluvian formations is accompanied by underwater slumping and white, coarse, fluid sand containing shells. The date of 10,600 B.C. ± 460 years on wood corresponds to that of "Loc. 34, 370 m. west, elevation 139 m." It corresponds also probably to R. Fairbridge dating on shell of 13,000 B.C. ± 300 years (I-533).

Locality 34 (formerly indicated as Locality 34 superior): Dibeira East district—El Ikhtiariya site. Here is a gravel bench at 149 m. elevation in the upper part of the slope, containing Industry C, Qadan. The dates of 9,250 B.C. ± 150 years and 9,460 B.C. ± 270 years on shells are possibly a little too young.

This is the only place where fluviatile gravel including Qadan material is at such a high elevation, so that interference of young tectonics can be suspected. At the back of the slope, at Locality 3401, an older silt aggradation still reaches 155 m. absolute elevation despite the strong erosion it suffered.

Localities 330 and 503: Sara-Faras East district. These two close localities are in slightly different environments, around 136 m. at 330 and 138 m. at 503, absolute elevations, and contain coarse, white, fluid sand with gravel. Shells have been dated 10,300 B.C. ± 200 years, which is acceptable.

Locality 343: Khor Musa district. Type-locality of Khor Musa vertisol. This one is covered by gravel at 149-150 m. absolute elevation and higher. Shells have been recovered in the gravel cover and in the fillings of open clefts of the top of the vertisol; this is evidence of a sudden sheet of water covering a former landscape.

Locality 501: Khor Musa district. Between Localities 440 and 443-1018. Outlier of the long ridge of sandy gravel going to the west, it sits at 150 m. absolute elevation and slightly above.

Locality 502: Khor Musa district. North of Localities 443-1018. This area is at the top of the long ridge of sandy gravel slightly above 150 m. absolute elevation and up to 153 m. Found *in situ* at a depth of 20-100 cm. At Locality 280, shells in similar position have been dated 4,040 B.C. ± 100 years, which is unacceptable.

Locality 81 inferior: Sahaba district. Shells are in a very poor state of preservation in the lowermost, hardened silt.

Localities D-5 and 509: Dibeira West district. The two localities are in the same stratigraphical and topographical position, slightly above 150 m. absolute elevation.

Locality 319: Dibeira West district. Same as above, this locality is two kilometers north; absolute elevation around 152 m. It has been dated 12,650 B.C. ± 100 years on shells, which is probably too young.

Locality 504: Airfield-Halfa Degheim district. Highest fluviatile molluscan association is at 157 m. absolute elevation, included in fine quartz gravel forming an old bench, probably just outside the old channel of the Nile itself. There is an absence of foreign lithological components.

Locality 235: Abu Sir-Buhen district. Symmetrical to Locality 504 on the left bank, this area is in similar gravel at 157 m. absolute elevation. It has been clearly shown that the gravel is included at the top of the Jer formation, silt containing an abundance of calcified roots. It has been dated 3,170 B.C. ± 100 years on shell, which is unacceptable.

Various localities situated outside the fossil Nile channel contain only *Zootecus insularis* (Localities 63, 505, etc.)

FORMATIONS AND STRATIGRAPHIC SUBDIVISIONS

The samples have been grouped according to their geomorphological and stratigraphical position.

Modern fauna: Present associations of dead shells, comparable to the fossil ones.

Arkin: Latest Nile aggradation, below 13 m. above modern floodplain.

Probable date of Locality 201: Around 8,050 B.C.

Probable range of the Arkin formation: 8,050 B.C. to 4,050 B.C.

Industries of the Arkin formation: Arkinian, late Mesolithic, and Neolithic.

Sahaba: Sandy and silty aggradation frequently around 20 m. above modern floodplain. Up to 28 m. above floodplain at Locality 34.

Probable range of the Sahaba formation: 14,050 B.C. to 9,550 B.C.

Industries of the Sahaba formation: Halfan, Qadan, and Sebilian.

Dibeira-Jer: Highest Nile aggradation, usually up to 30 m. above modern floodplain. Discordant datings made on shells.

Probable range of the Dibeira-Jer formation: More than 23,050 B.C. to 18,050 B.C.

Industry of the Dibeira-Jer formation: Khormusan.

Jer gravel: Lateral facies, very highest elevation of the edge of the Dibeira-Jer aggradation at 35 m. above modern floodplain, east and west of Halfa Degheim (Locality 504, east bank and Locality 235, west bank—both at 157 m. absolute elevation).

Probable date: 19,050 B.C. A date of 3,170 B.C. ± 100 years made on shells is unacceptable.

———

The land snail *Zootecus insularis* has not been included in the distribution chart as it does not appear in fluviatile formations. It is, however, an interesting species as it lives no more in the present environment to our knowledge and is abundantly represented in many subaerial profiles. It is usually associated with land surfaces and soils encased between Dibeira-Jer and Arkin formations.

SYSTEMATIC DESCRIPTIONS

Theodoxus niloticus (Reeve)
Figure 2, Number 1

SYNONYMY

Neritina nilotica Reeve, 1841, Con. Icon. IX, pl. XXXIV, fig. 157.
Neritina africana Reeve, 1841, Con. Icon. IX, pl. XXX, fig. 138.
Neritina (Neritaea) nilotica Reeve, Pallary, 1909, p. 68, pl. IV, figs. 30-33.
Neritina (Neritaea) nilotica Reeve, Pallary, 1924, p. 35.
Theodoxus niloticus (Reeve), Gardner, 1932, pp. 40-43, pl. III, figs. 87-122.
Theodoxus (Neritaea) africanus (Reeve), Bacci, 1951-1952, p. 17.

Localities

Modern: Second Nile Cataract, sandbanks below Locality 278 and below Abd el-Qadir.
Fossil: None.

Description

1. Locality below 278: There are 70 complete

specimens. Their size and number of whorls vary between a maximum of 8.5 mm. in height and 7.5 mm. in width with 2 3/4 whorls and a minimum of 2 mm. in height and 2.3 mm. in width with 1 1/2 whorls.

The test is subglobose. The greatest specimens present a more elevated spire because of the importance of the body-whorl.

The color, visible on few specimens, is yellowish, light brown with dark brown or purplish wavy stripes of irregular pattern.

The color of the apexes varies from frankly reddish orange to usually fading yellowish.

2. Locality below Abd el-Qadir: Except for one shell 5 mm. high and 6 mm. wide, the some thirty collected specimens are not much more than about 2 mm. high and 2.5 mm. wide with 1 1/2 whorls.

Remarks

The discrimination between the two following genera: *Neritina* Lamarck and *Theodoxus* Denis de Montfort relies on the shape of the radula (Pilsbry and Bequaert, 1927, p. 157), a characteristic upon which we cannot rely because of the lack of living specimens. *Theodoxus niloticus* is now abundant in the Nile.

Viviparus unicolor (Olivier)
Figure 2, Number 2

SYNONYMY

Cyclostoma unicolor Olivier, 1804, III, p. 68; Atlas, II, pl. XXXI, fig. 9a-b.
Vivipara unicolor (Olivier), Jickeli, 1874, pp. 235-239, pl. VIII, fig. 30.
Vivipara unicolor (Olivier), Pallary, 1909, p. 62.
Viviparus unicolor (Olivier), Pilsbry & Bequaert, 1927, p. 207, pl. XIX, fig. 1.
Viviparus unicolor (Olivier), Gardner, 1932, p. 27, pl. II, figs. 61-63.
Bellamya unicolor unicolor (Olivier), Mandahl-Barth, 1954, p. 27, fig. 4 a-f.
Viviparus unicolor (Olivier), Adam, 1957, p. 12, figs. 5-7.
Viviparus unicolor (Olivier), Adam, 1959, p. 7, figs. 1-2.

Localities

No modern specimen was found. Localities of fossil material are stated later in the discussion.

Description

This fossil species is rather rare. In spite of

their thick test, the shells are much damaged, rolled, and eroded. The first whorls are usually missing, and very few specimens are complete.

Complete shells vary in measurements from a maximum of 19.1 mm. in height and 13 mm. in width with 4 3/4 whorls to a minimum of 10 mm. in height and 8.6 mm. in width with 3 whorls.

The shape of the whorls is slightly variable— flat or more regularly rounded with sometimes a faint carination extending from the suture of the body-whorl to the last two whorls.

These individual variations are usually mixed in the same population (Localities 515, 506, 81, 3400, 330, and 503).

There are no carinated specimens at Locality 502.

Some tests have a double carination, slight but well visible, on the last whorl. This is the case of the only incomplete little form (maximum width, 11.5 mm.) from Locality 34; also of two specimens with missing upper part (maximum width, 14 mm.) from Locality 330.

The oval aperture is somewhat higher than it is wide or round.

The umbilicus is narrow but open, with a variable developed furrow.

Remarks

1. Taking the remark of Adam (1957, p. 12) into account, we chose, as he suggests, the genus name *Viviparus "sensu lato"* for these African fossil Viviparidae.

2. Following Mandahl-Barth's key (1954, p. 26), the discrimination between the subspecies of *Bellamya unicolor* is rather delicate in this case. Some tests could belong to *Bellamya unicolor unicolor* (Olivier, 1804); some others with very convex whorls and faintly developed furrow could belong to *Bellamya unicolor rubicunda* (von Martens, 1897). We are unable to discriminate between the subspecies in our material.

Lanistes carinatus (Olivier)
Figure 2, Number 3

SYNONYMY
Lanistes carinatus (Olivier), Gardner, 1932, p. 26, pl. II, figs. 52-54.
Lanistes carinatus (Olivier), Mandahl-Barth, 1954, pp. 49-50, fig. 19 a-b.
Lanistes carinatus (Olivier), Adam, 1959, p. 31, pl. 4, fig. 67.

Localities

Modern: None.
Fossil: Only Locality 504.

Description

There are two complete tests with short spire (respectively, 25.5 mm. high, 34.5 mm. wide and 27 mm. high, and 34.1 mm. wide), both with 4 1/2 whorls. The first whorls are very narrow with a sharp peripheral angle. The body-whorl is inflated with a carination all around the broadly open umbilicus.

Fig. 2

No. 1—*Theodoxus niloticus* (Reeve), Second Nile Cataract, modern sandbank below Locality 278, 1.5x.
No. 2—*Viviparus unicolor* (Olivier), Localities 506 and 330, 1x.
No. 3—*Lanistes carinatus* (Olivier), Locality 504, 1x.
Nos. 4, 5—*Valvata nilotica* Jickeli, Second Nile Cataract, modern sandbank below Locality 278, 3x.
No. 6—*Bithynia neumanni* (von Martens), Second Nile Cataract, modern sandbank below Abd el-Qadir, 2x.
No. 7—*Gabbia* cf. *walleri* (Smith), Second Nile Cataract, modern sandbank below Abd el-Qadir, 2x.
No. 8—*Melanoides tuberculata* (Müller), Second Nile Cataract, modern clefts of rocks, 1x.
No. 9—*Cleopatra bulimoides* (Olivier), on the upper line modern specimens of the Second Nile Cataract below Locality 278, on the lower line fossil specimens of Locality 201, 1x.
No. 10—*Bulinus truncatus* (Audoin), Ballana, 1.5x.
Nos. 11, 12—*Anisus planorbis* (Linné), Locality 516, 3x.
Nos. 13, 14—*Gyraulus costulatus* (Krauss), Locality 34 inf., 3x.
No. 15—*Ferrissia* sp. (Walker), Second Nile Cataract, modern sandbank below Locality 278, 2x.
No. 16—*Zootecus insularis* (Ehrenberg), Locality 505, 1.5x.
No. 17—*Caelatura aegyptiaca* (Cailliaud), on the left side modern specimens of the Second Nile Cataract below Locality 278, on the right side fossil specimens of Locality 235, 1x.
Nos. 18, 19—Hinges of fossil *Caelatura aegyptiaca* from Locality 235, 2x.
No. 20—Hinge of modern *Caelatura aegyptiaca* from the Second Nile Cataract below Locality 278, 2x.
No. 21—*Aspatharia hartmanni* (von Martens), Locality 34 sup., 0.5x.
No. 22—*Aspatharia cailliaudi* (von Martens), Locality 235, 0.5x.
No. 23—*Mutela ? nilotica* (Cailliaud), modern specimen of the Second Nile Cataract below Abd el-Qadir, 0.5x.

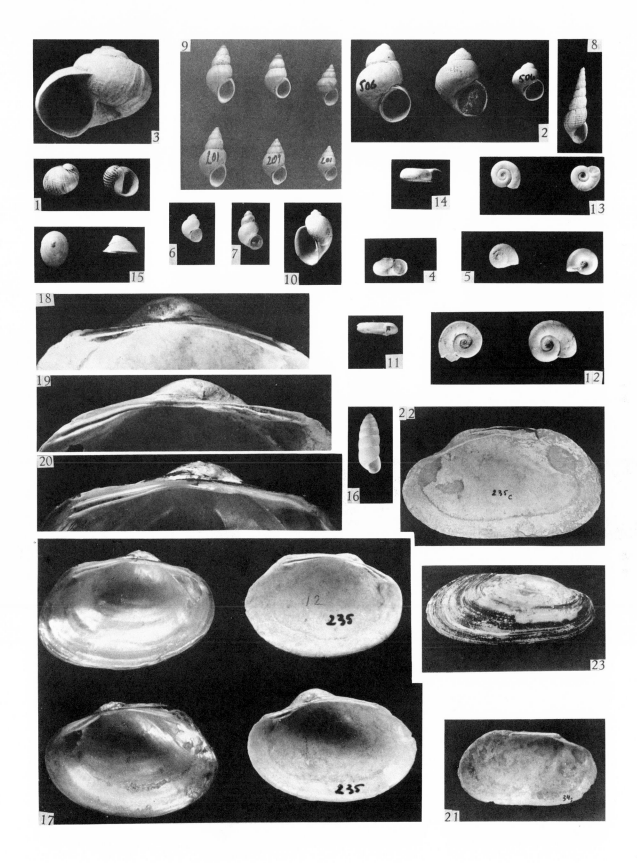

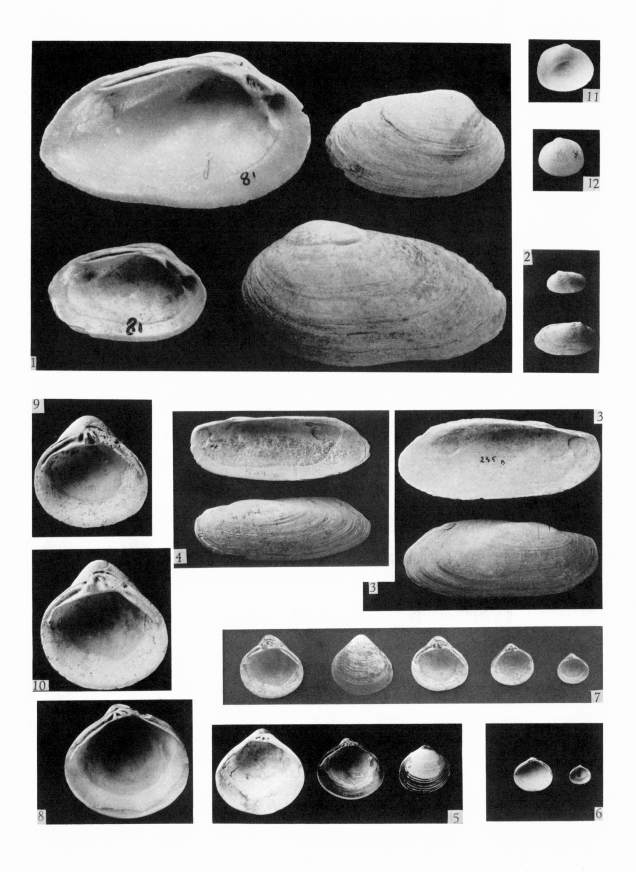

In addition, there is one fragment of body-whorl of 32 mm. width.

VALVATA NILOTICA Jickeli
Figure 2, Numbers 4, 5

SYNONYMY

Valvata nilotica JICKELI, 1874, p. 233, pl. VII, fig. 29.
Valvata nilotica Jickeli, PALLARY, 1909, p. 68, pl. IV, figs. 28-29.
Valvata nilotica Jickeli, GARDNER, 1932, p. 40, pl. III, figs. 135-136.

Localities

Modern: Second Nile Cataract, on sandbanks, 20 shells collected below Locality 278 and only one below Abd el-Qadir.

Fossil: Locality 515, about 12 specimens; Locality 81, about 30 specimens; Locality 3400, about 30 specimens; and Locality 516, about 20 shells plus 5 fragments. All the fossils are well preserved.

Description

Modern shells: The color which is visible on a few specimens, is yellowish or palish gray.

Fossil shells of Locality 516: The diameter of the test varies between 1.9 and 3.7 mm. and the height correspondingly between 0.9 and 2 mm. On ten measured tests, the diameter of the shell is 1.6 to 2.1 times the height and 3.8 to 4.1 times the diameter of the umbilicus. The largest shells have 3 1/2 whorls. The sutures and the umbilicus are deep. The aperture is almost circular.

Remarks

There is a close agreement between our modern and fossil shells of *Valvata nilotica* and the figures of Jickeli (1874).

BITHYNIA NEUMANNI (von Martens)
Figure 2, Number 6

SYNONYMY

Bithynia neumanni (von Martens), GARDNER, 1932, p. 36, pl. III, figs. 84-86.
Bithynia neumanni (von Martens), ADAM, 1957, p. 58.

Localities

Modern: Second Nile Cataract, on sandbanks, below 278 (about 100 complete tests) and below Abd el-Qadir (about 200 complete tests).
Fossil: None.

Description

The shells are obtusely conical and have a glossy and blunt apex. The young specimens look more globose than the old ones. The height goes from 2 to 4 mm.; it is 1.5 times the width for the greatest specimens which count 4 whorls. The whorls are very convex; the body-whorl is much developed and occupies at least half the total height. The narrow umbilicus is either open or covered by a part of the peristome. The aperture is large, with an angular upper part of the regularly rounded lower part; it is usually framed by a distinct edge; and its height is less than half the total height. The surface of the test is smooth with a metallic lustre. The color, rather rarely preserved, is gray.

Remarks

1. The operculum which is used for identification (Pilsbry & Bequaert, 1927, p. 213) is absent.

2. This Sudanese material agrees closely with *B. neumanni*, from Lake Rudolph (in the collections of the MRAC-Tervuren) and from the Chad (in the Dautzenberg collection of the IRSNB).

3. We compared the material with *B. tilhoi* (Germain) from Lake Albert (in the collections of the MRAC-Tervuren). This species looks thinner and shows a sharper apex. The first

FIG. 3
No. 1—*Unio abyssinicus* Martens, Locality 81, 1x.
No. 2—Young specimens of *Unio abyssinicus* from Locality 34 inf., 1x.
No. 3—*Mutela ? emini* (von Martens), Locality 235, 1x.
No. 4—*Mutela* cf. *rostrata* (Rang), Locality 504, 1x.
Nos. 5, 6—*Corbicula consobrina* (Cailliaud), Second Nile Cataract, modern sandbank below Locality 278, 1x.
No. 7—*Corbicula vara* Gardner s. l., Locality 504, 1x.
No. 8—*Corbicula consobrina* (Cailliaud), Second Nile Cataract, modern sandbank below Abd el-Qadir, 2x.
Nos. 9, 10—*Corbicula vara* Gardner s. l., Locality 504, 2x.
Nos. 11, 12—*Sphaerium hartmanni* cf. *mohasicum* Thiele, Second Nile Cataract, modern sandbank below Locality 278, 1.5x.

whorls are more elevated; the body-whorl is less important; and, for a same height, the number of whorls is greater. Only a few among our youngest specimens could perhaps fit the description of *B. tilhoi.*

4. By the way, we recall that Adam (1957, p. 59) has no definite opinion about the specific values of *B. tilhoi* and *B. neumanni.*

GABBIA (GABBIA) CF. WALLERI (E. A. Smith)
Figure 2, Number 7

SYNONYMY

Gabbia (Gabbia) walleri (E. A. Smith), MANDAHL-BARTH, 1954, pp. 51-52, fig. 20 a.

Localities

Modern: Second Nile Cataract, on sandbanks below Abd el-Qadir. (3 specimens).
Fossil: None.

Description

The height goes from 4.5 to 5.1 mm. and is 1.5 times the width. The spire is high with, at most, 4 1/2 strongly rounded whorls, with deep sutures between them. The umbilicus is open; peristome, well distinct from the body-whorl; and aperture, higher than it is wide; its height is less than half the total height. The test is whitish, semi-translucent.

Remarks

Gabbia cf. *walleri* seems to us the most likely determination, though this species is known only from Lake Albert (Mandahl-Barth, 1954, p. 52). There are still some slight differences with *G. walleri* from Butiaba (Lake Albert) determined by Mandahl-Barth in the collection of the Musée Royal de l'Afrique Centrale-Tervuren. The peristome of the specimens from Butiaba is more free, and the ratios of the aperture are more variable.

MELANOIDES TUBERCULATA (Müller)
Figure 2, Number 8

SYNONYMY

Melania tuberculata Müller, JICKELI, 1874, p. 251, pl. III, fig. 7; pl. VII, fig. 36.
Melanoides tuberculata (Müller), PILSBRY & BEQUAERT, 1927, p. 256, pl. XXI, figs. 1-7.

Melanoides tuberculata (Müller), GARDNER, 1932, pp. 31-32, pl. III, figs. 1-16.
Melanoides tuberculata tuberculata (Müller), MANDAHL-BARTH, 1954, p. 57, fig. 24 a-e.
Melanoides tuberculata (Müller), ADAM, 1957, p. 66, pl. I, figs. 13-15.

Localities

Modern: Second Nile Cataract, on sandbanks and in clefts of rocks below Locality 278 and on sandbanks below Abd el-Qadir.
Fossil: None.

Description

This species is rather rare; we found only 15 shells on the whole. The height goes from about 5 to 27 mm. On sandbanks, all specimens are discolored and much eroded, but the typical ornamentation is still visible. Several specimens found in clefts of rocks are fresher; their apex is preserved as well as their beige periostracum marked with darker ochre spots.

CLEOPATRA BULIMOIDES (Olivier)
Figure 2, Number 9

SYNONYMY

Cyclostoma bulimoides OLIVIER, 1804, p. 39, Atlas II, pl. XXI, fig. 7.
Cleopatra bulimoides (Olivier), PALLARY, 1909, p. 63, pl. IV, fig. 16.
Cleopatra bulimoides (Olivier), GARDNER, 1932, pp. 28-29, pl. III, figs. 23-27.
Cleopatra bulimoides cf. var. *richardi* Germain, GARDNER, 1932, p. 29, pl. III, figs. 28-32.
Cleopatra bulimoides et var. *bilirata* Germain, ROGER, 1944, p. 124.
Cleopatra bulimoides (Olivier), ADAM, 1957, p. 65.

Localities

Modern: Second Nile Cataract. (1) Below Locality 278, on silty beach between rocks and in clefts of rocks: 100 shells, first whorls broken; on sandy banks: 10 shells. (2) Below Abd el-Qadir, on sandy banks: 50 shells.
Fossil: Localities 201, 1027, above 278, 515, 506, 81, 3400, 330, 503, 501, 502, 319, and 81 inf.

Description

Modern material:
1. Below Locality 278: One hundred tests

show heights from 5 to 17 mm. On ten tests the height goes from 2.5 to 11 mm.

2. Below Abd el-Qadir: On 50 tests the height goes from 3.5 to 17.5 mm. The state of preservation is usually poor, except for the specimens collected on sandy banks. This species is easy to identify although it can vary in the following characteristics:

The ratio between the height and the width, the former being always greater than the latter.

The ratio between the whorls.

The aperture of the umbilicus, which is more or less covered by the expanded columellar margin.

The development of the nacreous edge around the upper part of the aperture.

The convexity of the whorls.

The color is dark or light brownish, sometimes greenish with darker reddish brown streaks.

The growth lines are generally thin and regular except on the body-whorl of the biggest shells.

Among modern specimens, there is usually no carination, except for three specimens from below Abd el-Qadir.

Fossil material:

The test is thick, yet much eroded; usually, the first whorl is lacking and the aperture is broken. One exception has to be made for the material from Locality 201, where the shells were well preserved between the valves of *Etheria*. In this case, a close comparison between the protoconchs of fossil and modern test is possible. These are similar, smooth and of about one whorl. One specimen of Locality 201 still presents a light yellowish periostracum.

At all sites where many shells could be collected (as at Localities 201, above 278, 515, 506, 81, 3400, 330, 501, and 502) the variation in size is great, ranging from 4 to about 17 mm. in height. There is sometimes a carination or a subsutural shoulder on some whorl of a shell.

We counted at least 80 tests from each locality.

From above Locality 278: about 10 per cent of the specimens have a strong subsutural angulation of the body-whorl; and about 1 per cent of the specimens have a double carina on the body-whorl, with the last and penultimate whorl simply carinated.

From Locality 330: about 6 per cent have a simple carination on the body-whorl.

From Locality 3400: about 1 per cent have a simple carination on the body-whorl.

From Locality 201, where we counted 300 specimens: 12 per cent have a simple carina on the body-whorl; 1 per cent have a double carina on the body-whorl; and 1 per cent have a simple carina on the body-whorl with the last and penultimate whorls doubly carinated.

The shells greater than 12 mm. never bear any carination.

Remarks

The variability of *Cleopatra bulimoides* is well known and has already been stressed by Gardner (1932, p. 28) for the Fayum collection. According to Mandahl-Barth (1954, p. 61), *Cleopatra pirothi* Jickeli could be no more than a geographical race of *C. bulimoides* (Olivier); in some instances there is a continuous variation between the typical carinated *C. pirothi* and the smooth *C. bulimoides*.

BULINUS TRUNCATUS (Audoin)
Figure 2, Number 10

SYNONYMY

Bullinus (Isodora) contortus Mich., PALLARY, 1909, p. 52, pl. III, fig. 39.

Bullinus contortus Mich., PILSBRY & BEQUAERT, 1927, p. 135.

Bulinus truncatus (Audoin), GARDNER, 1932, p. 23, pl. II, figs. 47-51.

Bulinus truncatus truncatus (Audoin), MANDAHL-BARTH, 1957, pp. 26-28, pl. XVIII, XIX, fig. 16.

Bulinus truncatus (Audoin), SPARKS & GROVE, 1961, p. 357, pl. I, figs. o, p-q.

Bulinus truncatus (Audoin), SPARKS & GROVE, 1963, p. 193, pl. I, figs. a-c.

Localities

Modern: Second Nile Cataract, on sandy banks, below Locality 278 (15 specimens) and below Abd el-Qadir (4 complete tests plus 2 broken specimens).

Fossil: Locality 81 (3 specimens), Locality 3400 (about 10 specimens).

Description

Mean height is about 6 mm. The number of whorls varies between 3 3/4 for shells 10.3 mm. high and 6.4 mm. wide and 2 for shells of 2.1 mm. high and 1.7 mm. wide. The whorls are well shouldered. The spire is quite low, more or less obtuse; the last whorls and the body-whorl expand rapidly. The body-whorl is inflated, the ratio between height and width of the test varying between 1.3 and 1.6. The shells from Locality 3400 show a more important variability going from 1.2 to 1.7. The ratio between the heights of the test and of the aperture varies from 1.2 to 1.5. The aperture is always higher than it is wide. The tests show well marked growth lines, which eventually develop a kind of costulate sculpture, especially on the body-whorl. The color preserved on the modern material is pale grayish-yellow.

Remarks

Mandahl-Barth (1957, p. 29, pl. XX, fig. 18) also described a *Bulinus truncatus rohlfsi* Clessin, subspecies of *Bulinus truncatus*. Being unable to distinguish between this subspecies and *Bulinus truncatus truncatus* (Audoin), we use only the species name: *B. truncatus*.

ANISUS PLANORBIS (Linné)
Figure 2, Numbers 11, 12

SYNONYMY

Planorbis planorbis (Linné), GARDNER, 1932, pp. 17-19, pl. II, figs. 25-34.
Anisus planorbis (Linné), ADAM, 1960, pp. 180-181, fig. 42.
Anisus (Tropidiscus) planoribis (Linné), THIELE, 1961, p. 481.

Localities

Modern: None.
Fossil: only Locality 516.

Description

About 12 shells were collected, their diameter ranging from 2.9 to 5 mm. The diameter of the shell is 2.9 to 3.3 times its height and is 2.2 to 2.7 times the diameter of the umbilicus. The whorls are gently increasing; their upper side is more rounded than their lower side. The central part of the upper side of the shell is a little more concave than the umbilicus. A sharp keel bounds the basal part of the last whorl. The aperture is transversely oval, obliquely descending and is higher than the last whorl.

Remarks

This species has been described by Gardner (1932, pp. 17-19) from the Fayum, where it has a wider variability in the positions of the carina.

GYRAULUS COSTULATUS (Krauss)
Figure 2, Numbers 13, 14

SYNONYMY

Planorbis (Gyraulus) costulatus Krauss, PILSBRY & BEQUAERT, 1927, p. 127, fig. 10.
Gyraulus costulatus costulatus (Krauss), MANDAHL-BARTH, 1954, p. 86, fig. 39a.
Gyraulus costulatus (Krauss), ADAM, 1957, p. 103, fig. 24.
Gyraulus (Caillaudia) costulatus (Krauss), HUCKRIEDE & VENZLAFF, 1962, p. 100, pl. II, figs. 6a-8b.

Localities

Modern: Second Nile Cataract, on sandy banks below Locality 278. (3 tests).
Fossil: Localities 81, 3400, 516 (about 12 tests from each locality, plus a few debris).

Description

The modern and the fossil tests have the same aspect. The shells are lenticulate. Usually, their diameter goes from 2 to 4.4 mm., except in Ballana terrace where one specimen reaches 5.2 mm. diameter. The ratio between the diameter and the height of the test lies between 2.3 and 3.1. The diameter of the test is 2.3 to 3.8 times the diameter of the umbilicus.

The depression of the umbilicus is wider than the central depression of the upper side.

The maximum number of whorls is 3 3/4; they are rapidly increasing, evenly rounded on both upper and lower sides. Most tests have no distinct keel.

The aperture is usually wider than the umbilicus but is very variable in position as well as in shape, in the same way that Jickeli (1874, p. 219, pl. VII, figs. 22-23) observed.

Normally, the ribbed growth lines are close-set.

The color of the modern tests is a light corneous grayish-yellow.

Remarks

Following Mandahl-Barth's key, we should have to refer most of the specimens to *G. c.*

costulatus (Krauss) and a few to *G. c. subtilis* Mandahl-Barth. The latter show a more depressed lower side and no distinct keel.

FERRISSIA SP.
Figure 2, Number 15

SYNONYMY
Ferrissia WALKER, 1903, XVII, p. 15.

Localities

Modern: Second Nile Cataract, on sandy banks below Locality 278 (about 40 tests) and below Abd el-Qadir (5 specimens).
Fossil: Only Locality 515 (1 specimen).

Description

The length of the test ranges from about 3 to 5.5 mm. The ratio between the length and the width of the test is rather constant—1.2 to 1.3. The ratio between the length and the height of the test is much more variable—from 1.6 to 3.

The tests are light and whitish, somewhat constricted at half-height. The apexes are symmetrical, translucent; all have been eroded so that the structure of the embryonal shell is nowhere visible.

The basal part of the test shows definite and irregular growth lines.

Remarks

Our material is not similar to that described by Walker (1914, pp. 126-130, pl. VI) and Mandahl-Barth (1954, pp. 119-120, fig. 59), or to that existing in the collection of the Musée Royal de l'Afrique Centrale-Tervuren and in the Dautzenberg collection (IRSNB). We are, therefore, unable to identify it as to species.

ZOOTECUS INSULARIS (Ehrenberg)
Figure 2, Number 16

SYNONYMY
Zootecus insularis (Ehrenberg), GARDNER, 1935, p. 487.
Zootecus insularis (Ehrenberg), SPARKS & GROVE, 1961, p. 360, pl. II, fig. g.
Zootecus insularis (Ehrenberg), THIELE, 1961, p. 554, fig. 637.

Localities

Modern: None.

Fossil: Localities 505, 343, 513, and top Inselberg 63. About 40 specimens from each locality, except for 10 at Locality 513.

Description

The material is not variable and fits in the description of Thiele. The length varies between 7 and 12 mm. The spire has 6 to 8 whorls, which are slightly and regularly increasing.

CAELATURA AEGYPTIACA (Cailliaud)
Figure 2, Numbers 17, 18, 19, 20

SYNONYMY
Unio aegyptiacus CAILLIAUD, 1823, Atlas II, pl. LXI, figs. 6-7.
Unio niloticus CAILLIAUD, 1823, Atlas II, pl. LXI, figs. 8-9.
Caelatura aegyptiaca (Cailliaud), GARDNER, 1932, pp. 46-47, pl. IV, figs. 1-9; pl. V, figs. 6-9.
Caelatura nilotica (Cailliaud), GARDNER, 1932, pp. 48-49, pl. IV, figs. 14-22.
Caelatura parreyssi var. *petrettinii* (Bourguignat), GARDNER, 1932, pp. 49-50, pl. IV, figs. 10-13.
Caelatura (Caelatura) aegyptiaca (Cailliaud), HAAS, 1936, pp. 69-70, pl. VI, fig. 4 a-d.
Caelatura aegyptiaca (Cailliaud), MANDAHL-BARTH, 1954, pp. 126-127, fig. 60.
Caelatura aegyptiaca (Cailliaud), ADAM, 1957, pp. 119-120.

Localities

Modern: Second Nile Cataract, below Locality 278, on muddy humid silt-bank; 75 per cent of the specimens are bivalves.
Fossil: Only Locality 235.

Description

Modern material:
The shells are elongated. The length goes from 25 to 50 mm.; its distribution is shown on Figure 4 upper.

This modern material is rather constant: dorsal and ventral margins are almost parallel, slightly converging in front. The hinge is formed by lamellate teeth; the lateral teeth are longer than the cardinal ones. The position of the umbo is given by the arithmetical mean $\frac{L_2}{L_1} = 1.90$; $\sigma = 0.23$; n = 50.

The growth lines are irregular, and a faint sculpture is limited to the beak.

The exterior of the valves is greenish-brown,

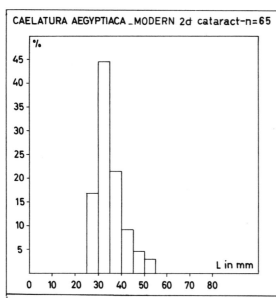

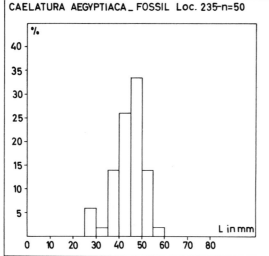

Fig. 4—Growth histogram of *Caelatura aegyptiaca*. Upper—Modern *Caelatura* of the Second Nile Cataract. Lower—Fossil *Caelatura* of Locality 235.

dorsally variegated to pinkish. The interior is pinkish or bluish.

Fossil material:

Around 100 well preserved though eroded tests were found in digging. The length goes from 29 to 55 mm. Figure 4 lower shows their size distribution.

The fossil shells are, as a whole, thicker than the modern ones (fig. 5), and they bear a more irregularly inflated beak.

A greater variability in the position of the umbo is a distinctive character of these fossil shells, compared with the modern ones. Their arithmetical mean $\frac{L_2}{L_1} = 2.1$; with $\sigma = 0.57$; $n = 50$.

Taking the range of both variabilities of modern and fossil shells into account, we find no reason to separate them into two different species.

About 20 per cent of collected tests from Locality 235 show strong irregularities of growth, which even influenced the nacreous layers.

Remarks

It seems to us that this material demonstrates the artificial character of the distinction between *C. aegyptiaca* (Cailliaud) and *C. nilotica* (Cailliaud) as it has already been suggested by Jickeli (1874, pp. 271-273, pl. X, figs. 1-9), Haas (1936, p. 69), and Adam (1957, p. 120).

UNIO ABYSSINICUS Martens
Figure 3, Numbers 1, 2

SYNONYMY

Unio abyssinicus MARTENS, 1866, p. 102.
Unio willcocksi NEWTON, 1899, p. 406, pl. XX, figs. 1-4.
Unio vignardi PALLARY, 1924, p. 40, pl. IV, figs. 16-18.
Unio fayumensis PILSBRY & BEQUAERT, 1927, p. 381.
Unio willcocksi Newton, GARDNER, 1932, p. 51, pl. V, figs. 17-18.
Unio fayumensis Pilsbry & Bequaert, GARDNER, 1932, p. 51, pl. V, figs. 10-16.
Unio abyssinicus Martens, HAAS, 1936, p. 88.

Localities

Modern: None.

Fossil: Localities 201, 1027, above 278, 506, 81, 3400, 34, 330, 503, 501, 502, 81 inf., D-5, and 319. This species is poorly represented by a few much eroded and damaged tests in the following Localities: 201, 1027, above 278, 506, 330, 503, 502, 81 inf., D-5, and 319. No specimens were found in the Jer gravels of Localities 504 and 235.

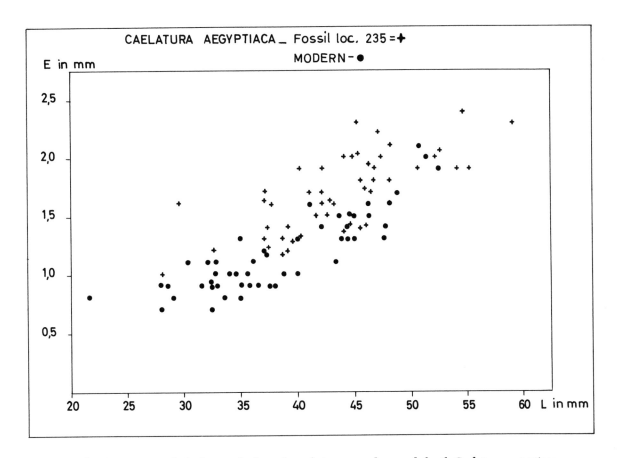

F<small>IG</small>. 5—Graph. Comparison of thickness of the valves between modern and fossil *Caelatura aegyptiaca*.

Description

The valves are elongated and thick. Their lengths vary from about 15 to 80 mm. Figure 6 shows the size distribution of the most important sites: Localities 81, 3400, and 34. The posterior part is more elongated than the anterior part which is much more shortly rounded. The ventral margin presents frequently a depression along which the test is flattened. Both of these characters are strongly expressed by the oldest specimens. The relation between the thickness of the test itself and its total length is expressed in Figure 7 by a curve, which translated in logarithmic coordinates becomes an allometric growth line. The beak projects slightly. The general shape of the tests and the position of the umbos are rather constant as Table 1 shows. Some valves, from Localities 3400 and 34, which are smaller than 30 mm. in length, show minute nodules on and around the umbo. The hinge is strong and thick. The anterior muscle scar is deep. The growth lines are strongly but variably developed, especially on the ventral part of the oldest specimens. Bivalves were found only in Locality 3400 (about 5 per cent of the specimens) and in Locality 81 (about 1 per cent of the specimens).

TABLE 1
M<small>EAN</small> V<small>ALUES</small> <small>OF</small> *Unio Abyssinicus*

Locus	n	$\overline{L}$ mm	$\overline{H}$ mm	$\overline{L}/\overline{H}$	$\overline{L_2}/\overline{L_1}$
81	100	58.3	33.3	1.7	3.4
3400	100	48.2	25.9	1.9	3.4
34(sup.)	100	45.6	25.6	1.8	3.2
330	7	62.5	35.4	1.8	3.4
503	18	53	29.6	1.8	3.4
502	18	48.9	28.0	1.7	3.3

There is to us no observable difference between the fossil specimens (*Unio willcocksi*) and the living species (*Unio abyssinicus*).

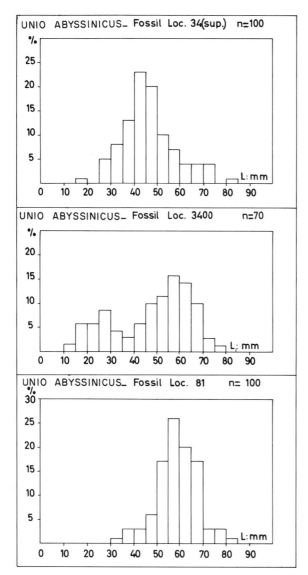

FIG. 6—Growth histogram of *Unio abyssinicus*. Upper—*Unio* of the Locality 34. Middle—*Unio* of the Locality 3400. Lower—*Unio* of the Locality 81.

ASPATHARIA HARTMANNI (von Martens)
Figure 2, Number 21

SYNONYMY

Aspatharia wahlbergi hartmanni (Martens), GARDNER, 1932, p. 53, pl. VI, figs. 6-9.
Aspatharia wahlbergi hartmanni Mts, CONNOLLY in ARKELL, 1949, p. 29.
Aspatharia hartmanni (v. Martens), ADAM, 1957, p. 131.

Localities

Modern: None.
Fossil: Locality 34.

Description

The tests are rather thin. One complete left valve is 77.5 mm. long, 45 mm. high, and has a diameter of 20 mm. The dorsal and the ventral margins are almost parallel, the line of the hinge being slightly curved. The notch and sinulus are distinct. One broken right valve is longer and is 53 mm. high. Two fragments are related, without any doubt, to the same species.

ASPATHARIA CALLIAUDI (von Martens)
Figure 2, Number 22

SYNONYMY

Aspatharia rubens var. *cailliaudi* Martens, GARDNER, 1932, p. 53, pl. V, figs. 29-30.
Aspatharia rubens, Lam. & var. *cailliaudi* Mts, CONNOLLY in ARKELL, 1949, p. 29.
Aspatharia rubens Lam., ARKELL, 1953, p. 10.
Aspatharia cailliaudi (von Martens), MANDAHL-BARTH, 1954, p. 150, fig. 79.
Aspatharia cailliaudi (v. Martens), ADAM, 1957, p. 129, pl. II, figs. 1-2; pl. IX, fig. 1.

Localities

Modern: None.
Fossil: Only Locality 235.

Description

One thick and complete bivalve was 112 mm. long and 63 mm. high, and had a diameter of 38.5 mm.

Remarks

The agreement with Mandahl-Barth's description is perfect (1954, p. 150).

MUTELA ? NILOTICA (Calliaud)
Figure 2, Number 23

SYNONYMY

Mutela nilotica (Cailliaud), PILSBRY & BEQUAERT, 1927, p. 436, pl. XLII, fig. 1.
Mutela nilotica (Cailliaud), MANDAHL-BARTH, 1954, p. 140.
Mutela ? nilotica (Cailliaud), ADAM, 1957, p. 132, pl. VIII, fig. 5.

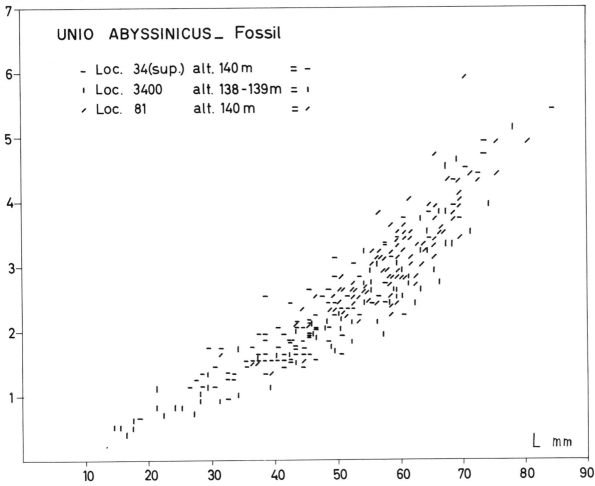

Fɪɢ. 7—Graph. Relation between the thickness of the test itself and the length of *Unio abyssinicus*.

Localities

Modern: Second Nile Cataract, below Abd el-Qadir (2 odd valves).

Fossil: Locality 34 (1 fragment). There are possibly some *M. nilotica* at Locality 235 where they are mixed with *M. emini*. We shall discuss the meaning of this assemblage under the heading of *M. emini*.

Description

Modern material: One complete right valve, solid, elongated, is 99 mm. long and 42 mm. high with a 27 mm. diameter. Its posterior part is higher than the anterior one. One incomplete left valve is smaller. Both specimens have a brownish-olive periostracum and a whitish slightly purplish interior.

Fossil material: One elongated fragment of the left valve was found at Locality 34. It probably belongs to *M. nilotica*.

Remarks

These specimens do not coincide exactly with *M. nilotica* (Cailliaud) "with an almost straight dorsal margin and a parallel basal margin, rising obliquely anteriorly" as described by Mandahl-Barth (1954, p. 140). They would be intermediate between *M. nilotica* (Cailliaud) and *M. emini* (von Martens) as interpreted by Mandahl-Barth (1954, pp. 140-142). On the other hand, Adam (1957, p. 132) states a great variability in the parallelism of dorsal and ventral margins, and he suggests that *M. emini* is no more than a subspecies of *M. nilotica*. As our poor material does not afford convincing proofs of identity, we keep both species names as valid.

Mutela ? emini (von Martens)
Figure 3, Number 3

SYNONYMY

Mutela emini (von Martens), Pilsbry & Bequaert, 1927, p. 435, pl. XLII, fig. 2-2a.
Mutela emini (von Martens), Roger, 1944, p. 141, pl. I, fig. 56.
Mutela var. *emini* (Martens), Franc, 1949, p. 177, fig. 6.
Mutela emini (von Martens), Mandahl-Barth, 1954, pp. 141-142, fig. 73.

Localities

Modern: None.
Fossil: Locality 235.

Description

The valves are solid and well preserved. The length varies from 88 to about 125 mm., and is about 2.4 times the width and almost 4 times the diameter. The specimens of this locality show a wide variability, reaching that of *M. nilotica*. Some wedge-shaped tests exhibit a widening of the posterior margin and a rather distinct inflection between the umbo and the anterior hinge. This is the case for three bivalves and two odd valves which have the typical shape of *M. emini*. In contrast, two other odd valves have almost parallel dorsal and ventral margins, so that they are like *M. nilotica*. Ten fragile fragments of the same locality are doubtful.

Mutela cf. rostrata (Rang)
Figure 3, Number 4

SYNONYMY

Mutelina rostrata Rang, Germain, 1911, p. 212, pl. III, fig. 7.
Mutela (Mutelina) rostrata (Rang), Roger, 1944, p. 142, pl. I, fig. 57.
Mutela rostrata (Rang), Mandahl-Barth, 1954, p. 143, fig. 5.
Mutela cf. *rostrata* (Rang), Adam, 1959, p. 60, pl. VIII, fig 5; pl. IX, figs. 1-2.

Localities

Modern: None.
Fossil: Locality 504.

Description

We collected two bivalves, three single shells, and thirteen fragments. The test is thin and elongated. The length is 2.7 to 3 times the height. Measurements of a complete bivalve are 101 mm. in length and 37 mm. in height, and the diameter is 22.5 mm. Three single valves have a length of about 90 mm.

The anterior margin is rounded, and the posterior one is slender. The ventral margin is slightly convex and sub-parallel with the dorsal margin. The beak is poorly developed. Our specimens best fit the figure of *Mutela rostrata* in Roger (1944, fig. 57).

Etheria elliptica Lamarck

SYNONYMY

Etheria elliptica Lamarck, Pilsbry & Bequaert, 1927, pp. 449-455, pl. XLVI, fig. 1-1a; pl. XXX, fig. 2-2a.
Etheria elliptica Lamarck, Mandahl-Barth, 1954, p. 156, fig. 84.
Etheria elliptica Lamarck, Adam, 1957, pp. 137-139, pl. VI, fig. 8.

Localities

Modern: Second Nile Cataract, below Abd el-Qadir (1 bivalve).
Fossil: Abundant material at Locality 201. This species is poorly represented by one or two fragments at Locality 1027, above Locality 278, and Locality D-5.

Description

Modern Material:
The bivalve (89 mm. long, 76 mm. wide) has a greenish-olive periostracum and a whitish interior. The upper valve is strongly convex. Tube-like prominences stand on both valves.
Fossil material:
The description is based on the fossils from Locality 201. The numerous shells grew close together and made compact banks. The valves are thick, heavy but loosely foliated. Their lengths range from about 50 to 100 mm. The ratio between length and width is very variable. The individuals of this population present two different shapes: about 60 per cent have a smooth surface and 40 per cent have tube-like prominences. The state of preservation does not allow

a very close calculation of their percentage. Such an association of two phenotypic adaptations is difficult to explain. It is usually admitted that smooth and flat valves are better adapted to rapidly running waters and that thorny and convex valves are adapted to calm waters (Franc, 1960, p. 2049).

CORBICULA CONSOBRINA (Calliaud) and CORBICULA VARA Gardner SENSU LATO
  Figure 3, Numbers 5, 6, 8; and Figure 3, Numbers 7, 9, 10

SYNONYMY OF *C. consobrina* (Cailliaud)
Cyrena consobrina CAILLIAUD, 1823, II, pl. LXI, figs. 10-11.
Corbicula consobrina (Cailliaud), PALLARY, 1903, pp. 8-9.
Corbicula artini PALLARY, 1903, p. 9, pl. I, fig. 4.

SYNONYMY OF *Corbicula vara* Gardner *s. l.*
Corbicula vara Gardner, GARDNER, 1932, pp. 58-60, pl. VII, figs. 1-11.
Corbicula artini (non Pallary), GARDNER, 1932, pp. 60-61, pl. VII, figs. 12, 15-22.
Corbicula consobrina (non Cailliaud), GARDNER 1932, pp. 61-63, pl. VII, figs. 25-42, 45-49.
Corbicula africana (non Krauss), GARDNER, 1932, pp. 63-64, pl. VII, figs. 50-54.

Localities of C. consobrina (*Cailliaud*)

Modern: Second Nile Cataract. (1) Below Locality 278 on modern silty beach, between rocks and in clefts of rocks, 131 single valves; on sandy banks, 60 valves, among which are about 20 per cent bivalve specimens. (2) Below Abd el-Qadir, on sandy banks, about 100 valves, among which are about 30 per cent bivalve specimens.
  Fossil: None.

Localities of C. vara *Gardner s. l.*

Modern: None.
Fossil: The material is abundant (over 100 valves) and usually well preserved at Localities 81, 501, 502, 34, D-5, 319, 504, and 235. About 20 per cent of the bivalves were collected at Locality 504 and about 1 per cent of them at Locality 235. At Localities 201, 1027, and in gravels above 278, the material is rare, much damaged, with umbo and growth lines corroded and more or less broken margins.

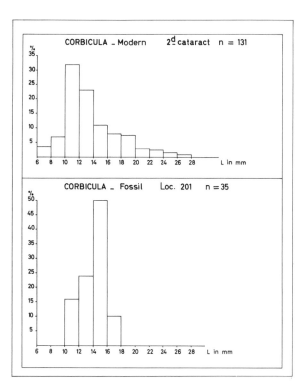

FIG. 8—Growth histograms of *Corbicula*. Upper—Modern *Corbicula* of the Second Nile Cataract. Lower—*Corbicula* of Locality 201.

Description of C. consobrina (*Cailliaud) and* C. vara *Gardner s. l.*

The modern and fossil *Corbicula* differ so much in shape that they can usually be separated at first sight. Thus we are apparently dealing with two different species, and that view has been confirmed by biometry. Both modern and fossil specimens have in common the following characteristics:

The anterior margin is regularly rounded and shorter than the posterior margin.

The distance between the consecutive growth lines increases toward the ventral margin; their total number and their development are strongly variable.

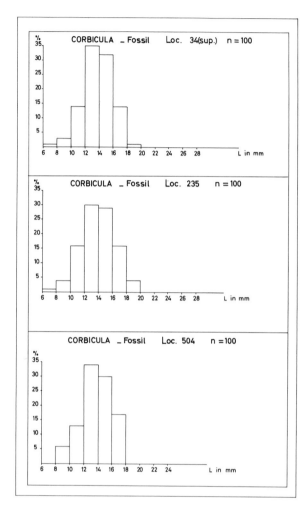

Main differences between the modern and the fossil groups of *Corbicula* are as follows:

Usually the fossils have an almost quadrangular shape. Few specimens are a little higher than they are wide or vice versa (7 to 18 mm. wide). The modern shells are typically wider than they are high (2 to 28 mm. wide). The growth histograms (figs. 8, 9) show the size distribution for some associations. The arithmetical mean of the length for fossil shells is between 12 and 14 mm., for modern shells between 10 and 12 mm. This can partly reflect different sampling conditions, young specimens being more abundant in the samples of modern shells.

The fossil valves are much more solid, thick, and arched than the modern ones. Table 2 shows clearly the differences between these two groups.

TABLE 2

RELATIVE CONVEXITIES OF *Corbicula*

Locus	n	Arith. mean $\dfrac{L}{C} \pm \sigma$
mod.	131	3.36 ± 0.33
81	100	2.60 ± 0.24
34(sup.)	100	2.59 ± 0.22
	67	2.53 ± 0.41
502	56[1]	2.65 ± 0.20
504	100	2.63 ± 0.24

[1] Without the young specimens which are particularly variable.

The umbo of the fossils is much more developed and projecting.

The hinges are similar, but those of the fossils are stronger. Table 3 gives the comparison of the arithmetical means of H_1 and H_2, respectively. The graphs of Figures 10 through 15 express also distinctly this difference and show the

FIG. 9—Growth histograms of *Corbicula*. Upper—*Corbicula* of Locality 34. Middle—*Corbicula* of Locality 235. Lower—*Corbicula* of Locality 504.

When preserved, the growth lines of the umbo are close and thin. The periostracum is never present on the fossils. On modern *Corbicula* the periostracum is greenish-olive to dark greenish-brown; the interior is smooth, bluish, more or less dark, with pinkish spots usually more developed near the umbo of the young specimens.

TABLE 3

MEAN VALUES OF *Corbicula*

Locus	n	$\overline{H}_1$ mm	$\overline{H}_2$ mm
mod.	131	12.8	1.8
201	35	13.1	3.3
1027	3	12.1	2.8
278	16	11.3	2.6
506	5	12.4	2.8
81	100	12.9	3.3
34(sup.)	100	12.9	3.2
343	12	13.0	3.2
502	67	12.6	2.7
504	100	12.9	3.2
235	100	13.0	2.8

TABLE 4
ALLOMETRY OF *Corbicula Vara* AND *Corbicula Consobrina*

Locus	n	$\overline{Y} \pm \dfrac{Sy}{\sqrt{n}}$	$\overline{X} \pm \dfrac{Sx}{\sqrt{n}}$	Sy	Sx	$\alpha \pm \sigma$	r_{xy}
mod.	131	1.061 ± 0.011	0.236 ± 0.012	0.122719	0.135787	0.904 ± 0.030	0.925807
81	100	1.101 ± 0.007	0.513 ± 0.010	0.071763	0.100498	0.714 ± 0.027	0.927242
34$_{(sup.)}$	100	1.104 ± 0.007	0.512 ± 0.010	0.073006	0.100050	0.730 ± 0.035	0.873788
502	67	1.064 ± 0.012	0.428 ± 0.018	0.100000	0.144913	0.690 ± 0.033	0.918056
504	100	1.106 ± 0.008	0.495 ± 0.013	0.078676	0.132211	0.595 ± 0.021	0.936667

TABLE 5
SIGNIFICANCE OF DIFFERENCES BETWEEN INCLINATIONS OF ALLOMETRIC GROWTH LINES OF *Corbicula*

Locus	mod.	81	34$_{(sup.)}$	502	504
mod.		xx 4.733443	xx 3.754011	xx 4.768846	xx 8.480274
81			0.351617	0.560814	xx 3.510561
34$_{(sup.}$				0.812941	xx 3.271666
502					x 2.412015
504					

x—significant test
xx—highly significant test

allometric growth lines in logarithmic coordinates. Table 4 gives the details of calculation to obtain these allometric growth lines. Table 5 gives the results of the test of discrimination between the obtained inclinations of these allometric growth lines.

Remarks

Taking into account our biometrical measurements, we have to state a specific difference between the modern and the fossil groups. As far as the modern group is concerned, it is undoubtedly *Corbicula consobrina* (Cailliaud). The possible synonymy with the Asiatic *Corbicula fluminalis* (Müller) remains a question mark. Concerning the fossil group and after considering the complex state of the synonymy, we choose *Corbicula vara* Gardner *s. l.* as the most appropriate name. It seems to us that *C. vara* Gardner *sensu stricto* applies to extreme specimens of a wide range of variations of the fossil population of the Fayum.

Therefore, *C. vara* Gardner *s. l.* should apply to four species formerly separated in Gardner (1932, pp. 58-64, pl. VII): *C. vara s. s., C. artini, C. consobrina, C. africana.*

The extreme phenotype of *C. vara* Gardner

s. s. is characterized by a very thick test, a strong hinge and a great elevation of the umbo. The measurements of *C. vara* as given by Gardner lie in the prolongation of the scatter diagram, established for our fossil material (figs. 11-15).

SPHAERIUM HARTMANNI CF. MOHASICUM Thiele
Figure 3, Numbers 11, 12

SYNONYMY

Sphaerium victoriae mohasicum Thiele, MANDAHL-BARTH, 1954, p. 167, figs. 87d, 88c.
Sphaerium hartmanni cf. *mohasicum* Thiele, ADAM, 1957, p. 146, fig. in text 25a, pl. II, fig. 8; pl. IV, fig. 2.

Localities

Modern: Second Nile Cataract, on sandy banks, below Locality 278 (8 specimens) and below Abd el-Qadir (2 fragments).
Fossil: None.

Description

We found only a few of these delicate, slightly inflated valves. Their lengths range from 5.6 to 10.2 mm. The ratio between the length and the width is constant: 1.2. Their periostracum is pale and yellowish, with faint growth lines and radial lines which are only visible under magnification.

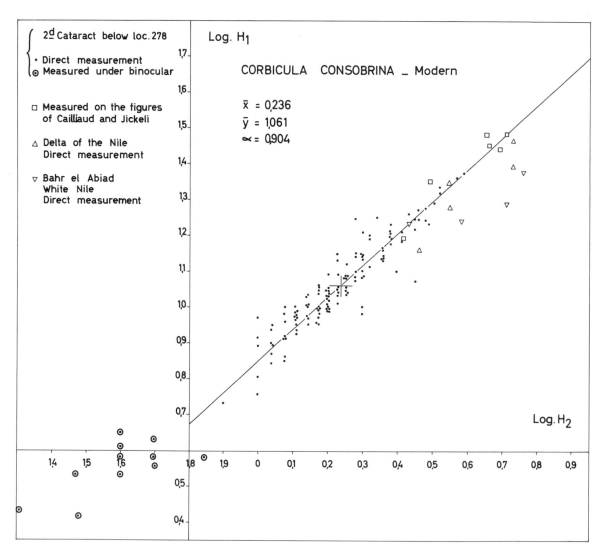

FIG. 10—Graph. Allometric growth lines of *Corbicula* in logarithmic coordinates. Modern *Corbicula* of the Second Nile Cataract.

Remarks

1. We thought at first that we had to deal with *Sphaerium pharaonum* Pallary which is known from Egypt *(Sphaerium (Corneola) pharaonum & Sphaerium (Corneola) teilhardi* Pallary, PALLARY, 1909, p. 74, pl. IV, figs. 26-27). We had at our disposal specimens of that species (Dautzenberg collection, belonging to IRSNB). They differ in the hinge shape, which is much weaker than in our material.

2. Our material agrees closely with the description of *Sphaerium victoriae mohasicum* according to Mandahl-Barth (1954, p. 167) and with the

description of *Sphaerium hartmanni* cf. *mohasicum* according to Adam. A direct comparison with the material of Adam and paratypes of Lake Mohasi (both in the collections of the IRSNB) does not disclose any difference.

CONCLUSIONS

The distribution of the various mollusks in the sites studied in Nubia is summarized in Table 6. The malacological association with which we have to deal is geologically a young one as none of the fossils is older than the Upper Pleistocene. A majority of Nilotic forms is mixed with Ethi-

TABLE 6

DISTRIBUTION CHART [1]

SPECIES [2]	MODERN FAUNA		ARKIN	SAHABA					81					KHOR MUSA			81					JER GRAVELS	
	RIGHT BANK	LEFT BANK	201	1027	278	515	516	506	SUP	3400	34	330	503	343	501	502	INF	AR-14	D-5	509	319	504	235
Theodoxus niloticus	r	c	–	-	-	-	-	-	-	-	-	-	-	-	-	-	-	-	-	-	-	-	-
Viviparus unicolor	-	-	-	-	-	r	-	rr	r	rr	rr	rr	r	-	-	rr	-	-	-	-	-	-	-
Lanistes carinatus	-	-	-	-	-	-	-	-	-	-	-	-	-	-	-	-	-	-	-	-	-	rr	-
Valvata nilotica	rr	r	-	-	-	r	x	-	r	c	-	-	-	-	-	-	-	-	-	-	-	-	-
Bithynia neumanni	c	c	-	-	-	-	-	-	-	-	-	-	-	-	-	-	-	-	-	-	-	-	-
Gabbia cf. walleri	rr	-	-	-	-	-	-	-	-	-	-	-	-	-	-	-	-	-	-	-	-	-	-
Melanoides toberculata	rr	r	-	-	-	-	-	-	-	-	-	-	-	-	-	-	-	-	-	-	-	-	-
Cleopatra bulimoides	c	c	c	cc	cc	cc	-	cc	cc	c	rr	cc	c	-	c	c	x	-	-	rr	r	rr	-
Bulinus truncatus	r	r	-	-	-	-	-	-	rr	c	-	-	-	-	-	-	-	-	-	-	-	-	-
Anisus planorbis	-	-	-	-	-	-	x	-	-	-	-	-	-	-	-	-	-	-	-	-	-	-	-
Gyraulus costulatus	-	rr	-	-	-	-	x	-	rr	r	-	-	-	-	-	-	-	-	-	-	-	-	-
Ferrissia sp.	rr	r	-	-	-	rr	-	-	-	-	-	-	-	-	-	-	-	-	-	-	-	-	-
Caelatura aegyptiaca	c	r	-	-	-	-	-	-	-	-	-	-	-	-	-	-	-	-	-	-	-	-	c
Unio willcocksi	-	-	rr	r	rr	-	-	rr	c	c	cc	c	c	x	rr	r	x	-	rr	-	r	-	-
Aspatharia hartmanni	-	-	-	-	-	-	-	-	-	r	-	-	-	-	-	-	-	-	-	-	-	-	-
Aspatharia cailliaudi	-	-	-	-	-	-	-	-	-	-	-	-	-	-	-	-	-	-	-	-	-	-	rr
Mutela nilotica	rr	-	-	-	-	-	-	-	-	rr	-	-	-	-	-	-	-	-	-	-	-	-	rr
Mutela cf. emini	-	-	-	-	-	-	-	-	-	-	-	-	-	-	-	-	-	-	-	-	-	-	r
Mutela cf. rostrata	-	-	-	-	-	-	-	-	-	-	-	-	-	-	-	-	-	-	-	-	-	r	-
Etheria elliptica	rr	-	cc	r	rr	-	-	-	-	-	-	-	-	-	-	-	-	-	rr	-	-	-	-
Corbicula consobrina	c	c	-	-	-	-	-	-	-	-	-	-	-	-	-	-	-	-	-	-	-	-	-
Corbicula vara	-	-	rr	r	r	r	-	rr	c	rr	c	-	r	x	cc	cc	x	cc	cc	cc	cc	cc	cc
Sphaerium hartmanni cf. *mohasicum*	rr	r	-	-	-	-	-	-	-	-	-	-	-	-	-	-	-	-	-	-	-	-	-

[1] Conventional notation for relative abundance: when the number of specimens reaches a minimum of 100, an approximate estimation of the relative abundance is possible, and is noted as follows: cc :> 50%; c : 10 to 50%; r : 1 to 10%; and rr :< 1%.

[2] Out of fluviatile formations. *Zootecus insularis* in many subaerial profiles and deposits.

opian forms. There is also a close relation with the Chad fauna.

Lanistes carinatus, Anisus planorbis, two species of *Aspatharia,* and two species of *Mutela* were found by us as fossils but not in the modern local fauna of the Second Nile Cataract. Yet, these species are living today in the Nile. It could be that better investigation might have revealed their presence. This assumption is reasonable if we consider the following faunistical lists: from the Egyptian Nile in Pallary (1909, 1924) and in Gardner (1932); from the White Nile in Haas (1936); from the Blue Nile in Bacci (1951); and from the Victoria Nile in Mandahl-Barth (1954).

Lanistes carinatus, prosobranch, essentially Nilotic (from Alexandria to North Uganda, known also in Somalia and Kenya) is characteristic of shallow and muddy waters.

Anisus planorbis, pulmonate of Mediterranean Palearctic affinity, is usually found in stagnant or slightly running waters.

Aspatharia cailliaudi is an Ethiopian essentially Nilotic form, living in rivers from Cairo to the Victoria Nile. It is of some interest to notice that this fossil was found among several other Pleistocene mollusks near the Murdi depression, Wadi Hawar, and Wadi Melik (Sanford, 1936, pp. 201, 202, 204, 206, 209, and 210).

Aspatharia hartmanni is also an Ethiopian form found in the Upper Nile, but it has a more Central African distribution.

Mutela emini, probably related to *M. nilotica,* is known today from Central Africa.

Mutela cf. *rostrata* has a wide Equatorial African distribution in the Niger-Chad area.

Two forms were found in the oldest deposits and in the modern fauna but not between them. They are *Caelatura aegyptiaca* (= *C. nilotica*) and *Mutela nilotica.* Both are essentially Nilotic bivalves. It is not certain that they were really absent in the intermediary levels, but they were at least much less frequent.

Forms such as *Mutela nilotica, M.* cf. *emini,* and *M.* cf. *rostrata,* which occur separately in equivalent Localities 235 and 504, are no more

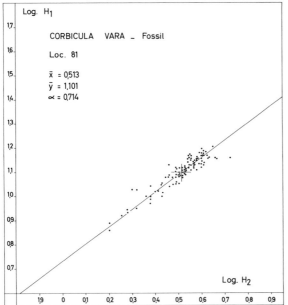

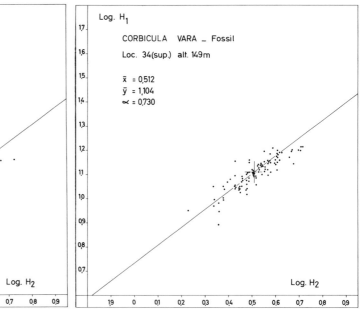

Fig. 11—Graph. Allometric growth lines of *Corbicula* in logarithmic coordinates, Locality 81.

Fig. 12—Graph. Allometric growth lines of *Corbicula* in logarithmic coordinates, Locality 34.

than very local adaptations and must be very closely related.

Unio abyssinicus is an abundant fossil in all Upper Pleistocene deposits, and is rare in the Arkin formation. It disappeared afterwards in this stretch of the Nile.

It occurs as fossil also in Fayum, at Kom Ombo, Edfu, Sebil, and Gebel Silsile. Fossil specimens have been usually identified as *Unio willcocksi* but the synonymy with *Unio abyssinicus* is beyond doubt. The lineage is now perpetuated in the colder water of Lake Tana only.

According to all evidence, the larger distribution of the fossils was favored by a lower temperature of the water in the course of the Blue Nile and downstream. Thus we are led to admit that this form has an explicit paleoclimatic meaning.

The fossil *Corbicula* of the Second Cataract area is quite different from the modern *Corbicula* of the same area. The variability of each group is slight, and statistical measurements justify a separation into two species: the fossil *Corbicula vara* Gardner *s. l.* and the modern *Corbicula consobrina* (Cailliaud).

We may not forget that the *Corbicula*, fossil and modern, taken as a whole, show an amazing variability, which is reflected in the great num-

ber of different species names proposed for African specimens.

We recall as most significant among them the following:

Corbicula consobrina (Cailliaud), originally described for a modern Nilotic shell (Cailliaud, 1823, II, pl. LXI, figs. 10-11).

C. artini Pallary, created for modern shells from the Upper Nile (Pallary, 1903, p. 9, pl. I, fig. 4).

C. lacoini Germain, first described for modern and subfossil shells of the Chad area (Germain, 1906, p. 241, pl. IV, figs. 13-14). This species corresponds probably to *C. tchadiensis* Germain.

C. fluminalis (Müller), originally described for specimens from the Euphrates (Müller, 1774, p. 205).

More or less related to our fossil *Corbicula* are the *C. saharica*, described by Fischer (1878, p. 77, pl. II, fig. 1), for thick, subquadrangulate tests from the Sahara area. They have not been included in the synonymy for lack of precision in the original description.

All the Fayum species described by Gardner (1932) have already been mentioned.

Two hypotheses can be considered:

In the hypothesis of adaptative radiation, different forms correspond to different conditions

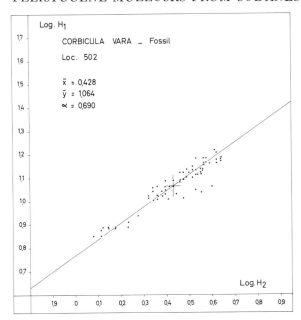

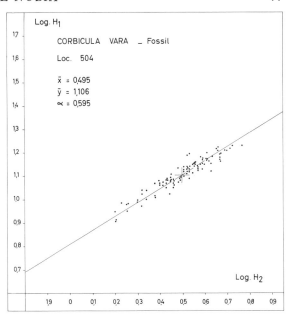

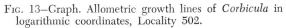

FIG. 13—Graph. Allometric growth lines of *Corbicula* in logarithmic coordinates, Locality 502.

FIG. 14—Graph. Allometric growth lines of *Corbicula* in logarithmic coordinates, Locality 504.

and are reversible. During the Upper Pleistocene, the waters of the Nile were probably colder (as already suggested by the presence of *U. abyssinicus*) and were also richer in carbonates; this would have induced a greater robustness of the *Corbicula* as well as *Unio* and *Caelatura*.

The hypothesis of a true evolution from *C. vara s. l.* to *C. consobrina* is also plausible, especially if we consider the progressive shift of the allometric growth lines shown in Tables 4 and 5.

Usually, the *C. vara* Gardner, *s. l.* are more abundant in Dibeira-Jer than in the Sahaba formations.

Cleopatra bulimoides has a wide Nilotic distribution today. It predominated in the Sahaba formation, where it was apparently accumulated in sand and gravel bars by current action.

Etheria elliptica is scarce as fossil except at the peculiar Locality 201 in the Arkin formation. It lives now in districts drained by the Nile, the Niger, and the Congo.

Viviparus unicolor is a prosobranch which now lives in Central African lakes (Victoria, Nyanza, Albert, Edward, and Chad) and also in the upper drainage basin of the Nile, where lacustrine conditions occur, as for instance in the Bahr-el-Ghazal (Roger, 1944, p. 121).

The fossils are represented by few specimens, usually in very bad shape, rolled, eroded, and seemingly transported from a long distance away. They indicate that lacustrine conditions prevailed somewhere upstream from the Second Cataract.

The following five modern species were not recovered by us as fossils, but some are known as such from elsewhere.

Their absence in the Pleistocene of the Second Cataract area is striking and stresses again the departure from present ecological conditions.

Bithynia neumanni is a prosobranch now frequent in the Chad, Niger, Lake Albert, and Abyssinia. It was found by Gardner in the Fayum (1932, p. 36).

Theodoxus niloticus is a North Ethiopian species, with rather Palearctic affinity. This species is common along the Nile of the present day and was found in the Fayum deposits by Gardner (1932, pp. 40-43) and by Blanckenhorn (1901, pp. 411, 444, 445, 463).

Melanoides tuberculata. This viviparous species is almost cosmopolitan in Africa. It was also widely distributed as fossil and was found in particular in Egypt (Blanckenhorn, 1901, pp. 397, 404, 413, 436, 444, 462, 466; Gardner, 1932, p. 490) and in Sudan (Arkell, 1953, p. 10).

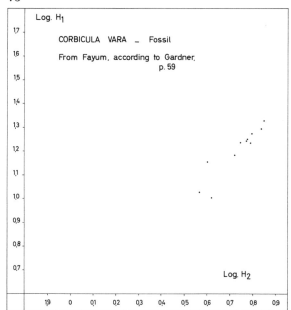

FIG. 15—Graph. Allometric growth lines of *Corbicula* in logarithmic coordinates, the Fayum (in Gardner, p. 59).

Gabbia cf. *walleri* is an uncertain identification for a rare species only mentioned today from Lake Albert (Mandahl-Barth, 1954, pp. 51-54).

Sphaerium hartmanni cf. *mohasicum* is mentioned in some central African lakes today.

The four following freshwater mollusks were found in both modern and fossil associations:

Valvata nilotica is a Nilotic prosobranch, probably of Palearctic affinity, living usually on water plants in stagnant pools.

Bulinus truncatus, this Ethiopian pulmonate of Palearctic affinity, can be found in North Africa.

Ferrissia sp. is a pulmonate living on aquatic plants, known in particular from North Africa.

Gyraulus costulatus is a pulmonate with a large African distribution.

These four little species were found as fossils in Sahaba formations only.

———

Zootecus insularis is abundant as fossil but seemingly absent in the area now. Its present distribution covers North Africa except in the northwest (rare in Egypt), the south of Abyssinia, Somali, Socotra, Arabia, and India. It is considered as a Palearctic element being absent in Central and South Africa. Although it is adapted to desert or semi-desert conditions, its implication in the present context is that it lived in more humid climatic conditions. It has been found in abundance far inland in the desert (Locality 505) and in soils at the top of many inselbergs (Locality 63) in conditions where no trace of vegetation can grow now. *Zootecus insularis* can be accepted as indicative of a main phase of climatic humidity in Nubia which can be approximately dated around 16,050 B.C.-8,050 B.C.

APPENDIX ON BIOMETRY

The symbols used here are the following; see Figure 16:

L = width: antero-posterior diameter

H = height: umbono-ventral diameter

C = convexity of one valve = half the diameter D of the bivalve

Ep = greatest thickness of the test itself; unless otherwise stated, it is measured just below the anterior muscle-scar

n = number of studied specimens

Concerning the *Corbiculas,* where two kinds of heights are measured:

H_1 = total height of the test: umbono-ventral diameter

H_2 = height from the top of the umbo to the base line of the hinge plate

Concerning the *Unio* and *Caelatura:*

L_1 = distance from the beak to the extremity of the cardinal teeth

L_2 = distance from the beak to the extremity of the lateral teeth

The measurements of the Gastropods were taken according to Mandahl-Barth (1954, pp. 20-21, fig. 1); their number of whorls were counted including the body-whorl (Mandahl-Barth, 1954, p. 21, fig. 2).

Biometry of *Corbiculas:*

Graphically, the relations between the arithmetical values H_1 and H_2 are expressed by an arc of curve. Transformed into logarithms, these relations are transformed into an allometric growth line, characterized by an inclination α.

The expression of this growth line is:

$$y = b.x^\alpha \qquad \text{(Teissier, 1937, p. 23)}$$

or $\log y = \log b + \alpha \log x$

or $Y = B + \alpha X.$

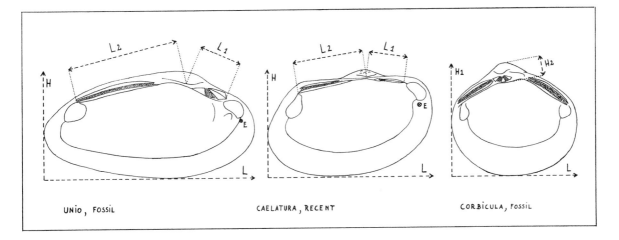

FIG. 16—Nile formations—Biometry of shells (fig. of fossil *Unio*, modern *Caelatura*, and fossil *Corbicula*).

In the present case:

$$Y = \log H_1$$
$$X = \log H_2$$

Variance and standard deviation of the arithmetical means X and Y are calculated by use of the following formulas:

$$S_x{}^2 = \frac{\Sigma X^2 - \overline{X}(\Sigma X)}{n} \qquad S^2{}_Y = \frac{\Sigma Y^2 - \overline{Y}(\Sigma Y)}{n}$$

$$S_x = \sqrt{S_x{}^2} \qquad\qquad S_Y\sqrt{S_Y{}^2}$$

The angular coefficient of the allometric growth line is:

$$\alpha = \frac{S_Y}{S_x} \quad \text{(Karmack \& Haldane, 1950, p. 31)}$$

The correlation between the two variables X and Y is expressed by a correlation coefficient:

$$r_{XY} = \frac{\Sigma XY - \overline{X}\Sigma Y}{n\, S_x\, S_Y}$$

The closer to the value 1, the higher is the correlation.

The variance of each angular coefficient is:

$$\sigma_{\alpha_i}{}^2 = \alpha_i{}^2 \left(\frac{1 - r_i{}^2}{n_i}\right)$$

(Charniaux-Cotton, 1957, p. 457)

The *Corbiculas* from the 81, 502, 34 sup., and 504 fossil layers and from the Second Nile Cataract were compared two at a time, using their respective angular coefficient of growth line.

The test of discrimination between two inclinations is:

$$\frac{\alpha_i - \alpha_j}{\sqrt{\sigma_{\alpha_i}{}^2 + \sigma_{\alpha_j}{}^2}} \quad \text{(Charniaux-Cotton, 1957, p. 440)}$$

where i, j, . . . correspond to the different layers.

Theoretical calculations show that a value of the test of discrimination higher than 2.6 means a highly significant difference between two groups and that a value higher than 1.96 is still significant.

MAMMALIAN REMAINS OF THE NORTHERN SUDAN AND SOUTHERN EGYPT

A. Gautier

(GEOLOGICAL INSTITUTE, STATE UNIVERSITY OF GHENT, BELGIUM)

INTRODUCTION

The literature on Pleistocene and subrecent fossil mammals from the Sudan is not very rich. A list and comments concerning most of the older references can be found in Bate (1949, description fauna Khartoum Mesolithic). Other important papers describe the faunal remains from Abu-Hugar and Singa (Bate, 1951: *Homoioceras singae*) and Esh Shaheinab (Bate, 1953, fauna Khartoum Neolithic). As for Egypt, the most important contribution to our knowledge of the Pleistocene fauna seems still to be the study of the Kom Ombo fauna (Gaillard, 1934).

The study of the present collection proved rather difficult, although most of the species present are rapidly recognized as being identical with, or very near to, extant forms. The material is extremely fragmentary. After the separation of unidentifiable and identifiable material only one fifth of the original collection was left. Another difficulty arose from the fact that our information regarding cultural and stratigraphical setting was second hand. One often gets a better idea concerning what questions the material can answer if one has at least seen the most important sites.

Some of the material, which was too fragmentary, could not be identified. The few rodents were handed over to W. Verheyen. Unfortunately, lack of time made it impossible for him to give more than a general identification.

We are indebted to D. A. Hooijer (Leiden), X. Misonne (Brussels), L. Cahen (Tervuren), D. Corbet, Mrs. Coryndon, and A. Sutcliffe (London), J. de Heinzelin (Ghent), and F. Wendorf (Dallas). They put at our disposal comparative collections of recent mammals or helped us in collecting the necessary information on the material.

ABBREVIATIONS

D.:   diameter

TR.D.:   transverse diameter
A-P.D: anteroposterior diameter
L.:   length
W.:   width
H.:   height
dist.:   distal
prox.:   proximal
ant.:   anterior
post.:   posterior
mc.:   metacarpal
mt.:   metatarsal
r.:   right
l.:   left
dex.:   dexter (right)
sin.:   sinister (left)
IRSNB: Institut Royal des Sciences Naturelles de Belgique (Brussels)
Reg.:   registered
spec.:   specimen

MATERIAL REMAINS

LEPUS sp.

Material

Complete left jaw with incisive and P$_2$-M$_3$: Site 1017-4. L. P$_2$-M$_3$: 15.8.
Fragment left jaw with broken incisive and P$_2$, part of alveoli P$_3$: Site 1021.

Remarks

The specimens were examined by W. Verheyen, who gave only a very general identification. According to Setzer (1956, pp. 472-477, fig. 3) the following rabbits occur in the Sudan: *Poëlagus marjorita* (two subspecies), *Lepus capensis* (four subspecies), and *L. victoriae*. If we judge by the present day distribution of rabbits in the Sudan, it seems probable to us that the specimens pertain to *Lepus capensis*.

CANIS AUREUS ? cf. SOUDANICUS Thomas
    Figure 1, Number 1

Material

Fragment right mandible with M₁ and alveoli for M₂ and M₃: Site 34C.
    L. M₁: 20.5[1]
    W. (across main cusp): 7.3
    Complete humerus: Site DIW-1 (r.)
    L.: ± 155
    TR.D. dist.: 35
    A-P.D. dist.: 27

Remarks

The jaw fragment was kindly identified by G. Ewer, who also gave a few comments. *C. aureus soudanicus* (Setzer, 1956, p. 550), the extant subspecies from the Sudan, is fairly small in comparison to the material from Site 34C. Modern large forms are *C. aureus algiriensis* (Algeria, Tunisia, Morocco) and *C. aureus lupaster* (Palestine, Egypt, Libya). The Site 34C material is about the size of *C. aureus lupaster*. The material of DIW-1 seems to fall within the range of *C. aureus soudanicus*.

On the basis of a single specimen it is difficult to equate the fossil material from Site 34C with *C. a. lupaster* (or *C. lupaster* as a distinct species). It may as well represent a large *C. a. soudanicus*, in which case it would indicate climatic conditions slightly different from those prevailing today.

CANIS MESOMELAS Schreber
    Figure 1, Number 2

Material

Fragment jaw with P₄, M₁ and alveoli P₂ sin.: Site 8905 (Locality D)
    L./W. P₄: ± 9.5/4.1
    L./W. M₁: 16.3/7.8
    Estimated L. M₂: ± 8
    Carnassial/molar ratio: ± 2.37

Remarks

From the measurements it is clear that this material cannot be lumped with *C. aureus* ? cf. *soudanicus*. Measurements and carnassial/molar ratio have been compared with analogous data in Ewer and Singer (1956, pp. 342-345) and

---

[1] The measurements are in millimeters.

Ewer (1956, pp. 62-63). The measurements are somewhat equivocal and indicate either small *C. adustus* or *C. mesomelas*. The ratio, however, falls within the range of *C. mesomelas*.

Setzer (1956, pp. 560-561) lists *C. mesomelas elongae* from the most southerly part of the Sudan. It is quite possible that *C. mesomelas* occurred as far north as Wadi Halfa, during the Upper Pleistocene. It would not have been influenced by the better climatic conditions, which may have influenced the size of the fossil *C. aureus* (see Remarks, *C. a.* ? cf. *soudanicus*). This might indicate that *C. mesomelas* found climatic conditions around Wadi Halfa much the same as those prevailing much farther south today.

EQUUS ASINUS cf. AFRICANUS (Fitzinger)
    Figure 1, Numbers 3, 4

Material

Cranium and upper dentition
    Fragment maxilla with right incisives I², I³: Site 1024
    Upper molariform teeth: Sites ANW-3 (M²/³ dex.); 287 (P³/⁴ sin.);
    1024 (M²/³ sin., fragments one complete right tooth)
    L./W. P³/⁴: 28/29
    L./W. M¹/²: 26/27
Mandible and lower dentition
    Fragment left with M₃ and M₂: Site 1017
    Fragment left jaw with alveoli and roots I₁, I₂: Site 1017
    Isolated molariform teeth: Sites ANW-3 (P₃/₄ sin., P₂ sin.); 1024 (M₃ dex., P₂ dex.)
    Fragments molariform teeth: Sites ANW-3 (dex.); 34 (M₃ sin.); 8873
    L./W. P₂: 31-32/16-17
    L./W. P₃/₄: 26-28/19-20
    L./W. M₁/₂: 26/16
    L./W. M₃: 28-30/14-16
    Fragments upper or lower molariform teeth: Sites 1017 (6); 8773 (several, originally one tooth ?)
    Root incisive: Site ANW-3
    The upper molariform teeth do not show a caballine fold. In the lower molariform teeth the lingual sinus between metastylid and metaconid forms a more or less pointed V. This feature can be used for

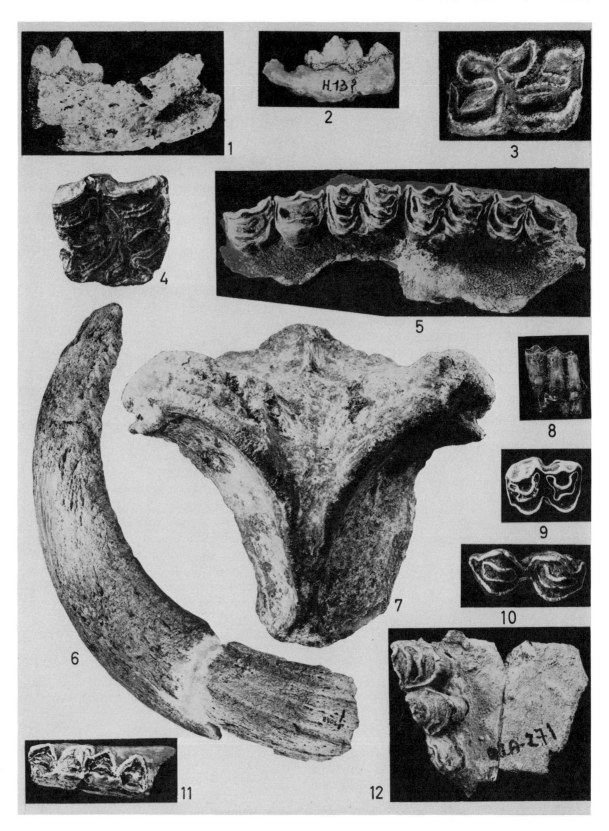

separating zebras and asses from true horses (Hopwood, 1936, p. 898).

Vertebrae

    Fragment axis: Site 1024

    Incomplete cervical vertebra: Site ANW-3

    Dorsal vertebra: Site ANW-3

    Various fragments: Site 1024(3)

    TR.D. anterior articular surface axis: 73

    Central body dorsal vertebra: 50

Humerus

    Fragmentary distal epiphysis: Site 1024(1)

TR.D. dist.: ±70

Tibia

    Distal epiphysis: Sites 440(r.); 1017(1)

    Fragment distal epiphysis: Sites 440(r.); 1017(1)

    Fragment distal epiphysis: Sites ANE-1 (l.); 1028(1)

    TR.D. dist.: 66

    A-P.D. dist.: 47

Calcaneum

    Complete specimen: Site ANW-3

    TR.D. prox. tuberosity: 30

    A-P.D. prox. tuberosity: 45

    Greatest TR.D.: 45

Cannon bone

    Distal shaft with complete epiphysis: Site ANW-3

The fossil cannon bone is certainly a metatarsus and has a strongly asinian index. It is heavier than the cannon bone of the female specimen *E. asinus somaliensis*.

First phalanges

    Fragments: Sites ANE-1 (1); 1017(2)

Second phalanges

    Complete specimens: Sites ANE-1; 1028

The fossil specimen is very probably an anterior phalanx. Its transverse distal diameter can be compared with analogous measurements for the two recent species. The indices are all caballine, for asinian second phalanges would have an average index of 0.825 and lower. A partial explanation for this anomaly may be the difficulty of measuring minimal transverse diameters on such compressed bone as second phalanges. Anyhow, the fact that the fossil phalanx has an index comparable to the one for *Equus a. somaliensis* indicates perhaps that it pertains to *Asinus* sp.

Remarks

Although equids form a difficult group to identify, most indications seem to prove that the fossil species is comparable to the recent *E. asinus africanus*. The estimated P_1-M_3 length and the length of separate teeth can be compared

	Fossil Cannon bone ANW-3	E. A. somaliensis (Stehlin and Graziosi, 1935, Table 2)		H. (Quagga) böhmi (IRSNB Reg. 12129)		E. asinus (Gaillard, 1934, Kom Ombo)
	mt.	mc.	mt.	mc.	mt.	mt.
TR.D. middle shaft	± 30	26	25.5	32	32	29
A-P.D. middle shaft	25	—	—	21	24	19
TR.D. dist. epiphysis	43	40	40	44	44	37
A-P.D. dist. epiphysis	36	—	—	—	—	—
$\dfrac{\text{TR.D. middle shaft}}{\text{A-P.D. middle shaft}}$	± 0.83	(0.60)	(0.80)	0.65	0.75	0.65

FIGURE 1

No. 1—*Canis aureus* ? cf. *soudanicus;* fragment right mandible with M_1; spec. 34-38; natural size.

No. 2—*Canis mesomelas;* fragment left mandible with P_4 and M_1; spec. 8905 cemented zone, hearth 13; natural size.

No. 3—*Equus asinus* cf. *africanus;* $P_{3/4}$ sin; spec. ANW-3-60; 4/3 natural size.

No. 4—*Equus asinus* cf. *africanus;* $M^{2/3}$ dex.; spec. ANW-3—?; 4/3 natural size.

No. 5—*Bos primigenius;* upper teeth row P^3-M^3 sin; spec. ANW-3 SE-section; 2/3 natural size.

No. 6—*Bos primigenius;* horn-core; spec. 8905; approximately 2/3 natural size.

No. 7—*Hippopotamus amphibius;* fragment post-orbital cranium; spec. ANW-3; 2/3 natural size.

No. 8—*Gazella rufifrons;* M_3 sin.; spec. 1017; 3/6 natural size.

No. 9—*Alcelaphus buselaphus* subsp.; M^1 dex.; spec. 34-1; natural size.

No. 10—*Alcelaphus buselaphus* subsp.; M_2 dex.; spec. 1028 (geological testpit 365); 4/3 natural size.

No. 11—*Gazella (Nanger)* sp.; fragment right mandible with M_1 and M_2; DIW-53; natural size.

No. 12—*Alcelaphus buselaphus* subsp.; palatal with P^2-P^4 dex.; spec. DIW-1 (DIA-271); natural size.

	Fossil Second Phalanx 1028	*E. asinus somaliensis* (Stehlin and Graziosi, 1935, Table 2)		*H. (Quagga) böhmi* (IRSNB, Reg. 12129)	
	ant.	ant.	post.	ant.	post.
Length	42	41.5	39.5	42	41
TR.D. prox.	46	44	42	45	44
A-P.D. prox.	30	—	—	—	—
TR.D. dist.	39	40	35.5	40	37
A-P.D. dist.	25	—	—	—	—
Min. TR.D.	37	36.5	35	36	35
$\dfrac{\text{Min. TR.D.}}{\text{Length}}$	0.89	0.88	0.87	0.86	0.86

with the same measurements in male *E. a. somaliensis* (Stehlin and Graziosi, 1935, pp. 6-7, figs. 5-6) and less well with female *E. a. africanus. Hippotigris (Quagga) böhmi* (IRSNB, Reg. 12129) which seems to have somewhat smaller teeth.

The fossil cannon bone can probably be compared with the cannon bone in the male *E. a. africanus.* Indeed female *E. a. africanus* seem to have about the size cannon bone as male *E. a. somaliensis.* Therefore, the female *E. a. somaliensis* should be much smaller than the male *E. a. africanus.*

According to Arambourg (1947, pp. 310-311) zebras and asses can be separated by the difference in the valleys between protostyle, mesostyle, and metastyle in the upper molariform teeth. In zebras the valleys would lie at the same height, but the posterior one would be tilted backward. In asses, both valley bottoms would be parallel, but the posterior one would lie nearer to the labial tooth side. This diagnostic feature can be seen on six of the eight molariform teeth of *E. a. sinus* figured in Stehlin and Graziosi (*ibidem*). Two of the fossil molars (Site ANW-3; Site 278) also show this feature; in the third incomplete specimen (Site 1024) it is much less clear.

E. asinus africanus seem to be extinct in the former range in Nubia. An intergrade *E. a. dianae* would live on the Eritrean Border as far south as the Atbara River and in the Red Sea Hills. *E. a. somaliensis* is confined to Ethiopia, Erithrea, and Somalia. The zebra species, *Hippotigris (Quagga) böhmi,* which was used for comparison occurs in the most southern part of the Sudan (Mackenzie, 1954, p. 20; Setzer, 1956, p. 569).

HIPPOPOTAMUS AMPHIBIUS Linnaeus
Figure 1, Number 7

Material (Table 1)

Cranium and upper dentition
  L. crista sagittalis: ± 100 mm.
  Max. D. upper C: ± 40
  Max. D.I^2: ± 30
  L. M^2: ± 55
  W. M^2: ± 51
Mandible and lower dentition
Circumference C: 180
  Max. D.C.: 62-70 (males; cf. Hooijer, 1950, p. 8)
  Min. D.C.: 39
  L. outer curve C: ± 280 mm. (Site 34)
  H. ramus at M$_2$: 125
  L. mandible (front-M$_3$): 400
  L. mandible (front-condyle): 530
  L. symphysis: ± 140
Radius
  TR.D. prox.: 99
  A-P.D. prox.: 62
Femur
  TR.D. trochlea: 81
  TR.D. condyles: ± 140
  A-P.D. dist. medial: 181
  A-P.D. middle trochlea to intercondyloid fossa: 108
Patella
  H.: ± 105
  TR.D.: ± 108
Tibia
  L. eminentia intercondyloidea-median dist. ridge: ± 350
  Min. TR.D. shaft: 16
  Min. A-P.D. shaft: 47

TABLE 1

IDENTIFIED FRAGMENTS OF *Hippopotamus amphibius* LINNAEUS AT DIFFERENT SITES

Hippopotamus amphibius LINNAEUS	Sites								
	440	ANW-3	443	34-C	ANE-1	8905	448	DIW-1	DIW-53
Cranium and upper dentition:									
a. Fragment post orbital cranium with sagital crest and part of occiput.		1							
b. Fragmentary canine		1							
c. Moiety I² (with fragments of mandible)				1					
d. More or less complete M²				1					
Mandible and Lower dentition: a. One poorly preserved complete left mandible and many fragments of not much worn molariform teeth.								1 many fragments	
b. Fragments lower canines				2 1R			1	1	
Upper and/or lower dentition a. Fragments upper or lower molariform teeth.		1	Many	1			1		1
Vertebrae: a. Cervical vertebra						1			
b. Fragment vertebra						1			
Radius: Proximal epiphysis with part of shaft	1R								
Femur: Distal epiphysis with part of shaft			1R						
Patella: Complete specimen		1L							
Tibia: Complete, poorly preserved specimen, proximal epiphysis not yet well fused. (cf. jaw of same site)								1	

TR.D. dist.: ± 90

A-P.D. dist.: ± 70

Remarks

The measurements for the femur have been compared with measurements of the recent individual at the IRSNB (Reg. 5129). The other measurements have been compared with those given by Hooijer (1950), who is rather skeptical with regard to the several subspecies established for *H. amphibius.* The distinguishing characteristics mentioned by older authors seem to be invalid for racial distinction and can be reduced to individual variation. Therefore, the material can be put on record simply as *H. amphibius.*

BOS PRIMIGENIUS Bojanus

Figure 1, Number 5; Figure 2, Number 1

Material (Table 2; see Atlas)

HORN-CORES

	DIW-1 55	DIW-1 235	8773	A	B	8905 C	D	E
Max. D/min. D.								
10 cm. from top	57/50	—	—	55/43	55/45	56/48	—	—
15 cm. from top	—	—	—	62/50	61/55	63/56	—	64/50
20 cm. from top	—	—	68/—	67/56	69/60	—	—	71/—
25 cm. from top	—	—	78/—	76/63	77/66	81/62	80/61	—
30 cm. from top	—	—	—	—	—	88/69	87/65	—
35 cm. from top	—	—	—	85/78	—	94/74	96/76	—
40 cm. from top	—	—	—	—	—	107/83	106/86	—
at base	—	74/49	—	—	—	±110/±90	±110/±90	—
L. top-middle base	—	—	—	—	—	±350	—	—
L. inner curve	—	—	—	—	—	±420	—	—
L. outer curve	—	—	—	—	—	590	—	—

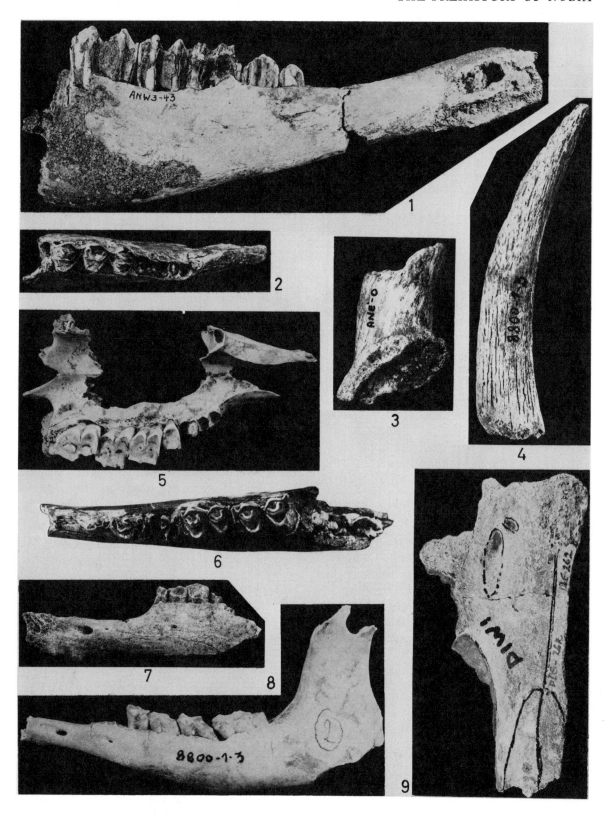

Cranium and upper dentition
Max. TR.D. nasalia: 98
L. nasalia: ± 250
L./W. $P^{2/3}$: 20-22/17-18
L./W. P^4: 20-22/17-20
L./W. M^1: 30-33/22-27
L./W. M^2: 33-34/24-28
L./W. M^3: 34-37/24-26
L. P^2-P^4: ± 60
L. M^1-M^3: 94-114
L. P^2-M^3: 154-174
Lower jaw and dentition
H. vertical ramus: ± 245
H. sigmoid notch/coronoid apophysis:
  ± 72-97
W. condyle: 44-57
A-P.D. below condyle: 62-81
H. ramus in front of P_4: 55
H. ramus behind symphysis: 37
L./W. m_3: 32-35/13-15
L./W. P_2: 15/10
L./W. P_3: 20-23/12-15
L./W. P_4: 24-25/14-17
L./W. M_1: 26-31/14-19
L./W. M_2: 32-36/15-20
L./W. M_3: 43-48/16-19
L. P_2-P_4: ± 58-61 mm.
L. $M_{.1}$-M_3: 103-111 mm.
L. P_2-M_3: 161-172 mm.
Vertebrae
TR.D. ant. articular surface atlas: 126
H. *idem*: 65
TR.D. post. articular surface atlas: 123
H. *idem*: 60
TR.D. greatest ant. atlas: ± 215
A-P.D. greatest post. atlas: ± 175
L. corpus vertebrae cervical vertebrae:
  ± 150
W. *idem*: 69-70
L. corpus vertebrae dorsal or lumbar vertebrae: 70-76

Scapulum
Min. D. articular surface: 54-65
Max. D. articular surface: 69-76
D. articular surface + notch: 82-90
Humerus
TR.D. dist.: 108-119
A-P.D. dist.: ± 110
Cubitus
A-P.D. above big sigmoid cavity: 25-32
H. big sigmoid cavity: 49
A-P.D. olecranon: 89
TR.D. prox. tuberosity olecranon: 40
Radius
TR.D. prox.: 88 (Site 8905)
A-P.D. prox.: 44-50 (Sites 8905; 8871)
TR.D. dist.: 83-98
A-P.D. dist.: 48-58
Unciform
TR.D.: 39
A-P.D.: 45
Magnum
TR.D.: 54
A-P.D.: 46
Pelvis
Max. D. acetabulum: 92-93
Min. D. *idem*: 71-74
Femur
TR.D. prox. head: 58-61
H. prox. head.: 54-60
TR.D. dist.: ± 105
A.-P.D. dist.: ± 140
Tibia
TR.D. dist.: 71-75
A-P.D. dist.: 56-58
Astragalus
Length: 70-95
TR.D.: 51-60
A-P.D.: 42-55
Calcaneum
Total L.: ± 170
TR.D. prox. tuberosity: 34-40

FIGURE 2
No. 1—*Bos primigenius;* left jaw with P_2, P_3, M_3, M_1, and M_2; spec. ANW-3; approximately 1/2 natural size.
No. 2—*Alcelaphus buselaphus* subsp.; fragment right jaw with M_3; spec. 1024-159; natural size.
No. 3—*Gazella rufifrons;* left male horn-core; spec. ANE-1; 2/3 natural size.
No. 4—*Gazella dorcas;* male horn-core; spec. 8800-1; natural size.
No. 5—*Gazella dorcas;* lower cranium with P^4-M^3 sin.; spec. 8800-1; natural size.
No. 6—*Adenota kob* ? cf. *leucotis;* fragment left jaw with P_2-M_2; spec. 448-6; natural size.
No. 7—*Gazella rufifrons;* left jaw with P_2-P_4; spec. 1017-4; 5/6 natural size.
No. 8—*Gazella dorcas;* left jaw with P_4-M_3; spec. 8800-1; 5/6 natural size.
No. 9—*Alcelaphus buselaphus* subsp.; frontal with part of nasal; spec. DIW-1 (DIE-262); 6/10 natural size.

A.-P.D. prox. tuberosity: 41-49

Naviculo-cuboid
    TR.D.: 64-83
    A.-P.D.: 60-74

Cannon bone
    A.-P.D. prox.: 65 (mt.) 36-40 (mc.)
    TR.D. prox.: 69-71 (mt.)
    TR.D. dist.: 68-88
    A.-P.D. dist.: 38-48

First phalanges
    L.: ± 65-82
    A.-P.D. prox.: 40-48
    TR.D. prox.: 32-41
    TR.D. dist.: 39
    A.-P. dist.: 31

Second phalanges
L.: 50-56
    TR.D. prox.: 36-40
    A.-P.D. prox.: 38-43
    TR.D. dist.: 31-36
    A.-P.D. dist.: 34-37

Hoofphalanges
    L.: 80-110
    H.: 45-64
    TR-D. articular surface: 25-32

A small hoofphalanx (L: ± 70 mm.) from the Neolithic Site 8822 still falls in the range of Libyan wild cattle (cf. Higgs (b), in press). It may represent a small female, a small breed such as *B. ibericus* from North Africa, *B. brachyceros* from Kom Ombo (Gaillard, 1934) or simply domesticated cattle of a much earlier date than the cultural contents of the site.

Upper sesamoids: Sites ANE-1 (3); 8905 (3)
Lower sesamoids: Sites 1017 (2); 8899

Remarks

There can be little doubt concerning the identity of the material described above. Most of it represents almost certainly *Bos primigenius*. There is no direct evidence of fossil buffaloes, such as *Homoioceras singae*, which has been found further south on the Blue Nile, or larger fossil buffaloes such as *H. antiquus* known from North Africa.

The 8905 horn-cores can be compared with those of European aurochs. Their measurements fall within the range of European specimens measured by Labaume (1909, Tables 6, 7). If one accepts that the collected horn-cores do not neces-

sarily represent female individuals, the measurements would indicate a somewhat smaller size for the Sudanese aurochs in comparison to his European counterpart.

In *H. antiquus* and *H. singae*, the upper molariform teeth are more compressed anteroposteriorly than in *Bos* (cf. Pomel, 1893, pl. II; Bate, 1951, p. 14). The collected upper molars fall within the range of *B. primigenius* upper molars. Their relative width is less than in *H. antiquus* or in *H. singae*. As to the less indicative lower molars, there is not much chance that only this collection contains buffaloes, as such remains almost certainly lack in the upper molar collection.

The postcranial skeleton measurements have been compared with measurements of European aurochs (Lehmann, 1949; our own measurements in the collections of the IRSNB) and North African bovids mostly representing *B. primigenius* (Higgs (b), in press). The North African aurochs would be somewhat smaller than its European counterpart. *H. antiquus* would be at least as large as this aurochs or somewhat larger (Higgs, *ibidem*). *H. singae* is slightly bigger than *Syncerus caffer*. Our postcranial collection falls within the range of the *B. primigenius*, which shows a rather pronounced variability in size according to age, sex, and individual. However, as for the horn-cores, there is an indication that the Sudan aurochs is somewhat smaller than European wild cattle. In this respect it agrees with the North African form.

One horn-core fragment is rather small (Site DIW-1). Labaume (1909) lists a female aurochs with very small horn-cores (83 x 70 mm. at the base). At the IRSNB, we found a horn-core measuring 71 x 58 mm. Gaillard (1934, pp. 33-35) identified wild *B. brachyceros* at Kom Ombo. Its horn-cores seem to be somewhat smaller than the one mentioned above (Site DIW-1-235). In North Africa another small *Bos* sp. has been identified as *Bos ibericus*. The existence of this separate wild small *Bos* species is not settled. It has been argued that in some cases it represents the female *B. primigenius*, in which the head is much less heavily built (Zeuner, 1963). For the time being, I rather include the DIA-235 horn-core in *B. primigenius* as a small female or a juvenile.

Some material included in *B. primigenius* comes from C-group sites. It is impossible to separate it from the material collected at older sites and certainly representing a wild bovid. Separation of domesticated cattle from wild cattle would only be possible in much larger collections (statistical analysis; cf. Higgs (b), in press), or with very characteristic material (horn-cores). The C-group horn-core fragment 8773-2 can be matched with the horn-cores from older sites. Therefore, there is no positive evidence of domesticated cattle in the collected material. If such cattle is present, it is probably akin to the Egyptian *B. africanus.*

It is not extraordinary that *B. primigenius* has been found in the Northern Sudan. The aurochs is well known from North Africa. It has also been identified at Kom Ombo (Gaillard, 1934). During Dynastic times, the Egyptians still hunted wild cattle. Probably the aurochs penetrated farther south along the Nile than has been established until now. The North African *Camelus thomasi* (Palikao) seems also to have lived as far south as Wadi Halfa during the Upper Pleistocene (Gautier, 1966).

ADENOTA KOB ? CF. LEUCOTIS (Lichtenstein & Peters, 1854)
Figure 2, Number 6

Material

Fragment jaw with P_2-M_2 sin. and alveoli P_2-M_1 dex.: Site 448
Moiety distal epiphysis cannon bone: Site 443
L./W. P_2: 6.5/4.5
L./W. P_3: 9/7
L./W. P_4: 11/8.5
L./W. M_1: 14.5/9
L./W. M_2: 16/9.5
L. P_2-M_3: ± 80
L. P_2-P_4: 27
L. M_1-M_3: ± 53
TR.D. dist. condyle cannon bone: 14 (total width dist. epiphysis: ± 32)
A-P.D. *idem*: ± 20

Remarks

According to Mackenzie (1954, pp. 10-11) three subspecies occur in Sudan: *A. k. leucotis,* *A. k. vaughni,* and *A. k. alurae.* According to Setzer (1956, p. 575), *A. k. vaughni* may be synonymous with either *A. k. leucotis* or *A. k. alurae.* *A. k. alurae* seems to be somewhat smaller than *A. k. leucotis* and could correspond to *A. k. thomasi* (Mackenzie, *ibidem*).

The fossil skull material is somewhat larger than recent *A. k. thomasi,* measured at the IRSNB. It could represent *A. k. leucotis* and synonyms or any form of about the same size. *A. k. leucotis* and *A. k. vaughni* are still very common in the southern Sudan and along the White Nile, while *A. k. alurae* only occurs in the region of Rhino Camp. The small fragment from Site 443 compares well with distal condyles of cannon bone in *A. kob;* it may represent this species.

ALCELAPHUS BUSELAPHUS subsp.
Figure 1, Numbers 9, 10, 12; Figure 2, Numbers 2, 9

Material (Table 3; see Atlas)

Cranium and upper dentition
Max. frontal: ± 65
TR.D. foramen magnum: ± 46
TR.D. condyle: ± 30
TR.D. condyles and foramen magnum: ± 85
L./W. m^2: 15.5/10.5
L./W. m^3: 18/12
L./W. P^2: $\frac{8}{6}$
L./W. P^3: $\frac{13}{9}$
L./W. P^4: $\frac{13}{11}$
L./W. M^1: $\frac{20\text{-}22}{13.5\text{-}14}$
L./W. $M^{2/3}$: $\frac{24\text{-}25}{14.5\text{-}16}$
L. M^2-P^4: 34 (calculated)
L. M^1-M^3: ± 68-72 (calculated)
L. P^2-M^3: ± 102-106 (calculated)
Lower jaw and dentition
L./W. m_3: $\frac{24.5}{8.5}$
L./W. P_2: $\frac{10.5\text{-}11.5}{5.5\text{-}6}$
L./W. P_3: $\frac{13\text{-}14.5}{7.5\text{-}8}$
L./W. P_4: $\frac{15\text{-}16}{9}$
L./W. M_1: $\frac{20\text{-}22}{10\text{-}12}$
L./W. M_2: $\frac{22\text{-}25}{10\text{-}12}$

L./W. M$_3$: $\frac{29\text{-}31}{10\text{-}11}$

L. P$_2$-P$_4$: 28.5-32

L. M$_1$-M$_3$: 71-78

L. P$_2$-M$_3$: 99.5-110

Vertebrae

    L. central body: 37-45

Ribs

Any rib with a width between 10 and 25 mm. has been included here. There may be some overlap with big ribs of *Gazella.* There is little chance that smaller equid ribs have been mixed in this lot, because the equid material is very limited in the whole collection.

Scapulum

    Min. D. articular surface: 34-37

    Max. D. articular surface: 44-47

    Max. TR.D. articular surface + notch: 55-57

Radius

    TR.D. prox.: 54.5-58

    A-P.D. prox.: 27-30.5

    A-P.D. dist.: 30-34

    TR.D. dist.: 41.5-44

Cubitus

    A-P.D. olecranon: 48

    TR.D. above great sigmoid cavity: 16.5-18

    A-P.D. prox. tuberosity olecranon: 39

    TR.D. prox. tuberosity olecranon: 18-20

Magnum

    TR.D.: 27-28 mm.

    A-P.D.: 27-29 mm.

Femur

    A-P.D. prox. head: 33

    TR.D. dist. epiphysis: 70

    A-P.D. dist. epiphysis: 90

    Max. TR.D. trochlea: 31-32

    TR.D. mesial condyle: 22-23

    A-P.D. mesial condyle: 41-44

    TR.D. external condyle: 26

    A-P.D. external condyle: 44

Tibia

    TR.D. prox.: ± 65

    A-P.D. dist.: 34-36

    TR.D. dist.: 44-46

Calcaneum

    A-P.D. prox. tuberosity: 28-32

    TR.D. prox. tuberosity: 22-23

    Max. A-P.D.: 41-44

    Max. TR.D.: 35-36

Astragalus

    Max. L.: 45.5-48

    A-P.D.: 26-28

    TR.D.: 27-31.5

Naviculo-cuboid

    A-P.D.: 34-35

    TR.D.: 39-43

    A-P.D.: 24-27

    TR.D.: 14-17

Cannon bone

    TR.D. prox.: 26 (mc.)

    A-P.D. prox.: 43 (mc.)-37 (mt.)

    TR.D. dist.: 28-29 (mc. or mt.)

    A-P.D. dist.: 43-46.5 (mc. or mt.)

First phalanges

    L.: 66-73

    TR.D. prox.: 20-23

    A-P.D. prox.: 24-28

    TR.D. dist.: 15-19

    A-P.D. dist.: 16-20

Second phalanges

    L.: 33-41

    TR.D. prox.: 17-20

    A-P.D. prox.: 26-27

    TR.D. dist.: 13-17

    A-P.D. dist.: 15-21

Remarks

As no horn-cores have been collected, it is difficult to say which (sub) species of *Alcelaphus* is present.

Following Ruxton and Schwarz (1929; cf. Allen, 1939) the *Alcelaphus*-group may be divided into *A. buselaphus, A. caama,* and *A. lichtensteini.* Within *A. buselaphus* twelve subspecies can be recognized divisible into five regional groups: *buselaphus, major, lelwel-jacksoni, tora-swaynei* and *cokei,* the remaining subspecies being by-forms of either *major* or *lelwel.*

According to Setzer (1956, pp. 577-578) the following *Alcelaphus*-forms occur in the Sudan: *A. buselaphus lelwel, A. b. roosevelti* (= ? *jacksoni* or *tora*), *A. b. tora,* and *A. b. tchadiensis* (= ? *lelwel*). He comments that any of the so-called races of *Alcelaphus* in the Sudan may in the end not stand critical examination, but will be shown to be synonymous with the older name *tora.* Mackenzie (1954, pp. 7-8) lists *A. b. lelwel, A. b. tora,* and *A. b. lelwel* X *tora* (= Neumann's Hartebeest).

The collected teeth compare very well with

those of specimens of *A. b. lelwel* and *A. b. lichtensteini* at the IRSNB (Reg. 12243, 12245, and 12048). They seem to be slightly larger than in the mentioned specimens, but this may be due to individual variation. The post-cranial skeleton can be compared with *Alcelaphus buselaphus* in Vaufrey (1955, pp. 378-379) and with *A. buselaphus* from Kom Ombo (Gaillard, 1934, pp. 40-44).

There is a chance that the material represents *A. b. buselaphus,* which became extinct in historical times. Indeed the material has been collected near the southern limit of the former range of this subspecies (cf. Wells, 1959). This form is smaller than *A. b. tora* or *A. b. lelwel.* We do not know how clearly this difference in size is reflected in the length of the teeth rows. If so, the fossil *Alcelaphus* would have about the size of *A. lichtensteini, A. b. tora,* or *A. b. lelwel.* On the other hand, it has been noted frequently that Pleistocene representatives of extant species are bigger than their living descendants (see also *Gazella rufifrons*). Therefore, the fossil hartebeest may either be a Pleistocene representative of *A. b. buselaphus* or rather belong to the *tora* (or *lelwel*) group.

GAZELLA DORCAS (Linnaeus)
Figure 2, Numbers 4, 5, 8

Material (Table 4)

Horn-cores
Male
A-P.D. base: ± 25
TR.D. base: ± 20
Horn-core index: ± 0.80
A-P.D. ± midway: 20-22-23
A-P.D. ± midway: 16-16.5-17
L. outer curve: ± 145
Female
A-P.D. base: 12
TR.D. base: 15
Horn-core index: 0.80
Cranium and upper dentition
L. P^2-P^4: 19
L. M^1-M^3: 30.5
L. P^2-M^3: 49-51
TR.D. palatal between M^1 and M^2: 22
$\dfrac{\text{L. } P^2\text{-}P^4}{\text{L. } M^1\text{-}M^3} \times 100 = 62.3$
L./W. M_3: 13.5/8.5

TABLE 4

IDENTIFIED FRAGMENTS OF *Gazella dorcas* (LINNAEUS)
AT DIFFERENT SITES

Gazella dorcas (LINNAEUS)

Material	8873	8800
Horncores		
a. Male, w/o base[1]	1	1
b. Fragments	2	2
c. Fragment cranium w/base		2 R. (female)
Cranium and Upper Dentition		
a. Almost\ complete lower cranium w/palatal		1
b. Fragments mandible w/ dentition		4
c. Fragment cranium		1 L. frontal
Lower Jaw and Dentition		
a. More or less complete, and fragments with teeth or alveoli		10 L, 7 R
b. Fragments vertical ramus		2 L, 4 R
c. Fragments jaw	2	
Fragments upper and lower		
Molariform teeth		± 200
Vertebrae and ribs		
a. Fragment atlas		2
b. Fragment dorsal vertebrae		1
c. Lumbar vertebrae		4
d. Rib fragments		4
Scapulum		
a. Complete specimens[2]		2 R
b. Fragments		1
Humerus		
a. Distal epiphyses w/fragment shaft		3 R.
b. Fragment shaft		1 L.
Radius		
a. Complete proximal epiphysis	1 L	1 L
b. Fragment proximal epiphysis		2 L, 1 R, 1?
c. Fragments shaft	1 R	1 L, 1 R, 1?
d. Distal epiphysis with part of shaft		1 L
Cubitus		
a. Complete specimens		3 L
b. Fragment proximal tuberosity		1 L
Femur, fragmentary distal epiphysis		1 L
Tibia		
a. Distal epiphyses		2 R, 3 L
b. Fragments shaft	1 R	3 R, 5 L
c. Fragments distal epiphysis	1 L, 1 R	
d. Fragments distal epiphysis[3]	1 L, 1 R	
Calcaneum		
a. Complete specimens		1 R, 2 L
b. Fragments	3 R, 1 L	
Astragalus, complete		1 R
Cannon Bone		
a. Complete metatarsal, distal epiphysis not fused, and missing		1 R
b. Fragmentary, distal part missing	L(mc)	1 R (mt), R (mc)
c. Fragments proximal epiphysis	1? (mt)	1 R (mc), 3 R (mt), 4 L (mt)
d. Fragments shaft	1	4
e. Distal epiphyses, with part of shaft	1	2
First Phalanges, complete		4

[1] One specimen base male horncore from Site 8906-B.
[2] Also one specimen (R) from Site 8702.
[3] Also one specimen (L) from Site 8702.
[4] Also one specimen from Site 8913.

Lower jaw and dentition
L. P_2-P_4: 16-20 (m_1-m_3: 22)
L. M_1-M_3: 33-37
L. P_2-M_3^3: 50-56
L./W. M_3: 16-17/6-7
H. condyle: 45-47
TR.D. condyle: 11-13
Total L. horizontal ramus: ± 120
Scapulum
Min. articular surface: 17-18.5
Max. articular surface: 18-21

D. articular surface + notch: 22.5-24.5

Humerus

    TR.D. dist.: 22-24

    A-P.D. dist.: 19-21.5

Radius

    TR.D. prox.: 20-21

    A-P.D. prox.: 12

    TR.D. middle: 12.5

    A-P.D. middle: 7

    TR.D. dist.: 19.5

    A-P.D. dist.: 14

Cubitus

    A-P.D. olecranon: 18-19

    A-P.D. prox. tuberosity olecranon: 16

    TR.D. prox. tuberosity olecranon: 6.5-8

    TR.D. big sigmoid cavity: 11-12.5

    TR.D. above big sigmoid cavity: 7-8

Femur

    TR.D. dist. epiphysis: ± 30

    Smaller TR.D. trochlea: 12

    Greater TR.D. trochlea: 15

    A-P.D. dist. epiphysis: ± 38

    TR.D. external condyle: 11.5

    A-P.D. external condyle: 20

    TR.D. mesial condyle: 12

    A-P.D. mesial condyle: 18

Tibia

    Total L.: ± 190

    TR.D.: middle shaft: 12-13

    A-P.D. middle shaft: 10-11

    TR.D. dist.: 19-20.5

    A-P.D. dist.: 15-16.5

Calcaneum

    A-P.D. prox. tuberosity: 14-15

    TR.D. prox. tuberosity: 11-11.5

    Max. A-P.D.: 19.5-21

    Max. TR.D.: 16-17.5

Astragalus

    Max. L.: 23.5

    A-P.D.: 13.5

    TR.D.: 14

    TR.D. neck: 12.5

Cannon bone

    L. without distal epiphysis: 137 (mt.)

    Total L.: ± 150 (mt. female ?)

    TR.D. prox.: 15-16 (mt.); 16-17 (mc.)

    A-P.D. prox.: 12-13 (mc.); 17-18 (mt.)

    A-P.D. middle: 8-10 (mc. & mt.)

    TR.D. middle: 11.5-13 (mc. & mt.)

    TR.D. dist.: 16-17 (mt.); 17-19 (mc.)

    A-P.D. dist.: 12-14 (mt.); 14-15 (mc.)

First phalanges

    L.: 36-41

    TR.D. prox.: 8-9.5

    A-P.D. prox.: 12-13

    TR.D. middle: 5.5-7

    A-P.D. middle: 7.5-8.5

    TR.D. dist.: 7-8.5

    A-P.D. dist.: 8-9

Remarks

All the material described under this heading has been collected at C-group sites, except the horn-core found at a Mesolithic Site 8906b. It is much eolized and has probably been collected on the surface. Therefore, it may be intrusive and date from a much later period than the cultural contents of Site 8906b.

The Gazella of the C-group sites is smaller than the form occurring at the older sites. Its horn-core index falls within the upper range of *Gazella dorcas* horn-cores (see Gentry, 1964, p. 357). Cross-sections of the horn-cores can be compared with the cross-section of *G. dorcas* figured in Gentry (1966, p. 63, fig. 7). According to Setzer (1956, p. 580), *G. dorcas* is represented in the Sudan by three subspecies: *G. d. isabella*, *G. d. littoralis*, and *G. d. osiris*. Mackenzie (1954, p. 13) gives approximately the same geographical distribution for two of these subspecies; *G. d. osiris*, however, seems to be *G. d. dorcas* in his census of Sudanese artiodactyles, as the area occupied by Setzer's *G. d. osiris* corresponds to the area occupied by Mackenzie's *G. d. dorcas*. It is practically impossible to separate these subspecies on osteological evidence, except maybe when several complete skeletons are present. Therefore, the C-group material has to be put on record as *G. dorcas*. It might represent either *G. dorcas littoralis* or *G. dorcas osiris*.

It is quite interesting that the C-group Gazella is different from the Gazella at the older sites. Gentry (1964, p. 354) suggests that *G. dorcas* could be the extension into North Africa of the Palearctic *G. dorcas* stock. Although the record of Gazellas around Wadi-Halfa during the Upper Pleistocene and Holocene is incomplete, it seems to corroborate this hypothesis. Probably *G. dorcas* arrived in the area when climatic conditions were deteriorating. This species seems to have much more resistance to drought than *G. rufifrons* or *G. thomsoni*, which are more typical savanna dwellers and representatives of the African Gazelline stock. When exactly *G. dorcas* replaced the larger Gazella known from the older sites is not known. The latest site containing *G. rufifrons* seems to be DIW-5, dated about 3,550 B.C. The C-group sites date from the period around 1,750 B.C.

GAZELLA RUFIFRONS Gray

Figure 1, Number 8; Figure 2, Numbers 3, 7

Material (Table 5)

Horn-cores

TABLE 5
IDENTIFIED FRAGMENTS OF *Gazella rufifrons* GRAY AT DIFFERENT SITES

MATERIAL	1017	1018	443	8859	1028	8899	ANE-1	34-C	8905	8905-A	8905-C	8905-D	DIW51	8957
Horncores														
a. Base male horncore w/part skull									1L					
b. Bases, male							3R, 1L	1(?)		2R			1	
c. Male horncores w/o base[1]			2(?)				1(?)				1			
d. Fragments		1					1(?)							
Mandible and Upper Dentition														
a. Fragment mandible w/teeth	2L				1R									
b. Isolated molars	1						1							
Lower Jaw and Dentition														
a. Fragments symphysis						1								
b. Fragments jaw in front of teeth					1R								1R	
c. Fragments jaw w/dentition	2				5			1						
d. Fragments ramus w/condyle	1R				1L		1R							
e. Isolated teeth	2				1		1	1			1			
Vertebrae and Ribs														
a. Central bodies		1					1							
b. Fragments cervical vertebrae				1			1							
c. Fragment rib												1		
Scapulum														
a. Complete specimen[2]														
b. Fragments							2L, 2R							
Humerus														
a. Fragments distal shaft										1R				1L
b. Fragmentary distal epiphyses					1L		1L				1L			
c. Complete distal epiphyses										2R				
Radius														
a. Fragment shaft w/proximal epiphysis												1R		
b. Distal epiphyses w/part of shaft							1L					1R		
c. Fragment shaft[3]														
Scaphoid, complete			1R											
Cubitus, fragments							2L					1R		
Pelvis, fragment acetabulum							1R							
Femur														
a. Fragment proximal head						1								
b. Fragment distal condyle					1									
Tibia														
a. Fragment proximal epiphysis							1L							
b. Distal epiphyses							2L	1L						
c. Fragment distal epiphysis					1R									
Calcaneum, fragmentary							1R				1L			
Astragalus, complete[3]										1R				
Cannonbone														
a. Distal epiphyses w/part of shaft							2R							
b. Fragments shaft[4]					1		1							
c. Distal epiphyses w/part of shaft			2		2									
d. Moieties and fragments distal epiphysis[5]			1		3	1	4			1	1			
First Phalanges														
a. Complete								1						
b. fragments epiphysis					2									
Second Phalanges														
a. Complete[4]			1		2									
b. Distal fragments							2							
Hoofphalanges, complete				1	2			1	1					

1. Also one left and one right from Site 440.
2. Also one right from Site Dibeira West 1.
3. Also one from Site 8905, Locality F.
4. Also one each from Site 34, Industry B.
5. Also one from Site 8899, Industry C.

A-P.D. base: 30-33
TR.D. base: 20-24
A-P.D. middle: 24-26
TR.D. middle: 17-18
Horn-core index (male): 66.6-72.7 (average: 69.6)
Mandible and upper dentition
  L. P^2-P^4: $\pm$ 22
  L. M^1-M^3: $\pm$ 33
  L. P^2-M^4: $\pm$ 55
  L./W. M^3: $\dfrac{11.5}{10}$
  Ratio $\dfrac{\text{L. P}^2\text{-P}^4}{\text{L. M}^1\text{-M}^3}$ x 100: 66.6
Lower jaw and dentition
  L. P$_2$-P$_4$: 17-20
  L. M$_1$-M$_3$: $\pm$ 41-43
  L. P$_2$-M$_3$: $\pm$ 58-61 (62.5)
  L./W. M$_3$: $\dfrac{17\text{-}18\ (19.5)}{7\text{-}7.5}$
  TR.D. condyle: 12.5-14

The M$_3$ of 34 is rather big (length: 19.5). Other material from 34 (distal fragment tibia) does not seem to be larger than comparable fragments from other sites. Therefore, it seems probable that the greater size of the M$_3$ from Site 34 does not indicate the presence of a larger species, but that it is rather due to individual variation.

Vertebrae and ribs
  L. corpus vertebralis: 19
Scapulum
  Min. D. articular surface: 19
  Max. D. articular surface: 21
  D. articular surface + notch: 27
Humerus
  TR.D. dist.: 26-27
  A-P.D. dist.: 24
Radius
  TR.D. prox.: $\pm$ 25
  A-P.D. prox.: $\pm$ 15
  TR.D. dist.: 23.5
  A-P.D. dist.: 16
Cubitus
  TR.D. above big sigmoid cavity: 9
Tibia
  TR.D. dist.: 22.5-23.5
  A-P.D. dist.: 18-19
Calcaneum
  TR.D. below prox. tuberosity: 8.5
  A-P.D. below prox. tuberosity: 17
Cannon bone

TR.D. prox.: 19.5 (mc.)
A-P.D. prox.: 14 (mc.)
TR.D. middle: 11 (mt.)
A-P.D. middle: 15 (mt.)
TR.D. dist.: 19.5-22 (mc. and/or mt.)
A-P.D. dist.: 14-16 (mc. and/or mt.)
First phalanges
  TR.D. dist.: 8.5-9.5
  A-P.D. dist.: 9-10
Second phalanges
  L.: 23-25
  A-P.D. prox.: 11-12
  TR.D. prox.: 8-10
  A-P.D. dist.: 10-11
  TR.D. dist.: 8-10
Hoofphalanges
  H.: 14-16
  TR.D.:7-8.5
  A-P.D.: 30

Remarks

The material was collected at sites older than those of the C-Group. The size of the remains indicates that this Gazella is about 10 cm. larger than *G. dorcas*. It would measure 65-75 cm. at the withers. This is about the size of *G. thomsoni* or *G. rufifrons*.

The horn-core indices fall within the range of *G. rufifrons* or *G. dorcas* (see Gentry, 1964, p. 357). The cross-sections, however, seem to be flattened somewhat more than in *G. dorcas* (Gentry, 1966, p. 63, fig. 7), although they are still subangular. The average horn-core index lies nearer to the mean value of *G. rufifrons* than to the one in *G. dorcas*. The difference in mean value between *G. rufifrons* and *G. dorcas*, however, is not statistically significant.

The absolute measurements of the horn-cores are larger than in *Gazella dorcas*, which we measured at the IRSNB, and in *G. dorcas* specimens from the Near East measured by Hooijer (1961, p. 47). Wells and Cooke (1956, p. 39) give average dimensions for horn-cores of *G. rufifrons*: 27 x 19 mm., and for those in *G. thomsoni*: 32 x 22 mm. Measurements of a specimen at the Natural History Museum (London), however, are comparable to those for the Sudanese fossil. It should also be mentioned that Hooijer (1961) records *Gazella* cf. *dorcas* from the rock-shelter at Ksâr'akil, of which the horn-cores are larger than those of the present day *G. dorcas* or *G. gazella*. This would conform to the general rule that Pleistocene representatives of extant species are often somewhat larger than their living descendants.

The estimated ratios of upper premolar length to upper molar length are again within the range of *G. dorcas* or *G. rufifrons*. The absolute measurements, however, rather favor the identification as *G. rufifrons*.

G. rufifrons laevipes is found today south of Khartoum along both sides of the Nile in arid acacia grassland to drier savanna country, while *G. thomsoni* (Mongalla Gazella) occurs only in the southeastern, more luxurious, savanna of the Sudan (Mackenzie, 1954, pp. 13-15; see also Gentry, 1964, p. 355).

It seems more reasonable to accept that during the Holocene *G. dorcas,* coming from the north, replaced the Red-fronted Gazella which withdrew to the south following the apparent shift south of the vegetation belts.

GAZELLA (NANGER) sp.
Figure 1, Number 11

Material

Fragments jaw with teeth: Site DIW-53 (subsurface) (M_1-M_2 dex.; M_2 dex.; P_4 dex.)
Isolated teeth: Site 1032 (M_1 size)
L./W. M_1: 16-17/8.5-10
L./W. M_2: 17.5-18/9.5-10

Remarks

The outline of the teeth can be compared with the figured molar of *G. granti* in Gentry (1966, p. 26, fig. 15). The size of the material agrees rather well with the measurements for *G. granti* given by Dietrich (1950, p. 26). The material has also been compared with *Gazella dama* at the IRSNB (Reg. 1383y), in which the transverse diameter of the teeth is slightly smaller.

Specimens of the subgenus *Gazella* (*Nanger*) in the Sudan are *G. granti*, *G. dama*, and *G. soemmeringi* (Mackenzie, 1954, pp. 13-15; Setzer, 1956, p. 582). More material is required in order to say which species is present. Probably the material represents *G. dama*, of which the subspecies *G. dama ruficolis* is still found west of the Nile between Dongola and Khartoum in desert to arid conditions (cf. Remarks *Gazella rufifrons*).

CAPRA HIRCUS (? or OVIS ARIES)

Material

Skull and dentition

Fragment upper jaw with not yet broken through P^2: Site 8800(r.)
Fragmentary molars: Sites 8702 (M_2); 8702 (M_2, M_3 dex.; M_3 sin.); 8866 (M^2)
Fragments molariform teeth: Sites 8848 (3); 8866 (4); 8702 (10)
L. M^2: 16
L./W. M_2: $\frac{14\text{-}16}{8.5\text{-}?}$
L./W. M_3: 23/8.5

Vertebrae

One central body of lumbar vertebra: Site 8800
L. corpus vertebralis: 32

Radius

Shaft juvenile radius: Site 8773 (r.)
Almost complete specimen, distal epiphyses not yet ankylosed and missing: Site 8773 (r.)
Proximal epiphysis with part of shaft: Site 8773 (2)
Fragment proximal epiphysis: Site 8800 (l.; r.)
TR.D. prox.: 35 (26)
A-P.D. prox.: 18-19 (14)
TR.D. middle: 16 (15)
A-P.D. middle: 10 (7.5)
The measurements for the smaller almost complete radius 8773 are given between parentheses.

Cubitus

Fragmentary specimen: Site 8873 (2)
TR.D. above great sigmoid cavity: 10.5

Calcaneum

Fragmentary specimen: Site 8773
A-P.D. below prox. tuberosity: 14
TR.D. below prox. tuberosity: 7.5
TR.D. max.: ± 21

Cannon bone

Complete metacarpal, distal epiphysis not yet fused and lacking: Site 8773 (l.)
Fragments proximal epiphysis: Sites 8773 (l.); 8773 (l. mc.); 8800 (2 r.)
Distal epiphysis: Sites 8773; 8848 (fragment of condyle)
Shaft of young individuals (epiphyses lacking): Sites 8773; 8800

TR.D. prox.: 27.5 mc. (30-32 mc.)
A-P.D. prox.: 18 mc. (20-21 mc.)
TR.D. middle: 16-18 (mc. or/and mt.)
A-P.D. middle: 11-14 (mc. or/and mt.)
TR.D. dist.: 31-33 (mc. or/and mt.)
A-P.D. dist.: 14 (mc. or/and mt.)
L. without distal epiphysis: ± 115 (mc.)
Total L.: ± 130 (mc.)

The measurements between parentheses are those for the proximal epiphyses from Sites 8773 and 8800. These are somewhat larger and may represent old individuals or males while the other material (measurements not between parentheses) may represent younger individuals or females.

Remarks

The material has been collected at sites from the C-group, except the tooth from Site 8866. This site is Mesolithic, but the collection was probably made on the surface. At Site 8848 a few tooth fragments and a fragment of a distal condyle would represent a small ruminant, comparable to the one from the C-group sites. This site is stated to be Neolithic, but the material comes from the surface. If the identifications are correct, one must accept that the material is probably intrusive at both sites.

Compared with the C-group *Gazella* material, the fragments described above are much less well preserved. This would be due to the more spongy texture of the bones, a condition often met with in domesticated animals.

The measurements for the teeth can be compared with those of the Neolithic goat "Hircus mambrica" from Toukh (Gaillard, 1934, p. 79). The metacarpus length compares with the analogous measurement in *Capra hircus mambrica* from the Dynastic period in Egypt (Lortet and Gaillard, 1903, p. 110).

Apart from "Hircus mambrica," another goat would be present at Toukh, described as "Hircus reversus" (Gaillard, 1934, p. 81). At Esh Shabeinab, Bate (1953) described a dwarf goat akin to the modern Sudanese dwarf goat and another small ruminant, goat, or sheep. This second animal was assigned to the Jericho-goat type by Zeuner (1963). According to Bate (1953) the Esh Shabeinab dwarf goat is quite different from the Toukh "Hircus reversus."

As the material is very poor, it can only be put on record tentatively. It might be a goat comparable to the large Toukh goat, the larger Esh Shabeinab goat, or represent still another form. There is also a probability that the material represents sheep. The rather low crown and the somewhat large transverse diameter of the lower teeth agree with the identification of the material as goat.[2] Sheep were known by the Fayum people, the Tarsians and the Badarians in Egypt. At Esh Shabeinab only a single horn-core suggests the presence of sheep.

UNIDENTIFIED MATERIAL

Small rodent

A small rodent is present at Site 8859. The material is rather fragmentary: two incisives, two jugal teeth, and a calcaneum. This material reached us at the end of the study and has been sent to R. Lavocat (Paris) for identification.

Small carnivore

Material
Fragment of left jaw with alveoli: Site 8800.
Remarks
As Site 8800 is a C-group site, the fragment represents very probably a species still living in the Northern Sudan.

Medium sized ruminant

A very incomplete lower molar of a ruminant might represent a calf of wild or domesticated cattle at Site 8800, but this identification is doubtful.

Large antelope

Material
First phalanx, proximal epiphysis lacking: Site ANE-1
L.: ± 50
TR.D. dist.: 26
A-P.D. dist.: 20
Lower sesamoids: Site 34 U.L. (2).
Remarks

---

[2] Since studying the material described above, the author has gained more experience with domestic sheep or goat. A more significant diagnostic feature is the ratio length / TR.D. diaphysis of the metapodals. The transverse diameter of the metacarpal from Site 8773 is 18 mm., although the specimen is not fully grown; therefore, it seems to have belonged to a large, subadult goat.

The lower sesamoids can be matched with the phalanx. Therefore, these isolated finds may represent one species. We compared the material with small *Taurotragus oryx* (IRSNB, Reg. 13946) and found that the fossil phalanx is only slightly smaller. *Taurotragus oryx* is still found in the southeastern part of the Sudan (Mackenzie, 1954).

PALEOECOLOGY

In Table 6 the sites are listed in the order in which the approximate age was known to us. Although the absolute (and relative) frequencies of the different species at each site vary markedly, we have not been able to detect any causal relationship between the quantitative composition of the collections per site and climatological or other factors of supraregional importance. The variation in the ratios of the most important species would be purely accidental or reflect the small size of the collections and the hazards of the hunting.

Most sites are divided into features. As with the sites, the features in each site yield quantitatively different assemblages; but again these differences are not likely to have much importance.

Three species seem to have been hunted regularly during the Upper Pleistocene and the early part of the Holocene: *Bos primigenius, Alcelaphus buselaphus,* and *Gazella rufifrons.* Two other species are less important: *Equus asinus* cf. *africanus* and *Hippopotamus amphibius.* Some other species occur sporadically: *Adenota kob* cf. *leucotis, Gazella* (*Nanger* sp.), *Canis aureus* cf. *soudanicus, C. mesomelas,* and *Lepus* sp. Several of these animals or comparable forms were still hunted during Dynastic times in Egypt: hippopotamus, aurochs, *Gazella dorcas,* the bubal (a hartebeest not necessarily identical with the Sudanese fossil form), and several other antelopes now only found along much more southernly latitudes.

The fact that *B. primigenius, A. buselaphus,* and *G. rufifrons* dominate the collected assemblages indicates that these species were probably very abundant game in the area. *A. buselaphus* is normally found in dry to more luxurious grassland or savanna. *G. rufifrons* still occur in the Sudan south of Khartoum. Wild cattle (aurochs) would prefer open arid grassland, dry bushland,

or even light woodland (cf. Higgs (a), in press). *Adenota kob* and *Gazella* (*Nanger*) sp. are found today in or near the southern Sudan, where savanna country prevails. The fossil *Canis* cf. *soudanicus,* which is rather big, might also indicate slightly better climatic conditions. *C. mesomelas,* the size of which agrees with the size of the extant form, occurs only in the southern Sudan. Perhaps the biotope of this jackal found around Wadi Halfa during the Upper Pleistocene did not differ very markedly from the one this animal lives in today.

B. primigenius is dominant within the group of the most frequent species. It is difficult to say if the aurochs was really the most abundant species during the Upper Pleistocene. Heavy bones have a better chance to yield identifiable fragments. Second, primitive man may have concentrated successfully on hunting this large animal instead of the smaller Hartebeest or *Gazella rufifrons.*

On the whole, one may conclude that during the period spanned by the sites older than those from the C-group, the region around Wadi Halfa and the Northern Sudan could support a much larger fauna than it could today without too much human interference. We would suggest that most of the time open dry grassland covered the area, while along the Nile and the wadis a more wooded and humid vegetation flourished. This type of country was probably also found along part of the Nile and its tributaries in Southern Egypt (cf. fauna of Kom Ombo; Gaillard, 1934). Such country can easily support large herds of wild cattle, together with less important populations of other ruminants.

The change of the vegetation into its present day state probably began during the C-group period. Along the Nile, it may even be directly related with the arrival of the domesticated animals, especially goat, of which the devastating influence on vegetation is well known (Zeuner, 1963). The replacement of *G. rufifrons* by *G. dorcas* in the C-group sites studied here seems to corroborate this tentative dating of the first changes of the vegetation towards very arid conditions. *G. dorcas* is much more resistant to drought than *G. rufifrons* and other African Gazellas.

The picture obtained is one of a shift to the

TABLE 6
FREQUENCIES OF IDENTIFIED FRAGMENTS OF EACH SPECIES AT DIFFERENT SITES

	Site	B. primigenius	A. buselaphus	G. rufifrons	E. a. africanus	H. amphibius	Goat (or Sheep)	Other Species and Remarks
	34 L.L.	1	4	—	—	—	—	
	1017	73	—	8	6	—	—	Lepus, sp. (1)
	34 U.L.	29	1	3	—	—	—	Large antelope (cf. ANE-1) (1)
	ANW-3	53	—	—	11	4	—	
	2004	2	—	—	—	—	—	
	440	48	—	2	1	1	—	
	1020	3	20	—	—	—	—	
	1018	13	40	2	—	—	—	
	624	1	—	—	—	—	—	
	443	114	97	6	—	1	—	Adenota kob ? leucotis (1)
	8859	2	1	3	—	—	—	Small rodent
	8867	8	15	—	—	—	—	
	8868	+	1	—	—	—	—	
	8871	5	2	—	—	—	—	
	1028	3	40	26	2	—	—	
	8956	1	5	—	—	—	—	
	8957	—	4	—	—	—	—	
	8899	19	1	3	—	—	—	
	1024	—	7	—	10	—	—	
	278B	—	—	—	1	—	—	
	34C	40	14	6	1	7	—	Canis aureus ? cf. soudanicus (1)
	ANE-1	140	134	28	3	1	—	Large antelope (cf. 34 U.L.) (1)
	8905	177	50	20	—	2	—	Canis mesomelas (1)
	8905a	5	1	+	—	—	—	
	8905b	—	—	1	—	—	—	Only one horn-core; probably
	8904a	1	—	—	—	—	—	G. dorcas and intrusive
	8864	2	1	—	—	—	—	
	448	15	4	—	—	1	—	Adenota kob ? leucotis (2)
	8895	+	1	—	—	—	—	
	DIW-1	10	14	1	—	3	—	Canis aureus ? cf. soudanicus (1)
	DIW-51	1	1	1	—	—	—	
	DIW-53	—	—	—	—	1	—	Gazella (Nanger) sp. (2)
	DIW-50	1	1	—	—	—	—	
	DIW-5	—	—	1	—	—	—	
	1021	2	—	—	—	—	—	Lepus, sp. (1)
	605	—	1	—	—	—	—	
	621	1	+	—	—	—	—	
	8908	1	—	—	—	—	—	
	8915	1	—	—	—	—	—	
	8822	1	—	G. dorcas	—	—	—	Only a few fragments bovid
C-group Nile	8913	—	1	—	—	—	—	
	8902	1ᵃ	—	—	—	—	—	
C-group Dungul	8800	—	—	135	—	—	7	Small carnivore; medium
	8773	2ᵃ	2	7	2	—	10	sized ruminant
	8702	2ᵃ	1	2	—	—	6	

ᵃ Probably domesticated cattle.

north of the vegetation belts as found today in the Sudan. However, it is still too early to explain this apparent shift in terms of Pleistocene climatological changes. The increase in precipitation in non-glacial regions (pluvials) is not necessarily directly linked with either higher or lower temperatures (glacial or non-glacial periods); much more has to be known about the general distribution of atmospheric pressure above Africa during the glacial, interstadial, or interglacial periods (see reconstructions, Van Zinderen Bakker, in press). Apart from this, such problems as, for example, the retardation and the presence of fossil ground water have to be taken into consideration when deducing climate from the faunal record and its interpretation in terms of vegetation.

The collected fauna can also be described in very general terms of present day or subrecent faunal distribution. *Adenota kob, Gazella (Nanger)* sp., and *Canis mesomelas* can be regarded as more typically "East African" elements; *Gazella rufifrons, Equus asinus africanus,* and *C. aureus* cf. *soudanicus* as more typical northern Sudanese forms; while *Bos primigenius* and maybe *Alcelaphus buselaphus* (? *buselaphus*) are Northern African invaders. There is also *C. thomasi* to provide a link with North Africa (Gautier, 1966).

The material from the C-group described under *B. primigenius* contains, very likely, remains of a large form of domesticated cattle, probably akin to the Egyptian *Bos africanus*. The small domesticated ruminant of these sites is probably goat. It seems that at the time of the C-group only *Gazella dorcas* was still hunted with considerable success. J. de Heinzelin has informed us that C-group people may have used a special hunting technique, based on driving the game towards a fence, interrupted by small passages, through which the animals could escape to be killed. This could explain the large amount of *Gazella dorcas* at Site 8800. The replacing of *Gazella rufifrons* by *Gazella dorcas* during the Holocene has been discussed already.

The fact that the C-group sites yielded only a few bones of domesticated animals should be mentioned. Normally sites of people with real Neolithic economic status yield large numbers of domesticated animal remains. Probably the so-called C-group sites studied here represent a peripheral population still relying on hunting for their needs, but in contact with the real C-group living along the Nile. Very likely this Oasis C-group obtained pottery and occasionally some domesticated animals from Nilotic settlements.

As a general conclusion one may say that the present study does not provide much information apart from the description of the collected mammals. During the Upper Pleistocene better climatic conditions prevailed in the region around Wadi Halfa, but the small amounts of material per site make it impossible to trace back possible fluctuations of the climate during that period.

FISH REMAINS
P. H. Greenwood
(DEPARTMENT OF ZOOLOGY, BRITISH MUSEUM, NATURAL HISTORY)

INTRODUCTION

Six, and possibly seven genera of fishes (representing seven or eight species and six families) have been identified from fifteen sites in Sudanese Nubia. Unfortunately, the fragmentary nature of these remains does not permit identification to the species level except in two cases. Nor, for the same reason, is it possible to use the material as a basis for comparison with populations of, presumably, the same species at present inhabiting the Nile. Nevertheless, this material is valuable since it adds another bit of evidence to the pitifully inadequate record of Quaternary fishes in Africa.

SITE REPORTS

SITE 1017 (Khor Musa; Khormusan industry, dated on charcoal 20,750 B.C. ± 280 years [WSU-203])

Family CLARIIDAE
CLARIAS sp.

Numerous fragments of *Clarias* are the only fish remains collected at this site. If judged by the size of the fishes present, and by the ornamentation of certain neurocranial bones, the species may be *C. lazera* (Val.), the commonest species of *Clarias* inhabiting the Nile today. The almost complete skull is about 170 mm. long, and thus could be from a fish of *ca.* 60 cm. standard length.

In addition to one almost complete neurocranium and a large portion of another, there are 60 fragments (some almost complete) of neurocranial bones, mostly from the roofing series.

Jaws are represented by two fragments (premaxillae), the pectoral girdle by three fragments of cleithrum (and one left pectoral fin spine), and the hyobranchial skeleton by three specimens (an epihyal and two branchiostegal rays). Only one vertebra can be identified as definitely being from a *Clarias*.

SITE ANW-3 (Anquash West; Khormusan industry, dates on charcoal 15,850 B.C. ± 500 years [WSU-215])

Three genera, and possibly a fourth, are recorded from this site.

Family CLARIIDAE
CLARIAS sp.

The genus is represented by one almost complete neurocranium, one damaged neurocranium and 43 neurocranial fragments. The larger and more complete skull is about 160 mm. long (from anterior tip of vomer to posterior tip of supraoccipital) and the smaller about 140 mm. long, thus being from fishes of *ca.* 60 and 55 cm. standard length respectively. Neurocranial ornamentation and the shape of the vomerine tooth patch in these specimens closely approach those of *Clarias lazera*.

The jaws (dentary and articular) are represented by three fragments (two from the right side, one from the left), the hyobranchial skeleton (epi-, cerato- and urohyal) by five specimens (one medial and two each from the left and right sides), the pectoral girdle by six fragments of cleithrum and coracoid, and by one right pectoral spine.

No *Clarias* vertebrae are present in the samples available.

Family MOCHOKIDAE
SYNODONTIS sp.

This genus is represented only by a fragment from the ventral margin of the right humeral process (a posterior plate-like extension of the cleithrum).

In addition, part of a dorsal fin spine is tentatively identified as being from a *Synodontis*.

Family CYPRINIDAE
BARBUS sp.

The sole remnant of this genus is part of the transverse process from the *pars sustentaculum* of the Weberian apparatus.

Family ? Centropomidae
? Lates sp.

A large fragment of a flat bone is thought, because of its shape and ridging, to be part of the right frontal from a large specimen of *Lates*.

Site 2004 (Gemai, south of Abka; Khormusan industry, age, based on typology, *ca.* 15,000-16,000 b.c.)

This site yielded the best preserved and most varied remains of *Barbus*, together with a very few fragments of *Clarias*.

Family Clariidae
Clarias sp.

Part of a left cleithrum (the ascending arm and part of the articular fossa) and a first vertebra are the only remains of this genus in the sample.

Family Cyprinidae
Barbus sp. cf Barbus bynni

From the viewpoint of species identification, the lower pharyngeal bones are the most useful elements available in this sample, especially when correlated with the two spine-like dorsal fin ray specimens. If judged by the stoutness of these ossified rays and by the morphology of the pharyngeal teeth, these bones are probably from specimens of *Barbus bynni* (Forsk.).

There are five almost complete pharyngeal bones (two left, three right), all from fishes with estimated standard lengths of between 35 and 45 cm., and two pharyngeal bone fragments (probably from the same bone). (See fig. 1, nos. 3 and 4.)

The vertebral column is poorly represented by one first vertebra (breadth of centrum, anterior face, 8 mm.; length 7 mm.), three caudal vertebrae (still articulated), and one almost complete and articulated caudal fin skeleton (the terminal and three preceding vertebrae, together with the proximal ends of the hypurals).

An almost complete left frontal and part of a basioccipital are the only neurocranial elements preserved. The hyobranchial skeleton is represented by a complete ceratohyal.

The supporting skeleton for the fins (besides the caudal skeleton mentioned earlier) is repre-sented by two first dorsal pterygiophores (both virtually complete and from fishes of the same size) and eight other pterygiophores whose serial position cannot be determined further than to say that they are from the anterior part of the dorsal fin. One pterygiophore fragment is thought to be from a dorsal fin support, and two other fragments are tentatively identified as parts of pterygiophores.

In addition to these dorsal fin supports there are remains of the rayed portion of that fin (the proximal part of the ossified second and third unbranched rays). These stout, well-ossified rays compare closely with similar rays in *Barbus bynni*. A group of nine closely approximated rays are thought to be from a pectoral fin.

Site 443 (Khor Musa, Halfan industry; dates on charcoal 14,550 b.c. ± 500 years [WSU-201])

Only two genera are present in material from this site, and the identity of one is tentative.

Family Clariidae
Clarias sp.

Clarias is poorly represented by thirteen fragments of neurocranial bones (mostly roofing elements) and one fragmentary pectoral fin spine. Judging from the different sizes of various skull bones, several fishes are represented by these remains.

Family ? Cyprinidae
? Barbus sp.

The inclusion of this family rests solely on a fragment of a fin spine thought to be from the distal end of the third unbranched dorsal fin ray of a large *Barbus* species.

Site 1018 (Near Site 443; Halfan industry, similar position)

Only *Clarias*, and poorly represented at that, is present at this site. There are two fragments of neurocranial roofing bones, and one vertebra.

Site 1020 (Near Sites 443-1018; Halfan industry, similar position)

Two fragments of *Clarias* neurocranial bones are the only fish remains from this site.

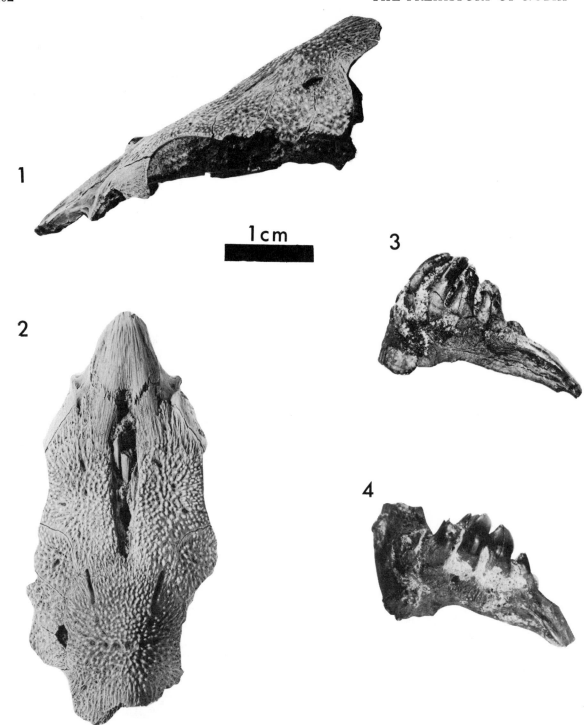

FIG. 1—Fish remains from Nubia.

No. 1—Neurocranium of *Synodontis clarias*, in lateral view. Specimen from Site Dibeira 18 (D-1).
No. 2—Neurocranium of *Synodontis clarias*, in dorsal view. Same specimen as in No. 1.
No. 3—Part of left lower pharyngeal bone (medial aspect) of *Barbus bynni*. Specimen from Site 2004.
No. 4—Part of left lower pharyngeal bone (medial aspect) of *Barbus bynni*. Another specimen, also from Site 2004.

SITE 440 (Khor Musa; unnamed industry, dated on charcoal 12,390 B.C. ± 500 years [WSU-290])

This site has yielded one of the largest aggregates of genera; five genera are identified with certainty, and a sixth genus is probably present.

Fish remains at this site came from two strata, viz., level 3 and level 4 of excavations made in 1963-1964 (which is equivalent to level 6 of the 1964-1965 season).

Level 3 yielded remains of *Clarias, Bagrus,* and *Lates;* while level 4 yielded remains of *Clarias, Synodontis, Lates, Tilapia,* and probably *Barbus.*

Family CLARIIDAE
CLARIAS sp. (Levels 3 and 4)

The neurocranium is represented by 224 fragments, mostly of roofing bones but including portions of the parasphenoid, derived from several fishes of various sizes.

Jaws (dentaries, articulars and premaxillae) are represented by seven specimens, the hyobranchial skeleton by three and the pectoral girdle by twenty-three specimens (mostly fragments of cleithra and coracoids). In addition there are eleven fragments of pectoral fin spines (three right, three left, and five indeterminable), and seven vertebrae (from both caudal and abdominal regions of the column).

Family BAGRIDAE
BAGRUS sp. (Level 3 only)

The only *Bagrus* fossil preserved is a fragment of cleithrum from that region of the bone contributing to the articular facet for the pectoral fin spine.

Two fragments from a fused vertebral mass (one from the anterior and one from the posterior part) are tentatively identified as being from a member of the Bagridae, probably *Bagrus.*

Family MOCHOKIDAE
SYNODONTIS sp. (Level 4 only)

Although this genus is well represented at Site 440, none of the specimens is sufficiently complete to permit specific identification, or close comparison with the shape and ornamentation of similar bones in living species.

Apart from one neurocranial fragment (part of an ethmoid) and two small fragments of humeral process, all the *Synodontis* material consists of portions of fin spines. There are twenty-four fragments from pectoral spines (two left, two right and twenty indeterminable), and twelve fragments from the third dorsal fin spine.

One small vertebra is tentatively identified as being from a *Synodontis.*

Family ? CYPRINIDAE
? BARBUS sp. (Level 4 only)

A large fragment from the proximal end of a fin spine (probably the third unbranched dorsal ray) is tentatively identified as being from a *Barbus* dorsal fin.

Family CICHLIDAE
TILAPIA sp. (Level 4 only)

This genus is included on the basis of three bones, viz., two large fragments from separate opercula, and an almost complete hyomandibula.

The large size, and certain morphological peculiarities of these fragments, effectively preclude their identification with any other genus of Cichlidae (especially *Haplochromis*); morphologically, the bones are clearly not referable to *Lates* (family Centropomidae) which is also present in this deposit.

Family CENTROPOMIDAE
LATES sp. (Levels 3 and 4)

Lates is fairly well represented at this site by several different skeletal elements.

There are many bones from the syncranium, including a still articulated occiput with parietals, supraoccipital, basioccipital, and otic region present but damaged. This neurocranium is thought to have been about 20 cm. long when complete. In addition, there are several fragments probably derived from this skull (? frontals), and three fragments from another. There is also one specimen each of a palatine, suborbital, and a quadrate; these bones cannot be associated positively with either of the neurocrania, nor can an isolated mesethmoid from a large fish. Two other fragments may be from the ethmoidal region of a *Lates.*

No jaw elements are preserved, but there are four fragments of preopercula, and some pieces of bone are thought to be branchiostegal rays.

Vertebrae are well represented by a total of eighteen specimens (one neural arch and spine from a first vertebra, two second and one fourth vertebrae, eleven abdominal and three caudal vertebrae). None is undamaged but it is possible to make measurements of the centrum on many specimens:

Abdominal vertebrae	Length (mm.)	Breadth (mm.)
	17.0	17.0
	17.0	18.0
	18.0	12.0
	20.0	23.0
	28.0	43.0
	32.0	45.0
Caudal vertebrae	13.0	12.0
	22.0	22.0
	25.0	23.0
Fourth vertebra	15.0	25.0
Second vertebra	10.0	23.0
	11.0	24.0

The fins are represented by five specimens of rays and spines, and one pelvic girdle; undoubtedly there are many more *Lates* fin rays among the generically unidentifiable fin ray material from this site. One piece of bone that cannot be identified with certainty could be from a pterygiophore.

Unidentifiable Material

Among the generically unidentifiable material from both levels at this site are several fin rays from percomorph fishes. Since most spines and all branched rays of *Lates* are not certainly distinguishable from those of *Tilapia*, no attempt has been made to assign these specimens to one genus or the other. However, their large size suggests derivation from specimens of *Lates*.

Other fin spine fragments are clearly from siluroid fishes, but generic or familial identification is impossible.

Part of a quadrate and two fragments of opercula can only be identified as being from percomorph fishes, while six pieces of flat, weakly ridged bone are thought to be from the pectoral girdle of a siluroid fish.

SITE 1028 (Ikhtiariya, Halfan industry; age, between 14,000-17,000 B.C. on typology)

Clarias is the only genus that can be identified with certainty from this site, but the cyprinid genus *Barbus* may also be present, and there is the possibility of a percomorph fish as well.

Family CLARIIDAE
CLARIAS sp.

The genus is fairly well represented by 43 neurocranial bones and fragments of neurocranial bone, especially roofing elements. There is also a fragment of pectoral girdle (cleithrum), and part of a pectoral fin spine.

Family ? CYPRINIDAE
? BARBUS sp.

Nine damaged vertebrae cannot be identified with any certainty, but resemble vertebrae of *Barbus bynni* more closely than they do vertebrae from any other genus which might be present in the area (comparisons were made with vertebrae from *Mormyrus, Hydrocynus, Alestes, Citharinus, Clarias, Bagrus,* and *Synodontis*).

Unidentifiable Material

The possible percomorph fish is represented by a single bone thought to be part of a preoperculum. However, we are unable to identify this specimen with the preoperculum from any genus or family of percomorph fishes likely to occur in the area.

SITE 34 (Ikhtiariya, Qadan industry; dates on shells 9,250 B.C. ± 150 years [WSU-106] and 9,460 B.C. ± 270 years [WSU-189]; possibly slightly earlier according to stratigraphy)

Only the genus *Clarias* is represented among the identifiable specimens from this site.

There are sixteen fragments of neurocranial bones, one left epihyal and one joined right epi- and ceratohyal, and one fragment of a pectoral fin spine.

Three fragments of vertebrae could not be identified even as to family.

SITE 448 (Khor Musa; not dated but possibly around 10,000-8,000 B.C.?)

Three genera, and tentatively a fourth, are recorded from this site.

Family CLARIIDAE
CLARIAS sp. (but see also note below)

The genus is particularly well represented by

173 neurocranial bones and fragments of bone, six elements from the jaw skeleton (two premaxillae, three articulars, and one quadrate), ten fragments of pectoral girdle (mostly cleithrum), six from the hyobranchial skeleton (one urohyal, the remainder epi- and ceratohyals), one operculum, and ten pectoral fin spines (two left, two right, and six indeterminable).

Once again, vertebrae are poorly represented at this site by eleven centra (mostly from the anterior abdominal region of the column) and one other specimen, part of the swimbladder capsule which is formed from the modified parapophyses of certain anterior vertebrae.

A number (17) of small, slender bones, almost cylindrical in cross-section, are thought to be fragments of *Clarias* branchioestegal rays.

Note: Among the neurocranial fragments is one vomer, the tooth patch of which resembles that of the related genus *Heterobranchus* more closely than it does that of *Clarias* (or the other clariid vomer found at this site). However, all the ornamented neurocranial bones from this site have the tubercle form and distribution pattern typical of *Clarias*.

Family MOCHOKIDAE
SYNODONTIS sp.

Only two specimens, the proximal part of a dorsal fin spine and the distal part of a pectoral spine, are referable to this genus.

Family ? BAGRIDAE
? BAGRUS sp.

A fragment from the distal end of a siluroid fin spine is tentatively identified as being from the spine of a *Bagrus*.

Unidentifiable Siluroid Fishes

Seven fragments of catfish fin spines cannot be identified further.

Family CYPRINIDAE
BARBUS sp.

A fragment of operculum is identified as being from a large species of *Barbus;* in addition, one other piece of bone is thought to be from a *Barbus* pharyngeal bone.

SITE DIW-1 (Dibeira West, Arkin formation; dated on charcoal 7,440 B.C. ± 180 years [W.SU-175])

Although only catfish remains are preserved at these localities, three and possibly four genera are present.

Family CLARIIDAE
CLARIAS sp.

This genus is poorly represented by two fragments of neurocranial bones and one almost entire neurocranial roof, a fragment of pectoral girdle, and one damaged anterior abdominal vertebra.

Family BAGRIDAE
BAGRUS sp.

From Locality E-55 there are four specimens (variously damaged and incomplete) of the fused vertebral mass associated with the Weberian apparatus, parts of two basioccipitals, and a fragment from a right cleithrum.

From Locality H-18 there is a somewhat more diverse collection of bones.

The skull is represented by two ethmoids, one of which is extensively damaged; the larger specimen is thought to be from a skull of about 15 cm. neurocranial length (ethmoid tip to posterior face of the basioccipital).

Apart from four fused vertebral masses, the vertebral column is not represented. The most complete fused vertebral masses are 27 and *ca* 23 mm. long; a more damaged specimen (but including part of a tripus and a small area of the fused parapophyses) is estimated to be *ca* 20 mm. long when complete, and the fourth specimen (consisting of the central mass and the base of one parapophyseal "wing") is about 30 mm. long.

Jaw elements consist of an incomplete articular, a fragment of right articular and the associated dentary from a small fish, and a similar but more damaged articular-dentary combination (also from the right side).

There is only one fragment of pectoral girdle (right cleithrum) definitely referable to *Bagrus,* but two other fragments (also right) are tentatively referred to this genus. The pectoral fin is represented by one complete left spine and a fragment from the articular head of a right spine. A small fragment is identified as being from the proximal end of a dorsal fin spine.

? CHRYSICHTHYS sp.

Two small pectoral fin spines (both left), each comprising the articular head and part of the spine, are tentatively referred to this genus. The curvature of the spines, and the large well-spaced serrae on their posterior faces, are more like those of the spines in Chrysichthys species than the spines of Bagrus or Clarias species. Both specimens are from Locality H-18.

Family MOCHOKIDAE
SYNODONTIS spp. (including S. CLARIAS [L.])

All Synodontis material is from Locality H-18, and includes some of the best preserved material from the entire collection.

Of special interest is an almost complete neurocranium lacking only the more ventral parts of the posttemporals, part of the nuchal shield and the anterior tip of the ethmoid; the lateral walls of the otic region are damaged. The cranial fontanelle is extensive and runs from the ethmoid to the point of contact between the supraoccipital and the frontals. When viewed laterally, the steep upward slope of the supraoccipitals and nuchal shield relative to the interorbital region is a most noticeable feature. (See fig. 1, nos. 1 and 2.) The skull shape and long fontanelle, together with the mixed reticulate-tuberculate ornamentation and the shape of certain neurocranial bones, are also found in the skull of Synodontis clarias, and seem to be characteristic for that species.

Certain measurements could be made on the fossil S. clarias skull:

Basicranial length
   (ethmoid to basioccipital facet)   ca 43 mm.
Length from anterior tip of ethmoid to the
   anterior tip of the supraoccipital   ca 29 mm.
Length from anterior tip of supraoccipital
   to the most posterior point   19 mm.
Estimated total length of neurocranium   ca 52 mm.
Least interorbital width   19 mm.
Length of fontanelle   19 mm.
Length of frontal   22 mm.

In addition to this almost complete neurocranium, there are two other and more fragmentary specimens of small Synodontis skulls. One is an almost complete nuchal shield (including the first, chevron shaped dorsal fin spine and part of its pterygiophore). The other is a laterally compressed specimen of the same skull region from a fish of about the same size. Neither specimen can be identified beyond the generic level.

Other remains of Synodontis from this deposit are:

1. A complete right humeral process including part of the cleithrum. The process is 27 mm. long and has a greatest depth of 9.5 mm. Its shape is such as to preclude identification with S. clarias; the proportions are nearest those of the humeral process in Synodontis schall.

2. A fragment from a right humeral process (ventral border and part of the shield) with proportions similar to specimen 1.

3. A fragment of right cleithrum (from the region of the articular fossa for the spine) together with the anterior part of the humeral process.

All three specimens are from fishes of about the same size.

Generically Unidentifiable Siluroid Material

Four vertebrae (Dibeira 55) are probably from siluroid fishes (possibly Synodontis or Bagrus); two fin spines (Dibeira 18) are definitely from catfishes but cannot be identified further.

SITE DIBEIRA 51 (Dibeira West, Arkin formation; Shamarkian industry, dates on charcoal 5,750 B.C. ± 120 years [WSU-176])

The only identifiable material from this site is referable to the genus Lates (Fam. Centropomidae). It consists of one caudal vertebra (centrum length 15 mm., breadth 15 mm.), and a single gill-raker.

A pelvic fin spine and the proximal end of a branched fin ray are definitely from a percomorph fish; if judged by the size of these specimens both should probably be referred to Lates.

SITE 1021 (Khor Musa; dated on charcoal 5,100 B.C. ± 210 years [WSU-213])

Identifiable fish remains from this site comprise only three specimens (two fragments of pectoral girdle, and a right pectoral spine), all referable to the genus Clarias.

SITE ANE-1 (Anquash East; Qadan, age estimated *ca.* 10,000 B.C. on typology)

Two genera are represented at this site.

Family CLARIIDAE
CLARIAS sp.

As in other deposits, the most numerous fragments are from the neurocranium (28 specimens). Jaws are represented by one incomplete left dentary, six articulars (two left and four right), and two quadrates (left and right). From the suspensorium there are a palatine and a fragment of pterygoid; and from the hyobranchial skeleton, two fragments of hyal bones. Only one vertebra (the first) is preserved.

Judging from the sizes of these various bones, several fishes are represented in the sample.

Family CYPRINIDAE
BARBUS sp.

Two bones are definitely referable to *Barbus*, namely, a fragment of the first vertebra, and an almost complete right dentary.

Two vertebrae, and parts of two opercula, are tentatively identified as being from a *Barbus* species.

SITE 8905 (Tushka, Egypt; Qadan industry, radiocarbon date on charcoal 12,550 B.C. ± 500 years [WSU-315])

Eight loci at this site yielded fish remains. With the exception of unidentifiable specimens, all this material can be referred to the genus *Clarias* (Clariidae).

Surface: The genus *Clarias* is represented by thirty-two fragments of neurocranial roofing bones (including one ethmoid) from several fishes of different sizes, and the heads of two pectoral spines (one left, one right). In addition, there are one fragment thought to be from a cleithrum and four badly damaged vertebrae tentatively identified as *Clarias.*

The pectoral spines and vertebrae are extensively eroded, and are very fragile, but the neurocranial fragments are well preserved.

Locality F (Surface): *Clarias* is represented by nineteen neurocranial fragments (including two ethmoids), six heads of pectoral spines (three left and three right), two anterior abdominal vertebrae, and two badly eroded bones ten-

tatively identified as articulars (one left and one right).

All specimens from this locus show some signs of erosion.

Locality F (Excavated): Fifty-three fragments are referred to the genus *Clarias.* These comprise two basioccipitals, two ethmoids, twenty-eight pieces of neurocranial roofing bones, one fragment of branchiostegal ray, five vertebrae still in articulation (from the anterior abdominal region of the column), five separate and badly damaged vertebrae, and ten pectoral spine fragments (five left and five right).

All these bones are extensively weathered and eroded, so that in the case of the neurocranial fragments the ornamentation is almost obliterated.

Three unidentifiable fragments are thought to be fish bones; one of these may be an eroded and weathered articular from a *Clarias.*

Locality D (Surface): Only *Clarias* remains were recovered from this locus. Of the sixty-two fragments examined, fifty are from the neurocranial roofing series (including one ethmoid), one is a fragment of ceratohyal, one is probably from the median part of the cleithrum, two are anterior abdominal vertebrae, two are left articulars, and six are extensively damaged pectoral spines (four left, two right). One badly eroded fragment is thought to be from the head of a right pectoral spine, and two others are tentatively identified as articulars (one left, one right) of *Clarias.*

Locality D (Excavated): Again, only remains of *Clarias* are preserved. There are seventy-five fragments of neurocranial bones (including eight ethmoids), one left operculum, two articulars (one left and one right, but from fishes of different sizes), a small fragment of cleithrum, two anterior abdominal vertebrae, and thirteen pectoral spine fragments from the head of the spine (nine left and four right spines).

Six fragments are tentatively identified as, respectively, three pieces of *Clarias* parasphenoid, and three fragments from the hyoid arch.

Locality E (Surface): *Clarias* is the sole genus represented at this locus by one left articular and one left pectoral spine (the head and proximal part of the spine itself). Both specimens are from small fishes.

Locality E (Excavated): As in the surface deposit at this locus, only *Clarias* is represented. There are two fragments of neurocranial roofing bones, one left operculum, one right articular, and one right pectoral spine (the head and proximal part of the spine). The spine is from a small individual, the other fragments from a larger fish (probably the same individual).

Locality A (Surface): Only four specimens from the locus were submitted to us. Of these, three cannot be identified with certainty even as fish bones. The fourth is undoubtedly part of a *Clarias* articular.

SITE 8956 (Ballana, Egypt; Ballanan industry, estimated to date between 16,000 and 12,000 B.C., on typology)

Only the genus *Clarias* is present in the collections, all from the surface. Among the identified were two pectoral spine fragments (one left and one right, but from fishes of markedly different sizes), a small fragment of ethmoid, eight fragments of neurocranial roofing bones, and one fragmentary right articular.

Addendum

As this paper was going to press, I received a small additional collection of fish remains. The material has not yet been studied in detail, but the following preliminary notes have been made:

SITE 8859 (Ballana, *ca* 16,700 B.C.)

Clarias: Numerous fragments of neurocranial bones.

Pectoral spine fragments: 51 right and 33 left; mostly from small fishes (*ca* 25-30 cm. standard length).

Fragments of premaxillary and vomerine tooth plates.

Articular (fragmentary): comprising 24 left and 19 right; from fishes of about 25-30 cm. standard length, and some larger individuals.

Quadrate: three fragments.

Urohyal: five damaged bones.

Vertebrae: 17, all from the anterior end of the vertebral column (32 other vertebrae are also probably referable to *Clarias*).

Barbus sp., cf. *B. bynni*: a single specimen, the crown of a major pharyngeal tooth.

? *Tilapia* sp.: one first vertebra is undoubtedly from a cichlid fish; from its size and general morphology it should probably be referred to this genus. Another cichlid vertebra was also identified.

? *Lates* sp.: a small fragment from the proximal end of a branched fin ray.

SITE 8899-C

Clarias sp.: one fragment of articular.

SITE 8905

The extra material also contained further material from *Site 8905* Locality B yielded numerous fragments of *Clarias* neuroncranial bones, representing (on the basis of mesethmoids preserved) at least nine large fishes. The largest individual is estimated to have had a head length (anterior tip of ethmoid to posterior tip of supraoccipital) of 24 cm.

From Locality D there are several fragments of *Clarias* pectoral spines (all from small fishes of about 15 cm. standard length), some anterior vertebrae from fishes of about the same size, and part of the operculum from a larger individual (head length, about 25 cm).

Also present in this sample are numerous unidentifiable vertebrae from small fishes, and a few fragments of branchiostegal rays thought to be from a large *Clarias*.

DISCUSSION

The occurrence of genera at different sites can be summarized as shown in the accompanying tabulation.

Two points emerge from this tabulation. First, the absence of certain genera which, on the basis of their present-day distribution, might be expected to occur in the region. Second, the few sites at which more than two genera are present.

Since the sites are all associated with human occupation, little ecological importance should perhaps be attached to the absentee genera. Selective factors associated with human activity might mean that these fishes were not caught, or were treated differently from those whose remains have been discovered. Such selection could well mask other and more biological ones such as the relative abundance of different species or their total absence because of inimical hydrobiological conditions. The most noticeable absen-

Genus	1017	ANW-3	2004	8859	443	1018	1020	440	1028	34	448	8956	8899-C	8905	1021	ANE-1	DIW-1	DIW-51
Clarias	X	X	X	X	X	X	X	X	X	X	X	X	X	X	X	X		
Bagrus								X			?							X
? *Chrysichthys*																		X
Synodontis		X						X			X							X
Barbus		X	X	X	?			?	?		X					X		
Tilapia				?				X										
Lates		?		?				X										X

X = Present

? = Identification tentative

tees are species of *Protopterus, Hydrocynus, Alestes, Citharinus, Mormyrus,* and *Polypterus.* Fishes of genera and species whose members do not reach as large a size as those found in the deposits (or noted for their absence) may not have been caught by the inhabitants, or may be too small for satisfactory subsequent preservation and collection.

The relative scarcity of postcranial skeleton elements, especially vertebrae, is noteworthy. At most sites (and for all genera except *Lates* and to a lesser degree *Barbus*) vertebrae are virtually unrepresented, even when the generically unidentifiable fragments are taken into account. Even for *Lates* and *Barbus* the picture is one of few vertebrae and fin rays in relation to the probable number of individuals preserved at the site. We can only conclude that this phenomenon is attributable to the habits of the contemporary humans who probably decapitated the fishes in one place and removed the bodies elsewhere.

Because of the possible human selective factors these fish remains cannot safely be used to compare hydrological conditions obtaining at the various sites and times. For those sites with several genera represented (ANW-3, 448, Dibeira 1, and, especially, Site 440) it is, however, reasonable to infer conditions similar to those of the present-day river. Since extant species of all the genera present as fossils occur both in the main river and in seasonally flooded swamps, the fossils could have lived in either type of habitat.

Those localities at which only *Clarias* are recorded (34, 1017, 1018, 1020, 1021, and 8905) could be of some significance if selective human factors are not involved. In this case the selective effect may be one of inefficient (or else highly specialized) fishing methods. But if this is discounted then the presence of *Clarias* species alone could indicate foul water conditions. All species of this genus have accessory breathing organs enabling the fishes to utilize atmospheric oxygen; indeed, some species may be obligatory air-breathers. Thus, *Clarias* species can and do inhabit water too foul and deoxygenated to support species with purely aquatic respiratory methods. This argument, of course, assumes that the samples of fossil fishes are fully representative of the species then present.

Sites at which both *Clarias* and *Barbus* species occur together (ANE-1 and 2004, possibly 1028) cannot be considered representative of adverse hydrological conditions. Extant *Barbus* species like *B. bynni* require well-oxygenated water, and are more common in fluviatile than in lacustrine habitats.

Finally it may be mentioned that apparently none of the fishes from Sudanese Nubian sites was of a particularly large size when compared with the known size range for species living in the Nile at present.

EARLY AND MIDDLE PALEOLITHIC SITES NEAR ARKIN, SUDAN

Waldemar Chmielewski

(INSTYTUT HISTORII KULTURY MATERIALNEJ POLSKIEJ AKADEMII NAUK)

ACHEULEAN SITE ARKIN 8

TO THE WEST of the village of Arkin, situated in the Nile valley, there is a plain built up of Nubia Sandstone. An escarpment 18 m. high forms the border between the valley and the plain. The area near the edge of the plain is covered by a thick deposit of quartz pebbles. The highest point of this formation is elevated 172 m. above sea level and 51 m. above the floodplain. The edge of the plain is dissected by numerous wadis. The wadis are transversal to the Nile valley, then are cut to a depth of about 15 m. near the edge of the plain, but this decreases gradually toward the West (Nubia Sandstone Plain) and very rapidly toward the East (Nile Valley). It is difficult to follow the courses of the wadis in the desert some 10 km. west of the escarpment.

The transversal profiles of the wadi valleys vary considerably along the courses of the wadis, ever changing within short distances. Near the escarpment the bottoms of the wadis are flat, sometimes 300 m. wide, and have stepped slopes. The wadis begin to narrow about 1.5-2 km. from the edge of the plain. There the bottoms are never flat and the slopes are less steep and not stepped. Nubia Sandstone forms the beds of the wadis in these parts of their courses, while near the escarpment the beds are composed of sand and gravel sometimes cemented with a lime crust. Xerophytic shrubs grow in a few places in the main beds of the wadis (fig. 2, A and B). Two or three wadis very often join their courses a few hundred meters upstream from the escarpment. Their lower and upper beds are additionally dissected by very short and shallow watercourses which are undoubtedly later than the main wadi beds and hang above the main depression. These have produced a root pattern drainage no longer utilized under contemporary climatic conditions of the area.

In the wadi terminating near the northern edge of the Shamarki village, R. Dougherty and P. Rice found a large concentration of Acheulean artifacts in March, 1963. They designated the locality as Site Arkin 8, and plotted it on the map. More than 100 tools, cores and flakes were collected at this time and given to J. and G. Guichard. On the basis of this collection the Guichards suggested a late Acheulean character for the site (Guichard and Guichard, 1965).

We visited this wadi and its sites first in February, 1964. Our reconnaissance showed that Arkin 8 was not a single extensive site but was composed of several different sites. Many of them were very much like the sites which were examined by J. and G. Guichard on the east bank of the Nile. Among them, however, existed an extremely rich and dense concentration of tools and artifacts made of quartz and some other kind of pebbles. This particular concentration we initially excavated in March, 1964. An additional collection and excavation were made in February, 1965, with the help of R. Schild. Sixty-four square meters, about one-eighth of the whole territory of the site, were excavated during both field seasons.

The other Acheulean sites in this locality were heavily eroded. Several handaxes made of ferrocrete, more or less eolized, formed the small concentrations, with cores of Levalloisian type and the waste by-products of cores and tools. These concentrations were lying on the surface, with no sediments below or with a scanty horizon of weathering Nubia Sandstone. In the lower wadi course only one small concentration has been found on the surface of the wadi deposits.

CONCENTRATION OF ARTIFACTS

The first study of the main Arkin 8 Site revealed the characteristic, unusually dense concentration of artifacts, as well as a sharply defined, clear-cut horizontal distribution of them. The artifacts were lying in the wadi deposit only

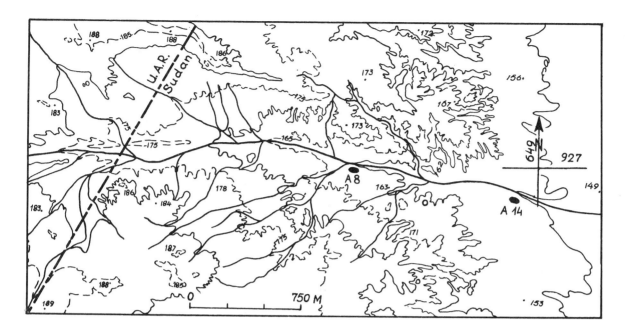

Fig. 1—Map of the wadi with Sites Arkin 8 and Arkin 14. Key: A8, Arkin 8; A14, Arkin 14; O, small Acheulean concentrations lying on the surface of the wadi deposit.

partly dismantled and dissected by later erosion. The raw materials which were used for the production of the tools were: pebbles of quartz, quartzite, igneous rocks, and slabs of ferrocrete. Such a variety of raw materials was not observed at the other known Acheulean sites between Wadi Halfa and Faras on both river banks. All these peculiarities were taken into account and influenced the decision to examine Site Arkin 8 more fully.

The Site is situated near the edge of the lower terrace of the wadi 60 m. below the point where the two large wadis join together and 1,200 m. west of the escarpment of the plain (figs. 1 and 3). To the west of the site an outcrop of Nubia Sandstone occurs. The site lies in a small depression filled by a sandy gravel deposit of the wadi. The territory of the site marked by a dense concentration of quartz pebbles, tools, and waste covers an oval area 40 m. long and 15 to 20 m. wide. Within this concentration eight subconcentrations were distinguished. Each of them was formed by an accumulation of the tools, pebbles, and flakes which formed a pile in the center and which was surrounded by similar artifacts covering an oval area 6 to 8 m. in diameter.

The outlines of the subconcentrations were not sharp, but the diminution in quantity of the artifacts near the edge of each subconcentration was easily visible, as shown by the plotting of each artifact on the map of the excavated part of the site (fig. 4).

The density of the artifacts laying *in situ* in the wadi deposits was greater than that observed on the surface. During the time of excavation it was noted that the layer filled with artifacts was 5 cm. thick. It lies some 5 cm. above the strongly weathered surface of the Nubia Sandstone and was covered by a 20 or 30 cm. thick wadi sediment composed of the sandy gravel deposit of the wadi slightly cemented by calcium carbonate. In the center of the subconcentrations the density of the artifacts was the greatest, and there the thickness of the layer containing the artifacts reached a depth of between 25-30 cm. and formed a small hill or pile about 1.5 m. in diameter. The tops of these hills were dismantled and eroded. In a few places small hollows have been observed. They are 30 cm. deep and are filled with gray sand, sometimes containing two or three artifacts. Near the edge of Subconcentration A, there were a few blocks of Nubia

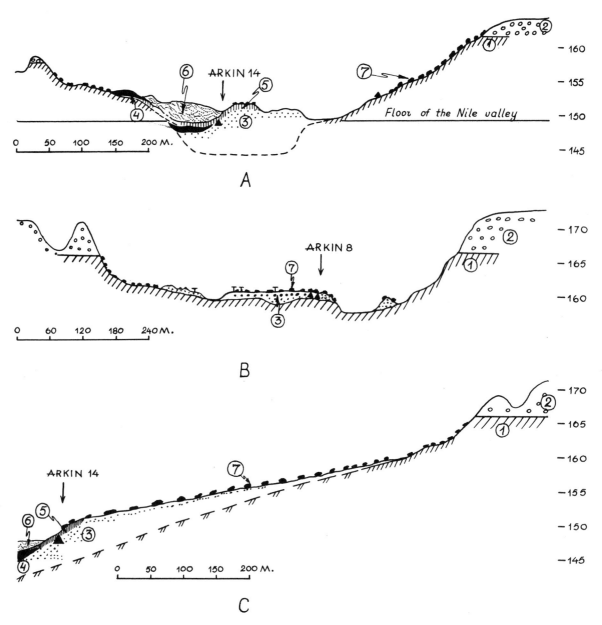

Fig. 2—Profiles of the wadi near Arkin 8 and 14. Key: A, transversal profile of the wadi with Arkin 14; B, transversal profile of the wadi with Arkin 8; C, length profile between Pre-Nile sediments south of Arkin 8 and Arkin 14: 1, Nubia Sandstone; 2, Pre-Nile gravels; 3, old wadi deposits; 4, Nile silt; 5, reddish soil; 6, younger wadi deposits; 7, pediment.

Sandstone, 25 to 40 cm. in diameter, forming a kind of irregular circle (fig. 4).

Two subconcentrations situated behind the main concentration were distinguished. They were designated as southern and western sub-concentrations on Figure 3. Both of them were dismantled by small wadis. Their dimensions and characteristics were the same as described above for the main concentration.

The sharp outline of the described concentration, the density of the tools and waste, the freshness of the edges of the tools and flakes which have been found in the deposit (not on the surface)—all these observations suggest that

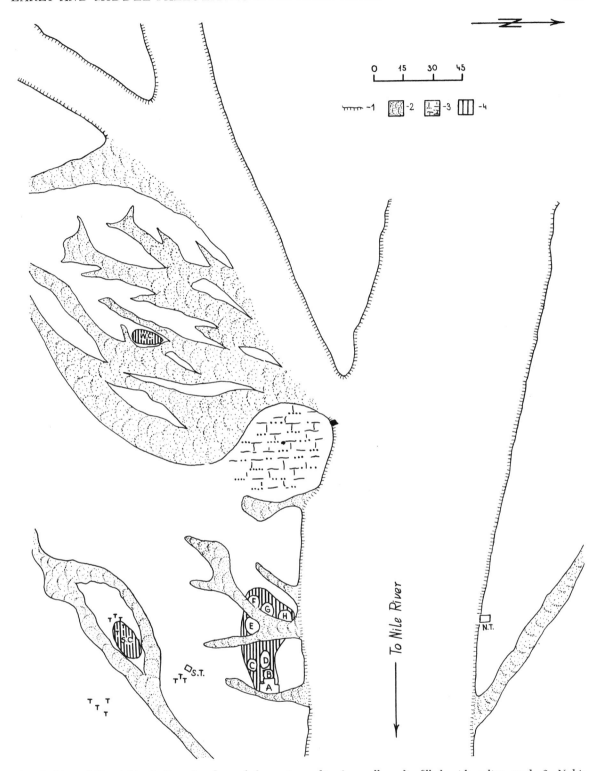

FIG. 3—Map of Site Arkin 8. Key: 1, edges of the main wadis; 2, small wadis filled with eolian sand; 3, Nubia Sandstone; 4, concentrations; A, excavated part of the site with A and B subconcentrations in it; B-H, subconcentrations; WC, Western concentration; SC, Southern concentration; ST, Southern trench; NT, Northern trench; T, calcic crusts.

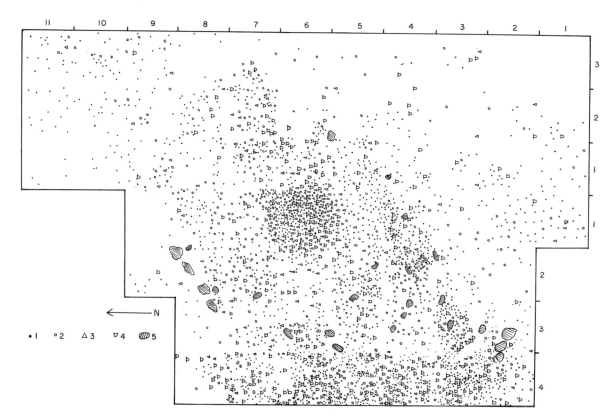

F‍IG. 4—Map of the distribution of artifacts on the excavated part of Arkin 8: 1, flakes; 2, ovates, choppers, chopping tools, discs and half-discs; 3, handaxes; 4, cores; 5, slabs of sandstone.

the site is a remnant of a prehistoric camp, with its living floor. This site was little disturbed by later erosion. A lack of fossil bones does not contradict such an interpretation taking into account the desert conditions.

Very close to Subconcentration H another interesting structure was found, probably connected with the camp activities. This structure was oval in shape, 1.8 m. long and 1.2 m. wide filled with a sandy gravel deposit. Three large slabs of sandstone were lying on the floor inside, surrounded by a wall built up of sandstone slabs. This wall was still preserved to a height of 30 cm. Two flakes and one core of quartz were found inside. This structure was found in the same wadi deposit as the artifacts forming Subconcentration H, near its northern edge. It was not seen on the surface of the site.

It was impossible to examine the whole territory of the site within the time limit we had for the excavation. Because of this only Subcon-

centrations A and part of B were excavated, although surface collections were taken from the other subconcentrations. The collection from the whole area of the site contains 3,409 artifacts. The description of the assemblage and the statistical calculations described in this report are based on the excavated collections from Subconcentrations A and B. They contained 2,500 artifacts.

The condition of the preservation of the artifacts varies according to the location in the sediments or on the surface. Those found on the surface were heavily eolized while those from the wadi deposits were extremely fresh. The type of stone used also influenced the state of preservation of the artifacts. The tools made of ferrocrete lying on the surface have sandblasted surfaces but they are hard, while those found in the sediment still retain their shapes but shatter in the hand.

The inhabitants of the site used pebbles for

the production of their tools. The only exception was the tools made of ferrocrete; they were prepared out of rock slabs. However, the quartz pebbles were much preferred, and this is a striking feature of the assemblage. The quartz artifacts form 76.6 per cent of the whole collection, while those made of ferrocrete are only 13.3 per cent. The remainder of the artifacts were made of: Precambrian rocks, 1.6 per cent; quartzite, 1.5 per cent; an igneous very fine crystallic rock similar to brownish chert, 0.9 per cent; and undefined rock, 5.8 per cent.

All the pebbles used for the artifacts were easily obtained in the territory surrounding the site. The banks of the wadi situated 200 m. to the south and 150 m. to the north of the site are built up of such pebbles, lying in the red matrix and designated by J. de Heinzelin (1964) as Pre-Nile sediments. Among the tools and cores which were found on the site there were a few made of very large pebbles which never occur among those of the Pre-Nile sediments. The deposits containing such pebbles occur probably in the Nile valley 2.5 km. east of the site covered by later deposits. They were reached at some depth below the old Nile sediments by the creators of a very large cemetery. Here the hills covering the graves are built up of such pebbles and reddish sand. The inhabitants of Arkin 8 probably got the raw pebbles for their large tools from somewhere in this area before the deposits in which they occur were covered· by later formations.

THE COLLECTION OF ARKIN 8

The collection of Arkin 8 is composed of the following seven groups of the artifacts: cores and flakes; choppers; chopping tools; discs and half-discs; ovates; handaxes; and tools made of flakes.

Cores and Flakes

The cores are divided into the following five types: A, cores with one striking platform; B, globular cores; C, discoidal cores; D, half-discoidal cores; and E, oval cores. (fig. 5, nos. 1-4, 6; fig. 6, no. 1).

A. Cores with one striking platform. This is a very simple type of core. All of them were made on pebbles. The striking platforms of those cores were prepared by the removal of one or two

flakes. These platforms form almost a right angle with the surface used for flake detachment. Most of the cores are medium in size (length x width, 70 x 55 mm. to 50 x 40 mm). The largest is 82 x 60 mm., and the smallest is 40 x 31 mm. Very often the natural surfaces of the pebbles are still preserved on part of the core.

The difference between these cores and chopping tools is defined by the angle between the striking platform and the surface used for flake detachment. This angle is very close to a right angle on the cores, while on the chopping tools it forms a sharp angle (about 60°). Another difference is the shape of the edge formed in the cores between the striking platform and the surface used for flake detachment and in the chopping tools between both flaked surfaces. This edge is more or less curved in the cores, while in the chopping tools it is straight or slightly zigzag. When these distinctions are not strongly expressed, identification can be difficult.

B. Globular cores. The striking platforms were not defined on these cores. The natural surface of the pebble was used very often as the striking platform, and the flakes were removed all round the pebble, in different directions. The natural surfaces of the pebbles are still preserved on parts of the cores. They are very much like the type *"boules polyédrique."* The diameters of those cores varied from 90 to 35 mm., but most often they lie·between 60 and 40 mm.

C. Discoidal cores. They are biconical in shape, but very often one of the cones is smaller than the other. The edge between the cones is uneven, very often having deep notches. The dimensions of these cores vary from 90 mm. in diameter and 45 mm. in thickness to 30 mm. and 15 mm. respectively (fig. 5, nos. 1-4, 6).

D. Half-discoidal cores. They are the most common core type in the assemblage. In this type part of the core has the shape of a biconical discoidal core, but part of it is always the original pebble surface. The largest core is 100 mm. long, 81 mm. wide, and 62 mm. thick, and the smallest is 35 mm. x 30 mm. x 24 mm. The most common dimensions lie between 70 mm. x 40 mm. x 34 mm. and 52 mm. x 40 mm. x 32 mm. (fig. 6, no. 1).

E. Oval cores. They possess prepared striking platforms surrounding all or the greater part of

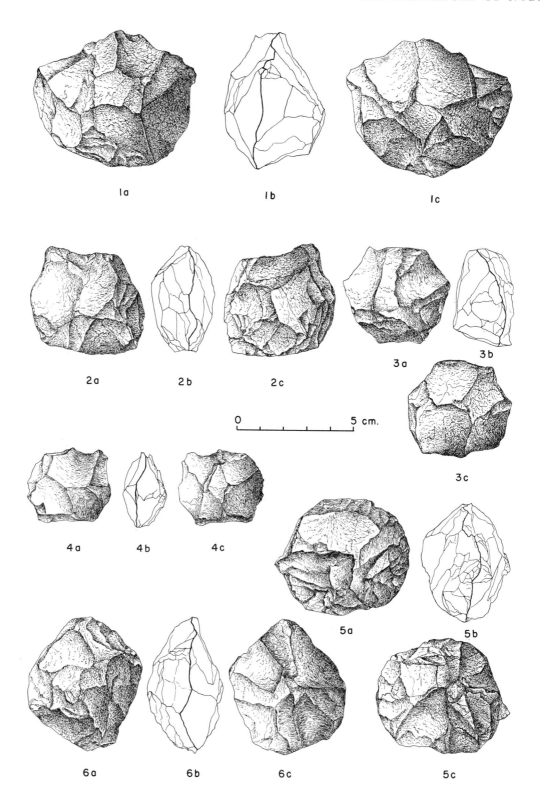

FIG. 5—Arkin 8: Nos. 1-4, 6, discoidal cores; 5, disc.

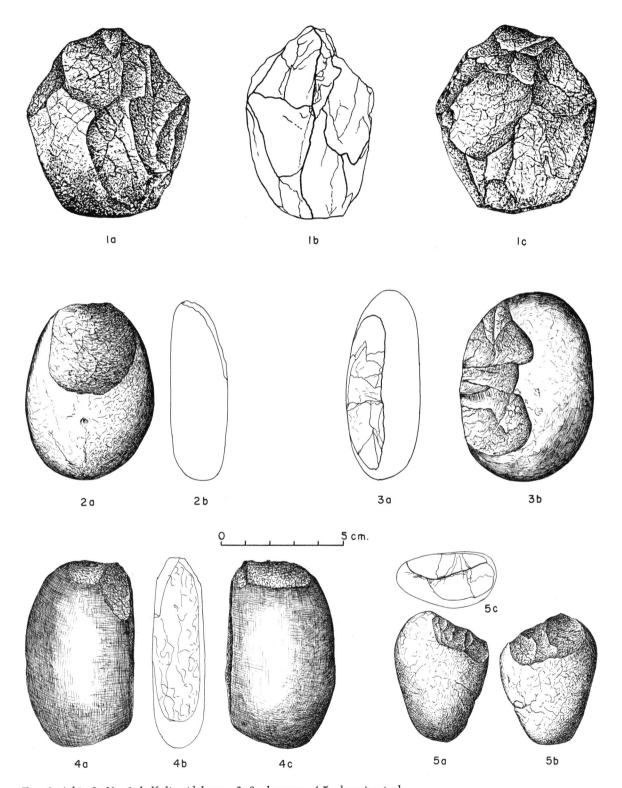

Fɪɢ. 6—Arkin 8: No. 1, half-discoidal core; 2, 3, choppers; 4-5, chopping tools.

the circumference of the core. The surface of detachment is flat, and the flakes are flaked radially. This type is very close to the Levalloisian type of core. In size these cores vary from 82 mm. in length, 60 mm. in width, and 31 mm. in thickness to 42 mm. x 30 mm. x 15 mm. respectively.

Flakes. The flakes found on the site are small to medium in size. Only three flakes are longer than 120 mm. Most of them have the pebble surface still preserved on their dorsal side. The flakes may exhibit one of the following butt types: with some pebble cortex still present; with one or two scars from the prepared core striking platform (*lisse* and *diédre*); faceted; and with a sharp thin edge. These butt types are present in about the same proportions in the flakes. Most of the flakes are broken. There were no more than 15 blades in the whole collection.

Choppers

This group of tools is divided into five types on the basis of the shape of the working edge and its position relative to the long axis of the pebble.

A. Choppers from which only one flake has been removed. They are represented by two examples. In both, the working edge is situated at the end of the long axis of the pebble (fig. 6, no. 2).

B. Transversal choppers. All these were made on flat pebbles. The working edge is situated transversally to the long axis of the pebble and is straight or slightly convex. The dimensions of these choppers vary from 85 mm. in length, 56 mm. in width, and 34 mm. in thickness to 35 mm. x 34 mm. x 16 mm. respectively.

C. Side choppers with a straight working edge situated parallel or slightly oblique to the long axis of the pebble. The largest is 76 mm. long, 55 mm. wide, and 24 mm. thick, the smallest measures 40 mm. x 36 mm. x 21 mm. (fig. 6, no. 3).

D. Side choppers with a convex working edge. This type is very much like the former, the only difference between them is the shape of the working edge.

E. Suboval choppers. In this type the working edge extends approximately three-quarters of the way around the circumference of the tool and is

oval in shape, while the remainder of the tool still has its natural pebble surface. It seems possible to interpret these choppers as unfinished handaxes, ovates, or discs. Their average dimensions are 55 mm. in length, 32 mm. in width, and 17 mm. in thickness.

Chopping Tools

The subdivisions in this group are based on the same principles as those used in the study of the choppers. These tools are very well represented in the collection and form, in fact, the most numerous tool group.

A. Chopping tools with a straight working edge transversal or slightly oblique to the long axis of the pebbles. Only one is 101 mm. long, 82 mm. wide, and 39 mm. thick. The most common dimensions vary between 82 mm. x 62 mm. x 39 mm. and 55 mm. x 50 mm. x 22 mm., but dimensions as small as 35 mm. long, 32 mm. wide and 12 mm. thick do occur. (fig. 6, nos. 4-5; fig. 7, nos. 1-2).

B. Chopping tools with a convex working edge transversal to the long axis of the pebbles. It is possible to distinguish three groups of the dimensions for this type: the large, which vary from 110 mm. x 75 mm. x 40 mm. to 95 mm. x 72 mm. x 45 mm.; the middle, from 83 mm. x 63 mm. x 28 mm. to 60 mm. x 47 mm. x 24 mm.; and the small about 45 mm. in length, 42 mm. in width, and 20 mm. in thickness. (fig. 7, nos. 3-4, 6; fig. 8, nos. 1, 3-4).

C. Chopping tools oval in shape with a very convex working edge on about three-quarters of the circumference of the pebbles. Their dimensions are in the middle and small groups in comparison with the former type. (fig. 8, no. 2).

D. Chopping tools with the sharp pointed end situated opposite the unflaked part of the pebble. Their dimensions are middle and small (fig. 7, no. 5).

E. Chopping tools with a straight or slightly convex working edge situated parallel to the long axis of the pebbles (fig. 9, no. 1).

F. Elongated chopping tools with a rounded end. They look like the handaxes and form a transitional type between the chopping tools and the latter. The differences lie in the shape of the working edge which is more convex in the chopping tools than in handaxes and in the type of

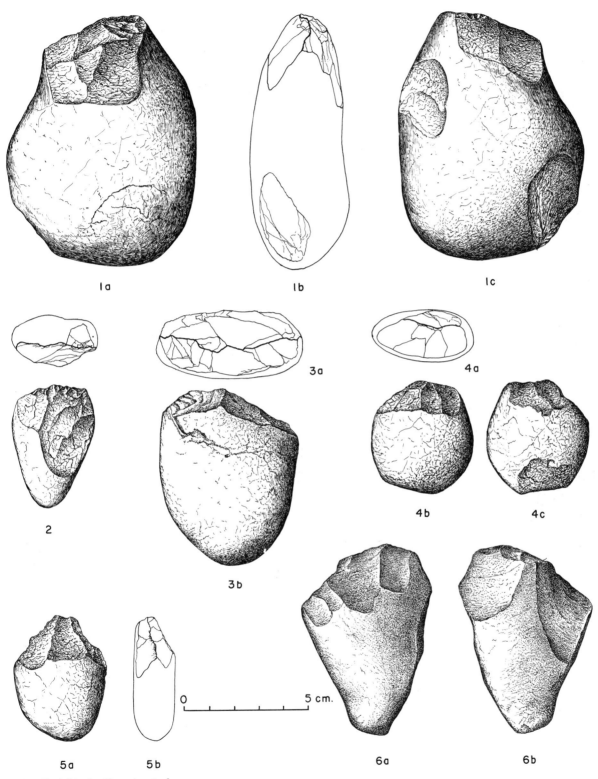

FIG. 7—Arkin 8: Chopping tools.

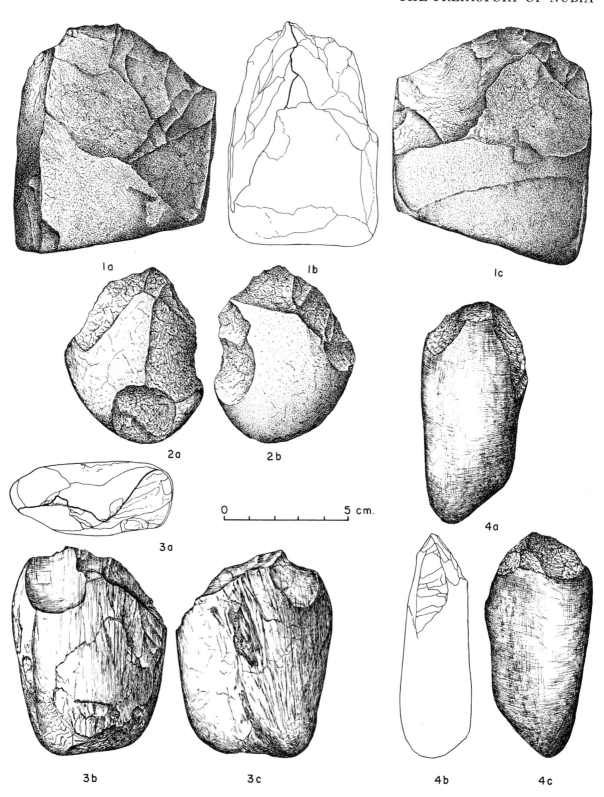

FIG. 8—Arkin 8: Chopping tools.

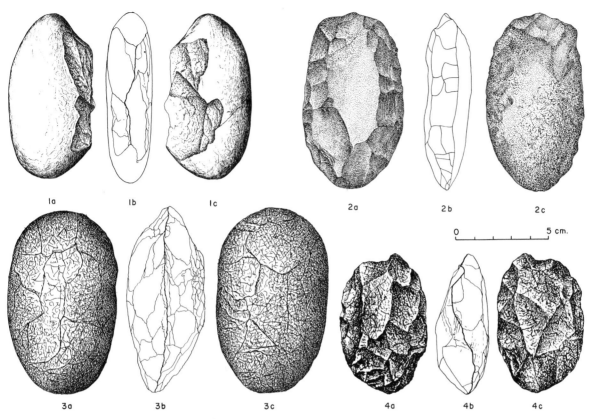

1a 1b 1c   2a   2b   2c

0   5 cm.

3a   3b   3c   4a   4b   4c

FIG. 9—Arkin 8: No. 1, side chopping tool; 2-4, ovates.

the retouch which never covers the whole surface of the tool in the chopping tools. Their
dimensions vary from 78 mm. in length, 85 mm.
in width, and 38 mm. in thickness to 30 mm. x
36 mm. x 16 mm. respectively.

Discs and Half-discs

A. Discs. These tools were made of pebbles
or of slabs of ferrocrete. They differ from the discoidal cores by a very regular, almost straight
edge. Their dimensions vary from 90 mm. in
diameter and 40 mm. in thickness to 30 mm. x
20 mm. respectively, but the most common are
ca. 60 mm. in diameter and 30 mm. in thickness.
(fig. 5, no. 5).

B. Half-discs. One half of the pebble is still
preserved in this type of the tool while the other
half is very carefully retouched like the discs. All
are made of quartz pebbles. Their dimensions
vary from 65 mm. in diameter and 35 mm. in
thickness to 30 mm. x 15 mm. This type is very
close to the chopping tools with a very convex

working edge, but is more round in shape than
the chopping tools.

Ovates

This type of the tool comprises a specific feature for the assemblage. It is represented by
numerous but very uniform examples. (fig. 9,
nos. 2-4; fig. 10). It is possible to distinguish only
two subtypes of these tools: (1) those retouched
on the one surface of the pebble and with very
little or no retouch on the other, and (2) those
bifacially retouched, which are more numerous.
The working edges of these tools are strongly
used and look like the edges of the cores or flakes
obtained by the bipolar technique of flaking or
like the surfaces of the hammerstones.

The dimensions of the ovates vary from 125
mm. in length, 83 mm. in width, and 48 mm. in
thickness to 65 mm. x 43 mm. x 29 mm. Together
with a few large handaxes they are the biggest
tools in the assemblage. Some of the side choppers and chopping tools with convex working

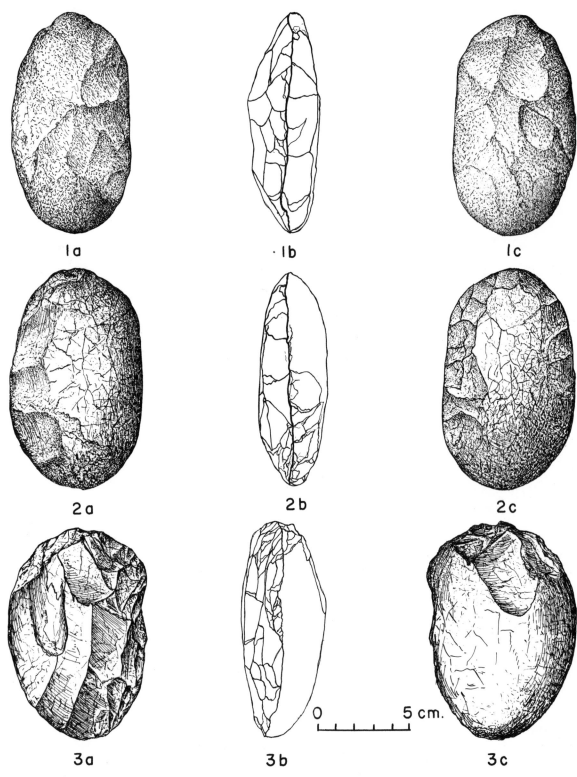

1a 1b 1c

2a 2b 2c

3a 3b 3c

FIG. 10—Arkin 8: Ovates.

edges were more than likely unfinished ovates.

Handaxes

The handaxes form another very characteristic group of the tools in the Arkin 8 assemblage. Sixty per cent of them are made of ferrocrete and 30 per cent of quartz pebbles. The characteristic feature of these tools lies in their dimensions, which are very small in comparison with other handaxes of the assemblages known from Nubia. Handaxes longer than 100 mm. in length are rare, but among the handaxes of the western subconcentration, one handaxe 234 mm. long was found. The dimensions of the handaxes and the length-to-width proportions are shown on a diagram (fig. 11).

The striking feature of this diagram is the homogeneity of the whole group of 81 hand-axes found in the excavated part of the site.

The most numerous group of handaxes form the cordiform specimens. They are subdivided into three subtypes: true cordiform (fig. 13), cordiform elongated, and cordiform with natural pebble butts (fig. 12, nos. 1-4).

Among 81 handaxes there are only seven specimens which are triangular or subtriangular. Their butts are natural surfaces of the pebbles or slabs of the ferrocrete, and their edges are straight, which gives them the triangular form. There is only one example with a flaked thin butt (fig. 13, no. 4).

The large group of 24 handaxes is classified as suboval and amygdaloidal forms. Some of them possess the pebble butts preserved to the half of their length (fig. 12, nos. 5-6; fig. 16; fig. 15, no. 2).

Ten specimens belong to the lanceolate type of handaxes (fig. 14). One of them looks like a leaf point, another one is plano-convex and looks like a pick (fig. 15, no. 1).

Two handaxes belong to the type known as the "shark tooth" form (fig. 17).

Only one large micoquian handaxe was collected from the surface of the western subconcentration.

Tools Made on Flakes

Thirty-seven tools made on flakes (fig. 18) form a very small group among the tools of the Arkin 8 assemblage. The most numerous are

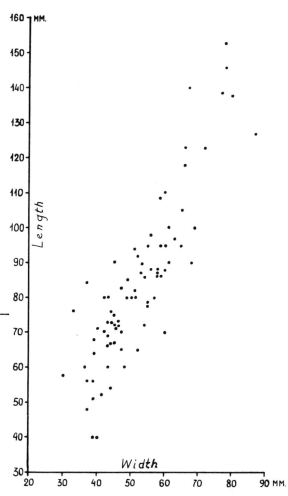

Fig. 11—Diagram illustrating the size and length-width proportions of the Arkin 8 handaxes.

scrapers (18 specimens) and the flakes with one or more notches on the edge (14 specimens). Two typical angle burins, one borer and two flakes with alternate retouch of the edges are represented in the collection.

Inventory of the Site

The inventory of the site, the proportions of the raw materials used for the production of the artifacts, and the proportions among the tool types are shown in the accompanying table.

Summary and Discussion

Summarizing the analysis and description of Arkin 8 assemblage we would like to point out its following characteristic features:

1. The predominance of the pebbles used as the raw material and the lack, or very scanty production, of the flakes as the base for further production of tools, as well as the absence of the true Levalloisian technique, characterize the technology utilized by the inhabitants of the site.

2. From the typological point of view the assemblage possesses its special affinities thanks to the nearly equal proportion of such typological groups of the tools as the handaxes, ovates, choppers, and chopping tools. Among these tools the ovates possess peculiar value as a very specialized type. The presence of the ovates, choppers, and chopping tools differentiates the Arkin 8 assemblage from other Acheulean assemblages known at the moment from the territory of Nubia.

Two questions arise with this recapitulation:

1. What is the age of the Arkin 8 assemblage

THE ARKIN 8 COLLECTION ACCORDING TO TOOL TYPES, PROPORTIONS, AND RAW MATERIALS USED

Tool Types	Raw Stone Used						No.	%
	Quartz	Ferrocrete Sandstone	Fine Crystallic[1] Rock	Fossilized Wood	Quartzite	Other Crystallic Rocks		
Cores								
A. With one striking platform	53		2			1	56	18.00
B. Globular	42	2	1	1			46	14.84
C. Discoidal	55	13	2			2	72	23.18
D. Half-discoidal	98	9	2				109	35.00
E. Oval with prepared striking platform	26	2					28	8.98
Total	274	26	7	1		3	311	
Per Cent	88.00	8.61	2.20	0.28	—	0.90	—	100.00
Flakes	1781	219	13	4	22	53	2092	
Per Cent	85.00	10.40	0.62	0.19	1.35	2.53	—	100.09
Choppers								
A. With one flake removed	2		1				3	6.38
B. Transversal	8	1	1				10	21.22
C. Side straight	15					1	16	34.00
D. Side convex	5						5	10.63
E. Suboval	12		1				13	27.67
Total	42	1	3			1	47	
Per Cent	89.20	2.12	6.38			2.12		9.61[2]
Chopping Tools								
A. Straight transversal	24		1	1			26	19.10
B. Convex transversal	20	5	2	1			28	20.60
C. Oval	17				1		18	13.24
D. With pointed end	13		1				14	10.30
E. Side	23	1	1	1		2	28	20.60
F. Elongated with rounded end	19	1			1	1	22	16.18
Total	116	7	5	3	2	3	136	
Per Cent	85.40	5.29	3.67	2.23	1.47	2.23		27.80[2]
Discs and Half-discs								
A. Discs	11	12					23	52.23
B. Half-discs	21						21	47.77
Total	32	12					44	
Per Cent	72.78	27.22						8.99[2]
Ovates								
A. Unifacially retouched	5	4		1			10	8.99
B. Bifacially retouched	40	40		1	3	1	85	76.50
C. Fragments	7	8			1		16	14.40
Total	52	52		2	4	1	111	
Per Cent	46.80	46.80		1.80	3.60	0.90		22.68[2]

[1] Brown in color and similar to chert.

[2] These figures show the proportion of the group of tools to total numbers of tools in the assemblage.

						Total	Per Cent	
Handaxes								
A. Lanceolate		9			1	10	8.82	
B. Cordiform	4	6			1	11	9.72	
C. Cordiform elongated	3	6			2	11	9.72	34.47[3]
D. Cordiform with pebble butts	11	4	1		1	17	15.03	
E. Triangular and subtriangular	2	3		1	1	7	6.33	
F. Suboval and amygdaloidal	8	16				24	21.20	
G. "Shark tooth"		2				2	1.77	
H. Unfinished and fragments	8	21	1		1	31	27.42	
Total	36	67	2	1	7	113		
Per Cent	31.82	59.20	1.77	0.88	6.33		23.15[2]	
Tools Made of Flakes								
A. Side-scrapers	6					6	16.20	
B. Side convex scrapers	2				2	4	10.80	
C. Transversal scrapers	1				1	2	5.40	48.60[3]
D. Double scrapers	3				1	4	10.80	
E. Convergent scrapers	2					2	5.40	3.68[2]
F. Flakes with notches	9	2	1		2	14	37.80	
G. Flakes with alternate retouch	2					2	5.40	
H. Burins	1			1		2	5.40	
I. Borer	1					1	2.70	3.88[2]
Total	27	2	1	1	6	37		
Per Cent	72.80	5.40	2.70	2.70	16.20		7.56[2]	

[3] These figures show the proportion of several important types to the numbers of tools of a given tool group.

in comparison with the age of the other Acheulean sites in the area?

2. What is the meaning of the differences in technology and typology of the Arkin 8 assemblage?

In a discussion of the first question, it is necessary to point out that we do not have direct superposition of two or more Acheulean assemblages within the area examined. The only possible answer to this question lies in the geological stratigraphy of the sites and in the typological comparisons. The observations of the first kind are very scanty, too, and very often are interpreted in a different manner.

The sites examined on the eastern bank of the Nile by J. and G. Guichard and partly by F. Wendorf were situated mainly on the tops of the jebels with the exception of Site 400 situated near the edge of the wadi and partially in its deposit (Guichard and Guichard, 1965). Very close to the last site another area of Acheulean remains was found in the slope of a stony deposit (Site 400-12) of the adjacent jebel.

On the western slope of the Nile valley there are very few Acheulean sites known up to now.

We mentioned a small concentration situated in the same wadi where Arkin 8 lies. Most of them occur on the surface of weathered Nubia Sandstone and one on the surface of the wadi deposits, between the site under discussion and the termination of the wadi. In this particular case it appears that the site containing handaxes made of ferrocrete sandstone only, accompanied by Levalloisian cores, is younger than the Arkin 8 assemblage. A similar site designated as Arkin 3 has been found 1,200 m. north by R. Dougherty and ourself. Here again it was on the surface of another wadi deposit.

In the vicinity of Arkin 8 two other sites containing Acheulean artifacts were found and examined. They are Arkin 14 and Dibeira 52. Both of them possess an interesting geological stratigraphy, which offers the possibility of examining the question under discussion.

The stratigraphy of Arkin 14 was described in our former report (Chmielewski, 1965). The additional work on this site, done in the 1965 field season, changed our former interpretation very much. It is now clear that the Nile silt described formerly as contemporaneous with the wadi de-

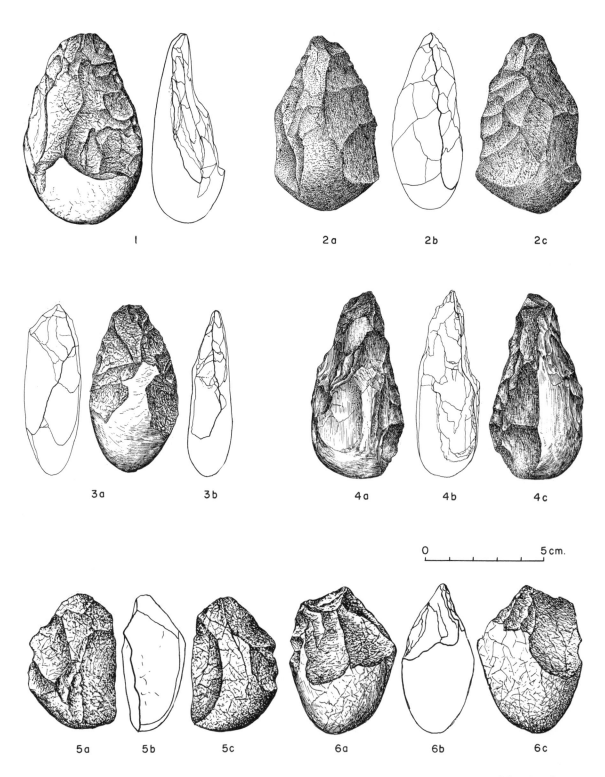

Fig. 12—Arkin 8: Nos. 1-4, cordiform handaxes with pebble butts; 5-6, irregular suboval or amygdaloid handaxes.

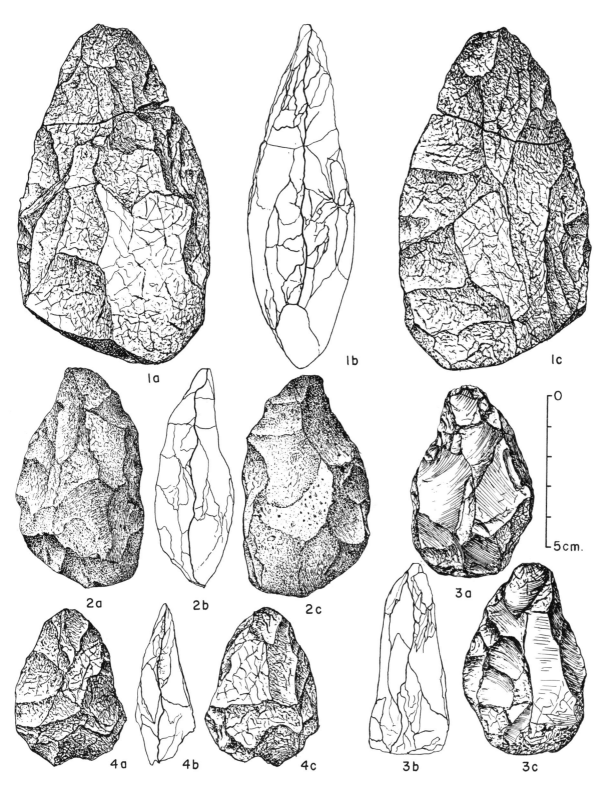

FIG. 13—Arkin 8: Cordiform and subcordiform handaxes.

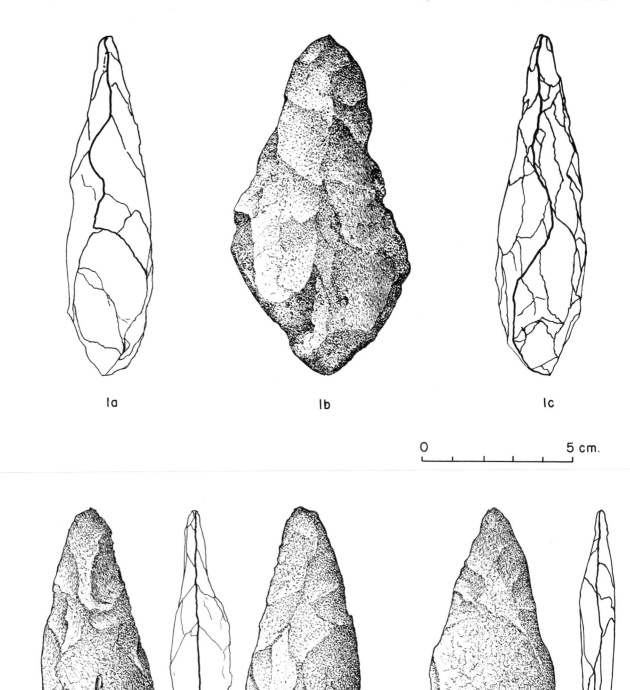

FIG. 14—Arkin 8: Lanceolate handaxes.

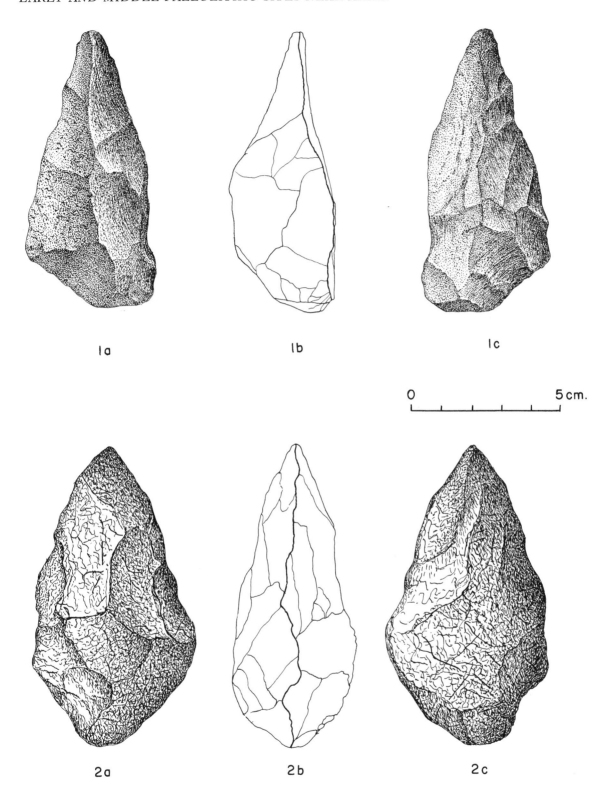

1a   1b   1c

0   5 cm.

2a   2b   2c

FIG. 15—Arkin 8: No. 1, pick-like handaxe; 2, amygdaloid handaxe.

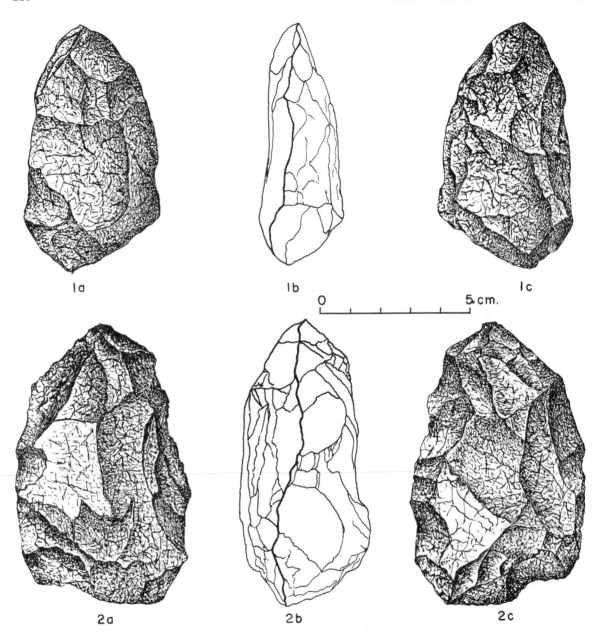

0 |———|———|———|———| 5 cm.

1a   1b   1c

2a   2b   2c

FIG. 16—Arkin 8: Suboval irregular handaxes.

posits containing Acheulean artifacts is in reality younger than the last sediment. It was observed that the silt has been covered by a slope of deluvial sand and small gravel deposit on which the reddish soil was formed. This soil was covered and dissected twice by young wadi deposits. Four hundred meters to the southwest of the site we observed an outcrop of the silt in the shape of a small island, situated about 6 m. higher than the silt of Arkin 14. A hard reddish soil was dismantled below this silt covering the weathered surface of Nubia Sandstone.

J. de Heinzelin suggested that both silts found in the vicinity of Arkin 14 belong to the same stage of the Nile siltation. It is difficult to accept such an interpretation. The very bottom part of the silt on Arkin 14 contains a large quantity of the gravels, showing that it was a transgressive

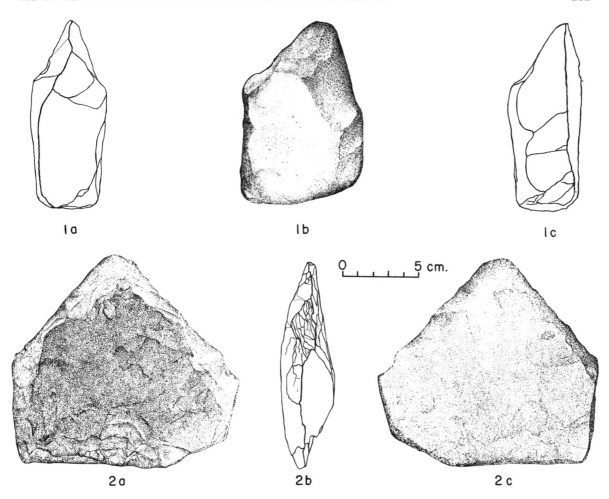

Fig. 17—Arkin 8: "Shark tooth" handaxes.

stage of the siltation. The top part of the silt is dissected by drying polygons. There is no dissection in the whole silt layer. All these facts show that this silt was deposited near the edge of the river and that the water was never much higher than the top of the silt. Because of this, we think that the silt found to the south of Arkin 14, and 6 m. higher than the site, represents another accumulation period—a true 30 m. siltation. The occurrence of the reddish soil below this silt and similar soil above the silt on Arkin 14 is another argument. Observed stratigraphy is illustrated in Figure 2, A and C.

A cordiform handaxe made of ferrocrete accompanied by a few quartz choppers, chopping tools, and flakes have been found in the top part of the wadi deposits below the reddish soil. The

handaxe (fig. 19) and choppers are very good analogies to the forms known from Arkin 8. At the same time no traces of Levalloisian technique were observed in this small assemblage.

Site Dibeira 52 is situated about 4 km. to the north of Arkin 14. The isolated hills covered by thick Pre-Nile gravel deposits are elevated there 162 m. above sea level. The eastern slopes of the hills are covered to the elevation of 152 m. above sea level by a sandy silt deposit of the 30 m. Nile siltation. A reddish soil was dismantled below this silt lying on a weathered surface of Nubia Sandstone and covered by a stony layer. In the latter sediment many flakes and cores made of quartz pebbles as well as of ferrocrete and one quartz cordiform handaxe with a natural pebble butt were collected. Some of the cores are Leval-

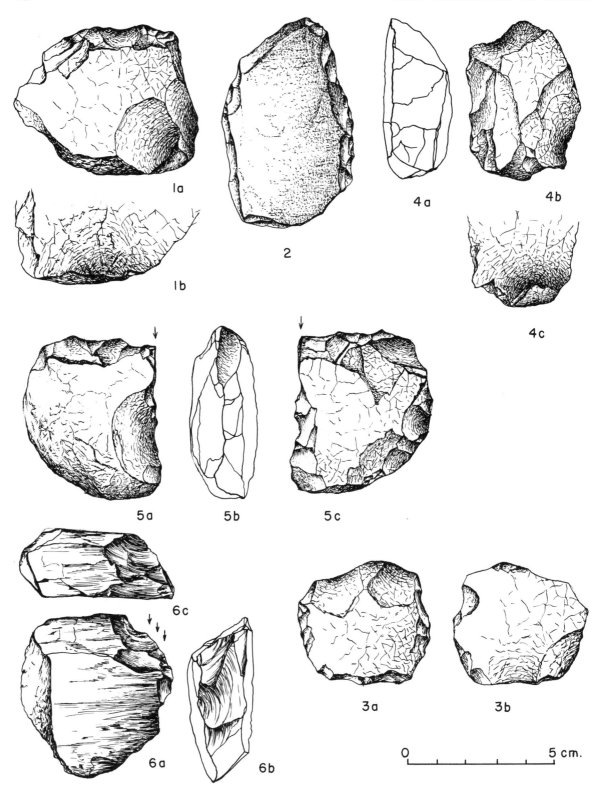

Fig. 18—Tools made of flakes: No. 1, transversal convex scraper; 2, double scraper; 3, alternate retouched flake; 4, straight side-scraper; 5, 6, burins.

loisian. Many artifacts and stones were rounded by wind action.

From a summary of the observations described, a preliminary supposition should be drawn; that is, that the Acheulean assemblages containing the Levalloisian elements of technology are younger in Nubia than those which do not contain them. In such a case the Arkin 8 and Arkin 14 assemblages are the oldest among known Acheulean assemblages in the Wadi Halfa area. The typology of these assemblages, and particularly the high percentage of the pebble tools in them, supports this interpretation, too.

Our knowledge about the connection of these assemblages with the formation of the Nile Valley is very small indeed. In a former report we suggested they were contemporary with the Nile silt represented on Arkin 14, which is a mistake in the light of the new observations. J. de Heinzelin's work on Site 440 during the 1965 field season has shown that there are traces of an older siltation which had taken place before the accumulation of the silt elevated 30 m. above the floodplain. Whether this siltation was contemporary with Acheulean assemblages or not, nobody knows at the moment. It is clear, however, that the wadis deposits containing Acheulean assemblages were connected with a depression or even with a river which has been situated somewhere in the Nile valley, but at a much lower elevation than the highest silt of this river. An additional argument for this is the occurrence of the very large pebbles in the Arkin 8 assemblage. The only place where such large pebbles occur *in situ* lies 2 km. east of the site in the elevation of about 135 m. above sea level, or about 15 m. below the highest silt of the Nile.

Discussing the second question facing us, we would like to point out the differences of all Nubian Acheulean assemblages when compared with other African assemblages. One is the lack of the cleavers in the former. The presence of the ovates in the older stage of Acheulean culture in Nubia is the second interesting factor.

The ovates were found in large quantity from the Acheulean Site of Khor Abu Anga in Omdurman, thanks to the work of A. J. Arkell (1949). The same author mentioned this type of tool from Sai Island about 200 km. to the south of Arkin. On the last site they were accompanied by quartz pebble tools and "undeveloped" handaxes. On the basis of this information, it seems to us that all these sites form a particular cultural group among the vast Acheulean complex in Africa. It is impossible at the moment to determine its exact geological age, its territory, and its place in the development of the Acheulean culture. On the basis of the observations described above, we suspect that this group falls into the middle stage of the development of Acheulean culture. J. D. Clark expresses the view that the differentiation of Acheulean culture began in its late stage in connection with the climatic changes (Clark, 1960, 1964). It is clear, however, that the climatic changes existed before the final stage of this culture too, and that the Arkin 8 assemblage together with similar sites have an old appearance and differ very much from the other Acheulean sites.

Site Arkin 8 has its own problems, too. Some of them were not solved during the time of the excavation. First among them is the question of whether or not all the recognized subconcentrations were contemporaneous. It seems more probable to us that each subconcentration was separated a little in time from the others. During the excavation, we noticed that on the territory between the Subconcentrations A and B the artifacts were lying in two slightly separated levels connecting with each other many times.

In describing the pattern of the distribution of the artifacts we noticed that the accumulation of the tools in the center of each subconcentration was in the form of a pile or a cairn. Similar cairns are known from the El Guetar site in Tunis (Gruet 1955, 1960). There they are interpreted as the offerings for supranatural beings connected with water (springs). Such an interpretation looks doubtful to us. We think that on both sites we have found traces of the designation of particular places that were very important for inhabitants. These cairns probably identified the ownership of the place where a given group of people camped together in the surrounding territory. This would designate these places for themselves as well as for other groups. If it was really so, those remnants should be interpreted as the very beginning of the custom still alive in Africa.

Another question is the presence or absence of camping accommodations. It was documented

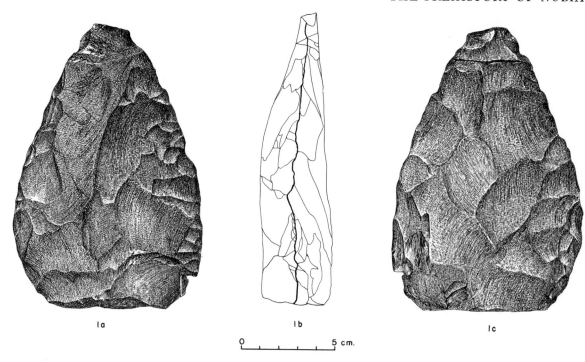

Ia   Ib   Ic

0 _____ 5 cm.

Fig. 19—Arkin 14: Cordiform handaxe.

during the excavation of Subconcentration A that it was lying in a small depression 25 cm. deep surrounded by large slabs of sandstone. Is this a remnant of a shanty or wind-shelter? We found another camp accommodation in the shape of a wind-shelter built up of stone slabs close to the Subconcentration H. Thus, we think that the circle of the stones surrounding Subconcentration A never served as the base or strengthened the wall of any construction. This circle looks too big for such a role. However, it should be noticed that a similar circle was described by J. D. Clark from the Kalambo Falls Acheulean layer, but it was without a big concentration of the artifacts inside as was the case at Arkin 8. (Clark, 1960).

If we accept the premise that the single subconcentration of Arkin 8 is a remnant of one camping community, it would seem that the group was a small one, judging from the size of each subconcentration. It is clear enough if we compare the size of these subconcentrations with the size of those discovered in the area and dated to later periods—Arkin 5 and Dibeira 1, for example. Those areas covered about 1,600 sq. m. compared with about 40 sq. m. for the Arkin 8 single subconcentration. About eight to fifteen

members of the community were probably the number of the people camping together. It is necessary, however, to note that such calculations need more careful and more detailed examinations of the sites for comparisons.

ASSEMBLAGES WITH FOLIATED POINTS— ARKIN 5, 6, AND 6A

The geomorphological situation of the sites containing the foliated objects in their inventory were described in a former report (Chmielewski, 1965). Three such sites were examined. They are Arkin 5, 6, and 6A, but among them only Arkin 5 was studied in detail. The description and interpretation of the assemblage of this site forms the main subject of this report.

The large quantity of the artifacts were lying on the surface which covered an oval area about 75 m. long in a southwest-northeast direction and 30 m. wide. The site was dissected by a shallow wadi (fig. 1). The artifacts lay among the slabs of ferrocrete sandstone forming a pediment. They were not transported after the site had been left by its inhabitants.

A trench 100 sq. m. in size was excavated in the southern part of the site to the depth of 50 cm. where the surface of Nubia Sandstone was reached. Within this trench three large subconcentrations of the artifacts were discovered. They were visible on the surface and documented on the map of the surface and subsurface (to the 5 cm. depth) distribution of the artifacts (fig. 2). They were clearer and well outlined in the depth between 5 and 40 cm. below the surface, as is shown on the second map (fig. 3).

These three subconcentrations were lying in the pits, each of about 3.5 m. in diameter. They were dug to the surface of the Nubia Sandstone by the inhabitants of the site. The most southern pit had the wall strengthened with the slabs of ferrocrete sandstone (figs. 3 and 4, B). The bottoms of the pits were covered by a 25 cm. thick layer of flakes, cores, and some tools mixed with reddish sand. The fill of the pits as well as the surrounding sediment were very hard, cemented by salt and gypsum concretions.

It is difficult to interpret correctly the pits and their fill. At the beginning we supposed that they are remnants of the camp building. But the character of their fill—mainly the vast products of the Levelloisian cores—seems to contradict such an interpretation. We think we are dealing with the remnants of the mining activity of a group interested in good slabs of ferrocrete. These thin slabs lying in their primary position were found in the northwest corner of the trench covered by colluvial reddish sand and a stony pediment layer (fig. 4, C). The workshops were situated in those pits after the slabs of the ferrocrete had been reached and removed. There were no traces which could suggest that such pits were covered by a roof made of organic material. Behind the waste of the Levalloisian core production some good tools as well as their fragments and unfinished and broken half-products were found. There are many Levalloisian cores for the production of the points in the collection, but no single point was found. Most of the Levalloisian flakes collected were broken, too. All these observations suggest the workshop and mining character of the site.

The typological analysis of the collections from workshop sites is difficult. Many of the tools are unfinished, very thickly flaked, and broken. We are dealing in reality with remnants of the site from which nearly all good tools were taken away.

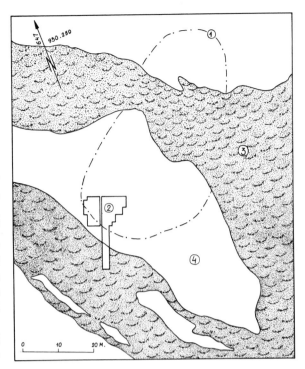

Fig. 1—Map of Arkin 5. Key: 1, limit of the concentration of the artifacts; 2, trench; 3, shallow wadis filled with eolian sand; 4, pediment.

The tools used in habitation sites are very poorly represented in the workshops like Arkin 5. We are faced with further difficulties when we start to compare such a site with others from the point of view of the cultural classification.

However, the collection of Site Arkin 5 makes it possible to examine the technology and typology of the mining and workshop site. Very little is known about this activity in the African Paleolithic cultures. For this reason, we think that the more detailed study of the Arkin 5 assemblage will be useful.

ANALYSIS OF THE TECHNOLOGY OF THE ARKIN 5 ASSEMBLAGE

The collection gathered during the time of the excavation contains 9,769 artifacts. All were made of the local ferrocrete sandstone. Of this number only 165 were tools, which equals 1.58 per cent of the whole collection. Such a small proportion of tools to the waste by-products seems to characterize it as a workshop site. An additional argument is that among the tools, we have many

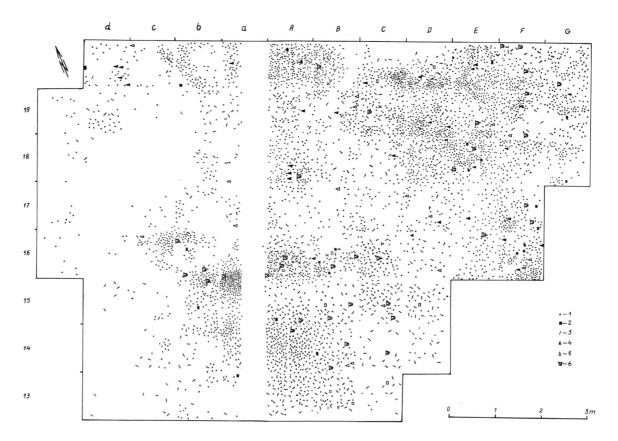

Fig. 2—Map of the redistribution of the artifacts on the surface and subsurface deposit in the excavated part of the
Arkin 5 site. Key: 1, flakes found on surface; 2, tools found on surface; 3, flakes found in subsurface deposit;
4, pointed tools found in subsurface deposit; 5, pointed tools found on the surface; 6, Levalloisian cores.

broken unfinished pieces as well as many raw
worked forms.

From the technological point of view the whole
assemblage is characterized by the occurrence of
the Levalloisian cores without a single core of
another type. We think that the calculation of
the Levalloisian Technological Index on the basis
of flakes does not express the real technology
used by the given population, because many
flakes of the non-Levalloisian type must be struck
off before the Levalloisian core was formed. The
calculation on the basis of the number of core
types is more accurate. Looking at the Arkin 5
assemblage in this manner we can say that it is
a full Levalloisian one.

All 93 Levalloisian cores found on Arkin 5
(fig. 5) belong to the "Nubian Levalloisian core,
Type I" according to the Guichards' classification
(1965). Their dimensions vary between 144 mm.

in length, 120 mm. in width, and 25 mm. in
thickness to 75 mm. x 66 mm. x 24 mm. The
Levalloisian points, flakes, and blades were detached from them. The following table gives an
idea of the quantities of artifacts which characterize the flaking technique.

Types	No.
1. Levalloisian cores, Type I	93
2. Levalloisian flakes (mainly fragments)	182
3. Blades (mainly fragments)	94
4. Flakes with cortex on the butt	910
5. Flakes with flat butt (*lisse*)	1430
6. Flakes with dihedral butt	497
7. Flakes with faceted butt: (a) flat	1426
(b) convex	121
(c) concave	78
8. Thin flakes with sharp butt (from the production of the bifacial tools and Levalloisian cores)	2233
9. Flake fragments	2540
Total	9604

The strict Faceting Index is 23.3 per cent. The

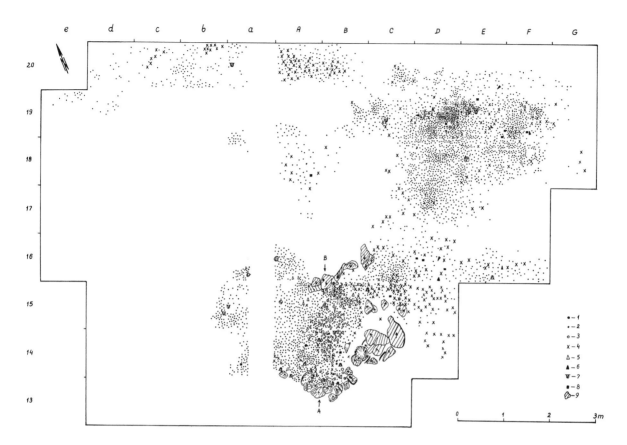

Fig. 3—Map of the redistribution of artifacts between 5 and 45 cm. depth from the surface in the excavated part of Arkin 5: 1, flake tools; 2, flakes; 3, flakes found below 30 cm. depth; 4, eolized flakes; 5, foliated handaxes and their half-products; 6, foliated points and knives, their fragments and half-products; 7, Levalloisian cores; 8, bifacially retouched slabs; 9, ferrocrete slabs forming a wall of the southern subconcentration; A-B, the line of the section shown on Fig. 4, B.

Levalloisian Technological Index calculated in the fashion of the F. Bordes system is lower than 4 per cent.

Nearly 62 per cent of the tools of the assemblage were produced by use of the bifacial technique of the retouch. These two techniques—Levalloisian for production of the flakes and bifacial for production of the tools—form very characteristic features of the assemblage.

TYPOLOGICAL ANALYSIS

The tools of Arkin 5 are subdivided into two main classes: (1) bifacially retouched tools, and (2) tools made of flakes. The first class forms about 61 per cent of all tools and must be subdivided into finished and unfinished forms. The last group is more numerous than the first. Many of the tools found were broken. The tools found

on the surface of the site are heavily eolized while those found inside the pits were extremely fresh.

The following types of the tools were distinguished: (1) foliated points and knives; (2) foliated handaxes and their half-products; (3) notched scrapers; (4) notched flakes; (5) denticulated flakes; (6) truncated flakes; and (7) atypical end-scrapers.

Foliated Points and Knives and Their Half-products

There are single specimens of the different subtypes of the leaf-like points and knives, very few of which belong to the same subtype. They are described as follows:

A. Elongated, thin, bifacially retouched point plano-convex in transversal section. The end is

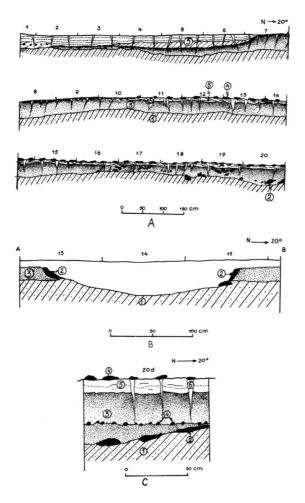

FIG. 4—The sections of the excavated part of Arkin 5. Key: A, length section in the trench; B, section of the southern pit; C, section in the NW corner of the trench; 1, Nubia Sandstone; 2, ferrocrete sandstone slabs; 3, colluvial reddish sand; 4, eolized sandstone fragments; 5, yellow sand; 6, wedges of desiccation.

sharp, the edges are convex, and the base, in the shape of a very short tang, is poorly separated from the edges (fig. 6, no. 4).

B. Thick bifacially retouched knife with rounded end, convex edges. Near the base a short notch on one edge forms a poorly expressed tang (fig. 6, no. 6).

C. Thin double ended, plano-convex bifacially retouched point with convex edges, asymmetrical to the long axis (fig. 6, no. 8).

D. Thin double ended plano-convex point, superficially retouched on the upper side only; the edges are convexly symmetrical to the long

axis. The length is 94 mm.; width, 38 mm.; and thickness, 12 mm.

E. Three thick double ended bifacially retouched points, symmetrical to the long axis and in transversal section (fig. 6, nos. 5, 9).

F. Three thick bifacially retouched points (or knives?), symmetrical in transversal section with sharp ends and rounded bases. The specimen illustrated (fig. 6, no. 2) was found broken in the northern subconcentration in two different squares. The two other specimens possess the following dimensions: length, 144 mm. and 150 mm.; width, 44 and 52 mm.; and thickness, 30 and 32 mm.

G. Two thick elongated bifacially retouched knives with rounded ends and bases (fig. 6, no. 7). They are symmetrical to the long axis and in transversal section.

Many fragments of the described subtypes, with the exception of subtype D, were found on the site. The thin bifacially retouched fragments of these objects are represented by nine specimens like that illustrated (fig. 6, no. 3), while the thick fragments are twenty in number. There are ten half-products of the foliated bifacial tools like those illustrated in Figure 8, Numbers 3, 7, 8. Their edges are uneven or have unretouched parts, and are very roughly flaked. It is interesting to notice the tendencies of forming of the tang on a few of these pieces (fig. 8, nos. 3, 7).

Foliated Handaxes

They are as numerous as the foliated points and knives but only one specimen (fig. 6, no. 1) is wholly preserved. It is impossible to exclude that they were not unfinished products of the pointed foliated objects of the former group. Their very regular almost straight edges and well formed ends contradict such an interpretation, while their fragmentation on the site makes it possible.

The difference between these tools and the true handaxes lies in the three following features: they are flatter and more elongated, and their edges are more convex than those observed on typical handaxes.

In addition to the foliated handaxe illustrated in Figure 6, Number 1, there are three others which are more completely preserved (fig. 7, nos. 1-3) and eleven fragments of these tools

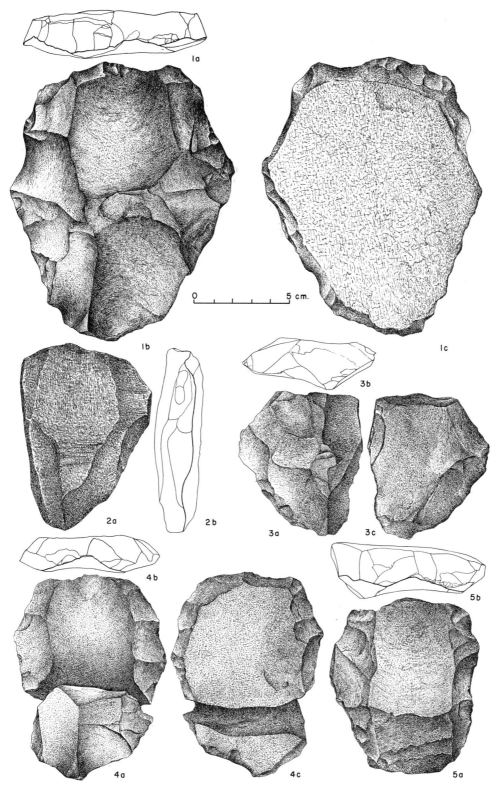

FIG. 5—Arkin 5: Levalloisian cores.

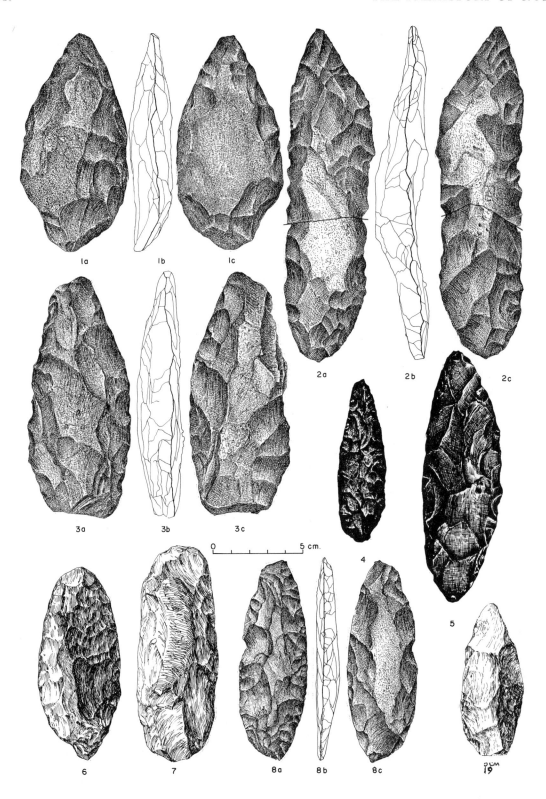

FIG. 6—Arkin 5: No. 1, foliated handaxe; 2-9, foliated points and knives.

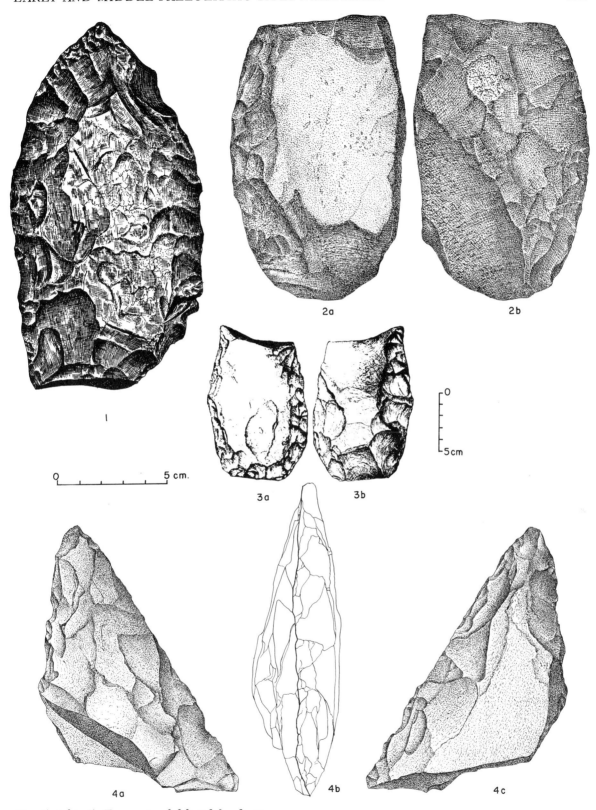

Fɪɢ. 7—Arkin 5: Fragments of foliated handaxes.

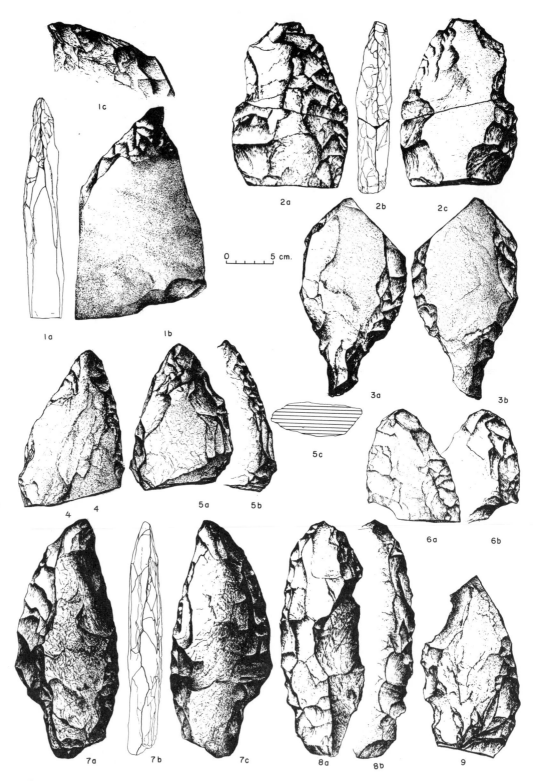

Fig. 8—Arkin 5: No. 1, bifacially flaked slab; 2, 5, 6, 9, half-products of foliated handaxes; 3, 7, 8, half-products of points and knives.

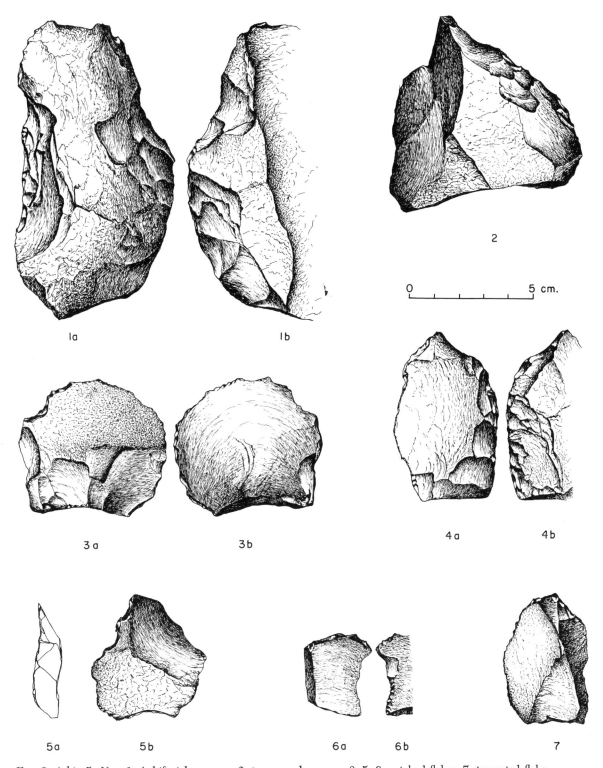

F<small>IG</small>. 9—Arkin 5: Nos. 1, 4, bifacial scrapers; 2, transversal scraper; 3, 5, 6, notched flakes; 7, truncated flake.

(fig. 7, no. 4). The fragments are parts of these tools—the bases, the middle parts, and the ends.

Thirty-six pieces look like the broken half-products of this type of tool (fig. 8, nos. 2, 5, 6, 9). Their edges are partly regular and well finished, and some are very roughly flaked. Some of them when taken separately, omitting the whole context of the site, would be classified as bifacial scrapers.

More than ten large plaquettes of ferrocrete were found with partial bifacial flaking of the edge. Their dimensions were greater than 30 cm. in diameter. The smallest one is illustrated (fig. 8, no. 1). They are not counted as tools, because they do not possess defined forms.

Scrapers

They are represented by twenty-two specimens and seven fragments. There are six pieces among the fragments which should be interpreted as broken, unfinished bifacial tools (fig. 9, nos. 1, 2, 4). The classification of the scrapers is given in the accompanying statistical table. Five specimens were made of Levalloisian flakes, eleven are on other flakes, and the others are on thin ferrocrete plates.

Notched Flakes

The notches are not typical; their retouch is low with the exception of one tool (fig. 9, no. 5). This type of the retouch could be accidental, produced by trample (fig. 9, nos. 3, 6). There is only one Clactonian notch. Four specimens were made of Levalloisian flakes.

Denticulated Flakes

They are atypical like the preceding type, and were probably produced by trample, too.

Truncated Flakes

Only six flakes with oblique truncation of the end were found, all made on Levalloisian flakes (fig. 9, no. 7).

End-scrapers

Atypical end-scrapers found were four in number: one on a Levalloisian flake and three on blades. Their retouch is very much like that observed on the notched and denticulated flakes.

The accompanying table gives the quantities of described tool types and the proportion of each to the total number of the tools in the assemblage.

Types	No.	%
1. Foliated points and knives	12	7.27
Fragments of foliated points and knives	29	17.57
Half-products of foliated points and knives	10	6.06
Group Total	51	30.90
2. Foliated handaxes	4	2.42
Fragments of foliated handaxes	11	6.66
Half-products of foliated handaxes	36	21.21
Group Total	51	30.29
3. Scrapers: transversal convex	5	3.03
side convex	3	1.81
side concave	7	4.24
side straight	6	3.63
bifacial	5	3.03
double	3	1.81
Group Total	29	17.55
4. Notched flakes	13	7.87
5. Denticulated flakes	11	6.66
6. Truncated flakes	6	3.63
7. Atypical end-scrapers	4	2.42
Total	165	99.32

DISCUSSION AND RESULTS

The interpretation of Arkin 5 as the mining and workshop site was given above. There are a few further questions that need clarification. The first question is whether or not they existed on the site in another section with a real living floor. Judging from the detailed survey on the whole surface of the site there was not such a place. Everywhere we found only the same Levalloisian cores, flakes, and rare bifacial tools scattered over the entire territory.

The supposition arises that the real living sites are situated somewhere in the vicinity of Arkin 5. The small excavations on Sites Arkin 6 and 6A were undertaken to answer this question. They resulted in the discoveries of other workshops and mines of the same character as at Arkin 5. Site Arkin 6A gave, besides the Levalloisian cores of Type I, three cores with clear indications that blades were detached from them, one elongated tool which served probably as a pick for digging, one good concave transversal scraper and two fragments of bifacial foliated points (fig. 10). The foliated handaxes were not found there. The artifacts lay in the pits which had been dug to the surface of Nubia Sandstone. Similar observations were made on the Arkin 6 site.

We do not know of other similar sites situated within the examined area. If we accept the above

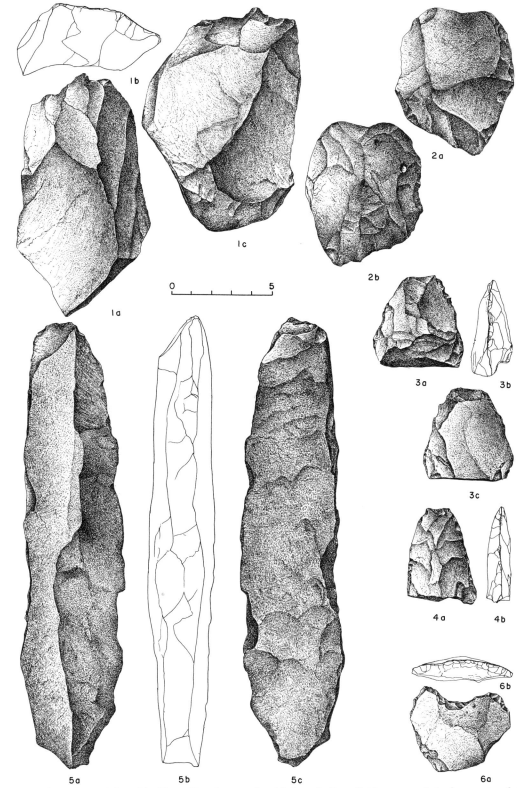

Fig. 10—Artifacts from Arkin 6A. Key: No. 1, core for blades; 2, Levalloisian core; 3-4, fragments of foliated points; 5, digging tool (pick ?); 6, concave scraper.

interpretation of Arkin 5 and 6 then we can suspect that the living sites connected with them will have the following appearance:

1. The quantity of the Levalloisian cores will be smaller than those observed on the workshop sites, but the Levalloisian points and flakes will occur more often.

2. There will be more well made foliated objects as well as other tools, mainly scrapers. It is suspected that the truncated flakes and blades will play an important role in these assemblages also. The frequencies of such tool types as notched and denticulated flakes are not clear.

The possibility exists that such sites were found within the Wadi Halfa area by J. and G. Guichard. They described a few sites with foliated objects, but not one of them was excavated. The comparison of the statistical figures published by those authors with those presented here are useless, because of the difference in sampling methods. However, the figure of about 60 per cent of the foliated objects found on the Site 420 is equal to that calculated for the Arkin 5 assemblage. Some of the foliated objects found on Site 420 form the best analogies to the foliated hand-axes of Arkin 5 (Guichard and Guichard, 1965, fig. 16, nos. 1-2). Again Site 420 is interpreted as a workshop.

It is possible to trace another analogy to Arkin 5 in the Brinikol assemblage published by the Guichards. There is one shouldered bifacial foliated object very much like the one illustrated (fig. 8, no. 7). All these observations show that the assemblages which are more or less similar to Arkin 5 are very numerous in Nubia. Maybe they are more numerous if we take into account the leaf points published by A. J. Arkell from Khor Abu Anga (1949).

The cultural classification of all these assemblages was discussed by J. and G. Guichard in the paper cited. They introduced the name "Nubian Middle Paleolithic with foliated objects" as the common one. It is as bad as the name "Sangoan" we used in our former paper for the Arkin 5 assemblage. We do not have a single assemblage within the region of Nubia which would give the name for the whole complex of sites where the leaf points and foliated objects were found. This is because all these sites are situated in places where the earlier or later ad-

mixture cannot be excluded, or they possess such peculiar characteristics like those of Sites Arkin 5 or 420.

It is true that the Sangoan culture contains a high proportion of the picks, which was noted by the Guichards as the difference between Sangoan culture and the assemblages with foliated objects from Nubia. But some of the rostrocarinate scrapers (or Nubian) are very much like the picks of the Sangoan culture, judging from the description of this type by J. D. Clark (1959, 1964), J. J. Janmart (1953), and L. S. B. Leakey (1945, 1949). The convex side-scrapers as well as the denticulated and notched tools characterize the Sangoan assemblages, and they are present in bigger or smaller proportions in Nubian assemblages, too. We mention all these points not because we think that Nubian assemblages with foliated objects belong to the Sangoan culture. They are, however, closer to it than to any other culture known at the moment from surrounding territories. As an additional remark we would like to point out that within the Sangoan complex there are several regional variants.

Those working on the problems of the assemblages with foliated points always mention the memorable lecture of G. Caton-Thompson (1946) in connection with her supposition about the genesis of the Aterian culture within the complexes with leaf points in tropical Africa. It will be very easy to accept that idea, but as long as we do not have well dated and typologically well defined assemblages in the territory of Nubia, this supposition must be kept as a working hypothesis only.

There is no good evidence for the determination of the geological age of the Arkin 5 assemblage and for similar assemblages from the region under discussion. It is clear that they are younger than the Acheulean assemblages and older than the assemblages situated in or above the highest siltation of the Nile. The Acheulean sites were contemporary with the wadis deposits and with the reddish soil formation covering them. Both of them are cut by the highest Nile deposits. The Arkin 5 assemblage lies on the colluvial sand with traces of soil formation in it. J. de Heinzelin observed the leached horizon in the top of colluvial sand which has been cut by one of the pits dug by inhabitants of Site Arkin 5. This colluvial sand with the soil traces in it is covered by the stony layer of the large pediment. The latter was probably contemporaneous with the occupation of the site. This pediment ends about 800 m. to the east of the site where it is cut by a poorly visible valley about 400 m. wide, filled with coarse sand and small gravel deposits. The elevation of this valley is about 155 m. above the sea level. We observed the same elevation of the highest silt near Arkin 14. Was this valley contemporaneous with this silt or not? We do not know, but the possibility must not be excluded. The pediment described above is older than the valley but the time difference was probably not a big one. On the basis of these observations we suspect that the Arkin assemblage immediately preceded the accumulation of the highest silt of this region.

CONTRIBUTIONS TO THE STUDY OF THE EARLY AND MIDDLE PALEOLITHIC OF NUBIA

Jean and Geneviève Guichard

(LABORATORY OF PREHISTORY, UNIVERSITY OF BORDEAUX)

Translated by Judith Friedlander

INTRODUCTION

IF OUR PREVIOUS WORK (Guichard and Guichard, 1965) is compared with the present work, it will be noticed that there are repetitions and, at times, even some contradictions. It should be recognized that our first publication was written solely to serve as a basis for discussion, with the explicit intention of encouraging further research (Third Expedition, etc. . . .). Numerical agreements between the tool frequency tables found in our previous work and those found here should not be sought. First, we had intentionally reserved the right to alter certain definitions which were somewhat hastily made in our previous work (Guichard and Guichard, 1965, p. 3); second, we have created sub-categories here. Furthermore, the material from many sites practically doubled by the close of the third season.

In the pieces illustrated, the flake tools are represented with the bulb of percussion at the bottom. The drawings initialed J.L. are by Josselyne Laurent. Those signed P.L. are by Pierre Laurent. The others are by Geneviève Guichard.

GEOLOGICAL CONSIDERATIONS:
RETREAT OF THE SANDY SLOPES AND THE DATING OF THE SLOPES' DEPOSITS

SLOPE EBOULIS

There are a prodigious number of Paleolithic sites in the zones of outlier buttes (*buttes témoins*). First, let us see how one of these jebels looks. The slopes of these inselbergs look confused and chaotic, nothing but a disordered accumulation of blocks which are in precarious equilibrium. They seem to have been broken up by falling one on top of another as they tumbled down from above. Sometimes they completely hide the slope under them, or else they simply cover up isolated well scoured slabs of *in situ* rocks. (Daveau, 1963, p. 16).[1]

Although these *gravity eboulis*, which are particularly common in the Sahara, have been described frequently, they "are with difficulty and only hypothetically dated . . . they represent a facies which is unusually hard to place in the quartinary chronology." (Chavaillon, 1964, pp. 321-322).

What is even more regretable is that the *gravity eboulis* exhibit conflicting influences of variations of temperature, wind, and water. (Daveau, 1963, p. 11). Mass wasting of ferruginous and Nubian sands is neither the only nor the major cause of the retreat of the slopes. More important is "the subterranean action of the water in the most delicate and porous layers. Then again, even more important, is the 'steam action.'" (Daveau, 1963, p. 30).

"The combined action of these processes result in a majestic stratification of forms which from top to bottom include the following . . . : the ledge; an eboulis with big blocks; a low slope covered with a blanket of debris (the Older Pediments of de Heinzelin); and, finally, the base of the slope (the Younger Pediments) joins a rocky bank which is at a slight incline or rather is submerged under a blanket of eolian sand" (Daveau, 1963, p. 30).

Thus, in the humid periods, there is a synchronism between the runoff leveling the pediments and the rise of the water table which corrodes them (the chemical action is very important) (Corbel, 1963, pp. 70-77 ff.), and the stream action which makes enormous detrital masses fall and slide along the slopes.

In dry periods (as in modern times, for example), the most unobtrusive mass-wasting is

---

[1] The 30 pages of this communication could serve, line for line, as the description of what we saw.

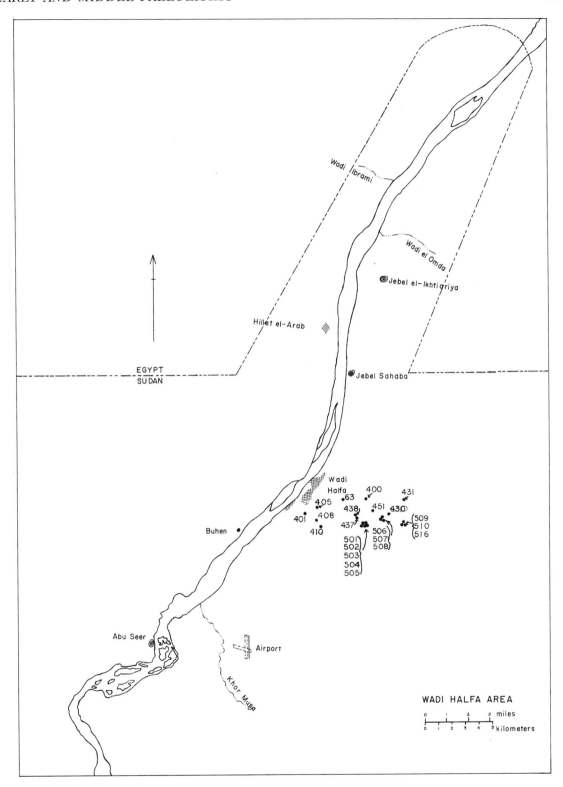

Fɪɢ. 1—Map of Wadi Halfa Area showing locations of Early Paleolithic and Middle Paleolithic sites discussed in the text.

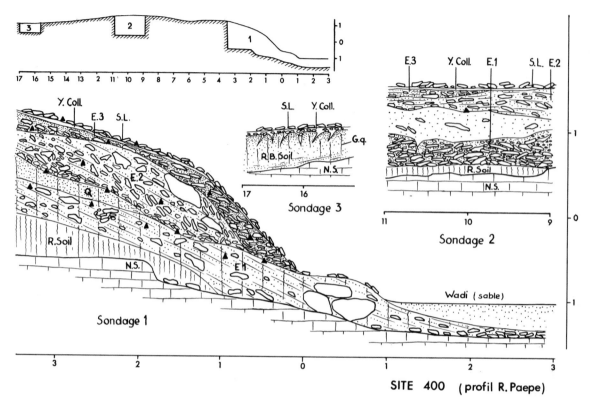

FIG. 2—The stratigraphy of Site 400-12.

deleterious. The lack of vegetation cover facilitates the action of the wind, and traces of this eolian erosion can be seen everywhere on the Nubia Sandstone in the form of parallel grooves or "yardangs." (Cailleux, 1965, p. 47). The plaques or slabs of harder ferruginous quartzite, found in overhangs above the Nubia Sandstone, are thus undermined and break and crumble away. The diurnal and nocturnal temperature variations, which tend to be extreme, favor this fragmentation and flaking of the rocks (heat broken cupules are common). This occurs to such an extent that many of these blocks of Nubia Sandstone are broken up at this point before ever reaching the foot of the slope where they would be moved away by the next stream action. Such is also the case for the quartzite plaques and plaquettes or slabs which, being more resistant, form the larger part of the "desert alluvium." Finally, the dryness, perhaps more than anything else (Cailleux, 1956, p. 45), favors rock fissure causing future breaks and diaclases. This

is the case to such a degree that it is possible to suggest that the arid phase prepares or sets up a situation which will necessarily cause massive erosion when the following humid sequence begins.

Thus, this prodigious countryside of jebels is once again presented as evidence of a powerful climatic rhythm. At first the question arose as to how we could date the area; now we know it is possible to date it by prehistory. Actually, in this zone, the slope eboulis contain artifacts when they are not entirely made up of them.[2]

PROFILE OF LOCALITY 400

Keeping what has just been said in mind, we are going to study Locality 400 (Guichard and Guichard, 1965, pp. 70, 80, 90 and map fig. 3 P 72) as an example (fig. 2).

We will examine the east slope from top to

---

[2] At Mouydir, the eboulis mentioned by H. Hugot are interesting due to the fact that they seal in prehistoric industries.

bottom; the other slopes would have a similar description:

1. Top: Flat structural surface of ferruginous quartzite on the edges and in places where Middle Paleolithic living camps or workshops were well delimited (20 x 10 m., 15 x 7 m., etc...), and in part destroyed (Localities 400-1-1, 400-1-2). At the center, a flattened mound (an old more or less eroded quartzite bench) in places covered with a thin deposit of yellow soil (Y. coll) (4 to 5 cms.) which is on top of some red soil lenses (Guichard and Guichard, 1965: 31).[3] On the yellow soil (and on the quartzite slabs which border it), we have the same Middle Paleolithic material as before (400-0).

2. Ledges: Formed by slabs of quartzite which are split parallel at the sides (Daveau, 1963, pp. 16-17, fig. 6 ff.). Next, they either become cracked or not, but eventually they break perpendicularly to their major axis. On and between these ledges, as is the case with subsequent fissures, the industry is the same as it is on the top.

3. Slope: The eboulis are uneven in size,[4] the fine pieces being often largely made up of the preceding Middle Paleolithic material; this is confirmed by a test pit in the lower third of the slope (400-2).

4. Bottom of slope: The eboulis form rubble cones. Same industry as above.

5. Pediment bank: Subhorizontal and occupies the small coomb at the foot of the jebel. This pebbly sloping bank (deformed when thick) is at a slight incline in the direction of the line of runoff and is cut by branched small ravines which form many micro-tributaries (Daveau, 1963, p. 12) of the large south wadi and the head of the north wadi. Locally reverse slopes are observed joined up not to the stationary rock but to particularly dense accumulations of debris. (Daveau, 1963, p. 12).

Archaeology

A. Near the rubble cones appears a "mixture"

of Middle Paleolithic and Acheulean material (at 400-2; IL = 45.85, cores especially of the Nubian "Mousterian" type plus 51 Acheulean bifaces).

B. A little farther away from the jebels, the mixture is the same but the proportion of the Middle Paleolithic decreases while that of the Acheulean increases.

C. From about 50 m. from the jebel slope: Only Acheulean material is found with no exception; 938 bifaces were collected from the surface.

Geology

A. Near the slope, the eboulis rest directly on the sandstone base.

B. A little farther away from the slope (400-3) their bases are found in a thin layer of very fine yellowish clayey sands (1 to 5 cm.). Next comes a red sterile soil (R. s) (5 to 45 cm.), then the substratum. Sometimes this same sequence is complicated by fissures and steps in the base; in addition, at contact with the red soil and at the top, there are inclusions of salt (400-4).

C. Farther still from the jebel slope, at the side of certain small ravines, the stratigraphy attains a depth of 2 m. Of primary importance, we noticed only one accumulation of Acheulean material.

The Middle Paleolithic Materials

Let us observe a Middle Paleolithic site which was partially in place at the side of a hilltop and partially on the surface falling down the slope (400-1-1 or 400-1-2; 400-2):

1. The entire industry was fashioned from slabs or plaquettes of quartzite (the cores reveal this); except, of course, for the material on silicified wood.

2. There exist at the top and *in situ* (400-1-1, 44-1-2) some "reserves" of unchipped cores: unworked slabs in more or less parallelepiped forms with unworn edges (eolization aside) in the middle of flaking debris. Sometimes, even these "precores" lie on a flat platform, also in quartzite of the summit which has remained intact and unfissured. They are, therefore, in a secondary position.

3. Such slabs could never come from the remains of an old dismantled high tier (there are a few of them around as at 400-0) because the quartzite blocks found on such places are com-

---

[3] The jebel top often has one or two depressions more or less filled with yellow or red soil (with shells of gasteropod: Loc. 401, 415, or even traces of industry: 401). "These forms lead one to think invincibly of a relief and circulation of the Karstitic type," with their holes, diaclases, etc. (Daveau, 1963, p. 18, pl. 11 ff.)

[4] At times with real eboulis being made (very localized).

pletely eroded and formless. In addition, although they could come from the slope, this was obviously not often the case; for to remove quartzite would leave numerous scars of crushing and flaking, and this is simply not the situation.

4. In contrast, the slabs are quite numerous at the top of the ledges.

5. These observations are applicable to all jebels east of Wadi Halfa.

The conclusions are obvious:

1. The "Mousterians" went to the top of the ledges where the slabs had broken away (that is, after an arid period), to look for "preformed" raw material and for cores which were nearly completely made. They took them and stored them in their camp site which was made as close as possible to this mine; in other words, at the top and on the side of an outlier butte.

2. Afterwards, when they had undoubtedly abandoned these places which had become dangerous because of the wearing away of the underlying sandstone, a period of tropical rains caused the partial or total destruction of their habitats. Thus, the rubble cone was formed, which is what we see now at 400-2.

Now, for the Lower Paleolithic in the old eboulis, all the bifaces and cores are fashioned out of slabs which are identical to the ones we have just described. It is legitimate to suggest, therefore, that the Acheuleans were forced to act in the same way as did the later Mousterians and for the same reasons. This very process may have been carried on all during Acheulean times up to the Late Middle Paleolithic following a certain climatic rhythm.

In summary, just as the nearness to springs and other sources of water has always been a necessary factor in man's existence, in Nubia the presence of these "pre-worked" quartzite quarries has been, likewise, an important consideration.

This theory explains why on "Acheulean pediment banks," that is, those not *in situ*, we most often find homogeneous industries on the surface.[5]

In effect, even in the case where it is imagined

that several tribes occupied the same place on top of a jebel: (*a*) In all probability, they followed each other gradually as the "pre-worked" slab quarry replenished itself; for it was precisely this raw material which attracted them there in the first place. (*b*) In other words, between the first and the second occupation, a "climato-sedimentary cycle" has taken place. When the second occupants arrived, the encampment of the first had already, at least in part, crumbled and slid off the side of the slope where it forms a rubble cone.

Thus the industries are pushed one after another, in order, onto the sides of the jebel, then onto the erosion slopes, while the slopes gradually retreat.

Of course, in this case, outside fringe areas where the industries are mixed will be found. But we think that with a detailed study of the artifacts in the field, it is possible to define the topographical limits of the mixed and pure area. Second, since we have good reason for thinking that these cycles were repeated a number of times during the Paleolithic—as often in Nubia as in the Sahara—and since during each cycle there was human occupation, we should expect to find a complete stratigraphy representing this entire period of time.

In the best examples, several cycles have passed between the two occupations. We would have liked to verify it at 400; yet because we do not have a great number of collected objects with which to define the Acheulean of 400-12, we do not know whether we are dealing with a single and unique deposit, which, after having crumbled, was stratified several times, or whether this is a matter concerning three different cultures.

However, in the most numerous cases, there was probably not more than one single occupation. In a total of 28 relatively important sites, the same succession of Acheulean-Middle Paleolithic is only seen three times (430 and 507,[6] 503 and 504, 439)—this is not including 400. Fifteen only have the Acheulean in pediment. All the Middle Paleolithic sites studied here only have "Mousterian" material. On two summits (63,

---

[5] That depends on the morphology of the outlier buttes. The "foot" of many of them is not "buried"; the rock is visible in a more or less slight slope. Obviously the industries cannot be stratified on this sandstone platform. They remain there "*à sec.*"

[6] Sites are numbered in the chronological order of their discovery. This explains why the top of the pediment of the same jebel can have two different numbers.

401), there are the contiguous occupations of the Acheulean and Middle Paleolithic, but fringes of mixing are visible. Contrary to the situation in the case of cave dwellings, which are always limited in number, in the case of open air sites in a region where raw material of the same quality is equally abundant everywhere the law of chance makes it unlikely that successive short occupations would be found in the same place.

In any case, by methodically repeating the "statistico-typologic" tests at a site and by very precise mapping of the area (the top as well as the pediment), one will inevitably come upon a vertiable harvest of material. (Daveau, 1963, particularly fig. 9, p. 25 and fig. 10, p. 27). Because of our not having understood the system immediately, and then because of our not having had enough time, we were able only to scratch the surface of what could be done here. Our observations are rather rudimentary in relation to the potential of the area.

Measuring and Dating the Retreat of the Slopes

This inseparable mass of geomorphologic-climatic and paleoethnologic facts allows us to attempt the dating and relative measuring of the retreat of the slopes. Referring to the map (Guichard and Guichard, 1965, fig. 3, p. 72): (1) The "Acheulean banks" are oriented according to the slope lines of the water. (2) It is easily seen that they come from the dismantling of the surrounding jebel (residual reliefs at the bottom and at the right of the map). (3) The erosion of the jebel is much greater in the horizontal plane than in the vertical.

In summary, the "Acheulean banks" are only detrital material pushed towards the slopes which limit them. The cubic content may be calculated, taking account of correction coefficients (transportation by wadis, chemical dissolution, etc.); and the order of size thus obtained permits the theoretic measure of the retreat of the slopes. At first sight, for the entirety of Acheulean times this can be calculated as some tens of meters.

The stratification of the Acheulean eboulis is horizontal or subhorizontal everywhere. It is complete.

The stratification of the Middle Paleolithic is vertical or subvertical (rubble cones). It is incomplete.[7]

There is no intermediary stratification.[8] There must have been a long "empty" time between the Acheulean and Middle Paleolithic.

Undoubtedly, during the last big Pluvial, the Middle Paleolithic material (which is late at 400-0, 400-1-1, etc.) began to collapse. The cubic content of its rubble cones should give the theoretic measure of the retreat of the slopes since this last episode. Its order of magnitude can be calculated in meters.

We have seen jebel walls with C-Group engravings. They are a bit disfigured or hidden by some blocks which have broken loose. We also had the chance from one field trip to the other to witness (at 401) the destruction of a ledge which had collapsed to the pediment between the two trips; thus erosion continues. However, the Middle Paleolithic rubble cones have never been covered up again, and from the point of view of the evolution of the countryside, we are in some ways "at the doors of death."

LOWER PALEOLITHIC

Introduction

Nowhere did we find anything resembling the Pre-Chellean of Olduvai or the faceted spheroids of Ain Hanech in stratigraphic context. At the approach of Mirgissa, at Sites 622 and 637, however, there seemed to be "concentrations" of very worn flakes and choppers, but we did not find an Abbevillian layer. Our study on the Lower Paleolithic is, therefore, only concerned with the Acheulean. Before beginning the subject, there are three points which need clarifying.

First, we have analyzed surface sites which seemed homogeneous and where there are: (1) sometimes worn forms (Abbevillian bifaces, trihedrals, picks, etc.) predominate in a striking manner; (2) sometimes, on the contrary, very "evolved" forms (lanceolates or Micoquian bifaces, etc.) are dominant; and (3) sometimes "intermediate" pieces are most numerous. We have accordingly called these industries Lower Acheulean, Middle Acheulean, and Upper Acheu-

---

[7] We consider the whole, i.e., the top plus the slope eboulis plus the pediment banks, as one stratigraphy.

[8] However, this is initiated at the foot of the rubble cones but only in one or two meters.

lean. This nomenclature is purely representative of a typological facies. Because of the absence of stratigraphy, we will make no statements as to its chronological value.

The second point is that we will describe each series in the most classical way; that is, by the study of the techniques, and by the study of the typology. However, in part because of the scarcity of tools other than bifaces, we will deal with this group first.

The third point concerns terminology. (Guichard and Guichard, 1965, p. 68). We temporarily identified as "Nubian" the tools which seemed unique to Nubia (specifically bifaces, side-scrapers, and particular cores). We are now assigning decriptive names to them: reniform biface, round-based Micoquian, ovaloid, etc.

STATISTICAL STUDY OF THE BIFACES

Working only with our own material from Nubia, we were able to analyze more than 3,000 bifaces representing the complete finds of 12 major sites. All were classified and studied by us. This is without a doubt the first time that so important a systematic sampling has been done in this way, and it is why we have tried to define the Acheulean facies by basing them largely on the statistical study of bifaces. It was possible to establish an exhaustive typological list. Many transitions between different classical types are found, but each of these new types is insufficient in number to be sure they respond to rational utilization, to the necessities of certain kinds of work.

We wish to emphasize that we are dealing with surface material. Experience—the essential foundation for the best work—leaves no doubt that it is more worthwhile to distinguish as carefully as possible the types of one collection that is known to be mixed than to rely on stratigraphic sites which have not been properly analyzed. We cannot compare our unsure and provisional results here with those obtained at Sidi Zin (Gobert, 1950) where the bifaces have only been classified according to three categories; or at Sidi Abderrahman (Biberson, 1953) where only four types are distinguished (the Chellean is rather vague); or at Olduvai (Leakey, 1951) where no classification has been undertaken. We regret-

fully note how much information we lack which would have been useful to us.

For the African material, however, we have relied especially on the work of Caton-Thompson (1952), Kleindienst (1962), and Tixier (1960).

Caton-Thompson and Kleindienst seemed to falter on a problem which held up our work for a long time. These authors distinguished bifaces at times by their contours (oval, circular, etc.); at other times by their sections (plano-convex, triangular, etc.); and yet in still other places by the utilization of the raw material (with reserved butt, on a slab, etc.). It seems to us that one should not pass indifferently from one of these criteria to the other as Caton-Thompson does.

In one single list, the author gives the percentages of lanceolates and ovaloids and immediately following this, percentages of "square-handled" and "V-shaped butted" (Caton-Thompson, 1952, p. 60). If the figures of the contours are referred to, it will be seen that the "square-handled" biface illustrated is a lanceolate with a reserved base, and the "V-shaped butted" is an ovaloid with a reserved base. A simple addition with the true lanceolates or the true ovaloids would give the total percentages of the lanceolate or ovaloid forms; and on the condition that we are correct in assuming that all the "square-handled" are lanceolates and all the "V-shaped butted" are ovaloids, this assumption is contrary to our experience. The lanceolates on slabs, like the ovaloids, have a great variety of base forms. We will return to this point later.

It is necessary to choose, or rather to set up for a single series, as many calculations as there are differing criteria; or, on the contrary, to present everything together with the aid of a table which allows for many entries.

In this work we chose to yield to the criterion of form, actually to that of volume determined both by contour and thickness. The latter only intervenes in some special cases: ovaloids and limandes, for example. (Bordes, 1961, pp. 62-63). We believe this criterion of form to be of prime importance; for a lanceolate biface can be conceived and realized as such be it on a slab, made with wood or stone, or with or without a reserved butt. It is recognized, of course, that other aspects are also extremely important, and we will treat them in the descriptive section.

Finally, the typological list of bifaces that we propose distinguishes 40 categories and is still far from being exhaustive. It is numbered according to an order which indicates a certain orthogenetic evolution of forms, but most important, the chronological (*sensu lato*) such as this has been delineated from all studies of either Africa or Europe.[9]

TYPOLOGICAL LIST

Group 1—The first group, from 1 to 7, takes in the "primitive" forms,[10] or those found in the lowest levels in the stratigraphy (in particular, the case of the trihedrals): (1) Abbevillian bifaces; (2) of Abbevillian style; (3) ficrons; (4) distorted ficrons; (5) picks; (6) globular amygdaliforms; (7) trihedrals; and (8) nucleiforms.

Group 2—The second group, from 9 to 18, includes the more elaborate forms. It is, perhaps, surprising to find cordiforms, ovaloids, and comparable forms. In fact these pieces in Nubia are rare and always quite crude. Contours aside, they do not in any way resemble cordiforms, etc., of the Mousterian of Acheulean tradition such as they are known in the Southwest of France, for example: (9) amygdaloids; (10) biface-*hachereau;* (11) shouldered bifaces; (12) cordiforms; (13) elongated cordiforms; (14) subcordiforms; (15) ovaloids; (16) elongated ovaloids; (17) ovals; and (18) limandes.

Group 3—From 19 to 28, these are the "refined" forms and in some way the culmination of style and technique. In Nubia these pieces are particularly beautiful; even the massiforms or pelecyforms: (19) lanceolates; (20) lanceolates with canted points; (21) lanceolates with incurved profiles; (22) lageniforms; (23) Micoquians; (24) Micoquians with oval bases; (25) Micoquians with circular bases; (26) massiforms; (27) pelecyforms; and (28) reniforms.

Group 4—From 29 to 33, these bifaces are always made on slabs in Nubia; except for some rare atypical triangular bifaces. They have been described at times as "unfinished bifaces"; the fineness of the retouching, the diversity of the forms of the points and *tranchets* categorically

contradicts this condemnation. Much to the contrary, as we will see later, they are forms which are well represented in the most evolved Acheulean.

Apparently a certain rigor of form was abandoned. At this stage, Paleolithic men seem no longer to adhere to archetypes. They rapidly adapted a simple slab to very diverse yet undoubtedly well defined activities. It creates an impression of great efficiency in a style which is deliberately casual.

In any case, this group seems to be especially valid for Nubia (perhaps due to the abundance of such raw material) if not for all of Africa: (29) atypical triangular bifaces; (30) ogival bifaces; (31) atypical shark tooth bifaces; (32) carinate bifaces; and (33) semi-circular bifaces.

Group 5—From 34 to 38, these types are only found in small numbers. They represent possibly a local facies. In other sites undoubtedly other rare forms could be found. Therefore, we consider this a "floating group." It would be easy eventually to change the nomenclature of this small group: (34) circular bifaces; (35) naviforms; (36) biface-borers; (37) ovals of the Khor Abu Anga type; (38) unclassifiables. Finally, (39) preforms (*ebduches*), and (40) fragments.

Before passing on to the definitions, we must again insist on one point: many of these bifaces of all types are worked on slabs. In this latter category, if one adheres to the contour of the working edge, it is possible to isolate (*a*) the "classic forms" (lanceolates, Micoquians, etc.), and (*b*) the original forms classed in the fourth group. However, since there are classic forms there, it would be abnormal not to mention them in their place with the others in virtue of the principle that a lanceolate is a lanceolate whether or not it is on a slab (a secondary characteristic).

In short, in order not to overburden the exhaustive tool frequency tables, we have not distinguished them from the others. Moreover, their numerical importance would seem to require a special study. A simple subtraction, category by category, will permit a separate valuation.

SOME DEFINITIONS

For most of the bifaces, we refer to the Traite

---

[9] Specifically the table of *longévité des principaux types d'outils.* (Bordes, 1861, p. 75).

[10] Not losing sight of the fact that an Abbevillian biface can, for example, be found in a Micoquian level.

de Typologie by F. Bordes (1961). However, several seem to merit some refinement, while others, designated by us, must be defined.

2. Bifaces of Abbevillian style. (Bordes, 1961, p. 69). We shall only specify that Abbevillian-like bifaces are like the archaic ones, but with a less sinuous profile. They tend towards crude and clumsy amygdaloids, nucleiforms, or cordiforms. There is little or no secondary retouching. We illustrate two (fig. 12, f-g) which are among the most elaborate; one subsequently served as a core (double patina).

4. Distorted ficrons. The section of the point is in a plane which is at an angle to the plane of the section of the body. They are generally big, thick, coarsely shaped and most often without secondary retouching (fig. 12, d, e).

6. Globular amygdaliforms. The globular or massiform body is set off from a short and solid point which at times takes the shape of a *bec*. In sum, the contour is that of an elongated amygdaloid tending toward a very squat lanceolate. The edge is sinuous at the point and often very sinuous at the base as well (fig. 13, f).

10. Biface-*hachereau*. (Bordes, 1961, pp. 63-64). A hypothesis has been proposed in which the biface-*hachereau* only represented one stage in the manufacture of bifaces (Goodwin, 1929, p. 12; Gobert, 1950, p. 19). Experience with tool making demonstrates that this is not the case. As with the bifaces on slabs with reserve butts, the biface-*hachereau* is a finished product (fig. 14, h).

11. Shouldered bifaces. They have an extremely asymmetric contour. One side is very often convex, sometimes subrectilinear; the other side is in a double concave curvature at the point and convex at the base thus creating a pronounced and characteristic shouldered side (fig. 14, g). (Guichard and Guichard, 1965, p. 79, fig. 11-c).

17. Ovals. It should be remembered that the limande, like the ovaloid, is widest at a point which is near the middle of the long axis. Yet the former is distinguished from the latter by its flatter sides, its thickness, and especially by its marked elongation. (Bordes, 1961, pp. 62-63). The oval itself is distinguished from the limande by its sides which are even flatter and only very slightly convex, at times being almost rectilinear

and symmetrical; also, by its greater width situated at the center and by a similarity of the radius of the curve at the proximal and distal extremities.

20. Lanceolates with canted points. These are lanceolates, one face of which has a slight concavity, that turns the point out at a strange angle (fig. 15, f). They are not, however, shouldered bifaces. Most of them are particularly well made.

21. Lanceolates with incurved profiles. One side is procurved in the style of a hog's back, chipped with rather rough retouching around a large area of cortex. The other surface, recurved like the "bowl of a spoon," has flat retouching with less cortex or sometimes a heat broken depression. This asymmetric shape creates a contour which is slightly though regularly denticulated. There is no doubt that in this particular case, all these peculiarities are the result of the nature of the raw material: very thin incurved slab (2.6 to 3.2 cm.). However, we do not know whether such a slab was chosen for this quality or whether, on the contrary, this is an accidental circumstance which imposes a particular form and style on this lanceolate. Perhaps it is simply a freak, even though it recurs quite often (fig. 15, c, g).

23. Micoquian bifaces. (Bordes, 1961, p. 57). Their form is very variable, sometimes their distal extremity is rounded, and sometimes it is so pointed that it turns the biface into a veritable "pointed weapon." The working edges are more or less concave, at times even subrectilinear. The curve of the dorsal and ventral surfaces is quite high. The base is more or less globular. By themselves, the Micoquian bifaces form a complex group, which will be studied later in an attempt to set up a meaningful internal classification, should one exist (fig. 16, a-b, in this figure we reproduced two notched Micoquian bifaces; fig. 16, h, k; and Guichard and Guichard, 1965, p. 79, fig. 11, e).

24. Micoquian bifaces with oval bases.[11] The base of this biface created an almost perfect oval shape. Starting eight- to nine-tenths of the distance from base to summit, a double symmetrical curve sets off a relatively short point, rather sharp, with a biconvex section. Biface is quite

[11] "Ovate acuminate" of Kleindienst (1962, p. 87).

flat with areas of cortex completely missing or limited (fig. 16, i, j).

25. Micoquian bifaces with circular bases.[12] The bases of this biface describe almost perfect circles. A double symmetrical curve sets off a relatively long point, rather sharp, with a biconvex section. In Nubia such bifaces are made on slabs with large areas of cortex remaining on the two faces (Guichard and Guichard, 1965, p. 7, fig. 11-a, e).

28. Reniform bifaces. In the shape of a kidney; one of the sides is concave, the other strongly convex and embodies the "point" and the "base" which are more or less symmetrical and blunt.

There also exists a rather strange subcategory of this type: the section of the upper half is in a plane which is at an odd angle in relation to that of the lower half. The distortion occurs in the middle of the piece. It is created by two very large alternating flake removals (not exactly Clactonian notches), one on the upper part of one of the edges of one face, the other on the lower part of the second face. As a result, there are on each side two unfluted working edges in a regular S form, both taking the same direction (fig. 17, h).

29. Atypical triangular bifaces. More frequently on thin or thick slabs than on smaller slabs. Their reserved bases are always flat; balanced, they can stand perfectly upright. In only two cases, the base is very slightly convex. They are often beautiful and well retouched (Guichard and Guichard, 1965, p. 81, fig. 13-b).

30. Ogival bifaces. The contour of the working surface of the slab forms an ogive, generally equilateral, sometimes wide. They are often very beautiful, with a great deal of secondary retouching which was done by removing flat overlying flakes (fig. 17, j).

32. Carinate bifaces. With partially oval contours. The profile has the shape of a keel. The dorsal surface is extremely convex.[13] The ventral surface is very concave, which makes the edge of the distal end thinner. This concavity is always produced by one or two large flake removals

perpendicular to the sides. They are made on slabs, most often rather thick ones. The base is variable (Guichard and Guichard, 1965, p. 81, fig. 13-3).

33. Semi-circular bifaces. The contour of the slab's working surface is in the form of a semi-circular arch. There is little or no secondary retouching (fig. 17, i).

37. Ovals of the Khor Abu Anga type. The bifaces are very singular, perhaps characteristic of a facies of the banks of the Nile. We only have a few specimens which were found in small, and, as yet, unstudied sites. The A. J. Arkell collection at the Khartoum Museum has around 30; they come from the upper levels (5 and 6) of Khor Abu Anga. Elsewhere, W. Chmielewski explored a site, Arkin 8, where numbers of them are found. We think that this piece constitutes a good "type-fossil" of the terminal Acheulean in Nubia.

Contour: regular oval. Cross-section: biconvex (convexity sometimes very marked). Retouch: not numerous, very seldom overlapping, "crude." They create an edge which zigzags slightly. Characteristics: "crushing" scars obliterate this edge. Because the series is so poor, it is impossible to tell whether the scars result from the technique of the primary flaking (bipolar? hammering?) or from use on hard material. Finally, at times retouch covers the entire piece; at other times it only partially does so on one side or end, and the object tends more toward being a chopper.

In addition, these bifaces are made sometimes out of ferruginous quartzite, and sometimes out of quartz. In the former case, they are completely corroded both at Khor Abu Anga and at Arkin 8. Retouching or other signs of flaking have totally disappeared. Nothing but a chunk of stone remains. This perhaps suffices to explain why A. J. Arkell, who illustrates two of them, sometimes describes them as hammerstones and sometimes as bifaces (Arkell, 1949).[14]

In summary, this is an instrument which has not been understood up till now and which

---

[12] We called them "Nubian bifaces" in Guichard and Guichard, 1965, p. 78.

[13] For the sake of convention, we have called the convex surface "dorsal."

[14] Drawing No. 1, pl. 10 is described on p. 8, line 40 as representing a hammerstone. Drawing No. 2, pl. 10 is described on p. 8 as a biface, line 27. Furthermore, perhaps the photos of specimens reproduced by Leakey (1951), pl. XXXI, XXXII and XXXIII represent objects which are similar in some ways. We know of no other figure showing comparable pieces.

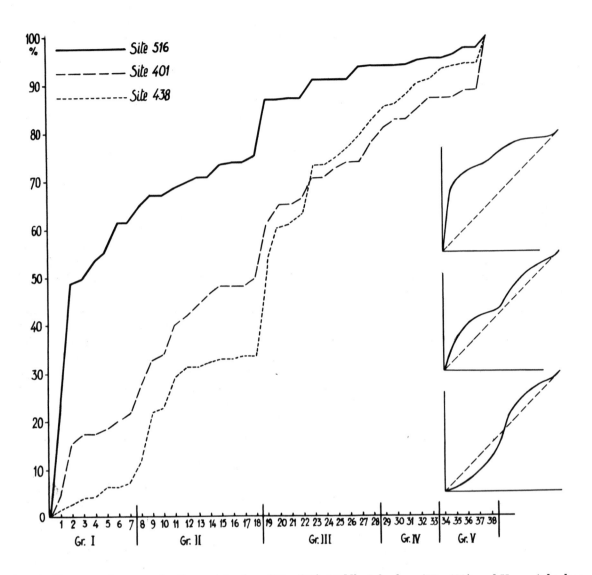

Fɪɢ. 3—Three cumulative graphs: Lower Acheulean (Site 516), Middle Acheulean (Site 401), and Upper Acheulean (Site 438).

would be able to be a "type-fossil" in the future. While waiting for Chmielewski's publication, we will provisionally call it the Khor Abu Anga type (fig. 18, a).

CUMULATIVE LINE GRAPHS AND HISTOGRAMS OF BIFACES

From the typological list we have drawn up some line graphs and histograms. By their slope we will first analyze three type sites which will

continually serve as points of reference: Site 516—Lower Acheulean; Site 401—Middle Acheulean; Site 438—Upper Acheulean.

Comparative Analysis of Sites 516-401-438

1. Cumulative line graphs (fig. 3). They are very different.

Site 516. Starting off with an extremely convex curve, with a major increase due to lanceolate forms which accentuates this convexity.

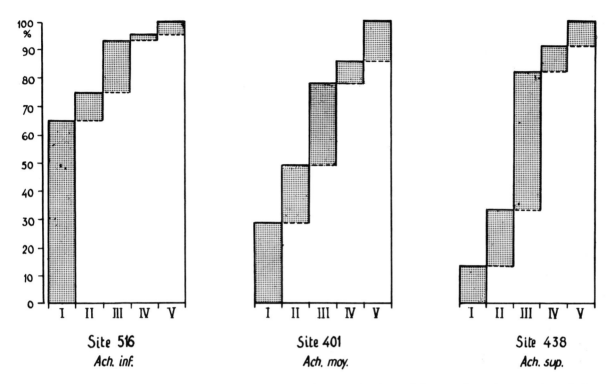

Fɪɢ. 4—Cumulative histograms of the Lower Acheulean (Site 516); the Middle Acheulean (Site 401); and the Upper Acheulean (Site 438).

Site 401. This is appreciably close to the diagonal line.

Site 438. In a drawn-out S which will become more defined for other sites of the same culture. The increased slope due to lanceolates, which was important in 401, is striking here.

2. Cumulative histograms (fig. 4).

Group I. In decreasing order respectively,[15] 65.12 at Site 516, 28.35 at Site 401, and 12.80 at Site 438.

Group II. From 9.94 at Site 516, it rises to 20.78 at Site 401, then decreases slightly at Site 438 with 18.76.

Group III. Ascending order: 18.49 at Site 516; 28.68 at Site 401; and 40.17 at Site 438.

Group IV. One would have thought that this group would be well represented at Site 516, but it does not go beyond 1.42. It reaches 8.29 at Site 401, and it is about the same at Site 438: 8.81. Let us note, however, that another Upper Acheulean locality, Site 451, holds the numerical record of 24.67 for slabs.[16]

[15] All following figures are given as percentages.
[16] We have already pointed that out in Guichard and Guichard (1965).

Group V. Low at 516 with only 4.98. This is due to the total absence of "variant" but elaborate forms (except for one very heavy crude naviform). Quite well represented at Site 401 with 13.90 which indicates a greater variety in the search for forms. It is a bit surprising to see it then fall down again to 9 at Site 438.

Finally, it should be remembered that the lanceolate bifaces even with some regular retouch are no more lacking in the Lower Acheulean than are the Abbevillian forms at Site 438. Possibly this is due to a slight contamination in the former case or to a beginning of a style and technique which was to develop later. At this stage of our research, we cannot determine which of these hypotheses is correct.

Comparative Analyses of the Middle Acheulean

We will examine Sites 401, 502, 505, 400-South 400-West, and 509. They are rather far from each other while belonging to a single restricted geographic zone. Beginning with Site 401 (map coordinates: 653.000/900.-915.000) one then finds: (1) At about 5 km. to the southeast and sepa-

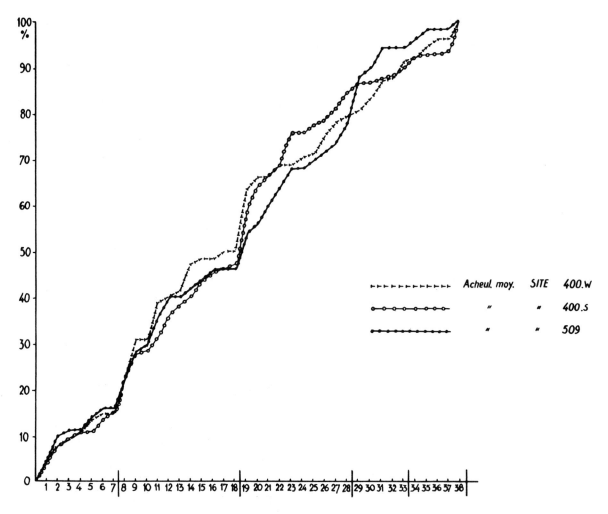

Fig. 5—Cumulative graphs of the Middle Acheulean (Sites 400-W, 400-S, and 509).

rated from one another from 2 to 3 km. are Sites 502, 505, and 509. (2) At about 4 km. to the northeast and separated by approximately 2 km. is the complex of Sites 400-South and 400-West.

1. Line graphs. They are remarkably similar. They are parallel or subparallel to the diagonal of the page and only turn towards the vertical at three points (fig. 5).[17]

From No. 4 to No. 9: 400-West, 400-South, and 509 all have a slightly smaller percentage of Abbevillian bifaces than do the other three. From No. 16 to No. 19: Generally low in ovals and similar forms. From No. 33 to No. 38: Relatively few of the variant bifaces (borers, naviforms, circular bifaces, etc.).

_____
[17] There are two superimposed curves.

The six line graphs show a clear increase because of the lanceolates.

2. Histograms (fig. 6). It is seen that the percentages for Group I vary between 18.54 and 28.35 (mean: 22.39), showing that this group is still well represented, but far below the 65.17 present at Site 516. Group II is much like the first group, with a percentage range between 20.78 and 30.10 (mean: 19.07) and, again quite different from Site 516, which stands at 9.94.

The percentages for Group III, from 28.68 to 45.97 (mean: 41.85), are higher than the preceding ones; the difference between Sites 401 and 505 being appreciable. In spite of its abrupt increase in the lanceolates which would make it similar to the Upper Acheulean, Site 505 remains

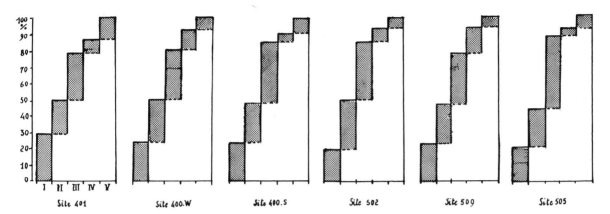

FIG. 6—Cumulative histograms of the Middle Acheulean (Sites 401, 400-W, 400-S, 502, 509, and 505).

in the Middle Acheulean. In effect, its percentage of Abbevillian forms is such that the cumulative line graph is pushed back to the left limit of the group. Group III presents a very sizable difference with Site 516 which has only 18.49.

Group IV is not negligible, percentages varying between 4.07 and 16 (mean: 10.30), while some of the sites have rather important local variations. Group V varies from 6 to 13.90 (mean: 8.99). The high percentage at Site 401 should be noted. As will be seen in the descriptive analysis, it is almost possible to arrange most of these "variant" bifaces in the forms of Abbevillian style, although they are still crude. The same can be done for the "unclassifiables" from Site 400-South (6.41 per cent of them alone).

TABLE 1

DATA FOR HISTOGRAMS OF THE MIDDLE ACHEULEAN
(PERCENTAGES)

Sites	Group I	Group II	Group III	Group IV	Group V
401	28.35	20.78	28.68	8.29	13.90
502	18.54	30.10	34.71	9.24	7.41
505	20.14	22.95	45.97	4.07	6.87
400-S	22.45	24.58	37.57	4.11	11.29
400-W	22.87	26.92	29.63	12.10	8.48
509	22.00	24.00	32.00	16.00	6.00

Comparative Analysis of the Upper Acheulean

We will examine Sites 438, 400-North, 430, 451, and 501.

As was previously the case, these sites, which are situated in a single rather restricted geographic zone, are well separated from one another.

1. Line graphs. Well grouped (fig. 7). The first half of the curve is concave and is situated at the right of the diagonal; it then crosses this threshold at the lanceolates, becoming extremely convex and even recutting the Middle Acheulean group.

2. Histograms (fig. 8). In Group I the percentages vary between 12.80 and 21.31 (mean: 15.83). It is noted that Site 430, with a percentage of Abbevillian bifaces reaching 6.71 and that of nucleiforms 10.31, makes the overall mean rise; this would normally be around 14. Lower Acheulean (Site 516): 65.17. Middle Acheulean: 22.39 (general mean).

In Group II the percentages vary between 15.27 and 22.57 (mean: 19.07). This group is coherent, lower than the Middle Acheulean with 24.88 (general mean), but higher than the Lower Acheulean with 9.94 at Site 516. In Group III the percentages vary from 31.93 to 47.07 (mean: 41.85). At Site 438, nearly half of the bifaces fall into the lanceolate group. On the other hand, at Site 451, this percentage is relatively low, as the slab group is heavily represented. This compares with the Lower Acheulean percentage of

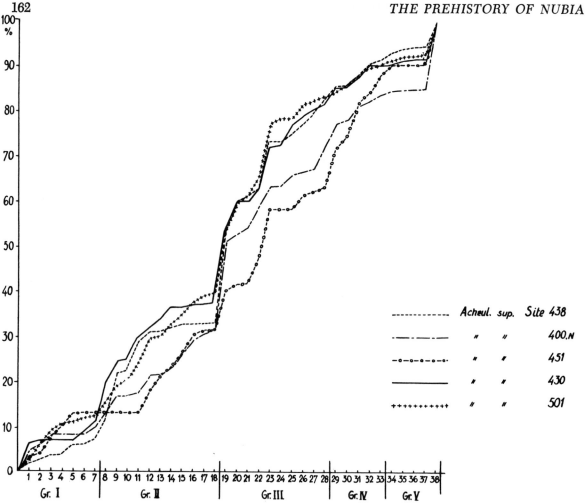

Fɪɢ. 7–Cumulative graphs of the Upper Acheulean (Sites 438, 400-N, 451, 430, and 501).

18.49 at Site 516 and in the Middle Acheulean which has a 29.86 (general mean).

In Group IV the percentages vary from 7.24 to 24.67 (mean: 12.50). There is an extraordinary increase of the slab group at Site 451, a relatively small site which is much enclosed and which has carefully worked material. This group only represents 1.52 in the Lower Acheulean (Site 516) and 10.30 in the Middle Acheulean (general mean). In Group V the percentages vary between 16.41 and 9.00 (mean: 11.75). In the Lower Acheulean (Site 516) this group accounts for 4.98, while the general mean for the Middle Acheulean is 8.99.

TABLE 2

Dᴀᴛᴀ ғᴏʀ ᴛʜᴇ Hɪꜱᴛᴏɢʀᴀᴍꜱ ᴏғ ᴛʜᴇ Uᴘᴘᴇʀ Aᴄʜᴇᴜʟᴇᴀɴ
(Pᴇʀᴄᴇɴᴛᴀɢᴇꜱ)

Site	Group I	Group II	Group III	Group IV	Group V
438	12.80	20.32	47.07	8.81	9.00
400-N	12.96	18.67	40.17	11.79	16.41
430	21.31	15.27	44.37	8.00	11.05
541	12.91	18.51	31.93	24.67	11.98
501	16.12	22.57	43.74	7.24	10.33

DESCRIPTIVE ANALYSIS OF THE
INDUSTRIES OF THE PRINCIPAL SITES

Although an exhaustive typological description of more than 3,000 bifaces, 1,000 cores, together with all the other artifacts, is impossible in the framework of this paper, we will try to discuss its most important aspects.

Lᴏᴡᴇʀ Aᴄʜᴇᴜʟᴇᴀɴ

Locality 516 (map reference 661.150/911.000)

The cumulative line graph and the histogram of the 209 bifaces from 516[18] confirmed our first

[18] The entire collection is at the Laboratory of Prehistory of Bordeaux.

Acheul. supérieur

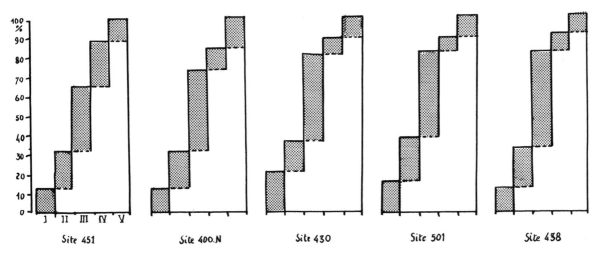

FIG. 8—Cumulative histograms of the Upper Acheulean (Sites 451, 400-N, 430, 501, and 438).

field impressions. In addition to a very high degree of eolization (an unusual occurrence since the site is situated in a narrow coomb which is sheltered from the winds), the large dimensions of the tools, and their massive and rude appearance, and the great quantity of debris and fragments, all cause us to classify this in a Lower Paleolithic context. We found some lanceolates, ovals, etc.; however, the majority of them can be considered proto-lanceolates or proto-ovaloids. They are coarse and poorly made and were formed using a hard hammerstone which produced deep flake-scars. Secondary retouching is rare and the edges are very sinuous.

Abbevillian bifaces (33). Large (12 to 27 cm.) and thick. They often have rather sizable flat surfaces (the edges of the slabs) and areas of cortex which have been heat broken or eolized with protuberances and deep depressions. This did not stop them from being utilized. Their extremely variable forms defy all rational classification. Seven of them are on regular slabs. One has its working edge in the form of a disengaged hose (11.5 cm.) and the body, on a non-retouched slab, is long (14 cm.); the base is V-shaped; a flake removal, possibly accidental, accentuates this form to the degree that it looks like a very pointed pick.

Twelve of them have "unretouched bases"; for

it cannot be said that they are either regular slabs or simple unshaped platform remnants. Two have been retouched to produce open V-shaped bases. They have, of course, enormous areas of cortex. The others present a further peculiarity: at first sight they resemble completely retouched bifaces. Actually, their bases are simply formed by fractured convex masses rounded by heat broken effects. From this "thermic mass,"[19] a point, frequently sizable, has often been worked. Finally, the general appearance is that of a "macromassiform." In two cases with such bases, there are some traces of flake removal subsequent to the heat broken formation.

A great quantity of the bifaces from this site were locally deformed by heat broken effects.

Of Abbevillian style (36). Scarcely better, however, tending towards more regular forms. Big, very thick, often gibbous. Like the preceding, they frequently preserve a large unretouched flat surface on one side (less often basilar) and large areas of cortex.

Twelve of them have reserved bases, two of which are U-shaped. Five tend towards the carinates; one disengages a large nose-shaped projection; it is short, squat, and globular. Four tend towards the lanceolates: they are slenderer,

[19] Since there are "thermic balls"; cf. especially Gobert, 1952, p. 224.

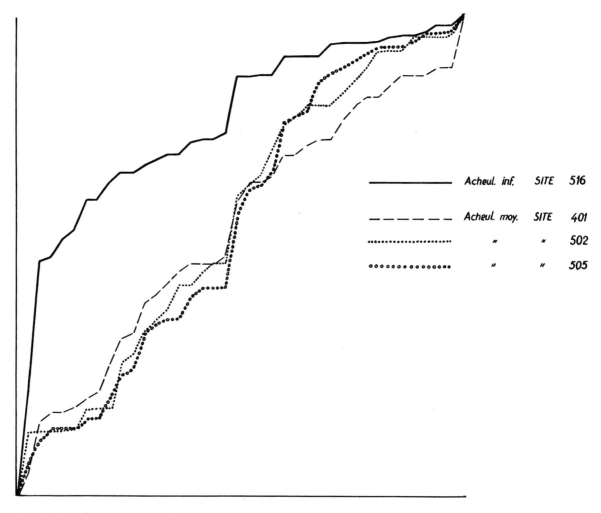

Fig. 9—Cumulative graphs of the Lower Acheulean (Site 516); compared with the Middle Acheulean (Sites 401, 502, and 505).

relatively narrow, with bases in a pointed or open V; one of the points is rather carefully done. Two tend towards Micoquian bifaces, one having its point canted to one side by a large and rather deep flake removal.

Finally, the last one possesses a pseudo-worked base, slightly re-formed at the end.

We were able to isolate two additional small series: (1) a sort of double-pick or enormous naviform, a little twisted with very sinuous edges, quite large and crude; and (2) robust, squat, but relatively narrow, chipped with large flakes removed and with little regular retouch. They do not have a functional point like the preceding ones: their contour is oblong.

Ficrons (1). Quite badly deformed by extreme eolization. It possibly has a reserved base.

Distorted ficrons (5). Three are on slabs and one of them is very saddle-shaped. The fourth is large and relatively flat. The last one has an excellent natural globular base. We will find this type right through the Upper Acheulean.

Picks (3). Extremely massive. Made on "bar-shaped," "ingot-like" slabs with square sections. The biggest (22.8 cm.) has unworked sides which are 17 and 18 cm. respectively. Its base is slightly oblique (natural break), and only 5.5 cm. of the ventral surface is retouched. Another one is very similar; however, its very short point is twisted into a different plane than that of the

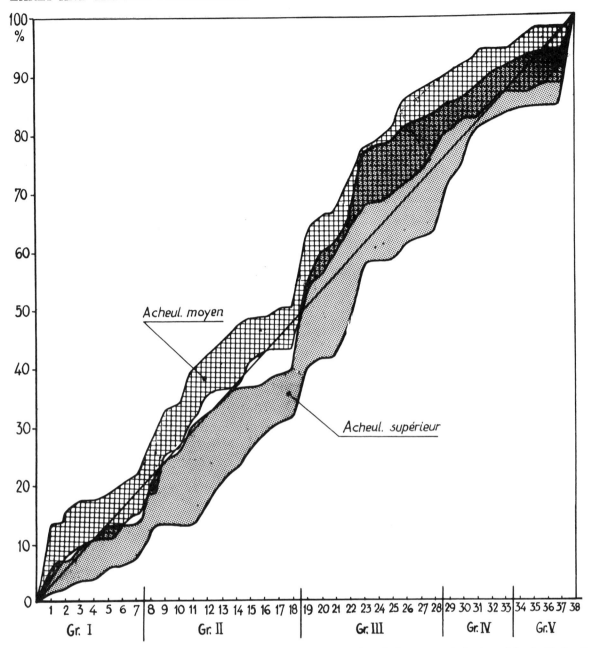

Fig. 10—Graph of the Middle Acheulean Cluster (checkered squares) and the Upper Acheulean (dots). Each of the two zones delimits the placing of the corresponding cumulative curves.

base. One of the four natural sides is unretouched and has a pointed butt. The third pick is shorter (non-retouched sides—10 cm.).

Globular amygdaliforms (8). In relation to the rest of the assemblage, they are relatively short (11.7-14 cm.), massive, and globular. Shaped in a most economical way.

Trihedrals (1). Atypical.

Nucleiforms (5). They fit into the range of Abbevillian style bifaces. Nevertheless, they are distinctive due to a certain degree of regularity. Two have suboval contours and a third is subcircular.

Amygdaloids (3). Appreciably better. One is made on a large flake. One, slightly atypical, has a large *bec*. This artifact is nearly oval but has a

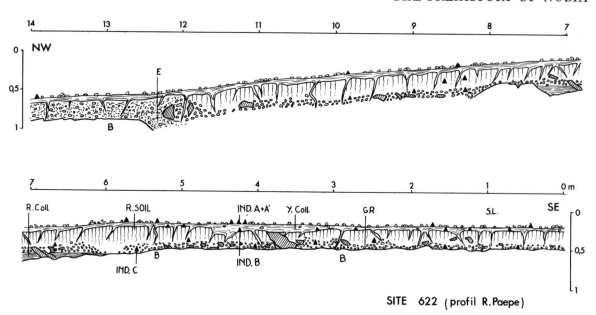

FIG. 11—The Stratigraphy of Site 622.

butt which tends to obscure this. The two last show traces of regularity; they are very carefully made.

Shouldered bifaces (2). Crude and atypical. One of them is extremely wind worn.

Cordiforms (1). Quite atypical with a basal "notch" (2). Much eolized with nonregular sides.

Ovaloids and elongated ovaloids (4). Atypical, tending towards the amygdaloids; they are very disfigured, and the sides are at best very slightly regular. One is rather globular.

Limandes (2). They are, rather, proto-limandes, thick and carelessly made.

Lanceolates (17). Rather large (18 to 23 cm.). Nine of them could have been included among those in the "Abbevillian style," because they are so crude, relatively thick and with little or no secondary retouching.

The eight others are better. Two have rather sharp points, slightly canted and with sizable butts (edges of the slabs). Two resemble Micoquians.

We note that two others are in Precambrian rock (that is to say, they come from a place approximately 20 km. to the south). They belong to a small lot which is more "evolved," secondarily retouched, well defined typologically (four lanceolates, two Micoquians, one pelecy-

form, two amygdaloids, and one elongated cordiform). Circumscribed in an area some meters square, we believe they are intrusive. Without a doubt they affect the cumulative line graph in a way that accentuates the rise caused by the lanceolates and evolved forms.

Pelecyforms (4). Also crude without secondary retouching.

Carinate and semi-circular bifaces (2). The carinate is relatively small; the semi-circular is atypical.

Naviforms (1). Big, crude with a very uneven edge.

Unclassifiables (6). Quite variable in appearance; almost always without regular retouch. They are not very numerous. Some could be classified with the Abbevillians yet they differ by the general form and their less sinuous edges. One of them is a pseudo cleaver-biface.

Preforms and fragments (30 and 38 respectively). Numerous although much of the debris was not collected. All the fragments belong to the Abbevillian bifaces. Certain "preforms" could be Abbevillian as well, but they have been so wind worn that one could only hazard a guess.

We have not mentioned the broken pieces (most frequently points, next bases, sometimes even sides). In actual fact, all the pieces share more or less the same characteristics except for the enormous typical Abbevillian bifaces.

Debitage. The recognizable flakes are large, extremely disfigured and rare. No Levallois flakes.

Cores. Rare, almost always formless and very big—of the globular type.

Flake tools. We have not recognized them. The "retouch" is not well defined; it is absolutely impossible to see if it is, or is not, intentional.

Site 516 in this group has suffered a great deal from eolization, heat broken effects, and time.

MIDDLE ACHEULEAN

Locality 401

This and Site 63 are the only *in situ* Acheulean sites on the summits. Altitude, 240 m. It is about 10 km. from the Nile.[20] Our description is based on 300 bifaces, 398 typical Levallois flakes, 133 atypical ones, 67 tools, and 319 cores.[21]

Abbevillian bifaces (16). Rather large dimensions, thick with sinuous sides. They do not reach the proportions of those of 516, however, and generally speaking, they are less crude. One of them is distinctive, due to the almost cylindrical section of its narrow but elongated body. It resembles the pseudo-picks of 516. Six others were subsequently reworked (double patina) into bifaces without, however, having been given any new well-definable form. Seven are on regular slabs.

Of Abbevillian style (25). Clearly better, but the shape remains Abbevillian. The edges are often very sinuous. Six of them form a small series; of sizable dimensions, and massive, they have a sort of large point which is very short and squat, yet they have nothing in common with the globular amygdaliforms. Another has an incurved profile and is rather keeled. Finally, another is shaped on a large flake with a dihedral talon.

Ficrons (6). Five have trihedral points. One is on a regular slab.

Picks (2). Both are on regular slabs; not very typical, rather crude.

Globular amygdaliforms (5). One has an un-

gainly appearance; it is at the very limit of the type. The others are better, with relatively sizable gibbosities. One of these had a surface flattened by large flake removals.

Trihedrals (4). They are atypical. One of them could figure among the Micoquians (very well made base) with a perfectly trihedral point. Two others resemble double-picks,[22] but one of their points is a true trihedron with two natural sides. The last one seems to have been formed on a large thermic ball; it is a three sided point worked by heavy blows.

Nucleiforms (17). Except for one which is quite large (15.5 cm.) with a lozenged cross-section, they are relatively small and rather globular. (fig. 14, d).

Amygdaloids (13). This is a very good series. They are almost all at the extreme limit of the cordiforms. One is truly crude, one is almost unifacial, and one is incurved.

Biface-cleavers (2). They are doubtful. They seem, strictly speaking, very similar to Type II of Tixier (Tixier, 1956; Bordes, 1961, pp. 64-66). One is particularly crude.

Shouldered bifaces (17). On the whole they are typical (except for five which are less so and one which was very rough). One possibly has a remade point, and one is on a regular slab.

Cordiforms (5). Quite crude on the whole, but typical. Rather small (fig. 14, f). Two of them were used as Levallois cores.

Subcordiforms (7). Relatively large and flat. Three are on flakes (dihedral butt, smooth lateral butt, "Clactonian" near lateral butt, respectively).

Ovaloids (4). Quite atypical, a little elongated and thick; one of them is disfigured by a great Clactonian notch which might have been accidental. This piece resembles a limande.

Limandes (3). With a rounded, slightly narrow distal extremity; one resembles a short lanceolate, the second is tiny and rather crude. The third, in contrast, is a little thick, but very beautiful and is covered with very fine retouch.

Lanceolates (30). They are nice specimens, often very carefully made, most of them with rectilinear edges. Seventeen are complete; four have reworked points; one is partial; its ventral surface is made up of a large oblique fracture

---

[20] We gave a detailed and comprehensive description of its sublocus and a small stratigraphic section in Guichard and Guichard, 1965, pp. 71, 74, 75, 76.

[21] The entire collection is at the Laboratory of Prehistory of Bordeaux.

[22] Such pieces have been described several times by Neuville and Rhulmann (1941).

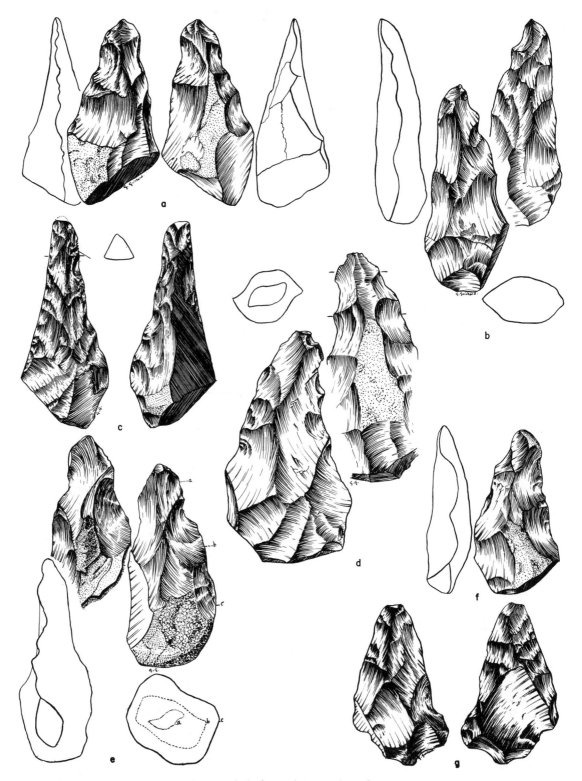

Fig. 12—Bifaces. a, Abbevillian biface (Site 510); b, ficron (Site 438); c, ficron (Site 400-12-1, *in situ*); d, atypical and distorted ficron (Site 502); e, distorted ficron (Site 516); f, Abevillian style biface (Site 438); g, Abbevillian style biface (Site 430). 1/3 natural size.

of the slab. It is large (23.5 cm.); three resemble Micoquian bifaces in having a slightly concave edge; one is on the much reworked ventral surface of a flake; the butt of the flake is half effaced due to a series of small removals; one is on a regular slab.

Lanceolates with canted points (11). This is the one important series of this type. One is partial, made on a flake; another tends toward the shouldered biface; still another has a base which is largely unworked; one is on a regular slab; and one is made out of sandstone.

Lageniforms (3). Atypical. One of them is on a regular slab.

Micoquians (12). They are dissimilar, either very crude or very beautiful. Five among them are complete; the others, like many of the lanceolates, have the extreme end of the point broken off without it being possible to determine whether this was due to accident or utilization (fig. 16, f).

Micoquians with circular bases (5). Rather typical, but more or less crude, except for the example illustrated (Guichard and Guichard, 1965, p. 79, fig. 11, a).

Massiforms (3). Very representative of this type, rather small.

Pelecyforms (1). Very eolized.

Reniforms (11). This is the single good series of this type; relatively small (10 to 13 cm.); sometimes on flakes (fig. 17, g).

Triangular bifaces (8). Three of them could, strictly speaking, be included with the triangulars (*sensu stricto*). However, this last type is practically unknown in Nubia (less than 10 from more than 3,000 bifaces). But perhaps they are more numerous and more obvious at Khor Abu Anga. In contrast, the triangular form (*sensu lato*) is quite well represented in the group of regular slabs.

Here, the five triangular bifaces on regular slabs are crudely made, but quite typical in form. Two are relatively flat, three are thick.

Ogival bifaces (2). One is a nearly finished preform; the simplified retouching does nothing but set off the working edges (4, 5, and 8 on 22 cm.); its base is U-shaped. The other one, on the contrary, is very well made; the working edges, which are better set off than in the former, extend to the base. It has been carefully evened.

Shark tooth bifaces (2). Rather coarse.

Carinate bifaces (5). Aside from one of them which is very typical and small (11 cm.), the others are large (17 cm. on the average) and thick (5 to 6.5 cm.). Four have convex bases. Another one, which is also very typical, has a "nose," thinned on the concave face by a large flake removal which is perpendicular to the tip. Its base is in a V.

Semi-circular bifaces (5). The ventral surface is disfigured by heat broken effects.

Naviforms (2). One is on a flake with a small butt and is in the form of a spindle (*fuseau*) with a clearly defined point (fig. 18, e). The other is small and also seems to be on a flake.

Unclassifiables (32). Seven are on regular slabs.

Preforms and fragments (9 and 28). Among the fragments, many are identifiable.

Technical indices. IL = 21.22, which is not negligible. IF^s = 39.78. IF^1 = 51.21. The Laminar Index is weak: 6.65.

Certain flakes are enormous and weigh up to 1 kg. Butts are sometimes dihedral, rarely faceted, often smooth. The blades, also, are sometimes very large (up to 27 cm).

Typological indices. The flake-tools seem too few for us to bother calculating.[23] Besides the 398 typical Levallois flakes and 133 atypical Levallois flakes which were systematically collected in well delimited areas (Guichard and Guichard, 1965, p. 30-32), we found only 73 other tools, as follows: Levallois points, 2; pseudo-Levallois points, 4; simple straight side-scrapers, 3; simple convex side-scrapers, 9; convergent convex side-scrapers, 1; typical end-scrapers, 2; atypical end-scrapers, 3; typical burins, 5; truncated flakes, 4; notches, 13; end-notches, 1; denticulates, 14; Tayac points, 3; push-planes, 1; choppers, 2; and variants, 6.

One of the choppers, which is of Precambrian rock, is comparable to the peripherally-worked pebbles of Sidi Zin (Gobert, 1950, p. 13, especially fig. 4).

Cores (319). Many partially flaked (81), form-

---

[23] These tools are not very different from their homologues in the Middle Paleolithic; certain ones are a little coarser; the majority is more eolized. They easily enter in the ordinary rubrics. In the present work, we will not describe them in greater detail. They will not even be illustrated. This holds true for all the Acheulean sites.

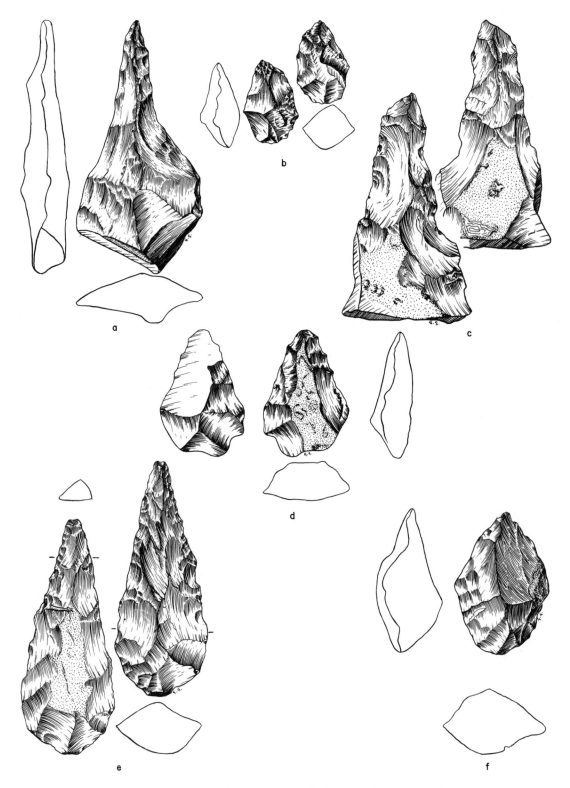

Fig. 13—a, pick (Site 438); b, amygdaloid (Site 438); c, pick (Site 515); d, amygdaloid (Site 501); e, trihedral (Site 515); f, globular amygdaliform (Site 400-S). 1/3 natural size.

less (54), globular (34), and variants (54). For the others, there is a predominance of Levallois flake cores (53), then discoids (30). Finally, three Levallois point cores (not at all comparable to those peculiar to the Middle Paleolithic of Nubia, but to those common in Europe); one para-Levallois, one "Acheulean," five with opposed flake removals, and one blade-core. We must draw attention to two cores which are in every way identical to those from Champlain (Algeria) and which L. Balout describes and figures under the rubric "Cores of the South African (Brandberg) type." (Balout, 1955, p. 233 and pl. XXXV).

Locality 400-South

This is the area of the "pediment banks" numbered 3, 4, 5, and 6 on the map (Guichard and Guichard, 1965, p. 72, fig. 3).[24] The analysis is based on 492 bifaces, 180 cores, etc.[25]

Abbevillian bifaces (19). Formless, not very globular; four are on regular slabs.

Of Abbevillian style (12). One is rather carinated and typifies a sort of large nosed pushplane. Another has a very short pick at the end of a slightly carinated nose. There is an oval worked by large and deep flake removals. Three others are on slabs, of which one has a gouge-shaped point.

Ficrons (7). They resemble picks. One of them is excellent, extremely pointed. Another is on a regular slab.

Distorted ficrons (3). One is on a regular slab.
Pick (1). Typical.

Globular amygdaliforms (11). They are good as a rule. One among them was used as a blade-core. The narrow point is often set off clearly by a large flake removal which notches the piece; this little *bec* is too thick to be considered a borer (fig. 13, f).

Trihedrals (6). One is on a regular slab.

Amygdaloids (21). Not always good, some-

times not easily definable, at the limit of the nucleiforms. Two tend toward pelecyforms.

Biface-*hachereau* (3). Two are rather crude. The third is very beautiful.

Shouldered bifaces (12). In the generally crude group, some are well made.

Cordiforms (18). Quite good, although some are at the very limit of the typical forms. Two are on flakes, two served as cores. One is flat and resembles the triangulars.

Elongated cordiforms (8). One of them is on a flake and served secondarily as a core.

Subcordiforms (6). Rather mediocre.

Ovaloids (14). One is very large and made on a flake. Another resembles a subcircular; two resemble amygdaloids; one, an elongated cordiform. Finally, one possibly received a *tranchet* blow.

Elongated ovaloids (7). Not very good except one which is beautiful. One is almost a proto-limande.

Ovals (4). Rather typical.

Limandes (3). One is a proto-limande and rather crude.

Lanceolates (44). They are almost all very good; often very beautiful. They are of all sizes (from 7 to 21 cm.) and they illustrate the great variety of the forms possible in this type: flat, or convex; almost globular; with rectilinear or slightly twisted sides; with round, slightly spatulate, or acuminate ends; sometimes with trihedral points; sometimes on a flake. A great number of them (15) resemble Micoquian forms because of slight concavity of one of their sides. Three are on regular slabs.

Lanceolates with canted points (20). One on a regular slab. On the whole, these are very typical of this site.

Lanceolates with incurved profiles (9). They are excellent; one, in spite of its curvature, resembles the pelecyform type (fig. 15, c).

Lageniforms (7). One atypical, two crude. One is on a regular slab; it is remarkably fine and elegant (Guichard and Guichard, 1965, p. 80, fig. 12, a).

Micoquians (29). Varying sizes (8.9 to 19 cm.); often very pointed (cross-section is either subcircular or remarkably flat). One tends toward a pelecyform, and another tends toward a

---

[24] If you refer to Guichard and Guichard (1965), you will notice that we have lumped several former sub-loci here. These subdivisions had only been made in the visibly homogeneous concentrations as controls. The percentages, the line graphs, and the histograms have well demonstrated that these were all the same group. That was, therefore, our conclusion.

[25] The entire collection is at the Laboratory of Prehistory of Bordeaux.

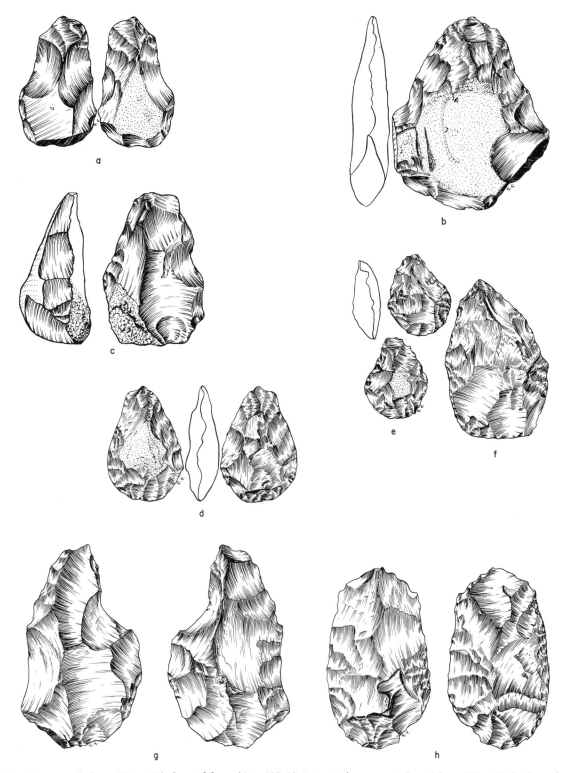

Fig. 14.—a, nucleiform (Site 410); b, cordiform (Site 400-12-1, *in situ*); c, atypical cordiform (Site 502); d, nucleiform (Site 401); e, cordiform (Site 400-O); f, cordiform (Site 401); g, shouldered biface (Site 502); h, biface *hachereau* (Site 400). 1/3 natural size.

lageniform. Two are on regular slabs (fig. 16, b-c).

Micoquians with a circular base (7). Rather typical. One of them was heat broken; only one longitudinal half remains. One was found *in situ* (Trench 400-4) (Guichard and Guichard, 1965, p. 75); its point has been reworked. This piece is slightly globular.

Massiforms (4). One is illustrated (fig. 17, a).

Triangular bifaces (8). Three of them are not on slabs; they could be placed at the extreme limit of the triangular group, analogous to those at 401; they are considered triangulars with the same reservations. One is on a thick flake. There are two flat ones; one is small (L = 11.3 cm.); the base is convex and formed by three natural flat surfaces (thickness: 1.9 cm.).

Shark tooth bifaces (3). One is small and elegant, another is a bit pointed.

Carinate bifaces (2). These are well-made and typical.

Semi-circular bifaces (3). One is slightly thick, it tends towards the carinates. The two others are mediocre.

Pelecyforms (9). They are good. One is disfigured by a deep lateral break, and one could be included with the borers.

Reniforms (14). Ten are distorted. On the whole, they are typical.

Naviforms (1). Rather crude.

Circular bifaces (3). One of them is rather typical, but a bit thick. Two are extremely atypical.

Unclassifiables (38). One resembles a cordiform, but is much too thick. The others are extremely varied in form. Thirteen, however, which are elongated and narrow, could be classified together in a single series.

Preforms and fragments (24 and 80). Many bases or points are recognizable. For example, two are certainly Abbevillian biface bases. One flat point, from a large biface, was used as a Levallois core. The rather sizable number of these fragments is certainly related to the fact that the industry fell and slipped down the slope of Jebel 400.

Technical indices. IL = 24.35 (against 21.22 at 401); IF^s = 45.25 (as opposed to 39.78 at 401); and IF^t = 55.09 (against 51.21 at 401). In contrast the Laminar Index is 12.23, almost

the double of its value at Site 401. Blades and flakes of large dimensions are less numerous here than at Site 401.

Typological indices. Flake tools are always very rare (except for 20 typical Levallois flakes and 74 atypical ones).[26] Other tools, totaling 14, are as follows: Levallois points, 1; Mousterian points, 1; simple straight side-scrapers, 2; simple convex side-scrapers, 1; concave side-scrapers, 2; typical end-scrapers, 1; typical burins, 1; denticulates, 1; pieces with retouch on the ventral surface, 1; pieces with bifacial retouch, 2; and *hachoirs*, 1.

Cores (180).[27] Many are partially flaked, formless or variant forms. As for the others, the predominant form is the Levallois core (47), followed by globular (31), "Mousterian" discoid (16), para-Levallois (4), with opposed flake removals (3), and blade-core (1).

Locality 400-West (Guichard and Guichard, 1965, p. 72, for coordinates and section)

This is right next to 400-South. Its cumulative line graph follows very closely that of the latter site. Actually, the study of 87 bifaces, cores, flakes, etc.[28] demonstrates a complete identity with 400-South. We illustrate a trihedral (fig. 15, e).

Locality 502[29] (map reference 659.100/911.800)

This very restricted little site is situated on a narrow pediment of a jebel on top of which is a Middle Paleolithic site, 503.

Even though some very rare unworn Levallois flakes are found in this Acheulean site which could have tumbled down from the top, the existence of Levallois debitage can nonetheless be established from the rare Levallois flakes which are eolized to an extent comparable to that of the bifaces (46). We illustrate the following: one distorted ficron (fig. 12, d); one shouldered biface (fig. 14, g); one atypical cordiform (fig. 14, c); one Micoquian with an oval base (fig. 16, l); and one biface-borer (fig. 18, d). In specific de-

---

[26] Always counted in delimited areas.

[27] In an area of 32 sq. m.

[28] The entire collection was sent to the Royal Museum of Tervuren.

[29] The collection sent from Wadi Halfa to the Museum of Khartoum was studied in a superficial way; i.e., one could draw, photograph, and take notes on it, but it was not the object of an exhaustive descriptive analysis.

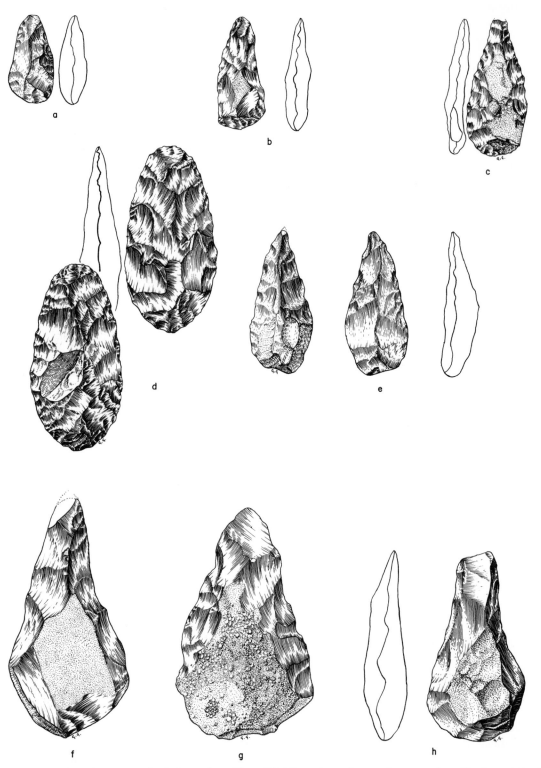

Fig. 15—a, lanceolate (Site 400-N); b, lanceolate (Site 400-N); c, lanceolate with incurved profile (Site 400-N); d, limande (Site 400-N); e, trihedral (Site 400-W); f, lanceolate with canted point (Site 513); g, lanceolate with incurved profile (Site 400-S); h, langeniform (Site 438). 1/3 natural size.

tails, the flake-tool assemblage here is analogous to that of 400-South.

Locality 505 (map reference 659.050/911.550).

We counted 107 bifaces.[30] The traces of Levallois technique are negligible. We illustrate: one pelecyform (fig. 17, c); one "Khor Abu Anga" oval (fig. 18, a). The flake tool assemblage does not differ much from those at 502 and 400-South.

Locality 509 (map reference 660.550/911.550).

We counted 63 bifaces.[31] The traces of Levallois technique are negligible. The assemblage is identical to those of 400-South, 502, and 505.

UPPER ACHEULEAN

Locality 438 (Guichard and Guichard, 1965, pp. 76 and 77 for map reference)

This site, which is a rectangle of about 100 m. x 50 m., produced 339 bifaces.[32] We divided the site into zones of pediment banks which were then subdivided according to whether they were closer to the slopes or to the wadi. Here again, the analysis revealed that we were dealing with a homogeneous group without any noticeable differences in the proportions of each type.

The tools are very evolved, certain pieces attaining actual perfection. They are almost always elegant, often perfectly symmetrical with considerable, carefully executed regular retouch. Lanceolates, Micoquian bifaces, and similar forms constitute about 50 per cent of the collection by themselves. There are few archaic forms.

Abbevillian bifaces (6). Except for one which is very large, they are most often small (from 12 to 17 cm.). There is one on a regular slab.

Of Abbevillian style (3). Rather regular shape (fig. 12, f).

Ficrons (3). One of these is very crude; the others are better (fig. 12, b).

Distorted ficrons (1). Rather atypical.

Picks (6). Three among them could conceivably be classed with the lanceolates or Micoquians; their bases and general shape are very

carefully made, but their points which are very long and thin leave no doubt as to what they were used for. Two others are on regular slabs, closer to the normal type (fig. 13, a).

Trihedrals (4). Two among them have one flat surface covered by small flake removals, the second is relatively convex, the third is natural. One of them is very eolized.

Nucleiforms (13). They are clearly more "evolved," with more retouch than those from the preceding sites. Many tend towards more defined forms (amygdaloids, subcordiforms, etc.).

Amygdaloids (29). This is a major series (a little less than 10 per cent). They are relatively varied. They range from a short, slightly globular form (7.5 cm.) as in Figure 13, b to a very flat elongated one (23.5 cm.) which resembles a limande with rather vast, "spectacular" proportions. We have only found the latter type in this site (see Guichard and Guichard, 1965, p. 80, fig. 12, d).

Biface-*hachereau* (3). Very mediocre and atypical, but certainly of this class.

Shouldered bifaces (17). Almost all are very beautiful. Among them, one stands out particularly, because of the fineness of the long retouch flakes which cover its surface. One is distinguished by its thinness (2.8 cm.), and a curved profile on an incurved slab; another is entirely covered with very narrow retouch. Only one does not have regular retouch. One other is atypical in that it is small, pointed, and carelessly made. Two are on regular slabs.

Cordiforms (5). Not very good except for one which is flat (3 cm.) and rather finely retouched. Only one is on a regular slab.

Elongated cordiforms and subcordiforms (3). Not very good.

Ovals and elongated ovaloids (4). One of the ovaloids is very beautiful, regular, symmetrical in relation to its major axis and carefully retouched. One elongated ovaloid tends towards a limande; it is short (9 cm.), a little thick, and on a flake (small, smooth butt).

Lanceolates (60). By themselves they represent 20.65 per cent of the collection of bifaces. They are very beautiful, sometimes even spectacular. Only eight of them have little or no secondary retouch.

Their section is generally biconvex, almost

---

[30] The collection was sent to Columbia University.

[31] The collection was turned over to Save Soderbergh for the Uppsala Museum.

[32] The collection is at the Laboratory of Prehistory of Bordeaux with the exception of 111 bifaces sent to Columbia University.

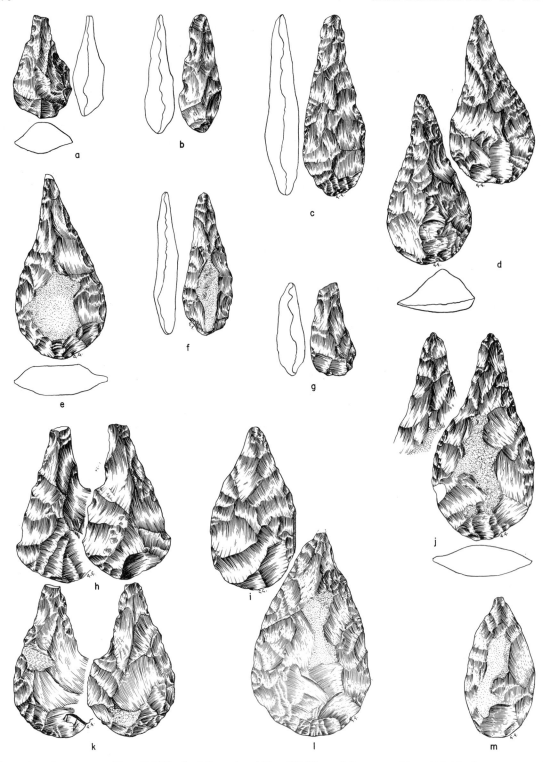

Fig. 16—a, Micoquian (Site 400-N); b, Micoquian (Site 400-S); c, Micoquian (Site 400-S); d, Micoquian (Site 511); e, Micoquian (Site 438); f, Micoquian (Site 401); g, Micoquian (Site 501); h, Micoquian with a notch (Site 511); i, Micoquian with oval base (Site 511); j, Micoquian with oval base (Site 439); k, Micoquian with a notch (Site 438); l, Micoquian with oval base (Site 502); m, Micoquian with oval base (Site ARW-8). 1/3 natural size.

cylindrical at certain points. Seven are very flat (2.66 to 3 cm. for a length of 18 to 21 cm.). Two are a little globular and asymmetric. They are big (between 13 and 25.5 cm.) and slim. The eolization is variable, and some are rather unworn. Others are practically smooth to the touch. In the latter case, some have very thin or "needle-like" conical points. Most are complete, and the others only lack the extreme end of the point.

Twenty-two resemble Micoquians. Two tend toward extremely elongated triangular bifaces. One, with a broken base, has a shortened point which was shaped into a poor end-scraper, and one is gibbous and has its point curved towards its flat surface. Another is the only one with a reserve base (8.5 cm. on a total length of 22 cm.); it has a large area of cortex (with a steep oblique slope); in all, it is poorly worked with nearly Abbevillian-like flaking.

One lanceolate (Guichard and Guichard, 1965, p. 79, fig. 11c, b) resembles a Micoquian and shows a possible accidental burin blow at the pointed end.

Lanceolates with canted points (18). The same elegant workmanship is present as in the preceding lanceolates. Two are on regular slabs, rather flat (3.3 and 3.5 cm.) and narrow (9 and 11 cm.). The points are set off rather high up (10.5/18 and 17/23.3 cm.); they are distinctly canted and pointed.

Lanceolates with incurved profiles (4). The areas of cortex are reduced, especially on the dorsal surface.

Lageniforms (4). One is very eolized, and its profile is curved. Its point seems to have received a *tranchet* blow on each surface, and the base is carelessly made. It is one of the crudest bifaces from this site (fig. 15, h).

Micoquians (30). They make up 10.31 per cent. Like the lanceolates, they are very beautiful. The body is generally globular, but the circumference of the base has been carefully evened and thinned. There are only two flat ones, 2.7 and 3.3 cm., the last one also being the smallest in the series, 16.3 cm. Aside from this exception, they are large, sometimes very large (18 to 29.5 cm.).

Their points are almost always cylindrical and pointed, often trihedral. The differences of eolization are the same as for the lanceolates. One is

globular and very finely retouched. Its base is perfectly thinned over its entire circumference; its point is sharp with a trihedral section. This is in a way the characteristic piece. One with moderate dimensions (fig. 16, k), but notched on one side, is illustrated with a biface found at Site 511, but because of its quality could belong to this series.

Micoquians with oval bases (1). Very eolized.

Micoquians with circular bases (4). Rather atypical; one is extremely eolized.

Massiforms (6). Two are mediocre (fig. 17, e).

Reniforms (7). Good as a whole, and typical (fig. 17, h). One (20 cm.) is the largest we found.

Triangular bifaces (8). Five are on slabs. One of these is flat, four are thick. The three others are atypical and crude.

Ogival bifaces (2). Rather successfully made.

Shark tooth bifaces (6). Good; one which is not regular is a little denticulated.

Carinate bifaces (6). Good except for one which is atypical.

Semicircular bifaces (4). They are very good (fig. 17, i).

Circular bifaces (5). Quite successfully made.

Naviforms (2). One is excellent, with a well-made point.

Unclassifiables (15). Almost all tend towards differentiated forms: subcircular bifaces; very atypical pelecyforms; and kinds of borers. Eight are on regular slabs.

Preforms and fragments (49). One of these preforms could be a rough out for one of the large flat amygdaloids which are found at this site; another, a naviform. Among the fragments, seven very pointed Micoquian or lanceolate points have been recognized. They are comparable to the most beautiful specimens.

Technical indices. IL = 11.22, very weak; the site is not "Levallois." $IF^s = 27.11$, $IF^l = 37.85$; they are very weak. The same goes for the Laminar Index which is 6.47. The flakes are relatively few in number.

Typological indices. We found no definite flake-tools.

Cores (64). Formless (16), variants (14), Levallois flake (12), discoids (6), with opposed flake removals (6), globular cores (5), "Acheulean" cores (4), and pyramidal cores (1).

In summary, this material stands out because

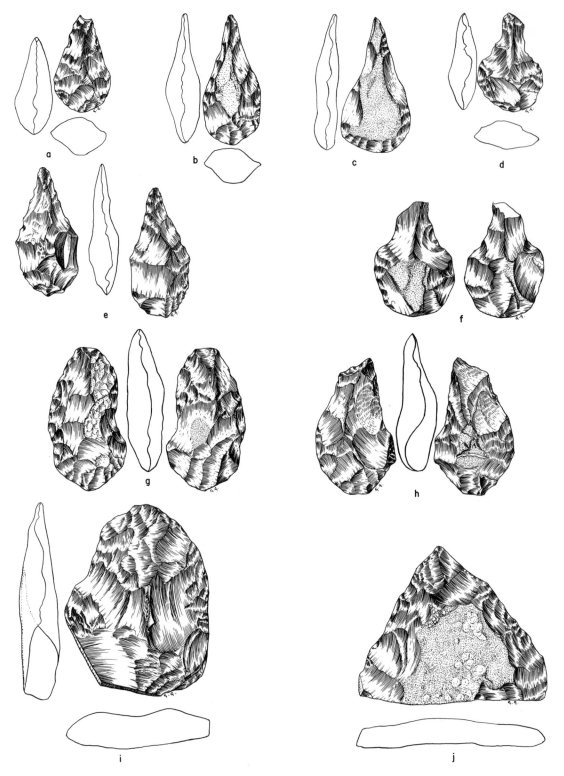

FIG. 17—a, massiform (Site 400-S); b, massiform (Site ARW-8); c, pelecyform (Site 505); d, pelecyform (Site ARW-8); e, massiform (Site 438); f, pelecyform (Site 430); g, reniform (Site 401); h, reniform (Site 438); i, semicircular (Site 438); j, ogival (Site 430). 1/3 natural size.

of its elegance, the perfection of its forms, and the fineness of the retouch. However, we find joined with a great mastery of the technique of biface production and to a variety of Micoquian facies, a non-Levallois debitage.

Locality 400-North

It is situated on the pediment banks (10 to 14) and produced 359 bifaces.[33]

Abbevillian bifaces (11). Formless, rather small, with two on regular slabs.

Of Abbevillian style (4). Small.

Ficrons (8). They are quite similar to those which come from Site 451. They clearly resemble regular and symmetrical picks. One, found *in situ,* is a little different. Its section is trihedral, and it resembles a ficron from Micoque.

Trihedrals (3). Very good. One is extremely eolized.

Nucleiforms (8). One is very large; another very crudely made.

Amygdaloids (9). One is very handsome and elongated; it has a slightly lateral platform remnant.

Shouldered bifaces (3). Very good, well finished; one has a very slightly twisted point.

Cordiforms (9). In general, good. One is small and typical with a notched base (this is not the only example of this sort). One example was found in level E-3, at 400-12 (fig. 14, b). In the same bed, but a little lower, we discovered a second one, almost the same, but its broken halves had been separated by several centimeters of sand.

One specimen resembling a triangular biface is very beautiful and remarkably well formed (Guichard and Guichard, 1965, p. 80, fig. 12, e). However, its point seems too low and the basal angles too largely convex to belong to the latter category, although it can actually be inscribed in an equilateral triangle with sides of 25 cm. (maximum length, 17 cm.; height, 18 cm.).

Subcordiforms (3). One of them is a little short.

Ovaloids (9). One is rather thick.

Elongated ovaloids (7). Rather elegant and regular. One example which was very flat was

found *in situ* at the end of beds E-1 and E-2 (400-12). One is on a flake; its ventral surface is partially retouched, its tip smoothed by small retouch.

Ovals (4). Quite typical, one of them is elongated.

Limandes (2). One is very well made (fig. 15, d).

Lanceolates (46). Often very beautiful. Smaller than at 438, they vary between 7.5 and 20 cm. Ten of them have a slightly saddle-shaped side. As at 400-South, sometimes they have rounded points, sometimes sharp points. This latter case is less frequent, however, than at 438 and 451. Two are on regular slabs; three are rather crude. One which is small (9.9 cm.) is almost a Micoquian. Another, one of the smallest from the site, is 7.5 cm. (fig. 15, b).

One excellent example is flat with a small very flat butt; its contour is a rather pointed ogive. It has been very finely retouched.

Finally, there are three very small lanceolate bifaces (about 7 cm.) which were formerly points of Micoquian or lanceolate bifaces. After breaking (in the course of fabrication or during utilization?), they were transformed into complete new bifaces by two or three careless flake removals which re-formed their bases. We have met with this situation elsewhere. The difference in the patina is not noticeable.

Lanceolates with canted points (4). One of these is on a regular slab.

Lanceolates with incurved profiles (4). One of them is very large (17 cm.) in relation to its thickness (3.1 cm.); it is very incurved. Another has, in addition, a canted point. One small example (fig. 15, c) is only slightly incurved, but the technique by which it was formed is rather representative.

Lageniforms (12). They are very good; one of them is on a plaquette.

Micoquians (11). Very well done, well finished, carefully retouched. One is particularly elegant with a regularly globular base, a very fine, slightly canted point. Another, on the contrary, is more elongated with a slightly expanding body, and its base is ovalized and thinned by numerous retouch flakes. The point on one piece is broken (fig. 16, a).

Micoquians with circular bases (6). Rather

[33] Stored in the Laboratory of Prehistory of Bordeaux except for 111 which were sent to the Royal Museum of Tervuren.

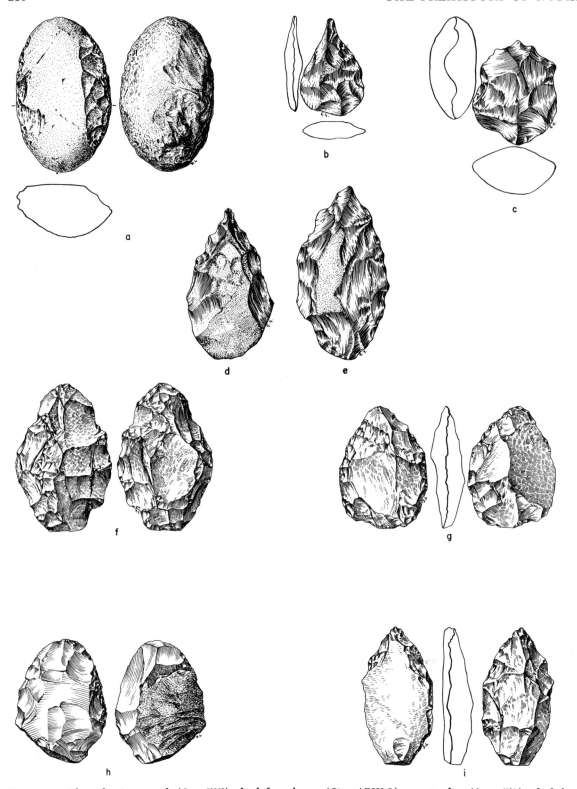

Fig. 18—a, Khor-Abu-Anga oval (Site 505); b, biface borer (Site ARW-8); c, circular (Site 451); d, biface borer (Site 502); e, naviform (Site 401); f, biface (A) (Site 622); g, biface (A¹) (Site 622); h, biface (A¹) (Site 622); i, diverse biface (C) (Site 622). 1/3 natural size.

good. One of them has a point broken almost flush with the convexity which sets it off.

Massiforms (2). Very good and typical.

Pelecyforms (2). Small (8 and 7.5 cm.).

Reniforms (11). Typical, but more or less well made.

Triangular bifaces (13). Seven flat, six thick. All well done.

Ogival bifaces (2). Very regular; however, the one found in the desiccation fissure which joins 400-12-1 and 400-12-2 at the top is less finished than the other.

Shark tooth bifaces (8). One is only a rather advanced preform. The other is boldly made and atypical (Guichard and Guichard, 1965, p. 81, fig. 13, c).

Carinate bifaces (6). One is a little pointed; the others, although unskillfully made, are more typical.

Semi-circular bifaces (4). Mediocre, but well typed except for one of them which is a bit pointed and tends to resemble an ogival.

Circular bifaces (3). These are more subcircular.

Naviforms (2). One of them is perhaps a little flat; the other, on the contrary, is very carinated.

Unclassifiables (34). Some are very well made with small fine retouch covering their surfaces, but their "whimsical" contour prevents any categorization. One is short, squat, and thick (L = 11 cm., W = 7.5 cm., T = 4.1 cm.); a sort of great notch sets off a steep nose; the base is heat broken. One is strange; one of the surfaces of the body is pyramidal with blade-like concentric removals; it is slightly shouldered due to a large notch near its point. One which is on a thick slab disengages a sort of duckbill shaped push-plane. Two others are partial, almost unifacial. Eight are on slightly regular slabs; one of these has a sort of carinated *tranchet*.

Preforms and fragments (110). Many of the fragments are identifiable: Micoquian butts with circular bases, lanceolate points (9 cm.), etc.

Technical indices. IL = 24.35; IF^s = 48.99; IF^1 = 57.04; Il = 3.62. Fewer Levallois than at 400-South; however, this site is more faceted and has many fewer blades.

Typological indices. Flake tools: rare; however, the following 108 tools are found: typical

Levallois flakes, 20; atypical Levallois flakes, 74; Levallois points, 1; Mousterian points, 1; simple straight side-scrapers, 2; simple convex side-scrapers, 2; simple concave side-scrapers, 1; typical end-scrapers, 1; typical burins, 1; denticulates, 1; pieces, retouched on ventral surface, 1; bifacially retouched pieces, 2; and *hachoirs*, 1.

Cores (70). Variants and formless (38); Levallois flake (15); Acheulean (14); globular (2); with opposed flake removals (1).

Locality 430 (no coordinates)

We have analyzed 201 bifaces[34] and about 800 flakes, cores, etc.

Bifaces. The collection is comparable to 400-North. Technical indices: IL = 15.58; IF^s = 22.85; IF^1 = 36.96; IL = 3.94. One of Abbevillian style (fig. 12, g); one pelecyform (fig. 17, f); and one ogival (fig. 17, j) are illustrated.

Locality 451 (map reference 658.200/913.100)

The analysis is based on 109 bifaces.[35] The Levallois debitage is far from negligible, compared with 430, and probably a little higher. Illustrations: one triangular biface (Guichard and Guichard, 1965, p. 81, fig. 13, b); one shark tooth biface (Guichard and Guichard, 1965, p. 81, fig. 13, a); and one circular biface (fig. 18, c).

Locality 501 (map reference 659.100/912.100)

Analysis based on 395 bifaces.[36] Levallois debitage is very rare. Illustrations: one amygdaloid (fig. 13, d); one Micoquian (fig. 16, g).

Other Sites[37]

These sites are represented by only a few bifaces, and, therefore, have not been subjected to a statistical analysis. Nevertheless, some are illustrated: Locality 510 (map reference 660.-800/910.100): Abbevillian biface (fig. 12, a). Locality 511: Micoquian biface (fig. 16, i). Locality 513: lanceolate with a canted point (fig. 15, f). Locality 515: pick (fig. 13, c); trihedral

---

[34] Most of the collection was sent to W. Chmielewski.

[35] A part of the collection sent to Columbia University, New York.

[36] The collection is at Southern Methodist University, Dallas, Texas.

[37] The material from Sites 504 (25 bifaces), 506 (20 bifaces), 510 (25 bifaces), 511 (28 bifaces), 513 (21 bifaces), 515 (43 bifaces), is at the Khartoum Museum.

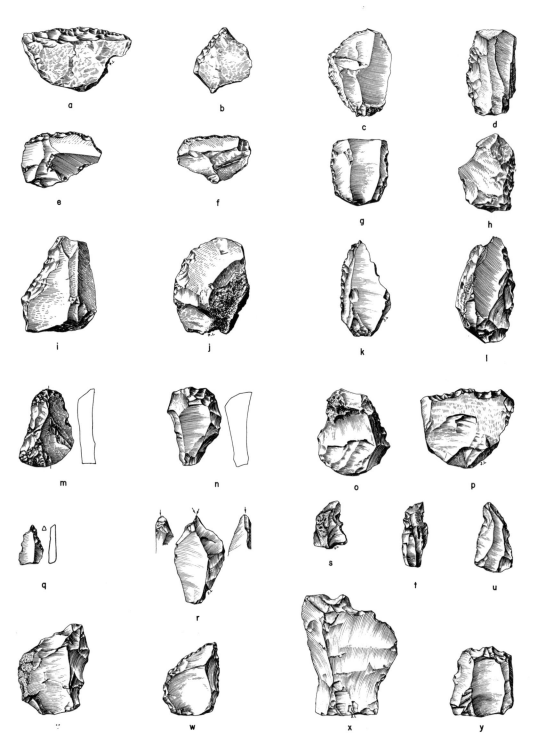

Fig. 19—a-l, denticulates and scrapers (Site 622); m-n, end-scrapers (Site 622); o-p, denticulates (Site 622); q, borer (Site 622); r, burin (Site 622); s-u, notches (Site 622); v, Tayac point (Site 622); w, Pseudo-Levallois retouched point (Site 622); x, y, distal end notches (Site 622); 1/3 natural size.

biface (fig. 13, e). Locality ARW-8 (map reference 646.500/927.000): massiform (fig. 17, b); biface-borer (fig. 18, b). Locality 439 (map reference 657.300/918.300): Micoquian with an oval base (fig. 16, j); carinate (Guichard and Guichard, 1965, p. 81, fig. 13, e). Locality 410: nucleiform (fig. 14, a). Locality 400-0 (map reference 659.500/915.000): cordiform (fig. 14, e). Locality 504 has not been illustrated.

CONCLUSIONS FOR LOWER, MIDDLE, AND UPPER ACHEULEAN

We wish to offer the following conclusions:

1. The analysis of the Acheulean assemblage has demonstrated that the collections from the surface sites are in themselves perfectly coherent. From the point of view of the typologist, it is hard to imagine how they can differ from the already known finds in stratigraphic context.

2. The statistico-typologic method may be usefully adapted to the study of surface sites. It permits us to determine whether or not we are dealing with mixed industries.

3. The Lower and Upper Acheulean are represented by very distinctive and characteristic cumulative curves and histograms (fig. 10).

4. The Middle Acheulean has an intermediate curve. Six sites have, with minor variation, the same graph. It is difficult to believe that the same mixing occurred six times in the same proportions. We experimentally "mixed" the Lower Acheulean of 516 and the Upper of 438. The result was a graph which differs greatly from the preceding ones, having a more accentuated S-shape. The abrupt rise (or rather the convexity) due to the "archaic" forms is greater in the case of the true Middle Acheulean. The situation is the same as regards the convexity due to the "evolved" forms.

5. It does not seem that it is necessary to postulate that the Nubian Acheulean is a young phenomenon. It appears to us to be of considerable age.

6. In every site, the polymorphism of the bifaces is considerable. We do not think this is unique to Africa. It would undoubtedly be the same in Europe on the condition that one could analyze series of as great numerical size.

7. Certain forms peculiar to Africa are com-

pletely missing here, like the cleaver-flakes.[38] The para-Levallois flaking technique is virtually unknown. In addition, for the sequences studied, trihedrals play a negligible role.

8. The utilization of crude slabs where retouching is only done on two-thirds of the piece, at most, is not a sign of great age. On the contrary, this type increases and culminates in a very evolved Upper Acheulean (Locality 451).

9. The Levallois debitage appears for certain in the Middle Acheulean (400-South, 400-West and 401). However, it is not an indication of evolution. There is a Micoquian facies with very slight Levallois debitage (Locality 438).

10. Tools on flakes are very rare, but they do exist.

11. In a word, especially because of the absence of cleaver-flakes, but also because of all the reasons detailed in the preceding paragraphs, Nubia, in Acheulean times, seems to have constituted a particular province,[39] an original enclave, in the interior of Africa. It is possible that this province extends, in the north, to Egypt, at least to Khartoum in the south, and perhaps to the Red Sea on the East—its limits in the West have not been defined. Thus, the exact boundaries of this province have yet to be made specific.

In conclusion, in each site the polymorphism of types is considerable, but there is regularity since the same shapes are found as in Europe, but they are, in Nubia, represented at this time in greater number. This polymorphism, this adaptation of a predebited material or preestablished forms, associated with rather diversified tools, sometimes of Levallois technique, extends into the Middle Paleolithic.

MIDDLE PALEOLITHIC

We suggest that there was a ramification of industries which in Nubia could be associated with the Middle Paleolithic (Guichard and Guichard, 1965, p. 84-111, specifically p. 86—Conclusion IV).

Actually, the presence or absence of certain

---

[38] There are none at Kharga; Leakey has illustrated those from Olduvai; they seem to be absent at Khor Abu Anga; Arkell gathered some to the east of Tibesti (Arkell, 1964, p. 11, fig. 15 and pl. 15 and 16 notably).

[39] "Province" in the sense of "paleontological provinces."

objects characteristic of the Middle Paleolithic in Nubia (bifacial foliate objects, particularly side- and end-scrapers, certain cores) permitted us to determine two large cultural manifestations:

1. Without bifacial foliate objects, particularly side- and end-scrapers and certain cores (Sites 401-B, 401-D, 113-A).

2. With these items, and in this latter case, we have recognized an evolutionary line and from that point have distinguished two subgroups according to the greater or lesser crudeness or, on the contrary, the more or less evolved aspect of these industries. This leads to the recognition of: (*a*) Nubian I "Mousterian"[40] (Brinikol, Abu Simbel 1 and 6); and (*b*) Nubian II "Mousterian" (Sites 400-0, 400-1-1, 400-1-2, 415, 420, 439, etc.).

In summary, we proposed to include all these in the Nubian Middle Paleolithic, and we suggested a definition (Guichard and Guichard, 1965, p. 111). In effect, at this point as during Acheulean times, Nubia appeared to be a separate province, although, strictly speaking, it can be shown that there are sometimes certain affinities with the Arterian, sometimes with the Sangoan, or even with the Stillbay.

All in all, our continued research in 1961 confirmed the point of view expressed in our Preliminary Report (Guichard and Guichard, 1965). In order not to lengthen the present work with repetitions from the earlier one, we suggest that the reader refer specifically to the text in the Report (Guichard and Guichard, 1965, pp. 84-111). We will limit ourselves to presenting only some further refinements. Next, therefore, we will describe a new facies of the Middle Paleolithic.

From a typological point of view, we gave definitions of Nubian Cores, Type I and 2 (Guichard and Guichard, 1965, pp. 68-69). These definitions are still fully accurate. However, in order to avoid any confusion and in view of some logical considerations, we add the following: (*a*) Levallois point core, Type I. This is the ordinary classic type which is most often illustrated by authors. Although common in Europe, it

seems to be rather rare in Nubia. (*b*) Levallois point core, Type 2. This is the one we formerly called "Nubian Core, Type 1" (fig. 22, f). It is exceptionally large, and the quality of preparation retouch is also absolutely remarkable (Guichard and Guichard, 1965, pp. 102-103, figs. 22-23). (*c*) Levallois point core, Type 3. This is our former Nubian Core, Type 2 (Guichard and Guichard, 1965, pp. 102-103, figs. 22-23).

We called end-scrapers of Aurignacian type "rostro or mucro carinates" (Guichard and Guichard, 1965, p. 68, and fig. 9, no. 10, fig. 19). According to F. Bordes, there is no reason not to give them the names which have been sanctioned by use, i.e., "carinated end-scrapers" or "nosed end-scrapers." We will henceforth follow this opinion. Moreover, the few carinated or nosed end-scrapers which we formerly described are somewhat reminiscent of the Aurignacian of Kom Ombo (Vignard, 1953), or even of the Jabrudian or pre-Aurignacian of Jabrud (Rust, 1950, pl. 12, no. 2 and 4, pl. 35, no. 7, etc.). Furthermore, is not the Aterian a slightly "Aurignacoid" culture itself?[41]

SITE DESCRIPTIONS

From the point of view of the new field research (field trip, 1964), the discovery of new sites confirms what has already been suggested. As an example, descriptions of Sites 507 and 410 follow:

Site 507 (map reference 913.800/660.900)[42]

This little deposit, which is very circumscribed, is situated on a narrow jebel that overhangs the Acheulean Site 451. The Levallois Index is 31.61; the Laminar Index, 15.9; and the broad and strict Indices of Faceting are 55.10 and 46.12 respectively.

There are only six bifaces, but they are finely made; specifically two amygdaloids (length, 9 and 10 cm.; thickness, 3.2 and 4.4 cm.). Twenty flake tools, six of which are rather good side-scrapers, were found. One of them is a conver-

---

[40] It should be remembered that the term "Mousterian," as used here and later, does not imply any chronologic, paleontologic, or stratigraphic meaning. It is simply a synonym for the Middle Paleolithic and only represents a lithic facies.

[41] Apropos of the type site, Bir el-Ater, Balout wrote: "End scrapers on massive elongated flakes or on the end of blades are often quite carinated and strongly resemble those of the Aurignacian." (Prehistoire de l'Afrique du Nord, p. 288.)

[42] The collection was sent to Columbia University, New York.

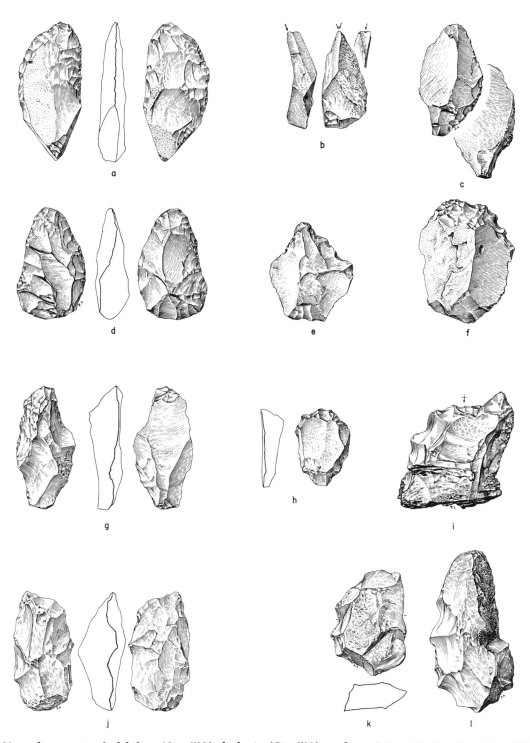

Fig. 20—a, diverse retouched biface (Site 503); b, burin (Site 503); c, divers (Site 503); d, biface (Site 503); e, Tayac point (Site 503); f, denticulated end-scraper (Site 503); g, divers (Site 622); h, denticulated end-scraper (Site 503); i, macrodenticulate (Site 622); j, biface (Site 622); k-l, macrodenticulate (Site 622). 1/3 natural size.

gent canted side-scraper with a rounded end. There are also twelve Levallois point cores (three of Type 2; nine of Type 3).

Site 410

Without a doubt, this is a workshop. Actually, among the thousands of flakes, we only found 19 tools, but they are among the best we found. The bifaces, which are rare, are paradoxically less good; yet this locality distinguishes itself by the skill of its flaking technique. Thus, the Levallois cores are remarkable for their exceptional dimensions and the mastery shown in their formation. In an area of 40 sq. m., we counted 85 cores; 66 are Levallois flake cores, 10 Levallois blade cores (7 of which are bipolar), 7 Levallois point cores of Type 2, and 2 of Type 3. No other deposit gave us similar proportions.

It should be noted that we found no points (Mousterian or Levallois); not even the pointed flakes drawn from the cores were discovered. This reinforces the impression that the site is a workshop rather than a habitation.

The Levallois Index is 39.07; the Laminar Index is 18.30 (this is rather high); the broad and restricted Faceting Indices are 55.11 and 47.04 respectively.

In addition, the discovery of new sites demonstrates that in these industries, when the number of bifaces increases, that of bifacial foliates decreases. They may even disappear completely as in the site we are going to consider. It is difficult to avoid using the term Mousterian of Acheulean tradition. However, it must be kept in mind that we are dealing here with a Mousterian of Acheulean tradition which is unique to Nubia. Its peculiarities include the presence of specific objects like side-scrapers with repeated retouch on both longer sides and on the curve of the oval top or, again, the Levallois point cores of Types 2 and 3. On the other hand, in the absence of stratigraphy, it is obviously necessary to guard against any chronological comparison with the European Mousterian of Acheulean tradition.

Site 503 (map reference 911.800/259.200)

It is located above Acheulean Site 502.[43] It is well delimited and rich. The Middle Paleolithic occupation is on the edges of the top of the in-

selberg, in places covering the Acheulean. On the slope below are many fresh pieces with Levallois debitage.

The importance of Site 503 is that it produced 56 bifaces, and in this respect, therefore, it is by far the richest of all those we examined.

Generally the pieces are small, thin, elegant, and extremely well retouched, although the lanceolates and cordiforms are poor and atypical. Ovalairs and amygdaloids, however, are perfect. All of the reserved base bifaces are well executed.

The "unclassifiable" series is interesting. Three of them have protruding short, solid backs, more or less carinate, made by notches on the base of the point.

We have also 14 bifaces which are a combination of a tool and a biface (but they are not flake-tooled with bifacial retouch): bifacial scrapers, 3; bifacial end-scrapers, 4; and bifacial ogival-scrapers, 7.

The ventral face of these pieces is sometimes plane or concave, sometimes slightly convex. The general outlines are ogival; the dorsal face is relatively carinate. They seem to approximate several scrapers of this site; but, for the latter (really scrapers), the ventral face of the flake is not retouched.

We have the following:

Nucleiforms (1). Almost circular (70, 65, 29 mm.).

Amygdaloids (4). These are excellent specimens.

Cordiforms (2). One has a notch, it is the largest, but very flat, 12, 85, 24 mm.

Subcordiforms (2). Short, solid and a little globular.

Ovalairs (2). Very beautiful, often the ventral face is partially flaked. Small and thin (26 mm.).

Lanceolates (3). Not beautiful. Atypical.

Reniforms (2). Very typical. Two of the best we have seen.

Shark tooth bifaces (3). Relatively good, always small. One of the thinner pieces from the site; like several others, is not more than 20 mm.

Carinate bifaces (7). Excellent specimens.

Semi-circular bifaces (1). Typical.

Bifacial scrapers (2). One is on a flake with cortex on the dorsal face, a little carinate, and with a little notch; the other is also good.

---

[43] The collection is stored at the Laboratory of Prehistory of Bordeaux.

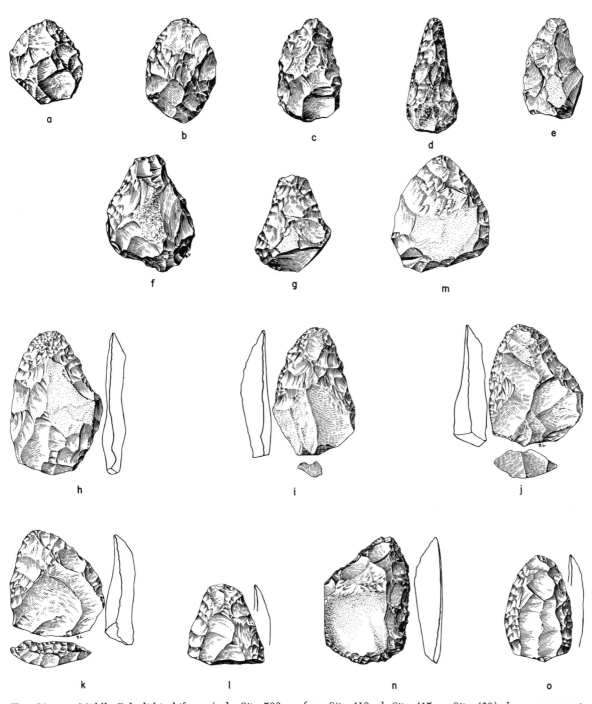

Fig. 21—a-g, Middle Paleolithic bifaces (a-b, Site 503; c, f, g, Site 410; d, Site 415; e, Site 420); h-o, convergent scrapers with rounded ends (h, Site 400-O; i, j, k, Site 503; l, Site 400-2; m, o, Site 415; n, Site 410). 1/3 natural size.

Bifacial ogival scrapers (7). Two of these are identical. One is 85, 80, 29 mm., the other 80, 85, 28 mm.

Bifacial end-scrapers (4).

Unclassifiables (8).

Fragments (5).

We note that the tools of this assemblage have rather small proportions and that 13 of them are with reserved bases.

The Levallois Index is 37.88; the Laminar Index is only 6.22; and the broad and restricted Faceting Indices 51.70 (dihedral butts dominate) and 36.52 respectively.

As always, the number of flake tools is not extremely important, but the specimens are really beautiful.

Sixty-seven flake tools, Levallois points, burins (rare), notches and denticulates, notches in ends, truncated blades or flakes, backs, end-scrapers; but the scrapers really dominate, either simple or double; denticulate side-scrapers; and the best, convergent convex side-scrapers with rounded ends.

Sixty-four cores were counted in an area of 16 m.; twenty-two are Levallois, four of which are point cores of Type 3.

The illustrated pieces are as follows: variant (bifacial tool) (fig. 20, a); reniform biface (fig. 20, d); convex side-scraper (fig. 22, a); simple straight side-scraper (fig. 22, c); denticulate blades (fig. 22, b, g); atypical end-scraper (fig. 22, d); burin (fig. 20, b); denticulated end-scraper (fig. 20, h); Tayac point (fig. 20, e); large atypical denticulated end-scraper (fig. 20, f); convergent side-scraper with rounded end (fig. 21, i, j); convergent side-scraper with rounded end (very faceted butt) (fig. 21, k); and bifaces (fig. 21, a-b).

Site 622 (map reference 603.500/298.500)

The most substantial contribution of the 1964 field trip was the discovery at Site 622 of a third original facies of the Nubian Middle Paleolithic.[44] The site, altitude 227 m., is about 2 km. from the Nile.

It is situated at the south of Mirgissa on the upper part of a slope oriented towards the west, which belongs to the system of sandy "hills"

---

[44] Collection at the Laboratory of Prehistory of Bordeaux.

---

which rise above the left bank of the Nile at the edge of the Second Cataract. Its area is about 150 m. x 80 m.

This site is of very great interest. It represents our only Middle Paleolithic site studied in a stratigraphic context in a solely desertic series of sediments.

We dug several test trenches at this site. The beds are the same everywhere; therefore, we will describe the longest trench (14 m.) which was dug in the direction of the slope. From top to bottom, the sediments are the following (fig. 11):

1. S.L.—Surface; coarse sand and gravels made up of Precambrian rocks and, in part, of Nubia Sandstone, containing eolized Middle Paleolithic industries (A and A¹ according to the degree of eolization).

2. Y. Coll.—Yellow colluvia, 7.5 YR, 8/4 to 7/4 sec., of fine clayey texture. The level is finely bedded, and contains rare pebbles. The base is regular, having desiccation fissures(F). Middle Paleolithic Industry (B).

3. R. Soil—Brown-red to dark brown soil, 5 YR, 5/3 sec.; 5 YR, 3/3, developed in a fine silty sand; rare pebbles, level finely bedded and stratified following the slope, cut by desiccation fissures. At the base are some pieces less rolled than those of A, A¹, and B; these seem to belong to the underlying industry (C).

4. G.R.—Coarse and angular gravel (Precambrian rocks and Nubia Sandstone). Some rounded pebbles probably come from the conglomerates found at the base of the Nubia Sandstone. Middle Paleolithic (C).

5. R. Coll.—Discontinuous red colluvia, between the gravels and the dismantled surface of the bedrock. Coarse stratification.

6. E—Coarse eboulis at the bottom of the slope, transitional, laterally to the red soil (R. Soil).

7. B—Bedrock, very irregular at surface.

It is convenient to remark before passing on to the description of the industry that A, A¹, B, and C evolve within a single industrial phylum (in the same way that there is an Aurignacian 1, 2, 3, etc., which always remains Aurignacian).

INTERPRETATION OF THE SECTION

1. The Red colluvia (R. Coll.), at the base of the cut are only found in hollows in the bedrock.

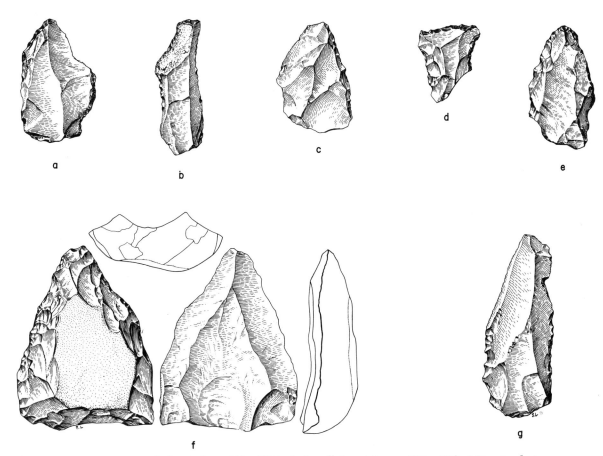

FIG. 22—a-e, g, scrapers and denticulates (Site 503); f, Levallois point core (Site 410). 1/3 natural size.

They give evidence of formation under vegetal cover and of washing, perhaps during sheet-flow (*écoulements en nappe*). As the colluvia have not been found anywhere else, it leads one to believe that they underwent a later phase of intense erosion which would have preceded the formation of the overlying gravel level (G.R.).

2. On the erosion surface thus formed, the first occupation dates from the Middle Paleolithic (Industry C). The conditions were semiarid then, as is shown by the deposition of these angular gravels (G.R.). During the end of this phase, the countryside must have undergone torrential tropical rains causing the deposits of debris and industry found at the bottom of the slope (E), and the gullying of its surface.

3. A red soil (R. Soil) formed at the top of the preceding horizon. This is the thickest deposit of the cut. It is of the Mediterranean type and, therefore, corresponds to a much drier climate than the former one. In fact, it gradually became totally arid. Actually, it is traversed by large desiccation fissures.

4. A second and without a doubt rather brief period of humidity: thin deposit of yellow colluvia. Very likely the second human occupation (Industry B) occurred during the period of transition from dryness to humidity.

Paleolithic man lived on the dissected surface of the red soil, and this is why their industry is found at the base of the Y. Coll.

5. A second arid period which has continued up to the present. New desiccation fissures (filled with yellow sand) develop which penetrate the yellow colluvia and extend downward to cut the older crevices in the red soil (these latter have been filled up with yellow colluvia). Industries A and A¹.

Unfortunately the typological interpretation of this material is difficult:

1. It does not resemble anything yet known.[45]

2. The distinction between A and A¹ (that is, according to the degree of eolization) gives no positive results.

3. There is a partial mixture between A and A¹ on the one hand and industry B on the other. This could be attributed as much to the excavator —we could not always distinguish very thin beds —as to the phenomena of deflation and perhaps of desiccation crevices.

4. The number of tools found in place in the 14 sq. m. area excavated is too small, for both B and C, to allow any calculation of representative indices.

5. The typological differences only appear in variations of percentages; the tools are the same from one bed to another. We are dealing here with a variation within a single group.

However, if we remain within prudent limits, it is possible to come to some extremely interesting conclusions for this collection. But first, since this lithic collection is not comparable to any other, what are the reasons for considering it a part of the Middle Paleolithic?

From a typological point of view the reasons are:

a. The presence of bifaces.

b. The absence of any intrusive piece which derives from a more recent culture (no truncated Levallois points of the Sebilian style, no microliths, no backed pieces, no grinding stones or pottery; insignificant blade debitage, etc.).

c. Although, at a distance of 1.5 km., there is an abundance of agate, jasper, flint, chert, etc., on the Nile "terraces," not one tool in these series is made out of these materials.

d. Although of different facies, the material shows a certain affinity with that of Brinikol in several details.

e. The industry cannot possibly be older than Middle Paleolithic. The bifaces are much too rare for the collection to be Acheulean, and, moreover, they are in the style of the Middle Paleolithic. It is impossible to consider them as belonging to the pebble culture either—the debitage is slightly Levallois and blades are present.

Finally there are some very advanced tools: burins; end-scrapers; etc.

We believe, however, that the strongest argument is the stratigraphic situation of Site 622. Although relationships with the terraces have not been followed or even established, the system of sedimentation cannot be recent. Formation of soils and colluvia of this nature at this altitude and location (without relation to the Nile or to a wadi) suggests considerable climatic variations which surpass in extent all that is known of those which affected the Upper Paleolithic, the Epipaleolithic, or the Neolithic in Nubia, Egypt, or in the Sahara.

DESCRIPTION OF THE FLAKE TOOLS

One of the unique characteristics of this strange industry is that it is fashioned out of a rather uncommon material. At first it was thought to be a very fine and hard quartzite (it cuts glass), in color from white to brown passing through a gold-yellow. The study of thin sections demonstrates that the light material is an entirely recrystallized rock, the quartz grains being completely joined together. The brown material is a resilicified argillite. The assemblage gives evidence of a powerful metamorphosis.

The three beds (A and A¹, B, C) have some rare tools in common; moreover, these are the most numerous ones and merit a precise description:

1. Macrodenticulates. Shaped on big, thick formless flakes with large areas of cortex. The flake removals are large (average length, 3 cm.; width, 3 cm.) and deep, often of Clactonian type. Generally, only one side of the flake is worked—it is tempting to say on one side of the "block." The flake removals are not numerous (from three to five) and set off sizable protrusions. Only some seem to have secondary retouching, but they might simply be utilization marks. As a whole, they are crude and coarse. We illustrate three (fig. 20, i, k, l), all from bed A.

2. Denticulated side-scrapers.[46] On a "true"

---

[45] It being understood that there are, nearby, innumerable and immense analogous deposits. They have never been described up to now.

[46] It is quite evident that the term "denticulated side-scraper" is only proposed in order to conjure up a typological image. From the point of view of its eventual utilization, such an instrument could not serve as a side-scraper; at best, it is a tearer.

denticulate, the notches, even contiguous ones, do not disengage a continuous working edge, only teeth. Moreover, a "real" side-scraper has a semi-cutting edge without notches or intentional denticulation. Here we have an intermediate type. The notches or denticulations, made by slightly abrupt retouching and sometimes arranged in a series of graduated depths, create a useful flat edge, slightly sloping and continuous, although the contours are more or less in a zigzag. When a side-scraper is made with a hard hammerstone without a number of precautions, such a tool is created as a first step and then it is evened with little blows (fig. 19, a, o, p).

It is seen that this transverse convex denticulated side-scraper has its important working edge set off by semi-covering retouch arranged according to graduated depth. For example, Figure 19, i, is a simple concave denticulated side-scraper, and Figure 19, f, is a "true" transverse convex side-scraper; the denticulation is only apparent and has been obviously caused by use.[47]

These tools are possibly comparable to the "denticulated end-scrapers" or the "spiny end-scrapers."

3. Flakes with ventral retouch. Numerous. In general the flake removals are sizable (length, 2.5 to 3 cm.; width, 2 to 2.5 cm., well marked negative bulb). They can be divided into three groups:

a. Denticulates, macrodenticulates, and denticulated side-scrapers on ventral flake surfaces.[48]

b. Variant objects, obviously finished, but unclassifiable (fig. 18, i). This is an important group.

c. Classic ventrally retouched flakes, the use of which is not discerned. Did they occasionally use them as tools? Abandoned preforms? (Bordes, 1961a, p. 45.)

COMPARATIVE STUDY OF THE THREE BEDS

Bed A and A^1. Crude, coarse debitage with huge, formless flakes which preserve a great deal of cortex. Thick butts often on the cortex, often convex with three flat surfaces overlapping con-

siderably on the sides of the flake. The assemblage is basically not Levallois (8.41 per cent). Some laminar flakes are found, but no blades. All the pieces are very much eolized.

Bed B. Some pieces are finer, specifically the Levallois flakes which are better made and sometimes better faceted. However, the Levallois Index remains quite small (9.3). The Laminar Index is 4. Thirty per cent of these objects are eolized, 70 per cent unworn.

Bed C. Fine debitage, thin flakes, some Levallois blades, two non-retouched bladelets. Strangely, two indices rise in parallel again—the Clactonian butts[49] (10.10) and the Levallois debitage (12.74). The Laminar Index is only 2.08. The industry is considerably unworn, the edges are still sharp.

In addition to these differences of appearance, disproportions in the division of tools among the beds are seen:

1. Bifaces—in the upper bed, A^1, some thick bifacial pieces with helicoidal profiles (fig. 18, g-h). In A, bifaces, often partial, are more finely retouched (figs. 18, f; 20, j).

2. Retouched Levallois points—one single specimen, bed B.

3. Retouched pseudo-Levallois points—two, in bed A. (fig. 19, w).

4. Side-scrapers—The proportions demonstrate a gradual impoverishment as you ascend in the stratigraphy: C, 12.79 per cent; B, 8.2 per cent; A and A^1, 6 per cent. On the whole, they vary little: simple straight, simple convex, simple concave, transversal convex, plain face, with abrupt retouch, with bifacial retouch, often denticulated; one example is a convergent canted scraper.

5. End-scrapers—Rare. Often atypical, sometimes having spines or denticulations on their working extremities (fig. 19, m-n) coming from A^1. However, in the lower level, one of them is very good.

6. Burins—Rare. Doubtful when they are on breaks. However, we have two in bed A on a concave retouched truncation (fig. 19, r).

7. Borers—only one (B).

---

[47] This last piece is very unworn; it comes from the deepest bed, C.

[48] They are not counted then under the category of "ventrally retouched flakes" but under denticulates, side-scrapers, etc. This is also true for the "variants."

---

[49] As a matter of fact, in these three beds, we found Clactonian butts in more important proportions than in other industries studied here. This percentage, however, does not go over 6.2 for A and A^1 or 7.04 for B.

8. Backed knives—only two and of mediocre quality (B and C).

9. Notches and denticulates—numerous. We illustrate a denticulate on the end of a flake (fig. 19, p); a denticulate on an atypical Levallois flake (fig. 19, o); three notches (fig. 19, s-u). All come from bed B. Finally, distal end notches (fig. 19, x, y), and some macrodenticulates (fig. 20, k-l).

It should be remembered that the "variant denticulates plus notches" block constitutes by itself 50 per cent of the A, A¹ and B assemblages, and 58 per cent in C. In this last bed, however, the notches clearly are the most numerous while they are of secondary importance in A, A¹ and B. The flakes with ventral retouch attain 13.07 per cent in A, A¹; 14.47 per cent in B; 24.13 per cent in C, where many tools, especially side-scrapers, are made on the ventral surface.

10. Bifacially retouched pieces—Rather rare, always found as part of a more characteristic tool.

11. Tayac points—Seven in A, none in either B or C. In general, they are good (fig. 19, v).

12. *Becs*—some. Rather good in A and B, absent in C.

13. Choppers and chopping tools—rather numerous, quite typical. Absent in C.

14. Variants—numerically this is an important group, especially in the upper beds.

15. Cores—Levallois cores are very rare in A, A¹; rare in B; and a little more numerous in C. The globulars and the "variants" predominate.

We surveyed some contiguous sites (Locality 627, in particular) which produced in an identical setting the same stratigraphy and tool assemblage.

In summary, then, this material gradually degenerates in quality as it evolves. The biface tradition maintains itself, but it becomes quite poor and "degenerate." In fact, this culture is original.

CONCLUSIONS FOR THE MIDDLE PALEOLITHIC

We have just distinguished three facies of the Nubian Middle Paleolithic:

1. The first is perhaps the oldest. The presence of rather crude bifacial foliate objects gives it some affinities with a middle Sangoan.

2. The second is more refined, particularly with respect to bifacial foliate objects and side-scrapers with repeated retouch on both longer sides and on the curve of the oval tip. Point cores of types 2 and 3, which are more numerous, have affinities, primarily technical, with the Aterian and, in fineness of retouch, with the Stillbay. In certain cases, with some reservations, it is possible to speak of this as Mousterian of Acheulean tradition.

3. The third is not yet comparable to anything known, and we are not able to assign it a chronological place in relation to the two preceding manifestations.

In summary, Nubia seems to have been a distinct province during the Middle Paleolithic, just as it was during Acheulean times.

However, we are aware that we have not exhausted the subject by any means. Undoubtedly, other facies do exist (Guichard and Guichard, 1965). We explicitly make reference to the numerous jebel tops covered over by an uninterrupted paving of flakes. These flakes are too thin, too regular, and too patterned to belong to the Acheulean. Incidentally, they are very old; their wear and position far from the Nile testify to this fact. Because of the lack of clearly identifiable tools in the midst of this profusion, we could not link them up to a given culture more precisely. But there is no question that they belong, *grosso modo*, to the Middle Paleolithic complex.

Sometimes these enormous concentrations contain groups of very small flakes and cores, from 1 to 2 cm. This poses the problem of a diminutive Mousterian. This has, at times, been defined by some people in the following way: "If one leaves the desert and walks towards the Nile . . . , it becomes apparent that the industries get smaller and smaller, more and more diminutive. And in proportion to the diminishing dimensions, the material becomes more recent."

This is, it seems to us, an unwarranted generalization. It is true that at the top and on the slopes of the jebels which are directly on the sides of the Nile, the beautiful Middle Paleolithic which has been described in the preceding pages is not found, and in its place is a "micro-Mousterian" which is definitely smaller. However, (1) in Neolithic and even Predynastic times, certain lithic elements are of large dimensions, and were generously shaped from huge cores. (2) In the desert, some 10 or 15 km. from the Nile, probably "diminutive Paleolithic" sites are far from rare and are often contiguous on a single hill top with one or several of the facies we have just described above. But, as far as wear can be trusted to give the age of pieces, they seem older than those we called the Nubian "Mousterian" II. We again deplore the fact that we did not find any definite flake tools.

Thus, the description of the diminutive Middle Paleolithic culture found near the Nile, and particularly studied by A. Marks, should fill in some details of the necessarily incomplete picture that we present here and which is only partially representative of the industries of the jebels in the zone which is now desert. It becomes clear, at least, that the question of the Middle Paleolithic industries of Nubia, from the point of view of typology alone, is more complex than anything which has been envisioned until now.

THE MOUSTERIAN INDUSTRIES OF NUBIA

Anthony E. Marks

(SOUTHERN METHODIST UNIVERSITY)

INTRODUCTION

THE DISCOVERY of Nubian Middle Stone Age sites began within the very first days of the initial field season, in October, 1961. Throughout the prehistoric research of the last few years in Nubia, the Nubian Middle Stone Age has almost constantly been studied, either in the field or in the laboratory. This report presents the results which were achieved by American teams during this work.

The sites reported here, however, represent only a small fraction of the total number of Nubian Middle Stone Age sites which were found in the area of Wadi Halfa, Northern Province, Sudan. Although survey, collection, and excavation were carried out over three field seasons, it was impossible to treat all sites systematically. The examination of the Nubian Middle Stone Age by the Combined Prehistoric Expedition was only part of an overall study of the whole prehistoric culture history of southern Nubia; hence, time permitted only a reasonable sampling.

Many lithic assemblages which belong to the Nubian Middle Stone Age closely parallel those of the Middle Paleolithic in Europe and the Near East. On the basis of typological and technological comparisons, these Nubian assemblages have been divided into a number of industries which fall within the larger Mousterian complex of the Middle Paleolithic.

During the course of this work, three preliminary reports were issued. The first (Solecki et al., 1963) noted the existence of Nubian Middle Stone Age sites (referred to as Middle Paleolithic), their gross distribution, and raw material employed and made some highly tentative comments on their typology and technology. The second (Wendorf, Daugherty, and Waechter, 1964) and third preliminary reports (Wendorf, Shiner, and Marks, 1965) gave more information on the typology and roughly grouped assemblages into industries. These reports were written

while laboratory studies were still in progress. Thus, certain observations made in them have had to be revised. Larger samples and a more rigorous application of typological criteria have resulted in the elimination of one entire group, which, a year ago, seemed to be similar to the European Typical Mousterian (Wendorf, Shiner, and Marks, 1965, p. xxii). On the other hand, greater distinctions are now made within other reported groups.

In this final report, every effort has been made to give all pertinent information and to illustrate as wide a range of tool and core types as possible.

HISTORY OF WORK AT NUBIAN MIDDLE STONE AGE SITES

The survey and collection of Nubian Middle Stone Age sites from the Egyptian border to the Third Cataract at Firka (figs. 1 and 6) were undertaken during the first three seasons of the Combined Prehistoric Expedition. During the 1961-1962 field season, preliminary survey was carried out in the Eastern Desert, near Wadi Halfa, and on the east bank of the Nile from Gamai to Firka. This survey established the presence of numerous living sites and flaking stations, particularly north of the Second Cataract (Solecki et al., 1963, pp. 73-80).

The second field season, 1962-1963, continued the survey by expanding to the west bank of the Nile, north of the Second Cataract (Wendorf, Daugherty, and Waechter, 1964, p. 14). Also, detailed studies were made on selected Nubian Middle Stone Age sites in the Eastern Desert, near Wadi Halfa (Guichard and Guichard, 1965, p. 63).

During the third field season, 1963-1964, additional work was done in the Eastern Desert, and detailed survey, collection, and excavation were carried out in the Eastern Desert, from Wadi Halfa north to Dibeira Station. Excavations were also carried out on the west bank of the Nile in

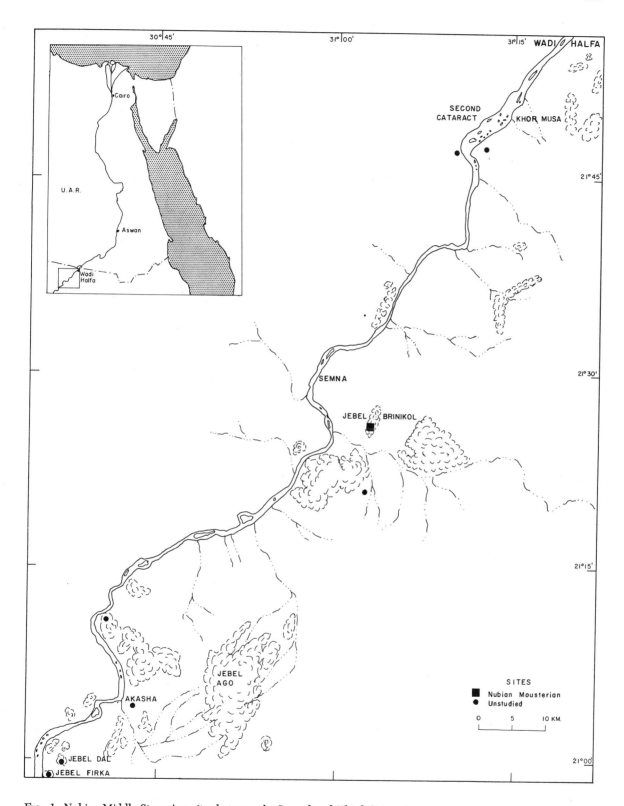

Fɪɢ. 1—Nubian Middle Stone Age sites between the Second and Third Cataracts.

the area of Dibeira West (Chmielewski, 1965).

Preliminary study of the sites surveyed during the 1961-1962 field season was undertaken at Columbia University, under the direction of R. Solecki. Those sites surveyed and collected in the Eastern Desert during the same and following season by J. Guichard and G. Guichard were studied at the Laboratory of Prehistory, Bordeaux, and a preliminary report was issued in 1965 (Guichard and Guichard, 1965).

The Guichards continued their work in the Eastern Desert during the 1963-1964 season, and the material collected at that time is at the Laboratory of Prehistory, Bordeaux. Those sites excavated by W. Chmielewski on the west bank of the Nile are under study at the Institute of History of Material Culture in Poland (Chmielewski, 1965).

Collections of material recovered by American teams of the Combined Prehistoric Expedition during the 1961-1962 and 1963-1964 seasons are at the Anthropology Research Center, Southern Methodist University, Dallas. Sample collections are also at the National Museum, Khartoum, and at Columbia University, New York City.

TECHNIQUES OF COLLECTION AND STUDY

As the majority of Nubian Middle Stone Age sites were found on the tops of sandstone inselbergs, without any stratigraphic or geological references, special techniques of collection and study were required. All surface sites reported in this paper were systematically collected. That is, all stone material was collected from an arbitrary area (1 to 100 sq. m.) without differentiating between a simple rock, a waste flake, or a finished tool. Two or more nearby areas within each site were normally collected in this way. These separate collections were then studied for technology and the results were compared. If the material was technologically homogeneous and if there was no other indication that the areas contained mixed assemblages (e.g., differential patination or weathering on artifacts within the areas), the collections were then combined and studied as a single unit. This was necessary because the number of finished tools in a limited area was usually quite small. Often, it was necessary to return to a site and expand the size of existing

collection areas, even though they may have been as large as 10 sq. m. each.

Subsurface sites were excavated by initial trenching followed by expansion of the trench following defined natural layers, if more than one occurred.

Laboratory studies of Nubian Middle Stone Age sites fall into two parts: the study of the stone-flaking technology and the typographical study of the finished tools. Technological studies include the ratio between Levallois and non-Levallois artifacts, the ratio of flakes to blades, and the percentage and type of butt preparation (Bordes, 1950). These observations are given in index form for each site. The following technological indices are used:

$$IL \text{ (Levallois Index)} = \frac{\text{total number of Levallois flakes, blades, and points x 100}}{\text{total number of flakes, blades, and points}}$$

$$IF \text{ (Faceting Index)} = \frac{\text{total number of convex, dihedral, and flat faceted butts x 100}}{\text{total number of recognizable butts}}$$

$$IFs \text{ (Restricted Faceting Index)} = \frac{\text{total number of convex and flat faceted butts x 100}}{\text{total number of recognizable butts}}$$

$$Ilame \text{ (Blade Index)} = \frac{\text{total number of blades x 100}}{\text{total number of flakes, blades, and points}}$$

These indices were formulated by F. Bordes of the Laboratory of Prehistory, Bordeaux, for the Mousterian of France (Bordes, 1953a, p. 277), but they are equally valid for the Nubian Middle Stone Age of the Northern Sudan. They have no cultural connotations but merely tabulate in simple form the numerous technological observations necessary in such a study.

Typological studies again follow the system and classification defined by Bordes (Bordes, 1950, 1954a, 1961a; Bordes and Bourgon, 1951). His type list, developed for the Mousterian of France, contains sixty-one tool types and a single category for all others.[1] The type list is not

[1] We wish to thank the Guichards, both students of Professor Bordes, who helped to clarify the actual application of the typology in a field situation.

meant to be complete but includes all tool types which have been found in significant numbers at Mousterian sites in France. In some cases, we have found that tools which occur in significant numbers in France either occur very rarely in the Northern Sudan or do not occur at all. These types have been left in the type list to facilitate graphic comparisons with European assemblages. In some cases, it has been found that variations occur at a given site which may be significant but which are not recognized by the type list. In these cases, the variations are described in the text, again, to avoid complications of graphic comparisons with European assemblages. The type list used for these studies is the following:

1. Levallois flakes, typical
2. Levallois flakes, atypical
3. Levallois points
4. Levallois points, retouched
5. Pseudo-Levallois points
6. Mousterian points
7. Mousterian points, elongated
8. Limaces
9. Side-scrapers, simple straight
10. Side-scrapers, simple convex
11. Side-scrapers, simple concave
12. Side-scrapers, double straight
13. Side-scrapers, double straight-convex
14. Side-scrapers, double, straight-concave
15. Side-scrapers, double biconvex
16. Side-scrapers, double biconcave
17. Side-scrapers, double convex-concave
18. Side-scrapers, convergent straight
19. Side-scrapers, convergent convex
20. Side-scrapers, convergent concave
21. Side-scrapers, *déjeté*
22. Side-scrapers, transverse straight
23. Side-scrapers, transverse convex
24. Side-scrapers, transverse concave
25. Side-scrapers, inversely retouched
26. Side-scrapers, abruptly retouched
27. Side-scrapers, thinned
28. Side-scrapers, bifacially retouched
29. Side-scrapers, alternately retouched
30. End-scrapers, typical
31. End-scrapers, atypical
32. Burins, typical
33. Burins, atypical
34. Borers, typical
35. Borers, atypical
36. Backed knives, typical
37. Backed knives, atypical
38. Natural backed knives
39. Raclettes
40. Truncated pieces
41. Mousterian tranchets
42. Notched pieces
43. Denticulate pieces
44. Bec burins
45. Inversely retouched pieces
50. Bifacially retouched pieces
51. Tayac points
52. Notched triangles
53. Pseudo-microburins
54. Pieces notched at the distal end
55. *Hachoirs*
56. Rabots
57. Pendunculate points
58. Pendunculate tools
59. Choppers
60. Inverse choppers
61. Chopping tools
62. Other tools (Varia).

In one place the typological list has been modified; we have eliminated types 46 through 49. These types include those flakes which have irregular, weak, or alternating retouch and are considered, at best, questionable tools (Bordes, 1961a, p. 45). Most of the assemblages from the Northern Sudan are surface concentrations with one flake piled on another. As the possibility that this irregularity of retouch was caused by natural disturbance is so high, it was felt that the inclusion of these types would introduce a potentially high error in the typological studies.

Within the type list of cores, we have added four core types which appear in significant numbers at Sudanese sites: Marginal cores (de Heinzelin, 1962, p. 8), including those cores which are struck in only one direction; para-Levallois cores (de Heinzelin, 1962, p. 9); Nubian Cores, Type I (Guichard and Guichard, 1965, p. 68); and Nubian Cores, Type II (Guichard and Guichard, 1964, p. 65). We have also found diminutive cores of all types, but these will be included under the general core types and will be described in the text.

A number of typological indices have been used. Again, these were developed by Bordes for the Mousterian of Western France (Bordes, 1953). The following indices are used:

IL^{ty} (Typological Levallois Index) = $\dfrac{\text{total number of Levallois flakes, blades, and points not made into retouched tools (types 1 through 4) x 100}}{\text{total number of retouched tools and unretouched Levallois pieces (types 1 through 62)}}$

$$IR \text{ (Side-scraper Index)} = \frac{\text{total number of side-scrapers (types 9 through 29) x 100}}{\text{total numbers of tools (types 1 through 62)}}$$

$$IC \text{ (Charentian Index)} = \frac{\text{total number of convex side-scrapers, limaces, and transverse scrapers (types 10, 8, 22-24) x 100}}{\text{total number of tools (types 1 through 62)}}$$

$$IA^u \text{ (Backed Knife Index)} = \frac{\text{total number of typical and atypical backed knives (types 36 and 37) x 100}}{\text{total number of tools (types 1 through 62)}}$$

$$IB \text{ (Biface Index)} = \frac{\text{total number of bifaces x 100}}{\text{total number of tools (types 1 through 62), plus bifaces}}$$

These same indices are again used for the restricted typology; that is, for the type list which counts only retouched tools. This eliminates unretouched Levallois pieces (types 1 to 3), and inversely retouched pieces (type 45). The indices are arrived at in the same manner as above but with the elimination of the types already mentioned.

In addition to the typological indices, there are four indices of "characteristic groups" (Bordes, 1953a), that is, those combined types which appear through experience to have major typological significance. They are as follows:

$$I \text{ (Levallois Group)} = \text{the same as } IL^{ty}$$

$$II \text{ (Mousterian Group)} = \frac{\text{types 5 through 29 x 100}}{\text{types 1 through 62}}$$

$$III \text{ (Upper Paleolithic Group)} = \frac{\text{types 30 through 37 x 100}}{\text{types 1 through 62}}$$

$$IV \text{ (Denticulate Group)} = \frac{\text{type 43 x 100}}{\text{types 1 through 62}}$$

The Characteristic Groups are also given for the restricted type list with the same deletions as those used in the restricted typological indices.

In addition to the complete and restricted typological lists, the Technological and Typological Indices, the Characteristic Group assemblages will also be shown in cumulative graphs.

These graphs facilitate gross visual comparisons between sites and will be based on the restricted typological lists.

GEOLOGY AND TOPOGRAPHY

The geology and topography from Firka to the Egyptian border have been described in detail in previous reports of the Combined Prehistoric Expedition (Solecki *et al.*, 1963; Guichard and Guichard, 1965; de Heinzelin and Paepe, 1965). Of particular concern to us is that part of the geology which predates the Nile silt deposits since no Nubian Middle Stone Age artifacts have ever been found, *in situ*, within them.

South of the Second Cataract, Nubian Middle Stone Age sites are extremely scarce. They are found on the tops of inselbergs in the Batn el-Hajar (Jebels Brinikol, Dal, and Firka), and along dykes of metamorphic rock (fig. 2). Both types of geological features are exceedingly rare in the Batn el-Hajar. The bulk of the landscape consists of granite and shale badlands, cut by wadis filled with eolian sand. Only on top of the inselbergs capped by ferrocrete sandstone and along the dykes is suitable material found for the manufacture of artifacts. It appears that wherever suitable raw material was available, it was utilized.

North of the Second Cataract, Nubian Middle Stone Age sites abound. The landscape is covered by inselbergs with ferrocrete sandstone present, an almost inexhaustible supply of raw material suitable for tool manufacture (fig. 3). The heavily desiccated sandstone landscape contains a series of features associated with the inselbergs: older rubble surfaces, younger pediments of 2.5 to 7.5 yellow/red colluvium, younger rubble surfaces, and a complex series of wadis and associated wadi terraces. The most important Middle Paleolithic finds occur on the tops of the inselbergs and, *in situ*, in the younger 7.5 yellow/red colluvium. Some sites have also been found on the older rubble surfaces at the foot of inselbergs, but these are not common and are not associated with the accumulation of rubble (fig. 4). Isolated finds of Nubian Middle Stone Age artifacts have been made on the younger rubble surfaces and in the wadis, but these are heavily wind abraded and rolled. No artifacts

Fig. 2—Dyke outcrop in the Batn el-Hajar.

were ever found *in situ* in or on the wadis or younger rubble surfaces.

While there are a vast number of inselbergs north of the Second Cataract, not all are capped by ferrocrete sandstone which is fine grained enough to be used in artifact manufacture. The quality of the ferrocrete sandstone varies from inselberg to inselberg. Generally, there are two main types of ferrocrete sandstone: a coarse, black, heavily weathered, porous stone quite unsuitable for tool manufacture, and a fine grained brown rock which fractures conchoidally. This latter ferrocrete sandstone was the preferred raw material used during the Nubian Middle Stone Age, although occasionally poorer qualities of ferrocrete sandstone were employed.

The brown, fine grained ferrocrete sandstone occurs in sheets, from 10 cm. to as much as 50 cm. in thickness. Normally, it is readily available

at the edges of the upper surfaces of the inselbergs (fig. 5). This type of ferrocrete sandstone is not present on all inselbergs. Its main outcrops occur in the Eastern Desert some 7 km. east of the Nile, and in smaller amounts on the row of inselbergs which fronts on the Nile in the area of Dibeira East. In this latter region, there is also a ferrocrete sandstone of poorer quality but which is still suitable for tool manufacture.

Other materials found at Nubian Middle Stone Age sites include small amounts of quartz pebbles and fossil wood, which are available in both the Eastern Desert behind Dibeira East and in the Western Desert behind Buhen.

Considering the distribution of the fine grained, brown ferrocrete sandstone in the Eastern Desert, it is not surprising that the inselbergs and older rubble surfaces, from 5 to 8 km. east of Wadi Halfa, are covered with Nubian Middle

FIG. 3—Inselbergs on the edge of the Eastern Desert.

Stone Age sites. The westernmost row of insel-bergs, facing the Nile on the east bank, south of Wadi Halfa, have few sites as there is little suit-able ferrocrete sandstone available. North of Wadi Halfa, however, this same row of insel-bergs does contain suitable raw material, and so, numerous sites are found in that area (fig. 6).

In short, Nubian Middle Stone Age sites are found only on the tops of inselbergs, on the older rubbles surfaces at the foot of the inselbergs, and occasionally, *in situ*, in the 5 to 7.5 yellow/red colluvium. These limited site situations may be accounted for in a number of ways.

The tops of inselbergs presented a potential threefold attraction: there was normally an im-mediately available supply of raw material for tool manufacture; the height of the inselbergs above the landscape brought a wide area into view; and the steep sides of the inselbergs per-mitted an easier defense of a camp site than if it were situated on the flat plain.

Sites on the older rubble surfaces were ad-

vantageous since they had suitable slabs of raw material, already broken into usable sizes, elimi-nating the necessity for actual quarrying of the ferrocrete sandstone cap.

Although only a few sites have been found, *in situ*, in the younger colluvium, they have all shown evidence of quarrying operations.

The relationship of these topographic features to other potential attractions has been obscured. It is quite impossible to reconstruct the old water sources or the distribution of vegetation, as today all is a heavily desiccated desert.

The advanced state of desiccation makes it impossible to say that during the Nubian Middle Stone Age man only lived in those localities where his sites are found today. There has been a radical change in environment since Nubian Middle Stone Age times, with the formation of countless wadis and a major deflation of the old land surfaces. Nubian Middle Stone Age sites which may have been situated on the then flat plain or near the major drainage systems would,

Fig. 4—Nubian Middle Stone Age site at the base of an inselberg, Eastern Desert.

by now, be scattered by deflation or by the occasional rains which result in flash floods in such an area.

The situations where the vast majority of Middle Stone Age sites have been found are exactly those which are least affected by flash flooding and wind deflation; thus, they are the most likely to survive intact.

Dating of the Nubian Mousterian

The placing of the Nubian Mousterian assemblages into a specific time range is a problem. Normally, dating of comparable Middle Paleolithic material is accomplished either through geological context or, more rarely, by radiocarbon age determination.

Unfortunately, the Nubian assemblages lack both stratigraphic position in the geology of the area and radiocarbon dates. Neither bone nor charcoal was ever found *in situ,* as the soil, being chemically acid, destroys organic materials. Most of the sites, however, were surface concentrations on the tops of inselbergs capped by ferrocrete sandstone. This typical site situation precludes any direct evidence for their absolute or even relative dating.

The single subsurface site, 1033, was within a 7.5 yellow/red colluvium on a low pediment near the Nile and cannot be accurately dated in relation to the whole geological picture nor even relative to the surface sites.

Therefore, it is quite impossible to use geological references for dating or for the ordering of the assemblages in time. The only possibility for dating the whole group of related assemblages is by typological and technological comparisons

Fig. 5—Natural slabs of ferrocrete sandstone at the edge of an inselberg (Site 1010-8).

with assemblages from other areas which have been, at least, relatively dated.

Paleoclimatic and Archaeological Evidence

The sites studied come from two areas: (1) in the pediments and on the tops of inselbergs which front on the east bank of the Nile; and (2) on the tops of inselbergs some seven kilometers east of the Nile, fully within the heavily desiccated Nubian Desert. These two areas have the greatest site density because of the availability of good raw material, but betweeen them there are sites on every inselberg which have raw material and even on many where suitable raw material is lacking.

As all these sites are either on the edge of, or fully within, what is now a total desert, it is implicit that they fall within a time when the local climate was different from that of today. Quite

apart from typological similarities with European material which roughly place these assemblages into a general time range, there is paleoclimatic and archaeological evidence for a terminal date.

The earliest silt deposits of the true Nile, the Dibeira-Jer formation, reach a maximum height of about 30 m. above the present floodplain at Wadi Halfa (Wendorf, Shiner, and Marks, 1965, p. xiii). Within this formation and directly under it, a series of sites have been found which form a distinct lithic industry, the Khormusan, more advanced than, but unlike, the Mousterian. A relatively early site in this sequence has been dated by radiocarbon at 20,750 B.C. ± 280 years (Wendorf, Shiner, and Marks, 1965, p. xxiv). On geological grounds it is estimated that the earliest phase of the Dibeira-Jer formation does not pre-date 30,000 B.C.

In spite of an extremely intensive survey of

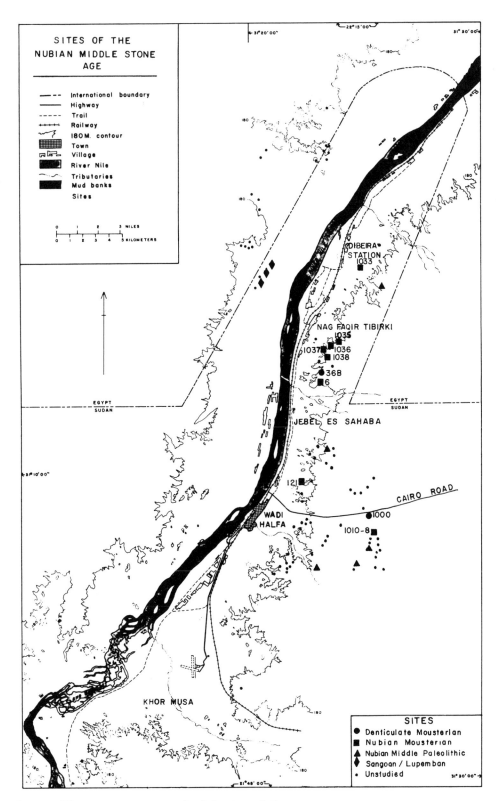

Fɪɢ. 6—Nubian Middle Stone Age sites north of the Second Cataract.

both the Nile silts and the surrounding Nubian desert, which took four years to complete, no Khormusan sites were ever found beyond the limits of the Dibeira-Jer formation, nor have any Mousterian artifacts ever been found within or directly under it. This differential distribution indicates a probable terminal date for the Nubian Mousterian in two ways.

As the Khormusan, which is well represented along the Nile, did not extend beyond the limits of the Dibeira-Jer formation, it is reasonable to assume that the surrounding area was already too dry to support man. The total absence of Mousterian artifacts directly under or in the Dibeira-Jer formation suggests that the Mousterian was no longer extant by 30,000 B.C. While this is somewhat recent, it is fully reasonable. Many Mousterian assemblages from other areas are known to date between 40,000 and 30,000 B.C. In Europe, at La Quina, France, Final Mousterian has been radiocarbon dated at 33,300 B.C. ± 530 years (Oakley, 1964, p. 166); and in the Levant the relatively late Levalloiso-Mousterian at Tabun has been dated from 38,000 to 37,500 B.C. (Garrod, 1962, p. 544). The latest date for the Mousterian in the Levant is 33,350 B.C. ± 500 years from Kebareh (Oakley, 1964, p. 166).

Thus, the evidence for an end to the Mousterian in Nubia prior to 30,000 B.C. only indicates that in its latter stages it may be generally synchronous with the Mousterian of Europe and the Near East. It is fully recognized that the evidence is purely negative. On the other hand, there is corresponding negative evidence from two unrelated industries. Perhaps more weight is given to this type of reasoning when it is considered that six major archaeological expeditions surveyed and excavated Paleolithic sites along the central Nile from 1961 until 1965, and there has not been one case where Middle Stone Age artifacts have been found directly associated with the Dibeira-Jer formation.

With the exception of a short time during the Neolithic, the Nubian Middle Stone Age is the last during which man inhabited the Nubian Desert. The desert conditions which today preclude human occupation possibly began somewhat before 30,000 B.C. If it is possible to follow Bernard (1959), strong interpluvial conditions

in the Sub-Equatorial regions began about 35,000 years ago. If this is correct, and the archaeological evidence from Nubia indicates that it is, the drying out of the Nubian Desert would have begun at this time. This is fully consistent with the probable end of the Mousterian in Nubia.

The process of desiccation must have been relatively slow. The presence of *Zootecus insularis* and termite nests in the paleosols associated with Nubian Middle Stone Age sites indicate a steppe environment. Sites found *in situ* in the Nile formations, up to 14,000 B.C., contain faunal remains including *Bos primagenius*, *Equus*, and Hartebeest. This suggests that some Savanna was still present at that recent date. On the other hand, the absence of sites in the desert during this period implies that there was not enough surface water available to support any prolonged human occupation.

The beginning of the Nubian Mousterian lacks all geological reference. A series of Acheulean stages have been recognized in the Nubian Desert (Guichard and Guichard, 1965), but there is no evidence for any temporal link between the late Acheulean and the Nubian Mousterian.

Therefore, any actual placement of the Nubian Mousterian assemblages into a temporal range, beyond the mere pre-30,000 B.C. date, can only be conjecture.

SITE REPORTS

As there are no stratigraphic or geological observations which might help group these assemblages into temporally similar units, it is necessary to rely on typological and technological studies without any internal time perspective.

A total of twelve assemblages from eleven sites were systematically collected and studied. In no case did any collection comprise the total number of tools and flakes from any one site. Sites were collected or excavated systematically to the extent that valid tool samples were obtained. One hundred retouched tools are considered a minimum valid sample by F. Bordes for the type of analysis employed here (Bordes, 1950, p. 23), and only those systematic collections containing at least that number of tools are fully reported.

Major technological or typological differences may be due to such factors as evolutionary change of one group through time or differences in activities performed at different sites by the same or different groups of people. Differences in typology and technology may also represent the traditions of distinctly different cultural groups.

Throughout the study of the Mousterian these factors are present. Unfortunately, it is only very recently that the first attempts to deal with these variables have been made. Techniques are still being evolved and sufficient work has not been done to make evaluation of the results possible.

Because of the unknown time range of the Mousterian in Nubia, the limited nature of the material evidence, and the total absence of a relative chronology, these variables cannot be dealt with satisfactorily. Typological and technological considerations must suffice in this study.

After extensive studies, the twelve Nubian Middle Stone Age assemblages have been placed into two major groups on the basis of their typological and technological attributes. One group has then been divided on the basis of the presence or absence of bifaces. The groups and the sites which represent them are as follows:

1. Denticulate Mousterian
        Sites: 1000
               36B
2. Nubian Mousterian
        Type A: without bifaces
               Sites: 1010-8
                      1035
                      1036
                      1037
                      1038
                      1033 Lower
                      1033 Upper
        Type B: with bifaces
               Sites: 6
                      121
                      Jebel Brinikol (?)

DENTICULATE MOUSTERIAN

SITE 1000

Site 1000 is situated on the top of a small inselberg some seven kilometers east of the Nile, on the southern edge of the Cairo Road (map ref. 658.4/196.1).[2] The inselberg is oval in plan

_____
[2] All map references are to Egypt—New Series 1:25,-000, printed by The Sudan Survey Department. April, 1960.

with a shelf around the whole perimeter near the top. Its upper surface comprises an area of about 1,000 sq. m. and is covered by very small fragments of a heavily weathered, black ferrocrete sandstone. These rest on, and partially in, a light tan, surficial powdery layer. On this surface, within a delimited area of 200 sq. m., there was a thick concentration of artifacts and debris made from a fine grained, brown ferrocrete sandstone.

The fine grained, brown ferrocrete sandstone is not found on the inselberg. The inselberg does contain ferrocrete sandstone, but, at its best, it is coarse, black, and poorly suited for tool manufacture. The fine grained material is available on inselbergs both to the south and north at a distance of less than 2 km.

Because of the heavy concentration of artifacts within a relatively small area, only a total area of 12 sq. m. was collected systematically. This was done in two adjacent 6 sq. m. areas located in the center of the concentration. The two areas produced a total of 1,042 pieces of fine grained brown ferrocrete sandstone. Of these, 184 were retouched tools, 565 were flakes or blades, 41 were cores, and the remainder consisted of debris, chips, and core manufacturing waste flakes.

Each systematic collection was studied separately and their technological indices were compared. When it was decided that they did, in fact, represent the same assemblage, they were grouped together and restudied both typologically and technologically.

TOOL TYPOLOGY

		No.	%	Restricted %
1	Levallois flakes, typical	33	17.9	
2	Levallois flakes, atypical	20	10.8	
5	Pseudo-Levallois points	2	1.1	1.6
10	Side-scrapers, convex	3	1.6	2.4
11	Side-scrapers, concave	1	0.5	0.8
25	Side-scrapers, inverse	4	2.2	3.2
28	Side-scrapers, bifacial	1	0.5	0.8
30	End-scrapers, typical	2	1.1	1.6
31	End-scrapers, atypical	1	0.5	0.8
33	Burins, atypical	1	0.5	0.8
34	Borers, typical	3	1.6	2.4
35	Borers, atypical	4	2.2	3.2
38	Cortex backed knives	5	2.7	4.0
39	Raclettes	1	0.5	0.8
40	Truncated pieces	1	0.5	0.8

		No.	%	Restricted %
42	Notched pieces	28	15.2	22.4
43	Denticulate pieces	60	32.4	48.0
44	Bec burins	2	1.1	1.6
45	Inversely retouched pieces	6	3.2	
53	Pseudo-microburins	2	1.1	1.6
54	Notched at the distal end	3	1.6	2.4
62	Varia	1	0.5	0.8
		184	99.3	100.0

Technological Indices

IL=14.3   IF=49.7   IFs=27.3   Ilame=13.9

Typological Indices and Characteristic Groups

IL^{ty}=28.7   IR=6.0   IC=1.6 IA^u=0.0   IB=0.0
I=28.7   II=7.2   III=5.9   IV=32.4

Restricted Typological Indices and Groups

IL^{ty}=0.0   IR=7.2   IC=2.4 IA^u=0.0   IB=0.0
I=0.0   II=9.6   III=8.0   IV=48.0

NOTES ON THE TYPOLOGY

Levallois flakes (53). Of the thirty-three typical Levallois flakes and blades recovered, only sixteen are complete (fig. 7, a-c, f). These are quite small and uniform in size: from 4 to 6.9 cm. in length.

Seven typical Levallois blades were found in this group. Only one flake even approaches a point in outline, but it certainly cannot be included in that category (fig. 7, d). Again, only one flake shows partial retouch (fig. 7, e).

Elaborate platform preparation does not seem to have been mandatory. Of the twenty-nine typical Levallois flakes which have their butts intact, eight are unfaceted.

The fourteen unbroken atypical examples show a greater range in size than do the typical Levallois flakes—from 3.3 to 8.2 cm.

Pseudo-Levallois points (2). Typical examples.

Side-scrapers, convex (3). The best shows a quality of retouch commensurate with the finest denticulates (fig. 7, h). The other two, however, are poor, with light marginal retouch along one lateral edge of broken flakes.

Side-scrapers, concave (1). The concave scraping edge is well formed by semi-steep retouch. The opposing edge is well denticulated. In effect, it is a convergent concave-denticulate scraper (fig. 7, g).

Side-scrapers, inverse (4). These form a poor group. There are one concave, one straight, and two convex side-scrapers. Retouch is semi-steep

but fairly light. No uniformity is apparent for these, except in their casual retouch.

Side-scrapers, bifacial (1). One fragment has flat retouch on one face and semi-steep retouch on the other. The scraping edge is markedly convex (fig 7, i).

End-scrapers (3). All three are nosed end-scrapers. One is on the distal end of the flake (fig. 7, j). One, made by inverse retouch, is on a lateral side of a flake, while the other is made on a projection of a rejected core.

Burins, atypical (1). This burin was made on the butt end of a false burin. A twisted burin spall was removed along the natural fracture plane of the false burin, forming a burin on a convex truncation. In this case, however, the truncation is no more than a section of the finely faceted butt of the original flake (fig. 8, d).

Borers (7). Four are short, heavy, pointed protrusions made by small notches and fine retouch at the distal ends of irregular flakes. One borer is on a core fragment (fig. 8, c), another is formed by inverse retouch (fig. 8, b), while the final one is rather large and made by careful retouch on a lateral edge of a large flake (fig. 7, k).

Cortex backed knives (5). All are on blades, the longest measuring 9.3 cm. (fig. 8, a).

Raclettes (1). A single example on a small flake.

Truncated pieces (1). An oblique truncation on a flake.

Notched pieces (28). Sixteen are micronotches, less than 1 cm. across. Of these, only two have been made by retouch, the remainder having been formed by single blows. Seven are inverse, nine obverse.

Twelve are macronotches, measuring over 1 cm. across. Of these, six have been formed by semi-steep retouch and six by single blows. All notches are relatively small, the largest not exceeding 1.5 cm. across.

Denticulate pieces (60). Denticulates are, by far, the most characteristic tool of this assemblage. With few exceptions, their retouch is of better quality than that of other tools. The most typical denticulate is made by retouch on one lateral edge of a flake or blade (figs. 8, f-h; 9, a, c). Other types also occur in some number as listed below (figs. 8, j-k; 9, b):

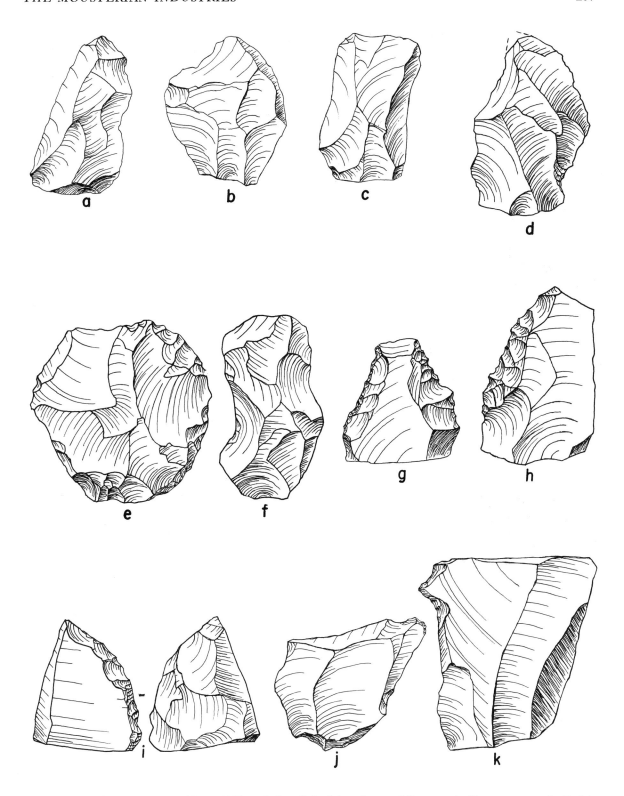

Fig. 7—Denticulate Mousterian (Site 1000): a-f, Levallois flakes (e, partially retouched); g, concave-denticulate scraper; h, convex scraper; i, bifacially retouched scraper fragment; j, nosed scraper; k, borer. 4/5 natural size.

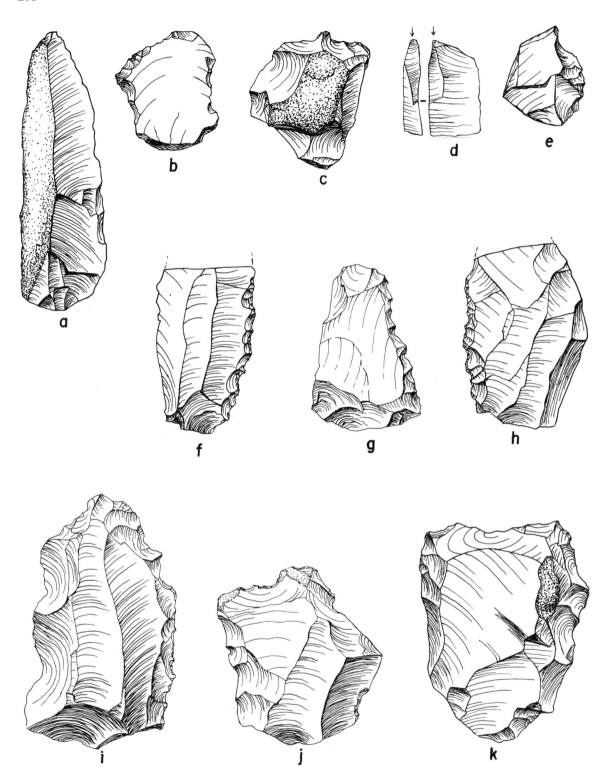

FIG. 8—Denticulate Mousterian (Site 1000): a, cortex backed knife; b-c, borers; d, burin; e, pseudo-microburin; f-k, denticulates. 4/5 natural size.

1. Lateral denticulates made by percussion, 19. Of these, eight are on blades and four are inverse.

2. Lateral denticulates made by retouch, 25. Twenty of these are microdenticulate, yet only five are inverse. All but six are made on flakes.

3. There are also three microdenticulates on cores; two bilaterally obverse, microdenticulates on blades; one inverse microdenticulate on a flake; seven denticulates on the distal ends of flakes; three convergent denticulates on flakes.

Only two denticulates have additional typological features. One lateral denticulate, on a large flake, has two macronotches formed by single blows on the edge opposite the denticulation (fig. 8, i). The other complex tool involving denticulation has been classified under concave side-scraper as this is the least common feature, although it also has a well retouched lateral denticulation (fig. 7, g).

Bec burins (2). Both are poor examples.

Inversely retouched pieces (6). All are flakes with part of one lateral edge inversely retouched. None shows strong enough nor consistent enough retouch to be classified as an inverse side-scraper.

Pseudo-microburins (2). Both are quite typical (fig. 8, e).

Notched at the distal end (3). One is an obverse micronotch made by a single blow. The other two are inverse micronotches, one made by a single blow, the other by retouch.

Varia (1). This tool is a heavy Levallois flake with a thick, square distal end. There is fine, flat, inverse retouch at the distal end and partially down one lateral edge. The retouch does not significantly thin the distal end.

CORE TYPOLOGY

	No.	%
Levallois		
Levallois blade	3	7.3
Levallois flake	17	41.4
Para-Levallois	3	7.3
Other		
Marginal	6	14.9
Discoidal	1	2.4
Unidentifiable	11	26.8
	41	100.1

NOTES ON THE TYPOLOGY

A total of forty-one cores and core fragments were collected. Two of these have been classified as denticulates but will also be considered here as their original function and form were that of cores.

Levallois blade (3). Only three were recovered. One, which was struck, measures 8 cm. in length and has had rough treatment of the lower surface but careful preparation of the upper surface. The other two are in the range of diminutive Levallois cores, measuring only 5.5 and 5.3 cm. in length and have typical tortoise backs. Neither has been struck and the upper surface preparation is rough, forming low convex tops.

Levallois flake (17). Seventeen Levallois flake cores were collected. These include struck, unstruck, and partially prepared cores. Finished Levallois flake cores, both struck and unstruck, account for fifteen of the total. Two quite distinct groups can be seen: ten are rectangular in shape with exceedingly flat upper surfaces (fig. 9, d); the other five are triangular in outline with rather steep convex upper surfaces (fig. 9, g). These may well be classified as Levallois point cores but there is no evidence of a successfully removed Levallois point. All had been struck but in every case the flake either had come off prematurely or had hinge fractured. Also, no Levallois points were found among the artifacts.

The size range on all the finished Levallois flake cores is from 4 cm. to 8 cm. Ten are diminutive, measuring under 5.5 cm. in length.

Para-Levallois (3). These are true Levallois flake cores but they have been struck across the long axis, instead of along it (de Heinzelin, 1962, p. 9). Of the three, two are particularly fine examples which show the removal of short, broad Levallois flakes (fig. 9, f). The third piece is quite rough and utilizes a natural fracture plane as a platform. These fall into the same size range as the Levallois cores described above, all measuring under 5 cm. in length.

Marginal (6). Six marginal cores were collected. These are fragments of ferrecrete sandstone with one natural fracture plane which is about 90° to one surface. The fracture plane has been used as a platform for the removal of a series of flakes, all struck in one direction. One measures 6 cm. in length but three others measure less than 4.5 cm. The longest example meas-

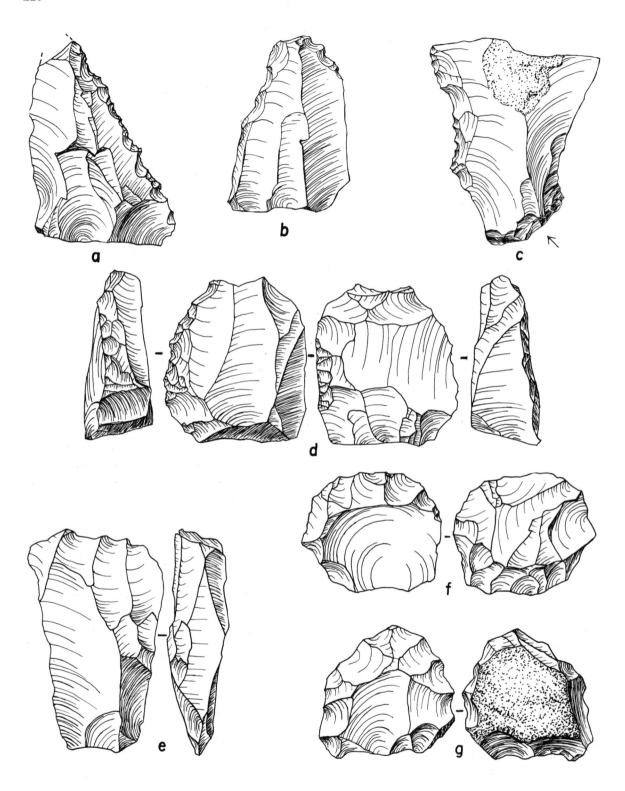

FIG. 9—Denticulate Mousterian (Site 1000): a-c, denticulates; d, g, Levallois cores (d, unstruck); e, marginal blade core; f, para-Levallois core. 4/5 natural size.

ures 7.5 cm. in length and shows the removal of a series of blades (fig. 9, e).

Discoidal (1). One rather large partial discoidal core shows bifacial flaking. It measures 7 cm. in diameter.

Unidentifiable (11). Various pieces of ferrocrete sandstone which have been flaked but which show no clear pattern.

SITE 36B

Site 36B is situated on a long inselberg which forms part of the line which fronts on the east bank of the Nile, north of Wadi Halfa. The inselberg is on the north edge of a large wadi which lies just north of Jebel es-Sahaba (map ref. 925.8/654.0).

When first visited during the 1961-1962 field season, the whole top of the inselberg was covered by clearly delimited areas of artifact concentration. During the 1962-1963 field season, the Guichards collected a large number of these (Guichard and Guichard, 1965, p. 98), but did not reach the southeastern area of the top. It was on this portion that Site 36B was located. It covered an area of about 200 sq. m. with an even and fairly dense concentration of artifacts. There was no evidence of any prior collecting within it. The site extended to the eastern edge of the inselberg, but very few artifacts were seen on the slope.

Two areas were collected systematically: one of 3 sq. m. and an adjacent area of 6 sq. m. These were studied separately and found to be the same technologically. In fact, in no case were the technological indices more than 3 per cent apart.

In the 9 sq. m. systematically collected, a total of 690 artifacts were collected. Of these, 164 were retouched tools, 439 were flakes and blades, 39 were cores, and the remainder consisted of chips, debris, and core manufacturing waste flakes.

TOOL TYPOLOGY

		No.	%	Restricted %
1	Levallois flakes, typical	13	7.9	
2	Levallois flakes, atypical	10	6.1	
5	Pseudo-Levallois points	2	1.2	1.5
9	Side-scrapers, straight	3	1.8	2.2
10	Side-scrapers, convex	4	2.4	2.9
11	Side-scrapers, concave	6	3.7	4.4

		No.	%	Restricted %
16	Side-scrapers, biconcave	1	0.6	0.7
17	Side-scrapers, convex-concave	1	0.6	0.7
23	Side-scrapers, transverse convex	1	0.6	0.7
25	Side-scrapers, inverse	5	3.0	3.6
29	Side-scrapers, alternate retouch	1	0.6	0.7
31	End-scrapers, atypical	5	3.0	3.6
33	Burins, atypical	2	1.2	1.2
35	Borers, atypical	4	2.4	2.9
37	Backed knives, atypical	1	0.6	0.7
38	Cortex backed knives	3	1.8	2.2
40	Truncated pieces	9	5.5	6.6
42	Notched pieces	24	14.6	17.5
43	Denticulate pieces	43	26.2	31.3
44	Bec burins	6	3.7	4.4
45	Inversely retouched pieces	4	2.4	
51	Tayac points	2	1.2	1.5
52	Pseudo-microburins	2	1.2	1.5
54	Notched at the distal end	6	3.7	4.4
62	Varia	6	3.7	4.4
		164	99.7	99.6

Technological Indices

IL=11.6   IF=33.6   IFs=20.6   Ilame=11.6

Typological Indices and Characteristic Groups

IL^{ty}=14.0   IR=13.3   IC=3.0 IA^{u}=0.6   IB=0.0
I=14.0   II=14.8   III=7.2   IV=26.2

Restricted Typological Indices and Groups

IL^{ty}=0.0   IR=15.8   IC=3.6 IA^{u}=0.7   IB=0.0
I=0.0   II=17.4   III=8.7   IV=31.3

NOTES ON THE TYPOLOGY

Levallois flakes (23). These are small and rather roundly prepared. Most of them tend to be short (fig. 10, a-b), although semi-elongated (fig. 10, d) and para-Levallois flakes also occur.

Pseudo-Levallois points (2). Two small, poor examples.

Side-scrapers, straight (3). All are on broken flakes and have mediocre, marginal retouch.

Side-scrapers, convex (4). Again, retouch is marginal and poor (fig. 10, c). Not one could be considered even an average example.

Side-scrapers, concave (6). These are mostly on broken flakes and the quality of retouch is only somewhat better than that on the convex scrapers. Two have inverse notches on the lateral edge, opposite the scraper (fig. 10, e).

Side-scrapers, biconcave (1). This piece is better made than most. Retouch is semi-steep and the scraping edges are well defined (fig. 10, g).

FIG. 10—Denticulate Mousterian (Site 36B): a-b, d, Levallois flakes; c, e, atypical side-scrapers; f, i, end-scrapers; g, biconcave scraper; h, j, inverse scrapers; k, borer; l, burin; m, basal truncation; n, truncated denticulate; o-p, double notches; q, notch. 4/5 natural size.

Side-scrapers, convex-concave (1). A poor example on a small, broken flake.

Side-scrapers, transverse convex (1). Slightly over half of the transverse edge has light retouch, while the other section of the same edge has a steep inverse retouch. The joining point, however, does not form a true bec burin.

Side-scrapers, inverse (5). There are three convex, one straight (fig. 10, j), and one concave scraper. All are on small flakes with rather flat retouch. One of the convex scrapers approaches an inverse angle scraper on an inversely truncated Levallois flake (fig. 10, h).

Side-scrapers, alternate retouch (1). This is a poorly made and broken converging convex scraper.

End-scrapers, atypical (5). End-scrapers are on small, irregular flakes and, in one case, on a blade (fig. 10, i). Retouch on all is marginal and somewhat irregular (fig. 10, f).

Burins, atypical (2). There is one burin *plan* on a snapped blade (fig. 10, 1), and a questionable angle burin on a flake fragment.

Borers, atypical (4). Two are roughly formed on the lateral edges of broken flakes by small retouched notches. Two others are on the ends of irregular flakes and formed by steep retouch (fig. 10, k).

Backed knives, atypical (1). This is a broken Levallois blade which has partial inverse and partial obverse backing along one lateral edge.

Cortex backed knives (3). Two of these are on flakes rather than blades.

Truncated pieces (9). There are three oblique truncations on flakes and one inverse, oblique truncation on a broken Levallois blade. In addition, there are three basally truncated flakes (fig. 10, m), one of which has some lateral inverse retouch and an inverse notch on the same edge. There are also three straight truncations, two of which are on thick blades. One of these blades has a light serrating retouch on one lateral edge and cortex on the other (fig. 10, n).

Notched pieces (24). Notches are a common feature in this assemblage. Inverse and obverse, single notches are about equal in number: nine inverse and twelve obverse. There are also three double notches on small blades (fig. 10, o). One of these also has some inverse marginal retouch on the edge opposite the notches (fig. 10, p).

Four inverse macronotches are made by retouch (fig. 10, q), and two by single blows. All five inverse micronotches are formed by single blows.

Seven of the twelve obverse notches are micro, that is, less than 1 cm. across. Four of these are formed by retouch and three by percussion. Two macronotches are formed by single blows and three by retouch (fig. 11, a).

As a group, the notches are well made and fairly deep. Only a very few could have been accidental.

Denticulate pieces (43). While the most numerous tool type, the denticulates are poorly made. Included in this group are some of the largest tools (fig. 11, k), and some of the smallest (fig. 11, c). One denticulate is on a fragment of fossil wood—the only non-ferrecrete sandstone tool in the assemblage.

Thirty-two denticulates are on one lateral edge of various sized flakes. Of these, eight are inversely formed by retouch (fig. 11, b-c), two are obversely retouched, and twenty-two are formed by obverse percussion (fig. 11, d-e, h, k). There are also five transverse denticulates, one bilateral, two lateral and transverse (fig. 11, f), and three at the distal end of flakes. None are truly macrodenticulate, but the serrations are, as a rule, quite irregular and poorly formed.

Bec burins (6). There are two good examples, one of which is on a large flake (fig. 11, 1), and four poorly formed examples.

Inversely retouched pieces (4). These are flakes which have a small amount of inverse retouch but where it is not consistent enough to form inverse scrapers.

Tayac points (2). Two very good examples (fig. 11, j).

Pseudo-microburins (2). Two typical examples, one of which was inversely notched.

Notched at the distal end (6). All are on small flakes and are formed by single blows.

Varia (6). There are four flakes with opposed notches, one example having opposed inverse notches (fig. 11, i). There is one broken flake which has a deep inverse notch, a bec burin, and inverse retouch, all on the same lateral edge. Another has unopposed notches, one on each lateral edge, and a partial oblique truncation and has been purposefully snapped.

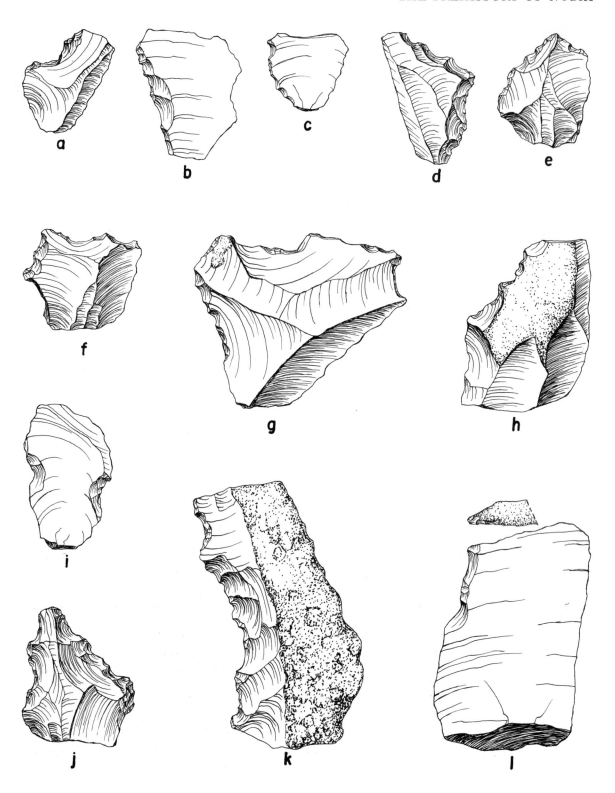

Fig. 11—Denticulate Mousterian (Site 36B): a, macronotch; b-h, k, denticulates; i, opposed, inverse notches; j, Tayac point; l, bec burin. 4/5 natural size.

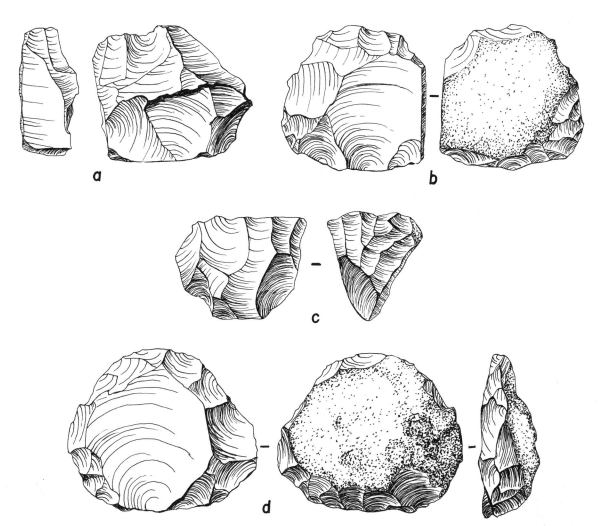

FIG. 12—Denticulate Mousterian (Site 36B): a, c, marginal cores; b, d, Levallois flake cores. 4/5 natural size.

CORE TYPOLOGY

	No.	%
Levallois		
Levallois blade	1	2.6
Levallois flake	9	23.7
Para-Levallois	6	15.8
Other		
Marginal	9	23.7
Globular	1	2.0
Unidentifiable	13	33.2
	39	101.0

NOTES ON THE TYPOLOGY

Levallois blade (1). A small, mediocre example.

Levallois flake (9). Most are quite small and short. They tend toward oval or pointed forms (fig. 12, b, d). Preparation is usually rough, although some good examples occur.

Para-Levallois (6). All are mediocre and quite small.

Marginal (9). These are small and all have been struck from opposing edges (fig. 12, a). One approaches a true blade core (fig. 12, c).

Globular (1). One small example.

Unidentifiable (13). These show no discernable pattern of flaking, although all have numerous flake scars.

NUBIAN MOUSTERIAN, TYPE A

SITE 1010-8

Site 1010-8 lies on a small finger of a large inselberg some 7 km. east of the Nile and 3 km. south of the Cairo Road (map. ref. c:115.3/659.6). The finger is no more than 8 m. long and less than 4 m. wide, extending toward the northwest. The site consisted of a very heavy concentration of artifacts on the surface of the finger, particularly on the western half. There were no artifacts on the jebel proper, directly adjacent to the finger. A small number were on the southwestern slope, indicating a certain amount of erosion of that area. Even considering this erosion of the edge, the site could never have occupied more than about 50 sq. m., bounded by steep cliffs on three sides. The artifacts were extremely fresh and were up to 4 cm. deep in a light tan surficial layer. Artifacts were made from a fine grained, brown ferrocrete sandstone, available at the edge of the finger.

This site is of interest because of its limited size and position which almost entirely ruled out any mixing of assemblages, and because it is in the area where numerous Nubian Middle Paleolithic sites were found. This assemblage did not appear to belong to that industry, and detailed study has placed it with those assemblages usually found closer to the Nile.

Initially, 2 sq. m. were collected systematically. This collection was used for the technological studies. Later, an additional 4 sq. m. were collected as the first tool sample was too small. In the first 2 sq. m. which were systematically collected, a total of 341 pieces of ferrocrete sandstone were collected. Of these, 50 were retouched tools, 175 were flakes, and 17 were cores, while chips, debris, and core manufacturing waste flakes made up the remainder.

TOOL TYPOLOGY

		No.	%	Restricted %
1	Levallois flakes, typical	15	8.7	
2	Levallois flakes, atypical	13	7.5	
3	Levallois points	1	0.6	
5	Pseudo-Levallois points	2	1.1	1.5
9	Side-scrapers, convex	6	3.5	4.5
10	Side-scrapers, concave	4	2.3	3.0
16	Side-scrapers, biconcave	2	1.1	1.5
17	Side-scrapers, convex-concave	1	0.6	0.8
19	Side-scrapers, convergent convex	1	0.6	0.8
21	Side-scrapers, déjeté	1	0.6	0.8
25	Side-scrapers, inverse	7	4.0	5.3
30	End-scrapers, typical	6	3.5	4.5
31	End-scrapers, atypical	7	4.0	5.3
32	Burins, typical	1	0.6	0.8
33	Burins, atypical	2	1.1	1.5
34	Borers, typical	5	2.9	3.8
35	Borers, atypical	5	2.9	3.8
39	Raclettes	1	0.6	0.8
40	Truncated pieces	13	7.5	9.8
42	Notched pieces	16	9.2	12.1
43	Denticulate pieces	24	13.9	18.2
44	Bec burins	8	4.6	6.1
45	Inversely retouched pieces	12	6.9	
51	Tayac points	2	1.1	1.5
54	Notched at the distal end	10	5.8	7.6
62	Varia	8	4.6	6.1
		173	99.8	100.1

Technological Indices

IL=25.4   IF=30.8   IFs=21.8   Ilame=3.5

Typological Indices and Characteristic Groups

IL^{ty}=16.8   IR=12.7   IC=3.5 IA^u=0.0   IB=0.0
I=16.8   II=13.8   III=15.1   IV=13.9

Restricted Typological Indices and Groups

IL^{ty}=0.0   IR=16.7   IC=4.5 IA^u=0.0   IB=0.0
I=0.0   II=18.2   III=19.7   IV=18.2

NOTES ON THE TYPOLOGY

Levallois flakes (28). There is a great variation in the size of the Levallois flakes. The largest measure between 8.5 and 9.6 cm. in length, while the smallest fall between 2.5 and 3 cm. As a group, they are thin, with rather flat bulbs of percussion (fig. 13, a-b). The larger examples, however, do have prominent bulbs and thick butts.

Levallois points (1). There is one extremely elongated point, measuring 11.5 cm. in length.

Pseudo-Levallois points (2). Two typical examples (fig. 13, e).

Side-scrapers, convex (6). These are well made and have mostly semi-steep retouch. One piece with flatter retouch is on a cortex backed knife (fig. 13, h). Four good examples are on Levallois flakes, one of which is also notched at the distal end. One partially truncated piece has both a convex and concave scraping section on the same edge, but the convex part predominates (fig. 13, f).

Side-scrapers, concave (4). The concave scrapers are poorly made by semi-steep retouch on rather large flakes. One has a deep notch on the opposite lateral edge (fig. 13, c).

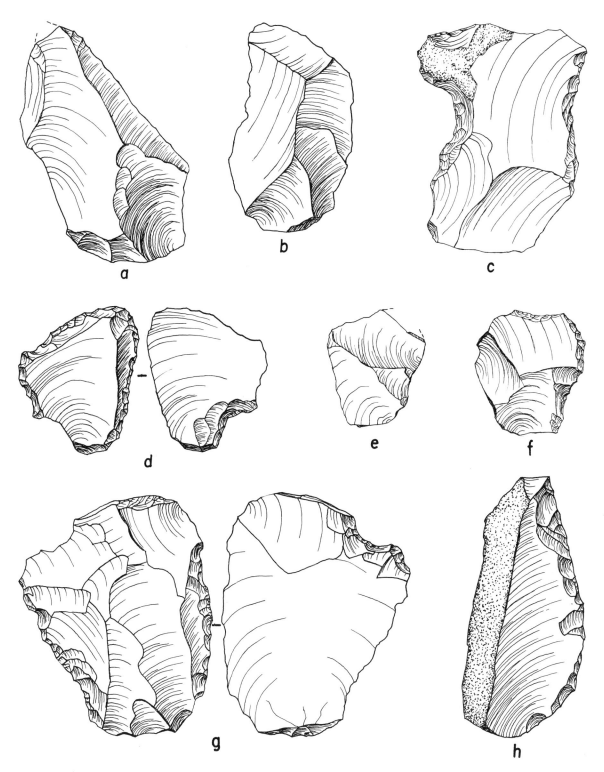

FIG. 13–Nubian Mousterian, Type A (Site 1010-8): a-b, Levallois flakes; c, atypical concave scraper with opposed notch; d, notched *déjeté* scraper; e, pseudo-Levallois point; f, h, convex scrapers; g, convex-concave scrapers, notched. 4/5 natural size.

Side-scrapers, biconcave (2). There are two with steep retouch on one edge and semi-steep retouch on the other (fig. 14, i). One has a bec burin on the end of the semi-steep retouched scraping edge.

Side-scrapers, convex-concave (1). This piece is a Levallois flake which, in addition to the scraping edges, is partially truncated and has an inverse macronotch located at its distal end (fig. 13, g).

Side-scrapers, convergent convex (1). This scraper has normal retouch on one edge and semi-steep retouch on the other. It approaches a Mousterian point but seems too thick at the butt to be a true point (fig. 14, a).

Side-scrapers, déjeté (1). One example is on a small flake which has a deep inverse notch by the butt. It approaches an asymmetric end-scraper but two sides are fully retouched (fig. 13, d).

Side-scrapers, inverse (7). The inversely retouched scrapers are on flakes which range in size from 2.7 to 7.6 cm. in length. There are four convex (fig. 14, c), and three concave examples. All retouch is semi-steep, forming generally even scraping edges. The smallest is on an intentionally snapped flake (fig. 15, b).

End-scrapers (13). End-scrapers form an important element in this assemblage. There are some exceedingly fine examples, but none is made on a true blade. There are two typical nosed scrapers (fig. 15, f), and four typical end-scrapers on flakes. One of these has a partially truncated base (fig. 14, b). Another has a denticulate edge adjacent to the end-scraper (fig. 14, f). The atypical examples include five partially formed nose scrapers and two irregular end-scrapers on flakes.

Burins (3). There is one typical burin on a straight, partial truncation (fig. 15, e), and two poorly made burins: an angle burin on a broken flake and a burin on a convex truncation. This latter piece is on a laminary flake and the burin spalls are both small and quite flat, almost forming a sort of burin *plan* on a truncation (fig. 15, c).

Borers (10). The borers mostly have short boring tips at the corners or ends of large flakes. There are four of this type made by inverse retouch, four by normal retouch (fig. 14, d), and

one by alternate retouch. In addition, there is one example with a long but fairly thick boring tip which approaches a long, thin nose scraper (fig. 14, g).

Raclettes (1). One concave scraper made by marginal retouch on a small flake.

Truncated pieces (13). Truncations are found mostly on rather small flakes, although one is on a flake 10.8 cm. long. There is one basal truncation; four straight truncations (fig. 16, b); five straight, oblique truncations; and three straight, oblique, inverse truncations.

Notched pieces (16). Notches occur mostly on large flakes. Of the sixteen notches, only three are micronotches: two obverse and one inverse, all formed by single blows. There are two particularly large notches, measuring between 3 and 4 cm. across. These have been initially formed by percussion but all show some use retouch (fig. 16, e). In addition, there are five retouched macronotches: three obverse and two inverse. There are also four inverse and two obverse macronotches formed by single blows.

Denticulate pieces (24). Denticulates are generally well made. They are on both flakes and blades, although those on blades are very rare. Denticulates range in size from 12.4 to only 3.5 cm. in length. Most of them, however, are not at the extremes. There are two main groups of denticulates: lateral and distal end.

Of the total seven are at the distal ends of flakes (fig. 16, c). The others are formed by percussion on the sides of thick flakes (fig. 16 a, d).

Bec burins (8). Bec burins are generally poor. One good example is a triple bec on a flake (fig. 15, d).

Inversely retouched pieces (12). Small amounts of inverse retouch which are not continuous enough or long enough to form true scraping edges.

Tayac points (2). One is on the lateral side of a triangular flake. Perhaps it is more of a lateral, converging denticulate (fig. 14, h). The other is more typical.

Notched at the distal end (10). There are four macronotches formed by retouch, three obverse and one inverse. There are also six obverse micronotches, all but one retouched.

Varia (8). There are five pieces with opposed

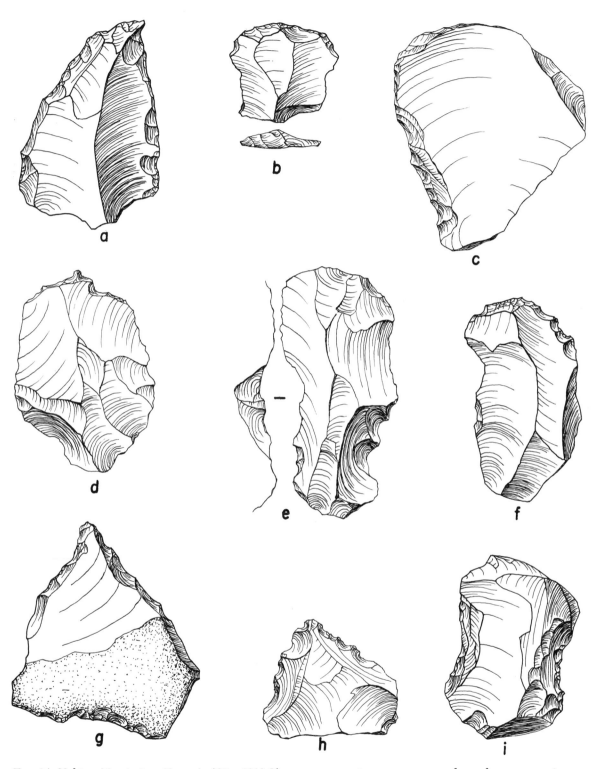

FIG. 14—Nubian Mousterian, Type A (Site 1010-8): a, convergent convex scraper; b, end-scraper; c, inverse scraper; d, g, borers; e, opposed notches; f, end-scraper—denticulate; h, Tayac point; i, biconcave scraper. 4/5 natural size.

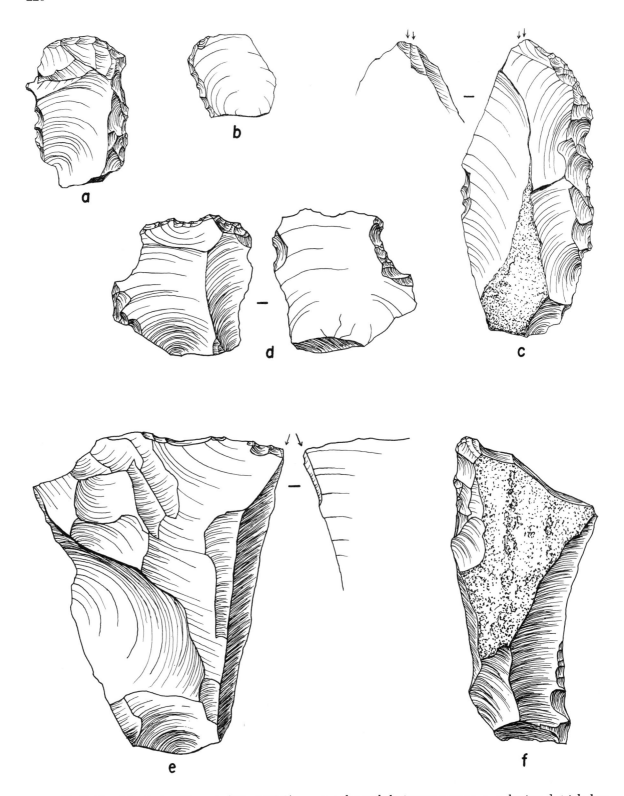

FIG. 15—Nubian Mousterian, Type A (Site 1010-8): a, complex tool; b, inverse scraper; c, e, burins; d, triple bec burin; f, nosed scraper. 4/5 natural size.

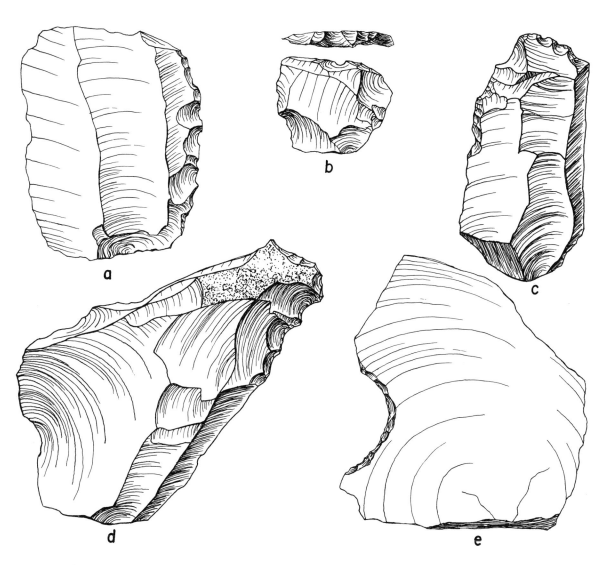

FIG. 16—Nubian Mousterian, Type A (Site 1010-8): a, c-d, denticulates; b, truncated flake; e, macronotch. 4/5 natural size.

notches. Two of these fall into the true strangled blade class. One of these is strangled by alternately retouched double notches (fig. 14, e). The other three examples do not really cut into the flakes sufficiently to strangle them.

In addition, there are three highly complex tools. There is a Levallois flake which is partially backed on one edge. It has a denticulate on the opposed edge and a large bec burin on the denti-

culated edge. There is also a short flake which has a typical end-scraper at the distal end, backing on one lateral edge and a denticulation and borer on the other edge (fig. 15, a). The third complex tool is a Levallois flake with an oblique truncation and an adjoining straight side-scraper, some inverse retouch on the opposed edge, a notch at the distal end, and a bec burin by the butt.

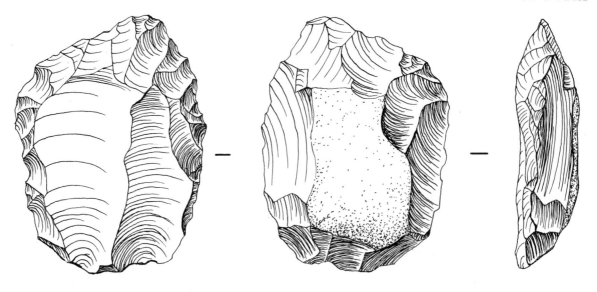

Fig. 17—Nubian Mousterian, Type A (Site 1010-8): Levallois blade core. 4/5 natural size.

CORE TYPOLOGY

	No.	%
Levallois		
Levallois blade	1	5.9
Levallois flake	5	29.4
Nubian, Type I	2	11.7
Para-Levallois	2	11.7
Other		
Marginal	1	5.9
Unidentifiable	6	35.3
	17	99.9

NOTES ON THE TYPOLOGY

In the 2 sq. m. collected for the technological study, only seventeen cores were recovered. In the additional four square meters which were collected systematically only for finished tools, more cores were found. These, however, are not included in the count below.

Levallois blade (1). There is one good example (fig. 17).

Levallois flake (5). These are well prepared on both faces (fig. 18, a-b). They range in size from 5.5 to 10.8 cm. in length, but the majority fall into the 8 to 9 cm. range. One is unstruck and shows careful preparation and an even, if marked, convex top.

Nubian, Type I (2). Two rather small examples, measuring 6.3 and 7.3 cm. in length. Both are struck, but neither shows the careful preparation typical of the Levallois flake cores.

Para-Levallois (2). These show less preparation on the under surface than the Levallois flake cores. They measure 6.5 and 7.6 cm. in length. Both were successfully struck.

Marginal (1). One large slab has a number of laminary flakes struck from a natural fracture plane.

Unidentifiable (6). Large cores which showed no particular pattern of flaking.

SITE 1035

Site 1035 is situated on the northwest finger of a large inselberg 1.4 km. southeast of Nag Faqir Tibirki, in the village of Dibeira East (map. ref. 927.4/654.6). The site is a surface concentration covering an area of some 100 sq. m. along the center of the finger. Few artifacts were found within two meters of the edges. The artifacts were in a sharply delimited concentration, but its density was not particularly heavy. The artifacts rested on, and in, a light tan, surficial layer.

An initial systematic collection was made from 24 sq. m. A subsequent systematic collection from 12 sq. m. was made as the number of finished tools from the first collection was inadequate. Thus, a total of 36 sq. m. was systematically collected.

All artifacts were made on a fine grained,

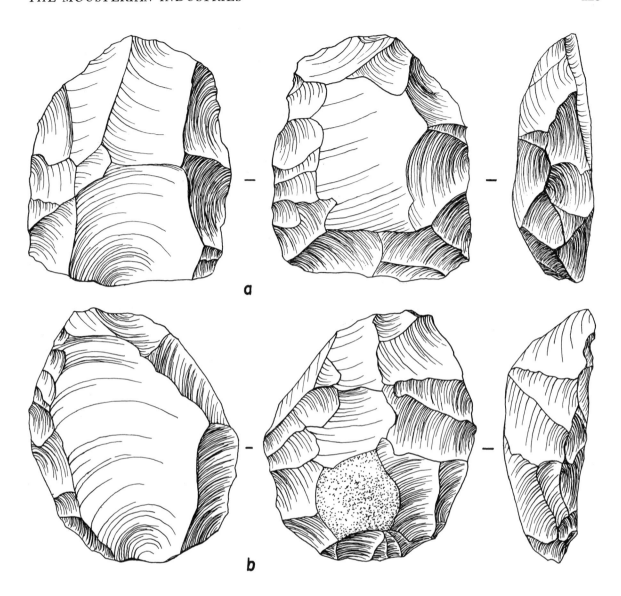

FIG. 18—Nubian Mousterian, Type A (Site 1010-8): a-b, Levallois flake cores. 4/5 natural size.

brown ferrocrete sandstone which was apparently unavailable on the inselberg. The only immediately available ferrocrete sandstone seen was coarse, black, and poorly suited for tool manufacture.

Even during the initial collecting of the site, it was obvious that the artifacts were quite different from the bulk of those associated with Nubian Middle Stone Age sites. The striking feature was the diminutive size of the flakes and cores, quite apart from their typological attrib-

utes. Later in the season, other sites with similar sized artifacts were encountered. This size problem will be discussed later as it forms one of the more puzzling aspects of the Middle Paleolithic studies in the northern Sudan.

A total of 841 pieces of ferrocrete sandstone were collected. Of these, 180 were retouched tools or Levallois flakes, 490 were flakes or blades, 138 were cores and core fragments, while the remainder were core manufacturing waste flakes and debris.

TOOL TYPOLOGY

		No.	%	Restricted %
1	Levallois flakes, typical	30	16.7	
2	Levallois flakes, atypical	34	18.9	
3	Levallois points	2	1.1	
5	Pseudo-Levallois points	2	1.1	1.8
9	Side-scrapers, straight	1	0.6	0.9
10	Side-scrapers, convex	3	1.6	2.7
11	Side-scrapers, concave	4	2.2	3.6
16	Side-scrapers, biconcave	1	0.6	0.9
19	Side-scrapers, convergent convex	1	0.6	0.9
21	Side-scrapers, *déjeté*	3	1.6	2.7
25	Side-scrapers, inverse	1	0.6	0.9
29	Side-scrapers, alternate retouch	4	2.2	3.6
30	End-scrapers, typical	2	1.1	1.8
31	End-scrapers, atypical	6	3.3	5.4
32	Burins, typical	2	1.1	1.8
33	Burins, atypical	1	0.6	0.9
34	Borers, typical	3	1.6	2.7
35	Borers, atypical	3	1.6	2.7
37	Backed knives, atypical	3	1.6	2.7
38	Cortex backed knives	2	1.1	1.8
39	Raclettes	1	0.6	0.9
40	Truncated pieces	12	6.6	10.8
42	Notched pieces	15	8.3	13.5
43	Denticulate pieces	22	12.3	19.8
44	Bec burins	6	3.3	5.4
45	Inversely retouched pieces	3	1.6	
51	Tayac points	1	0.6	0.9
53	Pseudo-microburins	1	0.6	0.9
54	Notched at the distal end	5	2.8	4.5
62	Varia	6	3.3	5.4
		180	99.8	99.9

Technological Indices

$IL = 21.7$ $IF = 69.3$ $IFs = 38.6$ $Ilame = 7.8$

Typological Indices and Characteristic Groups

$IL^{ty} = 36.7$ $IR = 10.1$ $IC = 2.2$ $IA^u = 1.6$ $IB = 0.0$
$I = 36.7$ $II = 11.2$ $III = 10.9$ $IV = 12.5$

Restricted Typological Indices and Groups

$IL^{ty} = 0.0$ $IR = 15.8$ $IC = 3.6$ $IA^u = 2.7$ $IB = 0.0$
$I = 0.0$ $II = 17.6$ $III = 18.0$ $IV = 19.8$

NOTES ON THE TYPOLOGY

Levallois flakes (64). The outstanding feature of these unretouched flakes in their diminutive size (fig. 19, a-c). They range in length from 2.5 to 5.2 cm. Only three pieces, however, measure over 5 cm. and only three measure under 3 cm. This clearly makes them diminutive in size. As a group they are well made. While the typical Levallois flake is quite thin, it also has a rather prominent bulb of percussion (fig. 19, d).

Levallois points (2). Only two diminutive examples were found. Both are somewhat atypical (fig. 19, e).

Pseudo-Levallois points (2). Both are typical and diminutive (fig. 19, h).

Side-scrapers, straight (1). A well made example on an elongated flake (fig. 19, f).

Side-scrapers, convex (3). Two are on broken flakes and one is on a snapped flake. Two are well made by semi-steep retouch (fig. 19, i), while the other has only marginal retouch.

Side-scrapers, concave (4). The concave side-scrapers have indifferent retouch. The largest example is just under 4 cm. in length.

Side-scrapers, biconcave (1). This example is on a snapped Levallois flake. Retouch is semi-steep and there is a micronotch made by percussion near the butt. It measures under 4 cm. in length.

Side-scrapers, convergent convex (1). This piece is not typical. It is actually a convergent convex-denticulate scraper on a Levallois flake. However, it has been placed here as the convex side is the determining factor. It is one of the largest tools, measuring 6.6 cm. in length.

Side-scrapers, *déjeté* (3). There is one typical example on a broken flake, measuring 2.5 cm. in length (fig. 19, g). The other two are atypical examples on elongated flakes, measuring 5.3 and 5.6 cm. in length.

Side-scrapers, inverse (1). There is one simple convex side-scraper made by semi-steep, inverse retouch on a diminutive, broken flake.

Side-scrapers, alternate retouch (4). Two are questionable *déjeté* scrapers made with alternate retouch on Levallois flakes (fig. 19, n) while the other two are convergent scrapers made by alternate retouch. These are also on Levallois flakes. The former measure under 5 cm., while the latter both measure 5.6 cm. in length.

End-scrapers (8). One typical example is on a complex tool. The scraper is a well formed nose scraper but there is also a convex denticulated edge (fig. 19, o). The other is also a typical, if somewhat wide, nose scraper. There are a number of atypical examples. There is one poorly made nose scraper and a series of roughly formed convex end-scrapers on odd shaped flakes. One, on a blade, measures 6.8 cm. in length, but the others are all on diminutive flakes.

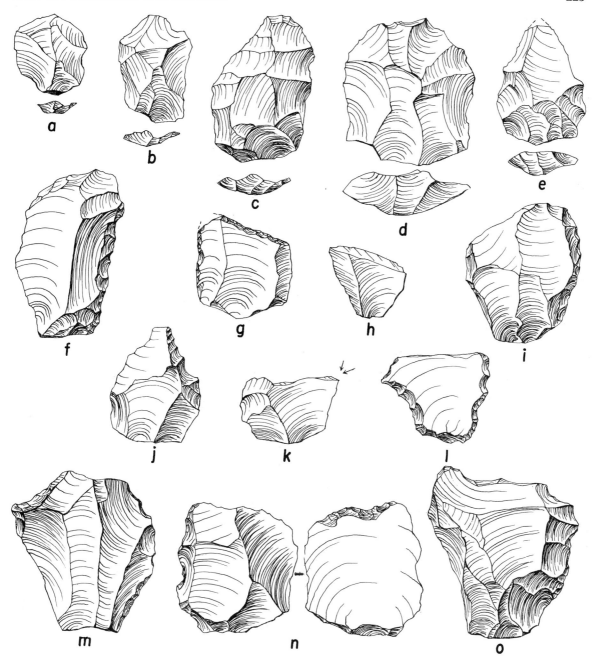

Fɪɢ. 19—Nubian Mousterian, Type A (Site 1035): a-d, Levallois flakes; e, Levallois point; f, straight scraper; g, *déjeté* scraper; h, pseudo-Levallois point; i, convex scraper; j, truncation; k, burin; l, borer-denticulate; m, borer; n, poor alternate scraper; o, end-scraper—denticulate. 4/5 natural size.

Burins (3). There is one quite typical dihedral burin (fig. 19, k), while the other typical example is a burin on a snapped blade. The atypical example is an angle burin on a broken flake, but it is poorly formed. All are diminutive.

Borers (6). Three are on the lateral sides of flakes, made by alternately retouched notches. One of these, on a snapped flake, has an inverse denticulate edge opposite the borer (fig. 19, 1). Another borer is on a flake measuring 6 cm. in length and is formed by two inversely retouched notches. Another is on a thick flake fragment. There is also one on a truncated flake and another on a Levallois flake which has a partial convex scraper on the opposed edge (fig. 19, m).

Backed knives, atypical (3). All are on short flakes. Retouch is steep to semi-steep. None is well made and each is somewhat questionable (fig. 20, g).

Cortex backed knives (2). Both are elongated flakes.

Raclettes (1). One transverse raclette was found.

Truncations (12). There are two basal truncations on Levallois blades (fig. 20, e). Three Levallois flakes have inverse concave truncations, one flake has a straight obverse truncation and one has an obverse concave truncation. In addition, there are five oblique truncations, one of which is reminiscent of a simple truncated Sebilian flake (fig. 19, j). All but three are diminutive.

Notched pieces (15). There are eight pieces with obverse macronotches and three with inverse macronotches, all made by single blows (fig. 20, a). There are also three retouched, obverse macronotches and one inverse, retouched macronotch. Only one notch is on a flake which measures over 5 cm. in length.

Denticulate pieces (22). The denticulates come closest to being normal sized tools. Of the twenty-two examples, nine measure over 5 cm. in length and two of these measure between 8 and 9 cm.

There are two convergent denticulates, one of which measures 8 cm. (fig. 20, i). The other converges laterally like a *déjeté* scraper and is formed by alternate percussion (fig. 20, k).

There are seven lateral, obverse macrodenticulates made by percussion (fig. 20, j), and six transverse macrodenticulates made by percussion, two of which are also notched (fig. 20, h). In addition, there are seven microdenticulates made by retouch; of these, four are obverse and three inverse.

Bec burins (6). There are six typical examples (fig. 20, b). One flake also has a transverse denticulate edge. All but one are diminutive.

Inversely retouched pieces (3). Small amounts of inverse retouch on odd shaped flakes.

Tayac points (1). One small example (fig. 20, c).

Pseudo-microburins (1). One typical example.

Notched at the distal end (5). There are two obverse macronotches and two obverse micronotches, all made by percussion. There is also one inverse micronotch made by retouch.

Varia (6). There are three strangled flakes, one of which is also truncated (fig. 20, d). There is also a flake with both basal and distal truncation in addition to a lateral inverse denticulation. Other pieces include a fragment of a backed and inversely retouched flake and a flake which has a deep, inversely retouched area near the butt and an obliquely denticulated edge joining the inverse retouch:

CORE TYPOLOGY

	No.	%
Levallois		
Levallois blade	2	1.4
Levallois flake	53	38.4
Levallois point	4	2.9
Nubian, Type I	29	21.0
Nubian, Type II	3	2.1
Para-Levallois	7	5.0
Other		
Marginal	3	2.1
Discoidal	5	3.6
Unidentifiable	32	23.2
	138	99.7

NOTES ON THE TYPOLOGY

Levallois blade (2). Two diminutive examples.

Levallois flake (53). There are two recognizable groups. One is roughly rectangular in shape with sharp corners, almost forming a square when seen from above (fig. 21, c), with upper surfaces well prepared and just slightly convex. The second group is triangular to pointed ovate (fig. 21, a).

Levallois point (4). These are some of the few typical Levallois point cores found in Middle Paleolithic context (fig. 21, b). Normally, points seem to have been produced on the Nubian Core, Type I.

Nubian, Type I (29). Again, the Nubian Cores, Type I, are diminutive. Only two of a total of twenty-nine measure as much as 5.3 cm. in length. The others vary from 2.6 to 5 cm.

Nubian, Type II (3). Only one is diminutive.

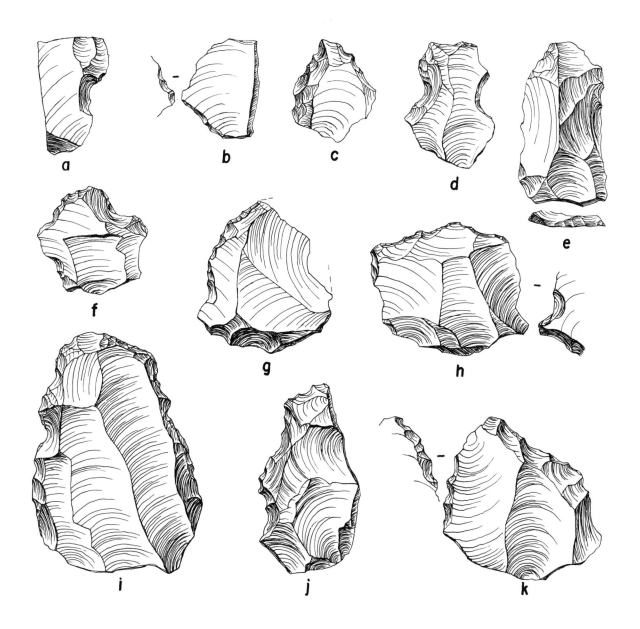

Fig. 20—Nubian Mousterian, Type A (Site 1035): a, notch; b, bec burin; c, Tayac point; d, strangled flake; e, basal truncation; f, denticulates; g, atypical backed knife; h-k, denticulates. 4/5 natural size.

Para-Levallois (7). Seven diminutive examples were found. They are all well prepared.

Marginal (3). Three typical, diminutive examples.

Discoidal (5). One large, partially bifacial core and four peripheral unifacial cores were recovered.

Unidentifiable (32). These cores showed no particular pattern of flaking, nor was there any similarity within the group itself.

SITE 1036

Site 1036 is situated on the southwest finger of a large inselberg 1.7 km. southeast of Nag Faqir Tibirki, in the village of Dibeira East (map ref. 927.3/654.6). It consisted of a loose surface con-

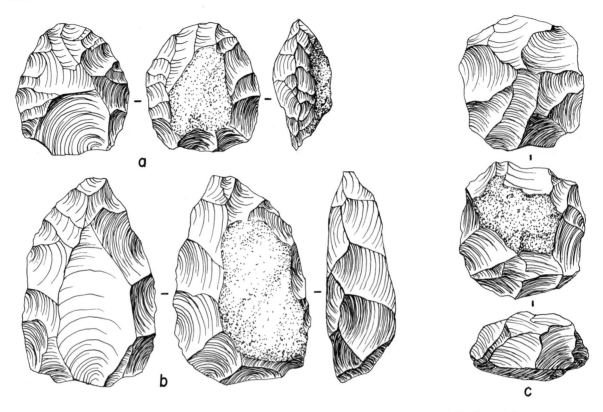

Fɪɢ. 21—Nubian Mousterian, Type A (Site 1035): a, c, Levallois flake cores (c, unstruck); b, Levallois point core. 4/5 natural size.

centration, without depth, covering an area of about 200 sq. m. This surface concentration covered most of the finger which is isolated from the main inselberg top by a narrow saddle. The saddle is some 40 m. in length extending eastward from the finger to the inselberg proper. Site 1037 is situated on the finger, but only on its most eastern part. Sites 1036 and 1037 are separated by no less than 30 m. of the saddle which was totally devoid of artifacts.

Initially, a 6 sq. m. area was systematically collected. As there was not a large enough tool sample in this collection, two additional collections were made. The second collection was systematically made over 20 sq. m. and the third covered 15 sq. m. Only the first two collections were used in the technological studies.

In the first two systematic collections artifacts totaling 1,101 were collected. Of these, 135 were tools, 717 were flakes, 45 were cores, and the remainder was debris, chips, and core manufacturing waste flakes. An additional 100 re-

touched tools and Levallois flakes were collected in the third area.

A striking feature of this site was the apparent small size of the finished tools. As a group they seemed to be among the smallest found and quite similar to those at Site 1035 which was situated on another finger of the same inselberg. An additional feature was the presence of very few tools made on heavily patinated Nile pebble, fossil wood, and quartz.

TOOL TYPOLOGY

		No.	%	Restricted %
1	Levallois flakes, typical	13	5.5	
2	Levallois flakes, atypical	11	4.7	
5	Pseudo-Levallois points	1	0.4	0.5
9	Side-scrapers, straight	4	1.7	2.0
10	Side-scrapers, convex	8	3.4	4.0
11	Side-scrapers, concave	6	2.6	3.0
12	Side-scrapers, double straight	1	0.4	0.5
13	Side-scrapers, double straight-convex	2	0.8	1.0
15	Side-scrapers, biconvex	2	0.8	1.0

		No.	%	Restricted %
17	Side-scrapers, double convex-concave	1	0.4	0.5
19	Side-scrapers, convergent convex	1	0.4	0.5
21	Side-scrapers, *déjeté*	4	1.7	2.0
22	Side-scrapers, transverse straight	1	0.4	0.5
25	Side-scrapers, inverse	13	5.5	6.6
29	Side-scrapers, alternate retouch	8	3.4	4.0
30	End-scrapers, typical	5	2.1	2.5
31	End-scrapers, atypical	7	3.0	3.5
32	Burins, typical	1	0.4	0.5
33	Burins, atypical	3	1.3	1.5
34	Borers, typical	8	3.4	4.0
35	Borers, atypical	7	3.0	3.5
36	Backed knives, typical	1	0.4	0.5
37	Backed knives, atypical	2	0.8	1.0
38	Cortex backed knives	4	1.7	2.0
39	Raclettes	4	1.7	2.0
40	Truncated pieces	20	8.5	10.2
42	Notched pieces	26	11.0	13.2
43	Denticulate pieces	24	10.2	12.2
44	Bec burins	10	4.3	5.1
45	Inversely retouched pieces	14	5.9	
53	Pseudo-microburins	6	2.6	3.0
54	Notched at the distal end	7	3.0	3.5
62	Varia	10	4.3	5.1
		235	99.7	99.4

Technological Indices

IL=4.9   IF=52.6   IFs=25.6   Ilame=3.2

Typological Indices and Characteristic Groups

IL^{ty}=10.2   IR=21.6   IC=3.8 IA^u=1.2   IB=0.0
I=10.2   II=22.0   III=14.4   IV=10.2

Restricted Typological Indices and Groups

IL^{ty}=0.0   IR=23.6   IC=4.5 IA^u=1.5   IB=0.0
I=0.0   II=24.1   III=17.0   IV=12.2

NOTES ON THE TYPOLOGY

Levallois flakes (24). Over half of these are broken, two perhaps intentionally. Of the ten whole examples, five are diminutive. As a group, butts are thick and there are large bulbar scars. The majority appear to be indifferently prepared (fig. 22, b), and for the most part are elongated (fig. 22, a).

Pseudo-Levallois points (1). One example which has a small amount of semi-steep retouch.

Side-scrapers, straight (4). All are diminutive with straight scraping edges made by marginal retouch. One has an additional, very weak oblique truncation (fig. 22, i).

Side-scrapers, convex (8). All but one are made on broken flakes (fig. 22, f). Retouch indicates that the scrapers were retouched after the breaking as it often encroaches on the broken edge (fig. 22, d). All are diminutive, made by semi-steep retouch.

Side-scrapers, concave (6). Again, all are on broken, diminutive flakes; of these three appear to have been intentionally snapped. Retouch is somewhat flatter than on the convex scrapers (fig. 22, c). One particularly nice example is on a heavily patinated flake of Nile pebble (fig. 22, e).

Side-scrapers, double straight (1). This piece is on a Levallois blade which also has a slightly irregular, partial truncation. The retouched scraping edges are somewhat irregular and retouch varies from semi-steep to normal.

Side-scrapers, double straight-convex (2). Both are intentionally snapped diminutive flakes. Retouch is weak and marginal.

Side-scrapers, biconvex (2). Both are on intentionally snapped, diminutive flakes. One has a slightly denticulated convex scraping edge on one side and a well formed convex scraping edge on the other. The other is formed by marginal retouch on one edge and by semi-steep on the other.

Side-scrapers, double convex-concave (1). One example on a snapped flake which has semi-steep retouch.

Side-scrapers, convergent convex (1). A slightly asymmetric example with somewhat ragged scraping edges (fig. 22, g).

Side-scrapers, *déjeté* (4). Four poor diminutive examples made by semi-steep retouch (fig. 22, 1). One has an inversely retouched micronotch on the unretouched lateral edge.

Side-scrapers, transverse straight (1). One diminutive piece which has a small borer on one end of the transverse edge (fig. 22, m).

Side-scrapers, inverse (13). Inverse side-scrapers are, by far, the most common scraper in this assemblage. They range in size from 2.6 to 6.9 cm. in length, with eleven in the diminutive range. Retouch varies from semi-steep to flat. There are two straight, eight convex (fig. 22, j), one concave and two questionably *déjeté* (fig. 22, h). Only four of the thirteeen are on broken flakes.

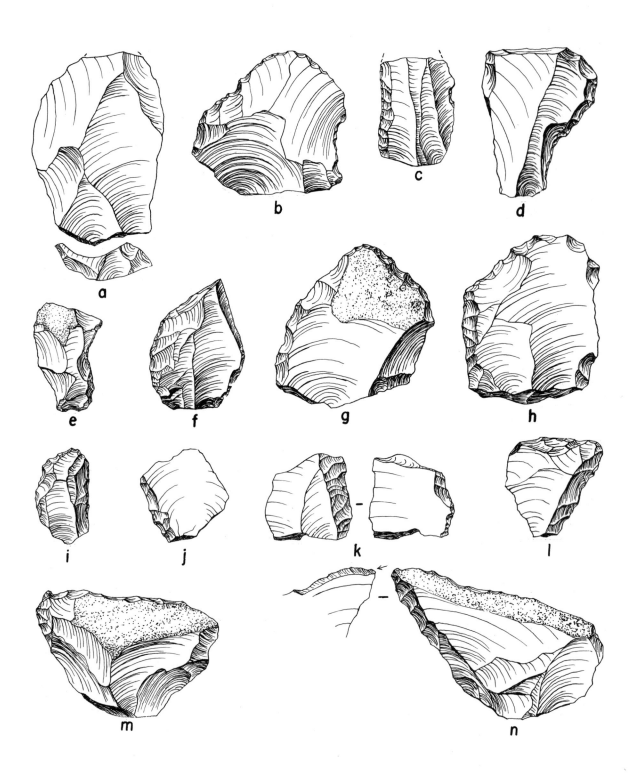

FIG. 22—Nubian Mousterian, Type A (Site 1036): a-b, Levallois flakes; c, e, concave scrapers; d, f, convex scrapers; g, convergent convex scraper; h, l, atypical *déjeté* scrapers; i, straight scraper; j, inverse scraper; k, alternate scraper fragment; m, transverse straight scraper; n, burin. 4/5 natural size.

Side-scrapers, alternate retouch (8). Five of the eight are on broken flakes and all but one are diminutive. This is a relatively poor group, including what appears to be scraper fragments (fig. 22, k).

End-scrapers (12). Typical end-scrapers include one carinated scraper on fossil wood (fig. 23, m), two thick nose scrapers, and two end-scrapers on flakes (fig. 23, c). Three fall into the diminutive range. Atypical examples include partially or poorly retouched end-scrapers; four thin nose scrapers and three end-scrapers on flakes. All but two are diminutive.

Burins (4). There is a typical transverse burin on a truncation (fig. 22, n), two poor burins on truncations and one questionable angle burin (single blow) on a short flake.

Borers (15). The typical examples are well made by retouch either at the distal end or the corner of diminutive flakes (figs. 23, g; 24, b). The atypical pieces are similar but not as well formed. Only one is on a flake which measures over 5 cm. in length.

Backed knives (3). The typical example is on a broken, elongated flake. The other two are on Levallois flakes (fig. 23, a). All measure between 5 and 6 cm. in length.

Cortex backed knives (4). Two are on blades and two on flakes.

Raclettes (4). There are two convex, one straight, and one concave raclette. All are formed by marginal retouch on flakes which measure under 1.9 cm. in length (fig. 23, f).

Truncated pieces (20). There are four with basal truncations (fig. 23, h); eight with oblique truncations (fig. 23, b), five of which are also notched; and eight with straight truncations. All but one are on diminutive flakes or blades.

Notched pieces (26). Notches are found on flakes and blades which range in length from 2.9 to 9 cm. With the exception of four blades, however, all are diminutive.

There are two inverse retouched and six obverse retouched micronotches. In addition, there are six obverse and six inverse micronotches made by single blows, as well as six inverse macronotches made in the same manner.

Denticulate pieces (24). Denticulates are generally roughly formed on odd shaped flakes.

They range in length from 2.6 to 7 cm. All but one are microdenticulates. There are four transverse denticulates, one of which was formed by retouch; fourteen lateral denticulates (fig. 23, d), of which five are inverse (fig. 23, k); three denticulates at the distal ends of the flakes; two lateral converging denticulates, one of which is formed by alternate percussion; and one double, lateral denticulate which also is formed by alternate percussion.

Bec burins (10). These are only fair. One large flake has a nice example on a corner of an inverse scraper (fig. 23, l). All but two are diminutive.

Inversely retouched pieces (14). A good number of flakes have small amounts of inverse retouch which is not continuous enough to form inverse scrapers. Ten have this retouch adjacent to the butt, often being concave, approaching notches.

Pseudo-microburins (6). Six typical examples.

Notched at the distal end (7). All are micronotches, two obverse and five inverse. One inverse and one obverse are made by retouch, the rest by single blows.

Varia (10). There are two strangled flakes, one of which has a borer at the distal end, and a strangled blade (fig. 23, e). There is a quartz flake with an inversely retouched, asymmetric point, and there is also an inverse angle scraper on a small flake.

In addition, there are a number of complex tools. There is one flake with basal and oblique truncations, a notch, and some flat inverse retouch at the point of juncture between the oblique truncation and the notched edge (fig. 24, c).

There is a Levallois flake with a convex side-scraper on one edge, a thin nose-like scraper and two wide retouched notches. The scraping edge and the notched edge converge (fig. 23, j). It is almost a converging convex-concave side-scraper.

There is a flake with inverse retouch, a bec burin, and a partial truncation and another which is similar but also has a denticulated lateral edge.

The final piece has two notches, an inversely retouched scraping edge and an obverse, convex scraping edge (fig. 23, i).

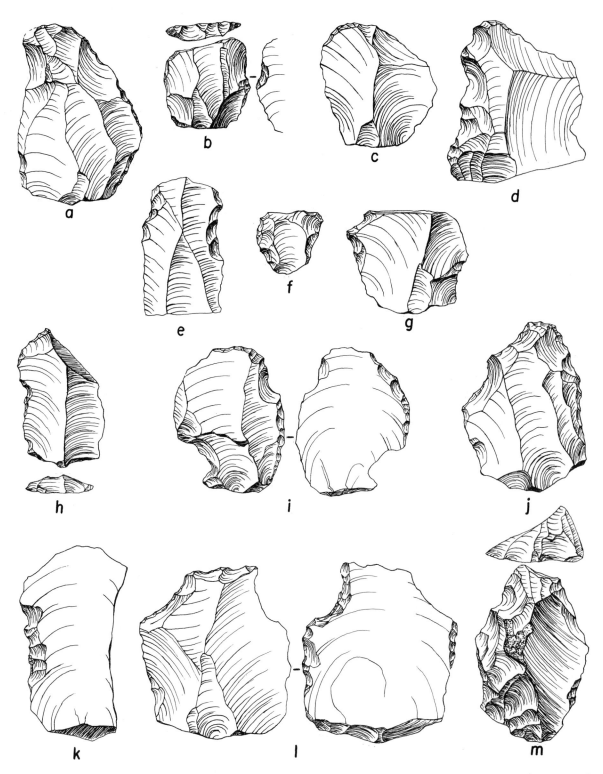

Fig. 23—Nubian Mousterian, Type A (Site 1036): a, backed knife; b, h, truncations; c, m, end-scrapers; d, k, denticulates; e, strangled blade; f, raclette; g, borer; i-j, complex tools; l, double bec burin. 4/5 natural size.

CORE TYPOLOGY

	No.	%
Levallois		
Levallois flake	14	31.4
Levallois point	1	2.2
Para-Levallois	3	6.6
Other		
Marginal	8	17.7
Discoidal	8	17.7
Globular	1	2.2
Isolated flake	1	2.2
Unidentifiable	9	20.0
	45	100.0

NOTES ON THE TYPOLOGY

Levallois flake (14). As a group they are roughly prepared. All are diminutive (fig. 24, a) and one is formed on a heavily patinated Nile pebble.

Levallois point (1). One very poor, diminutive example.

Para-Levallois (3). Diminutive examples (fig. 24, e).

Marginal (8). These are small; two are struck from opposed platforms (fig. 24, d), the others from single natural fracture planes.

Discoidal (8). There are four unifacial discoidal cores, three measuring between 6 and 7 cm. in diameter. Another is on a heavily patinated Nile pebble. The rest are broken but recognizable.

Globular (1). One diminutive example.

Isolated flake (1). One diminutive example.

Unidentifiable (9). These are all diminutive, showing no particular pattern of flaking. There are three, however, which have faceted platforms but no other preparation prior to the removal of the main flakes. Two unidentifiable cores are on fossil wood.

SITE 1037

Site 1037 is situated on an inselberg 1.7 km.

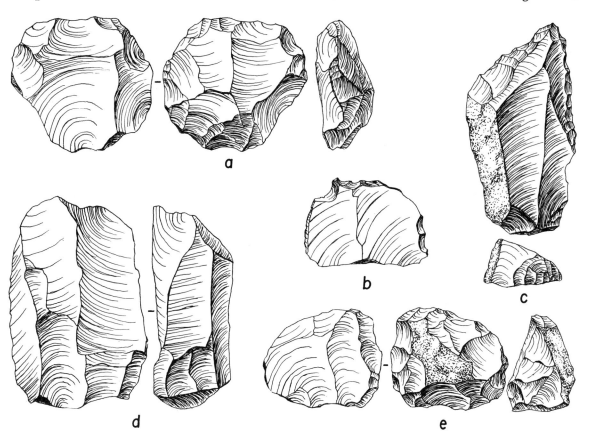

FIG. 24—Nubian Mousterian, Type A (Site 1036): a, e, Levallois flake cores; b, borer; c, complex tool; d, marginal blade core. 4/5 natural size.

southeast of Nag Faqir Tibirki, in the town of Dibeira East (map. ref. 927.3/564.8). The site is a surface concentration on a shallow saddle between the inselberg proper and a finger which extends toward the Nile.

The saddle was less than 10 m. wide and 40 m. long. The concentration covered an area of about 60 sq. m. on the eastern end of the saddle. There was an extremely dense concentration of artifacts and debris. The raw material was of a rather low quality ferrocrete sandstone which was available at the edge of the saddle in thin, natural slabs. The artifacts rested on the surface and were up to 6 cm. in a light tan surficial layer.

Because of the heavy concentration, initial systematic collections were made from only 2 sq. m. Subsequently, an additional area was systematically collected for only Levallois flakes and tools.

The initial impression of the material was that there were large numbers of thick short flakes and even a few tools made on natural fragments of ferrocrete sandstone. Technique of debitage appeared undeveloped, and Levallois flakes seemed to be rare. These observations were, for the most part, confirmed by detailed study, although retouched tools were quite similar to other Middle Paleolithic sites in the area.

The first systematic collections recovered 546 pieces of ferrocrete sandstone. Of these 99 were tools, 200 were flakes, 36 were cores, and the remainder consisted of debris, chips, and manufacturing waste flakes.

TOOL TYPOLOGY

		No.	%	Restricted %
1	Levallois flakes, typical	11	6.3	
2	Levallois flakes, atypical	6	3.4	
3	Levallois points	2	1.1	
9	Side-scrapers, straight	2	1.1	1.3
10	Side-scrapers, convex	5	2.8	3.3
11	Side-scrapers, concave	2	1.1	1.3
16	Side-scrapers, biconcave	1	0.6	0.7
17	Side-scrapers, double convex-concave	2	1.1	1.3
21	Side-scrapers, *déjeté*	6	3.4	3.9
24	Side-scrapers, transverse concave	1	0.6	0.7
25	Side-scrapers, inverse	6	3.4	3.9
26	Side-scrapers, abrupt	3	1.7	2.0
29	Side-scrapers, alternate retouch	8	4.6	5.3
30	End-scrapers, typical	6	3.4	3.9

		No.	%	Restricted %
31	End-scrapers, atypical	9	5.1	5.9
32	Burins, typical	3	1.7	2.0
33	Burins, atypical	5	2.8	3.3
34	Borers, typical	6	3.4	3.9
35	Borers, atypical	4	2.3	2.6
36	Backed knives, typical	2	1.1	1.3
37	Backed knives, atypical	6	3.4	3.9
38	Cortex backed knives	6	3.4	3.9
39	Raclettes	2	1.1	1.3
40	Truncated pieces	8	4.6	5.3
42	Notched pieces	18	10.3	11.2
43	Denticulate pieces	19	10.8	12.5
44	Bec burins	5	2.8	3.3
45	Inversely retouched pieces	5	2.8	
51	Tayac points	1	0.6	0.7
53	Pseudo-microburins	1	0.6	0.7
54	Notched at the distal end	7	4.0	4.6
62	Varia	8	4.6	5.3
		176	100.0	99.3

Technological Indices

IL = 11.6   IF = 43.0   IFs = 15.4   Ilame = 6.0

Typological Indices and Characteristic Groups

IL^{ty} = 10.8   IR = 19.8   IC = 3.4   IA^u = 4.5   IB = 0.0
I = 10.8   II = 19.8   III = 23.6   IV = 10.8

Restricted Typological Indices and Groups

IL^{ty} = 0.0   IR = 23.7   IC = 4.0   IA^u = 5.2   IB = 0.0
I = 0.0   II = 23.7   III = 26.8   IV = 12.5

NOTES ON THE TYPOLOGY

Levallois flakes (17). As a group, these are roughly prepared and most are struck slightly off the apparent prepared axis (fig. 25, n-o). Bulbs of percussion vary from flat to pronounced, while the butts are mostly well prepared. Six of the seventeen measure over 5 cm. in length, including one Levallois blade. Two appear to have been intentionally snapped, although it is very difficult to see this on even slightly eolized ferrocrete sandstone.

Levallois points (2). Both are very rough questionable examples.

Side-scrapers, straight (2). Both are on flakes covered by cortex. Retouch is relatively steep, verging on semi-steep (fig. 25, e, h).

Side-scrapers, convex (5). These show a pattern repeated in most tool categories: a mixture of diminutive and large pieces. One very rough example measures 9.3 cm. in length, while the others are all under 3.7 cm. Retouch is semi-steep and at least two are made on intentionally snapped flakes (fig. 25, b).

Side-scrapers, concave (2). One piece measures 6.3 cm. in length, while the other is only 2.9 cm. The large example is roughly retouched, but the smaller piece is well retouched and has a bec burin at one end of the scraping edge (fig. 25, a).

Side-scrapers, biconcave (1). One edge has a large concave scraper made by steep retouch, while the other lateral edge has a rather poor concave edge made mostly by marginal retouch. The scraper is on a thick primary flake which measures 5.5 cm. in length.

Side-scrapers, double convex-concave (2). Both are on intentionally snapped flakes. Retouch on both is semi-steep and the scraping edges are quite regular (fig. 25, g).

Side-scrapers, *déjeté* (6). These are quite rough, one approaching a nose end-scraper (fig. 25, c). The largest is 7.2 cm. and is inversely retouched. Two have their scraping tips broken and two are on short, wide flakes. Only the diminutive example is well made.

Side-scrapers, transverse concave (1). A rough example, measuring 5.8 cm. in length. Retouch is semi-steep, rather irregular and only covers about two-thirds of the transverse edge.

Side-scrapers, inverse (6). While these show great diversity in size—from 3.4 to 6.5 cm. in length—they are all well retouched. There are four convex and two straight examples. The convex scrapers are made by semi-steep retouch (fig. 25, d), and the straight examples have a rather flat retouch (fig. 25, m).

Side-scrapers, abrupt (3). Two are on elongated flakes and one is on a thick fragment of ferrocrete sandstone. Those on elongated flakes would be good examples of backed knives except that opposite the retouched edge is a cortex back in one case and a perpendicular plane of a false burin in the other. This latter piece also has a notch near the butt. The third example has a convex scraping edge on one side and cortex on the opposed edge (fig. 26, g).

Side-scrapers, alternate retouch (8). This is the most common type of side-scraper in the assemblage. Three of the eight are larger than 9 cm. but the others are diminutive. At least two

are on intentionally snapped flakes, one of which is partially truncated. There are three *déjeté* scrapers, two are double convex, one is double concave, and two are double convex-concave (fig. 25, f).

End-scrapers (15). The six typical examples show a number of types: four end-scrapers on flakes, one nose scraper, and one thumbnail scraper (fig. 25, k). The largest measures 8.4 cm. in length, but all the others are diminutive. In addition, there are nine atypical end-scrapers: three nose scrapers and six poorly formed end-scrapers on flakes.

Burins (8). This assemblage has a comparatively large number of burins for a Middle Paleolithic site in Nubia. They account for just over 5 per cent of all retouched tools, that is, about 3 per cent more than most other sites.

A typical example is an angle burin on a snapped flake (fig. 26, b), another is an angle burin (single blow), while the third is a transverse burin on a lateral truncation (fig. 26, k). There are five atypical examples. These either have odd forms or are poorly executed. There are two large angle burins (single blow) on irregular flakes, two transverse burins, one of which appears to be a reworked bec burin (fig. 25, l), and one burin on a very steep oblique truncation.

Borers (10). There are six typical examples, of which three are lateral, formed by retouch at the corners of flakes (fig. 26, f, h). Three others are at the distal ends of flakes and also formed by retouch. The four atypical pieces include those with short, stubby boring tips and those poorly formed.

Backed knives (8). There are two typical examples, one on a blade (fig. 26, l), and one on a flake (fig. 25, i). In addition, there are six atypical examples on flakes two of which are quite large (fig. 26, i).

Cortex backed knives (6). Four are on flakes (fig. 26, e), and two on blades.

Raclettes (2). There are two convex scrapers. One is formed by marginal retouch, while the other has semi-steep retouch. This latter piece, however, has a scraping edge only 1.7 cm. in length and is made on an intentionally snapped flake (fig. 26, c).

Truncated pieces (8). There is one basally truncated flake (fig. 26, j), four straight trunca-

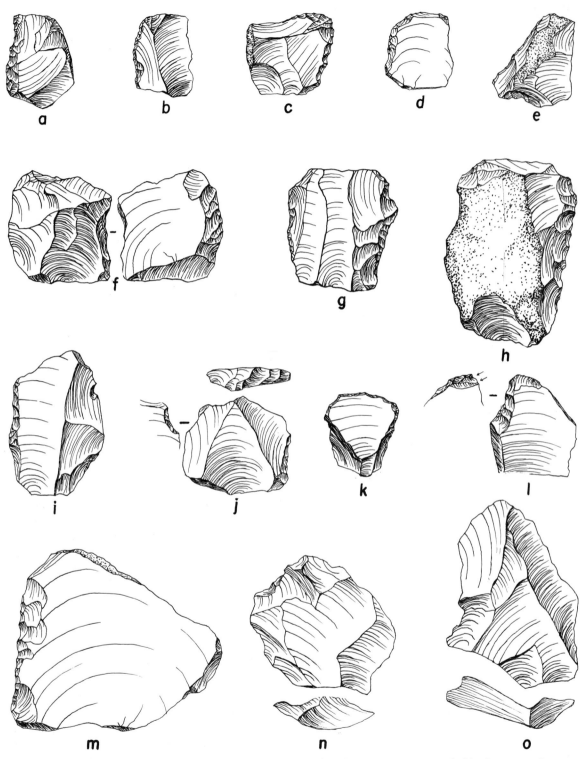

FIG. 25—Nubian Mousterian, Type A (Site 1037): a-b, simple side-scrapers; c, atypical *déjeté* scraper; d, m, inverse scrapers; e, h, straight scrapers; f, alternate scraper; g, convex-concave scraper; i, backed knife; j, truncation-
bec burin; k, end-scraper; l, burin; n-o, Levallois flakes. 4/5 natural size.

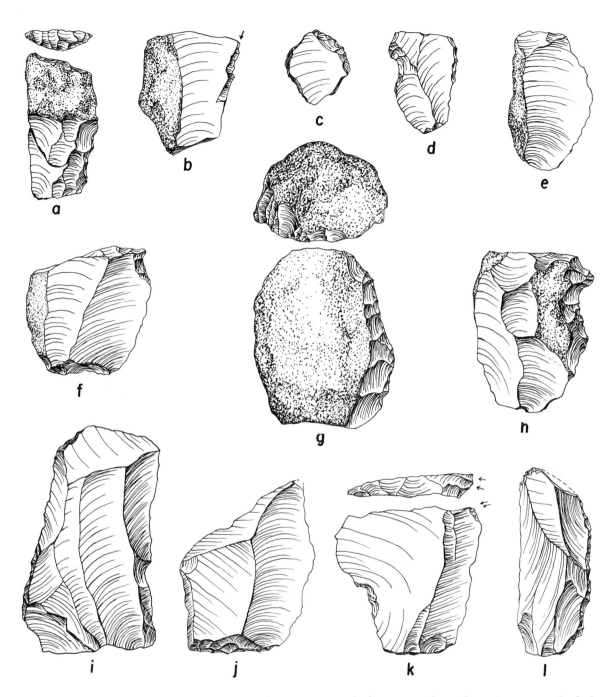

Fig. 26—Nubian Mousterian, Type A (Site 1037): a, truncation; b, burin; c, raclette; d, notch; e, cortex backed knife; f, h, borers; g, abrupt scraper; i, l, backed knives; j, basal truncation; k, transverse burin. 4/5 natural size.

tions on flakes, and three oblique truncations on elongated flakes (fig. 26, a). One piece has an inverse notch on one lateral edge, and another has a weak bec burin as well (fig. 25, j).

Notched pieces (18). There are nine obverse macronotches, three by retouch and six by single blows. In all cases, however, the single blow notches have additional retouch in the notch (fig. 27, a). Two of these are made on snapped flakes.

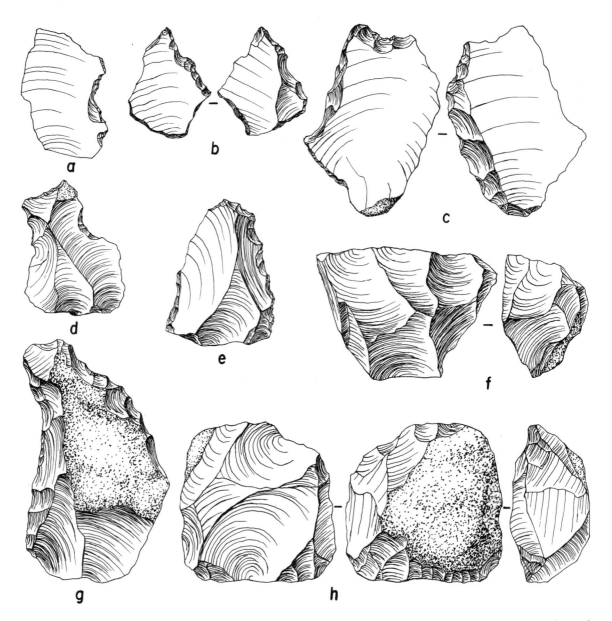

Fɪɢ. 27—Nubian Mousterian, Type A (Site 1037): a, notch; b, alternately retouched Tayac point; c, complex tool; d, opposed notches; e, g, denticulates; f, marginal core; h, Levallois flake core. 4/5 natural size.

There are nine inverse notches: two micronotches and seven macronotches. Six are formed by retouch (fig. 26, d), and three by single blows. These, too, show additional retouch in the notches. Flake size varies from 3.5 to 11.5 cm. in length.

Denticulate pieces (19). As a group, the denticulates are roughly formed on irregular shaped flakes. About half of them are on diminutive flakes, although many of these are quite thick.

There are four rough, obverse macrodenticulates at the distal ends of flakes, two inverse microdenticulates made by retouch on broken flakes, five lateral, obverse microdenticulates made by percussion, and eight lateral obverse macrodenticulates made by percussion (fig. 27, g).

Bec burins (5). Four are typical examples on

the corner of flakes. Two of these are beaked more than usual. The other bec is on a lateral edge of a thick flake. Only two are diminutive.

Inversely retouched pieces (5). Small amounts of inverse retouch on diminutive flakes.

Tayac points (1). This piece is formed by alternate percussion on a diminutive flake. The point is slightly off axis (fig. 27, b).

Pseudo-microburins (1). One typical, diminutive example.

Notched at the distal end (7). There are two inverse and three obverse micronotches made by single blows and two obverse macronotches made by retouch.

Varia (8). There are four diminutive strangled flakes, two of which are made by alternately retouched notches. The other two are made by obverse retouch and both are truncated (fig. 27, d).

In addition, there are a number of highly complex tools. There is a large flake with two bec burins at the distal end, a thick lateral borer, and an inversely retouched scraping edge (fig. 27, c). There is another large flake which has a nose scraper on one corner, and an inverse concave scraping edge on one lateral edge, and a bec burin on one end of the inverse scraper. There is also a short flake which has a straight truncation, a microdenticulate lateral edge, and a deep notch made by percussion near the butt. The final piece is truncated with a bec burin on the edge of the truncation and a macrodenticulate lateral edge.

CORE TYPOLOGY

	No.	%
Levallois		
Levallois flake	9	25.0
Levallois point	1	2.8
Nubian, Type I	1	2.8
Para-Levallois	2	5.6
Other		
Marginal	4	11.1
Discoidal	3	8.3
Unidentifiable	16	44.4
	36	100.0

NOTES ON THE TYPOLOGY

Levallois flake (9). Only three are diminutive but none measures over 6.6 cm. in length. They are indifferently prepared and most show cortex on part of the under surface (fig. 27, h).

Levallois point (1). This large example measures 9 cm. in length. Again the preparation is rough with the preparatory flake scars showing deep negative bulbs. There is cortex on part of the under surface.

Nubian, Type I (1). One example which is slightly more weathered than most of the other artifacts. The preparation is rough and the piece seems to be in accord with the general size and standard of manufacture of the other cores.

Para-Levallois (2). Two very roughly prepared examples, one of which has a natural fracture plane as a platform. The other has a cortex covered platform. Neither is diminutive.

Marginal (4). There are two struck from only one platform, and two struck from opposed natural platforms (fig. 27, f).

Discoidal (3). There are three large unifacial examples.

Unidentifiable (16). These are all small cores with numerous flake scars which show no particular pattern. Three, however, have faceted platforms but no additional preparation prior to the removal of the main flakes.

SITE 1038

Site 1038 lies on the southern edge of a large inselberg which faces the Nile, 1.9 km. southeast of Nag Faqir Tibirki in Dibeira East (map ref. 927.3/654.7).

The inselberg on which this site was found is of some note, as on its top four distinct sites were located: 1035, 1036, 1037, and 1038. Of the four sites, only Site 1038 contained flakes of a size typical of those found at the more westerly sites. Flakes from the other sites were either diminutive or verged on it.

The site consists of a surface concentration of tools and debitage, covering an area of about 200 sq. m. along the southern edge of the inselberg. All tools and debitage were made from a medium grained, dark brown ferrocrete sandstone which was present in natural slabs along that part of the inselberg edge. The artifacts rested, in most cases, on the ferrocrete sandstone of the inselberg surface but, in places, they were partially within pockets of a light tan surficial layer.

Two separate systematic collections were

made: one from a 5 sq. m. area some 6 m. from the inselberg edge and the other from a 2 sq. m. area along the edge. In the 2 sq. m. area, a total of 348 pieces of ferrocrete sandstone were collected. Of these, 70 were tools, 215 were flakes, 7 were cores, and the others were debris or core manufacturing waste flakes.

Each collection was checked separately for consistency and then put together and restudied as a single unit. The results of the separate studies showed a definite preferential area for the collection of Levallois flakes, but otherwise their technological indices were very similar.

TOOL TYPOLOGY

		No.	%	Restricted %
1	Levallois flakes, typical	46	20.4	
2	Levallois flakes, atypical	17	7.5	
3	Levallois points	7	3.1	
5	Pseudo-Levallois points	4	1.8	2.6
9	Side-scrapers, straight	3	1.3	1.9
10	Side-scrapers, convex	9	4.0	5.9
11	Side-scrapers, concave	2	0.9	1.3
20	Side-scrapers, convergent convex	1	0.4	0.6
21	Side-scrapers, déjeté	2	0.9	1.3
22	Side-scrapers, transverse straight	2	0.9	1.3
23	Side-scrapers, transverse convex	1	0.4	0.6
25	Side-scrapers, inverse	8	3.6	5.2
26	Side-scrapers, abrupt	1	0.4	0.6
29	Side-scrapers, alternate retouch	1	0.4	0.6
30	End-scrapers, typical	7	3.1	4.6
31	End-scrapers, atypical	10	4.4	6.5
32	Burins, typical	1	0.4	0.6
33	Burins, atypical	2	0.9	1.3
34	Borers, typical	6	2.7	3.9
35	Borers, atypical	4	1.8	2.6
37	Backed knives, atypical	2	0.9	1.3
38	Cortex backed knives	3	1.3	1.9
40	Truncated pieces	15	6.6	9.7
42	Notched pieces	19	8.4	12.4
43	Denticulate pieces	27	12.0	17.9
44	Bec burins	9	4.0	5.9
45	Inversely retouched pieces	2	0.9	
53	Pseudo-microburins	1	0.4	0.6
54	Notched at the distal end	8	3.6	5.2
62	Varia	5	2.2	3.3
		225	99.6	99.6

Technological Indices
$IL = 18.7$ $IF = 54.1$ $IFs = 30.1$ $Ilame = 11.0$

Typological Indices and Characteristic Groups
$IL^{ty} = 31.0$ $IR = 13.2$ $IC = 5.3$ $IA^u = 0.9$ $IB = 0.0$
$I = 31.0$ $II = 15.0$ $III = 14.2$ $IV = 12.0$

Restricted Typological Indices and Groups
$IL^{ty} = 0.0$ $IR = 19.3$ $IC = 7.8$ $IA^u = 1.3$ $IB = 0.0$
$I = 0.0$ $II = 21.9$ $III = 20.8$ $IV = 17.9$

NOTES ON THE TYPOLOGY

Levallois flakes (63). Unretouched Levallois flakes and blades form an important element of this assemblage. They range in size from 3.4 to 11.1 cm. but, for the most part, they are fairly large—34 per cent measure over 7 cm. in length. The flakes tend toward thickness, with prominent bulbs and bulb scars, although the smaller pieces are quite thin and fine. A few flakes are pointed, but the majority are rectangular or asymmetric in shape (fig. 28, a-c). There are eight Levallois blades in this group.

Levallois points (7). The Levallois points vary in quality (fig. 28, e), but most are typical examples. Two are partially retouched: one has a small notch and distal retouch (fig. 28, f), while the other is inversely retouched along both lateral edges adjacent to the butt.

Pseudo-Levallois points (4). All are quite typical, although one is notched.

Side-scrapers, straight (3). Two are fine examples made by semi-steep retouch. One straight scraper is on a complex tool. The scraping edge has a borer on one extremity, formed by two retouched notches, and the opposite lateral edge has both a retouched notch and a bec burin (fig. 29, e).

The presence of such complex tools is typical of this assemblage, but wherever a prime tool type is among the typological features, the piece has been placed with that tool type. Otherwise, a complex tool has been placed under type 62.

Side-scrapers, convex (9). The convex side-scraper is the most typical side-scraper of this assemblage. For the most part, they are the best made. Large flakes are carefully shaped by semi-steep retouch into even, broad convex side-scrapers (fig. 28, g). One example has a small nose along the distal portion of the scraping edge and approaches a déjeté scraper (fig. 29, a). Three other well formed examples have single notches close to the center of the scraping edges. All are on thick coarse flakes.

Side-scrapers, concave (2). Both are poor examples. Retouch on one is marginal, but on the other it is semi-steep (fig. 29, d).

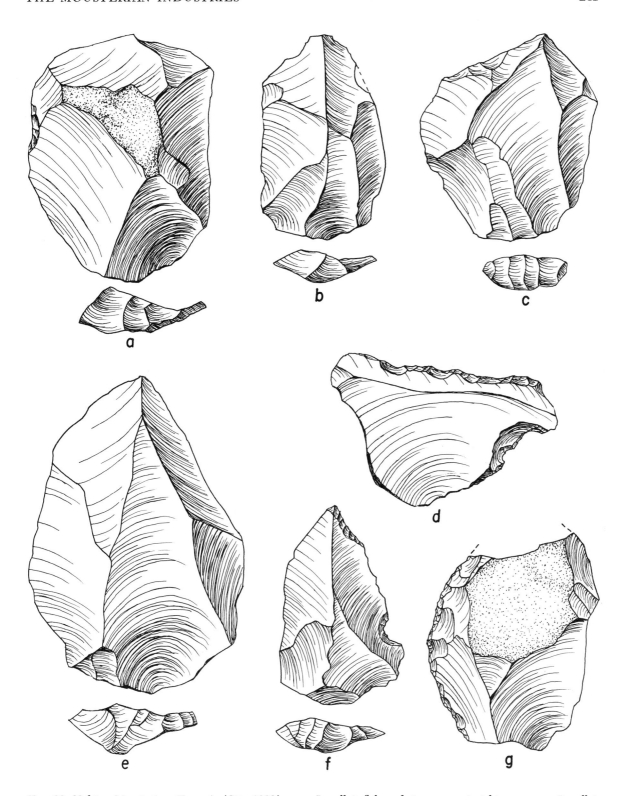

Fig. 28—Nubian Mousterian, Type A (Site 1038): a-c, Levallois flakes; d, transverse straight scraper; e, Levallois point; f, retouched Levallois point; g, convex scraper. 4/5 natural size.

Side-scrapers, convergent convex (1). An atypical example which verges on an ogival end-scraper.

Side-scrapers, *déjeté* (2). Both are on small flakes with generally poor marginal retouch on two edges. They are not equal in quality to the simple convex side-scrapers.

Side-scrapers, transverse straight (2). One has rather light marginal retouch on the scraping edge and a small amount of inverse retouch near the butt. The other piece has a slightly irregular scraping edge made by semi-steep retouch and has a macronotch on one side (fig. 28, d).

Side-scrapers, transverse convex (1). This scraper is formed by semi-steep inverse retouch. The scraping edge is somewhat irregular but not enough so to be a denticulate.

Side-scrapers, inverse (8). There are five convex, two concave, and one straight. Quality of retouch varies but most are well made by semi-steep retouch.

Side-scrapers, abrupt (1). This is an atypical example. It is formed on a thick, irregular core manufacturing waste flake. The scraping edge is slightly convex and does not extend the whole lateral length of the edge.

Side-scrapers, alternate retouch (1). The scraping edges are convergent, with marginal obverse retouch and flat inverse retouch. In addition, there is a macronotch made by percussion on one lateral edge near the butt and another macronotch made by inverse retouch on the opposite lateral edge (fig. 29, f).

End-scrapers (15). The distinction between typical and atypical end-scrapers shown on the typological list merely reflects variation in quality of workmanship. The most common form of end-scraper in this assemblage is the nose scraper. Seven of these were recovered. At their best, they are finely formed, but there are also rough examples. One particularly fine example has a bec burin on one lateral edge and a retouched notch on the opposed edge (fig. 29, e). Another piece, poorly made, also has a bec burin, while a third example is notched.

The remaining end-scrapers show a variety of forms. Four are typically convex (fig. 30, a), while the others are poorly executed and only roughly convex (fig. 29, g). Two pieces have additional notches and one typical example has a small borer on a lateral edge.

Burins (3). Even the typical burin is far from a fine example. Ferrocrete sandstone is relatively soft, and even light eolization tends to obscure burin facets. The typical example is a burin on a denticulate truncation (fig. 30, f). There is also a poor burin *plan* and a burin on a snapped flake, which also has a transverse denticulate section (fig. 30, e).

Borers (10). Borers are well made. Five are on the corners of irregular flakes and are slightly beaked. The remaining examples are straight. Of the total, six borers have additional typological features: one has a lateral, inverse macronotch made by percussion, two have double macronotches at their distal ends, and two have single obversely retouched lateral macronotches. The sixth is denticulated with a borer as the outstanding typological feature (fig. 30, b).

Backed knives, atypical (2). These are all questionable examples. One example is a thick, cortex backed flake which has received additional steep retouch along part of the cortex backed edge. The other piece has an irregularly retouched backing at the distal end of a cortex covered flake. The opposed side has a very light marginal retouch which appears to be due to use.

Cortex backed knives (3). Three quite typical examples (fig. 30, i).

Truncated pieces (15). Four are basally truncated. One of these also has a denticulated lateral edge (fig. 30, g). Of the eleven oblique truncations (fig. 30, c-d), eight are concave (fig. 30, h) and three are straight.

Notched pieces (19). Five flakes have inverse macronotches, three formed by single blows and two by retouch (fig. 31, d). Fourteen have obverse macronotches: nine by single blows (fig. 31, a), and five by retouch. While all notches measure over 1 cm. across, only one measures greater than 2 cm.

Denticulate pieces (27). Denticulates of this assemblage can be placed into two major groups: lateral side and distal end. It is of particular note that, of the sixteen denticulates at the distal ends of flakes and blades, ten are on short, wide, triangular flakes. These are truly transverse rather than distal end denticulates (fig. 31, g). Four

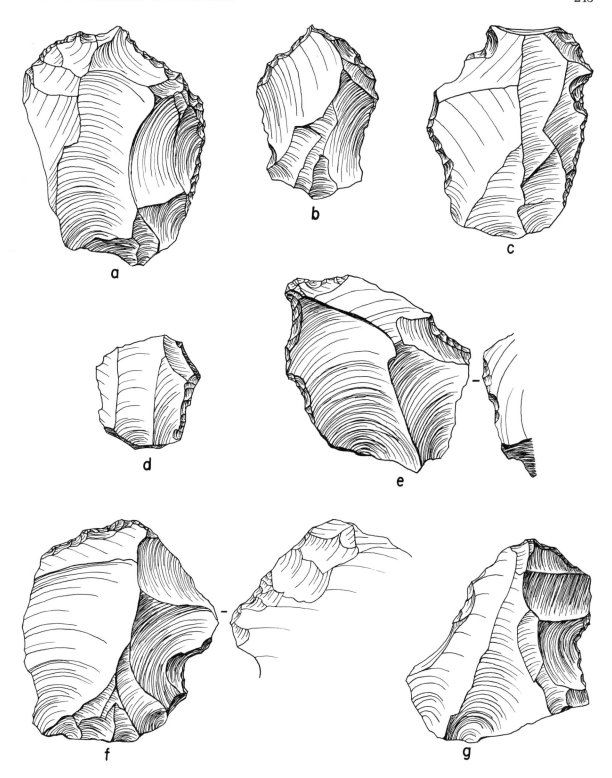

Fɪɢ. 29–Nubian Mousterian, Type A (Site 1038): a, convex scraper with spike; b, atypical converging convex scraper; c, complex tool; d, concave scraper; e, nosed scraper with bec burin; f, alternate scraper; g, atypical end-scraper. 4/5 natural size.

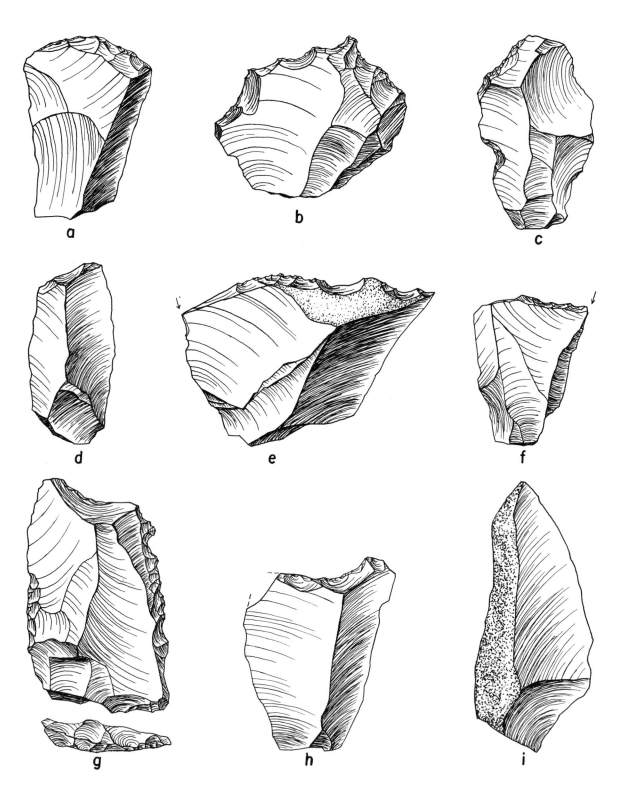

Fig. 30—Nubian Mousterian, Type A (Site 1038): a, end-scraper; b, borer; c-d, h, truncations, e-f, burins; g, basally truncated denticulate; i, cortex backed knife. 4/5 natural size.

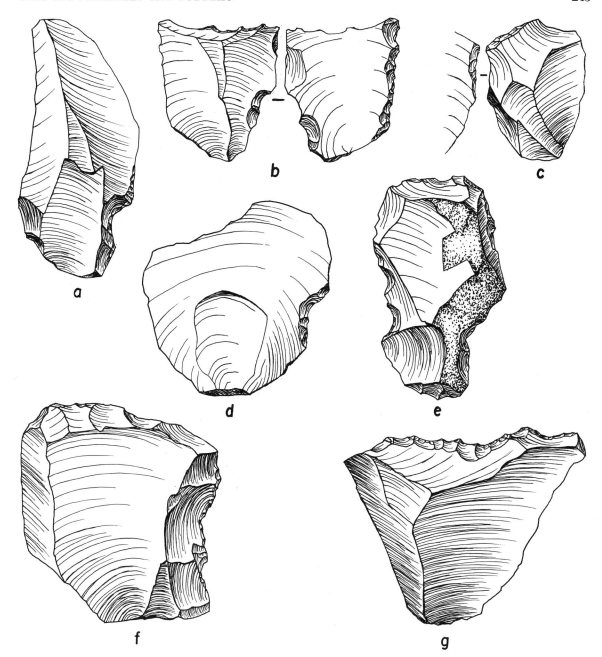

Fig. 31–Nubian Mousterian, Type A (Site 1038): a, d, notch; b, f-g, denticulates; c, bec burin; e, complex tool. 4/5 natural size.

denticulates are at the distal end of normal flakes and three are at the end of blades. All are made by percussion and only one is inversely formed. As a group, they are irregular, some areas being microdenticulate, with other areas of the same edge being macrodenticulate.

The lateral denticulates show more variety.

Two are inverse in microdenticulates formed by retouch, one is an inverse macrodenticulate made by percussion, five are obverse macrodenticulates made by percussion (fig. 31, f), and two are retouched obverse microdenticulates. In addition, there is one convergent macrodenticulate on a core.

The denticulates as a group are rough and poorly executed. One lateral example has a macronotch opposite the denticulate edge, but, otherwise, there are no complex typological features.

Bec burins (9). All are quite recognizable but most are rather indifferently produced. There are, however, a few excellent examples (fig. 31, c).

Inversely retouched pieces (2). Two odd shaped flakes with a small amount of inverse retouch.

Pseudo-microburins (1). A poor example.

Notched at the distal end (8). Two are inversely retouched macronotches, and six are obverse macronotches made by percussion. One has a small amount of marginal retouch near the butt.

Varia (5). There are two strangled flakes, one with an atypical end-scraper at the distal end and a basal truncation (fig. 31, e). One *déjeté* flake has a strangled extremity, and another piece has a deep concave thinning adjacent to the butt end which is too big to be a notch but too short to be a scraper. The final piece is a *déjeté* denticulate with an opposed macronotch (fig. 31, b).

CORE TYPOLOGY

	No.	%
Levallois		
Levallois blade	3	4.8
Levallois flake	16	25.1
Levallois point	1	1.5
Nubian, Type I	14	21.8
Nubian, Type II	1	1.5
Para-Levallois	14	21.8
Other		
Marginal	2	3.0
Discoidal	2	3.0
Unidentifiable	11	17.0
	64	99.6

NOTES ON THE TYPOLOGY

Levallois blade (3). These are moderately well prepared on the upper surface but are indifferently treated on the underside, all showing some cortex. The smallest measures 7.6 cm. in length, while the other two measure 9.4 cm.

Levallois flake (16). Six were unstruck, two hinge fractured and eight were successfully struck. Seven of the Levallois cores are squat, rather wide, approaching para-Levallois cores in

shape. They are roughly prepared, usually having cortex on the under surface (fig. 32, c). Nine flake cores are elongated, with prepared platforms across one short end. These for the most part are unstruck but the treatment is typical of a flake rather than a blade core. Again, the core preparation is rough.

Levallois point (1). One well made example (fig. 32, b).

Nubian, Type I (14). The Nubian Core, Type I, is well represented here but as with the normal Levallois cores, the Nubian Cores are roughly prepared. All have been struck, removing pointed flakes, but these are short, wide, and asymmetric (fig. 33). In nine examples, the two blades struck from the distal end are large, leaving deep scars on the cores. Only five examples are well made and these show a slight variation of the Nubian technique. While the two blade scars are recognizable, the core has also received additional lateral retouch along the blade scars which approach the tip. Nubian Cores, Type I, range in length from 5.2 to 8.3 cm., but eleven of them are between 7 and 8.3 cm.

Nubian, Type II (1). Only one unstruck example was found. It is well prepared, measures 8 cm. in length, and has a distal end which approaches a biface in form (fig. 32, d).

Para-Levallois (14). Again, like all the cores found at this site, the para-Levallois cores are roughly prepared and, when struck, show deep negative bulbs (fig. 32, a). As could be expected, their lengths are somewhat shorter than the other Levallois cores—from 4.5 to 7.1 cm. All but two measure between 5.1 and 7 cm.

Marginal (2). Two examples were found, one measuring 8.1 cm. in length and the other only 6.4 cm.

Discoidal (2). Both are peripheral, unifacial cores which show the removal of numerous flakes.

Unidentifiable (11). These show no recognizable pattern, although all have had more than one flake removed.

SITE 1033

Site 1033 lies on and in a pediment of 7.5 yellow/red colluvium, 0.5 km. northeast of the Dibeira Station (map ref. 993.5/656.4). This site was discovered by the Joint Scandinavian Expe-

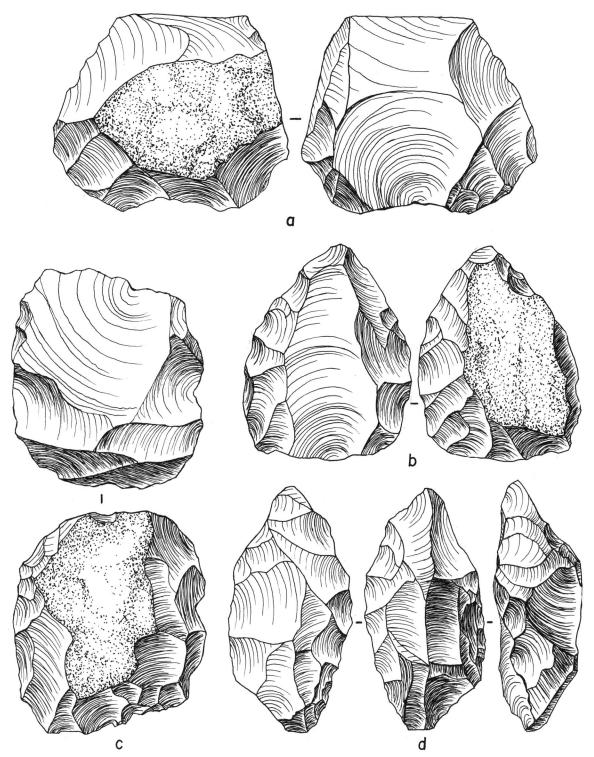

Fɪɢ. 32—Nubian Mousterian, Type A (Site 1038): a, para-Levallois core; b, Levallois point core; c, Levallois flake core; d, Nubian Core, Type II (unstruck). 4/5 natural size.

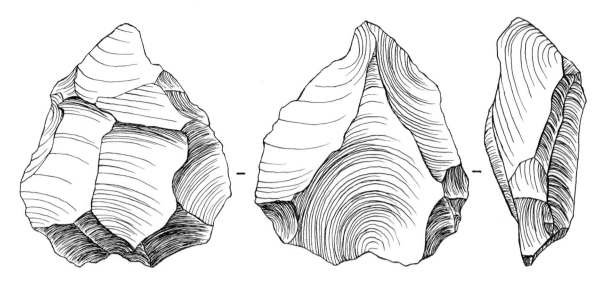

Fɪɢ. 33—Nubian Mousterian, Type A (Site 1038): a, Nubian Core, Type I. 4/5 natural size.

dition and test excavated by them. During the 1963-1964 field season, they kindly gave permission to the Combined Prehistoric Expedition to carry out additional excavations. These were deemed advisable because this was one of the very few Nubian Middle Stone Age sites which was subsurface, and thus could be placed in geological context.

The Combined Prehistoric Expedition work began at this site in January, 1964, and was concluded in the beginning days of February, 1964. As a good profile was available from the Joint Scandinavian excavation, it was possible to see clearly the stratigraphic position of the culture layer. Therefore, a grid pattern was laid out adjoining the old excavation trench. This older trench extended for a distance of 13 m., oriented east-west. The Combined Prehistoric Expedition's work extended the area of excavation mostly to the south, but also included additional trenches along the east-west line to give a clearer picture of the stratigraphy (fig. 34).

After the completion of the grid system, the first work deepened the Scandinavian trench to clarify fully the geological stratigraphy. This brought to light a second cultural layer. Thus not only was the site subsurface, but it was also culturally stratified.

Stratigraphy

The site rested in a pediment about 40 m. above the Nile and was marked by a surface concentration over 1,000 sq. m. in area. As there had been previous excavations, with the normal disturbance of the surface, it was not possible to see if there were distinct areas of heavy surface concentration or if it was a single loose concentration. Excavations indicated, however, that there should have been differential surface concentration as, in places, the cover of the upper cultural level was fully deflated. While absolute depth below the surface and the thickness of the sterile layers varied from area to area, the relative positioning of layers remained constant throughout the central section of the excavation.

A typical profile showed the following stratigraphy (fig. 35):

1. One to two centimeters of sand and small gravel with heavily sand-abraded artifacts on the surface.

2. Sterile layer 10 cm. thick of a sandy 7.5 yellow/red pediment with desiccation cracks.

3. A thin layer, usually only one stone thick, of fresh artifacts. A very few showed some eolization on one side. Upper Cultural Layer.

4. Twelve to twenty centimeters of sterile 7.5

Fig. 34—View of excavations at Site 1033, looking west.

yellow/red pediment which was less coarse and less oxidized than layer B.

5. Nine to sixteen centimeters of coarse and compact rubble. The base of this layer was rich in quartz gravels and the top contained fresh artifacts. Again, a very few showed some eolization. Lower Cultural Layer.

6. Sterile, coarse 7.5 yellow/red pediment. Similar to oxisol.

This was the typical stratigraphic layering at the site. On the western extreme, however, layer "B" rose to the surface, leaving only the artifacts from layer "C" and below in situ. Again, on the eastern edge of the old trench, artifacts from layer "E" stopped against the rubble layer which thickened at that point. Layer "D" was still present in this area as was layer "C" which, however, thickened to from 5 to 12 cm.

A total of 30.5 sq. m. were excavated to an average depth of 50 cm. Of this total area, 19

Fig. 35—Profile of stratigraphy at Site 1033.

sq. m. of the Upper Cultural Layer and 24.4 sq. m. of the Lower Cultural Layer were uncovered.

Upper Cultural Layer

Within the Upper Cultural Layer, 3,994 pieces of ferrocrete sandstone were excavated. Of these, 1,649 were flakes and blades, 66 were cores, 1,218 were debris, and 1,061 were core manufacturing waste flakes. Of the 1,649 flakes and blades, only 207 were retouched tools or Levallois flakes.

TOOL TYPOLOGY

		No.	%	Restricted %
1	Levallois flakes, typical	47	22.7	
2	Levallois flakes, atypical	42	20.3	
3	Levallois points	5	2.4	
5	Pseudo-Levallois points	3	1.4	2.8
9	Side-scrapers, straight	2	1.0	1.8
10	Side-scrapers, convex	4	1.9	3.7
11	Side-scrapers, concave	2	1.0	1.8
15	Side-scrapers, biconvex	1	0.5	0.9
17	Side-scrapers, double convex-concave	1	0.5	0.9
19	Side-scrapers, convergent convex	1	0.5	0.9
22	Side-scrapers, transverse, straight	1	0.5	0.9
23	Side-scrapers, tranverse convex	1	0.5	0.9
25	Side-scrapers, inverse	5	2.4	4.6
28	Side-scrapers, bifacial retouch	1	0.5	0.9
29	Side-scrapers, alternate retouch	4	1.9	3.7
30	End-scrapers, typical	4	1.9	3.7
31	End-scrapers, atypical	4	1.9	3.7
32	Burins, typical	1	0.5	0.9
33	Burins, atypical	2	1.0	1.8
34	Borers, typical	3	1.4	2.8
35	Borers, atypical	2	1.0	1.8
37	Backed knives, atypical	3	1.4	2.8
38	Cortex backed knives	2	1.0	1.8
40	Truncated pieces	9	4.3	8.3
42	Notched pieces	21	10.1	19.4
43	Denticulate pieces	12	5.8	11.1
44	Bec burins	7	3.4	6.5
45	Inversely retouched pieces	5	2.4	
54	Notched at the distal end	6	2.9	5.6
62	Varia	6	2.9	5.6
		207	99.9	99.6

Technological Indices

IL=7.0   IF=46.8   IFs=17.9   Ilame=9.5

Typological Indices and Characteristic Groups

IL^{ty}=45.4   IR=11.2   IC=3.4   IA^u=1.4   IB=0.0
I=45.4   II=12.6   III=9.1   IV=5.9

Restricted Typological Indices and Groups

IL^{ty}=0.0   IR=21.0   IC=6.4   IA^u=2.8   IB=0.0
I=0.0   II=23.8   III=17.5   IV=11.1

NOTES ON THE TYPOLOGY

Levallois flakes (89). Levallois flakes account for slightly more than 45 per cent of all tools. They are generally large, fairly thin, and show careful preparation. This extensive core preparation, however, did not always extend to the striking platforms, as about half the Levallois flakes have unfaceted butts. Over half are blades (fig. 36, e), laminary flakes, or flakes which have parallel or subparallel sides and approach laminary flakes (fig. 36, g). The others tend toward irregular, pointed ovates (fig. 36, c) or squat rectangles (fig. 36, b). As these flakes were absolutely fresh, it was somewhat surprising that exceedingly few showed any evidence of irregular edges which might have been attributed to use or accidental crushing.

Levallois points (5). All are rather atypical, as the classic scar pattern for a Levallois point is absent. In these, the flake scars are more complex. All are elongated (fig. 36, f, h).

Pseudo-Levallois points (3). Three typical examples, one of which has a small amount of retouch (fig. 38, b).

Side-scrapers, straight (2). Both are poor examples. One has marginal retouch and the other semi-steep retouch along part of an edge.

Side-scrapers, convex (4). These are among the best scrapers found. There is one with a denticulate on the edge opposite the scraper (fig. 37, b), and three are on large flakes (fig. 37, a).

Side-scrapers, concave (2). Both are fair examples made by semi-steep retouch (fig. 37, d).

Side-scrapers, biconvex (1). One, which is also truncated (fig. 36, a).

Side-scrapers, double convex-concave (1). This is without doubt a Nubian scraper (fig. 37, i), as defined by the Guichards (Guichard and Guichard, 1965, p. 68). It is interesting to note that in this assemblage it is not associated with Nubian cores or bifacial foliates.

Side-scrapers, convergent convex (1). A single, poor example.

Side-scrapers, transverse straight (1). A small piece made by marginal retouch.

Side-scrapers, transverse convex (1). A poor

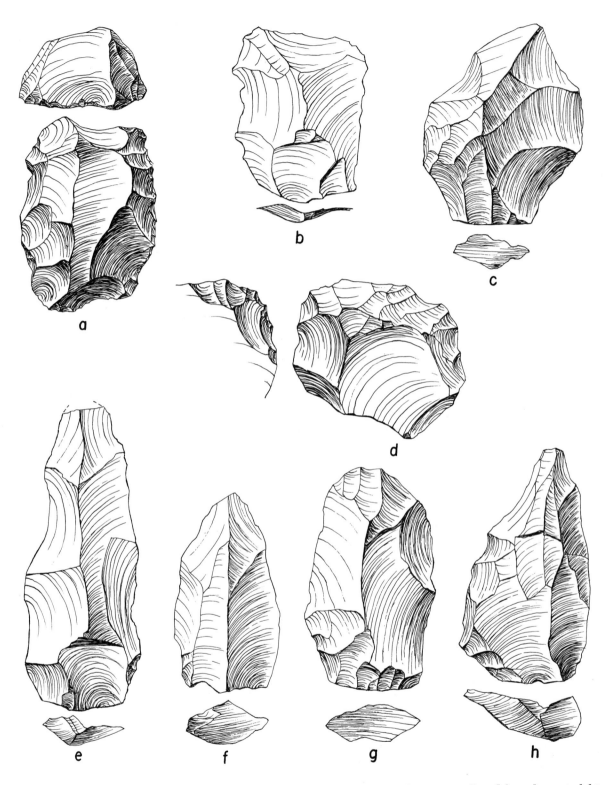

Fɪɢ. 36–Nubian Mousterian, Type A (Site 1033U): a, biconvex scraper; b-c, g, Levallois flakes; d, atypical bi-facial scraper; e, Levallois blade; f, h, Levallois points. 4/5 natural size.

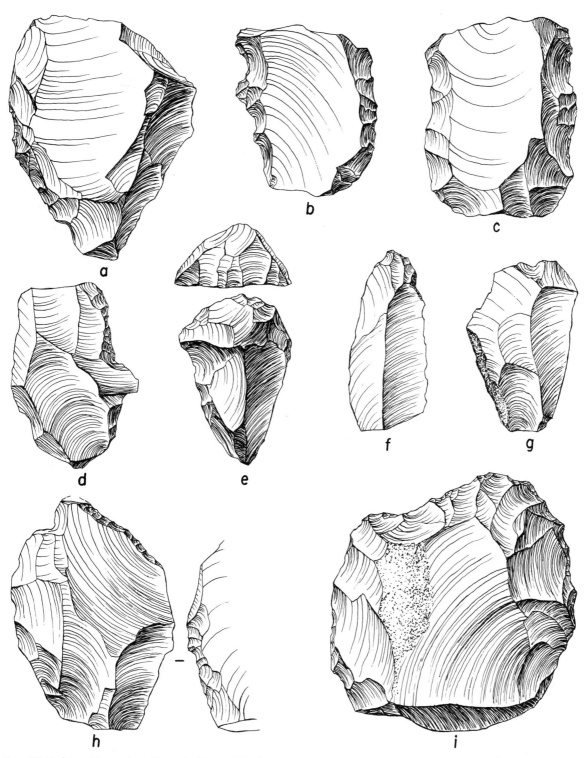

FIG. 37—Nubian Mousterian, Type A (Site 1033U): a, convex scraper; b, convex scraper—denticulate; c, convex-concave scraper; d, concave scraper; e-f, end-scrapers; g, cortex backed knife; h, alternate scraper; i, Nubian scraper. 4/5 natural size.

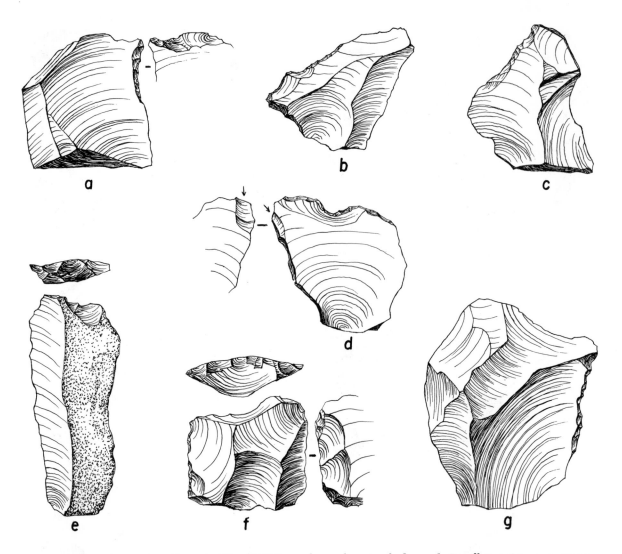

Fig. 38—Nubian Mousterian, Type A (Site 1033U): a, borer; b, retouched pseudo-Levallois point; c, e, truncations; d, burin; f, alternate *déjeté* scraper; g, atypical backed knife. 4/5 natural size.

example on a small flake, formed by inverse marginal retouch.

Side-scrapers, inverse (5). These are all poor examples. Retouch, in all cases, is marginal. The scraping edges include three straight, one concave, and one convex.

Side-scrapers, bifacial retouch (1). A very rough example where only part of the scraping edge is bifacially retouched (fig. 36, d).

Side-scrapers, alternate retouch (4). There is one with flat inverse retouch and semi-steep obverse retouch on a notched Levallois flake (fig. 37, h), two small *déjeté* scrapers made by alter-

nate retouch (fig. 38, f), and one double straight scraper made by alternate, marginal retouch.

End-scrapers (8). There are four typical examples: two on blades, and two on flakes. One of the latter is a carinated scraper (fig. 37, e). The atypical pieces have poor or incomplete retouch on both flakes and blades (fig. 37, f).

Burins (3). There is one burin on a notched, convex truncation (fig. 38, d), an angle burin on a snapped blade, and a questionable transverse, single blow burin at the distal end of a Levallois blade.

Borers (5). There are three typical examples,

one of which is made by alternate retouch (fig. 38, a). The two atypical examples are formed by retouched notches on the corners of flakes.

Backed knives, atypical (3). Three Levallois flakes have partial, irregular backing (fig. 38, g).

Cortex backed knives (2). Two Levallois flakes (fig. 37, g), one of which is also notched.

Truncated pieces (9). There are five oblique truncations (fig. 38, c), one straight truncation (fig. 38, e), one basally truncated flake with a denticulate lateral edge and two concave truncations on blades, one of which also has an inversely denticulated edge.

Notched pieces (21). There are three obverse and four inverse macronotches made by retouch. There are also five obverse and four inverse macronotches formed by single blows. In addition, there are four obverse and one inverse micronotch formed by single blows.

Denticulate pieces (12). Denticulates form a poor group. All are made by percussion on rather small flakes. Four are inverse, the remainder obverse. Only three are microdenticulate.

Bec burins (7). There is one double bec; there are six single becs. For the most part, they are on the lateral edges of small flakes.

Inversely retouched pieces (5). Small amounts of inverse retouch, one of which is on a blade.

Notched at the distal end (6). All are formed by single blows. Three are inverse, three obverse.

Varia (6). There are two flakes with opposed notches, three complex tools, and a fragment of a denticulated and backed tool. The complex tools combine bec burins, notches, and denticulates; and one even has a questionable burin. They are poor in that each tool type represented is indifferently executed.

CORE TYPOLOGY

	No.	%
Levallois		
Levallois blade	5	7.5
Levallois flake	25	37.5
Levallois point	1	1.5
Para-Levallois	2	3.0
Other		
Marginal	14	21.0
Discoidal	4	6.0
Globular	1	1.5
Isolated flake	7	10.5
Unidentifiable	7	10.5
	66	99.0

NOTES ON THE TYPOLOGY

Levallois cores predominate, and their preparation is generally rough. Flake scars from core preparation are prominent, and in many cases the point of percussion shows crushing. The pattern of Levallois core preparation is quite clear. In all cases, the under side was prepared first by the removal of a number of large flakes. The upper surface was then shaped into a slightly convex surface by peripheral flaking which removed the basal portions of the ventral flake scars. A platform was then prepared at one end, although at times opposing platforms were made. In struck cores, however, there is no evidence that more than one platform was ever utilized.

Levallois blade (5). Four are typical Levallois blade cores, but one is a circular core from which a number of Levallois blades have been removed. As a group, they are larger than the flake cores, ranging from 10.5 to 11.7 cm.

Levallois flake (25). These are rather small, averaging only 8.6 cm. in length, although the cores range in length from 5.8 to 13.5 cm. As with all the Levallois cores, the preparation is generally rough. The cores tend to be rectangular or elongate rectangular with very few ovoid examples. A few are formed on thick flakes (fig. 39, b).

Levallois point (1). There is one small Levallois point core which shows the removal of a Levallois point from both the dorsal and ventral sides.

Para-Levallois (2). Two small, rough examples.

Marginal (14). There are eight marginal cores made on blocks of ferrocrete sandstone which have had a series of parallel flakes removed from a natural platform or from a platform formed by the removal of a single flake. There are four marginal cores which are similar to the above, but the platform of each has been grossly faceted. Two atypical examples have a series of elongated flakes removed from opposite sides (fig. 39, a).

Discoidal (4). There are four unifacial Mousterian discoids, two of which have been flaked around only a part of the circumference.

Globular (1). One typical example.

Isolated flake (7). There are seven blocks of

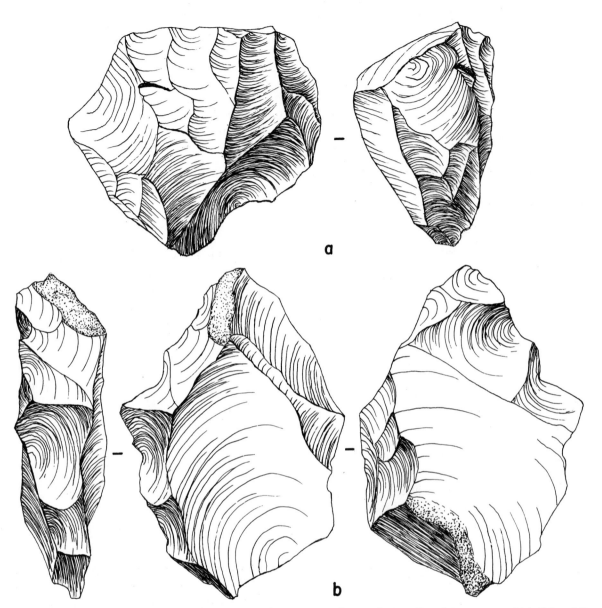

Fig. 39—Nubian Mousterian, Type A (Site 1033U): a, marginal core; b, Levallois flake core on thick flake. 4/5 natural size.

ferrocrete sandstone which have had only one primary flake removed from each.

Unidentifiable (7). These showed no particular pattern of flaking and none was extensively worked.

Lower Cultural Layer

Within the 24.4 sq. m. of the Lower Cultural Layer, 4,326 artifacts were excavated. Of these 1,569 were flakes or blades, 79 were cores, 1,541 were debris, and 1,137 were core manufacturing waste flakes. Of the 1,569 flakes and blades, 131 were Levallois and only 71 were retouched tools, including those made on Levallois flakes.

Distribution of artifacts across the 24.4 sq. m. was quite uneven. The main Lower Cultural Level was seen in a series of squares which ran 10 m. east-west and 1.5 m. north-south. At the extreme eastern end of these squares there were less than 50 flakes to each 1.5 meter square. At the far western end, however, there was an average of 295 flakes per 1.5 meter square. Throughout the line of squares, there was a gradual increase in flakes from east to west. However, the westernmost had more than double the number of flakes in other squares. This was due to the fact that these squares were situated at the edge of an artificial excavation some 30 cm. deep which the inhabitants had cut in order to quarry fresh slabs of ferrocrete sandstone. After the removal of the fresh slabs, the inhabitants filled the excavation with flakes and debitage.

As this level represents a workshop site, there are relatively few retouched tools, and these, for the most part, are poorly made. In fact, only seventy-one retouched tools were recovered. This is below the acceptable number for a systematic technological and typological study. Having come from the only stratified Nubian Middle Stone Age site, however, it was felt that it should be included in the study. It was hoped that it might throw some light on a relative chronology for the Nubian Mousterian. Unfortunately, as will be seen, both cultural layers are very similar and seem to represent the same stage of cultural development. This level is not only poor in tools, but their quality is very low, and almost all could have been rejected tools, not worth removing to a living site.

TOOL TYPOLOGY

		No.	%	Restricted %
1	Levallois flakes, typical	43	29.0	
2	Levallois flakes, atypical	28	18.9	
3	Levallois points	6	4.1	
5	Pseudo-Levallois points	1	0.7	1.4
9	Side-scrapers, straight	1	0.7	1.4
10	Side-scrapers, convex	2	1.3	2.8
11	Side-scrapers, concave	1	0.7	1.4
23	Side-scrapers, transverse convex	3	2.0	4.2
25	Side-scrapers, inverse	3	2.0	4.2
29	Side-scrapers, alternate retouch	2	1.3	2.8
31	End-scrapers, atypical	5	3.4	7.0
33	Burins, atypical	3	2.0	4.2
35	Borers, atypical	1	0.7	1.4
37	Backed knives, atypical	2	1.3	2.8
38	Cortex backed knives	5	3.4	7.0
40	Truncated pieces	4	2.7	5.6
42	Notched pieces	13	8.8	18.2

		No.	%	Restricted %
43	Denticulate pieces	16	10.8	22.4
44	Bec burins	1	0.7	1.4
54	Notched at the distal end	3	2.0	4.2
56	Rabots	2	1.3	2.8
62	Varia	3	2.0	4.2
		148	99.8	99.4

Technological Indices

IL=8.3   IF=43.7   IFs=15.2   Ilame=12.7

Typological Indices and Characteristic Groups

IL^{ty}=52.0   IR=8.0   IC=2.6   IA^{u}=1.3   IB=0.0
I=52.0   II=8.7   III=7.4   IV=10.8

Restricted Typological Indices and Groups

IL^{ty}=0.0   IR=16.8   IC=5.6   IA^{u}=2.8   IB=0.0
I=0.0   II=18.2   III=15.4   IV=22.4

NOTES ON THE TYPOLOGY

Levallois flakes (71). Over half are typical Levallois flakes. Their outstanding feature is the high tendency toward elongation. Out of seventy-one pieces, seventeen were Levallois blades (fig. 40, e, g), Most of the flakes are rather large, with parallel or subparallel sides (fig. 40, c). A number, however, are smaller and more typical of the rest of the Nubian Mousterian (fig. 40, a). Although rare, oval or nearly oval forms occur (fig. 40, f).

Faceting is more pronounced on the Levallois flakes than on non-Levallois, but it is still weak; just over half have faceted butts.

Levallois points (6). These are small, compared to the Levallois flakes. There are two elongate points, the others being short and broad. They are all poor, having somewhat irregular sides (fig. 40, b).

Pseudo-Levallois points (1). One point is present where the long axis does not coincide with the pointed end.

Side-scrapers, straight (1). A very poor scraper made by fine, uneven marginal retouch on a narrow flake (fig. 41, a).

Side-scrapers, convex (2). One is on a Levallois false burin. Retouch is normal, but there is a retouched macronotch toward the distal end of the scraping edge (fig. 41, h). The other is on an eolized Levallois flake. The eolization apparently took place during, and slightly after, the site was occupied. It was quite common to find flakes

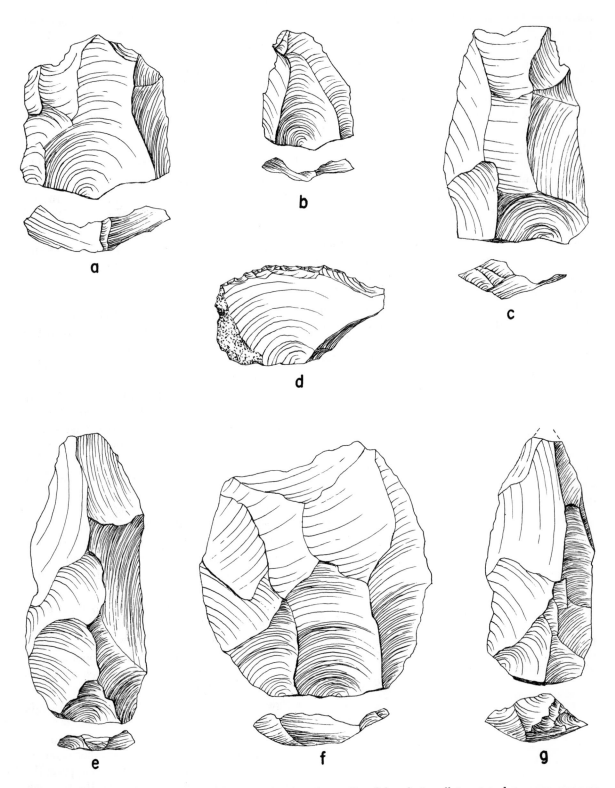

Fig. 40—Nubian Mousterian, Type A (Site 1033L): a, c, f, Levallois flakes; b, Levallois point; d, transverse convex scraper; e, g, Levallois blades. 4/5 natural size.

where one side was heavily eolized, while the other was fresh.

Side-scrapers, concave (1). This again is on a Levallois false burin. Retouch is marginal and the edge sinuous, with the concave section predominating.

Side-scrapers, transverse convex (3). One rather good example (fig. 40, d) and two atypical pieces.

Side-scrapers, inverse (3). There is a double inverse straight-convex scraper with a spike half way along the straight retouched edge (fig. 41, c). The other two are on large flakes and have flat retouch. One of these flakes also has a macronotch at its distal end.

Side-scrapers, alternate retouch (2). There is one large scraper on a broken Levallois flake. The obverse scraping edge is convex and marginally retouched. The inverse section is partially broken, but appears to have been straight and converging toward the distal end of the flake. The inverse retouch is semi-steep. There is also an alternately retouched *déjeté* scraper made by marginal retouch.

End-scrapers, atypical (5). This is a poor group. Retouch is irregular on odd sized flakes.

Burins, atypical (3). There is one heavy angle burin on a broken fragment (fig. 41, d) and another questionable example of the same type. There is also an unsuccessful burin on a retouched notch. At least three attempts were made to strike off a good burin spall, but they failed.

Borers, atypical (1). This is on a small fragment and is formed by steep retouch (fig. 41, b).

Backed knives, atypical (2). There is one on a cortex backed knife which has had a short backing in the form of an oblique truncation added to the cortex back (fig. 41, j). The other is a partially backed flake with only a very limited amount of backing.

Cortex backed knives (5). All are on laminary flakes.

Truncated pieces (4). There are three oblique (fig. 41, f), and one basally truncated flake.

Notched pieces (13). Notches are irregular and, for the most part, ill formed. There are seven micronotches made by percussion. Only two notches are inverse. Most are on flakes but two are on long blades.

Denticulate pieces (16). Denticulates are generally irregular. Of sixteen, only four are microdenticulate. All but one are lateral (fig. 41, i), and mostly made by percussion. There is one which approaches a converging denticulate (fig. 41, e). Four are inverse, the rest obverse. As a group, they are of mixed quality, size, and shape.

Bec burins (1). This bec is on a Levallois flake which has a slight oblique truncation as well.

Notched at the distal end (3). These three are macronotches, two formed by single blows and one by retouch.

Rabots (2). Both of these are convex scrapers on struck Levallois cores. The quality and amount of retouch along the scraping edges are quite different from the rest of the flaking done during core preparation. One is on a small Levallois core (fig. 41, g); the other has the only example of stepped retouch found at a Nubian Middle Stone Age site in Nubia.

Varia (3). There are two flakes with opposed notches, one heavily eolized retouched pseudo-Levallois point, and a blade with flat, inverse retouch at its distal end.

CORE TYPOLOGY

	No.	%
Levallois		
Levallois blade	8	10.1
Levallois flake	42	53.1
Levallois point	4	5.0
Para-Levallois	1	1.3
Other		
Marginal	10	12.6
Discoidal	3	3.8
Isolated flake	3	3.8
Unidentifiable	8	10.1
	79	99.8

NOTES ON THE TYPOLOGY

All cores found in the Lower Cultural Layer have generally rough preparation. Flake scars, whether from core preparation flakes or from the final Levallois flakes, have prominent negative bulbs and many show a slight crushing. It is quite apparent that a rather hard hammer was employed.

Cores vary greatly in size. The smallest is a Levallois flake core which measures under 5 cm., and the largest is also a Levallois flake core which exceeds 14 cm. in length.

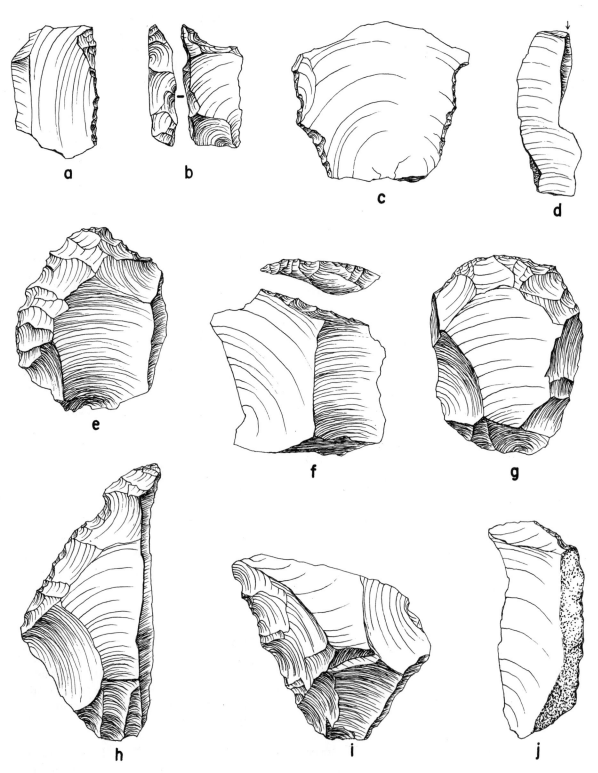

Fig. 41—Nubian Mousterian, Type A (Site 1033L): a, atypical straight scraper; b, borer; c, atypical inverse scraper; d, burin; e, i, denticulates; f, truncation; g, rabot; h, convex scraper; j, cortex backed knife. 4/5 natural size.

Levallois blade (8). As with all the Levallois cores, these are roughly made and show the same general pattern of preparation as described for the Levallois flake cores.

Levallois flake (42). These account for half of all cores. For the most part, dorsal preparation is rough and ventral shaping is minimal. Of the 42 examples, only 13 have well formed tortoise backs (fig. 42, b). Almost half are unstruck, and of those which were struck, eight have deep hinge fractures. Most of these cores are rectangular or elongate ovate; a few are circular or true oval forms.

Levallois point (4). There are two good examples but the other two are quite rough.

Para-Levallois (1). One poorly executed example.

Marginal (10). Four marginal cores were on small plaquettes of ferrocrete sandstone with single, unprepared striking platforms. One example was similar to those above, but the striking platform had been grossly faceted (fig. 42, a). Five marginal cores were utilized from opposed, unfaceted striking platforms. These, too, were made on rather small plaquettes.

Discoidal (3). There are one partially unifacial Mousterian discoid and two complete unifacial Mousterian discoids. All are small.

Isolated flake (3). Plaquette fragments with single flakes removed.

Unidentifiable (8). These had no discernable pattern of flaking and, for the most part, were only slightly utilized.

Nubian Mousterian, Type B

SITE 6

Site 6 is located on the top of a small but high inselberg north of the Cairo Road on the east bank of the Nile (map ref. 925.7/654.0). The inselberg is part of that series which fronts on the Nile, although, in this case, the inselberg is almost two kilometers from the present river.

The site was located during the 1961-1962 field season by Jean de Heinzelin and Roland Paepe and was systematically collected by them. The site consisted of a surface concentration covering the entire top of the inselberg—an area of about 500 sq. m. Artifacts were made from a locally available dark brown ferrocrete sandstone. In possible association with the surface concentration were four round cairns made of locally available natural rock slabs. A small test excavation failed to place these cairns in direct association with the artifacts, but, on the other hand, no evidence was found that they were definitely of a later date.

The surface collection was made over the entire area in five arbitrary sections. These were studied separately and found to be reasonably similar to each other. As no significant typological or technological differences were noted, they were placed together and restudied.

This site was of interest for a number of reasons. First, it was one of two sites to have bifaces located on the row of jebels which front on the Nile. Also, it was the only Middle Paleolithic site which contained burned ferrocrete sandstone. This came mostly from the southeastern area of the top, but some pieces were found in all sections of the site. Finally, this site appeared to have a very low Levallois Index and a rich variety of finished tools. After a careful study, the low Levallois Index was confirmed, but the number of finished tools turned out to be quite low compared with the total collection of artifacts and very low when compared with sites in the vicinity.

A total of 2,270 pieces of ferrocrete sandstone, one piece of fossil wood and one battered quartz pebble were collected. Of these, 291 were Levallois flakes or tools, 11 were bifaces, 100 were cores, 928 were flakes, 15 were hammerstones, and 925 were small fragments and core manufacturing waste flakes or debris.

TOOL TYPOLOGY

		No.	%	Restricted %
1	Levallois flakes, typical	35	12.0	
2	Levallois flakes, atypical	19	6.5	
3	Levallois points	6	2.1	
5	Pseudo-Levallois points	7	2.4	3.1
9	Side-scrapers, straight	8	2.7	3.6
10	Side-scrapers, convex	12	4.1	5.3
11	Side-scrapers, concave	5	1.7	2.2
12	Side-scrapers, double straight	1	0.3	0.4
19	Side-scrapers, convergent convex	1	0.3	0.4
21	Side-scrapers, *déjeté*	2	0.7	0.9
22	Side-scrapers, transverse straight	1	0.3	0.4

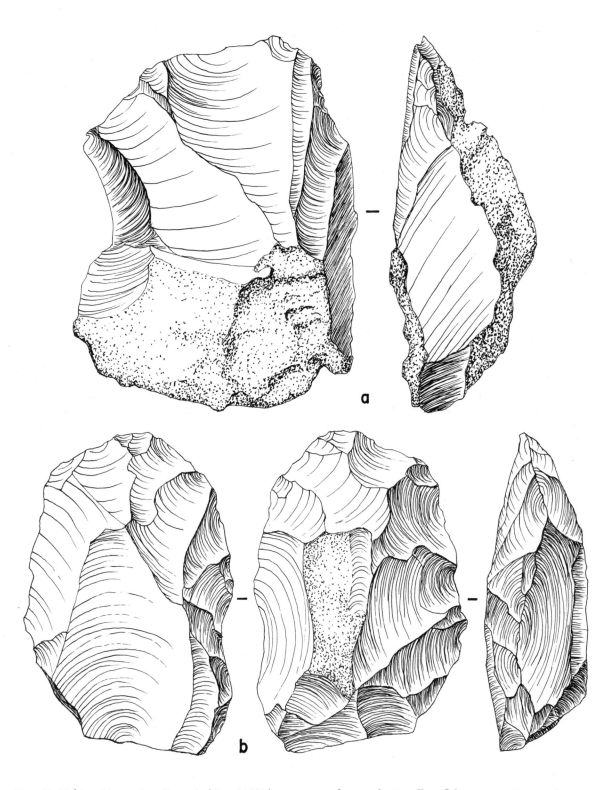

Fɪɢ. 42—Nubian Mousterian, Type A (Site 1033L): a, marginal core; b, Levallois flake core. 4/5 natural size.

		No.	%	Restricted %
23	Side-scrapers, transverse convex	2	0.7	0.9
25	Side-scrapers, inverse	13	4.5	5.8
29	Side-scrapers, alternate retouch	3	1.0	1.3
30	End-scrapers, typical	8	2.7	3.6
31	End-scrapers, atypical	8	2.7	3.6
32	Burins, typical	2	0.7	0.9
33	Burins, atypical	4	1.4	1.8
34	Borers, typical	5	1.7	2.2
35	Borers, atypical	5	1.7	2.2
37	Backed knives, atypical	4	1.4	1.8
38	Cortex backed knives	8	2.7	3.6
39	Raclettes	1	0.3	0.4
40	Truncated pieces	17	5.8	7.6
42	Notched pieces	45	15.5	20.1
43	Denticulate pieces	33	11.3	14.7
44	Bec burins	9	3.1	4.0
45	Inversely retouched pieces	7	2.4	
53	Pseudo-microburins	4	1.4	1.8
54	Notched at the distal end	7	2.4	3.1
62	Varia	9	3.1	4.0
		291	99.6	99.7

Cleaver	1
Disc	1
Pick	1
Biface subtriangular	1
Biface cordiform, elongated	1
Biface fragments	6
	11
Hammerstones	15

Technological Indices

IL=6.3   IF=44.1   IFs=32.8   Ilame≐10.5

Typological Indices and Characteristic Groups

IL^{ty}=20.6   IR=16.3   IC=4.8   IA^u=1.3   IB=3.3
I=20.6   II=19.1   III=13.2   IV=11.3

Restricted Typological Indices and Groups

IL^{ty}=0.0   IR=21.3   IC=6.6   IA^u=1.7   IB=4.2
I=0.0   II=24.4   III=16.0   IV=14.7

NOTES ON THE TYPOLOGY

Levallois flakes (54). As a group, the Levallois flakes are roughly shaped. Over half the typical examples are elongated, including six Levallois blades (fig. 43, h). The remaining typical examples are generally rectangular (fig. 43, i), although there is one typical para-Levallois flake as well (fig. 43, a). Platforms are usually faceted, but unfaceted pieces are not rare. The overall impression is one of a rather indifferent Levallois technology. There is no standardization of size, with flakes ranging from 3.5 to 8.5 cm. in length.

Levallois points (6). These are poorly formed and vary greatly in size from 2.8 to 5.5 cm. in length.

Pseudo-Levallois points (7). All typical examples (fig. 43, b).

Side-scrapers, straight (8). Straight side-scrapers are rare at Middle Paleolithic sites in Nubia. This assemblage has by far the largest number. For the most part, the scraping edges are somewhat ragged. Four are formed by marginal retouch, while the other four have semi-steep retouch. One straight scraper has an inverse notch at one end of the scraping edge, thus forming a type of bec burin (fig. 43, j).

Side-scrapers, convex (12). Four have marginal retouch, while the remaining examples are made by semi-steep retouch. Three well formed scrapers are on broken Levallois flakes (fig. 43, c), one is on a Levallois flake with a thinned butt, and the other four are on odd shaped flakes.

Side-scrapers, concave (5). Of the five found, four are well formed by semi-steep retouch. The other has marginal retouch. All are made on irregular shaped flakes of moderate size (fig. 43, f).

Side-scrapers, double straight (1). A poor example with marginal retouch on a broken Levallois blade.

Side-scrapers, convergent convex (1). Actually, this is a convergent convex-concave scraper with the tip broken. The convex side, however, is the determining factor in its being classed here.

Side-scrapers, *déjeté* (2). One is on a Levallois flake and has straight scraping edges made by marginal retouch. The other is made by semi-steep retouch, and the scraping edges are convex. It approaches an end-scraper (fig. 43, d).

Side-scrapers, transverse straight (1). The scraping edge has rather unequal retouch, some sections being marginal while others are semi-steep.

Side-scrapers, transverse convex (2). Both are on short, very wide flakes. One is partially retouched (fig. 43, g), while the other has semi-steep obverse retouch along half the scraping edge and flat, inverse retouch along the other half.

Side-scrapers, inverse (13). The most common inverse side-scrapers have convex scraping edges and are made by relatively flat retouch. There

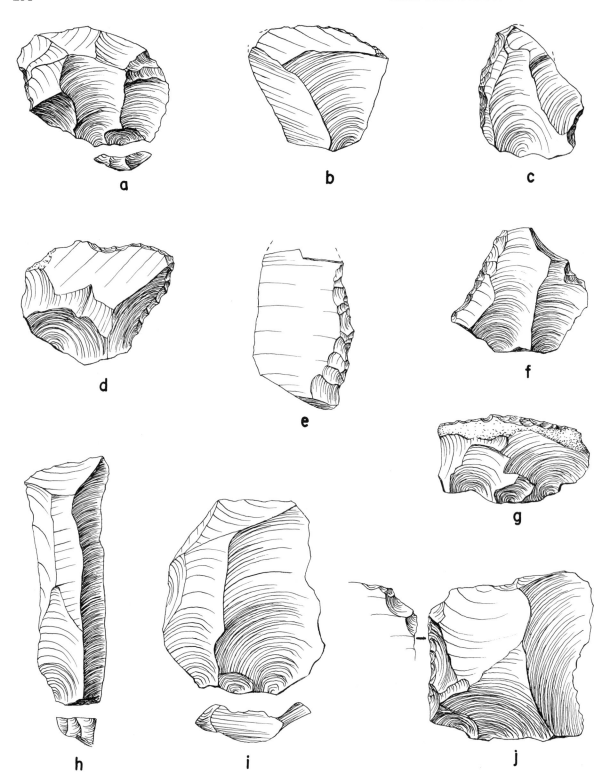

FIG. 43–Nubian Mousterian, Type B (Site 6): a, para-Levallois flake; b, pseudo-Levallois point; c, convex scraper; d, atypical *déjeté* scraper; e, inverse scraper; f, concave scraper; g, transverse convex scraper; h, Levallois blade; i, Levallois flake; j, straight scraper–bec burin. 4/5 natural size.

are nine such examples, the best of which has fine, flat retouch on a broken Levallois blade (fig. 43, e). There are also four straight scrapers with an almost semi-steep, inverse retouch.

Side-scrapers, alternate retouch (3). Each of the three is different. There is a double convex piece with semi-steep inverse retouch and marginal obverse retouch on a Levallois flake; a double convex-straight scraper made completely by marginal retouch on a Levallois flake; and a double convex-concave scraper made completely by semi-steep retouch on an irregular flake.

End-scrapers (16). There are three typical end-scrapers on small flakes (fig. 44, b), and five typical narrow nosed scrapers. Two of these are twisted to the right by deeply retouched notches which take the place of true shoulders (fig. 44, e). All are small, none exceeding 3.9 cm. in length. The atypical examples are poorly or only partially retouched.

Burins (6). One is a typical angle burin on a broken flake (fig. 44, g), while the other typical example is a dihedral angle burin on the tip of a false burin (fig. 44, k). The atypical examples are all poor single blow burins on the distal ends of thick flakes.

Borers (10). Three typical borers are made by inversely retouched notches and have short, pointed boring tips. One is made by alternate retouch on the corner of a broken flake, while the fifth typical example is made by inverse retouch on a partially truncated Levallois flake which also has a slightly denticulated sidescraper on one edge (fig. 44, h).

The five atypical examples have mostly short, rather stubby boring tips. All are made by retouched notches, although in two cases the notches are alternately retouched.

Backed knives, atypical (4). There is one nice example on an elongated Levallois flake. It is only partially backed, but the retouch is steep, although irregular (fig. 44, j).

Cortex backed knives (8). These are typical pieces, which range in size from 6.6 to 9.9 cm. in length.

Raclettes (1). This example is on a small, transverse flake and has a straight retouched, lateral edge (fig. 44, c).

Truncated pieces (17). There are one basally truncated flake, eight partial straight truncations, one partial concave truncation, and seven oblique truncations. As a group, they are poorly executed on irregularly shaped flakes, and some are, no doubt, questionable.

Notched pieces (45). One striking element is the rarity of retouched notches—only five out of a total of forty-five. There are two obversely retouched macronotches and three inversely retouched macronotches. One of the obverse examples is on a snapped flake.

There are thirteen additional inverse notches. These are made by single blows, of which six are micronotches and seven are macronotches.

The most common type of notch is an obverse notch made by a single blow. There are twenty-seven such examples, of which ten are macronotches and seventeen are micronotches. These micronotches are quite small, usually about 0.5 cm. across. Very few show any signs of use, and many may be accidental.

Denticulate pieces (33). Denticulates are generally well made, although there is a great range in form, size, and quality. The following types were recovered: (1) one macrodenticulate made by percussion on a core; (2) two microdenticulates made by percussion at the distal ends of small, thick flakes; (3) one bilateral microdenticulate made by alternate retouch on a Levallois flake; (4) four lateral, inverse microdenticulates made by retouch on blades, one of these blades being made of fossil wood; (5) nine obversely retouched microdenticulates on flakes (fig. 44, i); (6) one transverse, retouched microdenticulate; (7) two transverse macrodenticulates made by percussion; (8) three obverse macrodenticulates made by retouch, one of which is on a blade (fig. 45, c); and (9) ten lateral macrodenticulates made by percussion on flakes.

Bec burins (9). As a group, these are poorly made. Retouch is often light and in half the pieces, one part of the bec is formed by a notch rather than by a retouched edge. One bec has an additional notch near the butt.

Inversely retouched pieces (7). Inverse retouch on flakes which is not continuous enough to form true scraping edges.

Pseudo-microburins (4). Four small, typical examples.

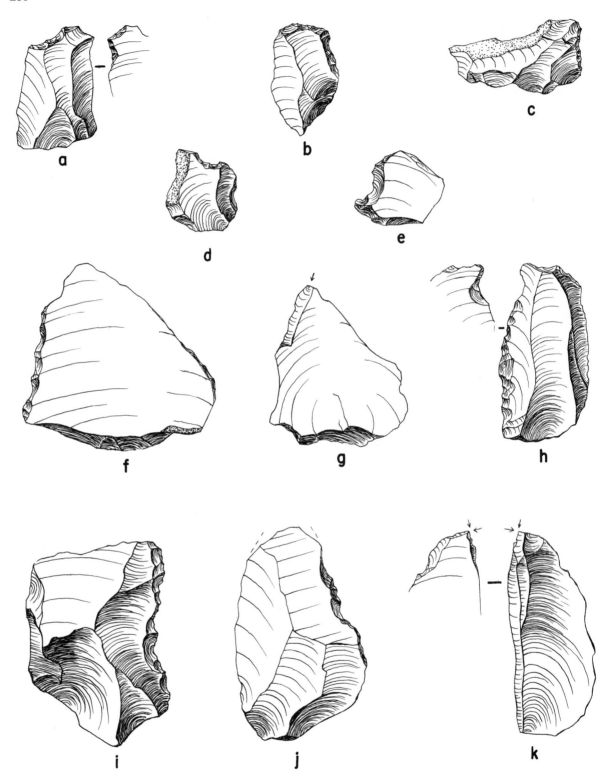

FIG. 44—Nubian Mousterian, Type B (Site 6): a, borer-truncation; b, end-scraper; c, raclette; d, end notch; e, nosed scraper; f, i, denticulates; g, k, burins; h, borer-scraper; j, atypical backed knife. 4/5 natural size.

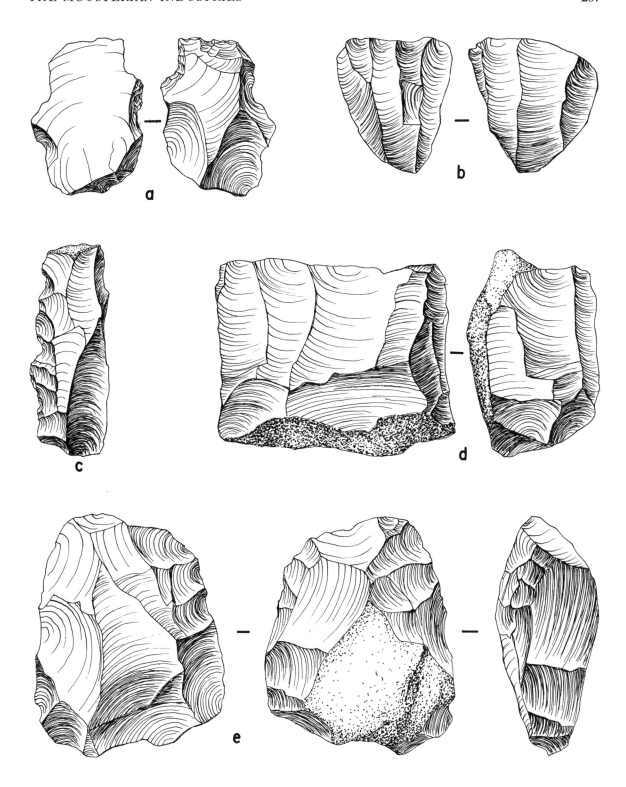

FIG. 45—Nubian Mousterian, Type B (Site 6): a, complex tool; b, blade core; c, denticulate; d, marginal core; e, Levallois core. 4/5 natural size.

Notched at the distal end (7). All are on small, thick flakes. They are all micronotches made by single blows, and all but one are obverse (fig. 44, d).

Varia (9). There are four strangled flakes, two of which are formed by alternately retouched notches. There is one inverse angle scraper on a large flake. The other four are highly complex tools.

There is one short flake with basal truncation, an atypical end-scraper at its distal end, a macronotch on one lateral edge, and an inverse microdenticulation made by retouch on the other lateral edge.

Another complex tool classed here has a large bec burin on each lateral edge, is truncated, and has a borer on one edge of the truncation (fig. 45, a).

One Levallois flake has a borer on the distal end, a short lateral, marginally retouched convex scraping edge, a deep inverse notch near the butt, and a flat, inverse scraping edge near the borer.

The fourth complex tool is a backed Levallois flake which has three large, inversely retouched notches on the side opposite the backing.

Cleaver (1). One fragment of a distal end (fig. 46, d).

Disk (1). One very nice example, measuring 7 cm. in diameter (fig. 46, a).

Pick (1). One large example on a plaquette. It is much more weathered than the rest of the artifacts and appears to belong to an earlier period.

Biface, subtriangular (1). One nicely made biface which is broken at the tip. At best, it could not have measured more than 8.5 cm. when whole (fig. 46, b).

Biface, cordiform, elongated (1). Again, this piece is well made, small with the tip broken (fig. 46, c).

Biface fragments (6). There are six fragments of biface tips. One appears to be from a triangular or subtriangular biface, while the others have rather blunt tips and convex edges.

Hammerstones (15). One unique aspect of this assemblage was the presence of fifteen battered wadi cobbles of ferrecrete sandstone. Each shows signs of use as a hammerstone on one or both ends. None shows full peripheral battering. They

measure from 5.5 to 8.5 cm. in length and many have short deep flake scars along with the battered edges. In addition, there was one battered quartz pebble. Five of these have beeen burned, either accidentally or for their color which rubs off as a red-brown powder.

CORE TYPOLOGY

	No.	%
Levallois		
Levallois blade	4	4.0
Levallois flake	19	19.0
Nubian, Type I	3	3.0
Para-Levallois	5	5.0
Other		
Marginal	16	16.0
Discoidal	10	10.0
Globular	5	5.0
Blade	2	2.0
Unidentifiable	36	36.0
	100	100.0

NOTES ON THE TYPOLOGY

Levallois blade (4). There are one unstruck and three struck cores. All are small, measuring betweeen 5 and 7.2 cm. in length. They are well made and are among the best prepared of all the cores from this assemblage.

Levallois flake (19). While there is great variation in quality of preparation and size, the typical Levallois flake core is of medium length and roughly prepared (fig. 45, e). Some might even be considered proto-Levallois cores, their preparation is so rough. Sizes range from 3.4 to 9.2 cm. although only two are diminutive. Less than half have been struck, all with indifferent results.

Nubian, Type I (3). Three quite typical examples were found. One is diminutive and all have been struck. In each case, however, the main flake was not a point but a simple Levallois flake.

Para-Levallois (5). There are two diminutive cores which are poorly prepared and have hinge fractured while being struck. There are also three other examples which are also roughly shaped.

Marginal (16). The greatest number of recognizable cores are of this type. For the most part, they are large and show a series of flakes or elongated flakes struck in one direction from a natural or unfaceted platform (fig. 45, d). Eleven

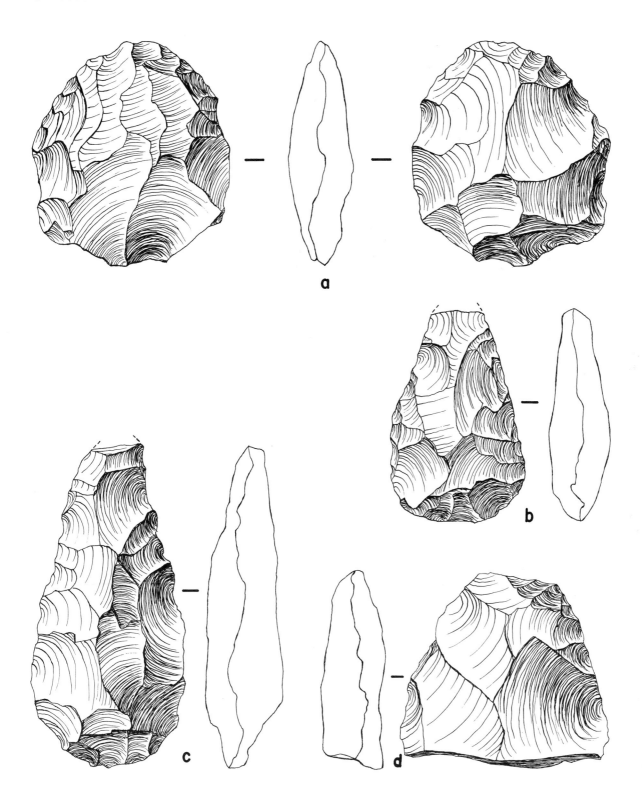

Fig. 46—Nubian Mousterian, Type B (Site 6): a, disk; b-c, bifaces; d, cleaver fragment. 4/5 natural size.

are formed in this way, while five have been flaked from opposing natural or unfaceted platforms. Only one is diminutive, while the largest examples are on natural slabs of ferrocrete sandstone measuring as much as 10 cm. in length.

Discoidal (10). There are three partial bifacial examples and seven complete unifacial cores. Three are diminutive, most are small, but one measures 11.5 cm. in diameter. They all show deep and irregular flake scars.

Globular (5). These have been flaked from all directions, leaving a globular shaped remnant. They are small, the largest measuring only 5 cm. in diameter.

Blade (2). These are two diminutive cores, one perimetrical and the other pyramidal (fig. 45, b). Neither is typical, but they are merely variations of the marginal type core.

Unidentifiable (36). Twenty-four show no noticeable pattern of flaking. There are twelve, however, which have faceted platforms and are struck, but show no other Levallois preparation. In effect, they are simple, faceted platform cores.

SITE 121

Site 121 is situated on the top of a small inselberg two kilometers north of the Cairo Road (map ref. 652/919.5). The inselberg is isolated from the main line, being closer to the Nile than any of the others. The top is composed of two small, oval platforms separated by a deeply eroded wedge. The site consisted of a dense surface concentration on the southern platform covering the whole surface but not extending onto the slopes or onto the northern platform. The platform was capped by a coarse, black ferrocrete sandstone which was unsuitable for tool manufacture. All artifacts were made on a brown ferrocrete sandstone which had to be imported from nearby inselbergs.

The southern platform covered an area of about 40 sq. m. and the total area was collected systematically. By completely collecting the site there were recovered a total of 984 pieces of ferrocrete sandstone. Of this total, 137 were tools, 604 were flakes, 76 were cores, and the remainder were fragments, chips, and core manufacturing waste flakes.

A striking feature of the assemblage was the small size of cores and core remnants, while a small portion of the flake tools were a good deal larger. This apparent inconsistency may well be explained by the fact that all usable raw material had to be brought to the site. Once there, it was utilized until too small to be of further value. Therefore, it was typical to get a few large flakes and many diminutive ones. In fact, the number of diminutive flakes and tools so outnumber the larger variety that this assemblage must be considered diminutive.

TOOL TYPOLOGY

		No.	%	Restricted %
1	Levallois flakes, typical	22	16.0	
2	Levallois flakes, atypical	15	10.9	
5	Pseudo-Levallois points	1	0.7	1.0
9	Side-scrapers, straight	3	2.2	3.2
10	Side-scrapers, convex	8	5.8	8.4
11	Side-scrapers, concave	3	2.2	3.2
17	Side-scrapers, double convex-concave	1	0.7	1.0
21	Side-scrapers, déjeté	1	0.7	1.0
22	Side-scrapers, transverse straight	1	0.7	1.0
25	Side-scrapers, inverse	5	3.6	5.3
29	Side-scrapers, alternate retouch	2	1.4	2.1
30	End-scrapers, typical	1	0.7	1.0
31	End-scrapers, atypical	5	3.6	5.3
32	Burins, typical	2	1.4	2.1
33	Burins, atypical	1	0.7	1.0
35	Borers, atypical	3	2.1	3.1
38	Cortex backed knives	6	4.4	6.3
39	Raclettes	1	0.7	1.0
40	Truncated pieces	6	4.4	6.3
42	Notched pieces	14	10.2	14.7
43	Denticulate pieces	16	11.7	16.8
44	Bec burins	5	3.6	5.3
45	Inversely retouched pieces	5	3.6	
51	Tayac points	1	0.7	1.0
53	Pseudo-microburins	2	1.4	2.1
54	Notched at the distal end	6	4.4	6.3
62	Varia	1	0.7	1.0
		137	99.2	99.5
	Biface fragments	1		

Technological Indices

$IL=7.9$ $IF=38.9$ $IFs=22.9$ $Ilame=6.9$

Typological Indices and Characteristic Groups

$IL^{ty}=26.9$ $IR=17.3$ $IC=6.5$ $IA^{u}=0.0$ $IB=0.7$
$I=26.9$ $II=18.0$ $III=8.5$ $IV=11.7$

Restricted Typological Indices and Groups

$IL^{ty}=0.0$ $IR=25.2$ $IC=9.4$ $IA^{u}=0.0$ $IB=1.0$
$I=0.0$ $II=26.2$ $III=12.5$ $IV=16.8$

NOTES ON THE TYPOLOGY

Levallois flakes (37). Levallois flakes in this assemblage were normally not retouched. Only seven of forty-four were made into retouched tools, and two of these were simple notches made by percussion. The unretouched Levallois flakes are generally small and indifferently prepared. There are, however, some fine examples (fig. 47, a). The majority—61 per cent of all complete pieces—are diminutive, measuring between 3 and 5 cm. (fig. 47, b-c). As a group, they are normally faceted and have rather prominent bulbs of percussion.

The atypical examples include many which are incurvate, similar to core manufacturing waste flakes. These, however, have well formed butts and show typical Levallois preparation.

Pseudo-Levallois points (1). One typical, diminutive example.

Side-scrapers, straight (3). Two straight scrapers are formed by semi-steep retouch on irregular shaped flakes. One of these has a slightly irregular scraping edge, two straight retouched sections on the same side which meet in a little bulge (fig. 47, k). The third example has marginal retouch. Two of the three are on diminutive flakes.

Side-scrapers, convex (8). Again, as at so many of the Middle Paleolithic sites in Nubia, the simple convex side-scrapers are the most numerous and are among the best made. Seven of the eight found in this assemblage are on diminutive, irregularly shaped flakes. Four are formed by semi-steep retouch (fig. 47, d) and four by marginal retouch.

Side-scrapers, concave (3). Three good examples are made by semi-steep retouch (fig. 47, f). All measure over 5 cm. in length.

Side-scrapers, double convex-concave (1). A well made piece on a partially truncated flake, measuring 5.4 cm. in length. The convex scraping edge is somewhat irregular but is not truly denticulate. Both scraping edges are formed by semi-steep retouch.

Side-scrapers, *déjeté* (1). This is a diminutive, *déjeté* scraper made by flat, inverse retouch. It has been classed here as its form is highly atypical for inversely retouched scrapers and is quite typical of the *déjeté* class (fig. 47, e).

Side-scrapers, transverse straight (1). A broken, diminutive example.

Side-scrapers, inverse (5). There is one straight scraper with bec burin on the opposite edge (fig. 47, j), two concave, and two convex, inverse scrapers. Four are on diminutive, irregularly shaped flakes, while one is on a broken Levallois flake, which measures over 5 cm. in length (fig. 47, i).

Side-scrapers, alternate retouch (2). Both are double concave scrapers on diminutive flakes. Retouch is, in all cases, semi-steep (fig. 47, g).

End-scrapers (6). There is one typical end-scraper on an elongated flake (fig. 47, h), and five atypical examples, two of which are on diminutive flakes.

Burins (3). There is a typical burin on a truncation and a burin *plan* on a partially truncated flake (fig. 48, d). The atypical piece is a poor dihedral burin on a core fragment. All are diminutive.

Borers (3). Two borers are made by alternate retouch on the side of diminutive flakes. The boring tips are short and quite wide at the base. The other borer is at the corner of a flake and is formed by a single retouch notch.

Cortex backed knives (6). These measure from 4.5 to 8.5 cm. in length and are quite typical (fig. 48, e).

Raclettes (1). The single raclette is on a flake measuring 1.7 cm. in length. The retouch is semi-steep and convex, but the size of the flake places it here rather than with the convex side-scrapers.

Truncated pieces (6). There are two oblique (fig. 48, c) and four straight truncations. Five of the six are diminutive in size.

Notched pieces (14). There are two obverse micronotches and three obverse macronotches made by percussion. There is also one obverse macronotch made by retouch on a Levallois flake. All are on flakes measuring under 5 cm. in length.

In addition, there are three inverse micronotches and three inverse macronotches made by percussion. There are also four inverse macronotches made by retouch. Only one inverse notch is on a flake measuring over 5 cm. in length (fig. 48, f).

Denticulate pieces (16). As a group, these are

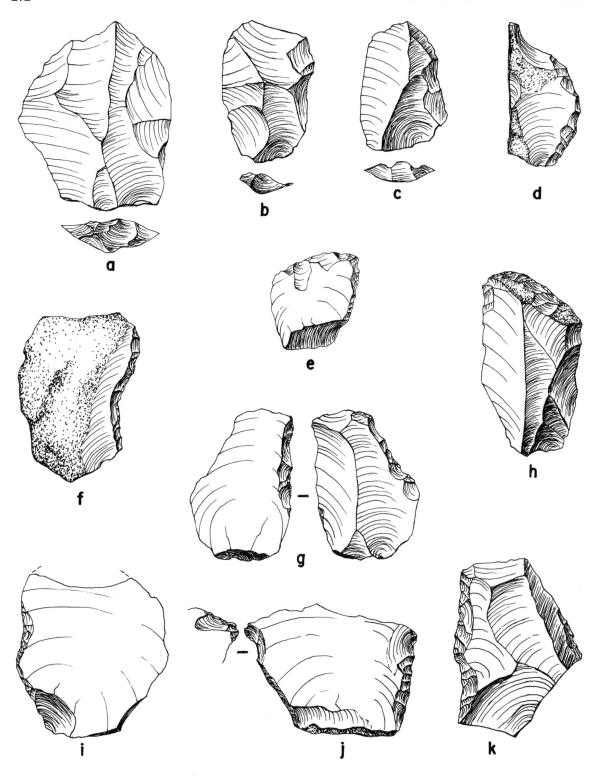

Fig. 47—Nubian Mousterian, Type B (Site 121): a-c, Levallois flakes; d, convex scraper; e, *déjeté* scraper; f, concave scraper; g, alternate scraper; h, end-scraper; i-j, inverse scraper; k, straight scraper. 4/5 natural size.

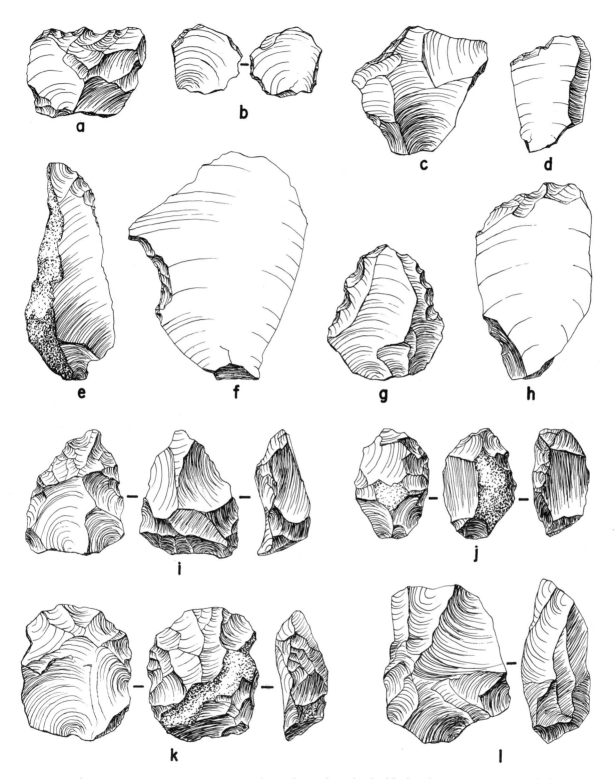

Fig. 48—Nubian Mousterian, Type B (Site 121): a, denticulate; b, double bec burin; c, truncation; d, burin; e, cortex backed knife; f, notch; g, Tayac point; h, varia; i, Levallois point core; j-k, Levallois flake cores; l, marginal core. 4/5 natural size.

on flakes which are larger than the average. They range in size from 2.6 to 9.2 cm., but ten of the sixteeen measure over 5 cm. in length.

There are one macrodenticulate on a core fragment, eight lateral macrodenticulates on flakes, and one macrodenticulate at the distal end of a flake; all are made by percussion. There are also two transverse macrodenticulates (fig. 48, a), two lateral, inverse macrodenticulates, and two lateral microdenticulates; all are made by retouch. They are generally rough and none shows really careful treatment.

Bec burins (5). Two are on the distal ends of thick blades, measuring over 5 cm. in length. The others are lateral examples on irregular, diminutive flakes (fig. 48, b). One of these flakes also has an inverse macronotch on the opposed edge.

Inversely retouched pieces (5). These flakes have small amounts of inverse retouch which is not continuous enough to form true scraping edges.

Tayac points (1). This is a convergent denticulate on a Levallois point. The denticulation is not particularly strong, and perhaps the piece should merely be classified as a denticulate (fig. 48, g).

Pseudo-microburins (2). Two typical examples on diminutive flakes.

Notched at the distal end (6). There are five micronotches made by single blows; two inverse and three obverse. There is also one inversely retouched macronotch. Only two of the six measure over 5 cm. in length.

Varia (1). This is a wedge shaped flake, 6 cm. long, which has a convex, semi-flat, inverse retouch on its distal end. Perhaps it might be considered an inverse end-scraper or a very light chopper (fig. 48, h).

Bifaces (1). One fragment of a distal end of a biface was found. It appears to be from an unfinished tool, as it is well retouched on one face but has only primary flaking on the other.

CORE TYPOLOGY

	No.	%
Levallois		
Levallois blade	2	2.6
Levallois flake	23	30.3
Levallois point	2	2.6
Nubian, Type I	1	1.3

	No.	%
Other		
Marginal	13	17.1
Discoidal	11	14.5
Globular	1	1.3
Unidentifiable	23	30.2
	76	99.9

NOTES ON THE TYPOLOGY

Levallois blade (2). Two struck examples, measuring 5 and 5.5 cm. in length.

Levallois flake (23). Twelve of the Levallois flake cores are diminutive. Of these, eight are unstruck and the rest are somewhat less than successfully struck (fig. 48, k). The smallest, which approaches a Levallois blade core in proportions, is only 3.5 cm. long (fig. 48, j).

Levallois point (2). Both are unsuccessfully struck diminutive examples (fig. 48, i).

Nubian, Type I. One unstruck fragment from a diminutive core.

Marginal (13). All are diminutive and mostly struck from only one platform. Cores struck from opposed platforms, however, are not rare; they account for about 40 per cent of all marginal cores (fig. 48, l).

Discoidal (11). There are three partial bifacial cores and eight unifacial examples. They are all diminutive.

Globular (1). One diminutive example.

Unidentifiable (23). These are all diminutive and show many sections of flake scars. They are truly remnants. The general impression of all the cores is seen here as well: while they were indifferently prepared, they were utilized until they were too small to work.

Jebel Brinikol

Jebel Brinikol is one of the three inselbergs capped with ferrocrete sandstone on the east bank of the Nile between the Second and Third Cataracts.[3] It stands massively above a wilderness of weathered granite and schist which form the typical landscape of the Batn el-Hajar. The inselberg is situated south of Semna, just west of the Wadi Halfa-Akasha road (long. 31° 05′/lat. 21° 25′). Jebel Brinikol consists of two platforms, in a north-south line, separated by a large, deeply eroded wedge (Solecki *et al.*, 1963, plate XIV, b).

---

[3] The other two are Jebel Dal, south of Akasha, and Jebel Firka, just north of the Third Cataract.

During the 1961-1962 field season, Jean de Heinzelin and Roland Paepe surveyed the southern platform. They discovered a large surface concentration of artifacts (Solecki *et al.*, 1963, p. 80). Because of the remoteness of the Jebel and its difficult access, three full days were required for making a systematic collection and transporting it down the inselberg.

Because of an unfortunate mistake, this systematic collection was split during packing so that part went to J. Guichard at the Laboratory of Prehistory, Bordeaux, and part to Columbia University and then to Southern Methodist University. Thus, neither collection constituted a systematic sample but rather a random sample taken from one which was initially systematic. Even this is not positive. The artifacts were labeled in the field, and it is not known if there was some form of unconscious sorting during this process. Therefore, a valid sample can be obtained only by combining the collections sent to Bordeaux and Dallas.

In 1964, the Guichards published a preliminary report on the collection in their possession (Guichard and Guichard, 1965, pp. 86-89). This current report will cover that material sent to America and incorporate the results reported by the Guichards. At the time, comparisons will be made between the two samples to show the extent of homogeneity.

Unfortunately, the Guichards did not publish a descriptive typology, although a type list and a number of drawings were included (Guichard and Guichard, 1965, pp. 86-89). Because of this, only general observations will be made on the tool types in this paper. The collection sent to New York was large enough, however, to permit technological and size studies. These will be dealt with in this and a later section.

The area systematically collected was not recorded, but the two collections may be divided into the following general types of artifacts:

	SMU		Laboratory of Prehistory	
	No.	%	No.	%
Bifaces	3	1.1	8	0.9
Flakes and blades	215	79.0	712	81.1
Cores, fragments, etc.	32	11.7	96	10.9
Debris, etc.	22	8.1	62	7.1
	272	99.9	878	100.0

The typology given below includes those tools sent to Bordeaux and to New York. The combined totals for each type in the collection sent to New York are given in parentheses immediately after.

Jebel Brinikol's position in the Nubian Mousterian, Type B, is somewhat open to question. In a previous report (Guichard and Guichard, 1965) it was classified as Nubian Middle Paleolithic I. This problem is fully discussed in a later section.

TOOL TYPOLOGY

		No.		%	Restricted %
1	Levallois flakes, typical	86	(15)	19.9	
2	Levallois flakes, atypical	78	(17)	18.0	
3	Levallois points	2	(2)	0.5	
5	Pseudo-Levallois points	3	(1)	0.7	1.2
6	Mousterian points	1	(1)	0.2	0.4
9	Side-scrapers, straight	8	(0)	1.8	3.3
10	Side-scrapers, convex	16	(5)	3.7	6.6
11	Side-scrapers, concave	10	(4)	2.3	4.1
15	Side-scrapers, biconvex	3	(0)	0.7	1.2
17	Side-scrapers, double convex-concave	1	(1)	0.2	0.4
19	Side-scrapers, convergent convex	2	(1)	0.5	0.8
21	Side-scrapers, *déjeté*	3	(3)	0.7	1.2
23	Side-scrapers, transverse convex	3	(3)	0.7	1.2
25	Side-scrapers, inverse	17	(11)	3.9	7.0
27	Side-scrapers, thinned	1	(1)	0.2	0.4
29	Side-scrapers, alternate retouch	2	(1)	0.5	0.8
30	End-scrapers, typical	2	(2)	0.5	0.8
31	End-scrapers, atypical	18	(7)	4.2	7.4
32	Burins, typical	1	(1)	0.2	0.4
33	Burins, atypical	3	(3)	0.7	1.2
35	Borers, atypical	13	(5)	3.0	5.4
37	Backed knives, atypical	6	(2)	1.4	2.4
38	Cortex backed knives	8	(8)	1.8	3.3
40	Truncated pieces	19	(7)	4.4	7.8
42	Notched pieces	17	(3)	3.9	7.0
43	Denticulate pieces	50	(18)	11.6	20.5
44	Bec burins	4	(3)	0.9	1.6
45	Inversely retouched pieces	20	(4)	4.6	
50	Bifacially retouched pieces	2	(0)	0.5	
54	Notched at the distal end	6	(6)	1.4	2.4
55	*Hachoirs*	1	(1)	0.2	0.4
62	Varia	25	(10)	5.8	10.3
		431	(146)	99.6	99.5
	Bifaces	3	(1)		
	Bifacial foliates	6	(0)		
	Picks	2	(2)		

Technological Indices

As the material in Bordeaux is described technologically in a series of indices, the material sent to New York will be compared with it in terms of the same indices. No attempt has been made to arrive at a single index for the total collection in any one observation. It should be noted, however, that the Blade Index is not valid for either collection as extra blades were collected in addition to the systematic collection (Guichard and Guichard, 1965, p. 88). The indices are as follows:

	SMU	Laboratory of Prehistory
IL	24.7	24.33
IF	50.0	51.23
IFs	37.1	43.20
Ilame	22.2	12.90

As can be seen above, there is a close similarity between the Levallois Indices and the Faceting Indices. The difference between the Strict Faceting Indices is apparently a normal variation within a single site.

The following typological indices are based on the total collection.

Typological Indices and Characteristic Groups

$IL^{ty}=38.4$　　$IR=15.2$　　$IC=4.4$　　$IA^u=1.4$　　$IB=2.2$
$I=38.4$　　　　$II=16.1$　　　　$III=10.0$　　　　$IV=11.6$

Restricted Typological Indices and Groups

$IL^{ty}=0.0$　　$IR=27.0$　　$IC=7.7$　　$IA^u=2.4$　　$IB=4.3$
$I=0.0$　　　　$II=28.6$　　　　$III=17.5$　　　　$IV=20.5$

NOTES ON THE SMU TYPOLOGY[4]

Levallois flakes. Levallois flakes are large, mostly elongate, with thick butts.

Levallois points. One large, atypical example.

Pseudo-Levallois points. All typical examples.

Mousterian points. Only one edge is truly retouched but the piece is quite pointed, although the retouched edge is slightly convex (fig. 49, a).

Side-scrapers, convex. These are on elongated flakes and have well formed semi-steep scraping edges.

Side-scrapers, concave. Two are large examples (fig. 50, c), and two are on small flakes.

Side-scrapers, double convex-concave. A broken example made by semi-steep retouch.

Side-scrapers, convergent convex. This approaches a Mousterian point.

Side-scrapers, *déjeté*. All are large and one has a spike in the center of each scraping edge (fig. 49, b).

Side-scrapers, transverse convex. Two have

---

[4] Numbers for each type are not given here because the notes refer only to those tools at SMU.

only poor marginal retouch, while the other is only partially retouched.

Side-scrapers, inverse. Most are on very large, thick flakes and have normal inverse retouch. One is a double side-scraper (fig. 49, d).

Side-scrapers, thinned. A convex side-scraper with rough thinning on the opposed edge.

Side-scrapers, alternate retouch. A small converging, straight-convex scraper.

End-scrapers. One nose scraper, but mostly wide scraping edges on flakes (fig. 50, d).

Burins. Aside from a small questionable burin *plan* on quartz, all burins are large, two are on oblique truncations, and one is a dihedral burin (fig. 49, c).

Borers. Short, thick boring tips on large flakes.

Backed knives. On blades which are only partially backed.

Cortex backed knives. These are both true blades and laminary flakes.

Truncated pieces. On large flakes or blades, similar to those published by the Guichards.

Notched pieces. All are macronotches made by single blows.

Denticulate pieces. All are macrodenticulates made by percussion, but many show retouch along the serrated edges (fig. 50, b). Two are inversely denticulated and one is *déjeté* made by alternate percussion.

Bec burins. Generally poor with some on small flakes.

Inversely retouched pieces. Small amounts of discontinuous, inverse retouch on flakes.

Notched at the distal end. All are macronotches made by single blows.

Hachoirs. One very small example (fig. 50, a).

Varia. These are all complex tools, involving a combination of scraping edges, notches, denticulates, borers, and bec burins.

Bifaces. One, small, thin ovate (fig. 51, a).

Picks. Two examples which are rather small (fig. 51, b).

CORE TYPOLOGY

	No.		%
Levallois			
Levallois blade	4	(2)	3.2
Levallois flake	44	(12)	35.2
Levallois point	10	(0)	8.0
Nubian, Type I	2	(1)	1.6

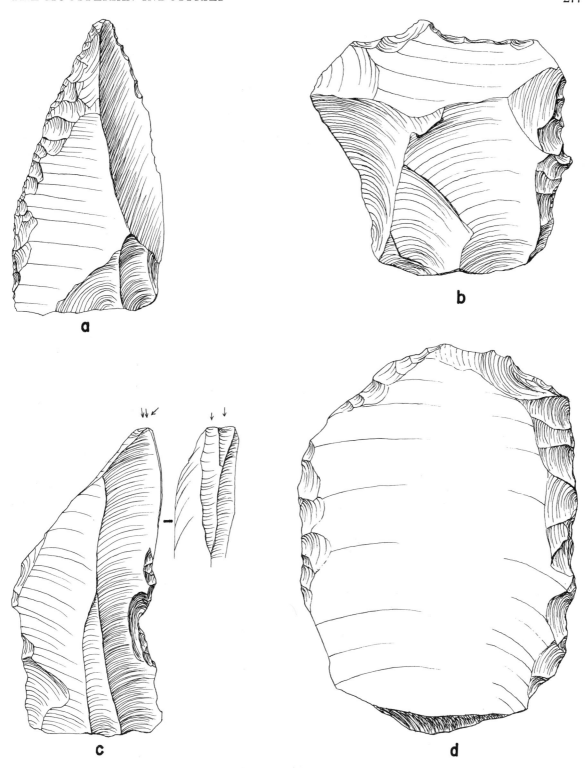

FIG. 49–Nubian Mousterian, Type B? (Jebel Brinikol): a, Mousterian point; b, *déjeté* scraper with spikes; c, burin; d, inverse scraper. 4/5 natural size.

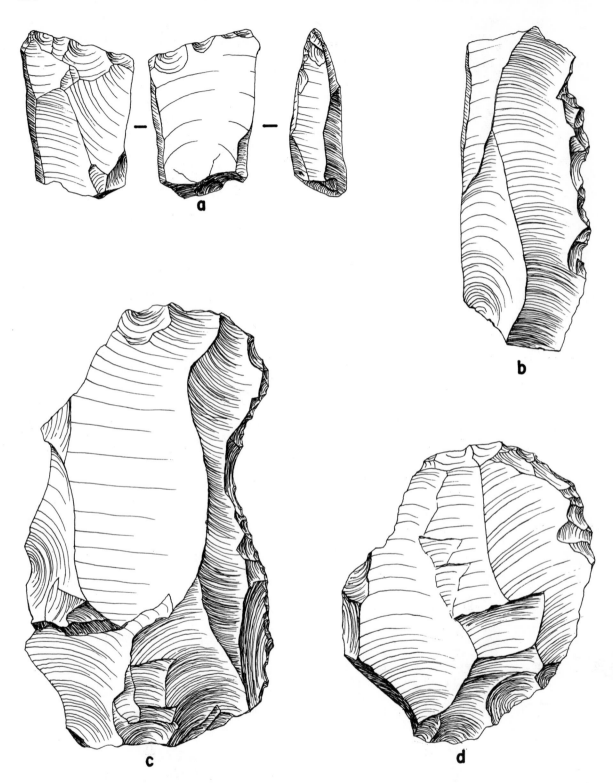

FIG. 50—Nubian Mousterian, Type B? (Jebel Brinikol): a, *hachoir;* b, denticulate; c, concave scraper; d, end-scraper. 4/5 natural size.

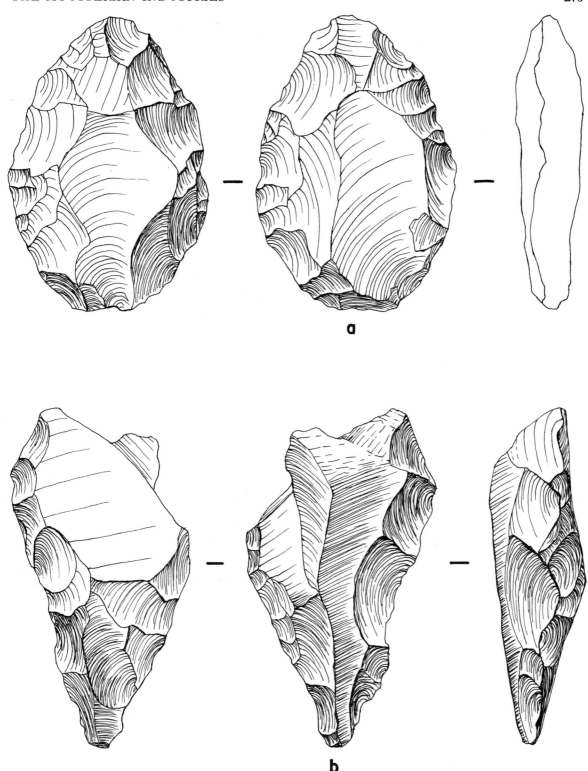

a

b

Fɪɢ. 51—Nubian Mousterian, Type B? (Jebel Brinikol): a, biface; b, pick. 4/5 natural size.

	No.	%
Nubian, Type II	9 (0)	7.2
Para-Levallois	2 (2)	1.6
Other		
"Acheulian"	3 (0)	2.4
Globular	3 (1)	2.4
Unidentifiable	48 (11)	38.4
	125 (29)	100.0

NOTES ON THE TYPOLOGY

Levallois blade. These are large and well prepared.

Levallois flake. For the most part, they are carefully prepared on both faces (fig. 52, a).

Nubian, Type I. A very large example has been struck twice.

Para-Levallois. Two large, roughly prepared cores (fig. 52, b).

Globular. A typical example.

Unidentifiable. Various cores showing no particular pattern of flaking.[5]

OTHER NUBIAN MOUSTERIAN SITES

During the 1961-1962 season, the Guichards surveyed and studied a number of Nubian Middle Stone Age sites (Guichard and Guichard, 1965, pp. 85-111). Most of these were classified as Nubian Middle Paleolithic—an industry which is reported to be technologically and typologically different from the Nubian Mousterian. They did, however, report three assemblages which they termed "non-Nubian" (Guichard and Guichard, 1965, pp. 84-86). Of these, only one assemblage, 401B, is reported in enough detail to permit comparisons.

Site 401B is situated on the top of an inselberg less than one kilometer south of Site 1010-8. A systematic collection was made from 16 sq. m., but only sixty-four retouched tools were recovered (Guichard and Guichard, 1965, p. 85). This sample was too small to permit a detailed typological study or comparisons with the Nubian Mousterian. On the other hand, the technological studies made by the Guichards are of value. The Levallois Index was among the lowest for any site they collected—15.5. Faceting Indices were high—IF = 54.5, IFs = 44.2; and the Blade

---

Index was low—4.7 (Guichard and Guichard, 1965, p. 85). Thus, technologically, this site fits well into the range of the Nubian Mousterian, as seen in Table 6.

The number of retouched tools was very small. They accounted for only 1.9 per cent of the total collection (Guichard and Guichard, 1965, p. 85). Assuming that the site was a workshop, this percentage correlates well with those from Site 1033, which were 2.8 and 1.6.

Sites 401B and 113A are too briefly described to permit comparison. In any case, the collection from 113A was not systematic and so, by definition, falls outside this type of study.

TECHNOLOGY AND TYPOLOGY OF THE MOUSTERIAN INDUSTRIES IN NUBIA

Each assemblage in the foregoing section is unique. No two are exactly alike. There are, however, certain typological and technological traits which show basic similarities within groups of assemblages and other traits which indicate differences between groups.

This section will compare the assemblages, showing how they are alike and how they differ. In the case of the Nubian Mousterian, a newly recognized Mousterian industry, a series of technological and typological limits will be suggested. Changes in these limits may well be necessary as more sites in adjacent areas are studied. Some limits may not have real industrial significance, but the total combination of typological and technological limits define the industry.

DENTICULATE MOUSTERIAN

Sites 1000 and 36B are both surface concentrations found on the tops of inselbergs. Site 1000 lies about seven kilometers east of the Nile, while Site 36B is in the range of inselbergs which fronts on the east bank of the Nile.

Apart from typological and technological considerations, these sites show many close parallels. Both are small; one covers an area of 150 sq. m., while the other is just under 200 sq. m. The density of artifact concentration at each site is between 80 and 90 per square meter. This was true in spite of the fact that raw material was locally available at Site 36B but had to be imported at Site 1000.

---

[5] There are numerous drawings of artifacts from this site in the Guichards' report (Guichard and Guichard, 1965, figs. 25-28).

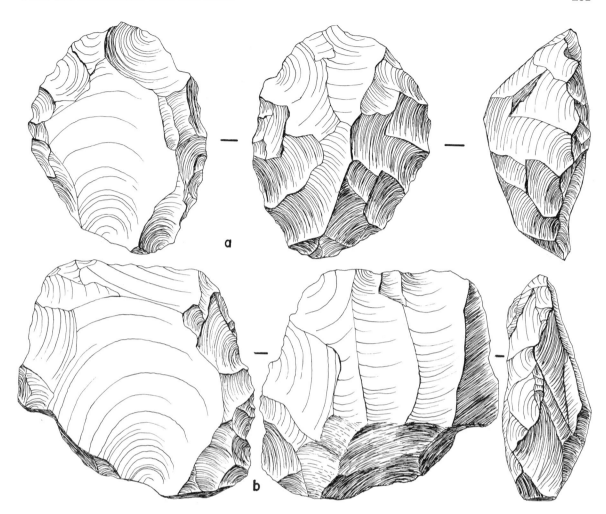

Fɪɢ. 52—Nubian Mousterian, Type B? (Jebel Brinikol): a, Levallois flake core; b, para-Levallois core. 2/3 natural size.

Both sites must be classified as living areas. While cores and debris were found in good number at each site, retouched tools accounted for 12.5 per cent of the total collection at Site 1000 and 19.8 per cent at Site 36B. This is somewhat above the average for all living sites studied, and contrasts sharply with those sites reported by the Guichards, where retouched tools were rare (Guichard and Guichard, 1965, p. 114).

The range in size of tools for both sites was from 2.4 to 9.7 cm. in length. The majority at both sites, however, fell between 3 and 6 cm., although those from Site 36B were on the average smaller than those from Site 1000. The general problem of artifact size will be dealt with in a later section.

Technologically, the assemblages are very similar, as shown in Table 1.

TABLE 1

DENTICULATE MOUSTERIAN: TECHNOLOGICAL INDICES

Site	IL	IF	IFs	Ilame
1000	14.3	49.7	27.3	13.9
36B	11.6	33.6	20.6	11.6

The differences in the Faceting Indices, while not large, are understandable when raw material is taken into account. At Site 1000, which has a higher proportion of faceted flakes, the raw material was a fine grain ferrocrete sandstone imported from a nearby inselberg. At Site 36B, the raw material was a rather coarse grain ferrocrete sandstone which verged on being marginal as a material for flake production. The raw material at Site 1000 is conducive to fine workmanship, while that from Site 36B resists it.

Typologically, both sites have a limited range of tool types. F. Bordes recognizes sixty-one significant tool types for the Mousterian of western France (Bordes, 1953b, p. 230). Of these sixty-one types, Site 1000 has only twenty and Site 36B only twenty-three. This compares with an average of twenty-nine types present at Nubian Mousterian living sites.

The Typological Indices, both complete and restricted, strongly reflect the paucity of tool types and the predominance of denticulate tools; see Tables 2 and 3.

TABLE 2

DENTICULATE MOUSTERIAN:
COMPLETE TYPOLOGICAL INDICES

Site	IL^{ty}	IR	IC	IA^u	I	II	III	IV
1000	28.7	6.0	1.6	0.0	28.7	7.2	5.9	32.4
36B	14.0	13.3	3.0	0.6	14.0	14.8	7.2	26.2

Two features stand out: the relatively high percentages of denticulate tools and the disparity between the percentages of side-scrapers. The Denticulate Index is comparable, but the "Mousterian" Group (Group II) shows that Site 36B is close to the upper limit for side-scrapers within a denticulate industry (Bordes, 1963, p. 44). This is more clearly seen in the restricted indices.

TABLE 3

DENTICULATE MOUSTERIAN:
RESTRICTED TYPOLOGICAL INDICES

Site	IL^{ty}	IR	IC	IA^u	I	II	III	IV
1000	0.0	7.2	2.4	0.0	0.0	9.6	8.0	48.0
36B	0.0	15.8	3.6	0.7	0.0	17.4	8.7	31.3

The major differences are in the percentages of Denticulate tools (Group IV) and "Mousterian" type tools (Group II). The denticulates, however, are both high, higher than is normal for other Mousterian industries. If notched pieces (Types 42 and 54) are added to the denticulates, these types dominate the assemblages. At Site 1000, they account for 72.8 per cent and at Site 36B for 53.2 per cent. At other Mousterian sites in Nubia, they never account for more than 37

per cent and normally they do not exceed 30 per cent.

The total configuration of tools is basically the same at both sites. This is clearly seen in Figure 53, which shows a cumulative graph for each assemblage taken from the restricted typological lists.

When significant cores are taken into account, there are some differences, but the general pattern is still similar, as can be seen in Table 4.

The table shows that the Levallois technology at Site 36B is less developed than at Site 1000. This may well be due to the difference in the quality of the raw material. If all Levallois cores are taken together, they total 56 per cent at Site 1000 and 42.1 per cent at Site 36B. Thus, the Levallois core element shows small quantitative as well as qualitative differences. The presence of more Marginal cores is understandable in that the raw material used at Site 36B was immediately available, while it had to be imported to Site 1000. This would tend to explain the higher proportion of relatively unprepared and slightly used Marginal cores at Site 36B as compared with those at Site 1000.

In short, there are no significant typological or essential technological differences between the two sites. The main difference lies in the quality of the tools. This is visually striking, but it is probably due to the limitations of the raw material used at each site.

NUBIAN MOUSTERIAN

The Nubian Mousterian is a typologically distinct industry which shows only a moderate amount of technological variation. For classificatory purposes, it has been subdivided into two typological facies: a facies without bifaces (Type A), and a facies with bifaces (Type B). This distinction goes beyond the mere presence or absence of a single tool type. A biface cannot be considered to be of the same order as a flake tool. It is not only different morphologically from a flake tool, but the production of a biface requires a different method of flaking and a quite different concept of a working edge. All Mousterian industries contain some bifaces, although their number varies considerably from industry to industry.

TABLE 4

DENTICULATE MOUSTERIAN: PERCENTAGES OF SELECTED CORE TYPES

| Site | Levallois | | | | Nubian | | | |
	Blade	Flake	Point	Para	Type I	Type II	Marginal	Discoidal
1000	7.3	41.4	0.0	7.3	0.0	0.0	14.9	2.4
36B	2.6	23.7	0.0	15.8	0.0	0.0	23.7	0.0

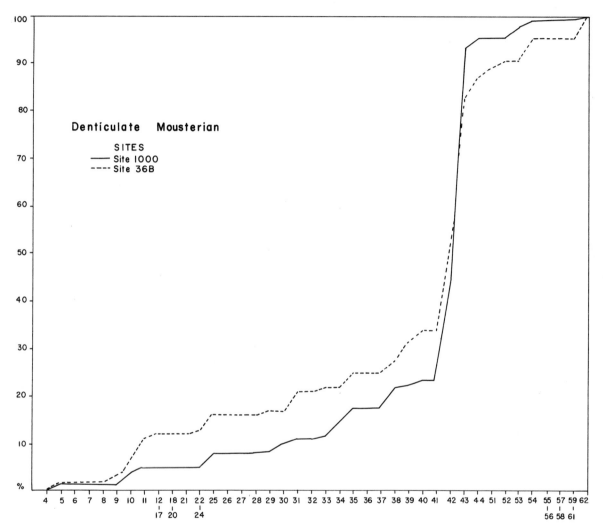

FIG. 53—Denticulate Mousterian: Cumulative graph of the restricted typology.

In the case of the Nubian Mousterian, bifaces are not commonly found in the assemblages. When they do occur, however, they are associated with a rather high side-scraper component and a relatively low "Upper Paleolithic" component. These, however, are not outside the range of the Nubian Mousterian, Type A, assemblages but tend to be at one extreme.

Therefore, as biface production utilizes a flaking concept different from flake tool production, as bifaces have been shown to be chronologically significant in certain Mousterian industries, and as those Nubian Mousterian assemblages with evidence of biface production all cluster toward one end of the defined typological range, it is felt that separate facies are justified. That is not to

TABLE 5

NUBIAN MOUSTERIAN, TYPE A: SITE AREAS, ARTIFACT DENSITY, AND
PERCENTAGE OF RETOUCHED TOOLS

Site No.	Area of Site in Sq. Meters	Density of Stone per Sq. Meters	Percentage of Retouched Tools
1010-8	50	170.5	14.6
1033 Upper	500+	210.0	2.8
1033 Lower	500+	172.8	1.6
1035	100	33.3	13.5
1036	200	42.3	11.1
1037	60	273.0	12.8
1038	200	174.0	14.3

say that these subindustrial facies will always be justified. More Nubian Mousterian sites may show that bifaces are not always associated with the other typological attributes noted above, but that they have a purely random occurrence. On the other hand, they may prove to have chronological significance or merely to be part of a true facies, an aspect of an industry which shows consistent but minor typological variation.

Until more Nubian Mousterian sites are found and studied, the two facies point to a possible significant difference between those Nubian Mousterian assemblages lacking evidence for a bifacial flaking tradition and those where that tradition is present but weak.

TYPE A

Over half of all the Mousterian assemblages studied fall into the Type A group. Seven assemblages out of a total of twelve (1010-8, both levels of 1033, 1035, 1036, 1037, and 1038) belong here. This larger sample may better illustrate the possible range in variation within a group than was the case with the Denticulate Mousterian. On the other hand, small differences may be due to normal evolutionary change or slightly different activities from site to site.

Of the six sites, all but 1010-8 are situated on the line of inselbergs which front on the east bank of the Nile in the area of Dibeira East. Four of them, Sites 1035 through 1038, are small surface concentrations on the same large inselberg. This is of interest as intensive survey disclosed that within two kilometers to the north and south, this line of inselbergs was devoid of other Mousterian sites. This particular inselberg did not have a higher quality ferrocrete sandstone than the others, nor was there any apparent topographic advantage in its specific locality.

Site 1033, a stratified subsurface site, is a few kilometers to the north, on a low pediment near the Nile which is still part of the complex of inselbergs which fronts on the Nile. The apparent motivating factor in the choice of this locality was the fine grain ferrocrete sandstone which the inhabitants quarried.

Table 5 shows the area, the density per square meter of all stone collected, and the percentage of retouched tools in the total collections for each site.

A number of similarities are at once obvious. With the exception of 1033, all sites are relatively small. The two smallest, 1010-8 and 1037, are situated on very narrow areas—a finger and a saddle—which, if nothing else, constricted their potential size. In both cases, the immediate area contained usable raw material. At both, there was an extremely dense concentration of artifacts but, at the same time, there was a high percentage of retouched tools in relation to the total collections. Because of this, it must be assumed that they were not primarily workshops but living areas.

Two sites stand out as having much lower density per square meter than the others—1035 and 1036. In spite of this, the percentage of retouched tools in proportion to the total collections is within the range of those sites with greater densities. A reasonable explanation is that these two sites were not occupied as long nor as intensively as were the others.

At Site 1033, both levels show the lowest percentages of retouched tools of any site. This is the one true workshop site listed, and retouched tools only account for about one-fifth of the proportion of tools found at living sites.

TABLE 6

NUBIAN MOUSTERIAN, TYPE A: TECHNOLOGICAL INDICES

Indices	1036	1033L	1033U	1037	1038	1035	1010-8
IL	4.9	8.3	7.0	11.6	18.7	21.7	25.4
IF	52.6	43.7	46.8	43.0	54.1	69.3	30.8
IFs	25.6	15.2	17.9	15.4	30.1	38.6	21.8
Ilame	3.2	12.7	9.5	6.0	11.0	7.8	3.5

Technologically, the Nubian Mousterian, Type A, shows certain internal variation (Table 6). This is particularly true of the Levallois Index, which rises from very little Levallois to a marginal Levallois facies level at two sites.

Perhaps the most striking aspect of the technology, with the exception of the generally low level of the Levallois Index, is the parallel low level of the Blade Index. The Faceting Index is reasonably similar at all sites, except at 1010-8 where it is low. The Restricted Faceting Index appears to be variable. In this case, it does not seem to be due to differences in the quality of raw material. Site 1037 has very low grade material, but Site 1033 has among the best found at any site. At 1033, however, the low Restricted Faceting Index may be due to the fact that it was a workshop where the inhabitants may have removed many of the finer flakes.

Typologically, these assemblages show great similarity within the restricted typology as the difference in the percentage of unretouched Levallois flakes varies considerably from site to site, as can be seen in Table 7. When compared with the indices for the restricted typology, listed in Table 8, it will be seen that the differences indicated by the complete indices are more apparent than real.

The most noticeable difference lies in the proportion of unretouched Levallois flakes. It is important to note that the highest percentage of these came from the two levels of Site 1033, a quarry and workshop site. This observation may well reflect on the sites reported by the Guichards as "classic" Middle Paleolithic and explains the extreme paucity of retouched tools which they encountered (Guichard and Guichard, 1965, p. 87). On the other hand, Sites 1036 and 1038 cannot be construed as workshops, as the percentages of retouched tools in the total collections are too high. These two sites appear to be intermediate between 1033 and the other living sites. The significance of this is obscure, although the IL^{ty} throughout seems variable.

A series of three pole graphs were employed in order to test the relationship between Levallois flakes and retouched tools, and to see if the variation in the indices is significantly different (Meighan, 1959). This system has normally been used as a means of temporal seriation of archaeological material, where three attributes are changing through time. It is just as effective, however, in testing whether there is variation in one attribute at a given time level, which causes percentage differences in two other attributes, or whether all three attributes are, in fact, variable.

For testing the significance of the variability of the IL^{ty} at Nubian Mousterian sites, three

TABLE 7

NUBIAN MOUSTERIAN, TYPE A: TYPOLOGICAL INDICES

Complete Indices	1033L	1033U	1035	1038	1010-8	1036	1037
IL^{ty}	52.0	45.4	36.7	31.0	16.8	10.2	10.8
IR	8.0	11.2	10.1	13.2	12.7	21.6	19.8
IC	2.6	3.4	2.2	5.3	3.5	3.8	3.4
IA^u	1.3	1.4	1.6	0.9	0.0	1.2	4.5
IB	0.0	0.0	0.0	0.0	0.0	0.0	0.0
I	52.0	45.4	36.7	31.0	16.8	10.2	10.8
II	8.7	12.6	11.2	15.0	13.8	22.0	19.8
III	7.4	9.1	10.9	14.2	15.1	14.4	23.6
IV	10.8	5.9	12.5	12.0	13.9	10.2	10.8

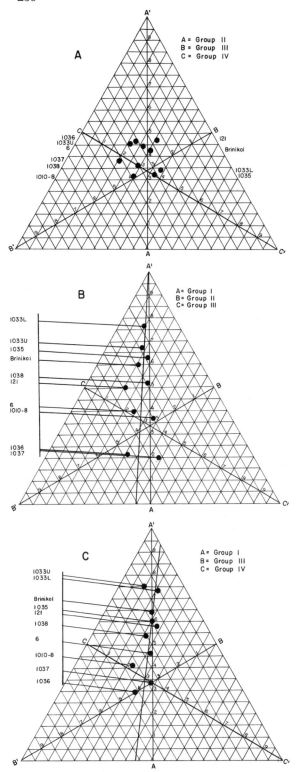

FIG. 54—Three pole graphs of the Nubian Mousterian:
a, Groups II, III, and IV; b, Groups I, II, and
III; c, Groups I, III, and IV.

separate graphs have been used. The first of these shows the internal relationship between the Typological Groups II, III, and IV (fig. 54, a); that is, the relationship between "Mousterian" tools, "Upper Paleolithic" tools, and Denticulate tools. The graph shows that all Nubian Mousterian sites cluster. Thus, the relationship between these three groups does not show any significant difference from site to site.

Once unretouched Levallois flakes become one of the attributes, however, we find a quite different graphic representation. In these cases, one of which includes Groups I, II, and III (fig. 54, b) and the other Groups I, III, and IV (fig. 54, c), the sites almost form along a straight line. This shows that the same single attribute is varying from site to site. On both graphs, it is the Levallois Group (Group I) which shows variation, other Groups retaining more or less even relationships to each other and to Group I.

Therefore, the total tool inventory shows no evidence for much internal variation within the Mousterian and Upper Paleolithic Characteristic Groups. The question arises whether the variation in the Levallois element is due to chance variation or to change through time. At present, there is no direct evidence pertaining to this point. On the other hand, the minimal change seen within the retouched tools suggests that no significant evolution of the industry took place.

In view of the above, it is best to look at the typological characteristics in terms of the restricted typology as it eliminates the factor of the unretouched Levallois flakes, and so deals only with more artifacts considered to be true tools.

The most noticeable feature here, seen in Table 8, is the standardly high proportion of "Upper Paleolithic" type tools (Group III). Not only is this significant in itself, but its relationship to the "Mousterian" type tools (Group II) is important. Three of the seven assemblages have proportionately more "Upper Paleolithic" type tools than "Mousterian" types, while at the four others, all "Upper Paleolithic" types are less than 8.1 per cent lower than "Mousterian" types.

Aside from a similarity within each assemblage of the Characteristic Groups II and III, it is important to note that these Groups are also very similar from assemblage to assemblage. Group

TABLE 8

Nubian Mousterian, Type A: Restricted Typological Indices

Indices	1033L	1033U	1035	1038	1010-8	1036	1037
IL^{ty}	0.0	0.0	0.0	0.0	0.0	0.0	0.0
IR	16.8	21.0	15.8	19.3	16.7	23.6	23.7
IC	5.6	6.4	3.6	7.8	4.5	4.5	4.0
IA^{u}	2.8	2.8	2.7	1.3	0.0	1.5	5.2
IB	0.0	0.0	0.0	0.0	0.0	0.0	0.0
I	0.0	0.0	0.0	0.0	0.0	0.0	0.0
II	18.2	23.8	17.6	21.9	18.2	24.1	23.7
III	15.4	17.5	18.0	20.8	19.7	17.0	26.8
IV	22.4	11.1	19.8	17.9	18.2	12.2	12.5

II shows a variation of only 7.5 per cent for all the assemblages and for Group III it is only slightly higher at 10.8 per cent. That is, the internal consistency within each assemblage and the consistency across assemblages are high. The same is true for all indices. In fact, there is no index for one assemblage which does not fit within a reasonable range for any other assemblage.

Perhaps the one discordant note is the total absence of backed knives at Site 1010-8. Backed knives, however, are always rare, and in the vast majority of cases they are exceedingly atypical. The total configurations of retouched tools from these assemblages form almost indistinguishable cumulative graphs, as can be seen in Figure 55.

Within the core typology, we find some strong differences which are not reflected in the tools. There are a few assemblages which have a high proportion of Nubian Cores, Type I, while others either have none, or their proportion is very low. Table 9 shows the percentages for significant core types.

The percentages for any one assemblage do not add up to 100. This is is because certain less significant types have been excluded, as have the

unidentifiable cores which, in all cases, account for a sizable percentage. The complete listings are given with the descriptive typology in the individual site reports.

Non-Levallois, Marginal, and Mousterian Discoidal cores are present in all assemblages. Their relative proportions, however, vary greatly. Only one site has more than 10 per cent Mousterian Discoidal cores, while four sites have more than 10 per cent Marginal cores. The relationship between the presence of Mousterian Discoidal cores and the other core types is not readily apparent, while the high percentage of Marginal cores fits a definite pattern. Those sites which have more than 10 per cent Marginal cores have few if any Nubian cores, while those sites with a high proportion of Nubian cores consistently have few Marginal ones.

Perhaps there is also more than a chance relationship between a high percentage of Nubian cores and a high percentage of para-Levallois cores. Unfortunately, the number of sites under consideration is small, and the evidence is not fully consistent even with the sample at hand.

It must be remembered that the Nubian Core, Type I, is really no more than a Levallois point

TABLE 9

Nubian Mousterian, Type A: Percentages of Selected Core Types

Sites	Levallois				Nubian			
	Blade	Flake	Point	Para	Type I	Type II	Marginal	Discoidal
1033L	10.1	53.1	5.0	1.3	0.0	0.0	12.6	3.8
1033U	7.5	37.5	1.5	3.0	0.0	0.0	21.0	6.0
1035	1.4	38.4	2.9	5.0	21.0	2.1	2.1	3.6
1038	4.8	25.1	1.5	21.8	21.8	1.5	3.0	3.0
1010-8	5.9	29.4	0.0	11.7	11.7	0.0	5.9	0.0
1036	0.0	31.4	2.2	6.6	0.0	0.0	17.7	17.7
1037	0.0	25.0	2.8	5.6	2.8	0.0	11.1	8.3

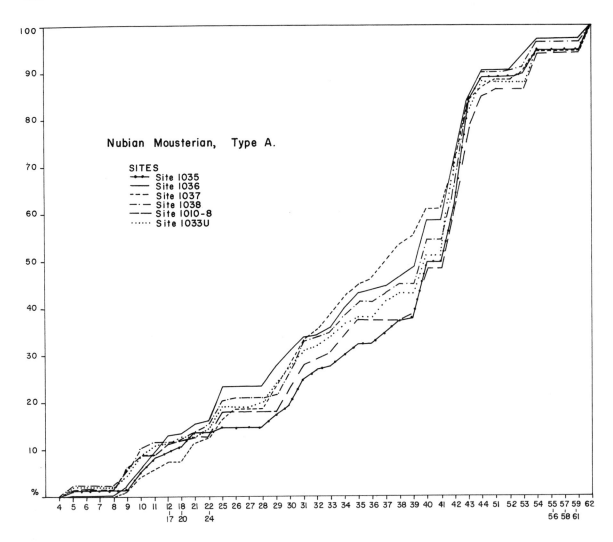

Fig. 55—Nubian Mousterian, Type A: Cumulative graphs of the restricted typologies.

core which has a slightly modified system of preparation. The same is true for the Nubian Core, Type II. If we take all Levallois cores as a group, it is clear that the dominant core technique is Levallois. At five of the sites, Levallois cores account for half or more of all cores and, at the other two, they never fall below one-third of all cores.

The relationship between the Nubian core technology and the typology will be examined later when comparisons are made between the Nubian Mousterian and the "Nubian Middle Paleolithic."

Of the technological and typological attributes perhaps three stand out as most significant: the low Levallois Index, the high proportion of "Upper Paleolithic" type tools, and the rather equal percentages of "Mousterian" and "Upper Paleolithic" tool types.

It must be remembered that the sample of assemblages is relatively small; but the typological consistencies are striking, and the technological attributes show only moderate variation.

TYPE B

Two assemblages have been termed Nubian Mousterian, Type B. These come from Sites 6 and 121. The distinction between Nubian Mousterian, Type A and Type B, mainly rests on the presence or absence of bifaces.

Sites 6 and 121 are both surface concentrations found on the tops of inselbergs which belong to the line which fronts on the east bank of the Nile. Site 6 is situated a little to the north of Jebel es-Sahaba and Site 121 a little to the south.

Site 6 was systematically collected during the 1961-1962 field season by the expedition geologists, before a uniform system of treatment was devised. Therefore, there is no information on the total area of the site or the total size of the systematic collection. This precludes information pertaining to artifactual density. The site did, however, contain 12.1 per cent retouched tools.

Site 121 covered an area of 40 sq. m., had an artifactual density of 42.5 per sq. m., and contained 10.1 per cent retouched tools.

Thus, the observations which are available for these sites place them fully within the range of Nubian Mousterian, Type A.

Sites 6 and 121 have the technological attributes shown in Table 10.

TABLE 10
NUBIAN MOUSTERIAN, TYPE B: TECHNOLOGICAL INDICES

Site	IL	IF	IFs	Ilame
6	6.3	44.1	32.8	10.5
121	7.9	38.9	22.9	6.9

The great similarity between the technology of these two assemblages is too obvious to warrant comment. As to their relationship to Nubian Mousterian, Type A, the Levallois Indices here fall within the lower range, and the Faceting

Indices are normal, as are the Restricted Faceting Indices. The Blade Indices, as well, fit fully within the Type A range.

Typologically, these two assemblages are unique in the presence of bifaces. Aside from this feature the assemblages are quite familiar. The Complete Typological Indices are given in Table 11.

There are only two differences apparent: the absence of backed knives at Site 121 and the relatively low index of "Upper Paleolithic" tool types also at Site 121. Group III, however, is not so low as to place it outside a probable normal range. It is only 4.7 below that for Site 6.

The Restricted Typological Indices tend, in this case, to accentuate the internal differences noted above. This can be seen in Table 12.

While the internal differences are accentuated, the Restricted Typological Indices minimize the differences between the two assemblages in Group III. Their overall similarity can be seen in the cumulative graph in Figure 56.

A comparison between the Restricted Typological Indices of the Nubian Mousterian, Type A and Type B, clearly shows that typologically they belong to the same industry. In Table 13, the range of selected Restricted Indices is given for Nubian Mousterian, Type A, and for Type B.

The only discernable difference rests in the slightly greater proportion of side-scrapers in Type B. While these account for a higher IR and Group II, they also produce the slightly lower range of Groups III and IV. In spite of this difference, there is, in all cases, a definite overlap, with Nubian Mousterian, Type B, in the upper range of the "Mousterian" types and in

TABLE 11
NUBIAN MOUSTERIAN, TYPE B: COMPLETE TYPOLOGICAL INDICES

Site	IL^ty	IR	IC	IA^u	IB	I	II	III	IV
6	20.6	16.3	4.8	1.3	3.3	20.6	19.1	13.2	11.3
121	26.9	17.3	6.5	0.0	0.7	26.9	18.0	8.5	11.7

TABLE 12
NUBIAN MOUSTERIAN, TYPE B: RESTRICTED TYPOLOGICAL INDICES

Site	IL^ty	IR	IC	IA^u	IB	I	II	III	IV
6	0.0	21.3	6.6	1.7	4.2	0.0	24.4	16.0	14.7
121	0.0	25.2	9.4	0.0	1.0	0.0	26.2	12.5	16.8

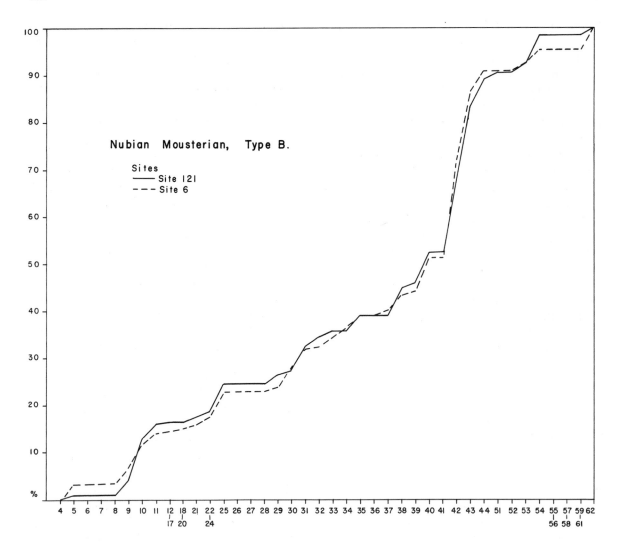

Fig. 56—Nubian Mousterian, Type B: Cumulative graphs of the restricted typologies.

TABLE 13

Nubian Mousterian, Types A and B: Selected Restricted Typological Indices

Nubian Mousterian	IR	IA^u	II	III	IV
Type A	15.8-24.6	0.0-4.6	17.6-25.1	15.4-26.2	11.1-22.4
Type B	21.3-25.2	0.0-1.7	24.4-26.2	12.5-16.0	14.7-16.9

the lower range of the "Upper Paleolithic" and Denticulate types. It is interesting to note that the individual Type A assemblage (1036) which is typologically closest to Type B is also the one which is most similar to it in the Levallois Index.

The extent to which the general configuration of tools from these two groups is similar is strikingly evident in the cumulative graph in Figure 57. This graph includes both Type B assemblages and three representative Type A sites.

The proportions of core types associated with Type B, unlike those of Type A, show a certain pattern (Table 14).

While Levallois cores are quite low at Site 6, those at Site 121 fall within the range of Type A. At both sites, Marginal and Discoidal cores are

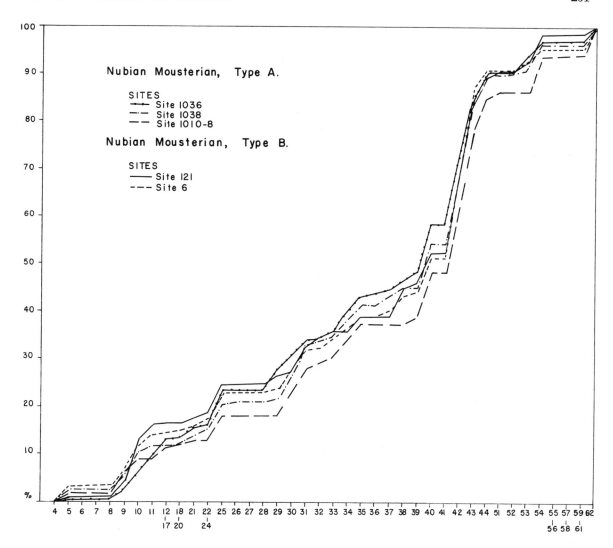

Fig. 57—Nubian Mousterian, Types A and B: Cumulative graphs of the restricted typologies.

high, which is again quite similar to Sites 1036 and 1037.

As bifaces are the main element which separates Type A from Type B, it is of importance to see what kinds are present and in what proportions. First, bifaces are rather rare at both sites. In actual number only one biface fragment was found at Site 121, while eight bifaces and biface fragments, one disk, one pick, and one atypical cleaver were found at Site 6. All examples are quite small, evolved, and cannot be confused with Acheulean forms. They are fully described and illustrated in the section dealing with individual site typologies.

TABLE 14

NUBIAN MOUSTERIAN, TYPE B: PERCENTAGES OF SELECTED CORE TYPES

| | Levallois | | | | | Nubian | | |
Sites	Blade	Flake	Point	Para		Type I	Type II	Marginal	Discoidal
6	4.0	19.0	0.0	5.0		3.0	0.0	16.0	10.0
121	2.6	30.3	2.6	0.0		1.3	0.0	17.1	14.5

TABLE 15

TECHNOLOGY OF THE DENTICULATE AND NUBIAN MOUSTERIAN

Type	IL	IF	IFs	Ilame
Denticulate Mousterian	11.6-14.3	33.6-53.3	20.6-22.3	11.6-13.9
Nubian Mousterian	4.9-25.4	30.8-69.3	17.9-38.6	3.2-12.7

In short, in every way, with the exception of the presence of bifaces, Nubian Mousterian, Type B, is within the range of Nubian Mousterian, Type A. It does not, however, correlate with the average Type A assemblage. Both technologically and typologically, Nubian Mousterian, Type B, fits best with those Type A assemblages which have the lowest Levallois Indices. There appears to be little question, however, that Nubian Mousterian, Type B, belongs within the same industry as Type A.

The Nubian Mousterian is clearly a unified industry. The question remains as to what relationship it has to the local Denticulate Mousterian. It has been well argued that in France, at least, the different Mousterian industries do not represent seasonal variations (Bordes, 1961, p. 807). The situation in Nubia, however, is somewhat different. There is not the same complexity of Mousterian industries, and there is also a lack of faunal evidence which adds much weight to Bordes' reasoning.

Denticulate Mousterian sites in Nubia are quite small and the density of stone material per square meter is rather low. The impression is that these sites were not long nor very intensively occupied. This permits the possibility that they represent, if not seasonal occupation, at least an occupation which might have emphasied a specific activity which called for the use of denticulates and notched pieces.

A comparison between the technological range of the Denticulate Mousterian and the Nubian Mousterian indicates that they both are within the same technological tradition (Table 15).

It may be argued that this similarity merely places both groups within the same broad Mousterian complex but not within the same industry. This cannot be refuted. The possibility exists, however, that the relationship is much closer. Still, until more concrete evidence can be found, the Denticulate Mousterian in Nubia must be considered, typologically, a separate industry within the Mousterian complex.

TYPOLOGICAL AND TECHNOLOGICAL DEFINITION OF THE NUBIAN MOUSTERIAN

On the basis of nine assemblages, it seems possible to give preliminary typological and technological limits to the Nubian Mousterian.

1. General
   a. Living sites are small, usually less than 200 sq. m.
   b. Density of stone concentration varies but is usually high, averaging 120 artifacts per square meter at living sites.
   c. Retouched tools, at living sites, usually account for between 10 and 14 per cent of all stone, but may be somewhat higher.
2. Technology
   a. The Nubian Mousterian generally shows a very poor quality of retouch, having many atypical or marginal tools.
   b. The Levallois Index is low, never exceeding 26.
   c. Faceting and Restricted Faceting Indices are variable.
   d. Blade Index is normally low.
   e. Levallois cores predominate. Nubian Cores, Type I, may or may not be present and Nubian Cores, Type II, are exceedingly rare.
3. Typology
   a. At living sites, the IL^{ty} is generally low, rarely reaching a level of 35.
   b. Side-scrapers never exceed 25 per cent of the restricted typology but do not fall below 15 per cent.
   c. Backed knives are present in small numbers and are generally very atypical.
   d. There is an almost total absence of Mousterian points and retouched Levallois points.
   e. "Upper Paleolithic" tool types (Group III) occur in large numbers, never falling below 14 per cent and can be as high as 26 per cent of the restricted typology.
   f. There is usually a close relationship be-

tween the percentage of "Mousterian" tool types (Group II) and "Upper Paleolithic" tool types (Group III).

g. There is a facies of the Nubian Mousterian which contains a low percentage of small, evolved bifaces. This facies tends to have more Mousterian Discoidal cores and Marginal cores as well as a slightly higher Side-scraper Index. This is not of Levalloisian type.

THE SIGNIFICANCE OF ARTIFACT SIZE

One of the criticisms of the system of study employed by F. Bordes is that the size of the artifacts is not taken into consideration. Of course, the size of artifacts may be due to many factors. The most obvious is that certain sites were situated in localities where only small pebbles or nodules were available. On the other hand, assemblages have been found which are diminutive, although a rich supply of large raw material was readily available.[6] In these cases, it must be assumed that the size of the artifacts was culturally determined, without any imposed environmental limitation.

The extreme size variation within the Nubian Mousterian must be due to pure cultural choice. The predominant raw material used was a ferrocrete sandstone which is found in large blocks on the edges of most inselbergs. Even today, the supply is almost limitless. There is no area where Nubian Middle Stone Age sites are found where an ample supply of good, large ferrocrete sandstone slabs is not obviously available in the immediate vicinity.

Any distinction between a normal sized flake and a diminutive flake must, by its very nature, be arbitrary. In the production of flakes and cores, control of the size of flakes is tenuous at best. Levallois core preparation will result in the removal both of large flakes during ventral shaping and of extremely small flakes in butt preparation. Therefore, measurements were not taken on the debitage. The production of retouched tools and Levallois flakes, on the other hand, calls for a selective choice of flakes on the part of the maker. All size flakes are available at a

workshop; those used for retouched tools, however, have been consciously chosen and so should reflect a desired cultural standard.

Thus, length measurements were taken on all unbroken, retouched tools and Levallois flakes found in all assemblages. A total of 1,482 pieces were measured from eleven assemblages. The measurements and their frequency distributions are shown as bar graphs in Figure 58. In order to put these measurements into readily comparable figures, it was decided to term any tool or Levallois flake 5 cm. or under diminutive. A Diminutive Index was chosen as the clearest way to see quickly size differences.

The Diminutive Index is arrived at by the following formula:

$$\text{Diminutive Index (ID)} = \frac{\text{all unbroken Levallois flakes and retouched tools 50 mm. or under} \times 100}{\text{all unbroken Levallois flakes and retouched tools.}}$$

Of the assemblages measured, the Diminutive Index ranged from a low of 7.3 to a high of 76.9. Table 16 shows the ID for each assemblage, the sample measured, the typological group involved, and whether raw material was immediately available at the site.

Through chance, if in no other way, it is to be expected that all assemblages would have some flakes which measure below 5 cm. and some which measure above 5 cm. Only when one or the other type predominates, however, does a clear picture emerge.

Overall, no fully consistent pattern emerges for all Mousterian assemblages measured. If only the Nubian Mousterian is considered, however, a definite pattern becomes apparent. Those sites situated on inselbergs without immediately available raw material have proportionately more small tools than those situated directly at the source of raw material.

It is difficult to go beyond this general observation. Nubian Mousterian assemblages are found at both extremes, and neither facies is limited to any portion of the total size range. It might be expected that the tools and Levallois flakes from the workshop at 1033 would be on the whole larger than those from living sites, when the vast amount of raw material available

---

[6] Micromousterian of level 5 at Jabrud I (Bordes, 1960, p. 95).

TABLE 16

DIMINUTIVE INDICES AND RELATIONSHIP TO TYPOLOGY AND AVAILABILITY OF RAW MATERIAL

Site	Number Measured	Diminutive Index	Presence of Raw Material	Typological Group
1036	178	76.9	no	Type A
1035	159	76.1	no	Type A
36B	99	73.7	yes	Denticulate
121	102	60.7	no	Type B
6	163	56.4	yes	Type B
1037	103	55.3	yes	Type A
1010-8	121	44.6	yes	Type A
1000	114	43.7	no	Denticulate
1038	115	24.3	yes	Type A
1033L	161	21.7	yes	Type A
1033U	167	21.5	yes	Type A
J. Brinikol	82	7.3	yes	Type B ?

and the relatively large number of unretouched Levallois flakes present at the site are considered. This observation is clear when we consider a workshop and gives some clue to an understanding of the assemblages with proportionately more large tools.

Those assemblages with the lowest Diminutive Indices (1038, 1033L, 1033U, and Jebel Brinikol), all have over 30 per cent unretouched Levallois flakes in their tool collections. While this might imply a simple cause and effect relationship, it is not fully the case. The assemblage from 1035 has an IL^{ty} of 36.7, yet its Diminutive Index is 76.1. Thus, no sure relationship can be made between those assemblages with a high proportion of large tools and those with a high percentage of unretouched Levallois flakes. There are indications that such a correlation may be generally valid, but the sample of assemblages is too small to consider 1035 as an aberrant exception to a proven rule.

Perhaps the most significant observation to come from this series of measurements is that there is no correlation between tool size and the Mousterian industries in Nubia. Neither the Nubian Mousterian nor the Denticulate Mousterian is limited to any demonstrable size range within the limits of the extremes of the available measurements. The Denticulate Mousterian sample is too small to warrant any definite conclusion, but conclusions may be reached for the Nubian Mousterian. Typologically, almost identical assemblages may be strongly diminutive or may contain almost no diminutive sized tools.

Again, it is felt that there is no demonstrable correlation between function and tool size. A burin with a working edge 5 mm. in width made on a flake 80 mm. long cannot be considered functionally different from another burin with the same width working edge made on a flake 40 mm. in length. Without doubt, there is a functional difference between a burin and convex side-scraper and, perhaps, even betweeen a convex and a concave side-scraper. Yet, the relative sizes of two convex side-scrapers, at this time, cannot be shown to result from differing functions. That possibility cannot be totally excluded, but the limited nature of the material evidence from Nubia precludes anything more than pure speculation. As there does appear to be a general correlation between tool size and immediate availability of raw material, this must take precedence over any explanation based on functional differences.

There is still one aspect of the size problem which is not explained by a mere statement that those assemblages found away from raw material have smaller tools than those where raw material is immediately available. Every site where raw material was unavailable was also less than a few hundred meters from a rich source of it on a nearby inselberg. Why then did people choose to live where they did and why, having chosen, did they make more smaller tools? The local topography has changed so radically since these occupations that the natural advantages of any one locality have been lost, but the problem of smaller tools can at least be considered.

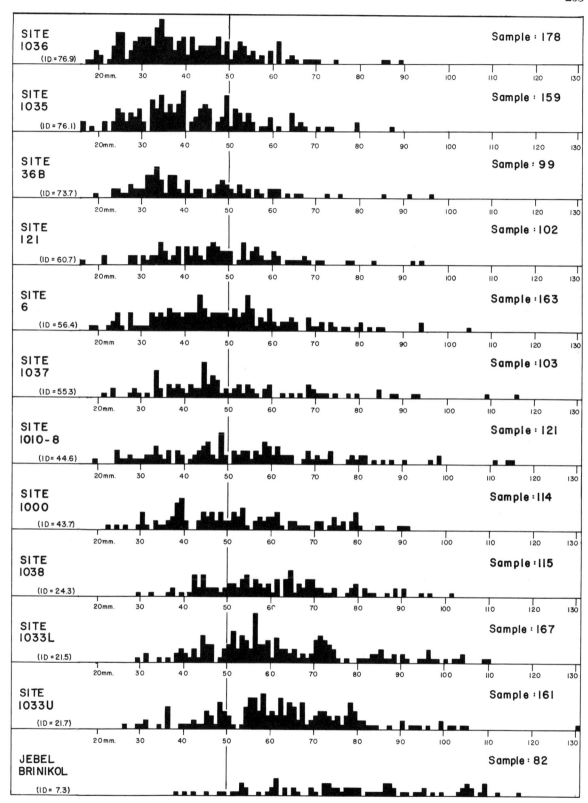

Fig. 58—Bar graphs of tool size at Nubian Mousterian sites.

From the percentages of tools to total collections and in the density of artifacts per square meter, it is clear that the people at Sites 1035, 1036, and 121 indulged in about the same proportional amounts of flaking and tool manufacture as did those people who lived directly on a source of raw material. They did not seem to import finished tools, but brought the untreated slabs of ferrocrete sandstone to their sites and then flaked them. Perhaps the greater effort involved in carrying loads of slabs up the steep inselberg sides caused them to select small slabs, smaller than they otherwise might have used, and to utilize them more fully.

From personal experience of carrying loads of artifacts down inselberg slopes, it seems fully understandable that they would want to carry as little as possible up the slopes. If this is the case, unprovable though it may be, it might suggest that any culturally conceived size preference for tools may well have been modified when people were faced with the necessity of innumerable trips up steep, scree-covered slopes with armfuls of rocks.

In short, the size studies show that, with the exception of the Denticulate Mousterian, there appears to be a direct correlation between tool size and the immediate availability of suitable raw material. There is also a tenuous correlation between assemblages with larger tools and those with proportionately more unretouched Levallois flakes. This, however, is not fully borne out by the available evidence, and because of the small sample of assemblages available, no fixed conclusion can be reached. Perhaps most important, it does seem that tool size varies greatly from assemblage to assemblage, while the types of tools present and their relative proportions in the typologies remain constant. This suggests that there was neither a strict overall tool size preference nor a functionally determined size preference for any tool from assemblage to assemblage.

THE NUBIAN MOUSTERIAN AND THE NUBIAN MIDDLE PALEOLITHIC

This report has not listed or described one new assemblage which belongs to the Nubian Middle Paleolithic. The Guichards' paper listed only one assemblage which is comparable to the Nubian Mousterian (Guichard and Guichard, 1965, p. 85). This is the result of intent, rather than chance. The assemblages described here were from sites which were specifically selected for their small size and their location. Effort was made to avoid workshops so that reasonable tool samples could be obtained.

One site, 1034, which fits the general pattern of the Nubian Middle Paleolithic was excavated by an American team. This site produced almost no tools in spite of a huge collection. No bifacial foliates were found *in situ*, but some fragments were recovered from the surface. Because of the poor typology and the already extensive coverage given to the Nubian Middle Paleolithic, it was decided not to do any more than mention its presence (Wendorf, Shiner, and Marks, 1965, p. xxii).

The problem of relationship between the Nubian Mousterian and the Nubian Middle Paleolithic must be discussed. The Guichards have defined the Nubian Middle Paleolithic as having the following attributes (Guichard and Guichard, 1965, pp. 98-110): (1) association of Nubian cores, Nubian scrapers, and bifacial foliates; (2) a high Levallois Index (over 40); (3) almost no para-Levellois technique; (4) generally high Faceting Indices; (5) low Blade Index; (6) prevalence of side-scrapers, particularly Nubian types; and (7) presence of bifaces of Acheulean type.

If we compare these attributes in tabular form with the Nubian Mousterian, we can see that there are both major technological and typological differences (Table 17).

Perhaps the most important difference lies in the total absence of bifacial foliate objects and the almost total absence of Nubian scrapers in the Nubian Mousterian. As the combination of Nubian cores, Nubian scrapers, and bifacial foliates is the prime definition of the Nubian Middle Paleolithic, it must be recognized that the assemblages of the Nubian Mousterian do not fit it. The one example of a Nubian scraper occurred at Site 1033 Upper, one of the few sites where Nubian cores were not present.

Although all the Nubian Middle Paleolithic

TABLE 17

COMPARISON OF NUBIAN MOUSTERIAN AND NUBIAN MIDDLE PALEOLITHIC TRAITS

	Nubian Mousterian (11 sites)	Nubian Middle Paleolithic (9 sites) (Guichard and Guichard, 1965, p. 99)
Nubian Cores	Present at 8 of 11 sites (2.8 to 24.2)	Present at all sites (0.9 to 20.9)
Nubian Scrapers	One example from Site 1033 Upper	Present at 5 of 9 sites
Bifacial Foliates	None	Present at 6 of 9 sites
Bifaces	Present at two sites (highly evolved)	Present at all sites
Levallois Index	4.9 to 25.4	38.2 to 52.6 (exception: Jebel Brinikol, 24.3)
Faceting Index	30.8 to 69.3	39.7 to 63.8
Restricted IF	15.4 to 38.6	29.5 to 53.6
Para-Levallois	Present at 9 of 11 sites	Negligible
Blade Index	3.2 to 11.0	3.7 to 15.0
IR (restricted)	15.8 to 25.2	25.0 to 55.5

sites do not have all three diagnostic types, they all have at least two. In the Nubian Mousterian, only the Nubian Core, Type I, is common, and no assemblage has more than one of these "index fossils."

Technologically, the most obvious difference rests in the Levallois Index. The Nubian Middle Paleolithic has a very high index, while at Nubian Mousterian sites it is very low. Only Jebel Brinikol has a Levallois Index which overlaps the Nubian Mousterian range. It must also be noted that only Jebel Brinikol represented a living site, with retouched tools accounting for 14.1 per cent of the total collection. This may indicate that the Levallois Indices of the Nubian Middle Paleolithic are artificially high, representing rejected flakes on workshop sites. In any case, the generally low range of the Levallois Index at Nubian Mousterian sites shows a quite different technological emphasis. This is again reflected in the difference between the occurrence of para-Levallois cores in these two industries.

Typologically, there are two distinct differences: the proportions of side-scrapers and the development of "Upper Paleolithic" tool types. In the Nubian Middle Paleolithic, side-scrapers

dominate the exceedingly poor typological lists (Guichard and Guichard, 1965, p. 110). In the Nubian Mousterian, side-scrapers occur in moderate percentage, from 15.8 to 25.2, but they never dominate the tool assemblage. This is due to the second discordant feature, which is the relatively strong development of the "Upper Paleolithic" tool types. With the exception of Jebel Brinikol, end-scrapers, borers, burins, and backed knives are exceedingly rare and atypical at Nubian Middle Paleolithic sites. This is not the case in the Nubian Mousterian, where side-scrapers and "Upper Paleolithic" tools often occur in almost equal proportions.

Similarities between the two industries can be seen only in certain of the technological indices. The Faceting Index has a similar range, as does the Restricted Faceting Index. The Restricted Faceting Index, however, tends to be somewhat lower in the Nubian Mousterian. Blade Indices are also similar and generally low.

It must be obvious that most of the differences between the Nubian Mousterian and the Nubian Middle Paleolithic are not strongly reflected at Jebel Brinikol. This poses something of a problem. Contrary to what the Guichards reported (Guichard and Guichard, 1965, p. 86), the part of the collection at Columbia University, and now at Southern Methodist University, contained artifacts from both the northern and southern areas. This part of the collection was made during the 1961-1962 season by J. de Heinzelin and R. Paepe. According to their notes, the collection was systematic, not random. It is probable that the Guichards made an additional collection during the 1962-1963 field season.

Since Jebel Brinikol is of importance, both the collection published by the Guichards (Guichard and Guichard, 1965, pp. 86-89) and the collection at hand have been treated together in the section on individual site reports. It will be seen that the two collections correlate closely on all levels, and there appears to be no basis for judging one to be less valid than the other. As they appeared to be the same technologically and typologically, they were put together so that an adequate tool sample could be obtained. The result of this is very interesting, although somewhat confusing.

The most obvious difference between Jebel Brinikol and the Nubian Mousterian is in the size of the artifacts. Jebel Brinikol has a Diminutive Index of only 7.4. On the other hand, it has been shown that artifact size appears to have no correlation either with other technological attributes or with typology.

In terms of the presence or absence of specific tool types, only bifacial foliates are unique to Jebel Brinikol. These, however, are poorly made (Guichard and Guichard, 1965, p. 89) and might even be termed marginal. Aside from this tool type, retouched tools from Jebel Brinikol easily fit into the Nubian Mousterian, Type B, assemblages. The presence at Jebel Brinikol of a large number of inversely retouched side-scrapers makes it quite different from the other Nubian Middle Paleolithic sites, where such scrapers are uncommon. The Nubian Mousterian, Type B, however, contains a high percentage of inverse side-scrapers, as does the Nubian Mousterian in general.

A comparison between Jebel Brinikol and the Nubian Mousterian, Type B, assemblages demonstrates that there are no essential differences as reflected in the restricted typological indices (Table 18).

TABLE 18

JEBEL BRINIKOL AND NUBIAN MOUSTERIAN, TYPE B:
RESTRICTED TYPOLOGICAL INDICES

Site	IL^{ty}	IR	IC	IA^u	IB	II	III	IV
Brinikol	0.0	27.0	7.7	2.4	4.3	28.6	17.5	20.5
6	0.0	21.3	6.6	1.7	4.2	24.4	16.0	14.7
121	0.0	25.2	9.4	0.0	1.0	26.2	12.5	16.8

Thus, the only typological difference between Jebel Brinikol and the Nubian Mousterian, Type B, is the presence at Jebel Brinikol of a small number of bifacial foliates. It must be asked what significance this has. Is it enough to place an otherwise technologically and typologically different assemblage into the Nubian Middle Paleolithic merely on the basis of one "index fossil"?

Unfortunately, the exceedingly low number of retouched tools at most Nubian Middle Paleolithic sites makes many of the Guichards' typological conclusions questionable. The high Sidescraper Indices shown for all Nubian Middle Paleolithic sites (Guichard and Guichard, 1965, p. 99) are based on invalid samples—either because of the small number of retouched tools or because of the uncertainties of random sampling. The association of three "index fossils" used to define the Nubian Middle Paleolithic also causes certain problems. Only at one site out of nine are all three, in fact, present (Guichard and Guichard, 1965, p. 99). Only the Nubian Core occurs at all sites and this type of core occurs at sites of the Nubian Mousterian as well.

The Nubian Middle Paleolithic I does not have Nubian Scrapers at all, only Nubian Cores and bifacial foliates. If the Nubian Core is excluded as a "type fossil," then it is merely the presence of bifacial foliates which form a typological basis for an industry distinction. As both the assemblages from Abu Simbel come from workshops, there is only Jebel Brinikol to give an idea of the typology of the Nubian Middle Paleolithic I. This has already been shown to be typologically the same as the Nubian Mousterian, Type B, with traits which do not fit within the definition of the Nubian Middle Paleolithic.

Therefore, it is suggested that Jebel Brinikol should not be considered Nubian Middle Paleolithic—in reality, it should belong within the Nubian Mousterian.

The presence of bifacial foliates poses a problem to this interpretation. As there is now ample evidence for a Sangoan (or Lupemban) in the immediate area (Chmielewski, 1965, pp. 157-158), the possibility of a mixing or of a typological overlap due to contact cannot be excluded. The Sangoan/Lupemban tradition in Angola has few flake tools until the Upper Lupemban (Clark, 1963, p. 185). In Nubia, they are present but rare (Chmielewski, 1965, p. 157). In terms of cultural development, it appears that the Sangoan/Lupemban industry came directly out of the African Acheulean without any Mousterian influences. Nubia, on the other hand, may well represent a border area where the northward expansion of the Sangoan/Lupemban peoples came in contact with peoples of the Mousterian tradition.

If this were the case, the presence of some foliates within the early Mousterian of Nubia would not be surprising, and their abandonment after a short time would also be understandable.

It has been assumed that the larger core tools of the Sangoan/Lupemban were developed in response to an adaptation to a forest environment (Clark, 1964, p. 177). Under the best of conditions, Nubia must have been very peripheral to the forest environment of West Africa and farther south in the Sudan. Any small change in climate would have affected Nubia first, and to a greater degree than other areas. In fact, there is evidence that Nubia, at this time, had a steppe environment. Thus, it is possible that large wood working tools were functionally extraneous and did not last for any length of time in Nubia. Needless to say, this is pure conjecture. Neither are there enough sites in Nubia which have been studied, nor is enough known about the northern expansion of the Sangoan/Lupemban to do more than postulate possibilities.

If this interpretation is correct, however, the Nubian Middle Paleolithic would represent a weak extension of a late Sangoan/Lupemban tradition, perhaps no more than Sangoan/Lupemban workshops, unrelated to the Nubian Mousterian, but occuring in the same general time range. Such a position disagrees with the Guichards' assumption that Jebel Brinikol is "archaic" and basal to the Nubian Middle Paleolithic (Guichard and Guichard, 1965, p. 89). There is,

without doubt, a massive appearance to the assemblage. This, however, seems more to emanate from its size rather than from the quality of retouch or its technology. It must be remembered that the raw material at Jebel Brinikol was a coarse grained ferrocrete sandstone which did not readily lend itself to fine flaking. This fact alone would give it a crude appearance and account for the number of thick flakes.

It must be admitted that without any stratigraphic evidence, the placing of any Nubian Middle Stone Age site into a specific evolutionary position is extremely hazardous. On the other hand, technological and typological studies make it possible to place Jebel Brinikol into a specific industry. It is felt that the overwhelming evidence points to its placement within the Nubian Mousterian.

THE SIGNIFICANCE OF NUBIAN CORES

Nubian Cores have been made an "index fossil" of the Nubian Middle Paleolithic (Guichard and Guichard, 1965, p. 98). Two types which are made by distinctly different processes have been defined (Guichard and Guichard, 1965, pp. 68-69). In spite of this, both types have been grouped together for a Nubian Core Index (Guichard and Guichard, 1965, p. 99), indicating implicitly that they are felt to have the same cultural significance. A study of the occurrence of the Nubian Cores, however, shows that this is not the case.

The problem of the significance of the Nubian Cores arose when they were found at Nubian Mousterian sites. If they were "index fossils" of the Nubian Middle Paleolithic, did this mean that the Nubian Mousterian was, in fact, Nubian Middle Paleolithic? As there were too many strong typological and technological arguments against this position, a re-evaluation of the Nubian Cores became necessary.

As the Nubian Cores, Types I and II, are made by different processes, each should be considered a separate core type. When this is done, certain distinctions became apparent.

At Nubian Middle Paleolithic sites, it is the Nubian Core, Type II, which occurs in significant numbers, while the Nubian Core, Type I is very rare (Guichard and Guichard, 1965, p. 87, table

4). As Nubian Cores, Type I, occur at Nubian Mousterian sites and at Mousterian sites in Europe and North Africa (Guichard and Guichard, 1965, p. 99), it seems more in accordance with the evidence to say that only Nubian Cores, Type II, are primarily characteristic of the Nubian Middle Paleolithic.

The Nubian Core, Type I, occurs in significant numbers at some Nubian Mousterian sites, while the Nubian Core, Type II, is exceedingly rare. At three sites, Nubian Cores, Type I, account for over 10 per cent of all cores, and at three sites, for under 3 per cent. At two sites, they do not occur at all.

Given this occurrence of Nubian Core, Type I, at both Nubian Middle Paleolithic and Nubian Mousterian sites, it is difficult to see the significance of this type core. Perhaps the most obvious difference is noted at certain Nubian Mousterian sites, where the Nubian Core, Type I, is common. This is never the case at Nubian Middle Paleolithic sites.

The opposite is also true—Nubian Cores, Type II, are common only in the Nubian Middle Paleolithic. With this in mind, it is possible to make a distinction between the Nubian Cores in these two industries. It becomes clear that the Nubian Core, Type I, cannot be used as an "index fossil" for the Nubian Middle Paleolithic, as it is present and forms a more significant element at some Nubian Mousterian sites. If there is any "index fossil" for cores in Nubian Middle Paleolithic, it must be the Nubian Core, Type II.

Beyond this observation, little can be said. The size of artifacts bears no relation to the presence or absence of the Nubian Core, Type I. Typologically, there is no discernable correlation with this core type, either. Therefore, it is questionable whether the Nubian Core, Type I, is diagnostic. The possibility remains, however, that it has some chronological value; but, if so, the typologies do not reflect it.

COMPARISON OF THE MOUSTERIAN INDUSTRIES IN NUBIA WITH INDUSTRIES FROM OTHER AREAS

Now that a typological and technological range for both the Denticulate Mousterian in Nubia and the Nubian Mousterian has been

established, it is essential to see to what extent these two industries are comparable with Mousterian from other areas. As most work has been done on the French Mousterian, an emphasis must be placed there. On the other hand, information on numerous sites in North Africa and the Near East has been published, and these also will be considered.

DENTICULATE MOUSTERIAN

Denticulate Mousterian assemblages have been reported from four countries: Spain, Italy, France, and Syria (Bordes, 1963, p. 48). Information on certain of these sites is not complete, but enough has been published to permit detailed comparisons. No Denticulate Mousterian has been published to date from either North or Sub-Saharan Africa.

The Denticulate Mousterian has been defined by F. Bordes (1963, p. 44) as having the following technological and typological attributes: (1) the presence of few side-scrapers (IR essential, from 3 to 20); (2) very few, if any, points (from 0 to 4.5 per cent); (3) few or no bifaces; (4) few or no backed knives and when present, highly atypical; (5) high percentage of notches (from 9 to 46 per cent); (6) high percentage of denticulates (from 20 to 48 per cent); (7) retouch usually mediocre; (8) variable Levallois and Faceting Indices; and (9) always more denticulates than side-scrapers.

As can be seen by referring to the type lists and indices, the industries from Sites 1000 and 36B fall within this definition.

In subdividing the European Mousterian, F. Bordes (1963, p. 46) recognizes the importance of both the Levallois and Faceting Indices. Denticulate Mousterian without Levallois debitage is defined as having a Levallois Index between 4.9 and 12.7. Although the Levallois Index at Site 1000 is somewhat above this limit (14.3), we consider it and Site 36B as belonging to the Denticulate Mousterian, non-Levallois debitage with faceting (*Moustérien à denticules, débitage non Levallois, faceté*).

Examples of this type of Denticulate Mousterian occur on the slope of Pech de l'Azé II in France, and at Romani Cave in Spain (Bordes, 1963, p. 46). Selected indices and tool percentages from these assemblages are compared with those from Sites 1000 and 36B in Table 19.

TABLE 19

Denticulate Mousterian: Comparisons of Selected Indices and Tool Percentages From European and Nubian Assemblages

	Pech de l'Azé II: slope	Ramani Cave	Site 36B	Site 1000
IL	6.7	9.7	11.6	14.3
IF	53.7	45.2	33.6	49.7
IFs	24.8	22.1	20.6	27.3
IR	14.7	13.6	15.8	7.2
Notches	20.0%	13.6%	21.9%	24.8%
Denticulates	35.8%	45.0%	31.3%	48.0%

A cumulative graph (fig. 59) shows the comparison between Sites 1000 and 36B and three Denticulate Mousterian assemblages from France. The French assemblages have been chosen to show the typological variation within the Denticulate Mousterian, and not necessarily because they were the most similar to the Nubian series. As can be seen, the Nubian assemblages fit within the published variation of the Denticulate Mousterian.

In short, we can find no significant difference between these European and Nubian assemblages. Without question, there is some variation, but no two assemblages are ever exactly alike. At this point, we feel that the industry of Sites 1000 and 36B should be considered true Denticulate Mousterian as defined for Europe and the Near East.

Denticulate Mousterian assemblages in Europe have been generally dated to Wurm I (Bordes, 1963, p. 44).[7] In the Sudan, unfortunately, both assemblages are without geological reference. Thus, there is no basis for judging even rough geological age. For the first time, however, a defined Denticulate Mousterian industry can be placed in Africa.

Nubian Mousterian

Any comparison of the Nubian Mousterian with Mousterian industries in other areas rests, to some extent, with the type of data available

concerning specific Mousterian assemblages. It is only recently that systematic studies of Mousterian technology and typology have been carried out. For many of the classic Mousterian sites, none such exist. Therefore, comparisons will have to be made on a variety of levels. Under ideal conditions, specific technological and typological comparisons can be made, but more often only general observations often based on incomplete data will be possible.

Four main areas will be considered: Egypt, North Africa, the Near East, and Europe. As Sub-Saharan Africa does not now appear to contain true Mousterian industries, it will be excluded from the study. This does not mean that the Mousterian is not present there, but merely that observations of the type made on the Fauresmith and the Proto-Stillbay emphasize specific African typological traits and rarely treat the technological aspects at all. So far, there is only one hint that the Mousterian may, in fact, occur in Sub-Saharan Africa. It has been tentatively suggested that the South African Fauresmith is no more than a Mousterian of Acheulean Tradition (Mason, 1959). Unfortunately, more specific data will be required before this possibility can be tested.

As the Nubian Mousterian, Types A and B, are almost typologically identical, they will be treated as a single unit in the comparisons. As must be expected, greatest emphasis will be given to those Mousterian industries which are fully described in a manner which permits detailed analysis. With the others, the analysis must be less satisfactory and the conclusions more tentative.

EGYPT

As Egypt is the most logical area in which to look for connections with the Nubian Mousterian, it is best to begin there. The prehistoric industrial sequence in Egypt which corresponds to the Nubian Middle Stone Age has, for the last twenty years, been termed Levalloisian (Caton-Thompson, 1946). Before that, isolated finds of artifacts had been called Mousterian (Sandford, 1934; Sanford and Arkell, 1933). Even since 1946, certain assemblages have beeen referred to as Mousterian or Levalloiso-Mousterian (Alimen, 1957, p. 92). The fact remains, however, that the

---

[7] Two levels at Jabrud I, 9, and 5 appear to be of Denticulate Mousterian type. Bordes would date these to the French Wurm III (Bordes, 1955b, pp. 504, 507).

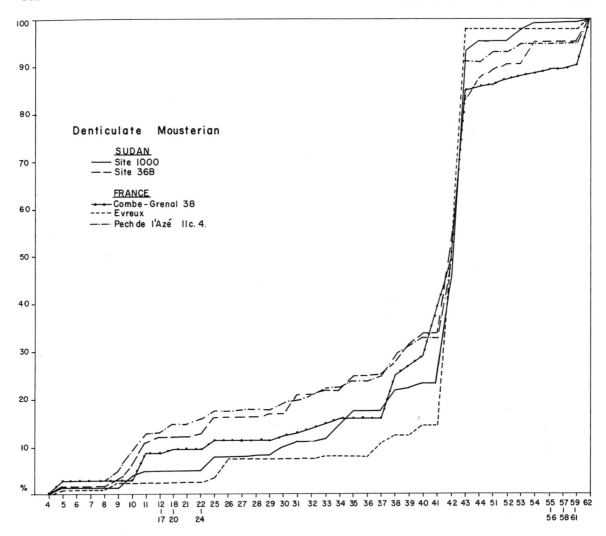

Fig. 59—Comparison of Nubian and French Denticulate Mousterian. Restricted typology.

Egyptian Middle Paleolithic sequence is normally called Levalloisian.

The Levalloisian has not been directly dated, but subsurface sites from Kharga Oasis were correlated with the local geological sequence and with a paleoclimatic history, inferred from the geological formations (Caton-Thompson, 1952, pp. 14-21). On the basis of these correlations and some typological studies, the Levalloisian was divided into an Upper and Lower, both of which are said to have occurred during the decline of the Second Pluvial at Kharga (Caton-Thompson, 1952, p. 20). This pluvial was correlated with the Second Pluvial of the Mount Carmel sequence, and, by association, with Wurm I in Europe. Specifically, the Levalloisian of Kharga

was correlated with the Levalloiso-Mousterian of Levels B and C at Mugharet et Tabun (Caton-Thompson, 1952, p. 20).

Recent radiocarbon dates show that if the Levalloisian is synchronic with Tabun B and C, then it is later in the European chronology than was at first thought. One radiocarbon date from Tabun B is 37,750 B.C. ± 800 years (GRN 2534), and one from Tabun C is 38,950 B.C. ± 1,000 years (GRN-2561) (Garrod, 1962, p. 544). A third radiocarbon date for Levalloiso-Mousterian in the Levant is 33,350 B.C. ± 500 years (GRN 2551) from level F at Mugharet el Kebareh (Oakley, 1964, p. 166). If we assume the correctness of the correlation between the Second Pluvial at Kharga and the Second Pluvial at

Mount Carmel, it would seem that the Levalloisian of Kharga is much more recent than Wurm I. This dating of the Levalloisian would place it within the later range of the European Mousterian (Movius, 1960, p. 374) as well as synchronic with the Levalloiso-Mousterian of the Levant.

Therefore, the Levalloisian of Egypt may be chronologically comparable to the Mousterian, and so it may be generally synchronic with the Nubian Middle Stone Age.

Before any direct comparisons can be made between the Nubian Mousterian and the Lower and Upper Levalloisian, it is first necessary to review Caton-Thompson's criteria for a discrete industry and to look at the specific evidence she presents.

The Levalloisian is defined in the following way:

> The Levalloisian is of normal Egyptian character, with a large production of admirable tortoise-cores of skilled technique, and a contradictory poverty in the range and retouch of flake implements until the latest phase . . . No handaxes or other bifacial tools have been found which could be attributed to it. (Caton-Thompson, 1952, p. 27)

The typological distinctions upon which the Upper Levalloisian is separated from the Lower are the following:

> . . . we find that the differences lie in their relative proportions rather than in any striking change in style or type. In both, well-shaped tortoise-cores, triangular or sub-triangular . . . occur with ovoid or discoidal forms . . . But if the evidence of two Upper Levalloisian sites may be trusted, oval and discoidal forms had largely ousted triangular shapes since the Lower Levalloisian period. (Caton-Thompson, 1952, p. 28)

An additional typological distinction has been made. In a comparison with the Mousterian industries of North Africa, it is noted that:

> The tortoise-core and flake industries of North-west Africa, moreover, frequently show a "Mousterian" typology and technique, on the whole absent in Egyptian groups, though sporadic examples are known in Upper Levalloisian context both in Kharga and Faiyum. (Caton-Thompson, 1946, p. 58)

It appears that the Levalloisian might simply be defined as an industry which employs tortoise cores for the manufacture of Levallois flakes but does not, until a late stage, make any significant number of retouched tools. The development of the Levalloisian is seen as a shift from triangular to ovoid Levallois cores and the first appearance of many retouched tools. There is also a certain differential in the thickness of flakes, with the Lower Levalloisian examples being heavier and not as well made (Caton-Thompson, 1952, p. 28).

This concept of a Lower Levalloisian virtually without retouched tools is rather strange. While Levallois flakes without secondary retouch may be used for cutting, they certainly cannot be used for scraping, boring, or graving; nor are they useful for any kind of wood working. Is it possible that the people who were responsible for the Lower Levalloisian did nothing but cut meat and soft fibers? It seems highly improbable. From where, then, does such a picture of the Lower Levalloisian emerge?

A short review of Lower Levalloisian sites at Kharga will point clearly to the basic problem. There are six Lower Levalloisian sites found *in situ* (Caton-Thompson, 1952, p. 28). Based on the very detailed site reports and the artifactual inventories which are available, Table 20 indicates the extent of the material which was recovered.

TABLE 20
TOTAL SAMPLE OF LOWER LEVALLOISIAN ARTIFACTS
FROM KHARGA OASIS
(CATON-THOMPSON, 1952, PP. 95-144)

Site	Cores	Flakes	Waste	Tools	Total
Refuf Pass					
Loc. IV	11	9	21	1	42
Loc. VI	4	2	0	0	6
Loc. VIII	6	3	15	0	24
Bulaq Pass					
Group I	3	10	6	0	19
Abu Sighawal Pass					
KO 18	14	14	63	1	82
Matana Pass					
Site F	5	5	0	0	10

As can be seen, no more than fifteen flakes were found at any site. Considering this sample, it is hardly surprising that there were few retouched flake tools. In fact, the flake sample is so small as to make it quite impossible to be sure whether retouched tools do not occur in reasonable number in the Lower Levalloisian. At workshop sites in Nubia, the occurrence of retouched tools never exceeds 3 per cent of all flakes (Guichard and Guichard, 1965, p. 114). With a total sample of only 43 flakes, two retouched tools is about all that might be expected.

In short, nothing is really known of the tool inventory of the Lower Levalloisian, not necessarily because it had none, but probably because of the size of the sample.

As cores have been made an important criteria in defining the Lower Levalloisian, the primary data must be examined. Forty-three cores make up the total Lower Levalloisian sample from Kharga. Of these, at least eighteen are non-Levalloisian cores (Caton-Thompson, 1952, p. 144). That leaves a sample of twenty-five possible Levallois cores. That is, just slightly over half of all cores are Levallois. Of the twenty-five Levallois cores, nine are described as being triangular and twelve either ovoid or discoidal (Caton-Thompson, 1952, pp. 95-144). Thus, it can hardly be said that triangular Levallois cores are particularly characteristic of the Lower Levalloisian. In any case, the core sample is so small—twenty-five Levallois cores from six sites—that its typological significance is limited.

After a review of the typological evidence for a Lower Levalloisian, it is necessary to concede that the sample size is so small that valid typological conclusions are impossible. The Lower Levalloisian may, in fact, exist as a discrete entity. It may differ from the Levalloiso-Mousterian industries of Northwest Africa and from the Nubian Mousterian; but, at present, there is not sufficient evidence to justify even the very vague definition now applied to it.

The Upper Levalloisian has somewhat more extensive primary data. Only two sites were attributed to this period at Kharga: Loc. VII at Refuf Pass and Site G at Matana Pass (Caton-Thompson, 1952, p. 28). A breakdown of the artifacts in Table 21 shows a slightly different result than that reported in the text. This is particularly true of Loc. VII, where illustrations make possible the inclusion of a number of "flakes" in the retouched tool class (Caton-Thompson, 1952, pl. 68-69).

TABLE 21
Total Artifact Sample for the Upper Levalloisian at Kharga Oasis (Caton-Thompson, 1952, pp. 95-143)

Sites	Cores	Flakes	Waste	Tools	Total
Refuf Pass					
Loc. VII	50	50	13	31	144
Matana Pass					
Site G	39	36	74	9	158

Typologically, the Upper Levalloisian becomes almost definable. From the typological list and illustrations, it is clear that the most common retouched tools are scrapers. Although only two tools are stated to be scrapers in the type lists for Loc. VII and Site G (Caton-Thompson, 1952, pp. 97-143), a number are illustrated (Caton-Thompson, 1952, pl. 72, nos. 1, 4, 5, 6). These appear to include both simple convex and converging side-scrapers, with thinning of the bulb of percussion.

Other illustrations (Caton-Thompson, 1952) of Site G and Loc. VII show two typical Mousterian points (pl. 72, no. 3 and pl. 69, no. 1), a denticulate point (pl. 68, no. 3), a cortex backed knife (pl. 68, no. 3), a pseudo-Levallois point (pl. 68, no. 4), and possibly a denticulated Levallois blade (pl. 68, no. 2). In addition, there are a good number of borers present at Loc. VII, although they are rare at Site G. Thus, the illustrated artifacts indicate that there may be few differences in the kinds of tools present in both the Upper Levalloisian and the Nubian Mousterian.

The core sample for the Upper Levalloisian is somewhat better than was the case for the Lower Levalloisian. A total of 89 cores were recovered. Of these, 81 apparently are Levallois cores of ovoid to discoidal shape. Without question, there are very few triangular cores, yet again, the sample is poor.

From the figure above, it appears that both Loc. VII and Site G were living rather than workshop sites.[8] As this does not seem to be the case at the Lower Levalloisian sites, it is really quite impossible to state that retouched tools come into their own during the later stage.

While it has been possible to show that the Upper Levalloisian has perhaps more retouched tools than were reported, the very nature of the

[8] The percentage of tools within the total collections ranges from 5 to 20 per cent, indicating living areas.

report makes it impossible to compare it typologically or technologically with the Nubian Mousterian. Needless to say, this is unfortunate. It should be expected that the Nubian Mousterian has connections primarily to the North, toward the center of the Mousterian complex. As there are no published sites from Egypt which have quantitatively valid artifact samples, it is at this time impossible to trace the Nubian Mousterian into that area. There seems to be little question, however, that such exists there. The presence at Abu Simbel of workshops of probable Sangoan/Lupemban affinities (Guichard and Guichard, 1965, p. 94) indicates that at least Egyptian Nubia is probably within the same culture area as Sudanese Nubia.

Since the Egyptian material cannot be usefully studied, it is necessary to go further afield for comparisons. This leads in two directions: to Northwest Africa and into the Levant.

NORTH AFRICA

It is quite out of place to compare the Nubian Mousterian with every reported Mousterian or Levalloiso-Mousterian assemblage in North Africa. On the other hand, general comparisons can be made, particularly with the Levalloiso-Mousterian of Libya.

True Mousterian sites are rare in North Africa, particularly west of Libya (Balout, 1965, p. 56). In this area, however, there appear to be two Mousterian industries: one of "European" facies, as at Retaimia (Dalloni, 1952); and one of "North African" or Levantine facies, as at Ain Meterchem (Balout, 1965, p. 54). Both have well made Mousterian points and side-scrapers. Their main difference appears to lie in the vastly overwhelming number of side-scrapers in the "North African" facies, as compared with the Mousterian of "European" facies. In addition, the "North African" facies is heavily Levallois in technology, with an exceedingly high percentage of faceted flakes (Balout, 1965, p. 54).

Neither facies seems to have developed in North Africa (Balout, 1965, pp. 56-57), but the Mousterian of "North African" facies seems to be very similar to that of the Levalloiso-Mousterian of Libya and the Levant.

In Libya, perhaps the best described Middle Paleolithic assemblage is from Sidi el Hajj Creiem, in Wadi Derna (McBurney and Hey, 1955, pp. 142-156). Unfortunately, even this assemblage is not fully reported, as only the Mousterian points and scrapers are described. The assemblage may, however, be characterized technologically by a fine flaking technique which resulted in very thin and relatively small flakes of both Levallois and non-Levallois types.

Typologically, the assemblage seems to be characterized by Mousterian points and side-scrapers. These types are so common in the total artifactual collection—some fifteen hundred pieces—that they accounted for just over 8 per cent. If we consider a typical Nubian Mousterian assemblage, all retouched tools—as many as 31 types—rarely account for more than 12 per cent of the total collection. The impression given by this is that either Hajj Creiem represents a living site with an abnormally high percentage of retouched tools or that side-scrapers and Mousterian points are, by far, the dominant retouched tools. As a complete type list is missing, this cannot be resolved, although the latter possibility seems more likely in view of the similar situation in the Levant.

On the basis of the published material, certain striking differences can be seen between the Levalloiso-Mousterian of Libya and the Nubian Mousterian. Perhaps the major typological difference rests in the high proportion of Mousterian points at Hajj Creiem and their almost total absence in the Nubian Mousterian. The same may be said for side-scrapers of all types; they are apparently very rich in variety and number in the Levalloiso-Mousterian, while occurring in only moderate proportions and in limited variety in the Nubian Mousterian. As no information is given concerning the numbers and types of "Upper Paleolithic" type tools from Hajj Creiem, direct comparisons cannot be made. On the other hand, it is reported that burins do not occur at all at Hajj Creiem. While they are not numerous in the Nubian Mousterian, a few do occur at every site.

The overall impression is that the Levalloiso-Mousterian of Libya is similar to the Mousterian of "North African" facies from farther west and that neither is strongly related to the Nubian

Mousterian. Certainly, there is much difference in proportional tool preference and a noticeably different technological emphasis.

As the Levalloiso-Mousterian of Libya is very similar to the Lower Levalloiso-Mousterian of the Levant (McBurney, 1960, p. 168), it is probable that this specific Mousterian manifestation extended along much of the edge of the eastern and southern Mediterranean, as far west as the Maghreb. Radiocarbon dates from Haua Fetah, in Libya (McBurney, 1960, p. 168), and Tabun, in the Levant, place this industry at about 40,000 B.C. McBurney suggests an African ancestry for the Levalloiso-Mousterian of Hajj Creiem and Tabun type (McBurney, 1960, p. 171). If this is the case, the Nubian Mousterian is a problem. Either the Nubian Mousterian is generically related to the Levalloiso-Mousterian (typologically unlikely), or the lithic development in Nubia did not take the same orientation as it did farther west and north.

At this time, it is hard to see a continuous development in Nubia from the Acheulean to the Mousterian. This is also true of the Mousterian of the Maghreb (Balout, 1945, p. 56). In the Levant, the Levalloiso-Mousterian occurs directly after the Jabrudian—a Mousterian of Quina affinities—without any typological transition. Therefore, there does not appear to be any demonstrable ancestor for either the Nubian Mousterian or the Levalloiso-Mousterian in North Africa or the Levant.

From the paucity of Mousterian sites of "North Africa" facies in the Maghreb, it would seem that the Maghreb represents the extreme western expansion of a more eastern tradition. With this in mind, it would be possible to trace the Levalloiso-Mousterian eastward across the North African littoral to its center of density in the Levant and, then, even northward into Anatolia. Yet, in no area can we find a progenitor for the Levalloiso-Mousterian. Perhaps, then, the origin of the Levalloiso-Mousterian lies outside the Mediterranean fringe in an earlier but related Mousterian industry. It might be possible to look to the East for such an ancestor. Both chronologically and typologically, an eastern origin of the Levalloiso-Mousterian is possible. The Mousterian of Iraq, particularly seen at Shindiar Cave,

has, generally, the oldest radiocarbon dates for any Mousterian in the Near East—about 48,000 B.C. and 44,000 B.C.—and these dates come from the very top of a thick deposit of Mousterian artifacts (Solecki, 1960, p. 189). In the Levant the earliest reliable dates are in the 35,000 to 40,000 year range for the Levalloiso-Mousterian, and at about 43,000 years in North Africa. Thus, the dates from the Mediterranean fringe are somewhat more recent than the most recent dates for the Mousterian in Iraq.

The Mousterian of Iraq is characterized by an extremely high percentage of Mousterian points (as high as 25 per cent), a very high percentage of side-scrapers (as high as 71 per cent), and a very low Levallois element (Skinner, 1965, pp. 64, 101, 104). Both industries are very low in "Upper Paleolithic" types, high in side-scrapers, and low in Quina retouch (so typical of the Jabrudian). Of particular interest is the very high Mousterian point content which is strongly paralleled in the retouched tools of the Levantine Levalloiso-Mousterian. While Mousterian points are a diagnostic feature of the Mousterian, the European varieties never have this large a proportion (Bordes, 1961b). Thus, this trait is common both to the inland Near East and to the eastern Mediterranean fringe, although somewhat more recent in the latter area.

There is no wish to overstress this position. It is merely noted as an alternative to an African origin for the Levalloiso-Mousterian. Only more excavation and more solid chronologies will solve this problem, if it is ever to be solved.

In short, the North African Levalloiso-Mousterian seems to be a western extension of the Levantine Levalloiso-Mousterian. It is not typologically similar to the Nubian Mousterian, nor can its origins be demonstrably placed in North Africa.

NEAR EAST

The Mousterian of the Near East may be divided into three types: Jabrudian, Levalloiso-Mousterian, and a third group typified by Shanidar D but found throughout Iraq and Iran (Skinner, 1965, p. 131). Each of these groups shows a specific character within the broad framework of the Mousterian tradition. Each differs from the others and all differ markedly from the Nubian Mousterian.

The Jabrudian is characterized by many *déjeté* scrapers of Quina type as well as simple scrapers also showing Quina retouch (Bordes, 1960, p. 94). In fact, it may be considered no more than a Near Eastern facies of the French Quina Mousterian (Bordes, 1955b, p. 488). The extreme difference between the Jabrudian and the Nubian Mousterian can be seen in terms of selected typological and technological indices in Table 22.

TABLE 22

COMPARISON BETWEEN SELECTED INDICES OF THE
NUBIAN MOUSTERIAN AND THE JABRUDIAN

| | Nubian Mousterian | | Jabrudian[1] | |
	1038	6	Jabrud I-25	I-22
Blade Index	11.0	10.5	7.3	7.1
Group I	31.0	20.6	1.2	0.9
IR (complete)	13.2	16.3	54.0	68.8
Group III (restricted)	20.8	16.0	5.3	3.2
Group IV (restricted)	17.9	14.7	12.1	8.1
Quina Index[2]	0.0	0.0	85.4	69.8

[1] Bordes, 1955b, p. 507.
[2] Quina Index refers to the percentage of Quina retouched pieces as compared with all retouched pieces (Skinner, 1965, pp. 127, 129).

The essential technological difference seems to rest in the presence of a Levallois technique in the Nubian Mousterian as compared with the Jabrudian. Typologically, the differences seem to be a much higher percentage in the Side-scraper Index (IR) and in the high percentage of Quina retouch in the Jabrudian. Quina retouch does not occur at all in the Nubian Mousterian.

The Mousterian of Iraq is again different from both the Jabrudian and the Nubian Mousterian. Levallois debitage occurs but not in sufficient amounts, while the Blade Index is much higher than in the Jabrudian. Table 23 compares selected indices from three Mousterian sites in Iraq with two Nubian Mousterian assemblages.

Again, a major difference can be seen in the extreme importance of the Mousterian Group in the Mousterian of Iraq as compared with the Nubian Mousterian. In this comparison, however, the Blade Indices are somewhat similar, although the Typological Levallois Indices are still very low in the Mousterian of Iraq. Quina retouch is certainly not as common in the Mousterian of Iraq, but it is still present. It is not present in the Nubian Mousterian.

The Levalloiso-Mousterian of the Levant is, perhaps, the best known of all Mousterian industries in the Near East. This is, unfortunately, strictly relative. Although Skinner has applied the Bordes system to the available collections from Mount Carmel, these collections cannot be considered complete as many tools now recognized as belonging to the Mousterian tradition (i.e., pseudo-Levallois points, denticulates) were apparently discarded in the field. Thus, the specific comparisons given in Table 24 must be viewed in that light.

While the differences between the Levalloiso-Mousterian and the Nubian Mousterian are not as extreme as those seen in the Jabrudian and the Mousterian of Iraq, they are still impressive. The average Typological Levallois Index is much higher in the Levalloiso-Mousterian than it is in the Nubian Mousterian and, again, the Quina Index, while low, is consistently present in the Levalloiso-Mousterian. Most important, the ratio between Group II and Group III in the Levalloiso-Mousterian is much higher than in the Nu-

TABLE 23

COMPARISON BETWEEN SELECTED INDICES OF THE NUBIAN MOUSTERIAN AND THE
MOUSTERIAN OF IRAQ

| | Nubian Mousterian | | Iraq[1] | | |
	1038	6	Bisitun	Shanidar D	Kunji
Blade Index	11.0	10.5	35.0	12.7	20.8
Group I	31.0	20.6	2.4	1.8	1.5
Group II (complete	15.0	19.1	94.0	79.4	94.0
Group III (complete)	14.2	13.2	4.6	11.3	1.9
Group IV (complete)	12.0	11.3	0.7	2.5	3.4
Quina Index	0.0	0.0	6.0	4.9	5.6

[1] Figures taken from Skinner (1965, pp. 61, 101, 104).

TABLE 24

COMPARISON OF SELECTED INDICES FROM THE NUBIAN MOUSTERIAN AND THE
LEVALLOISO-MOUSTERIAN

| | Nubian Mousterian | | Levalloiso-Mousterian[1] | | |
	1038	6	Tabun C	Tabun D	Tabun B
Blade Index	11.0	10.5	12.2	14.2	14.4
Group I	31.0	20.6	59.4	59.6	50.6
Group II (complete)	15.0	19.1	34.7	34.5	44.0
Group III (complete)	14.2	13.2	1.7	5.3	2.2
Group IV (complete)	12.0	11.3	1.3	0.0	0.0
Quina Index	0.0	0.0	7.4	8.6	9.5

[1]Figures taken from Skinner (1965, pp. 55, 71, 75).

bian Mousterian, where it rarely reaches two to one. This in itself serves to separate the two industries.

In short, throughout the Near East there are three distinct Mousterian industries, none of which is similar to the Nubian Mousterian.

EUROPE

The complex of Mousterian industries is best known from western France. The work of F. Bordes (1953a, 1953b, 1961a) has permitted a detailed typological and technological view of this complex. This work has resulted in the recognition of four distinct Mousterian industries (Bordes, 1961b). They may be summarized as follows:

1. Mousterian of Acheulean Tradition

This industry evolved out of the Final Acheulean of France. It shows a long development, beginning with a phase characterized by relatively many bifaces, including triangular and heart shaped forms. Other tools include normal Mousterian types, with side-scrapers accounting for between 20 and 40 per cent of all retouched tools. "Upper Paleolithic" types include a few backed knives, burins, end-scrapers, borers, and truncations.

By Wurm II[9] this industry passes into an evolved form. Bifaces become rare and triangular forms disappear. Side-scrapers also become rare (from 4 to 10 per cent), while backed knives increase to as much as 20 per cent of all tools and are now made on blades as well as flakes. Denticulate tools which were rare in the early

stage become more numerous, and true blades and blade cores begin to appear.

2. Typical Mousterian

The typical Mousterian is very similar to the early Mousterian of Acheulean Tradition, but bifaces and backed knives are either absent or very rare. Side-scrapers are typical and account for between 25 and 55 per cent of all retouched tools.

3. Denticulate Mousterian

There are few or no bifaces and backed knives in this industry, but when they occur they are highly atypical. Again, Mousterian points and side-scrapers are very rare. On the other hand, denticulate and notched tools abound. Taken together, they often account for as much as 80 per cent of all retouched tools.

4. Quina-type Mousterian

This industry is very different from the others. Very few or no bifaces and backed knives are found, but there are very many side-scrapers which account for as much as 75 per cent of all tools. Among the side-scrapers are normal, thin types, but there are also many on thick flakes which have unfaceted platforms. Their retouch is steep and "resolved." Normal Mousterian tools also occur and there are limaces as well. Quina scrapers can account for as much as one quarter of all scrapers.

In addition, there is a Ferrassie Mousterian very similar to the Quina-type. Here, however, there are few transverse Quina scrapers as this industry has many laminary Levallois flakes which are unsuited for transverse retouch. The Ferrassie Mousterian might be considered a Quina Mousterian with a relatively high Levallois element.

---

[9] This is the French chronology (Bordes, 1961b, p. 803).

Although this presents a very short and simplified definition of the various Mousterian industries, it is complete enough to see that certain industries of France are very different from the Nubian Mousterian.

It is at once apparent that the Mousterian of Acheulean Tradition has little in common with the Nubian Mousterian. Although two Nubian Mousterian assemblages do have bifaces, they are rare—never reaching the range of 8 to 40 per cent which is found in the early Mousterian of Acheulean Tradition (Bordes, 1961b, p. 804).

The evolved form of Mousterian of Acheulean Tradition is also very different from the Nubian Mousterian, but for other typological reasons. While bifaces have become rare, similar to the case in the Nubian Mousterian, backed knives on both flakes and blades assume a very important role. In the Nubian Mousterian backed knives are always rare and, for the most part, highly atypical. While side-scrapers occur only in moderate proportions in the Nubian Mousterian, they always account for more than 10 per cent of all tools, which is the upper range in the evolved Mousterian of Acheulean Tradition.

The Denticulate Mousterian has been recognized in Nubia at two sites and the problem of its relationship to the European variety has already been discussed in detail. It would serve little purpose here to contrast it to the Nubian Mousterian.

The Quina Mousterian also has traits which differ markedly from the Nubian Mousterian. Perhaps the most important typological trait of all is the presence of Quina-type side-scrapers in the Quina Mousterian and their total absence in the Nubian Mousterian. This is both a typological and a technological difference. The Quina side-scrapers normally are made on thick, unfaceted, platformed flakes. Within the Nubian Mousterian, this type of flake is rare and never used in scraper production. Not only are Quina scrapers absent in the Nubian Mousterian, but the overall percentage of side-scrapers is much too low to equate with the Quina Mousterian.

The Typical Mousterian poses more of a problem. Unlike the other Mousterian industries of France, it is not characterized by one or two major diagnostic tool types. Typologically, aside

from general cohesiveness in the overall tool proportions, the Typical Mousterian has very few, if any, bifaces or backed knives. In this sense, the Typical Mousterian and the Nubian Mousterian are similar. In fact, much the same tool types occur in both. Therefore, the similarities and differences between these industries must rest on the relative proportions of tools. This is certainly more subtle than the other comparisons, and the results are open to more varied interpretation.

The Nubian Mousterian, it may be remembered, is characterized by the presence of a moderate number of typical Mousterian side-scrapers, very few Mousterian points, few or no bifaces and backed knives, and a fairly large number of "Upper Paleolithic" type tools. Denticulates are variable and the Levallois Index also varies but is usually low.

In general terms this description of the Nubian Mousterian fits the Typical Mousterian except in one point: the relatively large numbers of "Upper Paleolithic" type tools. This difference can be seen in Table 25, manifested in the restricted Group Characteristics II and III from selected Typical Mousterian and Nubian Mousterian sites.

Within the Restricted Typological Indices and Characteristic Groups, it can be seen that the general range of Group IV (Denticulate) is comparable in both the Nubian and Typical Mousterian. It appears that this has little specific significance for comparative purposes, except that in both industries denticulates are not usually very common.

The extreme rarity of Mousterian points in the Nubian Mousterian is somewhat paralleled in the Typical Mousterian. Mousterian points usually occur in the latter industry, but they do not seem to form an important element in those assemblages where the data are available.

At the Typical Mousterian sites from Oissel and Houppville, Mousterian points account for less than 2 per cent of all tools in each assemblage (Bordes, 1952, p. 450), and at Moustier J it appears from its cumulative graph that there were no Mousterian points (Bordes and Bourgon, 1951, p. 7). Therefore, although the data are limited, it suggests that Mousterian points are not numerous in the Typical Mousterian.

It does seem, however, that a significant differ-

TABLE 25

RESTRICTED CHARACTERISTIC GROUPS OF THE TYPICAL MOUSTERIAN AND THE
NUBIAN MOUSTERIAN

Site	II	III	IV	IB
Typical Mousterian				
Moustier J	34.3	9.0	16.9	0.7
Peche de l'Azé 1, c.40[1]	c42.0	c7.0	c10.0	?
Nubian Mousterian				
1010-8	18.2	19.7	18.2	0.0
1036	24.1	17.0	12.2	0.0
1037	23.7	26.8	12.5	0.0
6	24.4	16.0	14.7	4.2
121	26.2	12.5	16.8	1.0

[1] The indices are derived from a cumulative graph and so, are only approximations (Bordes, 1963, p. 50).

ence can be seen in the ratio between Mousterian tools (Group II) and "Upper Paleolithic" tools (Group III). In the Typical Mousterian there always seems to be many more Mousterian tools than "Upper Paleolithic" tools. The ratio may, in fact, be quite high. At Peche de l'Azé, it is about six to one, and at Moustier J it is about four to one.

There is a somewhat different pattern in the Nubian Mousterian. The ratio between Mousterian tools and "Upper Paleolithic" tools averages about one to one. At one extreme, there are even slightly more "Upper Paleolithic" tools than Mousterian tools; while at the other, the ratio just reaches a two to one relationship with Mousterian tools predominating.

This range in the Nubian Mousterian shows perhaps a possible overlap with the Typical Mousterian. On the other hand, the general pattern is quite different. On this basis, the Nubian Mousterian shows a specific difference in type frequencies from the Typical Mousterian. This is not to say that they differ greatly, only that a clear area of consistent divergence is visible.

In general cultural terms this shows two rather distinct patterns of tool preference with the same range of utilized typological forms. Therefore, the Nubian Mousterian and the Typical Mousterian must be considered distinct industries.

In short, a review shows that the Nubian Mousterian is similar to some defined French Mousterian industries yet distinct from all. This is true for the Mousterian industries of the Near East, although the similiarities are less noticeable. Therefore, the Nubian Mousterian represents a newly recognized Mousterian industry located farther south than has been reported to date.

CONCLUSIONS

In previous sections the Nubian Mousterian has been described in detail and has been compared with other Mousterian industries in North Africa, the Near East, and Europe. On the basis of these comparisons it has been shown that the Nubian Mousterian is distinct from all, but similar enough to fall within the broad limits of the Mousterian tradition. The Nubian Mousterian shows one pattern of tool preference that places the various assemblages into a unified industry. The significance of this divergent but unified tool preference pattern may rest in many factors. It is not suggested that it will be possible to isolate the factors which account for a separate Mousterian industry in Nubia, but the general range of probable determinants should be considered. This necessitates an overall view of the development of the Mousterian and those attributes which unify the varied industries into a single cultural complex.

The position taken by F. Bordes is that at least three Mousterian industries in France had distinct and separate cultural progenitors: Mousterian of Acheulean Tradition evolving out of Upper Acheulean; Quina Mousterian, out of Tayacian or Clactonian; and the Typical Mousterian perhaps secondarily evolving from the early Mousterian of Acheulean Tradition (Bordes, 1961b, p. 807).

Implicit in Bordes' position is the view that the Mousterian does not represent the material culture of a stage in the continuous development of a single cultural tradition. It is conceived of as a general stage of typological and technological development reached by a number of separate cultural traditions. This, however, is not merely a stage in a unilinear scheme of Paleolithic evolution. It can be considered more a case of convergence.

The criteria for the Mousterian complex of lithic industries is not based on generic relationship, on future similar development, or even on contemporaneity. The Mousterian complex is based on typological and technological criteria which bring together the various Mousterian industries, whether they are found in Iraq at 60,000 B.C. or in France at 33,000 B.C.

A definition of the Mousterian complex, by the very nature of its material remains, must rest on technological and typological criteria which describe and delimit the range of techniques and tools found in the complex.

The initial step in this process was formulated by Bordes, when he listed sixty-one recognizably different types of tools as occurring more frequently than other tool types in the various Mousterian industries of France. This was based on a study of a large number of assemblages and had no more theoretical basis than the fact that well over 90 per cent of all tools from all Mousterian industries could be classified within his list of types.

No tool type in this list, however, has an a priori temporal or industrial significance. In defining either a single Mousterian industry or the complex as a whole, it is the proportional relationship of all the listed tool types that is diagnostic.

As has been noted before, the various Mousterian industries are characterized by quite different specific typological attributes and by strong divergences in the relative proportions of similar tool types. This can be seen in Figure 60, which shows typical cumulative graphs for the main Mousterian industries. Technologically, within any one industry there may be great variation in the technique employed in flake production, the size of the flakes produced, and the care taken in the flaking process. With these differences, and many more besides, what typo-

logical and technological attributes can define the Mousterian?

A definition of the Mousterian must rest with a number of traits, none of which is exclusive to the Mousterian, and, negatively, on a number of other traits and tendencies which are not normally found within the Mousterian. No one typological or technological trait is sufficient.

Those general attributes which are present in all Mousterian industries may be considered to be the following:

1. A typology based primarily on flake tools.

2. Typological emphasis placed on the elaboration in forms of side-scrapers, with even, well trimmed edges or with obviously denticulated edges.

3. Technologically, two main systems for flake production are employed: the Levallois technique and a non-Levallois technique based on discoidal cores. Neither technique is totally exclusive, however, in any Mousterian assemblage, and other types of cores may also occur.

4. There are always some tool types present which normally characterize the Upper Paleolithic blade industries. These are made either on flakes or on true blades.

5. When bifaces occur, which is rare, they are normally smaller and more evolved than those associated with the Acheulean and never dominate the tool inventory.

6. A number of other flake tools occur: notches, Mousterian points, Tayac points, bec burins, truncations, etc. The important consideration is that in the vast majority of Mousterian assemblages, most of these types are present.

Those traits which have been recognized in lithic traditions broadly contemporary with the Mousterian but seem to fall outside the essential Mousterian tradition are the following:

1. The tendency to work pebbles or cobbles into choppers and picks of rough form.

2. Typological emphasis placed on the elaboration of lanceolate and bifacial foliate points.

3. The tendency to make flake tools by rough, alternating retouch so that most tools have irregular, sinuous edges.

4. A dominance and elaboration of core tools, such as bifaces, cleavers, choppers, picks, axes, relative to flake tools.

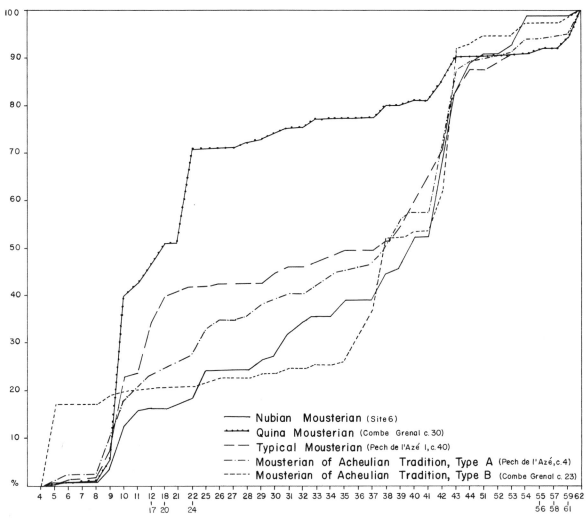

Fig. 60—Comparative cumulative graphs of various Mousterian industries.

5. The predominance of tools made on true blades with great elaboration and variation within each tool type.

This is not to say that pebble tools, lanceolate foliates, rough alternatingly retouched tools, and blade tools never occur in Mousterian context. When they do occur in the Mousterian, however, they are atypical of the industry in which they are found. Bifaces are typical of the early Mousterian of Acheulean Tradition, but they are proportionately few when compared with Acheulean assemblages.[10]

Thus, the Mousterian might be thought of as representing an aspect of one level of technological and typological preference and achievement in tool manufacture. In this definition, an emphasis would be placed on the concept of preference. While all Mousterian industries contain some "true" blades,[11] indicating at least a rudimentary technological competence to produce blades, the Mousterian toolmakers chose to make the overwhelming majority of their tools on flakes. All Mousterian industries have some bifaces, yet the biface was obviously not a pre-

---

[10] At Pech de l'Azé, where eight assemblages of Mousterian of Acheulean Tradition have been reported, the highest restricted Biface Index is only 10.98, and most others are much lower (Bordes, 1954b, 1955a).

[11] True blades are ones struck from cores which have been prepared for the removal of blades, rather than flakes.

ferred tool type as it had been during the Acheulean. While both the Mousterian and the Upper Paleolithic peoples made side-scrapers and end-scrapers, during the Mousterian there was a definite cultural preference shown for side-scrapers.

These are but a few examples of how choice determined the material culture of the Mousterian, in spite of a competence which would have permitted different emphases in typological and technological traits.

Within the range of usual Mousterian tools—some sixty-one types—each industry emphasized certain tools at the expense of others. This may have been due to different regional traditions, specific functional differences, changes and variations in local environments, or differences in time.

The Nubian Mousterian has been shown to be a typologically unified industry, similar to, but distinct from, the Typical Mousterian. The Nubian Mousterian fully fits within the typological definition proposed for the Mousterian and seems to correlate in time with some Mousterian industries in other areas.

As all industries are no more than typologically distinguishable stages of long lithic traditions, it is important to examine the potential progenitors of the Nubian Mousterian. Two possibilities exist: first, that it evolved locally out of the Upper Acheulean of Northeast Africa (with or without external influences) or, second, that it evolved outside Northeast Africa and moved in fully developed. If the first is true, then a position that it merely represents a regional specialization based on slightly divergent tradition within the Upper Acheulean would be theoretically acceptable. On the other hand, if the Nubian Mousterian evolved outside of the area and moved in fully developed, we should then expect to find similarities with Mousterian industries in adjacent areas.

Upper Acheulean is well represented in Nubia (Guichard and Guichard, 1965), and there are no other known pre-Mousterian industries in Nubia or adjacent areas. Therefore, if the Nubian Mousterian is locally derived, it must have come out of an upper Acheulean base.

There is one major problem with this hypothesis: no sites have yet been found in Nubia which can be considered truly transitional between the Upper Acheulean and the Nubian Mousterian. Only Site 6, of the Nubian Mousterian, Type B, has a reasonable sample of bifaces. These, however, are fully Mousterian in character. While it is possible that Nubian Mousterian, Type B, is transitional, there is no stratigraphic evidence, and very little typological evidence. Typologically, the mere presence of bifaces does not, a priori, make Nubian Mousterian, Type B, older than Nubian Mousterian, Type A. On the other hand, the biface tradition is exceedingly weak in the Nubian Mousterian, perhaps implying that Type B existed during a period before this trait was completely lost. Flake tools, however, are almost identical in the two Nubian Mousterian groups, indicating no other major typological evolution. Thus, while the possibility of Nubian Mousterian, Type B, being transitional cannot be excluded, specific stratigraphic and typological evidence is missing.

The second possibility, that the Nubian Mousterian moved into the area fully developed, has even less evidence behind it. If it did move into Nubia, from where did it come? There are only four possibilities: from the Sahara, from the southern Sudan, from North Africa and Egypt (and, by extension, from the Levant), or from the Red Sea hills. Both the southern Sudan and the Red Sea hills are almost totally unknown archaelogically and so, cannot be considered here. Enough excavation and survey has been carried out to suggest that the Mousterian does not occur in the Sahara. A Mousterian derivative, the Aterian, exists as far east as Dungul Oasis,[12] but it is so highly specialized that no serious comparison can be made between it and the Nubian Mousterian. Also, chronologically, the Aterian appears to be too young to have been an ancestor of the Nubian Mousterian, as it is evolved from the Levalloiso-Mousterian of North Africa (Clark, 1964, p. 175).

If the Nubian Mousterian moved into the Sudan from the north, there should be some indication in Egypt, North Africa, the Levant, or in

---

[12] Unpublished data of the Combined Prehistoric Expedition to Egyptian Nubia.

Nubia itself, of assemblages which are transitional between the Levalloiso-Mousterian or Jabrudian and the Nubian Mousterian. This is not the case. While one might expect to find radically different assemblages at the polar ends of a long development over time and space, one must insist on some material evidence for evolution or transitional change from the earliest to the latest, before postulating generic relationships.

Little can be said about Egypt, for reasons discussed in an earlier part of this paper. In North Africa, the most common Mousterian industry is the typical Levalloiso-Mousterian of the Levant, rich in tool types which are uncommon in Nubia. In the Levant, there are two major Mousterian industries: the Jabrudian and the Levalloiso-Mousterian. The earliest of these, and therefore the most logical one from which the Nubian Mousterian might have evolved, is the Jabrudian. While perhaps chronologically possible, typological considerations make such an evolution highly improbable.

The Jabrudian is a regional representative of the Quina Mousterian, characterized by large numbers of thick Quina scrapers and an almost total absence of "Upper Paleolithic" type tools (Bordes, 1960, p. 93). This contrasts too sharply with the Nubian Mousterian, where Quina scrapers do not occur at all and where "Upper Paleolithic" types are very numerous. It must be noted that, while Egyptian Middle Paleolithic is poorly known, there have been many scattered finds, none of which include Quina scrapers. Thus, it is felt that the negative evidence is too strong to support a hypothesis of generic connections between the Jabrudian and the Nubian Mousterian.

The Levalloiso-Mousterian, of North Africa and the Levant, is of more concern. Here again, however, typological considerations cast serious doubt on any demonstrable generic relationship with the Nubian Mousterian. The ratio favoring "Mousterian" type tools over "Upper Paleolithic"

type tools is even higher than in the Typical Mousterian. At Mount Carmel, the Lower Levalloiso-Mousterian has a ratio of "Mousterian" types over "Upper Paleolithic" types in the order of at least ten to one and even as high as twenty to one (Garrod and Bate, 1937, pp. 76-78). Upper Levalloiso-Mousterian has a ratio only slightly lower; from ten to one, at most, to eight to one in the youngest level at Tabun (Garrod and Bate, 1937, pp. 72-74). Considering the average Nubian Mousterian ratio of one to one, the extreme difference is clear. As pointed out in a previous section, this plus other factors made McBurney conclude that the North African Levalloiso-Mousterian was no more than a western extension of the Levantine Levalloiso-Mousterian.

Therefore, existing evidence points to two main Mousterian industries in the Levant, the Jabrudian and the Levalloiso-Mousterian, and mainly a Levalloiso-Mousterian in North Africa, although a "European" facies is known from the Maghreb. While hypothetically either of the two might be generically related to the Nubian Mousterian, there is no material evidence which documents any transitional stages.

Information concerning industries to the south of Nubia is lacking, but the hint that the Fauresmith may be a Mousterian industry opens possible links in that direction. Only further work in the southern Sudan, however, can clarify whether the Nubian Mousterian is related to more southern industries.

At this time, it is only possible to conclude that the Nubian Mousterian is a distinct industry, technologically and typologically within the larger Mousterian complex. Evidence does not permit generic linking of the Nubian Mousterian with any other known Mousterian industry. This does not preclude the possibility of such linking at a future date, but leads to a hypothesis that the Nubian Mousterian is basically a local development, perhaps influenced by the diffusion of ideas and techniques from outside Nubia.

THE KHORMUSAN: AN UPPER PLEISTOCENE INDUSTRY IN SUDANESE NUBIA

Anthony E. Marks

(SOUTHERN METHODIST UNIVERSITY)

INTRODUCTION

THE DESIGNATION of a new late Upper Pleistocene industry along the Nile, in Nubia, is not done lightly. The Khormusan industry, named after the type site 1017 in a bank of the Khor Musa, is represented in the archaeological record by five sites, all *in situ*, which are rich in chipped stone tools and faunal remains and contain rare examples of worked bone and ground hematite.

Technologically and typologically, the Khormusan industry exhibits at each site unifying characteristics which set it apart from other industries and which demonstrate that these sites represent a single lithic tradition.

A clear chronological order of Khormusan sites has been established. It is based on their geological position in the known sequence of Nile sedimentation and erosional phases and on associated radiocarbon dates. These dates place the Khormusan in time from about 25,000 B.C. until 14,000 B.C. Thus, not only is there a clear picture of a typologically and technologically unified industry, but the dynamics of change within the Khormusan can be traced and documented. Information concerning site distribution, site size, and artifact distribution within each site is also available.

The relationships between the Khormusan industry and temporally comparable industries from other areas have been considered. While there are certain technological similarities, there is no question that the Khormusan is typologically unique in its total tool configuration and in many of its technological attributes. Therefore, it cannot be viewed as a mere variant of any other known industry.

In order to achieve a maximum clarity in a definition of the Khormusan, the author has organized this paper into sections which discuss major traits as units, rather than as fragments within the individual site reports. These sections will point out any sites where atypical traits occur, and will emphasize those common factors which define the industry and show how these develop and change through time. Near the end of the paper are individual site reports which include detailed typological and technological descriptions of each assemblage. The final sections will discuss the relationships between the Khormusan and those temporally comparable industries in adjacent areas.

During the early work of the Combined Prehistoric Expedition, Khormusan sites were discovered, but their significance was not fully recognized. Excavated samples were too small to give valid pictures of assemblages, and, to some extent, preconceptions of overall Nilotic prehistory prevented the recognition of the fact that this was a new and distinct lithic industry.

Certain preliminary reports on Khormusan sites have already been published. The first—Solecki (1963)—recognized that the assemblage at Locality 34 (34A) was of "Upper Paleolithic" type and, at the same time, was unknown elsewhere in Nubia. The second report dealing with a Khormusan site was published by Waechter (1965) as part of a paper entitled "A Preliminary Report on Four Epi-Levallois Sites." In this paper, test excavation and surface material from Site ANW-3 was described. Unfortunately, insufficient sampling led to a tentative erroneous grouping together of unrelated sites.

The third report (Wendorf, Shiner, and Marks, 1965) recognized for the first time the presence of the Khormusan industry at two sites, 1017 and ANW-3, and gave a very basic definition of the typological attributes of the industry.

Subsequent excavations have added two new sites, 34D and 2004, and have recovered *in situ* a sample from 34A which permitted a true view of the typological and technological attributes of that assemblage. The results of this last excavation made clear that 34A belonged within the Khormusan tradition.

Thus, to date, five Khormusan assemblages are

known: 34A, 1017, 34D, ANW-3 and 2004. These sites were excavated during a number of field seasons by various personnel. Table 1 lists the persons who excavated at each site and the dates of the excavations.

TABLE 1

HISTORY OF WORK AT KHORMUSAN SITES

Site	Excavator(s)	Date Excavated
2004	A. Marks	2/65
ANW-3	J. Waechter	2/63
	A. Marks	2-3/64
34D	W. McHugh	2-3/64
	A. Marks and F. Wendorf	1/65
1017	A. Marks	11/63
34A	R. Stigler and A. Marks	2/61
	W. McHugh	3/64
	A. Marks and F. Wendorf	1/65

Work carried out by McHugh consisted of the excavating of geological test pits, the making of surface collections, and the mapping of the area surrounding Site 34. Work done by Waechter at ANW-3 consisted of minor test excavating and surface collecting. Stigler and Marks made both test excavations and surface collections from the eastern section of Site 34. Marks and Wendorf carried out intensive excavations at Site 34, and Marks made intensive excavations at Sites 2004, ANW-3, and 1017.

The result of all this work is a detailed picture of the existence and development of a new and artifactually rich industry of the late Upper Pleistocene in the northern Sudan.

TECHNOLOGICAL AND TYPOLOGICAL STUDIES

A word should be said about the system of technological and typological studies employed during laboratory analysis. As all Khormusan assemblages contain an important element of prepared cores and flakes, the technological treatment used is that developed by F. Bordes, at the Laboratory of Bordeaux, for the technological description of the Mousterian complex (Bordes, 1950). This in no way implies any direct generic link with the Mousterian but merely utilizes a system which permits simple quantitative observations on the various aspects of Levallois flake production. These are given as a series of Technological Indices derived as follows:

$$IL \text{ (Levallois Index)} = \frac{\text{total number of Levallois flakes, blades, and points x 100}}{\text{total number of flakes, blades, and points}}$$

$$IF \text{ (Faceting Index)} = \frac{\text{total number of dihedral, convex, and straight faceted flakes, blades, and points x 100}}{\text{total number of flakes, blades, and points with recognizable butts}}$$

$$IFs \text{ (Restricted Faceting Index)} = \frac{\text{total number of convex and straight faceted flakes, blades, and points x 100}}{\text{total number of flakes, blades, and points with recognizable butts}}$$

$$Ibl \text{ (Blade Index)} = \frac{\text{total number of blades x 100}}{\text{total number of flakes, blades, and points}}$$

In addition, there are a number of typological indices used to facilitate comparisons between assemblages. These indices describe the major tool classes in the complete typologies—those with unretouched Levallois flakes, blades, and points—and, also, in the restricted typologies—those which exclude unretouched Levallois flakes, blades, and points. The complete indices are derived from the complete typological lists, as follows:

$$IL^{ty} \text{ (Levallois Typological Index)} = \frac{\text{total number of unretouched Levallois flakes, blades, and points x 100}}{\text{total number of tools listed in the complete typology, including unretouched Levallois pieces}}$$

$$Ibu \text{ (Burin Index)} = \frac{\text{total number of burins x 100}}{\text{total number of tools listed in the complete typology, including unretouched Levallois pieces}}$$

$$Ident \text{ (Denticulate Index)} = \frac{\text{total number of denticulates x 100}}{\text{total number of tools listed in the complete typology, including unretouched Levallois pieces}}$$

Iendscr (End-scraper Index) = total number of end-scrapers x 100

total number of tools listed in the complete typology, including unretouched Levallois pieces

Isscr (Side-scraper Index) = total number of side-scrapers x 100

total number of tools listed in the complete typology, including unretouched Levallois pieces

The Restricted Typological Indices are arrived at in the same way, but unretouched Levallois flakes, blades, and points are excluded from the restricted typological lists.

In the typologies for each site, a number of points need explanation. Levallois blades include all typical blades taken from Levallois blade cores as well as laminary Levallois flakes which are more than twice as long as they are wide. The latter are, by far, the most common.

Burins are both numerous and varied in the Khormusan. Not all are typical; but where possible they have been classed in those types defined by D. de Sonneville-Bordes and J. Perrot (de Sonneville-Bordes and Perrot, 1956a). Certain modifications have been made, however. As most burins occur on short flakes or cores, it was felt that the primary feature was the form of the working edge rather than the type of artifact on which it was made. Therefore, they have been classified as to the form, and the type of piece on which they were made is noted in the text.

A few atypical forms of burins occur which are not listed by de Sonneville-Bordes and Perrot. A distinction has been made between angle burins which are formed on the edges of snapped pieces and those which are formed by single blows on the naturally perpendicular edges of flakes and cores. This includes those single blow burins struck from the butts of flakes. There are two types of single blow angle burins: those which are normally parallel to the long axis of the piece, and those which are transverse to it. Each type is listed separately.

Denticulates form an important element in the Khormusan, so they have been typologically subdivided according to the placement of the denti-

culate edge or edges. They are also classified as to whether they are macro- or microdenticulate. In a macrodenticulate the notches between teeth are more than 1.0 cm. across, and in a microdenticulate they are less than 1.0 cm. across.

The last category, "varia," is meant to apply to all retouched tools which do not belong in the other list types. These are not numerous, and any one type rarely occurs in more than one assemblage.

Aside from these observations, all tools are classified as defined in the literature of de Heinzelin (1962); de Sonneville-Bordes and Perrot (1954, 1955, 1956a, 1956b); and Bordes (1950, 1961).

STRATIGRAPHIC CRITERIA FOR THE KHORMUSAN CHRONOLOGY

The chronological ordering of Khormusan sites is primarily based on their position in the sequence of aggradational and erosional phases of the Nile. Corroborative information was obtained from radiocarbon age determinations and technological and typological seriation of individual assemblages. These systems produced results which are in full agreement with each other.

The sequence of Nile aggradations and erosions near Wadi Halfa, Sudan, has been reconstructed both by large geological trenches and by a series of associated radiocarbon dates. A preliminary report of the results, with radiocarbon dates, has already been published (Wendorf, Shiner, and Marks, 1965, pp. xiii-xv). In summary, the earliest Nile aggradation is represented by the Dibeira-Jer formation,[1] which rises to a normal, absolute elevation of 156 m., or 35 m. above the present floodplain. This phase was followed by a major erosional period, the Ballana formation. The following aggradational phase is called the Sahaba formation, and it reaches a maximum absolute elevation of 147 m., or 26 m. above floodplain. This ends about 10,000 B.C. and is followed by the Birbet formation, a period of minor erosion. The Arkin aggradational phase begins about 8,000 B.C., and reaches a maximum elevation of 135 m., or 14 m. above floodplain. This phase is followed by a series of receding

---

[1] This was originally referred to as the Dibeira formation (Wendorf, Shiner, and Marks, 1965).

beach lines which can be dated up to early historical times.

The Khormusan assemblages have been found stratigraphically just under the Dibeira-Jer formation, within the middle and upper stages of the Dibeira-Jer formation, in the Ballana formation, and, perhaps, in the base of the Sahaba formation. Table 2 shows this relationship. Radiocarbon dates associated with these assemblages have added greatly to the absolute dating of these early Nile stages.

TABLE 2

RELATIONSHIP OF KHORMUSAN SITES TO THE
NILE SEQUENCE WITH RADIOCARBON DATES

Sites	Stratigraphic Position	Radiocarbon Dates
2004	Base of Sahaba	
ANW-3	Ballana formation	15,850 B.C. ± 500 years (WSU-215)
34D	Top of Dibeira-Jer	
1017	Middle of Dibeira-Jer	20,750 B.C. ± 280 years (WSU-203)
34A	Ikhtiariya formation	

SITE 34A

The earliest of the Khormusan assemblages was found just east of the village of Nag el-Ikhtiariya in Dibeira East (fig. 1). It was present both on the deflated surface and within a sand dune covered by fluvial sands and silts of the Dibeira-Jer formation. Of particular note in one area, this assemblage was stratigraphically below another Khormusan assemblage, 34D. As the tool sample was obtained in situ in this area, it will be discussed as being typical of the general stratigraphy of the site.

The area, excavated as Features 200 through 213, was on the middle of the slope of the deflated Dibeira-Jer formation at an absolute elevation of 149 m. In this area, part of the cover of the Dibeira-Jer formation was still intact in the form of about 20 cm. of sands with artifacts covered by partially deflated silts. Below these was an extensive sand dune which, in other parts of the site, formed the deflated surface. The top 10 cm. or so of the dune was sterile, containing no artifacts. A few artifacts were present in the next 10 cm., but the main concentration of 34A occurred between 19 and 21 cm. below the surface

of the sand dune. Occasional artifacts were found below this layer, but these appeared to have been walked into that part of the dune (fig. 2).

In various geological test pits, it was possible to trace in situ the position of 34A eastward for a distance of 100 m. At the extreme eastern end of the site, fresh artifacts of this assemblage were resting on a sandstone shelf covered by silts of the Dibeira-Jer formation. The sand dune has been estimated to date back to about 25,000 B.C.

SITE 1017

Site 1017 is situated in a branch of Khor Musa, southwest of the Wadi Halfa airport (fig. 1). Excavations revealed a living floor in fluvial sand, covered by partially deflated silts of the Dibeira-Jer formation. The living floor was on the top of a fluvial sand, covered by an additional 27 cm. of other fluvial sand, and from 25 to 70 cm. of silt (fig. 3). The surface of the silt was at an absolute elevation of from 144 to 145 m., or from 23 to 24 m. above floodplain. This places the living floor just under 143 m. absolute elevation; that is, within the middle of the Dibeira-Jer aggradation. A charcoal sample from the living floor gave a date of 20,750 B.C. ± 280 years.

SITE 34D

The assemblage of 34D was found both on the deflated surface and stratigraphically above 34A at Nag el-Ikhtiariya, at an absolute elevation of 149 m., or 28 m. above floodplain (fig. 1). The sample occurred in situ in a loose fluvial sand layer which showed a weak soil formation. At the eastern extreme of the excavated area, this zone was covered by a thin layer of silts. These silts were truncated a short way down the slope to the west. Its position, however, is seen in the profile in Figure 2. These silts represent a very late stage of the Dibeira-Jer aggradation. The absolute elevation, which appears somewhat high, has been affected by local tectonics. The result is an overall rise of the Dibeira-Jer formation deposits here by some 6 m.

SITE ANW-3

ANW-3 is situated behind the village of Angash, on the west bank of the Nile (fig. 1). It consists of a massive silt remnant of the Dibeira-Jer formation which has erosional cracks on its

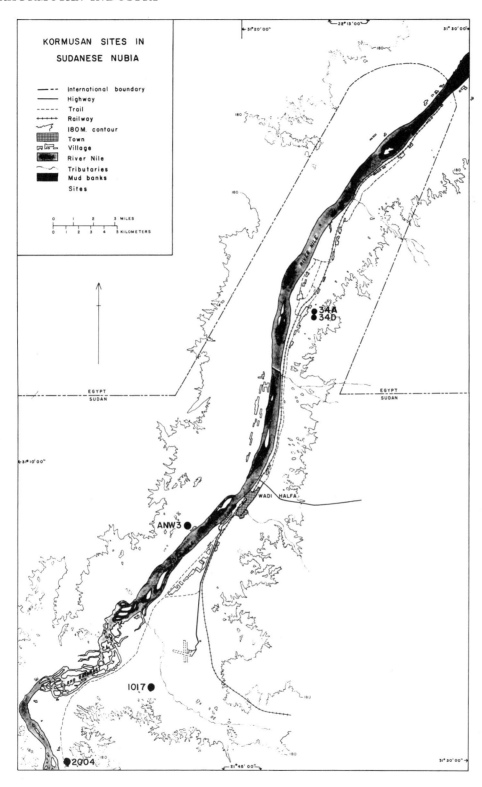

FIG. 1—Map of Khormusan sites in Sudanese Nubia.

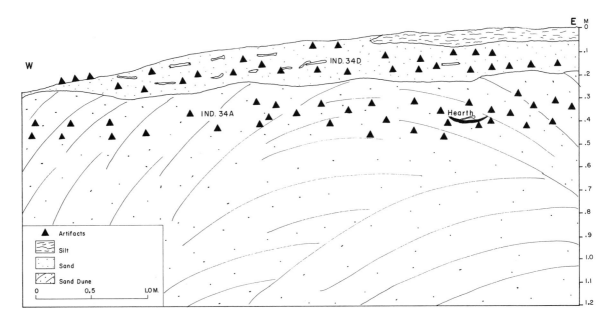

FIG. 2—East-west profile of excavations at Site 34A.

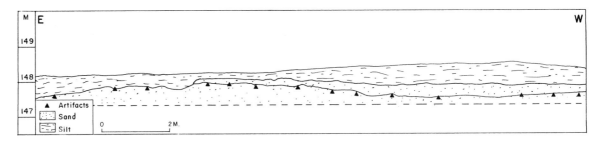

FIG. 3—East-west profile of excavations at Site 1017.

surface, shallow mud pools on its western side, and a sharply eroded old Nile bank with slumped silt blocks at its eastern edge. A sand dune is banked against this old Nile bank, rising above it and covering sections of it in the northern part of the excavated area. Khormusan artifacts were recovered from within this dune, in dune sand in the erosional cracks, and in dune sand resting on the mud flats to the west.

The sand dune was covered by a thin layer of fluvial sand and silt pebbles, which in turn was covered by a sterile layer of fluvial sand. Within the erosional cracks and on the mud pools, the same stratigraphic sequence was present. Covering the whole site was a thin colluvium which

is present over the whole landscape in this area (fig. 4). The sand dune was at an absolute elevation of 138 to 139 m., or 17 to 18 m. above present floodplain.

The extremely well preserved bank of the Nile indicates a rapidly falling water level which remained low while the sand dune accumulated. It was during this period of the Ballana formation that people lived on the dune and the deflated and cracked silt block behind it. The thin layer of silt pebbles indicates that a brief flood covered the dune, which, then in turn, was covered by fluvial sand of the Sahaba aggradation to an elevation of 20 m. above floodplain. A carbon sample from the artifact bearing dune sand

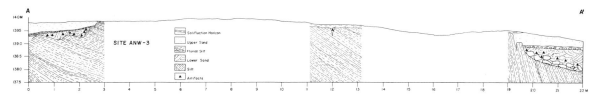

Fig. 4—East-west profile of excavations at Site ANW-3.

above the mud pools gave a date of 15,850 B.C. ± 500 years.

SITE 2004

Site 2004 is south of the Second Cataract, within the village of Gemai East (fig. 1). Artifacts were found, *in situ*, on a living floor 4 cm. under the top of a fluvial sand deposit, covered by partially deflated silts, at an elevation of 8 m. above present floodplain (fig. 5). The low elevation of the site indicates that the fluvial sands and silts represent a basal level of the Sahaba aggradation. The site, however, is south of the Second Cataract, and a direct correlation between these deposits and those below the Cataract is not positive. It is possible that these sands are contemporary with the final phase of the Ballana formation north of the Second Cataract.

Thus, no Khormusan sites were found in stratigraphic position later than, perhaps, the base of the Sahaba formation. On the basis of stratigraphy and radiocarbon dates, the sequence of assemblages is clear. With minor extensions, the Khormusan industry is clearly associated with the aggradation and erosion of the Dibeira-Jer formation.

DISTRIBUTION OF KHORMUSAN SITES

Khormusan sites were located along a 50 km. stretch of the Nile, from Gemai East to Nag el-Ikhtiariya in Dibeira (fig. 1). All sites were found within reasonable proximity to the Nile and were always associated with formations of the present Nile.

One site, 2004, was south of the Second Cataract at Gemai in the Precambrian badlands of the Batn el-Hajar. Another, 1017, was found in the Khor Musa which forms the boundary between the Batn el-Hajar and the Nubian Sandstone Desert to the north. Three sites, ANW-3, 34A, and 34D, were found north of the Khor

Musa on the edge of the Nubian Sandstone Desert.[2]

Although an intensive survey was carried out in the desert areas, no Khormusan sites were located beyond the Nile silt deposits. This distribution of sites shows that choice of site location was governed by the immediate presence of the Nile. The total absence of Khormusan sites beyond the silt deposits indicates that the surrounding country may have been too dry to support prolonged human occupation.

SITE SITUATIONS

Two types of site situations were seen. Three of the five sites rested on fluvial sand deposits, which were covered by additional fluvial sands of the same stage of aggradation as those upon which the sites rested. Two sites were in dune sand and covered by sands of the same dunes.

Those sites on fluvial sand—1017, 34D, and 2004—because of the generally continuous nature of the sand deposits below and above the sites, apparently were originally sand bars at the edge of the Nile. Those sites on sand dunes, 34A and ANW-3, are oriented parallel to the Nile and probably were situated within a very short distance of the river itself.

SIZE OF KHORMUSAN SITES

Compared with sites of other industries found along the Nile, Khormusan sites are extremely large. As all the sites were mostly *in situ*, it was impossible to judge accurately the total area of each site. Enough material was present on the surface of each site, however, to make rough estimates of total area of occupation.

Site 34A was traced, *in situ*, over 100 m. east-west, and surface material was thickly spread

---

[2] An additional Khormusan site was found by the Colorado Expedition at Murshid, about 10 km. south of Gemai (unpublished).

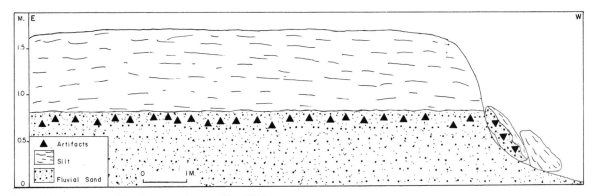

Fig. 5—East-west profile of excavations at Site 2004.

over a distance of 95 m. north-south (fig. 6). Thus, the probable total area occupied at this site was over 9,500 sq. m.

Site 1017 was present along an old Nile shore for about 250 m. The width of the site, on the other hand, was just less than 8 m. in the excavated area. In this area, it is apparent that the site was situated on a narrow sand bar between two silt exposures (fig. 7). In this case the site was most definitely oriented lineally along an old Nile shore, covering a possible total area of 2,000 sq m.

Site 34D showed a surface concentration which extended only 30 m. east-west but was still basically oriented along the edge of the river, covering over 2,100 sq. m. in area (fig. 6).

Site ANW-3 was traced for a distance of one-half kilometer parallel to the Nile. Along some of the way, massive fluvial sand deposits of the Sahaba formation covered most surface indications. There was, however, a thin scattering of artifacts every few meters. At its widest this site was no more than 18 m. from east to west. That is, it was very definitely oriented along the old Nile shore, covering at most 9,000 sq. m. and at least 1,000 sq. m. in the intensively studied area.

Evidence for site size at 2004 is less reliable. Only a small area was exposed. This could be traced *in situ* for no more than 100 sq. m. On the other hand, large areas to the east were covered by massive silts and houses. Wherever there were pits, however, there were some Khormusan tools on the surface. The general impression, which could not be fully tested, was that the site was large—at least 100 m. north-south and perhaps as much as 15 m. east-west.

The large size of these sites poses a number of questions. Either populations were very large during occupation, or the sites represent areas which were revisited again and again by small groups of people.

The density of artifacts is rather low in comparison with that at Nubian Mousterian sites. It seems reasonable, therefore, to assume that these sites represent a series of short occupations by small roups of people over relatively long periods of time. The single exception to this is Site 1017. Within the excavated area—only 176 sq. m.—the artifactual distribution was very thin. Many cores could be reconstructed, and a number of broken tools fit back together as the pieces were right next to each other. The impression was that the area had been occupied for only a very short period; so short, that almost no disturbance of the living floor had taken place. In fact, less than 110 retouched tools were recovered in the area excavated. Site 1017 truly represents "a moment in time" in the Khormusan development, if we consider the total span of perhaps 10,000 years during which there is evidence of its presence in the area.

The concept of numerous short occupations is reinforced at a number of sites where there were distinct artifactual concentrations around fire burned areas, with little in the spaces between them. This will be described in detail in the individual site reports.

ARTIFACTUAL CONTENT

Although extremely large in area, Khormusan sites have a relatively low density of artifacts. Within excavated areas, a total of 16,945 artifacts

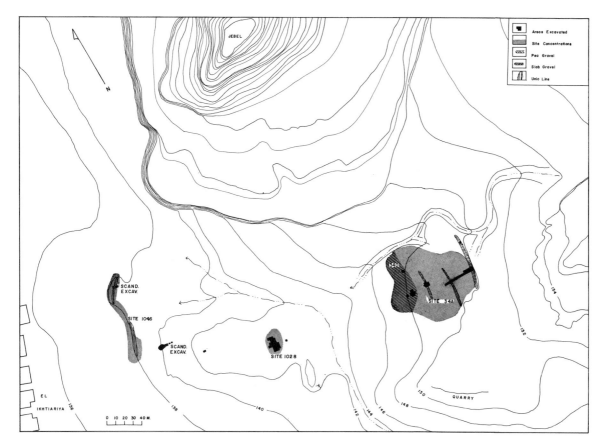

FIG. 6—Topographic map of Nag el-Ikhtiariya, showing areas of artifact concentrations.

was obtained from five sites. No sample contained under 1,500 artifacts or over 4,500. Within each site, however, excavated areas produced few artifacts per square meter. Table 3 shows this information.

TABLE 3

TOTAL ARTIFACTS AND ARTIFACTS PER SQUARE METER
AT KHORMUSAN SITES

Site	Area Excavated	Total Artifacts	Artifacts Per Sq. M.
2004	30 sq. m.	1525	50.8
ANW-3	254 sq. m.	3444	13.5
34D	76 sq. m.	4478	58.8
1017	176 sq. m.	4472	25.4
34A	78 sq. m.	3046	39.0

Initially, artifacts were divided into gross classes. This included the following groups: (1) tools, all retouched tools, and Levallois pieces; (2) unretouched non-Levallois flakes and blades; (3) cores; (4) primary flakes;[3] and (5) debris,

including chips, unidentifiable fragments, core manufacturing waste flakes, core trimming flakes, etc.

It was hoped that this might give some indication of seasonal activity or, at least, intensity of flaking at each site. The results, however, showed that, from site to site, there was no appreciable difference in the proportions of these types (fig. 8).

Two points are noticeable, however. At Site 1017, there is a very low percentage of primary flakes—only 1.9 per cent. This is from one-quarter to one-tenth of the proportions at other sites. Cores, on the other hand, are average for all sites. This indicates that primary flaking of cores at 1017 took place outside the site area, perhaps in the wadis where the raw material was collected.

At ANW-3, there is a much higher proportion of primary flakes than is typical at other sites.

[3] These have cortex covering one-half or more of the upper surface (de Heinzelin, 1962, p. 13).

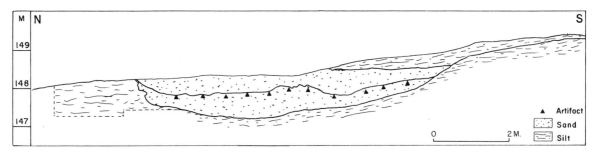

Fig. 7—North-south profile of excavations at Site 1017.

This is also the site with the highest percentage of chert cores and with, by far, the highest percentage of all cores. It is apparent that the higher number of flaked cores resulted in a higher number of primary flakes. Yet, there is not a corresponding increase in the number of flakes and debris. This means that each core was utilized to a lesser extent than at other sites. The fact that chert pebble cores require less primary shaping than Precambrian or ferrocrete sandstone cobbles may explain this difference.

A third observation may be made. At the two most recent Khormusan sites, ANW-3 and 2004, unusable debitage (debris and primary flakes) account for 55.5 and 56.9 per cent of the total collections. At the three earlier sites, however, they account for between 70.2 and 81.5 per cent. This can probably be correlated with the greater size and preparation given to Levallois cores at the early sites and the tendency to rework the same rocks into smaller and smaller Levallois cores.

In short, while some variation occurs, the proportions of gross classes of artifacts remain rather standard and show a definite overall pattern which is present throughout the whole development of the Khormusan.

UTILIZATION OF RAW MATERIALS FOR LITHIC ARTIFACTS

Within the general area of the Second Cataract, there are a number of types of locally available stone which can be used in the manufacture of tools.

Basically, there are five types of usable rocks, each with a slightly different areal distribution. They may be summarized as follows:

1. Ferrocrete sandstone: Available in natural slabs on the edges of most inselbergs in the Eastern and Western Deserts, north of the Second Cataract. It is also available in small quantities as cobbles on the floors of the major wadis at the Second Cataract.

2. Precambrian rocks: These include quartzites, riolites, dyke exposures of metamorphic rocks, shales, etc. They are available in the wadis of the Batn el-Hajar, south of Khor Musa, and on the west bank, as dyke exposures near the Second Cataract.

3. Quartz: Available in the Batn el-Hajar as outcrops and as pebbles on the pre-Nile plain and the major wadis. Also, rarely as pebbles deposited by the Nile on the Dibeira-Jer formation.

4. Chert and Agate: Mainly available as pebbles deposited by the Nile on the Dibeira-Jer formation. Also, small numbers are available in remnants of a sandstone conglomerate. This latter source was seen only in two small localities.

5. Fossil wood: Available as large trunk fragments in the Eastern Desert, directly behind Dibeira East, and in the Western Desert, some kilometers behind Buhen. There are also occasional cobbles of fossil wood in the wadi bottoms of the Second Cataract area.

One of the characteristics of the Khormusan industry is the utilization of all these types of rocks. During its earliest known stage, at 34A, the choice of raw material strongly reflects a Nubian Middle Stone Age tradition, although major changes are already apparent. At typical Nubian Middle Stone Age sites, at most, less than 0.5 per cent of any class of artifact is made on nonferrocrete sandstone material. At 34A, while only 6.6 per cent of the tools are made on other rocks, 27.3 per cent of the cores are made on fossil wood, quartz, or chert (fig. 9). The exceedingly

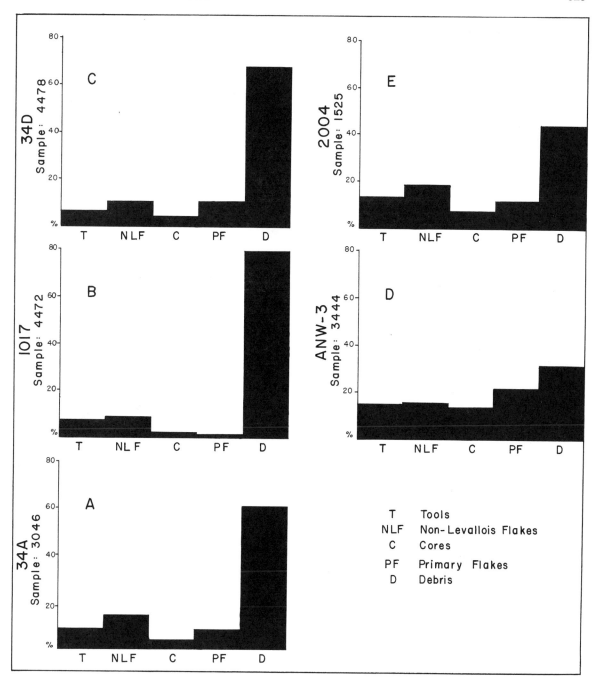

FIG. 8—Percentages of gross artifact classes.

low level of Precambrian rock may be explained by its unavailability in the immediate vicinity.

From this stage of experimentation with a wide range of rocks, the use of non-ferrocrete sandstone materials grows rapidly. By about 21,000 B.C., Site 1017, ferrocrete sandstone is a relatively small element in all artifacts, while remaining an important element in tool manufacture. At this stage, the use of Precambrian rocks becomes dominant, and chert makes its first significant appearance. The following stages, as seen at 34D and ANW-3, show a progressive in-

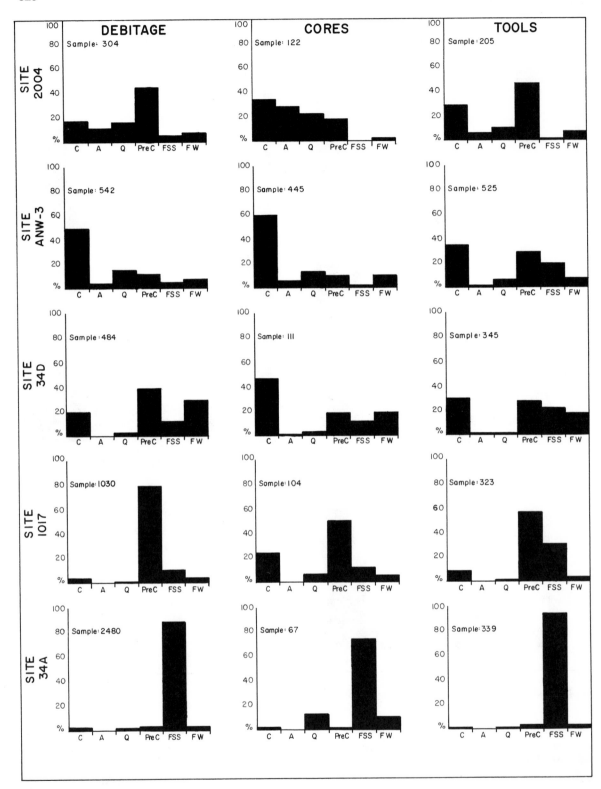

Fɪɢ. 9—Utilization of raw materials in debitage, cores, and tools: C=chert; A=agate; Q=quartz; PreC=Precambrian; FSS=ferrocrete sandstone; FW=fossil wood.

crease in the use of chert, a drop in Precambrian rocks, and a further small decrease in ferrocrete sandstone (fig. 9).

The latest known stage, 2004, poses something of a problem. As the site is south of the Second Cataract, there is a different distribution of available raw materials. In particular, chert is not as readily found, and ferrocrete sandstone is not present at all in the immediate vicinity. This has resulted in a re-emphasis on Precambrian rocks.

As must be expected, site situation and immediate availability of specific raw materials affected the proportions of utilized raw material. The relatively high proportion of fossil wood at 34D, ferrocrete sandstone at 34A, and the above mentioned predominance of Precambrian rock at 2004 are examples of utilization of immediately available material beyond what might normally be expected. In spite of this factor, it should be noted that 34A and 34D are located in the same place, yet a definite change has taken place in raw material preference.

In a very simplified way, it might be said that the major change in the choice of raw materials is a shift in the ratio between ferrocrete sandstone and Nile chert, with a replacement of the former by the latter (fig. 10).

One of the more interesting aspects in the utilization of raw materials is that different materials were often used for different types of tools. The most striking difference is seen in a comparison of Levallois flakes and burins. Although changes occur through time in both groups, they are made, for the most part, from different types of rock.

Levallois flakes call for the preparation of a core which, in turn, necessitates a rather large natural slab or cobble. These usually occur only in ferrocrete sandstone or Precambrian rocks. Chert, agate, and quartz are generally available only as small pebbles. Therefore, it is not surprising to find that the vast majority of Levallois flakes are made on ferrocrete sandstone or Precambrian rocks. As the flake size of the industry decreased, however, the smaller sized materials were also utilized, but never as commonly as in other classes of tools (fig. 11).

Burins are one of the most common tools of the Khormusan industry. In the early stages, there is a direct correlation between burins and

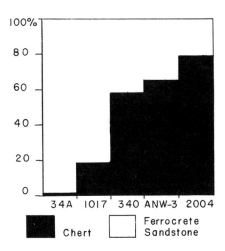

Fig. 10—Relationship of ferrocrete sandstone to Nile chert at Khormusan sites.

chert. At 1017, where chert first occurs in significant amounts, it is used almost exclusively for the manufacture of burins. Other tools on chert, a truncation and a notch, may well be unfinished burins. Burins are also made on Precambrian rocks and fossil wood, but only at 34A are any found on ferrocrete sandstone (fig. 11).

The relationship between burins and chert is functionally clear. Chert is harder than the other available rocks, and the making of burins calls for no elaborately prepared flakes or even large flakes. The almost exclusive utilization of chert for making burins at 1017 indicates that the advantages of its natural attributes were appreciated and utilized, although at 1017 still a minority of burins are on sandstone.

Even more than in Levallois flakes, there is a rapid increase in the use of chert for burins and a total disappearance of ferrocrete sandstone for the same purpose. Even Precambrian rocks are used less and less (fig. 11).

Other classes of tools (denticulates, scrapers, notches, etc.) may be successfully made on any type of lithic material. Again, the only restriction depends on the desired size of the tool being made. As more small tools occur through time, there is an increasing utilization of agate and chert at the expense of other lithic materials (fig. 11).

SIZE OF KHORMUSAN TOOLS

Studies were made of the lengths of all com-

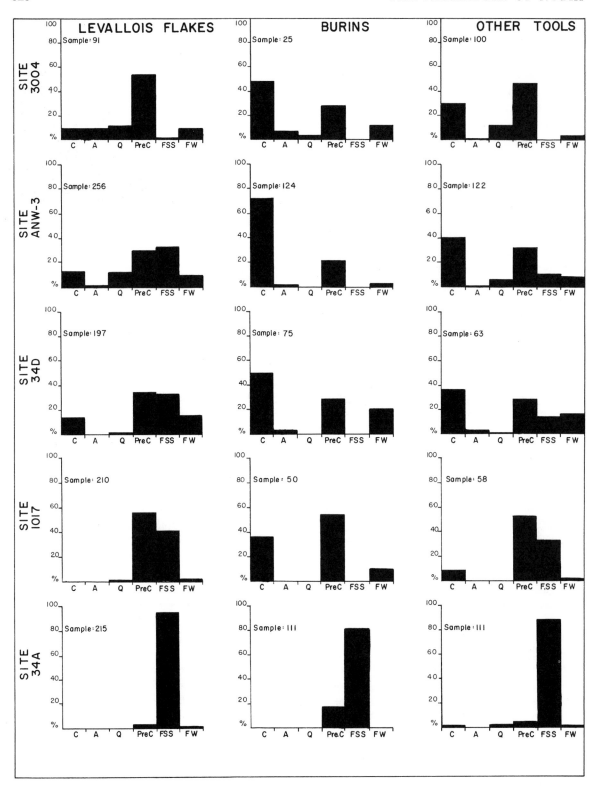

FIG. 11—Utilization of raw materials for Levallois flakes, burins, and other tools: C=chert; A=agate; Q=quartz; PreC=Precambrian; FSS=ferrocrete sandstone; FW=fossil wood.

plete Levallois flakes and retouched tools at each site. The result shows that there is a decided trend toward an overall diminution when comparing early ones with late ones. The mean lengths of all tools decrease through time, although the change is neither very great nor wholly consistent. The two earliest sites, 34A and 1017, have almost identical mean lengths: 43.8 and 44 mm. At 34D, however, there is a major drop to 31.4 mm. Site ANW-3 somewhat reverses the trend but only to a very small extent at 36 mm. There appears to be a significant shift in size between 1017 and 34D, with all assemblages after 34D falling within the same general range.

This pattern is very clear when only retouched tools are considered. In such a case, bar graphs for 34A and 1017 are very similar, yet quite different from those for 34D, ANW-3, and 2004. The latter three are almost identical, as can be seen in Figure 12.

These graphs indicate that the actual change in tool size is the result of an increase in the number of tools under 30 mm. in length and a sharp decrease in those over 50 mm. in length. Throughout the whole sequence, those measuring between 30 and 50 mm. remain constant—from 39.5 to 44.3 per cent of all retouched tools.

Once the tool size reached the level seen at 34D, it remained almost constant, although changes continued to take place in the utilization of raw materials, technological attributes, and typology.

CHARACTERISTICS AND DEVELOPMENT OF THE KHORMUSAN INDUSTRY

The Khormusan industry, as known from excavations, spans over 10,000 years of the Upper Pleistocene, beginning about 25,000 B.C and ending some time after 15,000 B.C. Throughout this long period, the Khormusan retains its essential character, although certain changes do occur.

The development of the Khormusan may be traced through a number of changes in its typology and technology. Yet, within general limits and discounting minor changes, the Khormusan may be defined as having the following technological and typological attributes:

Technological:

1. The Levallois flake tradition is strong.

2. There are a few true blades but a number of laminary flakes.

3. The percentage of flakes with faceted butts, both Levallois and non-Levallois, is very high.

4. Levallois cores show extremely careful preparation.

5. Levallois cores of oval to pointed oval shape predominate.

6. A wide range of raw materials is utilized.

7. Different raw materials are often used for different types of tools.

8. There is often a wide range in tool size.

9. The Khormusan has basically a unifacial flaking tradition, with bifacial retouch exceedingly rare.

Typological:

1. The industry is characterized by the dominance of three tool types: Levallois flakes, burins, and denticulates.

2. During the main stages of the Khormusan, end-scrapers and side-scrapers are not common, although always present.

3. Unretouched Levallois flakes account for almost half to three-fifths of all tools.

4. Very few notched flakes or simple truncated flakes occur.

5. The following tool types are not found at Khormusan sites: (a) borers, (b) backed blades or backed microblades, (c) backed knives, (d) backed points, (e) geometrics, and (f) large bifacial core tools—bifaces, foliates or lanceolates, picks, etc.

Aside from typological and technological attributes, Khormusan sites have a number of other features in common:

1. All are large, covering thousands of square meters.

2. All seem to have been close to the Nile and lineally oriented along it on sand formations.

3. Sites appear to represent a series of small artifact concentrations around hearths, rather than a uniform scattering of artifacts over the entire site.

While the Khormusan may be defined by a number of attributes, it is not static. Numerous changes take place; some are apparently without pattern, while others show definite trends. It is this latter group which best demonstrates the direction of development of the Khormusan industry.

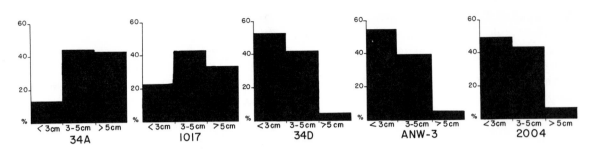

F‍ɪɢ. 12—Size of retouched tools at Khormusan sites.

Changes take place in both the technology and the typology. The technological changes are of a number of types, but all show a consistency and degree of change which goes beyond mere chance variation in sampling.

Within the technological sphere, the Levallois Index shows an erratic but definite drop through time. The level of faceting remains constantly high throughout the sequence, and the percentage of complex faceted butts remains relatively level. Blades and laminary flakes are rare throughout, and no trend toward blade production can be seen in Table 4. There is no question that the Khormusan is predominantly a flake industry.

TABLE 4

T‍ᴇᴄʜɴᴏʟᴏɢɪᴄᴀʟ A‍ᴛᴛʀɪʙᴜᴛᴇꜱ ᴏꜰ ᴛʜᴇ
K‍ʜᴏʀᴍᴜꜱᴀɴ I‍ɴᴅᴜꜱᴛʀʏ

	34A	1017	34D	ANW-3	2004
IL	34.0	36.6	23.2	30.1	18.8
IF	63.8	78.3	74.2	69.7	67.4
IFs	42.3	50.5	50.5	40.1	43.3
Ibl	8.1	14.1	9.0	14.1	11.7

The differential utilization of lithic raw materials has already been discussed. The only additional observation is that as the use of chert pebble became more common, there was not a corresponding decrease in tendency to facet cores, although there was a drop in Levallois flake production (table 4).

The size of Khormusan tools has also been discussed. The pattern which emerges is a slow decrease in the average size of tools because of a decrease in the number of tools which measure over 5 cm. in length and their replacement by microlithic tools. The number of tools in the intermediate range of 3 to 5 cm. stays constant.

The differential utilization of raw materials for specific artifact types is more clearly seen in the early stages—1017 and 34D—than in the later stages. This is due, in large measure, to an ever increasing use of chert for all types of tools. The discrepancy at site 2004 may be accounted for by its location and the difficulty of obtaining chert pebble south of the Second Cataract.

Bifacially retouched tools occur only sporadically. When present, they are rare and atypical. They seem to represent a holdover from an early pre-Khormusan stage in the lithic development.

The overall impression of the Khormusan technology is one of relative stability. This is also the case in the typology. Here, however, certain traits show progressive changes, although these are small.

At Site 34A, we are faced with an assemblage which is just recognizable within the Khormusan industry. As an assemblage, it is least like other Khormusan sites. This is particularly true in the rich variety and high percentage of side-scrapers. These are more typical of the Mousterian sites of the Nubian Middle Stone Age than they are of the Khormusan. A distinct difference is, however, apparent. Retouch on the side-scrapers at 34A is usually very flat and fine, a trait rarely seen in the Nubian Mousterian.

Another typological attribute which is unique is the high percentage of strangled blades. These do not really occur in the Nubian Mousterian; neither are they common in the later part of the Khormusan. Their number and fine workmanship indicate that they are not a new, developing type, but that they must have had a background during some unknown stage just prior to the beginning of the Khormusan industry.

Clearly distinct from those of the Nubian

Mousterian, however, are the number and variety of burins. These are intermediate between the Nubian Middle Stone Age assemblages and the Khormusan proper. Their connection with the Khormusan becomes stronger when we consider that a number of these were on materials other than ferrocrete sandstone.

Another element which removes 34A from the Nubian Middle Stone Age is the absence of a number of tool types: borers, backed knives, and bec burins. Also, a number of artifact types—cortex backed knives, notched pieces, and truncated pieces—are rare at 34A, while common during the Nubian Middle Stone Age. These minor occurrences fit fully within the whole development of the Khormusan, where these types are never of importance.

The overall picture of 34A is that of a stage during which the prime traits of the Khormusan industry are already apparent but have not developed to any degree. It is hard to conceive of an earlier stage which could still be referred to as Khormusan.

The large number of scrapers and the preference for ferrocrete sandstone seem to indicate that 34A has a base somewhere within the Nubian Middle Stone Age or a corresponding stage in an adjacent area. There is, however, a major gap present, and so it is impossible to state firmly from where it sprung.

From the beginning of the Khormusan industry, the basic traits develop rapidly. These. are all present at Site 1017 and thereafter. Development of these traits usually shows clear patterns, although it seems difficult to divide the Khormusan into discrete periods. This is due to the overall gradual changes and, to some extent, to the rather limited number of sites available for study.

As the Levallois element is one of the major typological and technological attributes of the Khormusan, it is best to begin a study of its development there. The Levallois element may be viewed from three points: the proportion of Levallois flakes to the total assemblages (Levallois Index); the proportion of unretouched Levallois flakes to the total tool collections (Typological Levallois Index); and the proportion of Levallois cores to all cores. The Levallois Index has already been discussed; it shows a general, al-

though erratic, decrease. The other two categories, however, show a clear trend away from the Levallois tradition (table 5).

TABLE 5
DECLINE OF LEVALLOIS TECHNOLOGY

	34A	1017	34D	ANW-3	2004
IL^{ty}	63.3	65.9	59.7	51.4	44.3
Levallois cores (all)	65.8	56.6	49.1	44.5	40.4

It is recognized that, although the Levallois element decreases steadily, it remains at a very high level. It is still exceedingly important at Site 2004 when compared with the bulk of Nubian Mousterian sites.

The study of cores shows one of the major typological changes during the development of the Khormusan. As was seen in Table 5, the percentage of all Levallois cores steadily decreases through time. In reality, only Levallois flakes and point cores consistently occur in each site. Nubian (Type I), blade, opposite end, and para-Levallois occur only sporadically.

The other main types of cores are the single unfaceted platform, the single faceted platform, the opposed platform, and the discoidal core. Other types are rare and do not occur at all sites. These typical non-Levallois cores show decided trends in occurrence during the development of the Khormusan. Particularly, there is a major increase in the percentage of single, faceted platform cores and a steady decrease in the single, unfaceted platform cores. Discoidal cores increase erratically, and opposed platform cores show no regular change (table 6).

The single discordant note is the core typology from 34A. Here, it still reflects an earlier Middle Stone Age tradition, particularly in the number of discoidal cores.

TABLE 6
PERCENTAGES OF SELECTED CORE TYPES

	34A	1017	34D	ANW-3	2004
Levallois flake	48.8	53.0	40.7	32.1	34.1
Levallois point	12.2	1.2	1.7	2.3	2.1
Single, unfaceted platform	9.8	9.9	8.5	6.6	4.2
Single, faceted platform	0.0	13.6	13.5	22.7	34.1
Opposed platform	0.0	8.6	18.6	9.4	12.8
Discoidal	19.5	1.2	1.7	6.8	4.2

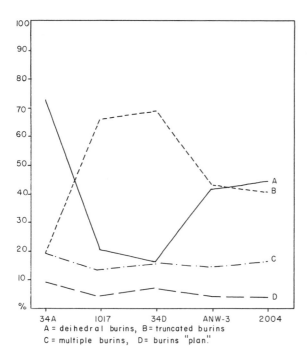

A = deihedral burins, B = truncated burins
C = multiple burins,   D = burins "plan."

Fɪɢ. 13–Frequency of burin types at Khormusan sites.

Burins, which form the most important tool element, are more complex in their development. Of great interest is the rich variety present at all Khormusan sites. Although only 8.8 per cent of all retouched tools are burins at Site 34A, there are seven types present. At any Nubian Mousterian site, rarely more than two types occur.

It is perhaps within the burins that the greatest typological elaborations can be seen. Development is rapid and reaches a height at ANW-3, becoming poorer both in number and types at 2004 (table 7).

TABLE 7

Oᴄᴄᴜʀʀᴇɴᴄᴇ ᴏꜰ Bᴜʀɪɴs ᴀᴛ Kʜᴏʀᴍᴜsᴀɴ Sɪᴛᴇs

	34A	1017	34D	ANW-3	2004
Ibu (restricted)	9.6	46.3	53.5	50.7	21.9
Number of types	7	12	14	17	12

The great number of types of burins is quite atypical for an African industry. Of particular interest is the significant number of transverse burins. Two basic kinds occur: those on lateral or concave lateral truncations, and those "single blow" burins which are transverse. The latter type can be considered generally accidental, as they are extremely rare. Those on truncations, however, are important. They occur at three sites: 1017, 34D, and ANW-3. These sites form the central part of the Khormusan sequence; they are also those sites where the elaboration of burins is taken to its highest level. These transverse burins are all quite typical. It must be remembered, however, that Khormusan burins are on flakes and not blades. Thus, the direction of the burin facets in regard to the long axis is not of much functional importance. The flake may be held or mounted equally well from the butt end or from one side.

The significance of the transverse burins lies in their presence, for none have been reported from other sub-Saharan sites. They do occur in North Africa at Hagfet ed Dabba, in Libya (McBurney and Hey, 1955, p. 200). These, however, are on blades and the burin facets are made by a very special form of preparation rather than by simple flaking (McBurney, 1960, p. 197). Although they are generally contemporary in age with the Dabba material beginning earlier, they cannot be considered directly related to it in more than a mere gross typological sense.[1]

The internal distribution of some burin types throughout the Khormusan shows changes which are not readily understandable, while other types remain rather uniform. Multiple burins and burins *"plan"* remain in constant proportion at each site (fig. 13). The relationship of dihedral burins to burins on truncations (including transverse types) is another matter. At Site 34A, simple and multiple dihedral forms predominate. If we view them as the beginning of a burin technology, this is not surprising. At Sites 1017 and 34D, however, there are about three times as many burins on truncations as there are dihedral forms. This changes abruptly at Site ANW-3, where both dihedral and truncated forms occur in about the same proportions. This continues to be the case at 2004 (fig. 13). This radical shift in a short period cannot be explained, except that there is a gradual decrease in the number and quality of the more complex tools as the Khormusan reaches its last known stage.

The change in the character of the Khormusan during the final stages is not great but is noticeable. It may be seen in an increase in the number of simple retouched flakes, end-scrapers, and rather atypical side-scrapers (table 8). The side-scrapers at 34A differ to some extent from those which occur later in the sequence. At 34A, they are well made by flat retouch, while those at other sites are marginally retouched on irregular flakes and are generally poor—little better than the simple retouch flakes.

TABLE 8

RESTRICTED PERCENTAGES OF SELECTED TOOL TYPES

	34A	1017	34D	ANW-3	2004
Retouched flakes	11.3	2.7	4.3	8.2	16.7
End-scrapers	3.2	1.8	5.7	6.3	8.4
Side-scrapers	24.1	1.8	3.6	3.9	5.3

The high percentage of retouched flakes at 34A reflects its early stage of development. Many flakes in this class were probably unfinished scrapers. This was not the case at later sites, where the retouch was always marginal and very light.

Denticulates, the third characteristic tool of the Khormusan, do not exhibit any clear pattern of change. Lateral denticulates predominate throughout, although converging denticulates and denticulate points are present in significant numbers in the middle part of the sequence.

Only core denticulates seem to have chronological significance; they occur only at ANW-3 and 2004. At both sites, however, they are rare.

Another late typological feature is the multiple tool, including combinations of burins, with scrapers and denticulates. In no case are they common, but they indicate a general decline in the quality of retouched tools as seen in all other types, particularly denticulates.

In short, the development of the Khormusan shows a rapid increase in the variety and number of burins and denticulates, while at the same time side-scrapers occur in number only at the very beginning. Once the full Khormusan character is established, there is a slow increase in less typical tools and a general drop in the quality of all tools in the later stages.

While it is felt that 34A represents the first recognizable stage of the Khormusan, Site 2004 does not seem to be a logical ending point in its development. While they are definitely on the decline, Khormusan traits still dominate the as-semblage. At the same time, there is no indication that the Khormusan is developing toward the other later industries in the area: Halfan and Gemaian/Qadan. Thus, it must be stated that the final Khormusan, or its transitional stage to another industry, has not been found.

As the Halfan and Qadan seem to have relations to the north, it is possible that the movement of peoples from northern Nubia forced the Khormusan peoples from the Second Cataract into the Batn el-Hajar.

SITE REPORTS

SITE 34A

Site 34, at Nag el-Ikhtiariya in Dibeira East (map ref. 830.1/655.2),[4] was first discovered during the 1961-1962 field season. After three field seasons of excavation, the general pattern of the site is now known. It is a very rich site, containing five distinct assemblages (fig. 6), and is further complicated geologically by local tectonics. The site comprises the area east of the village, on the upper slope of the deflated Dibeira-Jer formation. A large portion of this slope was covered by a surface concentration of ferrocrete sandstone artifacts. Within the same area, differential deflation left the artifactual bearing level in situ. The first of these was discovered by trenching in 1961 (Solecki, 1963, p. 85). Additional areas were uncovered in 1963-1964 during geological test excavations. The main area of concentration, however, was not found until the 1964-1965 field season. During that final season, 78 sq. m. containing artifacts in situ from the assemblage now called 34A were excavated. The exact stratigraphic position of these artifacts has already been described, as has the total site area.

The stratigraphic position of the artifacts was clear; they rested within a large sand dune which underlay sands and silts of the oldest silt aggradation, the Dibeira-Jer formation (fig. 2).

While artifacts were in situ, they were weathered somewhat by chemical action. This was very clear on the surface artifacts which had been uncovered by deflation. The weathering affected the edges of the flakes, often obscuring

---

[4] All map references are to Egypt-New Series 1:25,000, printed by the Sudan Survey Department. April, 1960.

whatever retouch had been present. Those *in situ*, however, were only slightly weathered, and all retouch was clearly visible.

Within the 78 sq. m. excavated, a total of 3,046 artifacts of various types were recovered. These are broken into classes (fig. 8). The vast majority were made on ferrocrete sandstone which was immediately available at the base of the inselberg to the west. Some other materials were utilized, and the proportions of these have been previously noted (fig. 9), as has artifact size (fig. 12).

DISTRIBUTION OF ARTIFACTS

Within the excavated area, there was an uneven distribution of artifacts. The area was excavated in 4 sq. m. units. Density of artifacts ranged from 40 to 288 per excavation square. Two areas of dense concentration were seen: one on the northern side of the excavation, and one, somewhat lighter, in the southwestern area (fig. 14, a). In the latter area, there was also evidence of an amorphous fire pit, with burned bone and blackened sand.

Distribution by artifact type showed that a relatively high percentage of tools came from those squares adjoining the fire pit. In one square, where only 40 artifacts were recovered, ten were tools. In this general area, from 11 to 25 per cent of all artifacts were either retouched tools or Levallois flakes. This contrasts with percentages of other squares where they ranged from 5.4 per cent to a very few with as much as 12.5 per cent (fig. 14, b).

Distribution of Levallois flakes shows a concentration around the fire pit (fig. 14, c), as does the distribution of retouched tools (fig. 14, d). The pattern of distribution, however, does not show any specific distribution of any one tool type.

NON-LITHIC ARTIFACTS

A small number of burned bones were found within the area of the fire pit, and one small piece of ground hematite was recovered in the same area. The presence of ground hematite is typical of the Khormusan, and it is present at all sites. No bone tools, ground stone, or architectural features were found.

TOOL TYPOLOGY

	No.	%	Restricted %
Levallois flakes	196	57.8	
Levallois blades	10	2.9	
Levallois points	9	2.6	
Pseudo-Levallois points	6	1.8	4.8
Burins, dihedral *déjeté*	1	0.3	0.8
Burins, dihedral angle	1	0.3	0.8
Burins, angle "single blow"	3	0.9	2.4
Burins, transverse	1	0.3	0.8
Burins, on concave truncations	2	0.6	1.6
Burins, *plan*	1	0.3	0.8
Burins, multiple angle	2	0.6	1.6
End-scrapers	4	1.2	3.2
Side-scrapers, straight	3	0.9	2.4
Side-scrapers, convex	8	2.4	6.4
Side-scrapers, concave	11	3.2	8.9
Side-scrapers, convergent convex	1	0.3	0.8
Side-scrapers, *déjeté*	1	0.3	0.8
Side-scrapers, transverse straight	1	0.3	0.8
Side-scrapers, transverse concave	1	0.3	0.8
Side-scrapers, inverse	4	1.2	3.2
Notched pieces	17	5.0	13.7
Converging denticulates	2	0.6	1.6
Transverse denticulates	2	0.6	1.6
Lateral denticulates	17	5.0	13.7
Bilateral denticulates	1	0.3	0.8
Lateral and transverse denticulates	2	0.6	1.6
Retouched flakes	14	4.1	11.3
Truncated pieces	3	0.9	2.4
Cortex, backed knives	1	0.3	0.8
Strangled pieces	10	2.9	8.0
Varia	4	1.2	3.2
	339	100.0	99.6

Technological Indices

$IL = 35.0$ $IF = 63.8$ $IFs = 42.3$ $Ibl = 8.1$

Typological Indices

$IL^{ty} = 63.3$ $Ibu = 3.6$ $Ident = 7.1$

$Iendscr = 1.2$ $Isscr = 8.9$

Restricted Typological Indices

$IL^{ty} = 0.0$ $Ibu = 9.6$ $Ident = 19.3$

$Iendscr = 3.2$ $Isscr = 24.1$

NOTES ON THE TYPOLOGY

Site 34A is typologically dominated by unretouched Levallois flakes, side-scrapers, and denticulates. Unlike the Nubian Mousterian, however, it also contained a good number of burins. These four types of tools may be generally characterized in the following way:

1. Levallois flakes, blades, and points in the vast majority are fragmentary. Of the complete examples, most are typical and fall between 3

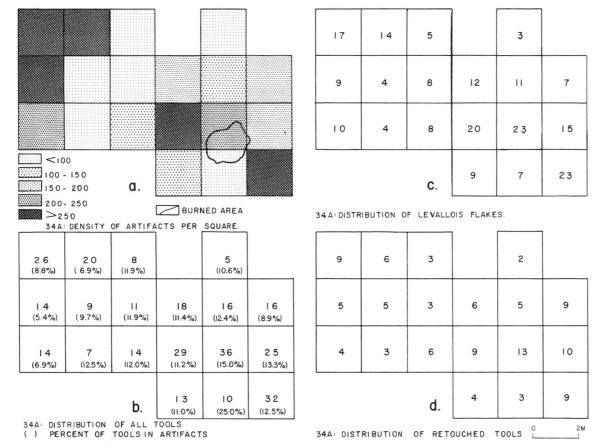

a.

<100
100 - 150
150 - 200
200 - 250
>250

BURNED AREA

34A: DENSITY OF ARTIFACTS PER SQUARE.

26 (8.8%)	20 (6.9%)	8 (11.9%)	5 (10.6%)		
14 (5.4%)	9 (9.7%)	11 (11.9%)	18 (11.4%)	16 (12.4%)	16 (8.9%)
14 (6.9%)	7 (12.5%)	14 (12.0%)	29 (11.2%)	36 (15.0%)	25 (13.3%)
			13 (11.0%)	10 (25.0%)	32 (12.5%)

b.

34A: DISTRIBUTION OF ALL TOOLS
( ) PERCENT OF TOOLS IN ARTIFACTS

c.

17	14	5		3	
9	4	8	12	11	7
10	4	8	20	23	15
			9	7	23

34A: DISTRIBUTION OF LEVALLOIS FLAKES.

d.

9	6	3		2	
5	5	3	6	5	9
4	3	6	9	13	10
			4	3	9

34A: DISTRIBUTION OF RETOUCHED TOOLS   0   2M

Fig. 14—Artifact distributions at Site 34A.

and 5 cm. in length. The large flakes measure between 7 and 7.5 cm., although some broken flakes and blades appear to have been originally even longer.

2. Burins, for the most part, are poorly fashioned on ferrocrete sandstone. Simple types prevail: "single blow," multiple "single blow," and angle burins on snapped flakes. The great elaboration seen at later Khormusan sites is absent here, but burins are much more common and show more variety than at any Nubian Mousterian site.

3. Unlike the situation at later Khormusan assemblages, side-scrapers on ferrocrete sandstone dominate the typology here. There are numerous types, but the simple concave side-scraper is the most common. This large element of side-scrapers gives the assemblage a Nubian Mousterian look. There are differences, however, between these side-scrapers and the typical Nubian Mousterian

types. The most noticeable difference is in the retouch. The best examples at 34A have a very flat obverse retouch which is absent in the Nubian Mousterian but occurs at later Khormusan sites in a slightly different form. Another difference rests in the thinness of the flakes used for scrapers here as compared with the Nubian Mousterian types. There seems to be little question, however, that the scrapers have their ultimate origin in a Mousterian-like tradition.

4. Of the 24 denticulates, all but two are on ferrocrete sandstone. One is on a quartz flake, and one is on Precambrian rock. There is a large range in size, and quality varies markedly. Denticulates are not as developed in either number or quality as they are at later Khormusan sites.

Levallois flakes (196). Flakes vary in size, shape, and quality. One hundred and eight are broken. The vast majority are on ferrocrete sandstone, but eight are on Precambrian rock and five on fossil wood. The larger examples are generally atypical (fig. 15, b, i). Smaller examples are usually rectangular to oval (fig. 15, c-d, j).

Levallois blades (10). There are three blades which measure over 7 cm. in length (fig. 15, k), and seven small examples, mostly fragmentary.

Levallois points (9). All are small and rather poor (fig. 15, a).

Pseudo-Levallois points (6). All are small and typical.

Burins, dihedral *déjeté* (1). A large, poorly made example on a thin, natural slab of ferrocrete sandstone.

Burins, dihedral angle (1). A nice example on a thick ferrocrete sandstone flake (fig. 15, f).

Burins, angle "single blow" (3). Three atypical "single blow" burins on odd fragments of ferrocrete sandstone (fig. 15, m).

Burins, transverse (1). This is a highly atypical type on a Precambrian flake. It is a single blow burin with the burin spall struck from a thick outer edge, transversely along a broken plane. There is also a small amount of retouch on the other edge (fig. 15, h).

Burins on concave truncations (2). Both are on ferrocrete sandstone. Notches are poorly formed, but the burin facets are clearly visible (fig. 15, g).

Burins, *plan* (1). One poor example on ferrocrete sandstone.

Burins, multiple angle (2). A small flake fragment of Precambrian rock with two burin facets, one on each side of the same edge (fig. 15, 1). The other piece has two well-made burins on the same snapped flake (fig. 15, e).

End-scrapers (4). All are on ferrocrete sandstone flakes. There are three rather typical end-scrapers on small flakes, all of which have broken along one lateral edge. Thus they look similar to burins on convex truncations, but they are clearly not burins (fig. 16, d). The fourth example is an unfinished convex end-scraper on a large, elongate flake.

Side-scrapers, straight (3). All are small with regular retouch along one edge. One example is also notched near the butt (fig. 16, c).

Side-scrapers, convex (8). These range from flake fragments with flat retouch to Levallois flakes with normal to semi-steep retouch (fig. 16, a). There is one flake which also has a concave denticulate edge (fig. 16, h). Of the eight, one is on fossil wood and the others are on ferrocrete sandstone.

Side-scrapers, concave (11). These include some very large examples, equal in length to the largest of the strangled pieces. One long, wide blade with both a concave and convex scraping edge measures 13.5 cm. (fig. 16, i) while another, a simple concave scraper, measures 10.5 cm. in length (fig. 16, j). Retouch varies from exceedingly flat to semi-steep, but normal retouch predominates. Aside from the large examples, there are five small scrapers, one of which is made on a quartz flake.

Side-scrapers, convergent, convex (1). A beautiful example made by fine, flat retouch on a Levallois flake (fig. 16, b).

Side-scrapers, *déjeté* (1). A good example made by fine, flat retouch on a Levallois flake.

Side-scrapers, transverse straight (1). An excellent example with semi-steep retouch (fig. 16, e).

Side-scrapers, transverse concave (1). An excellent example on a small para-Levallois flake, made by fine, flat retouch.

Side-scrapers, inverse (4). There are two concave and two convex scrapers. Retouch is flat only on one piece, marginal on two, and normal on one.

Notched pieces (17). Ten lateral notches are made by retouch. Of these, six are micro (under 1 cm. across) and three macro (over 1 cm. across). There are also seven made by single blows, two of which are end micronotches. Only two notches are on Precambrian rock, the rest are on ferrocrete sandstone.

Converging denticulates (2). There is one on a Levallois flake and a small asymmetric example on a thick flake, which is typologically a Tayac point (fig. 17, c).

Transverse denticulates (2). One is a denticulated end-scraper, reworked on a weathered flake (fig. 17, b). The other has a microdenticulate straight edge on a Levallois flake.

Lateral denticulates (17). For the most part, these are rough, covering only part of one lateral edge. Some, however, are more regular (fig. 17, i). The majority are macrodenticulate formed by percussion (fig. 17, a), although microdenticulates occur (fig. 17, b).

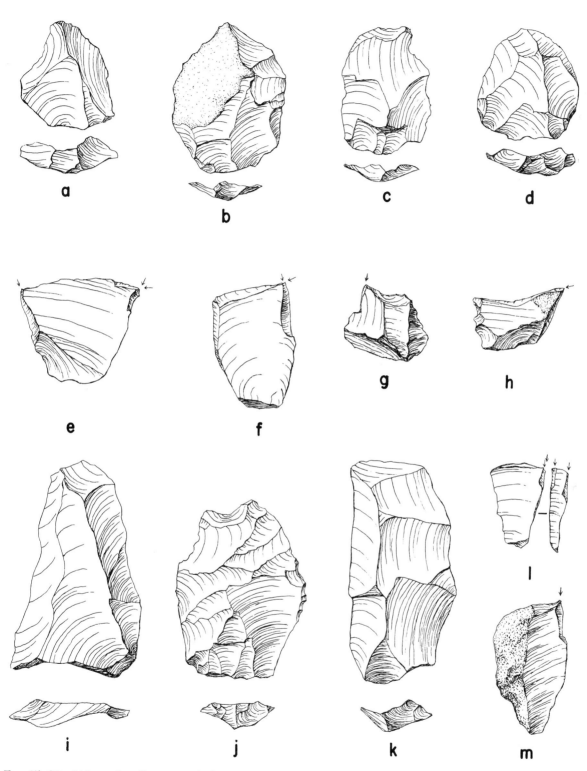

FIG. 15—Site 34A: a, Levallois point; b-d, i-j, Levallois flakes; e-h, l-m, burins; k, Levallois blade. 4/5 natural size.

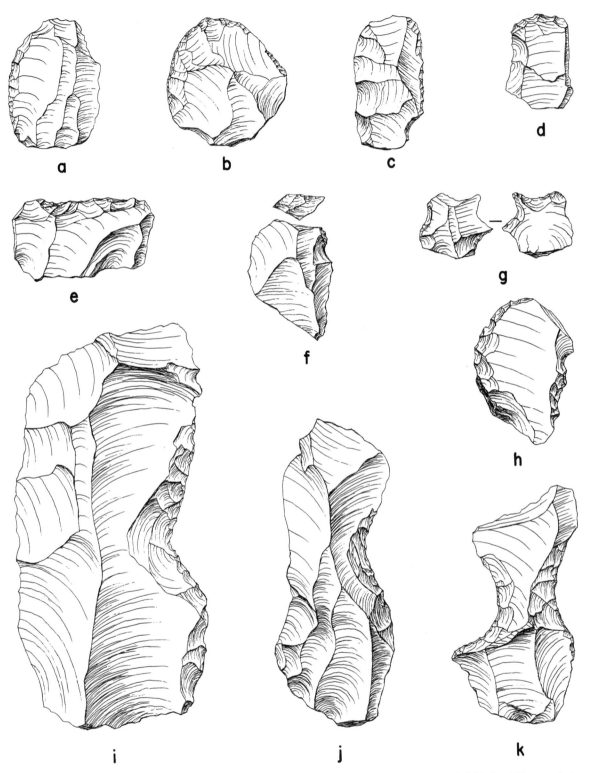

Fig. 16—Site 34A: a-c, e, h-j, side-scrapers; d, end-scraper; f, truncation; g, borer; k, strangled blade. 4/5 natural size.

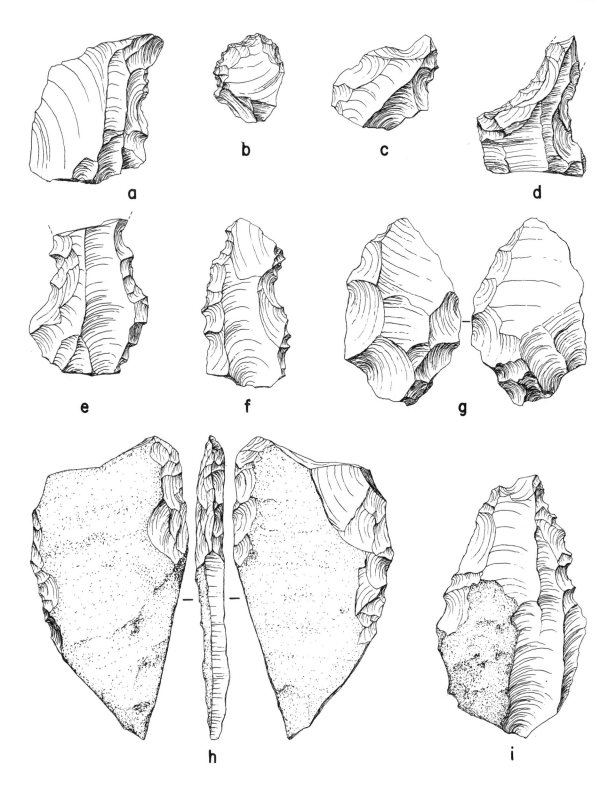

FIG. 17—Site 34A: a-c, f, i, denticulates; d-e, broken strangled pieces; g, bifacial point?; h, bifacially retouched plaquette. 4/5 natural size.

Bilateral denticulates (1). A well made piece on a Levallois blade (fig. 17, f).

Lateral and transverse denticulates (2). One poorly formed example and one alternately retouched piece on a Levallois flake.

Retouched flakes (14). These are ferrocrete sandstone flakes and fragments which have a small amount of retouch which is not consistent enough to form true scraping edges. Four have flat, inverse retouch, and ten have marginal retouch. Two of the former are on Levallois flakes as are four of the latter (fig. 15, j).

Truncated pieces (3). One Precambrian flake not only has a straight truncation but is also purposefully snapped (fig. 16, f). Another ferrocrete sandstone flake has a concave truncation, and a third has an oblique truncation.

Cortex backed knives (1). This one is an elongated ferrocrete sandstone flake.

Strangled pieces (10). Strangled pieces form a relatively small but very characteristic element of this assemblage. In a normal Nubian Mousterian assemblage, strangled flakes are really no more than opposed notches which barely "strangle" the flake. Here, on the other hand, these pieces are carefully made and are truly "strangled."

While the excavated area produced mostly fragments, the surface examples and one piece *in situ* shows that, when whole, they were very large. The largest was found in 1961 and measured 13.5 cm. in length (Solecki, 1963, p. 87, fig. 6, a). The one complete example *in situ* measures 8 cm. long (fig. 16, k). This is longer than most tools in the assemblage and, in fact, larger than any excavated core.

Retouch is normally steep and serrated (fig. 17, e), although many examples have even edges (fig. 17, d). Perhaps the serrations on the broken examples indicate that they were broken during manufacture.

One is made on a broken fossil wood blade, and one is on Precambrian rock, but all the others are on ferrocrete sandstone.

Varia (4). There is a thin, broken ferrocrete sandstone slab which has partial, bifacial retouch along both edges (fig. 17, h). Another piece might best be described as a very crude, partially bifacial point; perhaps unfinished (fig. 17, g).

The remaining two pieces pose something of a problem. Both are borers, one a multiple made on chert pebble by a fine, steep retouch (fig. 16, g). They are completely out of character with the rest of the assemblage, yet there is no question that they were found *in situ* with the other tools. The possibility had to be considered that they came from the upper layer, 34D. This, however, was not the case. Both have the typical dune sand adhering to them and they would have been just as out of character in 34D as in 34A. Borers do not occur in the Khormusan. These are the only two found in a total of 1,763 tools from five assemblages. They appear to be typologically more at home in a Neolithic context but, as stated above, there is no question about their stratigraphic position.

CORE TYPOLOGY

	No.	%	Restricted %
Levallois flake	20	16.7	48.8
Levallois point	5	4.2	12.2
Nubian, Type I	1	0.8	2.4
Para-Levallois	1	0.8	2.4
Marginal (single platform)	4	3.3	9.8
Discoidal	8	6.7	19.5
Bipolar	1	0.8	2.4
Isolated flake	1	0.8	2.4
Unidentifiable	79	65.9	
	120	100.0	99.9

NOTES ON THE TYPOLOGY

Within the excavated area, 120 cores were recovered. They were evenly distributed over the sand dune, showing no area of concentration. The vast majority was made on ferrocrete sandstone although a few quartz, fossil wood, chert, and Precambrian cores were also found.

The most striking feature of the cores is their size as compared with the associated tools. The largest core—which has received only preliminary preparation—measures 8.7 by 8.5 cm. This is a full 5 cm. shorter than the larger blades. Most utilized cores, however, measure under 7 cm. in length, and many measure as little as 4.5 cm. One obvious explanation for this contradiction is that cores were prepared, struck, and prepared again. This process was continued until they were too small to be of further use. This is also seen at Site 1017 where more than one Levallois flake can be assigned to the same core.

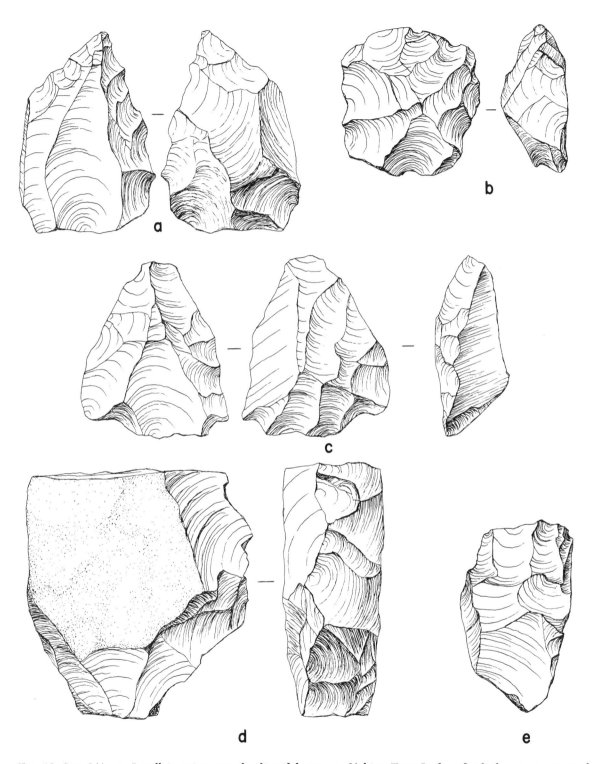

Fig. 18—Site 34A: a, Levallois point core; b, discoidal core; c, Nubian Type I; d, unfinished core; e, marginal core (opposed platform). 4/5 natural size.

Fig. 19—Photo of Site 1017 from the north.

Levallois flake (20). Of these, only seven have been struck. The rest show a rough preparation on the upper surface and, in many cases, hinge fracturing is visible. This may well account for their being unstruck. Seven unstruck examples measure under 4.5 cm. in length. The struck cores usually show minimal preparation of the ventral surface.

Levallois point (5). These are the most carefully prepared of all Levallois cores (fig. 18, a), although they are not commensurate with the extremely fine preparation of Levallois cores at Site 1017. Again, three of the five are unstruck. All measure under 7 cm. in length.

Nubian, Type I (1). This type has been defined by the Guichards for the "Nubian Middle Paleolithic" (Guichard and Guichard, 1965, p. 68). This is a good example (fig. 18, c).

Para-Levallois (1). One small example.

Marginal (single platform) (4). Three of the four are single platform cores on small fossil wood fragments. There is also one on ferrocrete sandstone (fig. 18, e).

Discoidal (8). Again, these are all small. Three are on quartz pebbles, the remainder on ferrocrete sandstone (fig. 18, b).

Bipolar (1). One on an elongate quartz pebble. It is highly atypical for the Khormusan.

Isolated flake (1). One small quartz pebble has had a primary flake removed.

Unidentifiable (79). These include some ferrocrete sandstone slabs which show only the first steps of core preparation (fig. 18, d).

In one case, the ferrocrete slab is 3.5 cm. thick, a full centimeter thicker than any prepared core. This piece shows a series of flat flakes struck toward the center of the slab along one side. The margin of the platform was then flaked, forming a series of facets perpendicular to the upper surface. Thus, instead of the upper and lower surfaces being flaked alternately, one plane at a time was flaked.

FIG. 20—Photo of Site 1017 from the south.

The remaining cores include two quartz pebbles and two cores on fossil wood. None of these cores show any discernable pattern of flaking, or they are in such an early stage of preparation that the intended type could not be judged.

SITE 1017

Site 1017 was the first Khormusan site recognized as belonging to a new industry. It represents a type site for the industry as a whole and for its early stages in particular. It was located on a side branch of the Khor Musa (fig. 1) during the final days of the 1962-1963 field season by J. de Heinzelin and R. Paepe (map ref. 903.8/642.3). Early in the following season, the site was revisited, and excavations were begun in December, 1963.

This site was located by a thin scattering of artifacts on a deflated slope of sand in front of a large, sand covered rock outcrop (figs. 19,

20). The artifacts formed a clear line where the sand met a partially eroded silt cover (fig. 21). Test trenching showed that the artifacts rested on a living floor in the sand, which in turn, was covered by more sand and silt. The living floor was at an absolute elevation of 148 m., or 27 m. above present floodplain. This placed the silts within the middle of the Dibeira-Jer formation, during the period of aggradation.

A total of 176 sq. m. was excavated, and from an additional 200 sq. m. surface material was systematically collected. Within this area, a total of 4,472 artifacts of which over 4,000 were from the living floor was recovered. The vast majority of these was small chips and other debris, however, and rather few finished tools were recovered.

The relative proportions of tools to other classes of artifacts has already been noted, as has the size of the tools which were recovered. It need only be added that in both areas, these

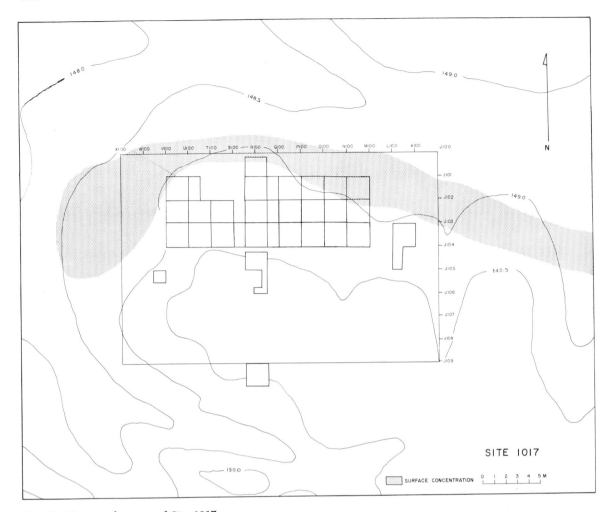

F𝗂𝗀. 21–Topographic map of Site 1017.

were consistent with the rest of the Khormusan industry.

Within the main area of excavation, there were four amorphous fire pits (fig. 22, a). These were more like lenses of charcoal with associated concentrations of burned bone than like carefully shaped pits. A few large rocks were found near the easternmost fire area, but these failed to show any clear pattern in relation to the burned area.

Distribution of artifacts across the living floor showed definite preferential areas for certain classes of tools and debitage. Two distinct areas of artifactual concentration were seen: one large concentration in the middle of the excavated area and a smaller one, just touched on, at the extreme western edge (fig. 22, a). The distribution of tools and Levallois flakes followed the same general pattern, although there is a more restricted concentration of tools around the central fire pits (fig. 22, b). The tool which shows a clearly distinct distribution is the burin. While the concentration of burins is strong around the central and western fire pits, it is of some significance that they were very rare in the other areas of the site, particularly near the eastern fire pit (fig. 22, c). In fact, the small number of finished tools and Levallois flakes near the eastern fire pit contrasts sharply with the rather large number of debitage in the same area. This perhaps indicates that this section of the site was used as an area for core preparation as compared with the central and western sectors, which seemed to have been used for both core prepara-

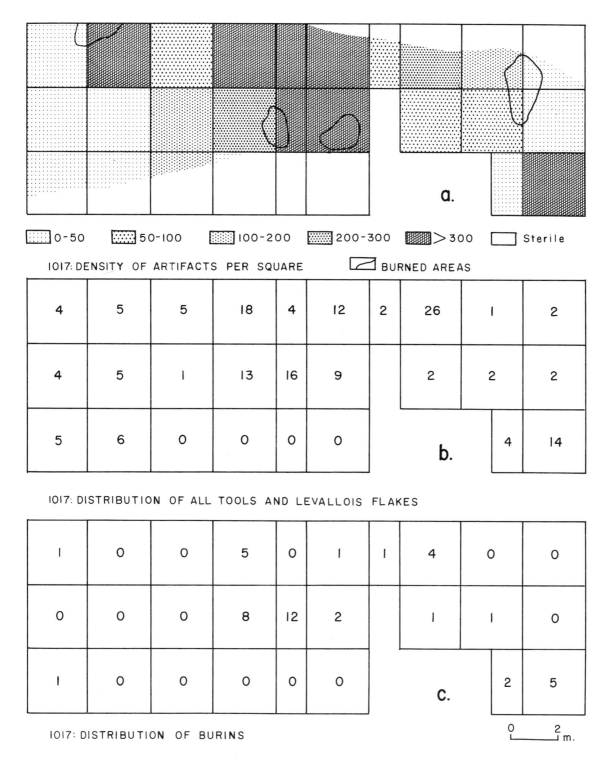

FIG. 22—Artifact distributions at Site 1017.

tion and the manufacture and use of finished tools.

Faunal remains were numerous throughout the excavated area, particularly around the fire pits. Preservation was extremely good, as evidenced by the recovery of even rodent bones. A number of the bones had incised lines but these showed no pattern. In consideration of the importance of burins in the typology, it is surprising that the bone showed so little work. There is no question that bone tools were unknown during this period of the Khormusan.

The only artifacts not in the stone tool class found during excavation were five pieces of ground hematite. These all showed grinding on one or more surfaces, which resulted in rectangular tablets of less than 5 cm. in length.

LITHIC ARTIFACTS

The vast majority of finished tools and Levallois flakes came from the excavated living floor. A few examples were also found on the surface, where the living floor had been uncovered by deflation. Since there was no question of their association with the artifacts, *in situ*, they were included in the typological studies.

TOOL TYPOLOGY

	No.	%	Restricted %
Levallois flakes	171	52.9	
Levallois blades	37	11.5	
Levallois points	5	1.5	
Levallois flakes, distally thinned	2	0.6	1.8
Pseudo-Levallois points	2	0.6	1.8
Burins, straight dihedral	2	0.6	1.8
Burins, dihedral *déjeté*	2	0.6	1.8
Burins, angle on snapped flakes	4	1.2	3.6
Burins, angle "single blow"	3	0.9	2.7
Burins, transverse "single blow"	1	0.3	0.9
Burins, on oblique retouched truncations	9	2.8	8.2
Burins, on convex retouched truncations	4	1.2	3.6
Burins, on concave retouched truncations	10	3.1	9.0
Burins, transverse on lateral truncations	5	1.5	4.5
Burins, transverse on concave truncations	4	1.2	3.6
Burins, *plan*	2	0.6	1.8
Burins, multiple mixed	5	1.5	4.5
Burins, multiple on retouched truncations	2	0.6	1.8

	No.	%	Restricted %
End-scrapers	2	0.6	1.8
Side-scrapers	2	0.6	1.8
Notched pieces	5	1.5	4.5
Converging denticulates	12	3.7	10.8
Transverse denticulates	4	1.2	3.6
Lateral denticulates	17	5.3	15.3
Bilateral denticulates	1	0.3	0.9
Lateral and transverse denticulates	1	0.3	0.9
Retouched flakes	3	0.9	2.7
Truncated pieces	3	0.9	2.7
Cortex backed knives	4	1.2	3.6
	324	99.7	100.0

Technological Indices

$IL = 36.6$ $IF = 78.3$ $IFs = 50.5$ $Ibl = 14.1$

Typological Indices

$IL^{ty} = 65.9$ $Ibu = 15.8$ $Ident = 10.8$
$Iendscr = 0.6$ $Isscr = 0.6$

Restricted Typological Indices

$IL^{ty} = 0.0$ $Ibu = 46.3$ $Ident = 31.5$
$Iendscr = 1.8$ $Isscr = 1.8$

NOTES ON THE TYPOLOGY

Unlike Site 34A, the typology here lacks a developed side-scraper component. The main tool types are unretouched Levallois flakes, burins, and denticulates. In broad terms, they may be described as follows:

1. The most noticeable characteristics of the Levallois flakes are their great size range and the variety of raw materials used in their manufacture. On the other hand, there is uniformly high quality for all Levallois pieces, reaching a particularly excellent standard in the larger examples. Flakes are more numerous, by far, than either blades or points.

2. Burins form a rich and varied tool class, including a number of complex forms. Only three types of rock were utilized in their manufacture: Precambrian, fossil wood, and chert pebble. The strong Levallois tendency of the industry is even apparent here where 33.3 per cent of all burins are made on Levallois flakes. Most burins are well made and many show evidence of resharpening. There is a tendency for some burin facets to be slightly oblique to the flake plane, but very few are truly *plan*. Burins are made on flakes, primary flakes, and core fragments but rarely on blades or laminary flakes.

3. Generally, denticulates are made on large Levallois flakes. Teeth are prominent and denticulated edges are well formed, both by percussion and retouch. Numerous types occur, but the most common are lateral and converging denticulates.

Levallois flakes (171). These may be roughly divided into two groups. The most impressive, comprising 51 examples, are large well prepared flakes, usually with massive convexly faceted butts (fig. 23, f-j). They range in size from 4 to 8 cm. with most measuring between 5 and 7 cm. Their butts range in thickness from 1 to 1.5 cm., and may be as much as 5.5 cm. in length. This type of Levallois flake was used for making denticulates and scrapers and was often snapped prior to burin production.

The 120 examples of the second group are much smaller with thin faceted butts (fig. 23, b-d). They were rarely retouched. They range in size from 4.5 cm. to as small as 2.5 cm. in length. There is no question that they came from prepared cores and are Levallois, but it is somewhat questionable whether they were thought of in the same way as the larger examples. Their production may be the result of the exceedingly fine and extensive preparation given many Levallois cores and of the habit of reworking Levallois cores for the removal of more than one major flake.

Levallois blades (37). Like the Levallois flakes, these are both large and small examples. The majority measures between 5 and 6 cm. in length, although longer blades occur (fig. 23, e).

Levallois points (5). All are good examples (fig. 23, a), although one has a tip which is slightly off the long axis.

Levallois flakes, distally thinned (2). This type is rare but quite distinctive. A Levallois flake is flaked by a very flat inverse retouch from the distal end. The results are hardly ever satisfactory as the tips tend to break. Neither of these pieces was successfully thinned. One, a large Levallois flake, broke on one edge, although some inverse thinning is still visible. A smaller flake shows two minor breaks and a number of flake scars (fig. 24, m).

Pseudo-Levallois points (2). Two typical examples on ferrocrete sandstone.

Burins, straight dihedral (2). One poor ex-

ample is on a laminary flake and one is on a primary chert flake.

Burins, dihedral *déjeté* (2). Both are on chert, one on a primary flake and one on a laminary flake (fig. 24, a).

Burins, angle on snapped flakes (4). Two are on Levallois flakes (fig. 24, k) and two on flake fragments. All are typical and well formed.

Burins, angle "single blow" (3). All are atypical forms on flakes. In each case a single burin spall has been struck from one corner of the butt, removing a major portion of the flake.

Burins, transverse "single blow" (1). A rare and atypical type on chert.

Burins, on oblique retouched truncations (9). This is one of the more common types. Six are on Levallois flakes (fig. 24, f), two on non-Levallois flakes, and one on a small primary chert flake. One burin has been resharpened by a blow which formed a straight dihedral burin, but the original truncation is still visible; in fact, four have been resharpened. One fossil wood Levallois flake has had the burin edge sharpened three times, each time by the removal of a large burin spall (fig. 24, i).

Burins, on convex retouched truncations (4). Two are on Levallois flakes and two are on core trimming flakes. On one, resharpening has formed a dihedral angle burin but the original convex truncation still shows.

Burins, on concave retouched truncations (10). Two are on Levallois flakes (fig. 24, c, j), one is on a primary chert flake (fig. 24, e), four are on normal flakes, and three are on core fragments. One of the latter is chert; all are well made and typical.

Burins, transverse on lateral truncations (5). As a group, these are not well made. In two cases, the burin facets are weak, and in one it is almost *plan*. Three are on primary, Precambrian flakes, two on normal flakes, one of which is chert.

Burins, transverse on concave truncations (4). One is on a chert, primary flake (fig. 24, h), and three are on Levallois flakes. Before striking off the burin spalls, the Levallois flakes were snapped (fig. 24, b).

Burins, *plan* (2). One is on a primary chert flake with an oblique truncation, and the other is a transverse burin on a laterally truncated Levallois flake.

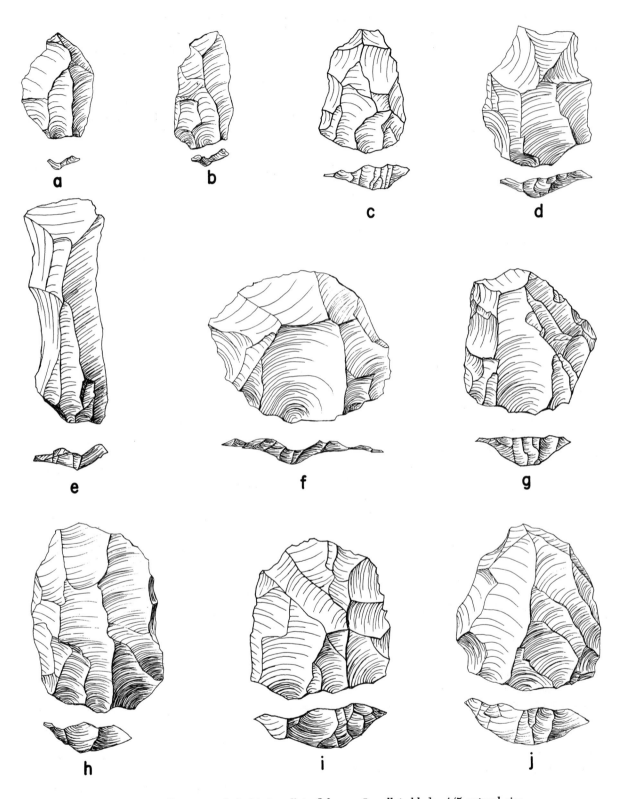

Fig. 23—Site 1017: a, Levallois point; b-d, f-j, Levallois flakes; e, Levallois blade. 4/5 natural size.

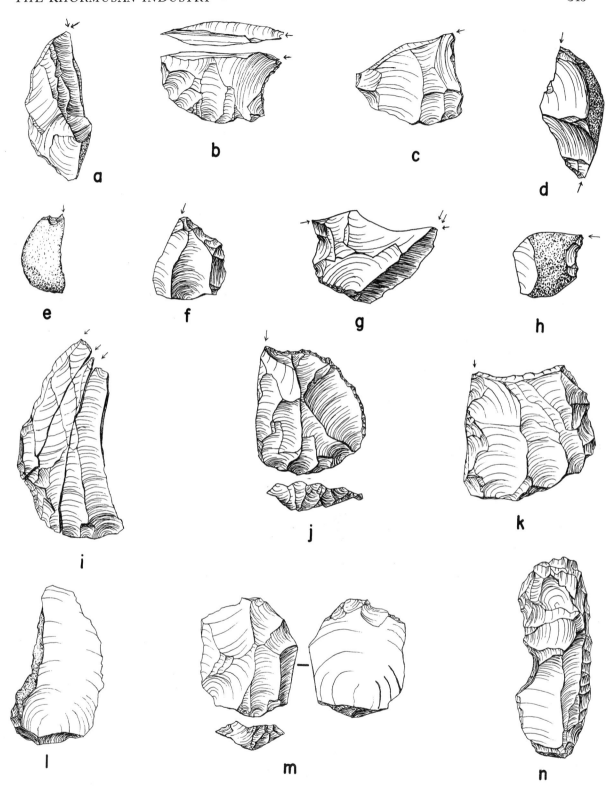

FIG. 24—Site 1017: a-k, burins; l, cortex backed knife; m, distally thinned Levallois flake; n, notched blade. 4/5 natural size.

Burins, multiple mixed (5). Three are on non-Levallois flakes (fig. 24, g), one is on a Levallois flake, and another is on a primary chert flake. In all cases, one burin is on a concave retouched truncation, while the other is some form of angle or dihedral burin.

Burins, multiple on retouched truncations (2). Both are double burins on convex truncations. One is on a core fragment, the other on a laminary flake of chert (fig. 24, d).

End-scrapers (2). Both are extremely poor examples. One, on a primary chert flake, has a slightly convex scraping edge with retouch which is little more than might be expected from use. The other is a fragment with a partially retouched end-scraper at one end (fig. 25, b).

Side-scrapers (2). These are very similar. Both are inverse side-scrapers made by very flat retouch on Levallois flakes (fig. 25, a). One is almost a converging, inverse side-scraper, but the retouch on one edge is not continuous along most of the edge (fig. 25, c). While these are rare, they are very well made, and the flatness of the retouch is typical of the scrapers found at Site 34A.

Notched pieces (5). There are three macronotches made by percussion (fig. 24, n), one retouched micronotch at the distal end of a microlithic flake, and a lateral retouched micronotch on a primary flake.

Converging denticulates (12). Nine are on large Levallois flakes, one each on a blade and non-Levallois flake, and one microdenticulate is on a small primary flake. Those on Levallois flakes are carefully prepared and well serrated (fig. 25, i). One could almost be considered a denticulate Mousterian point (fig. 25, e).

Transverse denticulates (4). These are on large flakes and similar in quality to the converging denticulates. Only one is on a Levallois flake (fig. 25, g).

Lateral denticulates (17). These are usually not as well made as the other types of denticulates (fig. 25, f). Only three are on large Levallois flakes (fig. 25, d). While some are fine examples (fig. 25, h), many are microdenticulated by light retouch.

Bilateral denticulates (1). A broken, non-Levallois flake with straight, retouched denticulate edges.

Lateral and transverse denticulates (1). A good example on a large primary flake of ferrocrete sandstone. Again, this indicates that ferrocrete sandstone was not always quarried on the jebels but was also collected as cobbles from the major wadis.

Retouched flakes (3). These are all broken Levallois flakes which have some retouch, one with a flat retouch and two with marginal. The breaks prevent further typological placement, although by the retouch it would seem that the one with a flat retouch might have been a scraper.

Truncated pieces (3). There are two concave oblique truncations which are snapped at one end. Perhaps they could be considered in the microburin class, although they are quite large. It is probable that they were intended for burins but were not finished. Another flake has a small oblique truncation near the distal end which is too small to be typical of burin truncations.

Cortex backed knives (4). Two are laminary flakes (fig. 24, 1), and two are blades. One measures almost 9 cm. in length.

CORE TYPOLOGY

	No.	%	Restricted %
Levallois flake	43	42.2	53.0
Levallois flake, opposite end	1	1.0	1.2
Levallois blade	1	1.0	1.2
Levallois point	1	1.0	1.2
Single platform, unfaceted	8	7.8	9.9
Single platform, faceted	11	10.7	13.6
Opposed platform	7	6.8	8.6
Discoidal	1	1.0	1.2
Ninety degree	1	1.0	1.2
Isolated flake	7	6.8	8.6
Unidentifiable	21	20.6	
	102	99.9	99.7

NOTES ON THE TYPOLOGY

Cores vary greatly in size and material. Over half are on Precambrian rock, but chert, fossil wood, quartz, and ferrocrete sandstone are also represented. The Levallois flake core is the most typical, while other forms of Levallois cores are rare.

Detailed descriptions of core types are given in the report for Site ANW-3, as the sample there was the largest and most varied.

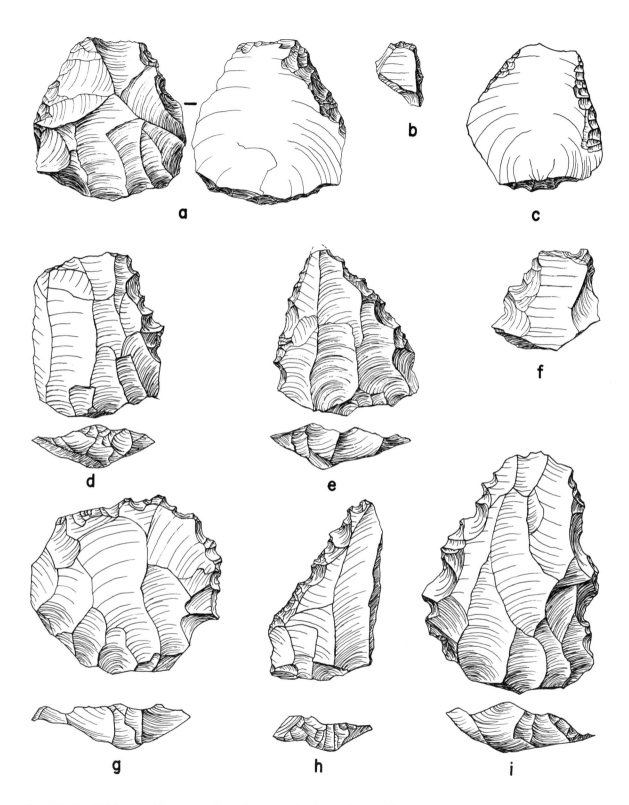

FIG. 25—Site 1017: a, c, side-scrapers; b, end-scraper; d-i, denticulates. 4/5 natural size.

Levallois flake (43). The most common material used was Precambrian rock, which was found to occur 28 times; then ferrocrete sandstone, 13; and finally quartz, 2. No chert was employed.

Most Levallois flake cores are particularly well made by intensive preparation through the removal of numerous small flakes from both faces. This is best seen on a large, unstruck example of Precambrian rock (fig. 26, d).

Levallois cores are quite uniform, most being oval to pointed oval in shape (fig. 27, b), although circular cores occur.

In quality, these are some of the finest prepared cores seen in Nubia (fig. 26, a). Infinite care was taken in preparation, and good material was often reworked so that smaller and smaller Levallois flakes could be removed from the same core. This is evident from the flakes themselves as well as from the size variation of the cores and flakes. The largest Levallois core, one in an advanced stage of preparation, measures 9.8 cm. in length; while the smallest, also unstruck, measures only 3.8 cm. Both represent extremes. Most cores measure between 4 and 6 cm.; three between 3 and 4 cm. in length; nineteen between 4 and 5 cm.; fourteen between 5 and 6 cm.; five between 6 and 7 cm.; and two which measure over 7 cm.

Quite obviously, there are few cores found which, in their present size, are large enough to have produced the larger sized Levallois flakes.

Levallois flakes, opposite end (1). This is a Levallois core which is prepared mostly from two directions and has a single large flake removed. This example is not typical but is on a large chert pebble.

Levallois blade (1). A typical example.

Levallois point (1). The negative point scar indicates that it verged on a flake (fig. 27, a).

Single platform, unfaceted (8). Five are on chert and three are on chunks of Precambrian rock. The latter are more typical of the cores on plaquettes than of the pebble cores of later periods.

Single platform, faceted (11). As might be expected, eight are on chert pebble (fig. 27, d). They are all typical, although none has been extensively flaked.

Opposed platform (7). All have two faceted platforms: five on chert, one on fossil wood, and one on Precambrian rock. They are all poor examples and only slightly utilized.

Discoidal (1). A flat discoidal core similar to the typical Sebilian type (fig. 27, c).

Ninety degree (1). A chert pebble which has two flaked surfaces which are perpendicular to one another. This is a rare type in the Khormusan (fig. 26, b).

Isolated flake (7). Cobbles of fossil wood and pebbles of chert and quartz which have had a single primary flake removed.

Unidentifiable (21). Cores which show no discernable pattern of flaking. Almost half are chert, the remainder Precambrian rock.

Site 34D

Site 34 was the most stratigraphically complex and had the greatest variety of lithic assemblages of any site found in Nubia. Only after three seasons of excavation was it possible to separate the assemblages and place them with assurance into the geological stratigraphy. The site, located at Nag el-Ikhtiariya (map ref. 930.1/655.2), has been described in this paper in reference to the assemblage 34A.

The Khormusan assemblage designated as 34D was noticeable over a wide area of the middle and upper slope of the partially eroded Dibeira-Jer formation but, at first, could not be clearly distinguished from the assemblage of 34A, which was also Khormusan. It was only during the final field season that a small area was located where both 34A and 34D occurred *in situ* in stratigraphic position. In this area, 34D was within a fluvial sand deposit, which, in places, was covered by a thin layer of Nile silts. The assemblage of 34A was found beneath the fluvial sand layer, in a thick layer of dune sand (fig. 2).

During the 1964-1965 field season, an area of 78 sq. m. was excavated. In this area, artifacts from 34A and 34D were present in stratigraphic position in all but 2 sq. m., where only 34A material was present.

During the 1963-1964 field season, a number of test pits which produced small amounts of artifacts, *in situ*, from 34D were excavated. After careful checking, the artifacts from four of these were added to the overall study in order to

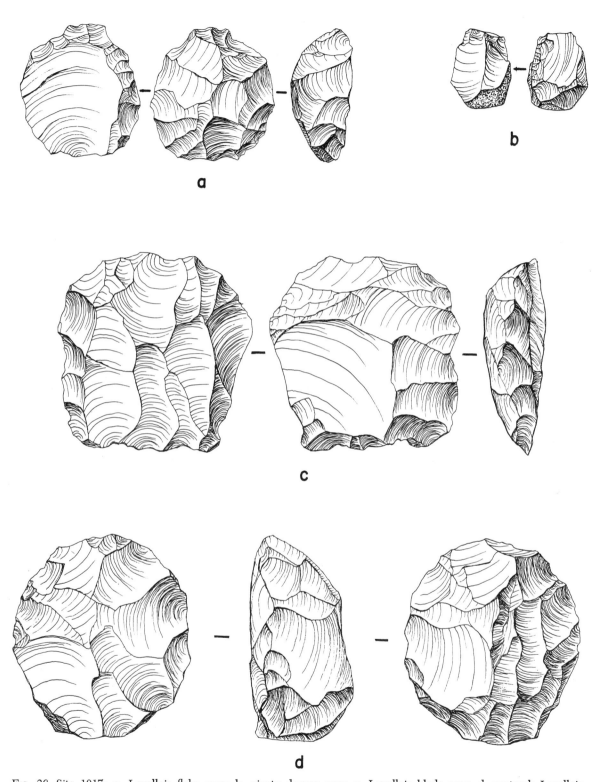

FIG. 26—Site 1017: a, Levallois flake core; b, ninety degree core; c, Levallois blade core; d, unstruck Levallois flake core. 4/5 natural size.

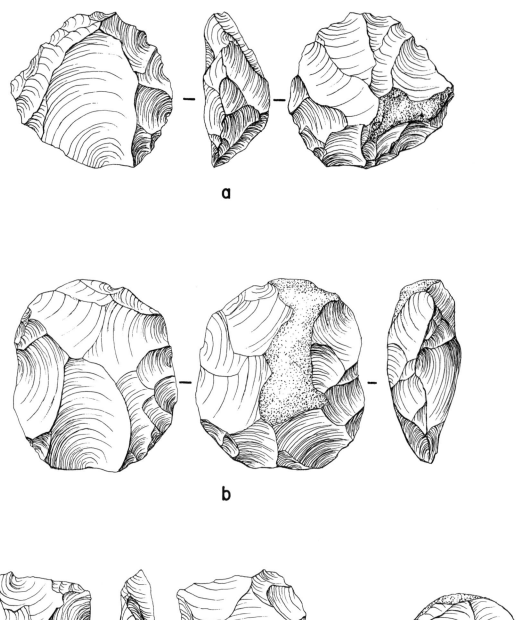

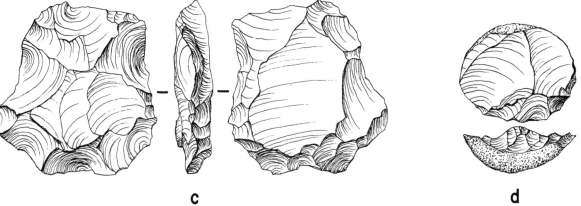

FIG. 27—Site 1017: a, Levallois point core; b, Levallois flake core; c, discoidal core; d, faceted, single platform core. 4/5 natural size.

enlarge somewhat the available tool sample, *in situ.*

There was a large surface concentration of artifacts of 34D type to the west and north of the excavated area (fig. 6). Because of their proximity to surface material from 34A, however, it was impossible to be absolutely sure whether any artifacts, particularly if made on ferrocrete sandstone, belonged to 34D rather than to 34A. Thus, while the surface material was collected, it was felt that it could not be included in the typological studies. As the tool samples from the excavations—345 Levallois flakes and retouched tools—were more than sufficient, no need to use the surface material arose. It was only after obtaining the excavated sample that it was possible to check the consistency of the surface finds. This showed that there were no types present *in situ* that were not present on the surface and that no types occurred on the surface which were not also present *in situ.* The surface collection also contained technological attributes and proportions which fully correlated with those *in situ.* This indicates that, if there was overlap between the surface concentrations of 34A and 34D, it was minimal.

The excavation area produced 4,478 artifacts. Observations on raw materials, size of artifacts, and gross proportions of the assemblage have already been discussed.

The total density of artifacts per square meter was rather low, but there was a definite differential distribution across the excavated area. Over half the squares yielded less than 200 artifacts. On the other hand, four squares produced from 400 to 800 artifacts per square. Figure 28, a, shows the density of distribution per square for all artifacts recovered. While the heaviest concentration was at the northern end of the excavation, there was not a fully corresponding distribution of tools (fig. 28, b).

In the southern section of the excavations, there was a disproportionately high number of tools to all artifacts in each square. This was within and around a rather amorphous burned area. Retouched tools and Levallois flakes account for only 6.3 per cent of all artifacts at the site; yet in those squares around the burned area, they account for between 9.7 and 15.9 per cent. The majority of tools, however, is found in the

heavy concentration at the northern end, but in each of those squares they account for less than the overall average of tools for the whole site (fig. 28, b). Thus, we can see in the southern area, at least, a direct association of a tool concentration with a probable fire pit.

With the two most common tool types, Levallois flakes and burins, this pattern of concentration is fully reflected. Levallois flakes occur in every square, but the majority is concentrated around the fire pit and at the northern end (fig. 28, c). Burins have a much more limited distribution. They are heavily concentrated at the northern end, although there is a minor concentration around the fire pit. The area between is almost devoid of them (fig. 28, d).

Aside from the one rather clear area of burned bones and blackened sand, there was another smaller area which appeared to contain the scattered remains of a fire pit (fig. 28, a). The fire pit in the southern area covered about 2 sq. m., but the original shape was completely lost in the very loose fill.

NON-LITHIC ARTIFACTS

As bone preservation was poor in the artifactual bearing level, only a few burned bone fragments were recovered. One small fragment of ground hematite was found in the southern fire pit, but there was no evidence of worked bone or ground stone.

TOOL TYPOLOGY	No.	%	Restricted %
Levallois flakes	187	54.2	
Levallois blades	15	4.3	
Levallois points	4	1.2	
Levallois flakes, distally thinned	1	0.3	0.7
Burins, straight dihedral	3	0.9	2.1
Burins, dihedral *déjeté*	1	0.3	0.7
Burins, dihedral angle	5	1.4	3.6
Burins, angle on snapped pieces	3	0.9	2.1
Burins, on straight truncations	4	1.2	2.9
Burins, on oblique truncations	14	4.0	10.0
Burins, on convex truncations	6	1.7	4.3
Burins, on concave truncations	13	3.6	9.3
Burins, transverse on lateral truncations	2	0.6	1.4
Burins, transverse on concave truncations	5	1.4	3.6
Burins, *plan*	5	1.4	3.6
Burins, multiple dihedral	1	0.3	0.7
Burins, multiple mixed	3	0.9	2.1

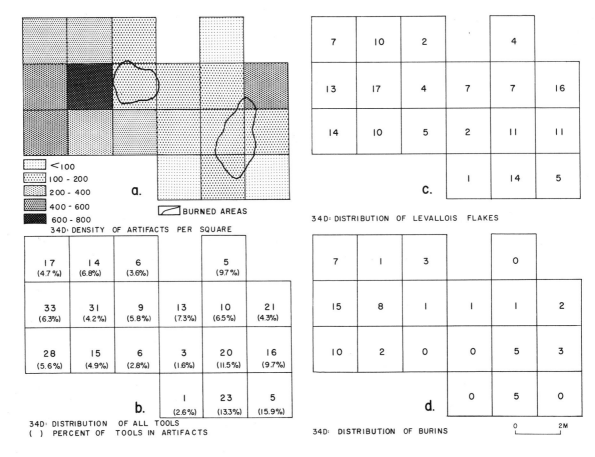

FIG. 28—Artifact distribution at Site 34D.

	No.	%	Restricted %
Burins, multiple on retouched truncations	8	2.3	5.7
Burin—Denticulates	2	0.6	1.4
End-scrapers	8	2.3	5.7
Side-scrapers	1	0.3	0.7
Core scrapers	4	1.2	2.9
Notched pieces	4	1.2	2.9
Converging denticulates	3	0.9	2.1
Transverse denticulates	4	1.2	2.9
Lateral denticulates	12	3.5	8.6
Bilateral denticulates	5	1.4	3.6
Transverse and lateral denticulates	1	0.3	0.7
Denticulate points	3	0.9	2.1
Retouched flakes	6	1.7	4.3
Truncated pieces	3	0.9	2.1
Cortex backed knives	7	2.0	5.0
Varia	2	0.6	1.4
	345	99.9	99.2

Technological Indices

$IL=23.2$ $IF=74.2$ $IFs=50.5$ $Ibl=9.0$

Typological Indices

$IL^{ty}=59.7$ $Ibu=21.5$ $Ident=8.8$
$Iendscr=2.3$ $Isscr=1.5$

Restricted Typological Indices

$IL^{ty}=0.0$ $Ibu=53.5$ $Ident=21.4$
$Iendscr=5.7$ $Isscr=3.6$

NOTES ON THE TYPOLOGY

Again, as at Site 1017, unretouched Levallois flakes, burins, and denticulates characterize this assemblage. While Levallois flakes are the most numerous type, burins become the dominant retouched tool. The main points concerning these tool types follow:

1. Levallois pieces are made from all types of available raw material except agate. By far the most common raw materials used, however, were ferrocrete sandstone and Precambrian rocks. Together, they account for 73 per cent of all Leval-

lois flakes, with each accounting for over 35 per cent. Both Levallois blades and points are rare.

2. As at Site 1017 burins are the dominant retouched tool and account for over 50 per cent of all such tools. Roughly half of them are made on chert from Nile pebbles, the remaining half are evenly split between Precambrian rock and fossil wood. Only two examples are on agate, while there are no burins on ferrocrete sandstone. As at all Khormusan sites, burins show great elaboration, including many multiple varieties. Burins are made on blades, flakes, cores, simple fragments, and primary flakes. As there was apparently no preference shown for any of these artifacts, burins made on cores are not considered a separate class but are classified by the type of burin present on the core. By far, the most common class of burin is that made on truncations, including transverse forms. They account for well over half of all burins. This is similar to the situation at Site 1017 but is markedly different from that at Site ANW-3.

3. As expected at Khormusan sites, denticulates are very common. At this stage, however, they do not nearly match the number or quality of the burins. This particular assemblage has a denticulate tool type not seen in the other Khormusan assemblages—the denticulate point. It is rare even here but is a logical step, considering the number of converging denticulates at earlier sites and the overall trend toward diminutization of retouched tools.

Levallois flakes (187). There is a great size variation, but the larger examples are scarce and rarely measure over 60 mm. in length (fig. 29, n, q). As at Site 1017, the larger examples have wide, convexly faceted butts and prominent bulbs (fig. 29, n). The smaller examples have rather thin butts but are mostly faceted (fig. 29, g, o).

Although many of the Levallois flakes are broken or irregular in shape, a tendency toward rectangular forms can be seen. There is apparently no difference in this from material to material. It is true of fossil wood, Precambrian rock (fig. 29, n), and ferrocrete sandstone (fig. 29, o). Other, more irregular shapes also occur (fig. 29, g).

Levallois blades (15). Levallois blades were made on a variety of raw materials. The com-

ments made for Levallois flakes also apply here. All are rather small, none exceeding 55 mm. in length (fig. 29, l, p).

Levallois points (4). These are small and rare, considering the large number of Levallois flakes.

Levallois flakes, distally thinned (1). This single example was only partially successful. The tip is broken, but the inverse side shows two flat flake scars at the tip made during the thinning process (fig. 29, m).

Burins, straight dihedral (3). Typical examples (fig. 30, d).

Burins, dihedral *déjeté* (1). Typical on a primary flake.

Burins, dihedral angle (5). Two are simple "single blow" types on overpassed flakes, while the other three have at least two converging burin facets (fig. 30, e).

Burins, angle on snapped pieces (3). One has a notch on the opposed lateral edge, while another shows some inverse retouch.

Burins, on straight truncations (4). Rather thick examples, often with only partial truncation (fig. 30, b).

Burins, on oblique truncations (14). The most typical type in the assemblage. On four examples, the burin spall has twisted, which results in a burin facet which is almost *plan* (fig. 30, a). The other examples are more typical (fig. 29, i).

Burins, on convex truncations (6). Rather typical, well made examples (fig. 29, j), one of which is on a small Levallois flake (fig. 30, g, h).

Burins, on concave truncations (13). Three are on core fragments, while the others are on irregular flakes. All are typical with well retouched concave truncations.

Burins, transverse on lateral truncations (2). One is on a snapped Levallois flake, the other demonstrates a typical system of burin preparation used in the Khormusan. A flake is first given both a lateral and an end truncation. The burin spall is then struck from the meeting point of the two truncations. In this case, the spall was struck transversely (fig. 30, f). Burin spalls often show a fine steep retouch along one edge, indicating that the original truncations covered most, if not all, of the flake edges.

Burins, transverse on concave truncations (5). Two are notched by inverse retouch (fig. 30, c), while the remaining examples are wholly typical.

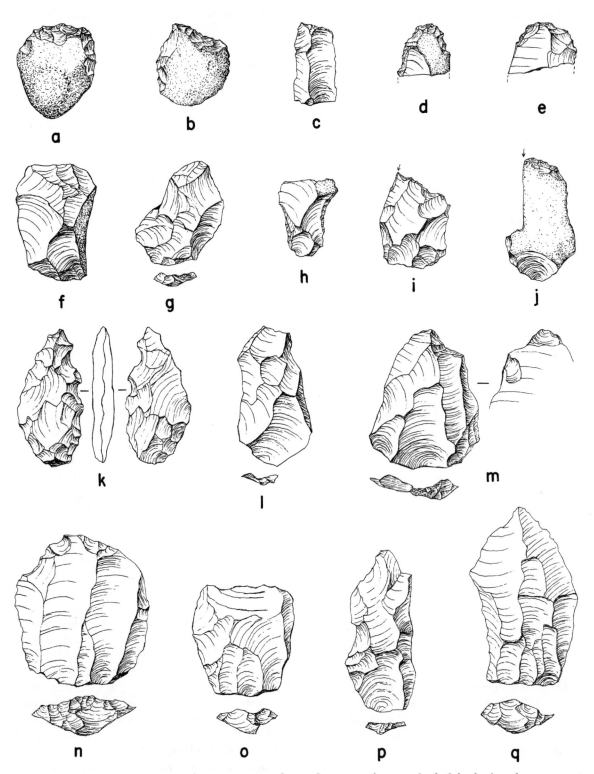

FIG. 29—Site 34D: a, core scraper; b-c, truncations; d-e, end-scrapers; f, cortex backed knife; h, side-scraper; i-j, burins; k, bifacial point; g, l, n-o, q, Levallois flakes; m, distally thinned Levallois flake; p, Levallois blade. 4/5 natural size.

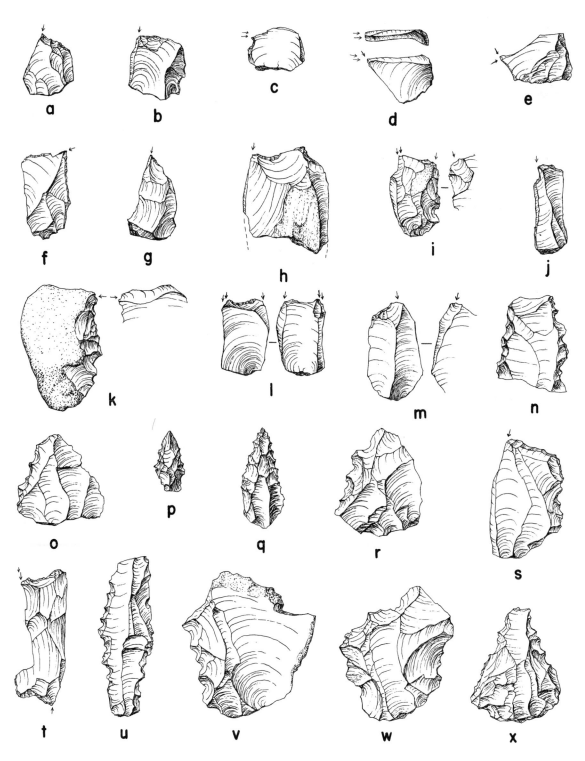

FIG. 30—Site 34D: a-j, l-m, t, burins; k, s, burin—denticulates; n-o, r, u-x, denticulates; p-q, denticulate points. 4/5 natural size.

Burins, *plan* (5). One large example is on a concave lateral truncation, another is on a convex truncation. The other three are on oblique truncations (fig. 30, m).

Burins, multiple dihedral (1). This is a small agate fragment with two angle burins on the opposite ends of the same snapped section, and a "single blow" burin taken on one of the other burin facets. The result is a triangular piece with a burin at each apex.

Burins, multiple mixed (3). In this case all have one burin on a retouched truncation and one angle burin on a snapped segment (fig. 30, i).

Burins, multiple on retouched truncations (8). Six have opposed burins (fig. 30, 1), while two have burins faceted at both ends of the same truncations (fig. 30, t).

Burin—Denticulates (2). There is one transverse burin on a laterally denticulated edge (fig. 30, k), and one burin on an oblique truncation which also has a lateral denticulation. This piece is on a well made Levallois flake of fossil wood (fig. 30, s).

End-scrapers (8). End-scrapers are poorly developed. There are three indifferent examples on ferrocrete sandstone flakes, four on broken chert flakes (fig. 29, e), and one on a primary flake from a chert pebble. They all tend to have irregularly retouched scraping ends, some even approaching end denticulates (fig. 29, d).

Side-scrapers (1). A single example. It is a biconcave scraper made by rather flat retouch on a snapped chert blade (fig. 29, h).

Core scrapers (4). There is a slightly nosed scraper on a split chert pebble (fig. 29, a), and a slightly convex scraper on the striking platform of a single platform microblade core. In addition, there are two Levallois cores which have had fine retouch added to a section of their edges, forming convex scrapers.

Notched pieces (4). One chert and three fossil wood flakes have deeply retouched micronotches.

Converging denticulates (3). There is one asymmetrically converging microdenticulation on an agate blade and a Levallois flake which has converging denticulate edges which end at a square tip (fig. 30, k). There is also a small fragment of fossil wood which shows an alternately retouched, converging denticulation.

Transverse denticulates (4). These are rather small and generally indifferently produced. Only one piece is well made and is, by far, the largest example.

Lateral denticulates (12). Microdenticulates are in the majority, although a few pieces have good macrodenticulates (fig. 30, r, v). One Levallois point has a denticulated edge (fig. 30, o). As a group they are poorly made, not nearly as fine as the denticulates from Site 1017.

Bilateral denticulates (5). Three are on broken flakes, but all show careful retouch (fig. 30, n). One is on a long fossil wood blade (fig. 30, u), and another is on a ferrocrete sandstone flake. On all pieces denticulations are small and made by retouch.

Transverse and lateral denticulates (1). A well made example on ferrocrete sandstone (fig. 30, w).

Denticulate points (3). These have been distinguished from the converging denticulates by their small size. There are two on chert flakes which are unifacially retouched (fig. 30, p-q). Another is a bifacially retouched point on ferrocrete sandstone (fig. 29, k).

Retouched flakes (6). Small irregular flakes which have a minor amount of flat retouch along a portion of one edge.

Truncated pieces (3). There are two obliquely truncated blades (fig. 29, c) and one thick primary flake which has converging oblique, convex-concave truncations. Conceivably, it could be considered a scraper, but at the point of convergence there are two unsuccessful attempts to strike off burin spalls (fig. 30, b).

Cortex backed knives (7). These range from flakes (fig. 29, f) to long blades. As a group they are among the largest tools.

Varia (2). There is an unretouched flake which approaches a point and a broken blade which has two retouched notches on an oblique truncation.

CORE TYPOLOGY

	No.	%	Restricted %
Levallois flake	24	13.5	40.7
Levallois point	1	0.6	1.7
Para-Levallois	4	2.2	6.7
Single platform, unfaceted	5	2.8	8.5
Single platform, faceted	8	4.5	13.5
Opposed platform	11	6.2	18.6
Discoidal	1	0.6	1.7
Ninety degree	1	0.6	1.7

	No.	%	Restricted %
Bipolar	2	1.1	3.4
Globular	2	1.1	3.4
Unidentifiable	118	66.6	
	177	99.8	99.9

NOTES ON THE TYPOLOGY

While a small majority of all cores is on chert pebble (fig. 31, a), those made on Precambrian rocks and ferrocrete sandstone tend to be more completely utilized and made into more complex types. Of all cores, only 59 were complete or classifiable into recognizable types. The remaining 118 were either fragments or unidentifiable.

Levallois flake (24). All are small and well prepared (fig. 31, f). Six unstruck examples show extensive preparation of both upper and lower surfaces (fig. 31, b). Levallois cores on chert are rare and not as fully prepared. Most are oval to pointed oval in shape (fig. 31, a).

Levallois point (1). One small example on fossil wood.

Para-Levallois (4). Compared with the Levallois flake cores, these are roughly prepared (fig. 31, e).

Single platform, unfaceted (5). Mostly chert pebbles which have had flakes or short blades removed (fig. 31, d).

Single platform, faceted (8). These have one faceted platform which has been utilized without any other core preparation (fig. 31, g).

Opposed platform (11). Odd sized cores from the removal of flakes or blades struck from opposite ends of a pebble or a small piece of fossil wood.

Discoidal (1). A good unifacial example on a chert pebble (fig. 31, c).

Ninety degree (1). A poor example.

Bipolar (2). These small examples are highly atypical for this industry.

Globular (2). Two small core remnants.

Unidentifiable (118). Mostly chert pebbles which have been minimally flaked in no discernable pattern.

SITE ANW-3

Site ANW-3 covers an extensive area behind the village of Angash, on the west bank of the Nile just north of Buhen[5] (map ref. 913.9/645.2). The site extends for about 500 m. north-south, but is quite narrow east-west (fig. 32). The total size of the site and its stratigraphic position have been described in detail in earlier sections.

The site was discovered by J. Waechter during the 1962-1963 field season. At that time he carried out test excavations and made surface collections from a number of areas (Waechter, 1965, p. 124). He recognized two main areas which he designated Localities 2 and 3 (Waechter, 1965, p. 124). Locality 2 fell somewhat outside the main site and artifacts from it differed from those in the main part of the concentration (Waechter, 1965, p. 124). The majority of tools recovered during the 1962-1963 field season came from Locality 2. Unfortunately, only 39 retouched tools and Levallois flakes were found, and of these, only 31 were *in situ*.

The results of this work indicated that more excavation was needed and that the possibility of obtaining a large collection from *in situ* was good. In February, 1964, work was resumed on the site. This work was restricted to the area called Locality 2. A detailed surface study indicated that Locality 3 did not represent part of the same site as Locality 2. Therefore, all references to Site ANW-3 are to Locality 2, as described by Waechter.

The initial excavation of ANW-3 during 1964 was concerned with clarifying the geological stratigraphy and placing the cultural material within it. Although it proved to be necessary to remove a great deal of loose sterile sand, the stratigraphic position of the artifacts was firmly established.

Artifacts rested on and in a sand dune which was banked against a remnant of the Dibeira-Jer silts. The dune was covered by a thin layer of fluvial sand and silt pebbles which, in turn, was covered by more fluvial sand of the Sahaba formation. This placed the site as having been occupied in the period of low Nile during the erosion of the Dibeira-Jer formation.

Artifacts were found in three areas: in dune sand filled cracks in the Dibeira-Jer silts, on dune sand banked against an eroded bank of the Dibeira-Jer silts, and in dune sand resting on

---

[5] This is referred to as "Buhen Village" by Waechter but is listed on the map as Angash.

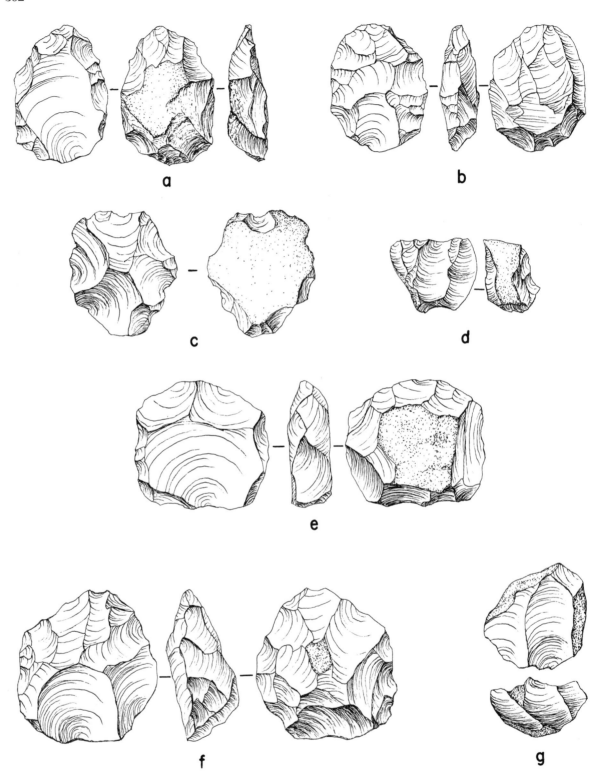

FIG. 31—Site 34D: a-b, f, Levallois flake cores; c, discoidal core; d, unfaceted, single platform core; e, para-Levallois core; g, faceted, single platform core. 4/5 natural size.

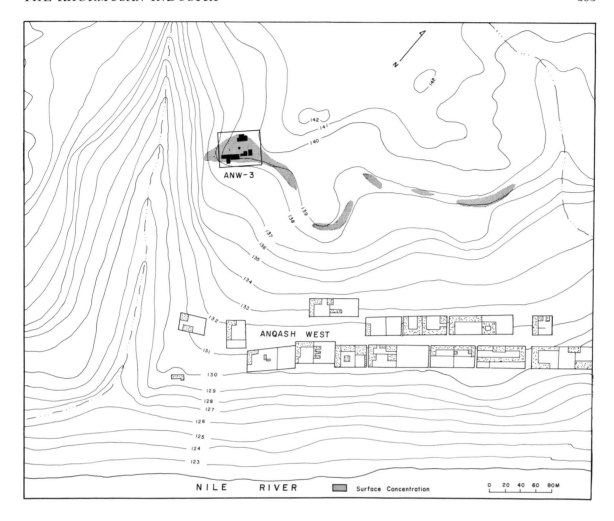

Fig. 32—Topographic map of Site ANW-3.

mud pools on the eastern edge of the Dibeira-Jer silts (fig. 4).

After the stratigraphic position of the artifacts was clear, two areas were more fully excavated: along the eroded bank of the silts and in the area of the mud pools (fig. 33). A total of 254 sq. m. was excavated in 2-m. square areas. Of this, 184 sq. m. were excavated along the eroded silt bank and 60 sq. m. in the area of the mud pools. In the dune sand above the latter, a charcoal sample gave a date of 15,850 B.C. ± 500 years.

NON-LITHIC ARTIFACTS

Six pieces of ground hematite were recovered *in situ*. They are small, measuring usually about 5 cm. long, and are rectangular in shape. On one

surface of each are grinding marks which indicate that they were rubbed against a hard surface from one direction only (fig. 34). They come from all three excavated areas.

In addition, two bone tools were found *in situ*. One is a poor boring tool, polished to an uneven tip (fig. 34); the other is a small spatulate tool (fig. 34). Both came from the sand dune along the silt bank. These are the only bone tools found in association with Khormusan artifacts and represent probably the oldest bone tools found in Nubia.

FEATURES

No true fire pits were discovered, but there are a few areas where burned sand and bone

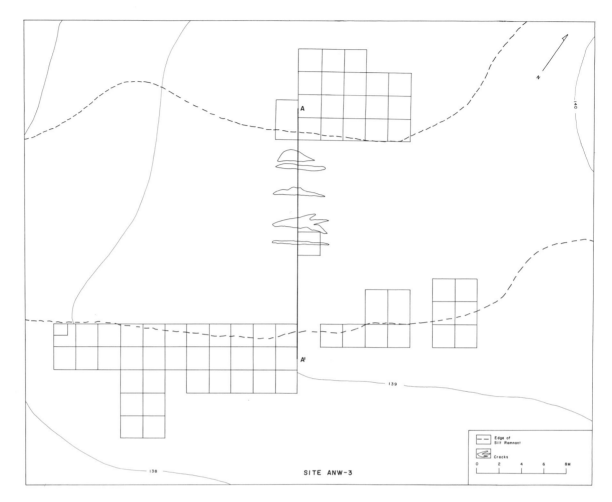

FIG. 33—Detail map of excavation area at Site ANW-3.

were present (fig. 35). There is no indication that fire pits were lined in any way. More likely, fires were built on the surface or in small depressions in the dune. The remains were quickly scattered, as is seen by the lack of any heavy concentration of bone and an almost total absence of charcoal. The small amount of charcoal recovered was found in the dune sand associated with a number of artifacts but not within a heavily burned area.

LITHIC ARTIFACTS

A total of 3,444 artifacts were recovered in all excavated squares. No difference was seen between the artifactual content of the two main areas, nor in the artifacts found within the ero-

sional cracks. By far, the majority of artifacts came from those squares adjacent to the silt bank. The utilization of raw materials and the major classes of artifacts found have already been described in earlier sections. It need only be said that these were consistent within the Khormusan tradition.

DISTRIBUTION OF ARTIFACTS

Three main areas were excavated. At most, they were only 18 m. apart. Major excavation, however, took place along the eroded silt bank. A series of 2-m. squares were dug for a distance of 32 m. north-south, and in places as much as 10 m. east-west. The excavation did not attempt to encompass fully the total site, but merely to

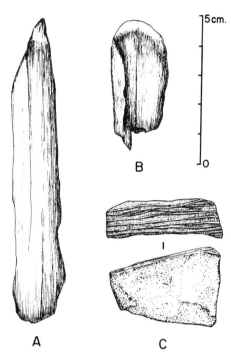

Fig. 34—Site ANW-3: a-b, bone tools; c, ground hematite. 4/5 natural size.

coming from the southern side of the main concentration.

TOOL TYPOLOGY

	No.	%	Restricted %
Levallois flakes	203	38.7	
Levallois blades	49	9.3	
Levallois points	18	3.4	
Levallois flakes, distally thinned	4	0.8	1.6
Burins, straight dihedral	13	2.4	5.1
Burins, dihedral *déjeté*	8	1.5	3.1
Burins, dihedral angle	12	2.3	4.7
Burins, angle on snapped piece	10	1.9	3.9
Burins, angle "single blow"	3	0.6	1.2
Burins, transverse "single blow"	4	0.8	1.6
Burins, busque	1	0.2	0.4
Burins, on straight truncations	4	0.8	1.6
Burins, on oblique truncations	6	1.2	2.4
Burins, on convex truncations	3	0.6	1.2
Burins, on concave truncations	19	3.6	7.4
Burins, transverse on lateral truncations	9	1.7	3.5
Burins, transverse on concave truncations	10	1.9	3.9
Burins, *plan*	5	0.9	2.0
Burins, multiple dihedral	3	0.6	1.2
Burins, multiple mixed	12	2.6	4.7
Burins, multiple on retouched truncations	4	0.8	1.6
Burin—Denticulates	3	0.6	1.2
End-scrapers	16	3.0	6.3
Side-scrapers	10	1.9	3.9
Notched pieces	15	2.8	5.9
Converging denticulates	6	1.2	2.4
Transverse denticulates	5	0.9	2.0
Lateral denticulates	26	4.9	10.2
Bilateral denticulates	3	0.6	1.2
Core denticulates	2	0.4	0.8
Retouched flakes	21	3.9	8.0
Truncated pieces	2	0.4	0.8
Cortex backed knives	13	2.4	5.1
Strangled pieces	1	0.2	0.4
Varia	2	0.4	0.8
	525	100.2	100.1

Technological Indices

IL=30.1   IF=69.7   IFs=40.1   Ibl=14.1

Typological Indices

IL^{ty}=51.4   Ibu=25.0   Ident=8.6
Iendscr=3.0   Isscr=1.9

Restricted Typological Indices

IL^{ty}=0.0   Ibu=50.7   Ident=17.8
Iendscr=6.3   Isscr=3.9

sample it. As a result, full distributional information is lacking. A general pattern which fits within what would be expected at a Khormusan site can be seen in the excavated area.

Artifactual density is low, ranging from 6 to 138 per square. That is, at most there are only 34 artifacts per square meter, the average being less than a third of that.

The distribution of artifacts over the excavated area was not uniform. There is one main area of concentration with parts of two other areas showing on the ends of the excavation (fig. 35, a). Cores show a distribution slightly different from that of the tools (fig. 35, c-d), while debitage and tools show a similar pattern (fig. 35, b).

The overall impression is that the site is made up of a number of small areas with relatively heavy artifactual concentration, separated from each other by a loose scattering of artifacts. This is reinforced by the distribution of faunal remains and burned sand. They occur to some extent all over the excavated area, but there are only three concentrations. These coincide with the artifactual concentrations, the largest number of bones

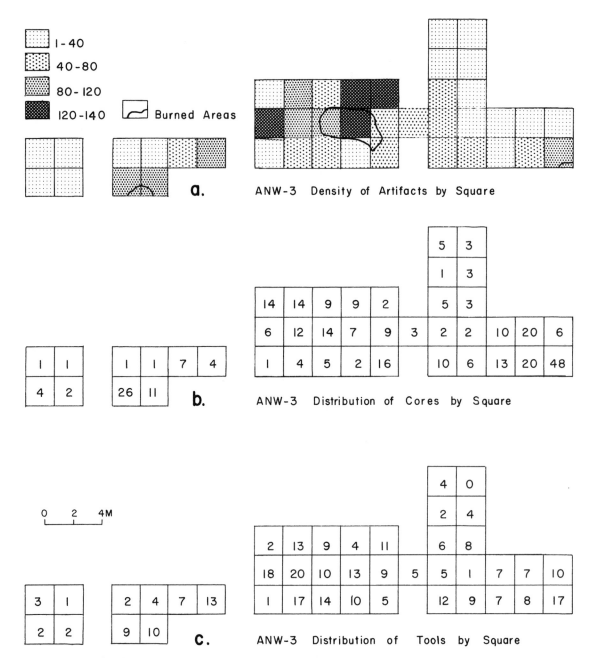

Fig. 35—Artifact distributions at Site ANW-3.

NOTES ON THE TYPOLOGY

Again, Levallois flakes predominate followed by burins and denticulates. The trend toward smaller tools is visible in every tool type and the amount of chert used in tool manufacture in-creases at the expense of ferrocrete sandstone. These three classes of tools may be characterized in the following way:

1. As at all Khormusan sites, the standard of Levallois technology is very high. Almost all ex-amples are typical, although in every category

they tend to be smaller than those from preceding Khormusan assemblages.

2. Burins are exceedingly numerous. Most are made on chert flakes, often on primary chert flakes. Precambrian and fossil wood flakes were also utilized. There is a wide range in types, sizes, and quality. In many cases burin facets are intermediate between *plan* and normal forms. Few burins, however, are truly *plan*. Burins were usually made on flake and core fragments, with burins on blades being exceedingly rare. Burins range in size from a few which are more than 4.5 cm. long to many microlithic burins and multiple burins as small as 1.6 cm. in length.

3. Denticulates are generally well made by percussion on fairly thick flakes or flake fragments. The majority is on Precambrian rocks. But denticulates also occur on fossil wood, quartz, ferrocrete sandstone, and chert.

Levallois flakes (203). Levallois flakes were found in all shapes and sizes and made from all types of material. For the most part, they are smaller than those from 1017 but larger than those from 34D. Preparation is careful, and flakes are thin with well faceted butts (fig. 36, c, f, i, k-m). There are a number of smaller examples made on chert with butts which are not always elaborately faceted (fig. 36, d-e).

Levallois blades (49). These are mostly laminary flakes, although true Levallois blades occur. A good number are made of either quartz (fig. 36, j) or fossil wood (fig. 36, h).

Levallois points (18). There are two which are slightly off axis (fig. 36, a) but the rest are typical (fig. 36, g). There are a few which have slightly more complex scar patterns than is usual (fig. 36, b).

Levallois flakes, distally thinned (4). This special Khormusan technique is most clearly seen here, although it is never widely used. It is possible to see on one flake the desired effect. The under side of the Levallois flake is treated by very flat, inverse retouch struck from the distal end (fig. 38, o). It would appear that it serves little or no purpose but may be effective for thinning overpassed flakes. Four have been treated this way, but only one successfully. At best, this technique is difficult and, more often than not, results in the breaking off of a large piece of the distal end.

Burins, straight dihedral (13). Eight are on flakes (fig. 37, b), three on primary flakes, and one on a core fragment. All are typical.

Burins, dihedral *déjeté* (8). There are four on flakes (fig. 37, b). three on primary flakes, and one on a core remnant.

Burins, dihedral angle (12). Seven are on flakes (fig. 37, d), one on a primary flake (fig. 37, c), and four on core fragments (fig. 37, e).

Burins, angle on snapped flakes (10). Nine are on flakes or flake fragments (fig. 37, f), and one is on a primary flake.

Burins, angle "single blow" (3). Two are on flakes and one is on a core. One of these on flakes is struck from the butt.

Burins, transverse "single blow" (4). These are single blow burins which have transverse burin facets. They are not typical and only barely successful.

Burins, busque (1). An atypical example on a primary flake.

Burins, on straight truncations (4). These are all on core fragments but the burins are quite well formed.

Burins, on oblique truncations (6). All are on flakes, four of which were Levallois (fig. 37, g-h).

Burins, on convex truncations (3). One is on a very small primary flake, and two are on core fragments. They are a rather rare type in the Khormusan, although all burins on truncations predominate in many assemblages.

Burins, on concave truncations (19). The most numerous type found in the assemblage. Three are on cores, seven on primary flakes (fig. 37, k), and nine on regular flakes (fig. 37, i).

Burins, transverse on lateral truncations (9). Three are on primary flakes (fig. 37, l), five on flakes, and one on a blade (fig. 37, m).

Burins, transverse on concave truncations (10). Again, transverse burins are numerous. This type is generally more typical than those on lateral truncations. The concave truncations range from deep notches to truncations which are only slightly concave. A few have burin facets which verge on *plan* (fig. 37, n). Two are on primary flakes (fig. 37, r), and eight on normal flakes (fig. 37, q).

Burins, *plan* (5). There is one on a convexly truncated flake, and four are on concavely truncated flakes (fig. 37, j).

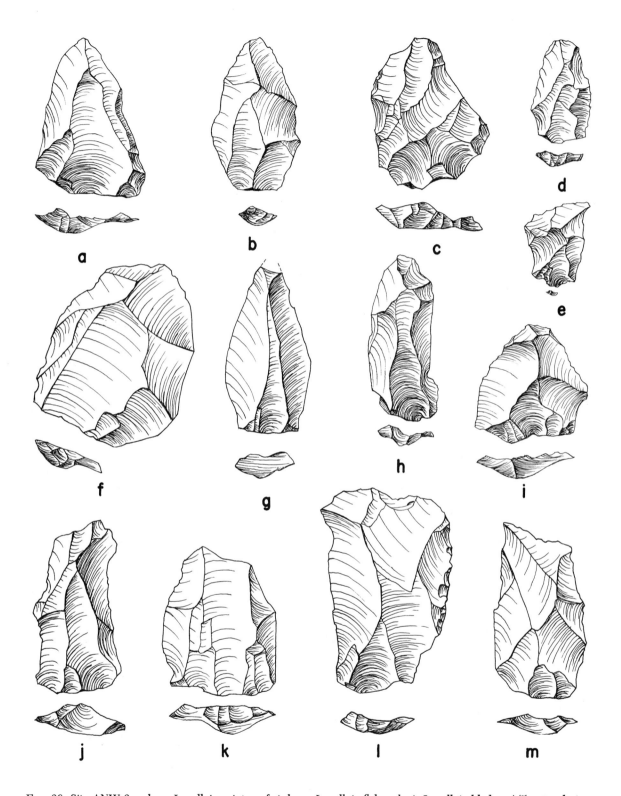

Fig. 36—Site ANW-3: a-b, g, Levallois points; c-f, i, k-m, Levallois flakes; h, j, Levallois blades. 4/5 natural size.

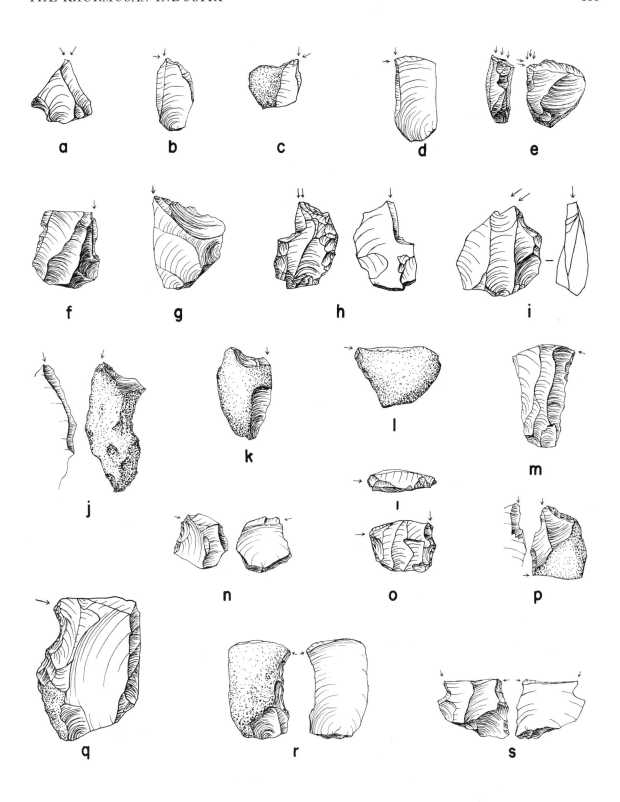

FIG. 37—Site ANW-3: a-s, burins. 4/5 natural size.

Burins, multiple dihedral (3). One multiple dihedral is on a very small flake. There are two multiple angle burins on snapped microlithic chert flakes, with the facets of both burins struck off opposite ends of the same snapped edge.

Burins, multiple mixed (12). All but two are on flakes (fig. 37, o, s). One is on a primary flake, the other on a core fragment.

Burins, multiple on retouched truncations (4). One is on a core fragment, and three are on primary flakes. One on a primary flake has a transverse burin on a lateral truncation and a burin *plan* on a concave truncation (fig. 37, p).

Burin–Denticulates (3). There is a transverse burin on the end of a microdenticulated blade; an angle burin on a snapped flake which has a denticulated edge; and a burin on a convex truncation on a Levallois flake with a micro-denticulated edge.

End-scrapers (16). The majority is on short thick flakes and have well formed convex scraping edges (fig. 38, a-b). A number are atypical with only sections of the end retouched (fig. 38, c), or the retouch is irregular and very steep (fig. 38, d). At least one had an unsuccessful burin spall struck from one end of the retouched scraping edge.

Side-scrapers (10). These are mostly poor examples. One is a large slightly convex side-scraper on a fossil wood core (fig. 38, m); one is a good inverse, convex side-scraper on a flake (fig. 38, e); one is a biconvex, inverse side-scraper on a flake; and one is a good convex side-scraper on a flake. Six are rather bad examples with semi-steep retouch. These may represent poor lateral truncations for intended transverse burins.

Notched pieces (15). Notches are on a variety of blades and flakes. There are six end notches, six side notches, and three side notches near snapped edges which appear to be the first step in the manufacture of transverse burins on concave truncations. One of the latter examples even shows an unsuccessful attempt to remove a transverse burin spall.

Converging denticulates (6). There is one asymmetric, microlithic Tayac point, but the rest are on large flakes or flake fragments (fig. 38, g), all but one, Levallois. The largest has two minute transverse burin spalls on the distal end, perhaps caused accidentally during retouch (fig. 38, n).

Transverse denticulates (5). These are not as well made as are the other types (fig. 38, j); only one, on a primary flake, has small even teeth (fig. 38, h).

Lateral denticulates (26). There is a great range in quality among these. Ten are on Levallois flakes, two on blades (fig. 38, f), and fourteen on non-Levallois flakes and flake fragments (fig. 38, l) and primary flakes. The denticulations are, at times, weak; and all of them are micro-denticulate.

Bilateral denticulates (3). One is formed by alternate retouch on an elongated Levallois flake, and two are made by simple retouch on non-Levallois flakes. One of these is on quartz (fig. 38, i).

Core denticulates (2). One is on the side of a single platform core, while the other is on one edge of a flat, struck Levallois core. Both are microdenticulates.

Retouched flakes (21). There is retouch on twelve Levallois flakes, three Levallois blades, and six non-Levallois flakes. Retouch is normally marginal but regular. Some of these closely approach scrapers, but the retouch is lighter than that on scrapers.

Truncated pieces (2). There is a concave truncation on a small Levallois flake and one inverse convexly truncated flake.

Cortex backed knives (13). All are on laminary flakes or blades which show evidence of some use retouch along the sharp edge (fig. 38, p). Most are on Precambrian rock, but three are on quartz.

Strangled pieces (1). This is a single fragment on ferrocrete sandstone.

Varia (2). One side of a pointed Levallois flake has been scaled, with most retouch showing on the inverse face (fig. 38, k). There is also a microburin on a microlithic flake, which is apparently accidental.

CORE TYPOLOGY

	No.	%	Restricted %
Levallois flake	113	23.9	32.1
Levallois flake, opposite end	25	5.6	7.1
Levallois blade	1	0.2	0.3
Levallois point	8	1.8	2.3
Nubian, Type I	7	1.6	2.0
Para-Levallois	6	1.3	1.7
Single platform, unfaceted	23	5.1	6.6

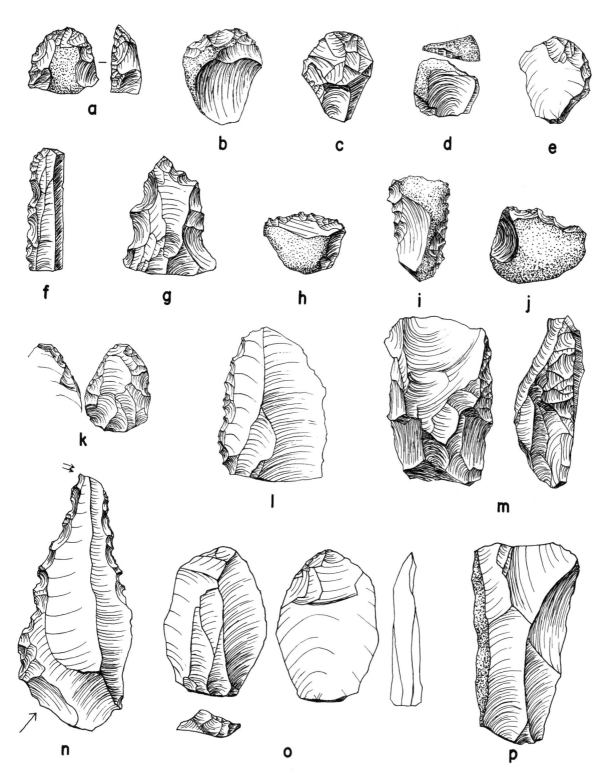

FIG. 38—Site ANW-3: a-d, end-scrapers; e, m, side-scrapers; f-j, l, n, denticulates; k, scaled piece; o, distally thinned Levallois flake; p, cortex backed knife. 4/5 natural size.

	No.	%	Restricted %
Single platform, faceted	81	17.8	22.7
Opposed platform	33	7.2	9.4
Discoidal	24	5.3	6.8
Globular	1	0.2	0.3
Ninety degree	8	1.8	2.3
Isolated flake	21	4.6	5.9
Unidentifiable	104	22.8	
	455	99.2	99.5

NOTES ON THE TYPOLOGY

As ANW-3 has the largest and most varied core sample, it seems appropriate to go into more detail here than in the other Khormusan assemblages.

Khormusan cores are diagnostically important, for in the core typology can be seen the kind and degree of technological change which takes place during the Nubian Upper Stone Age. This takes the form of an adaptation to the use of small chert pebbles with the resulting modification in types of core preparation.

The Khormusan industry is characterized by a heavy, although decreasing, emphasis on the production of Levallois flakes. Levallois flakes are obtained from Levallois cores which are carefully and extensively prepared. As has been noted, Levallois cores from 34A and 1017 are made on ferrocrete sandstone, fossil wood, or Precambrian rock. All are found either as large slabs or sizable wadi cobbles of irregular shape. Relatively extensive preparation and shaping of the upper and lower faces is necessary in order to arrive at the basic tortoise shape desired in Levallois cores. This is as true of Levallois cores on these materials at 34A as it is at 2004.

On the other hand, the introduction of chert pebbles made available a raw material which was not only too small for extensive preparation but was also generally shaped like a tortoise core in its natural state. At first, chert pebbles were considered too small to be used for prepared flake production. At 1017, where they first appear in significant number, they were exclusively used for the manufacture of burins. These, of course, need be neither large nor made on flakes with elaborate preparation.

As the general size of tools and Levallois flakes decreased, however, chert pebbles began to fall within a desired size range for Levallois flakes.

At this stage, Levallois cores on chert pebble exhibit all the characteristics of those on other materials, namely elaborate preparation of both surfaces. Apparently, through time, the Khormusan people realized that such preparation was not necessary. It was possible to get a regularly controlled flake from a pebble core with a minimum of preparation because of the pebble's natural shape. This was particularly true of the under surface which is naturally convex. The problem remained, however, to remove the cortex from the upper surface. This is relatively difficult without some side preparation, for it is hard to remove a series of primary flakes from a rounded pebble.

This fact called for a compromise between the normal Levallois core preparation and the obvious fact that the chert pebble initially had the desired shape. Since a workable surface on the pebble was desired, platforms were made at both ends, and initial primary flakes of the upper surface were directed from the platforms. Once this had been done, a small amount of side preparation followed, using the natural cortex as a platform. The resulting core was truly Levallois on the upper surface but, as seen from below, it appeared to be basically opposed platform.

At Site ANW-3, another variation which might be considered an advance in simplifying core preparation appears. As pebbles have a generally oval shape to begin with, preparation of the sides of a Levallois core on pebble is not always necessary. Thus, a number of cores show careful preparation from both platforms, but only minimal or no preparation on the sides. These are still within the Levallois type as only one large flake was struck from the core, while a number of small, preparatory flakes were first removed from the opposed platforms.

Beyond this point, cores cease to be Levallois. There are two varieties which seem to derive from the simplification of the Levallois preparation: the opposed, faceted platform core and the single faceted platform core. The first is very similar to the last stage in the decline of Levallois preparation, except flakes of equal size are struck from the opposed platforms without any one flake predominating. The second type, the single faceted platform, is very common at ANW-3, almost equal in number to Levallois flake cores. Their name is purely descriptive; there is a faceted platform at one end from which a few large flakes are struck off along the long axis of the pebble. Apparently, the first two were primary flakes, but the third flake was free of cortex.

There are a number of other core types, both specialized Levallois cores and non-Levallois types. These are all obvious types which occur in other areas and in other periods in Nubia, but in the Khormusan they never attain much importance.

In general, the Khormusan shows a development of cores from a typically Middle Stone Age typology, through a highly developed Levallois phase, into a period of decline in classic Levallois forms. The decline is characterized by a replacement of Levallois cores with abbreviated varieties and non-Levallois forms.

Levallois flake (113). Sixty-seven are made on Nile pebble. The vast majority of these is on chert, but a few occur on agate. Over half the pebble Levallois cores show only preparation of opposed platforms on the under surface. The remaining 30 examples have more extensive preparation of the under surface, although some cortex is present on most (fig. 39, e-f). All are microlithic, ranging in length from 2.7 to 5 cm. Most, however, fall between 3 and 4 cm.

There are a number of unstruck examples which show careful preparation of the upper surface (fig. 39, b).

The remaining 46 Levallois flake cores are made on ferrocrete sandstone, Precambrian rock, fossil wood, or quartz. As a group, they are larger than the chert Levallois cores and more carefully prepared on both surfaces (fig. 39, e). The largest measures just under 10 cm. in length (fig. 39, d) while the smallest measures 3.5 cm.; the majority range between 4.5 and 6 cm.

Levallois flake, opposite end (25). This type has been defined above. All but one are on chert pebbles and demonstrate the same size range as the typical chert Levallois flake cores (fig. 40, c-d).

Levallois blade (1). One small example on a chert pebble.

Levallois point (8). These are all small, ranging from 2 to 4.9 cm. in length. They are similar to the Nubian Core, Type I, but the blows

which define the tip are not oriented toward the butt (fig. 39, a). They are intermediate between a typical Levallois point core and the Nubian variety.

Nubian Core, Type I (7). The type was first defined for the Nubian Middle Stone Age (Guichard and Guichard, 1965, p. 68). They are Levallois point cores which have the tip formed by the removal of just two elongated flakes struck from the tip toward the butt. This leaves a definite ridge between the flake scars. At ANW-3, these fall within the same size range as the chert Levallois flake cores. For the most part, they are indifferently made, but some are quite fine. They tend to have rather prominent tips caused by deep blows off the distal end. This is not usually seen on Nubian Cores, Type I, of the Nubian Middle Stone Age, although a few have been found in Nubian Mousterian context.

Para-Levallois (6). Rather poorly made with the para-Levallois flakes usually unsuccessfully struck.

Single platform, unfaceted (23). These are rather rare. All have *lisse* platforms, and most are flake cores, although a few microblade cores occur in sub-pyramidal forms. The largest measures just under 6 cm. in length, but most are microlithic.

Single platform, faceted (81). Next to Levallois flake cores, this is the most numerous type. As described above, this type seems to be a modification of the Levallois technique taken to a point where it can no longer be considered a true prepared core (fig. 40, e). Only two measure over 5 cm., and the remainder falls within the size range of the chert Levallois flake cores. All but eight are on chert pebbles, the others are on fossil wood.

Opposed platform (33). This type is often made on fossil wood where flakes usually follow the grain. Here, seven are on fossil wood, two on quartz, one on Precambrian, and the remainder on chert pebble. Most platforms are faceted, although various combinations exist. For the most part, they are flake cores (fig. 40, a) and fall within the typical size range for chert cores.

Discoidal (24). These tend to have rather small flakes removed. Some may really be cores which were in the first stages of preparation, although most are clearly discoidal (fig. 40, b).

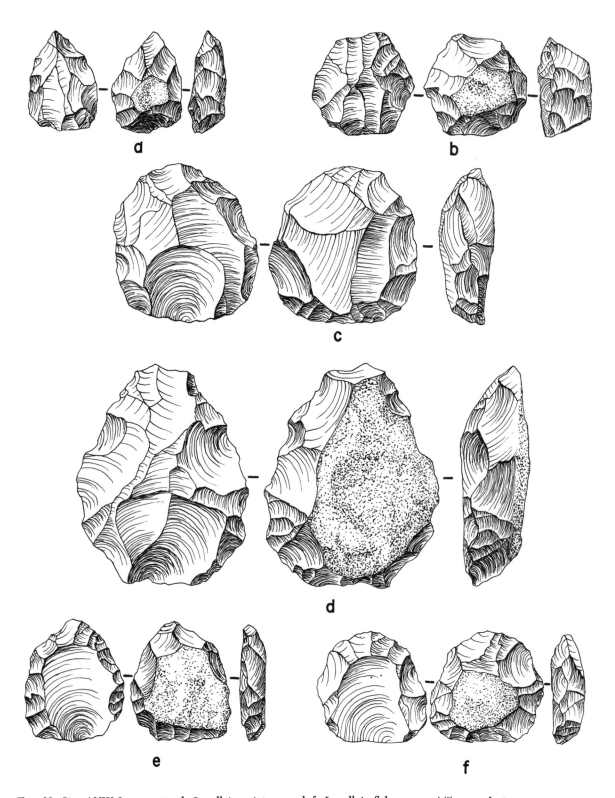

FIG. 39—Site ANW-3: a, unstruck Levallois point core; b-f, Levallois flake cores. 4/5 natural size.

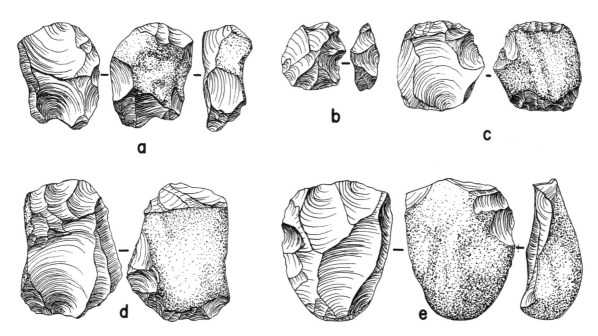

Fɪɢ. 40–Site ANW-3: a, opposed platform core; b, discoidal core; c-d, Levallois flake cores, opposed end preparation; e, faceted, single platform core. 4/5 natural size.

Globular (1). A single example on Precambrian rock.

Ninety degree (8). Quite atypical for the industry. They are poor examples and may owe their form as much to chance as to intent.

Isolated flake (21). These are pebbles which have had one or two primary flakes removed.

Unidentifiable (104). Various cores and core fragments which show no discernable pattern of flaking.

Sɪᴛᴇ 2004

The village of Gemai East is situated at the southern end of the Second Cataract, in a wide silt filled plain (lat. 21° 45′/long. 31° 12′). At the southern end of the town the houses rest on silt exposures which rise to a height of some 15 m. The villagers mine the silt for material to use in house construction, leaving large pits in the flat silt banks. In one area, there is a major exposure of geological profiles where the cover of silt has been removed and the underlying fluvial sand blown away leaving small cliffs (fig. 41). In one of these profiles a number of artifacts was seen under the silt and within a fluvial sand layer.

Thirty square meters were excavated on what turned out to be a living floor in the fluvial sands. This floor occurred some 10 cm. below the top of the sands and under a meter of silts, the top of which was deflated. The living floor was at an elevation of 8 m. above the present floodplain. The total site area was masked by the village, but a reasonable estimate has been made elsewhere.

The living floor contained numerous artifacts, including a large riolite slab which showed indications of some polishing. This did not, however, modify the shape of the rock, nor did it cover more than 20 cm. of the center of one face. It is, however, the only evidence that there was any polishing or grinding on stone at Khormusan sites. In consideration of the small number of bone tools at Site ANW-3, perhaps this piece is best explained as being used for fashioning bone artifacts.

Scattered evenly over the living floor were fragments of burned fish bones and a very few bones of large mammals. No evidence was found of even amorphous hearths.

There was a somewhat differential distribution of artifacts across the living floor, but it did not

Fig. 41—Site 2004 from the north.

show more than one irregular concentration (fig. 42, a). Whereas other Khormusan sites indicated special areas for certain classes of tools, such was not the case here. Tools, Levallois flakes, cores, and even burins merely followed the distributional pattern seen for all artifacts; they occurred in greatest number in those squares which possessed the greatest overall artifact content (fig. 42, b-d).

NON-LITHIC ARTIFACTS

Four pieces of ground hematite were recovered, but neither bone tools nor other non-lithic artifacts were found.

LITHIC ARTIFACTS

A total of 1,525 artifacts of chipped stone were recovered. Materials and classes of artifacts have

already been described. Typologically, the assemblage represented a very late and degenerate stage of the Khormusan, although all Khormusan traits were present.

TOOL TYPOLOGY

	No.	%	Restricted %
Levallois flakes	77	37.5	
Levallois blades	6	2.9	
Levallois points	8	3.9	
Pseudo-Levallois points	1	0.5	0.9
Burins, straight dihedral	1	0.5	0.9
Burins, dihedral *déjeté*	1	0.5	0.9
Burins, dihedral angle	1	0.5	0.9
Burins, angle on snapped piece	5	2.4	4.4
Burins, angle "single blow"	1	0.5	0.9
Burins, on straight truncations	2	1.0	1.7
Burins, on oblique truncations	2	1.0	1.7
Burins, on convex truncations	4	1.9	3.5
Burins, on concave truncations	1	0.5	0.9
Burins, *plan*	1	0.5	0.9

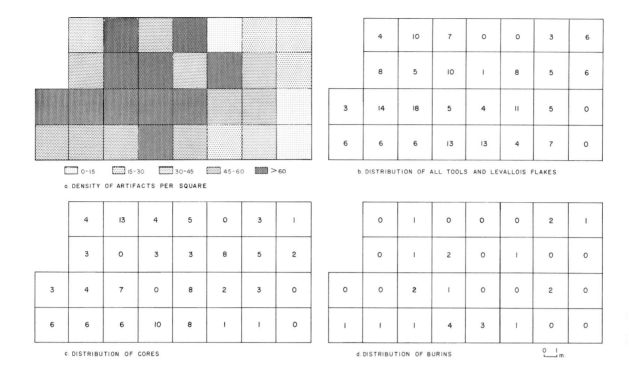

a. DENSITY OF ARTIFACTS PER SQUARE

☐ 0-15   ☐ 15-30   ☐ 30-45   ☐ 45-60   ■ >60

b. DISTRIBUTION OF ALL TOOLS AND LEVALLOIS FLAKES

4	10	7	0	0	3	6
8	5	10	1	8	5	6
3	14	18	5	4	11	5	0
6	6	6	13	13	4	7	0

c. DISTRIBUTION OF CORES

4	13	4	5	0	3	1
3	0	3	3	8	5	2
3	4	7	0	8	2	3	0
6	6	6	10	8	1	1	0

d. DISTRIBUTION OF BURINS

0	1	0	0	0	2	1
0	1	2	0	1	0	0
0	0	2	1	0	0	2	0
1	1	1	4	3	1	0	0

0 1 m

FIG. 42–Artifact distributions at Site 2004.

	No.	%	Restricted %
Burins, multiple on retouched truncations	1	0.5	0.9
Burins, multiple on snapped flakes	2	1.0	1.7
Burin–Denticulates	1	0.5	0.9
Burin–End-scrapers	2	1.0	1.7
Denticulate–Side-scrapers	1	0.5	0.9
End-scrapers	8	3.9	7.0
Side-scrapers	5	2.4	4.4
Notched pieces	11	5.3	9.6
Converging denticulates	1	0.5	0.9
Transverse denticulates	9	4.4	7.9
Lateral denticulates	17	8.3	14.9
Bilateral denticulates	2	1.0	1.7
Lateral and transverse denticulates	1	0.5	0.9
Core denticulates	1	0.5	0.9
Retouched flakes	19	9.3	16.7
Truncated pieces	5	2.4	4.4
Cortex backed knives	5	2.4	4.4
Strangled pieces	1	0.5	0.9
Varia	2	1.0	1.7
	205	100.0	100.0

Technological Indices

IL=18.8   IF=67.4   IFs=43.3   Ibl=11.7

Typological Indices

IL^{ty}=44.3   Ibu=12.3   Ident=16.2
Iendscr=4.9   Isscr=2.9

Restricted Typological Indices

IL^{ty}=0.0   Ibu=21.9   Ident=29.0
Iendscr=8.4   Isscr=5.3

NOTES ON THE TYPOLOGY

Site 2004 is situated south of the Second Cataract, in the Batn el-Hajar. In this area there is no ferrocrete sandstone available and very little chert pebble. This affected the proportions of raw materials and also, perhaps, the overall quality of retouch. Levallois flakes are still the most numerous tool type but there are many fewer here than at earlier Khormusan sites. Burins are still important, but denticulates are now more numerous. These types may be generally characterized as follows:

1. Unlike the rest of the Khormusan sites, there is a definite decline in the quality of the Levallois technology. As at the others, however, there is still a strong Levallois tradition and a large

number of unretouched Levallois flakes. As always, Levallois blades and points are comparatively rare.

2. Burins are common in this assemblage and account for about one-fifth of all retouched tools. Yet, like all tool types here, they are not as well made as at earlier sites. Simple burins are in the majority, although there is still a wide variety of types present.

3. Denticulates are the most numerous retouched tools in the assemblage. They occur on flakes, blades, cores, and core fragments. As a group, they are indifferently retouched, in no way commensurate with those from earlier Khormusan assemblages. Denticulates occur on all kinds of rock but most typically on Precambrian or quartz.

Levallois flakes (77). Compared with the other Khormusan assemblages, these Levallois flakes are rather poorly prepared. This may be due in part to the late stage involved, but it is also probably affected by the coarse grained Precambrian rock employed for many of the larger flakes. The large flakes are rare but tend to be irregular (fig. 43, n). Smaller flakes, made on chert, agate, and fine grained Precambrian rock are better prepared (fig. 43, a). A number of the smaller pieces are elongate but not truly laminary (fig. 43, b-c).

Levallois blades (6). All of these are fragmentary.

Levallois points (8). These are small and not very good examples (fig. 43, d).

Pseudo-Levallois points (1). One typical example.

Burins, straight dihedral (1). One mediocre example on a thick flake fragment.

Burins, dihedral *déjeté* (1). This is made on an overpassed Levallois flake (fig. 44, a).

Burins, dihedral angle (1). A small, mediocre example on a core fragment.

Burins, angle on snapped flakes (5). This is the most common type. Four are snapped flakes and one is on a snapped blade. All are typical (fig. 44, b), and one has some retouch on the edge opposite the burin (fig. 44, h).

Burins, angle "single blow" (1). One typical example on a rectangular flake fragment. The burin spall is struck off a weathered surface.

Burins, on straight truncations (2). A poor example on a core fragment and another poor one on a primary flake.

Burins, on oblique truncations (2). One is on a primary chert blade with an inverse truncation (fig. 44, i). The second is more complex. Originally, it was a dihedral *déjeté* burin, but during resharpening a truncation was made and a second, almost a *plan* burin facet, was added (fig. 44, e).

Burins, on convex truncations (4). There is one on a small chert core fragment, one poor example on a Precambrian flake, one on fossil wood (fig. 44, g), and one on a convexly denticulated flake (fig. 44, f).

Burins, on concave truncations (1). A good example on a flake.

Burins, *plan* (1). A rather poor example of an atypical type of burin.

Burins, multiple on retouched truncations (1). A good example on fossil wood. Both burins are on the same concave truncation, one of them being *plan* (fig. 44, k).

Burins, multiple on snapped flakes (2). Two good examples on flakes are these burins which are made on opposite ends of the same snapped edge (fig. 44, c).

Burin—Denticulates (1). This is an oblique microdenticulate on a flake with a single blow burin at its distal end. The burin is poor, but the denticulation is fine and regular.

Burin—End-scrapers (2). One, on an agate primary flake fragment, has a well made end-scraper at one end and a transverse burin on a retouched notch at the other (fig. 44, d). The second piece is a primary chert flake with a wide convex end-scraper which has a burin *plan* on one edge (fig. 44, l).

Denticulate—Side-scrapers (1). A well made piece on a primary chert blade. Retouch is semi-steep, with both the scraping and denticulate edges well defined (fig. 43, k).

End-scrapers (8). These are generally poor. Retouch is normally marginal with irregular scraping edges on small flakes or blades. There are two end-scrapers on blades (fig. 43, h) and two on flakes. There are three mediocre, thin nose scrapers on flakes (fig. 43, g). Also there is one end-scraper on a large Precambrian flake.

Side-scrapers (5). There are three inverse side-scrapers: one concave and two convex (fig. 43,

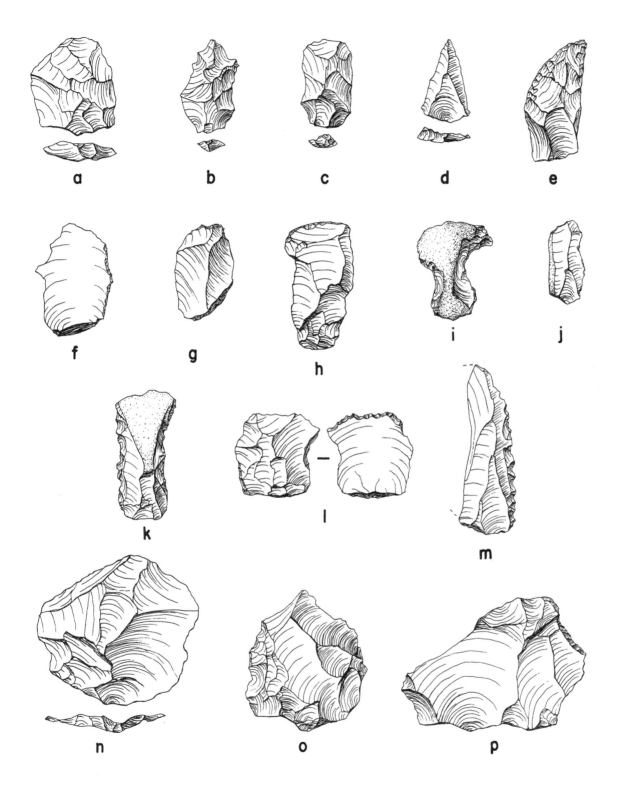

FIG. 43—Site 2004: a-c, n, Levallois flakes; d, Levallois point; e-f, side-scrapers; g-h, end-scrapers; i, strangled piece; j, cortex backed knife; k, denticulate—side-scraper; l-m, o, denticulates; p, truncation. 4/5 natural size.

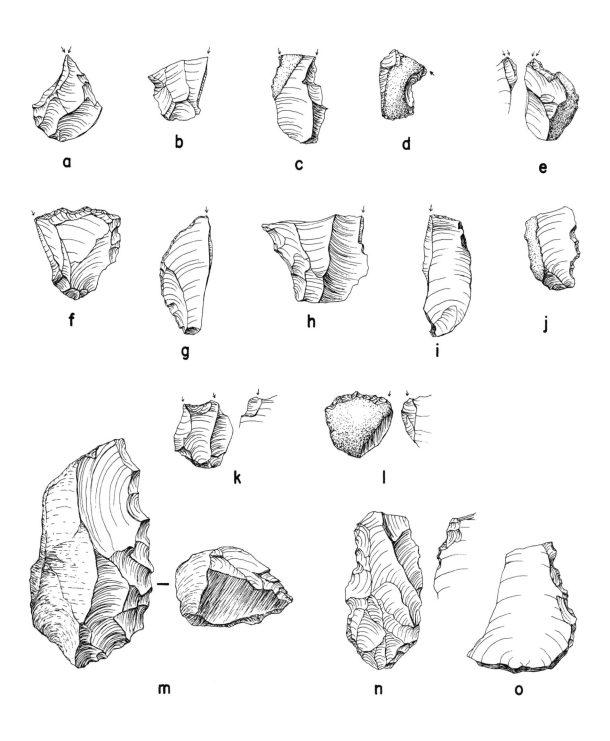

Fig. 44—Site 2004: a-c, e-i, k, burins; d, l, burin—end-scraper; j, m-o, denticulates. 4/5 natural size.

f). Retouch is either flat or marginal. There is also one straight side-scraper made by marginal retouch, and one convex example which has both inverse and flat obverse retouch on adjoining sections of the same edge (fig. 43, e). All scrapers are small and rather atypical.

Notched pieces (11). Notches are on various odd shaped flakes. There are three retouched micronotches, four retouched end micronotches, and three lateral macronotches made by percussion. None of the latter are over 1.5 cm. across.

Converging denticulates (1). A poor example with irregular teeth on a small, thin flake.

Transverse denticulates (9). These range from some large, generally well made examples (fig. 43, o) to some formed by marginal retouch (fig. 43, l).

Lateral denticulates (17). These include some of the best made examples (fig. 43, m), although most have irregular teeth (fig. 44, j, o).

Bilateral denticulates (2). Both are on quartz. One well made piece is alternately retouched, although the inversely retouched edge is only partially denticulated (fig. 44, n). The other is a poor example on a short flake.

Lateral and transverse denticulates (1). A large rough example on a thick Precambrian flake.

Core denticulates (1). This is somewhat atypical. The serration is irregular but mostly microdenticulate. It has been formed by stepped retouch, a technique not usual in the Khormusan (fig. 44, m).

Retouched flakes (19). Most of these flakes have small amounts of marginal retouch which verges on use retouch. A few are fragments with stronger retouch, but they are too small to be assigned to any other tool type.

Truncated pieces (5). There are four oblique truncations, one of which is on a large Precambrian flake (fig. 43, p). In addition, there is a convexly truncated cortex backed blade.

Cortex backed knives (5). All are small blades with cortex backing. Two are fossil wood. All show some use retouch (fig. 43, j).

Strangled pieces (1). A well made example on a primary chert flake (fig. 43, i).

Varia (2). A fragment of a quartz flake with bifacial retouch and a small fossil wood blade fragment with steep retouch along one edge.

CORE TYPOLOGY

	No.	%	Restricted %
Levallois flake	16	12.7	34.1
Levallois point	1	0.8	2.1
Nubian, Type I	2	1.6	4.2
Single platform, unfaceted	2	1.6	4.2
Single platform, faceted	16	12.7	34.1
Opposed platform	6	4.8	12.8
Discoidal	2	1.6	4.2
Globular	1	0.8	2.1
Bipolar	1	0.8	2.1
Unidentifiable	79	62.6	
	126	100.0	99.9

NOTES ON THE TYPOLOGY

Most cores are quite small. The larger examples are exclusively on Precambrian rock. Quartz is common and agate occurs in a higher percentage than at any other Khormusan site.

Levallois flake (16). These occur on all material except ferrocrete sandstone. All are small, ranging in size from 2.2 to 5.6 cm. in length. Of the sixteen, seven are unstruck. Some of these show very careful preparation and only very slightly convex upper surfaces. One excellent example is of quartz, a generally intractable material (fig. 45, g). Those on chert are usually less carefully prepared with little or no treatment of the undersurface (fig. 45, e).

Levallois point (1). A roughly prepared example on Precambrian rock.

Nubian, Type I (2). One fragmentary example and a highly unusual one on a chert pebble (fig. 45, a).

Single platform, unfaceted (2). These are small flake cores on chert pebbles.

Single platform, faceted (16). One of the most common types in the assemblage. An elaborate convex platform is prepared without any preparation of the upper surface of the core (fig. 45, b-c). In the majority of cases, flakes were struck from the cores, but occasionally blades were also removed. In one example, the core has had a flake removed perpendicularly to the main platform as if a new orientation were planned (fig. 45, d).

Opposed platform (6). These are all poor or atypical pieces. The one on quartz is rather unique as it almost approaches some form of wedge shaped tool (fig. 45, f).

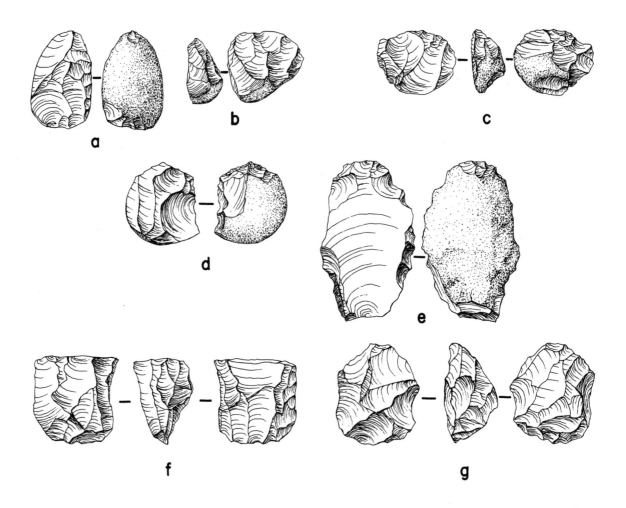

Fɪɢ. 45—Site 2004: a, Nubian Core, Type I; b-d, faceted, single platform cores; e, g, Levallois flake cores; f, opposed platform core. 4/5 natural size.

Discoidal (2). Two rather flat Precambrian cores which are among the largest in the sample, having diameters of about 5 cm. each.

Globular (1). The small example is of fossil wood.

Bipolar (1). This very small agate core is, perhaps, accidentally bipolar.

Unidentifiable (79). Most of these are fragmentary cores of chert or quartz which show no discernable pattern of flaking.

COMPARISON OF THE KHORMUSAN WITH OTHER INDUSTRIES

There are numerous industries with which the Khormusan could be compared. It is only meaningful, however, to deal with those which are generally contemporaneous with the Khormusan, or those undated industries from adjacent areas, which superficially appear to be similar.

The Khormusan is technologically characterized by, among other attributes, a dominant Levallois flake tradition. This is basically a technological trait, considered to be less affected by seasonal occupation or by varying environmental conditions than typological attributes. The one factor which may affect a Levallois technology is the availability of suitable raw materials. In a Levallois tradition, however, this may perhaps cut down the amount of Levallois preparation but should not, theoretically, eliminate it entirely. Therefore, those industries which have been called "Levalloisian" or "Epi-Levalloisian" would seem, at first glance, to warrant comparison with the Khormusan.

Use of the criteria of a strong Levallois tradition along with contemporaneity makes it necessary to deal with industries in Nubia, the southern Sudan, Egypt, and East Africa. In most cases, comparisons can only be made on a very general level. This is due to both the limited or incomplete publication of primary data for some industries and to small or poorly described samples for others. It is extremely uncommon to find complete type lists of tools in publication, and the description of debitage and cores is even more rare.

In the southern Sudan, the "industry" of Singa will be considered. In Egypt, those industries termed "Levalloisian" will be reviewed, with the exception of the Sebilian sequence which does not, in any way, even superficially resemble the Khormusan. As some comparisons have already been made between site ANW-3 and certain East African industries (Waechter, 1965, p. 144), these, too, will be considered.

Nubia

The most obvious place to begin comparisons is in Nubia. The basic problem concerns what connections the Khormusan has with other industries of the Second Cataract.

Chronologically, the Khormusan appears in Nubia between 30,000 B.C. and 25,000 B.C. and lasts until some time after 15,000 B.C. It fills the gap between the Nubian Middle Stone Age industries and those microlithic industries of the late Nubian Upper Stone Age and Nubian Late Stone Age. There are two industries which are, at least, partially synchronic with the Khormusan: the Halfan and the Gemaian.

The Halfan is of particular interest as there are radiocarbon dates from two sites which would tend to place a developed phase of the industry at about 17,000 B.C.: Site 2014 at 17, 200 B.C $\pm$ 375 years (WSU-332) and Site 8859 at 16,650 B.C. $\pm$ 550 years (WSU-318). These assemblages are about midway in the Halfan sequence, indicating that earlier Halfan assemblages are even

older if the dates are correct, perhaps as early as 18,000 B.C.

Therefore, some of the Khormusan development took place in Nubia at a time when another industry was also evolving there. Considering the extremely small area under consideration—a mere 50 km. along the central Nile—it is somewhat surprising how different the Halfan is from the Khormusan. These differences extend to all areas of study: the types of sites technology, and typology. It is impossible and quite out of place to describe the Halfan in detail here; a separate monograph is in preparation on the Halfan.[6] Table 9, however, will give a good idea of certain areas of difference, enough to show that the Halfan and Khormusan are distinctly separate traditions. The general developmental trends are also quite different. The Khormusan develops towards smaller tools but always those which are typical of the industry as a whole: Levallois flakes, burins, denticulates, etc. At the same time, there is a corresponding decline in the quality of tool manufacture. The Halfan, on the other hand, develops from a microflake industry, characterized by Halfan flakes and backed microflakes, to a true microblade industry with backed microblades as the dominant tool. On this basis alone, the Khormusan and the Halfan must be considered as belonging to discrete and unrelated traditions.

The same conclusion must be reached when considering the relationship between the Khormusan and the Gemaian. Although no radiocarbon dates are available for the Gemaian, it is found *in situ* in the base of the Sahaba formation;[7] that is, it perhaps overlaps in time with the end of the Khormusan. Again, on all levels of study, the Gemaian shows marked differences from the Khormusan. In terms of general development, the Gemaian changes into the Qadan, which is characterized by smaller tools, lunates, and truly thick convex side-scrapers. The Gemaian has a large number of retouched leaf-shaped points, a feature totally missing from the Khormusan, as shown in Table 9.

[6] A preliminary discussion of the Halfan appears in Wendorf, Shiner, and Marks, 1965, pp. xxvii-xxxi.

[7] Site 278 is now included in the Gemaian. While the Gemaian has not been fully reported, the stratigraphic position of 278 is clear (Wendorf, Shiner, and Marks, 1965, p. xvii).

TABLE 9

Comparison of Khormusan, Halfan, and Gemaian Attributes

ATTRIBUTES	KHORMUSAN	HALFAN: STAGE II	HALFAN: STAGE IV	GEMAIAN
General				
Site area	1,000 + sq. m.	c. 250 sq. m.	c. 250 sq. m.	c. 400 sq. m.
Hearths	Amorphous fire pits	Earth ovens	Earth ovens	None found
Site shape	Lineally oriented along Nile	Small, oval	Small, oval	Oval
Technology				
Raw materials	Numerous types, up to 23% chert	91.4 to 94.5% chert	96.8 to 98.3% chert	74 to 96% chert
Levallois Index	18.8 to 36.6	Less than 1	Less than 1	2 to 8.6
Blade Tool Index	Less than 1	12.8 to 16.0	70.8 to 71.7	7.7 to 21.6
Microlithic Tool Index	17 to 49	81.2 to 84.5	95.8 to 96.2	36.0 to 47.4
Typology[1]				
Burin Index (restricted)	21.9 to 53.6	6.2 to 6.5	1.1 to 1.5	1.3 to 4.8
Denticulate Index (restricted)	17.8 to 31.8	7.0	1.5 to 2.0	13.1 to 26.2
Halfa flakes	None	52.5 to 56.0%	0.5 to 1.4%	None
Backed pieces	None	3.4 to 8.9%	82.5 to 83.8%	0.0 to16.2%
Leaf shaped points	None	None	None	8.7 to 39.7%
Thick Side-scrapers	None	None	None	1.0 to 19.0%

[1] Site 34A is not included as it is barely within the industry and predates the Halfan and Gemaian.

At this time, it appears that during the later part of the Dibeira-Jer and the earlier part of the Sahaba formations, there were three typologically and technologically distinct lithic industries centered around the Second Cataract.

SOUTHERN SUDAN

Although extensive prehistoric research has been carried out in Sudanese Nubia, very little is known about the prehistory of the rest of the Sudan. It is almost 1,200 km. from Wadi Halfa, in Nubia, to the southern border of the Sudan. Within this area, only three prehistoric sites have been extensively excavated and published: Early Khartoum (Arkell, 1949a); Shaheinab (Arkell, 1953); and Khor Abu Anga (Arkell, 1949b). Both Early Khartoum and Shaheinab are Neolithic in age and thus fall outside any possibly meaningful comparisons with the Khormusan. Khor Abu Anga contains Acheulean and Sangoan/Lupemban industries and also falls well outside the time range of the Khormusan.

A few other sites have been briefly visited and there are occasional short reports dealing with them. One of these is at Singa, south of Khartoum. The "industry" from Singa has been described as having "Levalloisian affinities" and so must be viewed for possible connections with the Khormusan.

There are only two primary publications on the site: one is a study of the Singa calvarium by A. S. Woodward (1938), and the other is a discussion of a recent visit to the site by A. J. Arkell (1949b). On the other hand, information concerning the lithic artifacts and stratigraphy comes from Alimen (1957) and Arkell (1949b). This information is, at best, disappointing.

The site of Singa is of interest due to the find of a human calvarium of dubious affinities (Cole, 1963, p. 170). The calvarium was found in derived position (Alimen, 1957, p. 342) along with some stone artifacts, presumably also derived. While the calvarium was derived, it was felt that the layer in question was perhaps of "ancient Nile alluviums" (Alimen, 1957, p. 342). Thus, while not dated accurately, the artifacts could be from the period of the Khormusan. They could be earlier, or even later. In any case they have been reported to have "Levalloisian affinities."

The artifacts themselves also pose something of a problem. Arkell, on a visit to the site, found no artifacts *in situ* and only one flake on the surface in the general vicinity of the site (Arkell, 1949b, p. 46). Alimen, on the other hand, reports, in reference to the Singa calvarium, that "the associated industry consisted of flakes (without any retouching) of Levalloisian affinity . . ." Alimen, 1957, p. 342). On the basis of this unnumbered series of unretouched flakes, S. Cole writes, "the skull was associated with a rather indeterminate industry that may be Proto-Stillbay . . ." (Cole, 1963, p. 170).

These references make it somewhat difficult to compare the "Singa industry" with the Khormusan. Even assuming that some or perhaps many of the flakes mentioned by Alimen were Levallois, it is still quite out of the question to give such a collection an industry status. Levallois flakes occur in all Middle Stone Age industries as well as in many Late Stone Age industries both in East Africa and on the Nile.

Thus, in actuality, nothing is known of the artifacts found at Singa, except that they were in the same layer as the calvarium (although not necessarily of the same age) and that some of the flakes may be Levallois. Whether of age or typology, comparison with the Khormusan is obviously out of the question. Therefore, there are no sites in the Sudan, south of Nubia, which fit either the time range or the typology of the Khormusan. It must be emphasized that this is probably due to the fact that very little prehistoric research has been done in the Sudan.

EGYPT

In Egypt, there are a number of industries which are either broadly contemporaneous with, or are superficially similar to, the very early Khormusan. The later Khormusan, from 21,000 B.C. onward, seems not to have any direct connections with Egypt. This is based on the very important part burins play in the Khormusan typology. Burins are very rare at Paleolithic sites in Egypt, with the exception of a single site near Nag Hammadi (Vignard, 1920). These burins, however, are on blades and are felt to be of Predynastic Age (Alimen, 1957, p. 101).

Therefore, any connections with industries in Egypt will have to rest either with assemblages which are contemporaneous with the Khormusan, Site 34A, or with those which may be ancestral to it.

To date, only a single industry appears to be possibly connected in any way with the Khormusan, the Levalloisian. The Levalloisian poses something of a problem. The industry is firmly entrenched in the literature, but its typological and technological basis must be regarded as tenuous at best.

Levalloisian artifacts have been reported all along the Nile (Sandford and Arkell, 1933), in the Faiyum Depression (Caton-Thompson and Gardner, 1934), and at Kharga Oasis (Caton-Thompson, 1952). In most areas, no more than isolated flakes or cores have been found. Along the Nile, there is not one recorded example of a sizable Levalloisian assemblage. At Kharga Oasis, however, eight sites were found *in situ*, six of which are considered Lower Levalloisian and two, Upper Levalloisian.

The Levalloisian of Kharga Oasis has not been firmly dated. The sites have been placed into the geological sequence of the Oasis, however, and a paleoclimatic history of the Oasis has been reconstructed from the geological formations (Caton-Thompson, 1952, pp. 14-21). On the basis of this history, the Levalloisian, from the end of the Second Pluvial at Kharga, has been correlated with Wurm I of the European glacial sequence, via a correlation with the Mount Carmel chronology (Caton-Thompson, 1952, p. 20).

If it is possible to accept this rather involved series of correlations,[8] the Levalloisian then dates at least prior to 30,000 B.C. and, conceivably, could be ancestral to the Khormusan.

The two-fold division of the Levalloisian into Lower and Upper is based both on stratigraphic position and on certain typological observations. While there is little question as to the relative stratigraphy, the typology is another matter. The Lower Levalloisian at Kharga is based on six sites. The total artifact sample consists of 43 cores, 43 flakes, 2 retouched tools, and a small amount of waste material, no one site having

---

[8] Recent radiocarbon dates from et Tabun in the Carmel, 37,750 B.C ± 800 years (GRN-2534) and 38,950 B.C. ±1,000 years (GRN-2729) (Garrod, 1962) indicate contemporaneity of the Levalloiso-Mousterian with Wurm III rather than with Wurm I.

more than a total of 28 cores, flakes, and tools (Caton-Thompson, 1952, p. 144). At the present stage of prehistoric studies, it is not necessary to comment further on the validity of such a sample as a basis for a lithic industry.

Additional scattered finds of Lower Levalloisian flakes and cores have been made on the Nile in association with a series of terraces. The question of these materials will be discussed later. It need only be said here that all finds are isolated and do not represent meaningful assemblages.

The Upper Levalloisian has a somewhat firmer footing. While found only at two sites in Kharga, the samples are larger and average 150 artifacts per site (Caton-Thompson, 1952, p. 143). The Upper Levalloisian contains many ovoid and discoidal cores, plus a very few triangular forms. Also, there is an unstated number of Levallois flakes and blades. Flakes are reported to have a high Faceting Index (Caton-Thompson, 1952, pp. 20, 142).

Typologically, the number of reported retouched tools is small but the illustrations show a number of tools which are unrecognized in the type lists presented in the Kharga Oasis study. These include converging and simple sidescrapers (Caton-Thompson, 1952: pl. 72, nos. 1, 4, 5, 6); Mousterian points (pl. 69, no. 1; pl. 72, no. 3); denticulates (pl. 68, no. 8); and a cortex backed knife and a pseudo-Levallois point (pl. 68, nos. 3, 4). A number of borers were also found (Caton-Thompson, 1952, p. 97).

A series of measurements of cores and flakes to help define the technological limits of the Levalloisian was also presented, but the samples are so small—rarely exceeding 20 pieces—that they are of no significance.

Certain tentative comparisons between the upper Levalloisian and the earliest stage of the Khormusan may be made with this concrete data, little as it may be. It is, of course, recognized that all specific comparisons made below are only as good as the data available from Kharga Oasis.

Points of technological similarity are as follows:

1. Both appear to have a dominant Levallois technology.

2. Levallois cores at both tend toward oval forms, although triangular forms (Levallois point cores?) occur as well.

3. Faceting Indices are high at both; higher than normally would be expected in the Nubian Middle Stone Age.

The extent of the Levallois Index cannot be judged for the Upper Levalloisian. Technologically, this is a vital factor in judging possible connections. On the other hand, that technological data available from Kharga do not seem to differ in any significant way from the early Khormusan.

Typologically, both are dominated by sidescrapers. On the other hand, 34A contains burins and strangled pieces, but lacks Mousterian points and borers. Thus, there are certain differences in the presence or absence of tool types. As the sample for the Upper Levalloisian is so small, there is no reason to assume that the total range of tools of the Upper Levalloisian was found.

In short, it is conceivable that the Upper Levalloisian is either ancestral to, or is contemporary with, the Khormusan since it shows possible generic links. Unfortunately, the available data from Kharga do not permit more definite conclusions.

The Levalloisian material reported from the Nile terraces must be totally disregarded. A large number of scattered finds have been reported and brought together by Caton-Thompson (1946). Miss Caton-Thompson relies heavily on the work of Sandford and Arkell in assigning these finds to specific Nile terraces (Caton-Thompson, 1946, p. 83).

It is quite impossible to go into the whole problem of Sandford and Arkell's interpretation of the Nile terraces (1933, 1934), however, it is now apparent that they were almost totally incorrect in naming their higher platforms terraces (Solecki, 1963, p. 79; Butzer and Hansen, 1965, p. 82), and in their dating of the lower terraces (Butzer and Hansen, 1965, p. 81). Correlation between Sandford and Arkell's terraces and the recent results attained by Butzer, Hansen, de Heinzelin, Said, Paepe, and others is almost impossible owing to the lack of excavated profiles in the earlier work.

Artifacts found by Sandford and Arkell in their 3 to 4 m. and 8 to 9 m. terraces termed Levalloisian by Caton-Thompson (1946, p. 83) may be Khormusan or may merely be derived Nubian Middle Stone Age artifacts. It is quite impossible to tell.

SUB-SAHARAN AFRICA

The time range of the Khormusan, about 25,000 B.C. to about 15,000 B.C. corresponds broadly with that of two major Sub-Saharan lithic traditions, the Stillbay and the Lupemban. The Lupemban is characterized by core tools, totally missing in the Khormusan. They seem to have been an adaptation to a forest environment (Clark, 1963, p. 210). Thus, there is no need to compare it with the Khormusan. On the other hand, the Stillbay shows rather gross similarities, at least technologically, and it has already been claimed that at least one Khormusan site shows more than superficial relationship to it. One suggestion is that the assemblage from ANW-3 is developing toward Stillbay and perhaps might be considered to belong to "the Stillbay group" (Waechter, 1965, p. 144). This reasoning was based on the presence of a single, unifacially retouched Stillbay-like point and a dominant Levallois technology (Waechter, 1965, p. 143).

As tentative as this suggestion may have been, serious objections to it must be taken, on both general and specific grounds. Site ANW-3 and the other sites which constitute the Khormusan are situated around the Second Cataract, just south of the Egyptian border. That is, they are well over 1,000 mi. north of the nearest claimed Stillbay site. As has been mentioned, no comparable sites are known within the whole of the Sudan or in the border areas of adjacent countries. Thus, in terms of the reported distribution of Stillbay, the Khormusan lies far away, totally isolated by an enormous area which is unknown archaeologically. This in itself does not, a priori, exclude the possibility that ANW-3 (by extension, the whole Khormusan) belongs within "the Stillbay group." It would, however, seem to demand extremely careful consideration and ample specific evidence. Only after detailed comparisons might it be acceptable to enlarge so radically the Stillbay area on the basis of a single isolated site.

Quite apart from its application to ANW-3, the term Stillbay poses something of a problem.

Stillbay has been reported from the Harrar to South Africa and ranges in time from at least 30,000 B.C. to about 9,000 B.C.[9] Twenty thousand years and many thousands of square miles seem to be somewhat too large a time-space unit for a single, typologically unified lithic industry. However, since it has been reported to cover so long a time and so extensive an area, it is necessary to look at its definition and see how it might be applied to the Khormusan.

The Stillbay has been defined as an industry adapted to savanna and grasslands, characterized by "light cutting, piercing and projectile tools of stone" (Clark, 1964, p. 177).

More specifically, the Stillbay seems to be recognized by the presence of two traits: both bifacial and unifacial pressure flaked points and a developed Levallois technology. However, a few small bifaces also occasionally occur (Waechter, 1965, p. 143). On the negative side, burins are exceedingly rare, and blades do not occur until a relatively late stage of development (Waechter, 1965, p. 143).

As there appear to be no complete type lists available for Stillbay assemblages, it is very difficult to judge just how similar any two assemblages are, or whether, in fact, there is even a true distributional or overall typological continuity to the Stillbay.

In terms of the recognized Stillbay typology, one must admit that certain traits considered to be diagnostic are shared by industries now considered to be generically unrelated, particularly the dominant Levallois technology. Strong Levallois tradition occurs in almost every African industry during the Middle Stone Age, and even during the First Intermediate Period. In North Africa are found the Levalloiso-Mousterian and the Aterian. In East and South Africa is the Stillbay; and in the Congo and Angola is the Sangoan/Lupemban—all of which have been reported to be strongly Levallois in flake production. Along the Nile and in the Oasis, the "Levalloisian" and now the Khormusan also have important Levallois elements. Therefore, in itself, the presence of a Levallois technology is not

---

[9] Stillbay has been dated at 31,000 B.C. at Malewi Gorge and a late local variant at Petersberg to 9,600 B.C. (Clark, 1964, p. 177; Howell and Bourliere, 1963, p. 629).

diagnostic of any one industrial tradition. It is, in fact, no more than a technique of flake production, occurring in varying degrees in unrelated industries, and seemingly in vogue throughout all of Africa for a very long period.

In terms of specific tool types, the Stillbay is noted for its unifacial and bifacial points, a few small bifaces, and a paucity of burins. Burins, however, are rare or absent in many African Middle Stone Age industries, making their absence questionable as a specific industrial indicator. Small bifaces occur in the Fauresmith as well as Stillbay and form, perhaps, a typological link although their relative occurrence in the two traditions is markedly different. Thus, only bifacial and unifacial retouched points remain as unique diagnostic tools. Even these, however, are not solely restricted to the Stillbay as they also occur at some Magosian sites. However, if we accept a combination of many retouched points, a few small bifaces, a paucity of burins, and a dominant Levallois technology as a very general typological definition of the Stillbay (of perhaps many Stillbays, in the Mousterian sense), we are faced with the fact that the Khormusan does not begin to fit this definition (table 10).

Specifically, at ANW-3—that site used by Waechter for his observations—the typology shows little in common with the definition of the Stillbay. It is true that Levallois flake production dominates the technology and that Levallois flakes are an essential element of the assemblage. As pointed out above, however, this by itself has little comparative value. While burins are rare in Stillbay, they are the single most common tool at ANW-3 and account for just over half of all retouched tools. Small bifaces are totally absent, not only from ANW-3 but also from all other Khormusan sites. On the other hand, denticulates are numerous in the Khormusan. At Site ANW-3 they account for over 16 per cent of all retouched tools. Denticulates, however, seem to be rare in the Stillbay, although they occur to some extent in the Somaliland Stillbay (Clark, 1954, p. 191). It is already quite apparent that the Khormusan, and Site ANW-3 in particular, is very different from the Stillbay.

The major, and perhaps most important, typological trait of the Stillbay is the retouched point, either bifacial or unifacial. It is not only diagnostic due to its mere presence but also due to the number found in each Stillbay assemblage. If the site of Porc-Épic is any indication, they tend to be quite numerous (Bruiel, 1951). Excavations at Site ANW-3 recovered over 550 retouched tools and Levallois flakes. Of these, only one was a retouched point. All Khormusan sites produced over 1,700 retouched tools and Levallois flakes, yet only one unifacial and one bifacial point were found among them. On the basis of these occurrences, one can hardly consider retouched points significant, much less diagnostic, in the Khormusan.

It is true that in the Khormusan there are numerous converging denticulates—in effect, denticulated points. Some converging denticulates of this type occur at Hargeisa in the Lower Somaliland Stillbay, but they are always asymmetric (Clark, 1954, p. 193).

In summary, it is clear that while the Khormusan and the Stillbay both contain an important Levallois technology, typologically they appear to be quite distinct. On this basis, plus the great distance separating the Khormusan from any Stillbay site, it must be recognized that there is no justification for considering the Stillbay and Khormusan to be generically related. At best, they converge in gross appearance, because of similar technological habits; although in specific adaptation as seen through their lithic typologies, they differ greatly.

CONCLUSIONS

While the foregoing sections have emphasized the unique features of the Khormusan as compared with contemporary industries in adjacent areas, there has been no intent to overstress this point. Without question, the Khormusan is typologically distinct and warrants a new industry designation. It has been defined temporally, typologically, and distributionally. It is assumed, however, that with more archaeological work in immediately adjacent areas the distribution of the Khormusan will be expanded. The same may be said for the temporal limits of the Khormusan, which may be wider than the evidence now indicates. On the other hand, all Khormusan assemblages studied so far show excellent unity, with change, in both their typology and technology.

Yet, with the exception of the importance and variety of burins, the Khormusan has much in common with other contemporary industries in Africa.

Of prime importance is the presence and advanced development of the Levallois technique of flake production—a widespread trait throughout Africa at this time. Another technological feature of the Khormusan shared by many other industries is the paucity of true blades and the emphasis on flakes both in primary production and as blanks for making finished tools.

Typologically, the Khormusan lacks heavy core tools, a trait shared by the industries of the Nile and of East Africa. Yet, the Khormusan also lacks the distinct points of the East African industries and the backed tools of the later West African and Sebilian industries. The Khormusan is specialized typologically. This takes the form of a heavy emphasis on two tool types, burins and denticulates.

The differences seen in the tool kit of the Khormusan as compared with the Stillbay or the Sebilian industries of later times must reflect a different way in which the Khormusan people utilized their environment. While all evidence of non-material culture, by the very nature of archaeological evidence, must be indirect, it is still possible to reconstruct, to some extent, the life of the Khormusan people.

Such a reconstruction is based on a number of observable material remains, including site situations, typological content, internal distribution of artifacts within sites, utilization of raw materials, artifact size, faunal remains, etc.

The first step in reconstructing the life of the Khormusan peoples is the recognition of the environment in which they lived. Evidence from site distribution and from faunal remains gives a rather clear picture of the environment of Nubia from 25,000 B.C. until about 15,000 B.C. Of primary importance was the Nile, higher than at present, still fluctuating, but perhaps not as much as today. From fish remains it appears that the temperature of the Nile was about the same then as it is today, and all fish remains were of types which are still present. Along the banks of the Nile we might expect to find more of the reeds and vegetation typical of that region, but the relatively recent intensive collection of firewood,

the grazing of goats, and the irrigation of the alluvium have tended to displace most natural vegetation from the bulk of the alluvium. The presence of Hippo remains indicates that there was, at times, fairly quiet water, perhaps as shallow bays or swamps in the vicinity of the Second Cataract, though there is no evidence that these were always present or extensive when present.

The major difference between the environment during late Pleistocene times and today would seem to rest in the area adjacent to the Nile alluvium. Faunal remains of Equus, Hartebeest, and Bos indicate the presence of a savanna in areas which are today fully desert. Yet from site distribution, it would appear that there was relatively little surface water away from the Nile, preventing prolonged occupation of the savanna by Khormusan peoples.

Thus, during the late Pleistocene, the area of the Second Cataract included two micro-environments: the heavily vegetated fringe of the Nile, including the Nile itself, which provided a wealth of plants, fish, and small animals; and a savanna of unknown extent, where numerous large herbivores lived and could be hunted. Remains at Khormusan sites indicate that both of these micro-environments were utilized.

On the basis of internal artifact distribution within the very large Khormusan sites, it appears that the Khormusan peoples were organized into small bands. These bands were restricted in their wandering, returning time after time to the same immediate areas for their camp sites. From the artifacts, however, there is no indication that choice of any particular locality was governed by special seasonal activity; the same tools occur in much the same proportions at all sites. How restricted their wanderings were is not known, but there is no question that they stayed close to the Nile, as no Khormusan sites have been found beyond the Nile alluvium.

There is ample evidence that the Khormusan peoples knew well the area of the Second Cataract. This may be seen in their utilization of lithic materials. They traveled to the jebels, back from the Nile, to obtain ferrocrete sandstone. They knew the source of quartzites in the bleak Precambrian badlands and took much care in the selection of exotic examples. They were also aware of the limited occurrences of fossil wood in the Eastern and Western Deserts, and they slowly developed a working knowledge of the chert and agate pebbles brought downstream by the Nile.

Faunal evidence shows that the Khormusans were hunters and fishers, fully as capable of successfully killing the large herbivores of the savanna as of the smaller rodents and birds of the Nile edge. They were not, however, specialized hunters but killed whatever they could from Hippo to birds. At most sites, fishing seems to have played a relatively unimportant part in the economy of the people, but fish did on occasion make up the bulk of the nonvegetal diet, as seen at Site 2004.

No vegetal remains have been found at Khormusan sites. This in itself does not mean that the Khormusan peoples were not gatherers as well as hunters. There is, however, indication by the lack of grinding stones that whatever was collected was not ground. In fact, to tell what part the gathering of vegetable matter played in their diet is quite impossible.

There is little question, however, that the Khormusan peoples used wood and perhaps reeds, and used them extensively. The evidence for this is indirect but fairly sure. Burins are the dominant tool of the Khormusan, yet there is little evidence of their use on bone, although literally thousands of bones were recovered during excavations. In fact, only two bone tools were found, showing how minor a role they played in the Khormusan.

If burins were not normally used on bone, what then was their purpose? They could have been used only on wood and reeds, both of which we assume to have been readily available along the Nile. While by process of elimination it is possible to say that the burins were used on wood and reeds, it is not so simple a matter to suggest exactly what wooden and reed objects were made. There is no direct evidence for any wood or reed structures, and the seemingly transitory nature of the hearth areas within sites gives weight to the idea that, if the Khormusan peoples built structures at all, they were very flimsy—perhaps no more than wind shelters.

We must assume that the hunting tools were mostly made of wood. The stone material gives no indication of light projectile points or barbs which might have been used as arrows, implying that the Khormusan peoples used spears. These might have been tipped with large denticulate points or with unretouched Levallois points. The size of the denticulate points, however, would indicate that in most cases they were no more than converging denticulate scrapers, while Levallois points are quite rare in the assemblages. Thus, it is possible that spears were not usually tipped with stone or that stone tips were no more than irregular, unretouched flakes or flake fragments.

Smaller wooden weapons such as throwing sticks and clubs may well have been made, but there is no evidence of them. It is assumed, however, that while they would have been capable of killing small animals, at least a spear would have been required in the hunting of the larger herbivores.

Fishing was another occupation that called for special tools. It may have been carried out with simple spears in the shallow pools of the Cataract, or perhaps traps of wood and reeds were used. While there is no direct evidence of either system, the number of burins in the Khormusan implies a wood- and/or reed-working industry far in advance of the limited technological skills needed to make simple spears for hunting and fishing.

The suggestion is made that the emphasis on burins reflects an intensive use of the special wood and reed material available along the Nile, rather than any adaptation for use on normal savanna vegetation. This might well give a framework for explaining the relative importance of burins at this period along the Nile as compared with their paucity in the savanna areas of East Africa.

The presence of many denticulates in the Khormusan may be viewed two ways: they might have been used for cutting wood and reeds, or they might have been used for scraping skins. While they would have been poor for final cleaning of skins, they certainly would be very appropriate for removing the tough sinews and fats which adhere to the inside of skins. The rarity of scrapers implies that while skins were processed, true scrapers were not extensively used. It is altogether probable, however, that denticulates served both as cutting tools and rough

TABLE 10
COMPARISON OF STILLBAY AND KHORMUSAN TRAITS
(Shading shows areas of major difference)

TRAITS	STILLBAY	KHORMUSAN
Levallois Technology	high	high
Flakes	dominant	dominant
Blades	rare	rare
Pressure Flaking	present	absent
Unifacial Points	numerous	one example
Bifacial Points	numerous	one example
Small Bifaces	present	absent
Burins	very rare	abundant
Denticulates	rare ?	abundant
Scrapers	rare	rare
Backed Tools	rare	absent

scrapers, equally adaptable for work on wood, reed, or flesh.

The stone material also indicates that wood must have been used for hafting of certain tools, particularly in the later stages of the Khormusan. End-scrapers, when they occur, and most burins are very small—too small to have been effectively used held by hand. Hafting may well have been accomplished by first making a groove in the end of a piece of wood with a burin and then fixing the end-scraper or microlithic burin into the groove with the sap of the Acacia tree. This is most common in the savanna and semi-desert which borders on the Nile today only a few hundred kilometers south of the Second Cataract and is still found in small numbers as far north as the Egyptian border, if not farther north.

In addition to purely technological and economic uses of raw materials by the Khormusan peoples, we also see some evidence of "luxury" pursuits. Every Khormusan site contained some ground hematite. It is assumed that this was used for body decoration. As no burials were found,

it is impossible to say whether the coloring was meant for the living or the dead, yet it may well be that it was used for both. Hematite is only found at the base of Jebel el-Sahaba, which is over 15 km. from the Khormusan sites near the Second Cataract. This indicates that its source was known and exploited, even by bands who were encamped quite some distance from its source.

In short, we arrive at a picture of the Khormusan peoples which shows them to be small bands of hunters and fishers who indulged in limited wandering but who had a definite sense of territoriality, knowing and extensively exploiting both the mineral and animal resources available to them along the central Nile. They entered the area of the Second Cataract about 25,000 B.C., already possessing a basic, if undeveloped Khormusan tool kit, and were forced out of the area by the expansion of more northernly peoples about 15,500 B.C. From where they came and to where they went can only be guessed until more of the archaeology of the adjacent areas is known.

THE HALFAN INDUSTRY
Anthony E. Marks
(southern methodist university)

INTRODUCTION

DURING THE 1961-1962 field season of the Combined Prehistoric Expedition, R. Fairbridge discovered a surface concentration of microlithic tools north of Wadi Halfa, Sudan. Prominent among the artifacts were backed microblades, tools which were unknown up to that time in the area of the Second Cataract. Subsequently, other sites with numerous microblades were found, including some which also contained flakes from highly specialized prepared cores. The relationship between these sites was not immediately apparent, and it was only after intensive excavation and study that industrial unity and chronological sequence were discovered.

The industry represented by these sites was typologically unlike any in the Second Cataract area and was also quite different from all published sites from anywhere along the Nile. This newly discovered industry was given the name Halfan after the town of Wadi Halfa in the Sudan.[1] In order to achieve maximum consistency in terminology, the typologically new specialized flakes were named Halfa flakes, and the cores from which they came were named Halfa cores.

Within the concession area of the Combined Prehistoric Expedition in Sudan, six Halfan sites were located and either systematically collected or excavated. The newly discovered Halfan is important for two reasons: it documents the earliest microblade industry in Africa, and it also illustrates a clear technological transition from a microflake industry to a true microblade industry.

The six Halfan sites were excavated over a period of three field seasons by various personnel. As can be seen in Table 1, the excavation of Halfan sites was very much a joint effort.

During laboratory analysis of the artifacts,

TABLE 1
HISTORY OF WORK AT HALFAN SITES

Sites	Excavator(s)	Date
1020	J. Guichard and J. Waechter (surface collection)	12/1962
	P. Evans (excavation)	11/1963
1018	A. Marks (excavation)	12/1963 2/1965
443	J. Guichard (surface collection and test pit)	12/1962
	A. Marks (excavation)	11-12/1963
624	W. McHugh (surface collection and test pit)	2/1964
2014	J. Shiner (collection)	2/1965
1028	J. Shiner (excavation)	3/1964

three reports were issued which mentioned Halfan material (Waechter, 1965; Wendorf, Shiner, and Marks, 1965; and Wendorf et al., 1965).

Although all publications have the same date, the first report was based solely on the surface collection made in 1962 from Site 1020.[2] This report mistakenly grouped Site 1020 with unrelated sites, under the term Epi-Levallois (Waechter, 1965). Perhaps because of an insufficient sample, the Halfa flakes were not recognized as being distinct from simple Levallois flakes.

The term Halfan, as applied to this material, was first suggested in Wendorf, Shiner, and Marks (1965, p. xxviii), and the general typological attributes of the Halfan industry were discussed. These initial observations have been only slightly modified in this paper, although much more is now known concerning stratigraphy, detailed typology, and chronology.

This current study represents a final report. Therefore, each site has been described as fully as possible, relationships between sites are dis-

---

[1] The names Halfan, for the industry, and Halfa flake and core for specific typological forms were decided upon jointly by the Combined Prehistoric Expedition and H. Erwin of the University of Colorado Expedition during the 1963-1964 field season.

[2] This report (Waechter, 1965) referred to Site 1020 as 443A.

cussed, and comparisons are made with other industries in Nubia and adjacent areas. An attempt has been made to illustrate as many Halfan tools as possible. Certain sites, however, considered type sites for their stages of development have received greater coverage and illustrations than others. The illustrations, drawn by Miss M. B. Stokes and Mrs. G. D. Addington, add appreciably to the typological descriptions.

TYPOLOGICAL AND TECHNOLOGICAL STUDIES

While the Halfan seems to have been in the area of the Second Cataract for only a relatively short time, major typological and technological changes took place. So that these could be documented, it has been necessary to rely on a very detailed typology of both tools and debitage.

A series of technological indices has been devised in order to facilitate comparisons. They include the following:

$$\text{Microlithic Tool Index} = \frac{\text{total number of tools measuring 30 mm. or less x 100}}{\text{total number of tools}}$$

$$\text{Chert Tool Index} = \frac{\text{total number of tools made on chert x 100}}{\text{total number of tools}}$$

$$\text{Chert Core Index} = \frac{\text{total number of cores on chert x 100}}{\text{total number of cores}}$$

$$\text{Flake Tool Index} = \frac{\text{total number of flake tools x 100}}{\text{total number of tools}}$$

$$\text{Blade Tool Index} = \frac{\text{total number of blade tools x 100}}{\text{total number of tools}}$$

$$\text{Core Tool Index} = \frac{\text{total number of core tools x 100}}{\text{total number of tools}}$$

In addition to these, a number of other observations will be given as percentages in the summaries of each site report and in later sections.

DEFINITIONS

Within this report, there are references to a number of tool and core types. Many of these are well known, defined by other workers (de Heinzelin, 1962; de Sonneville-Bordes and Perrot, 1954, 1955, 1956a, 1956b; Bordes, 1961). On the other hand, there are a few types which have not been previously described. These will be defined below. In addition, there are a number of terms which may be unfamiliar in English, which are not commonly used, or which have been used to mean different things by different workers. These too, are defined below.

Retouch

Obverse or normal retouch: Small flakes which are removed from a flake or blade to regulate a working edge. Their flake scars are present on the dorsal surface of the retouched piece.

Inverse retouch: Small flakes which are removed from a flake or blade to regulate a working edge. Their flake scars are present on the ventral surface of the retouched piece.

Flat retouch: Retouch which results in flake scars which are almost parallel to the surface of the retouched piece. The scars are usually short and broad, with ill defined negative bulbs of percussion. Flat retouch may be obverse or inverse. In the Halfan, it is more commonly inverse.

Marginal retouch: Retouch which is normally weak. The flake scars do not encroach much upon the original shape of the retouched piece.

Backing: Retouch which is steep and has a blunting effect on a lateral edge or edges of a flake or blade. A backed edge has flake scars which are perpendicular to the plane of the flake or blade. The backing need not greatly alter the original shape of the backed piece.

Truncation: The same as backing but the retouched area is either perpendicular or oblique to the long axis of the flake or blade. Truncations may be basal or distal, and convex, straight, or concave.

Debitage, Debris, and Size

Debris: All chips, core trimming flakes, heavily burned fragments; that is, those lithic artifacts which were not considered as potentially useful for tool manufacture.

Debitage: In this paper debitage refers to all flakes and blades which could have been used in tool manufacture but were not.

Primary flakes: A form of debitage. Flakes which are the first to be removed from a piece of weathered rock; normally Nile pebble in the Halfan. Their dorsal surface is at least half covered by cortex or other evidence of an unmodified, weathered surface. In French, these are termed *éclats d'épannelage* (de Heinzelin, 1962, p. 13).

Microblades: Blades which are 30 mm. or less in length.

Microflakes: Flakes which are 30 mm. or less along both the long and short axes.

Micronotch: A notch which is less than 5 mm. across. If more than 5 mm. across it is a macronotch (de Heinzelin, 1962, p. 39).

Microdenticulate: A serrated edge where the individual teeth are less than 5 mm. apart. If they are more than 5 mm. apart, they are referred to as being macrodenticulate (de Heinzelin, 1962, p. 40).

Halfa Flakes and Cores

As Halfa flakes and their associated cores are not only newly recognized types but also appear in significant quantity at Halfan sites, as full a definition as possible will be given below.

The technological bases of a new tool type either must be due to a radically new approach in working stone or must involve a recombination and modification of already existing techniques and forms. In this instance the technological process of manufacture of the Halfa flake and its final typological form represent a recombination and modification of a series of technological processes which were well known along the Nile.

Because of a large sample, it has been possible to define typologically the Halfa flake and to follow every step of its production.

The raw material normally used was a small, roundish Nile River pebble of chert or agate. Chert was by far most common; at Site 1018 chert accounted for 96.6 per cent of the Halfa cores and 96.1 per cent of the Halfa flakes.

The technological process involved a number of distinct steps which followed in a predetermined order. If any step was not successfully completed, the core was usually abandoned without further work. The first step called for the placing of an unfaceted or straight faceted platform on one end of the pebble (fig. 1, a). This platform was usually formed at an angle between 50° and 75° to the flaking surface. Out of 40 finished cores at 1018—some successfully, many unsuccessfully struck, in the final step—one has

an angle of over 75°, while only three have angles under 50°.

If a satisfactory platform was achieved, a series of parallel or subparallel microblades were struck from this platform (fig. 1, b). If poorly executed, they would be microflakes. These numbered anywhere from three, in the case of microflakes, to seven, where the microblades were well struck. The most common number was six microblades per core. These microblades were normally less than 10 mm. in length, although some might be longer.

Prior to the removal of the microblades, a wide dihedral faceted platform was formed on the other end of the pebble, opposite the original platform (fig. 1, b). This second platform was normally at an angle between 60° and 80°. A number of flakes were then removed from this platform, stripping the cortex left on the upper core surface (fig. 1, c). Occasionally, a few flakes were also struck from the lateral edges of the core, adjacent to the dihedral platform, both to straighten the sides and to remove cortex from the upper surface. The effect of this flaking was to give the upper surface a slightly convex shape and to give it the appearance of a Levallois core on one half and that of a microblade core on the other.

If this step was successfully completed, the dihedral platform was then transformed into a convex faceted platform by fine retouch.

The next flake struck was taken from the newly formed convex faceted platform. This flake was normally short and wide, removing most flake scars from the upper surface. The bulb of percussion was pronounced, leaving a deep reverse bulb on the flaked surface. The flake, however, normally did not encroach upon the microblade flake scars on the far half of the upper core surface. Occasionally, it would remove the very ends of these scars, but this was rare.

The convexly faceted platform would then again be treated, the convex faceting retouched to bring it back to shape, often in the form of a *chapeau de gendarme*.

At this point, the upper surface of the core showed a series of parallel microblade scars extending from the distal platform on one side and one large flake scar from a convex faceted platform on the other side (fig. 1, d). A few ex-

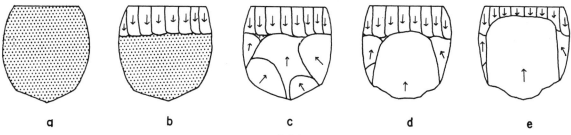

a   b   c   d   e

FIG. 1—Steps in the technology of the Halfan core and flake.

amples show small flake scars from the lateral edges near the convexly faceted platform as well as the main flake scar. The core was then fully prepared and the next flake, if successful, would have the desired form of the Halfa flake. The core would then show a major flake scar at one end and partial microblade scars at the other, the main flake scar being larger than in the preceding step (fig. 1, e).

The striking of the Halfa flake resulted in one of three types of flakes, two of which were unsuccessful. In one case, the resulting flake would remove too much of the core, including part of the distal platform. These "overpassed" flakes were quite common and are valuable to the study of the technology as they show the final stage of the upper core surface. The second type of flake from a Halfa core, which also must be considered unsuccessful, is one which was too short, leaving the upper core surface before it had reached the parallel microblade scars. All these have faceted platforms, pronounced bulbs of percussion, and pronounced reverse bulbs on their upper surface, and are short and wide. There is no evidence that they were ever used.

The truly successful Halfa flake has one of two shapes: it is either generally rectangular with a square tip or it has a fairly pointed top. This would appear to depend on the blow which removed the flake. There are no pointed Halfa cores. The square tipped Halfa flake is by far the most typical. The square tip is exceedingly thin, caused by the convergence of the ventral surface of the flake with the dorsal parallel microblade scars. The tip end was never retouched but was, without question, the working edge.

Occasionally, the lower lateral edges of the Halfa flake would be backed. Often, the backing is only on one lateral edge. This has the effect of both straightening and dulling that part of the lateral edges nearest the butt.

The distal ends of Halfa flakes never show any indication that they were used for scraping. Occasionally, there is a minute amount of use retouch on both faces, but there is never any large amount on only one face. This fact, combined with the tendency to back the lower lateral edges, seems to indicate that these flakes were hafted and used as points. The tip end is exceedingly sharp and may be compared to the edge of a transverse arrow. Instead of a meeting of two planes at an extremely acute angle as in the transverse arrow, the Halfa flake has a meeting of one major plane with a series of parallel planes, effecting an extremely acute angle. Another indication of possible hafting is the thin nature of the butt. This is achieved by first removing a waste flake from the core surface and then striking the Halfa flake from directly below the reverse bulb of the waste flake.

Functionally, there is no indication of any Halfa flakes being used for cutting or scraping. Also, no successful Halfa flake has received additional retouch in the form of a notch, denticulation, inverse retouch, etc.

All these observations do not prove that the Halfa flake was, in fact, hafted and used as a point; they do, however, indicate that there is a good possibility that they were so used.

Tool Types

Most of the tool types referred to here are well known types, fully defined in other works (Bordes, 1950; de Heinzelin, 1962; de Sonneville-Bordes and Perrot, 1954, 1955, 1956a, 1956b). Most works referring to these tool types are not in English, and occasionally the English term equivalents used here are not completely obvious.

Levallois flake: This type of flake is well defined (Bordes, 1950, p. 21). Although this term is not normally applied to flakes from Africa, it is felt that the mere designation "faceted platform flakes" is not satisfactory as both Levallois and non-Levallois flakes may be either faceted or unfaceted.

Scaled piece: This is the same as the *pièce esquillée,* as defined by de Heinzelin (1962, p. 22) and de Sonneville-Bordes and Perrot (1956b, p. 552).

Nosed scraper: This type is the same as the *grattoir plat à museau ou à épaulement* (de Sonneville-Bordes and Perrot, 1954, p. 332). In the Halfan there are only thin nosed scrapers: *grattoir plat à museau.*

Carinated scraper: Although this term is used to describe two examples, they are not true carinated scrapers but have a superficial resemblance to this type (de Sonneville-Bordes and Perrot, 1954, p. 332).

Core scraper: In the Halfan, these are not always true rabots (de Sonneville-Bordes and Perrot, 1954, p. 332). In most cases these are formed on wedge cores and the angle of the scraping edge is, therefore, always very acute.

Denticulate core scraper: This is a new type. It is merely a denticulate made on a core or a core fragment. It has the same attributes that a normal core scraper has, but the working edge is purposefully serrated.

Cortex backed knife: This is a type taken from the Middle Paleolithic typology of Bordes (1961). In the Halfan, they are small cortex backed microblades without intentional retouch but which show indications of use retouch. They may be considered quasi-tools.

The remaining tool types mentioned in this report are already well defined and are used here without any modifications of the accepted definitions.

Cores

Some important changes during the development of the Halfan are best seen in a change in frequency of core types. Therefore, core typology has been made fairly complex, with eleven defined types. Some of these are in general usage, while others are not. The terms prismatic and pyramidal are not used as emphasis is placed on the system of flake removal, particularly in the type of platforms used.

Halfa cores: These have been defined above, in conjunction with Halfa flakes. As far as is known, this core type is found only on the Nile.

Levallois cores: Already fully defined in the literature (Bordes, 1961; de Heinzelin, 1962, p. 8).

Single platform, unfaceted: In the Halfan, this type of core is made on a Nile pebble. The platform is formed by the removal of a single primary flake from one end of the long axis, which leaves a single, flat flake scar. This scar is then used as a striking platform for the subsequent removal of flakes or blades on one face of the pebble along the long axis (fig. 2, a). The best examples are microblade cores, but often, because of hinge fracturing, it is impossible to tell whether flakes or blades were intended.

Single platform, faceted: These cores are similar to the single platform, unfaceted variety except that the striking platform is formed by the removal of a series of flakes, resulting in a convex or dihedral faceted striking platform. Unlike the unfaceted type, these are mainly flake cores, although they, too, are only worked on one face (fig. 2, b).

Opposed platform: This core type is also formed on a Nile pebble. In this case, however, two platforms are formed, one on each end of the long axis. Flakes or blades are then removed from both platforms (fig. 2, c). As on the other types above, only one face of the pebble is flaked.

Ninety degree: This type is relatively rare. It consists of a pebble with two platforms. On one face of the pebble, flakes, or blades are removed along the long axis, while on the opposite face, flakes or blades are removed along the short axis. This results in two series of flaking scars which are perpendicular to one another (fig. 2, d).

Wedge: This type derives its name from its profile. First a primary flake is removed from one end of a pebble at an acute angle to the pebble surface to be flaked. A series of microblades are then taken off from the platform. These never extend the whole length of the core, leaving the lower part of the pebble unworked. Once these microblades have been removed, a second series is struck off, using the base of the microblade scars as platforms from the other side of the

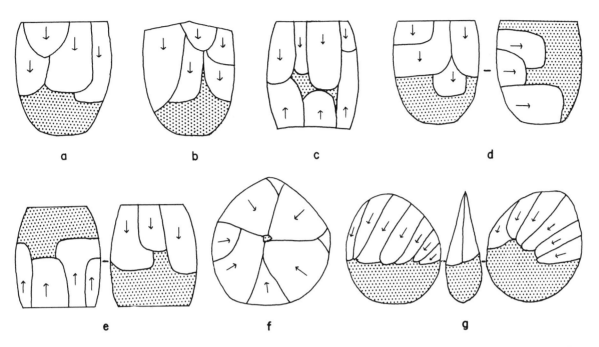

Fig. 2–Diagram of selected core types: a, single platform, unfaceted; b, single platform, faceted; c, opposed platform; d, ninety degree; e, opposite side; f, discoidal; g, wedge.

pebble. This results in a core which looks like a wedge. The platform angle of the second series of microblades is always below 50° and often as low as 30° (fig. 2, g).

Bipolar: Already well defined in the literature (de Heinzelin, 1962, p. 10).

Opposite side: These are opposed platform cores where, rather than only one surface being flaked, opposed surfaces are flaked with each platform used for the removal of flakes or blades from only one surface (fig. 2, e).

Discoidal: This does *not* refer to a Levallois core which is discoidal in shape. A discoidal core is flaked around the periphery so that the series of flake scars meet at the center of the core. The under surface is not prepared, although on occasion, thinly faceted platforms are made around the periphery prior to flake removal. Each flake is of approximately the same size, and it is assumed that each is meant for future modification into a tool (fig. 2, f). This type is often referred to as a Mousterian core (de Heinzelin, 1962, p. 8).

Globular: Already well defined (de Heinzelin, 1962, p. 8).

Isolated flake: A pebble which has had one or two primary flakes removed from one or both ends (de Heinzelin, 1962, p. 8).

In addition to these types, there are cores termed unidentifiable. Unidentifiable cores are either large fragments or whole cores which do not show any observable pattern of flaking. Small core fragments are not included in this group. They are listed but are not placed in the typology.

STRATIGRAPHIC CRITERIA FOR THE HALFAN CHRONOLOGY

The chronological ordering of Halfan sites was achieved by combining three systems: geological position within the known sequence of Nile silt aggradation and erosion, radiocarbon age determination, and typological seriation. While there is some problem with absolute dating, the relative sequences based on stratigraphy and typological situation are in agreement.

Four of the six Halfan sites (1020, 1018, 443, and 2014), were located in a branch of the Khor Musa, southwest of the Wadi Halfa airport. This made it possible to arrive at a relative sequence for these sites based on their position in the geological history of the wadi branch. One surface site, 624, was found on the west bank of the Nile, near Buhen, and was placed in the industrial sequence by typological seriation. The final site, 1028, was located north of Wadi Halfa on the east bank of the Nile and was fitted into the cultural sequence both by geological position and typological seriation (fig. 3).

Geologically, the Khor Musa contains a number of features. As all Halfan sites found there are in close proximity to one another, it is best to view the geological stratigraphy from an idealized cross-section (fig. 4).

The sequence of geological events, beginning with the deposit of the Dibeira-Jer formation, was the following:

1. Deposit of the Dibeira-Jer formation to an absolute elevation of 153 m., or 32 m. above present floodplain. At another locality in the Khor Musa, a late part of this deposit has been dated to 20,750 B.C. ± 280 years (WSU 203).

2. Erosion of the Dibeira-Jer formation in the wadi to below absolute elevation of 140 m., or 19 m. above floodplain, with a minor pause at 144 m.

3. Concurrent with the erosion, there was a deposit of eolian sands of the Ballana formation, which reached an absolute elevation of 147 m. along the edge of the eroded Khor Musa formation.

4. The Nile slowly dropped, with seasonal flooding of the wadi. At this time, Site 1020 occupied part of the upper slope of the west edge of the silts. The alternate wetting and drying of the silts formed a vertisol which incorporated artifacts from 1020 within it.

5. During the final drying out of the vertisol, Site 1018 occupied a sand dune on the very edge of the vertisol. At this time, a hard, calcarious crust formed under the surface of the dune, cementing in some of the cultural material. This phase is viewed as part of the final vertisol formation. Thus, Site 1018 is only slightly younger than Site 1020.

6. After the formation of the hard cap, there was additional deflation of the whole surface and the occupation of Site 443 on the surface of the calcarious hard cap on a nearby dune. For this area to have been habitable, there still must have been occasional flooding of the wadi and vegetation, fed, perhaps, by ground water.

7. The slow recession of the Nile meant less and less flooding of the wadi. At this point, Site 2014 was occupied on the edge of the now dormant vertisol, at an absolute elevation of 142 m. or 20 m. above floodplain. This point is viewed as being generally synchronous with the occupation of Site 443, but perhaps slightly later.

8. Subsequent to the final drying out of the vertisol, there was a long period, lasting to the present time, of wind deflation which spread a thin layer of eolian sand over all older features.

Sites 624 and 1028, found outside the Khor Musa, showed no clear geological placement. Site 624 was fully deflated and rested on a silt remnant of the Dibeira-Jer formation. Site 1028, also heavily deflated, was partially in the silts at an elevation of 21 m. above floodplain. The area, however, was affected by local tectonics, and the precise time of occupation is unknown.

Site 624 was placed into the Halfan Sequence between Sites 1018 and 443 by typological seriation, the bases of which will be discussed in detail later. Site 1028, on both geological and typological grounds, is felt to be later than any Halfan site in the Khor Musa, and, thus, the youngest Halfan site known at present.

ABSOLUTE DATING OF THE HALFAN

While the relative stratigraphy of the Halfan assemblages is clear, particularly those from the Khor Musa, there is a decided problem with ascribing an absolute date to any Halfan assemblage. This problem rests on two factors: a conflict in radiocarbon dates for almost identical assemblages and an acceptance of specific dates for the Halfan in the light of the whole pattern of dated geological features along the Nile in Nubia.

Three radiocarbon dates were obtained from Halfan sites. Two of these came from Sites 443 and 2014 in the Khor Musa, and a single date was obtained from a Halfan site, 8859, at Ballana, Egypt. Typologically, all these sites contain assemblages which are almost identical, all belonging to Stage IV of the Halfan sequence. This stage is quite characteristic and cannot be confused with either earlier or later stages. Therefore, typologically, these three sites should all date from just about the same time. Unfortunately, this was not what the radiocarbon samples

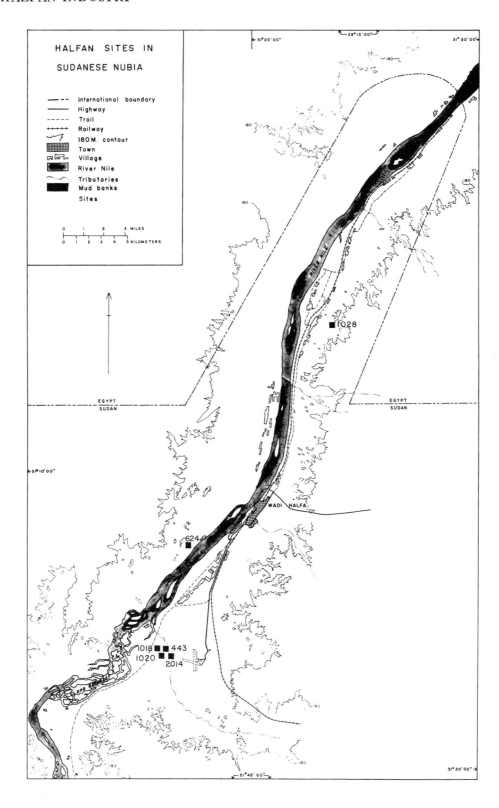

FIG. 3—Map of Halfan sites.

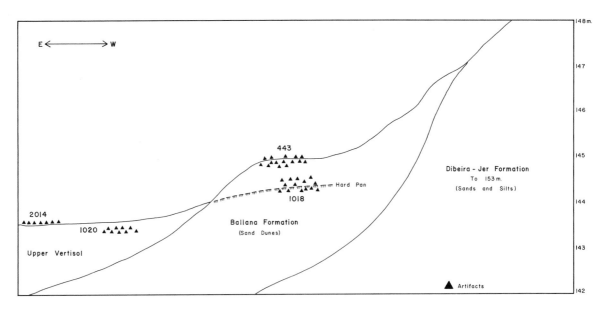

Fig. 4—Profile of Halfan sites in Khor Musa.

indicated. The dates obtained are the following:

1. Site 443. Khor Musa.
    14,550 B.C. ± 500 years (WSU-201)
2. Site 2014. Khor Musa.
    17,200 B.C. ± 375 years (WSU-332)
3. Site 8859. Ballana.
    16,650 B.C. ± 500 years (WSU-318)

Thus, while the dates from Sites 2014 and 8859 are in agreement, the date from Site 443 appears to be about 3,000 years too young. This date was obtained from small bits of charcoal, and the radiocarbon laboratory considered it to be a minimal date. It would seem, therefore, that there is really no conflict and that the correct absolute date for Stage IV of the Halfan should be placed at about 17,000 B.C.

Before it is possible to accept this, however, it is necessary to look at the overall dated geological sequence and the relationship of the Khor Musa stratigraphy to it. Each of the dated Halfan sites occurs in or on sand dunes of the Ballana formation. The main part of this formation occurs after the Dibeira-Jer silt aggradation and during the succeeding episode of erosion, before the Sahaba silt aggradation (Wendorf, Shiner, and Marks, 1965). Sites within the Ballana formation have been dated by radiocarbon from 17,200

B.C. to 15,800 B.C. Therefore, there is no conflict between the stratigraphy from Khor Musa and Ballana.

The sequence of Halfan sites also is typologically consistent. There is clear development along a number of typological and technological lines, as is discussed in detail in later sections.

Generally, it can be said that Stage IV of the Halfan was present in Nubia between 17,000 B.C. and 16,000 B.C., and this may be tied to the stratigraphic sequence as shown in Table 2.

TABLE 2
STRATIGRAPHIC POSITION OF HALFAN SITES

Site	Stratigraphy
1028	Silt of unknown age
443	On top of Ballana formation
2014	Same as Site 443
1018	Within Ballana formation on dune
1020	Substage of Dibeira-Jer erosion, in vertisol

HALFAN LITHIC DEVELOPMENT

The relative stratigraphic position of the Halfan sites gives a basis for studying changes in Halfan technology and typology. These sites, however, do not appear to be evenly spaced throughout the total span of Halfan occupation of the Second Cataract.

Sites 1020 and 1018 are more or less contemporary, although Site 1020 may be somewhat earlier stratigraphically. Again, Sites 443 and 2014 appear to have been occupied during the same general period. Sites 624 and 1028 are not directly tied to the other sites by stratigraphy, but geologically Site 1028 is younger than all the others.

The chronology of sites inferred from their relative stratigraphy is fully substantiated in the stage of typological development seen at each site. While detailed typological and technological attributes are given for each site, certain observations seem to have special value in documenting lithic change, while others show consistencies throughout the sequence or demonstrate uniformity within certain groups of sites.

TECHNOLOGICAL CHANGE

Technological change may be seen through a number of attributes. They are size, material used, relative proportions of debitage, and the ratio of flakes to blades.

The earliest known Halfan assemblage is already decidedly microlithic. There is, however, an increasing trend toward a larger percentage of microlithic tools throughout Halfan development (table 3). It must be emphasized that this tendency begins at an extremely high microlithic level, although Sites 1020 and 1018 have about 10 per cent fewer microlithic tools than all the later assemblages.

TABLE 3

HALFAN MICROLITHIC INDICES

	1020	1018	624	2014	443	1028
Microlithic Index	84.5	81.2	91.7	95.8	96.2	96.3

All known Halfan assemblages have an overwhelmingly high proportion of chert from Nile pebble used in tool manufacture. Again, there is an increase in this attribute, so that at most later Halfan sites, well over 90 per cent of all tools are made on chert (table 4).

TABLE 4

UTILIZATION OF CHERT PEBBLE AT HALFAN SITES

	1020	1018	624	443	2014	1028
Tools	91.4%	94.5%	95.0%	98.3%	96.8%	89.3%
Cores	93.9%	88.2%	96.2%	95.3%	92.9%	80.9%

While there is a certain uneven variation in percentages of chert tools and cores, all Halfan sites have a much higher occurrence of chert than is true at Khormusan sites, which is always less than 40 per cent of all tools (Marks, 1966b).

The relatively high percentage of other materials at 1028 is due to a large amount of fossil wood which was available in the immediate vicinity of the site and to a relatively high percentage of agate tools.

As might be expected, every Halfan site has very much the same pattern of artifact types. With the heavy use of chert from Nile pebble, there is a corresponding high proportion of primary flakes (fig. 5). By far the most common artifact may be considered debris: chips, small fragments, etc.

While all Halfan sites are similar, it is noticeable that the earliest Halfan sites, 1020 and 1018, are almost identical. In fact, only in the core category is there a difference of more than 2 per cent (fig. 5).

The only noticeable change of these types within all Halfan development, where data are available, is an increase in the percentage of tools after Site 1018. Sites 1020 and 1018 each have less than 3 per cent tools—2.2 and 2.7. Beginning with Site 624, there is a jump to 4.1 per cent, a level which then remains more or less constant, although declining at Site 1028.

One of the significant changes within Halfan development is an increase in the proportions of blades to flakes. This is not readily visible in the gross categories of artifacts because at later Halfan sites a high percentage of all tools are made on microblades rather than flakes.

If the ratio of flakes to microblades is considered, including all retouched and unretouched pieces, there is a constant change (fig. 6). While data are not available for Site 2014, there is little question that in the Halfan sequence there is a decided decrease in the ratio of flakes over microblades, and by Site 443, microblades and flakes are almost equal in number. By Site 1028, microblades are in the majority, with a ratio of 1.5 to 1 over flakes. Thus, by the latest known stage of the Halfan, and perhaps even somewhat earlier, the technology passes into a predominantly microblade industry. It is interesting to note that this change is gradual and is not fully reflected in the tool typologies.

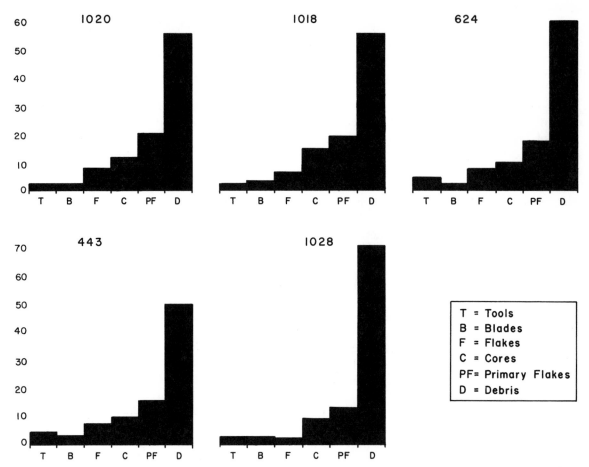

FIG. 5—Gross artifact classes at Halfan sites. Key. T=tools; B=blades; F=flakes; C=cores; PF=primary flakes; D=debris.

In short, the Halfan shows the gradual development of a microblade technology based primarily on the use of chert from Nile pebbles, an increase in the microlithic content, and in the percentage of chert used in tool manufacture. Only within the size range can we see a clear grouping of sites. Sites 1020 and 1018 both have significantly lower Microlithic Indices than the later assemblages.

TYPOLOGICAL CHANGE

While the Halfan has complex typological attributes because of a radical shift in tool types through time, it is possible to say that, overall, it is characterized by three main tools: Halfa flakes, backed microflakes, and backed microblades. It is only during a transitional stage that all three occur in significant amounts, but all types do occur in every assemblage.

The most general typological observation, one which also directly relates to the technology, is the relative proportions of flakes, microblades, and cores chosen for retouch (fig. 7). This, obviously, reflects both the tools desired in each assemblage (i.e., Halfa flakes vs. backed microblades), and the degree of the development of the microblade technology (i.e., backed flakes vs. backed microblades). It is quite apparent that a shifting pattern is visible. This pattern which groups together Sites 1020 and 1018, makes 624 transitional, groups Sites 443 and 2014 together and finally shows further development of overall trends at Site 1028. This is also fully reflected in the relative stratigraphy, in the typology, and to some extent in the technology.

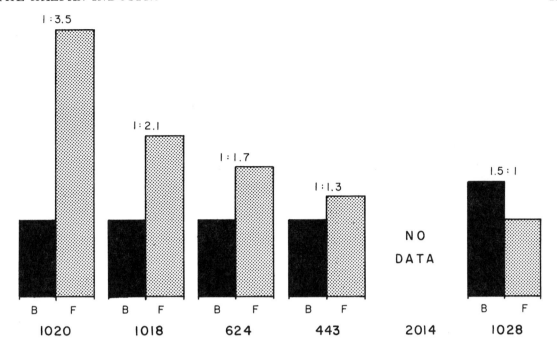

Fig. 6—Ratio of flakes to blades at Halfan sites: B=blades; F=flakes.

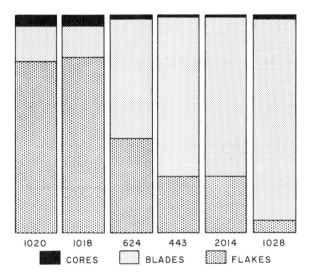

Fig. 7—Proportions of flake, blade, and core tools at Halfan sites.

Core typology shows a number of changes. Although twelve types of cores have been recognized, only a few seem to have chronological significance. Globular, discoidal, isolated flake, bipolar, ninety degree, and Levallois cores either occur only sporadically or show no significant variation from site to site. On the other hand,

Halfa cores, wedge cores, unfaceted single platform, and opposed platform cores seem to show patterns of occurrence directly related to the relative stage of development of the assemblage in which they occur (table 5).

TABLE 5
PERCENTAGES OF SELECTED CORE TYPES AT HALFAN SITES

Core Types	1020	1018	624	443	2014	1028
Halfa	43.1	45.3	15.8	4.4	3.2	0.0
Wedge	0.5	3.2	9.9	16.2	5.3	1.0
Single platform, unfaceted	11.8	15.9	21.2	39.7	59.4	60.7
Opposed platform	13.9	13.2	11.6	7.8	3.2	14.7

By far the clearest progressive change can be seen in the Halfa cores. It is the most common type at Sites 1020 and 1018, is still significant at 624, is barely present at Sites 443 and 2014, and has completely disappeared by Site 1028 (fig. 8).

Wedge cores show a different pattern. They are present at all sites but reach a peak of popularity at Site 443, then drop off markedly at Site 2014. Only one example is present by Site 1028.

Single platform unfaceted cores gain in popularity throughout. They occur in significant numbers even at the earliest Halfan site, and by the later part of the sequence dominate the core

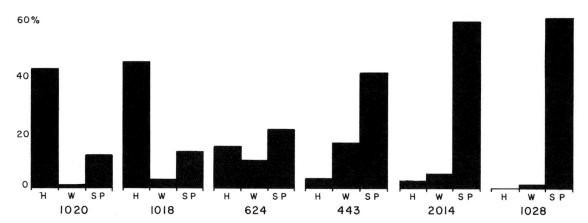

Fig. 8—Occurrence of Halfan cores (H), wedge cores (W), and single platform, unfaceted cores (SP) at Halfan sites.

typology. The slight drop in unfaceted, single platform cores at Site 1028 can be accounted for by the resurgence of opposed platform cores, a type which shows a gradual decrease in popularity until that time. There is no obvious way, however, to account for this new recurrence in force of opposed platform cores at 1028. The tendency has been clearly toward a decrease. As only one site of this stage is now known, how typical this situation is cannot be judged.

It is interesting to note that Sites 1020 and 1018 again show traits which are within the range of variation for a single site. This, however, is not fully the case for Sites 443 and 2014, the other sites which are so closely linked stratigraphically and typologically. It may be judged from this, that changes seen in the core typology reflect changes which become typologically discernible at a later date.

Typologically, three tool types dominate the Halfan: Halfa flakes, backed flakes, and backed microblades. It is through these tools that the radical shifts in preferred tools may best be seen (fig. 9).

It is at once apparent that Site 1020 and 1018 are, again, almost identical. It is possible, however, to note a slight increase in the percentage of backed microblades at 1018. The following Site 624, shows radical changes from 1018. Halfa flakes have dropped sharply, although they still account for a significant percentage of the total tool inventory. There is a marked increase in the percentage of both backed flakes and backed microblades. This results in a pattern which

shows little modification until Site 1028. At 624, however, backed microblades do not assume the importance they will have later.

Sites 443 and 2014 are also very similar. The only significant difference, in terms of trends, is that backed microblades have become the dominant tool, although backed flakes still retain their importance.

The tendency toward backed microblades is fully realized by Site 1028. There was only one Halfa flake and only two backed flakes present, compared with 259 backed microblades of various types.

Thus, while there is a major change in the overall pattern between Sites 1018 and 1028, all Halfan sites are typologically linked by the presence of Halfa flakes, a highly specialized tool type. Sites 1020 and 1018, while dominated by Halfa flakes, are linked to the later sites by the presence of backed flakes and backed microblades. There is little question, however, that a major gap exists between 1018 and 624, which must represent the main transitional period from the manufacture of Halfa flakes to backed flakes and backed microblades.

Beginning with Site 624, the major typological forms are either backed flakes or backed microblades. While numerous typological changes take place in the later part of the Halfan sequence, the treatment of these backed pieces remains relatively constant and helps to define the Halfan.

Backed flakes were always microlithic. On the other hand, there are some backed blades which measure over 30 mm. in length. These are, how-

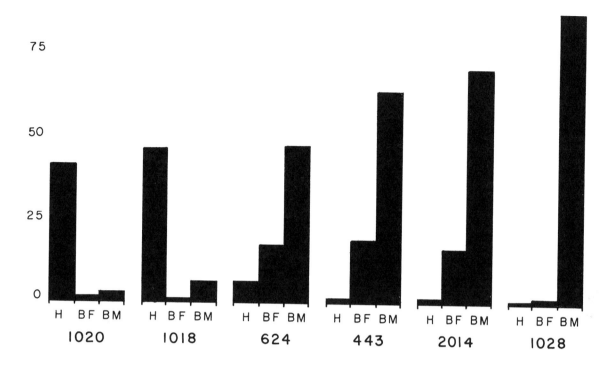

FIG. 9—Percentages of Halfan flakes (H), backed flakes (BF), and backed microblades (BM) at Halfan sites.

ever, very rare, and the backed microblade is by far the most typical. Microblades also have a definite character. For the most part, they are poor, with many showing cortex on their upper surface. A typical microblade in the Halfan is relatively short, is somewhat irregular in outline, and is incurvate. This last trait is strong at all sites. At Site 1020, where very few microblades were backed, all are incurvate. By Site 624, however, backed microblades are typologically very significant, and there 66 per cent are incurvate. This percentage increases to 82.9 at Site 443, and is 78.3 at 2014. By 1028, however, there is an increase in flat microblades, but still 64.7 per cent are incurvate.

Backing shows a uniformity in treatment. Backing is normally very fine and light and is always obverse. There is a distinct preference as to which edge of the microblade or flake was to be backed. At Site 624, where backing becomes important, 63.7 per cent of all backing is on the left edge. This remains constant at Site 443, with

65 per cent, and at Site 2014, with 62.4 per cent. At 1028 there is a decided increase in this standard, where 87.8 per cent have left edge backing.

An important aspect of the later Halfan assemblages is the tendency to make tools on backed microblades. Thus, at Site 443, there are backed microblades which have been truncated, denticulated, notched, and retouched; and there are even some with retouched borers opposite the backed edge. These forms do not occur in any number, and combined they never account for more than 10 per cent of all tools. They are significant, however, by their presence.

These complex backed tools also have a rather typical pattern of treatment. Backing is always obverse, and the other retouched typological feature is normally inverse. From 63.7 per cent to 77.5 per cent of all backed, complex tools have the secondary typological feature made by inverse retouch. This is somewhat at variance with retouch on unbacked tools, where obverse retouch is typical. In fact, inverse retouch never accounts for more than 30 per cent of these re-touched tools, and it is more common to find it accounting for no more than 20 per cent.

Aside from backed tools and Halfa flakes, the Halfan has a very poor typology. It is not so much that other types are not present, but when present, they occur only in very small numbers. Significant types include scrapers, burins, denticulates of various forms, notches, truncated flakes, and scaled pieces. With the exception of scaled pieces, every type is as common, or more common, in the early Halfan assemblages than in the later. The pattern of occurrence is shown in Table 6.

TABLE 6
PERCENTAGES OF SELECTED TOOL TYPES FROM HALFAN SITES

Types	1020	1018	624	443	2014	1028
Scrapers (end, side, core)	6.0	6.4	5.1	2.8	2.7	1.6
Burins	6.5	6.2	2.1	1.1	1.5	1.5
Denticulates (flake, core)	7.0	7.0	2.3	1.5	1.6	2.0
Notches	6.5	4.7	4.8	2.2	2.1	1.0
Truncations (flake)	2.5	2.3	4.3	0.9	0.5	0.0
Scaled pieces	0.0	0.0	1.0	0.8	2.1	1.0

In terms of assemblage groupings, it is apparent that, again, Sites 1020 and 1018 are almost identical. Only in one category, notches, is there as much as one-half of one per cent difference between them. At these early Halfan sites, scrapers, burins, denticulates, and notches all occur in significant numbers, although none can be considered a major element in the assemblages.

It is also possible to see the extremely close parallel between Sites 443 and 2014. With the exception of scaled pieces, no category differs between sites by more than 0.6 per cent. Here, however, there is not such a distinction between 443 and 2014 when compared with 624 which precedes them, or with 1028 which follows them.

Site 624 can be seen as typologically transitional between Sites 1020/1018 and Sites 443/2014. In certain categories 624 is similar to the earlier group (scrapers and notches), while in others it is similar to the later (burin, denticulates, and scaled pieces). Only the rather high percentage of truncated flakes differs from all other sites. It should be noted that 624 seems

somewhat more like the Halfan sites which follows it than like those which come before. The presence of scaled pieces is, perhaps, particularly significant as that type does not occur at either 1020 or 1018. Scrapers at 624 are intermediate between earlier and later assemblages and notched pieces match with the earlier assemblages, but all other types are fully within the very narrow range found in later Halfan assemblages. This would imply that 624, while transitional, is closer in development to 443 and 2014 than it is to the earlier assemblages of 1020 and 1018. This only reinforces what was already observed on other typological and technological criteria.

Site 1028 obviously is closely related to Sites 443 and 2014. The pattern which emerges there shows even less emphasis on non-backed tools so that no type occurs in significant number.

SITE REPORTS

SITE 1020

Site 1020[3] lies 3 km. west of the Wadi Halfa airport (fig. 3) in a side branch of the Khor Musa (map ref. 642.5/904.7).[4] The site is situated on a long slope on the southern side of a large Precambrian rock outcrop which rises to a height of 152 m. The slope itself is about 80 m. in length, extending from 147 m. at its top to 141 m. at the wadi bottom. The site was recognized by a large surface concentration of some 2,000 sq. m., evenly spread, 50 m. north-south along the middle section of the slope and some 40 m. east-west across the slope (fig. 10). It is probable, however, that there were originally a number of small concentrations which were subsequently dispersed by deflation.

Test excavations showed the slope to consist of a 5 to 10 cm. thick cover of eolian sand which rested on a deep deposit of vertisol. The total depth of the vertisol was not discovered, but half way up the slope, it was over 1.5 m. in depth. The vertisol, resting on a sand and covered by another eolian sand, pinched out at the 145 m. elevation. This upper sand, in turn, was covered

---

[3] This site was originally referred to as 443A, and reported by Waechter as 443 (1965).

[4] All map references are to Egypt-New Series, 1:25,-000, printed by the Sudan Survey Department, April 1960.

FIG. 10—Site 1020, looking east across site.

by a weathered zone and a surface sand accumulation (fig. 11).

Artifacts were found in all geological zones except for the lowest eolian sand. By far the greatest number of artifacts came from the vertisol—to a depth of 75 cm. below the surface. Because of the large cracks and slide planes in the vertisol, however, no meaningful stratigraphy was possible. Quite apparently, the original occupation of the site took place at the edge and on top of a silt deposit prior to its formation into a vertisol. During this process, most artifacts were swallowed by the soil, while others remained near the surface and were subsequently incorporated into the loose sand deposits which covered the entire slope.

As Site 1020 is situated within a short distance of three other sites, two of which are also Halfan, the chance of a mixture of the surface material was fairly high. Therefore, although much surface material was collected, it is not included in this study. Only those artifacts recovered from within the vertisol are used for the technological and typological studies which follow.

Excavations were carried out at various points along a north-south line by P. Evans during December of 1963. Initially, 1 sq. m. test pits were excavated at the base and top of the slope. It was found that the lower 25 m. of the slope did not contain *in situ* sufficient artifacts to warrant intensive excavation, but that the upper portions of the slope contained a fairly dense concentration. Therefore, most excavation took place about three-quarters of the way up the slope at a surface elevation of 144 to 145 m. A total of 28 sq. m. was excavated; 23 of them were within the latter area.

Features

During excavation, portions of three earth ovens were uncovered. These were in an east-west line about three meters apart. They were recognizable by concentrations of burned rock, bone, and thermal fractured artifacts, although the earth ovens could only be seen clearly in profile. They were not visible in the loose surface cover but became noticeable within the first few centimeters of the vertisol. The largest was 2.5

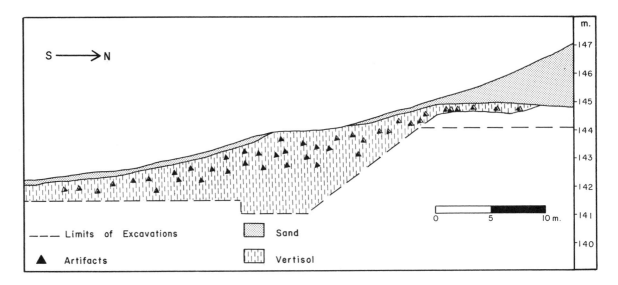

Fɪɢ. 11—Profile of Site 1020.

m. long by 1.5 m. wide. The smallest was roughly circular and less than 1 m. in diameter. Each earth oven was approximately 50 cm. deep and filled with fire-cracked rock, bone, and artifacts. There was, however, no difference between the artifactual contents of the earth ovens; thus, all artifacts found within them were treated as belonging to the square in which they were found.

Lithic Artifacts

A total of 8,794 artifacts were recovered from the vertisol. The vast majority was debris or debitage, including 4,906 pieces of debris, 1,787 primary flakes, 519 unidentifiable core fragments, 499 cores, 689 flakes, and 194 blades. The remaining 200 artifacts were classifiable as tools. Tools, therefore, accounted for only 2.2 per cent of all artifacts recovered. While density of artifacts must be considered not only in terms of a single plane, but also in depth, it is significant to note that there was a high concentration per square meter: 313.9. That is much higher than at sites of the Khormusan industry (Marks, 1966b).

Chert from Nile pebble was used extensively in tool production. Other materials occur but always only in small numbers. The proportions of the different rocks utilized are shown in Table 7.

TABLE 7

Uᴛɪʟɪᴢᴀᴛɪᴏɴ ᴏꜰ Rᴀᴡ Mᴀᴛᴇʀɪᴀʟs ᴀᴛ Sɪᴛᴇ 1020

	Cores	Tools
Chert	93.9%	91.4%
Agate	4.2%	5.6%
Quartz	1.3%	0.4%
Fossil wood	0.3%	0.9%
Precambrian	0.3%	1.7%

TOOL TYPOLOGY

	No.	%
Halfa flakes, unretouched	81	40.5
Halfa flakes, retouched	24	12.0
Levallois flakes	4	2.0
End-scrapers	5	2.5
Core scrapers	4	2.0
Side-scrapers	3	1.5
Borers	1	0.5
Burins, dihedral angle	1	0.5
Burins, angle on snapped pieces	6	3.0
Burins, on cores	6	3.0
Denticulates	12	6.0
Denticulate core scrapers	2	1.0
Notched pieces	13	6.5
Truncated flakes	5	2.5
Cortex backed knives	7	3.5
Partially backed flakes	4	2.0
Backed microblades	3	1.5
Partially backed microblades	1	0.5
Backed microblades, truncated	1	0.5
Truncated microblades	3	1.5
Retouched microblades	4	2.0
Retouched flakes	9	4.5
Varia	1	0.5
	200	100.0

NOTES ON THE TYPOLOGY

As this site represents basically the same stage of development as that at Site 1018, the descriptions of the artifact types will not be as detailed as in the site report that follows. It should be emphasized that this material does not differ in any appreciable way from that at Site 1018.

Halfa flakes, unretouched (81). The vast majority has some form of convexly faceted butt. Of the total, 38 have *chapeau de gendarme* butts and 30 have simple convexly faceted butts. The remaining examples include five broken pieces, two unidentifiable, four dihedral and two plane faceted.

They range in size from 15 to 33 mm. in length. Most, however, fall between 19 and 27 mm., being somewhat larger than those at 1018.

There is a wide latitude in the quality of the Halfa flakes, but most are quite successful (fig. 12, d-h, j-k). The only noticeable difference between these and those at Site 1018 is the slightly lower proportion of *chapeau de gendarme* butts at 1018.

Halfa flakes, retouched (24). Eleven have simple convexly faceted butts, one has a dihedral butt, and twelve are *chapeau de gendarme*. Size range is the same as for unretouched examples, except for one atypical Halfa flake which measures 39 mm. in length—the largest Halfa flake found (fig. 12, i).

Only four have bilaterally blunted edges near the butt (fig. 12, a, i, m) while the remainder have been dulled on only one side (fig. 12, b-c, l).

Levallois flakes (4). These are all atypical and are, due to their small number, possibly accidental.

End-scrapers (5). Four are on primary flakes (fig. 13, o), only one showing a well formed scraping edge (fig. 13, m). The other example is on a very small microblade and has a fine working end which approaches a truncation.

Core scrapers (4). Two are on Halfa cores, while the third is on a rather large pebble (fig. 13, r), and the fourth is on a core fragment.

Side-scrapers (3). There is one well made inverse side-scraper with semi-steep retouch (fig. 13, s), but the others are poor examples. All are on thin flakes, with convex retouch which is not much better than simple retouched flakes.

Borers (1). A questionable example on a flake.

Only one side of the tip is retouched, the other shows no more than use retouch.

Burins, dihedral angle (1). A rough example on a fragment (fig. 13, u).

Burins, angle on snapped pieces (6). Four are on microblade fragments (fig. 13, f), while the others are on thick flakes.

Burins, on cores (6). These include four burins on weak truncations and two single blow burins, one on a split pebble (fig. 13, v) and one on a Halfa core (fig. 13, q).

Denticulates (12). On the whole, these are not as well made as those from 1018, although all are microdenticulate. Only three are on microblades, while the rest are on a variety of flake types (fig. 13, t). Ten are lateral denticulates, one fragmentary example showing serration as regular as any from 1018 (fig. 13, k). In addition, there is an end denticulate (fig. 13, l), and a bilateral example on an overpassed Halfa flake (fig. 12, n).

Denticulate core scrapers (2). Both are microdenticulate on unsuccessful Halfa cores.

Notched pieces (13). While they are the most numerous retouched tool type, these lack quality. Four are micronotches made by percussion on microblades, three inverse and one normal. The rest are on irregular flakes. All are micronotches. All but two are made by percussion (fig. 13, j).

Truncated flakes (5). Three are on primary flakes, two oblique convex and one straight. In addition, there is an oblique concave example (fig. 13, h) and a Halfa flake which has been obliquely truncated (fig. 13, g).

Cortex backed knives (7). All are incurvate microblades with cortex forming a blunted back along one edge and showing some evidence of use on the other. None has been intentionally retouched.

Partially backed flakes (4). Very fine backing on irregular microflakes. One has backing cut into a rather thick cortex edge (fig. 13, e), a trait rather typical of the Halfan.

Backed microblades (3). Three incurvate microblades have been backed. One backing is straight (fig. 13, b), one convex (fig. 13, d), while the backed edge of the third is somewhat irregular (fig. 13, a).

Partially backed microblades (1). A single incurvate microblade with typical, very light, partial backing.

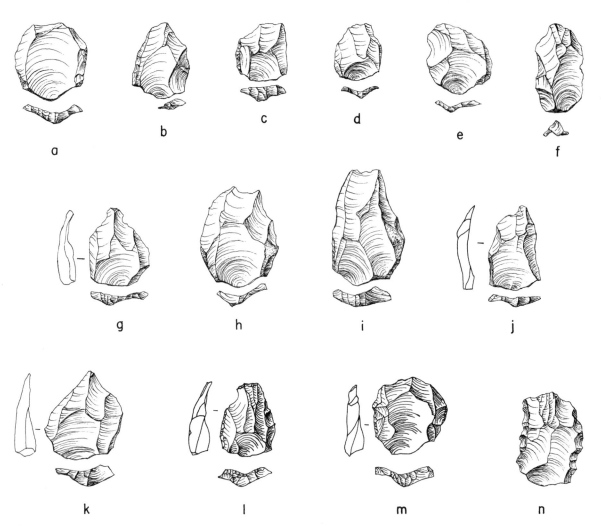

FIG. 12—Site 1020: a-m, Halfa flakes, retouched and unretouched; n, denticulate on an overpassed Halfa flake. 4/5 natural size.

Backed microblades, truncated (1). A fine example on a relatively long, although incurvate, microblade (fig. 13, c).

Truncated microblades (3). Two are cortex backed knives with oblique truncations, while the third is a microblade with a straight truncation.

Retouched microblades (4). Retouch is light and only partial. One is inversely retouched (fig. 13, p). As in all microblades at this site, these are incurvate.

Retouched flakes (9). Small amounts of light retouch on irregular microflakes. Two have inverse retouch and approach oblique basal truncations, but the retouch is not steep (fig. 13, i).

Varia (1). This is a large ferrocrete sandstone

cobble—105 mm. by 79 mm. by 37 mm.—which has been flaked into a rough denticulated core scraper. There is no evidence that it was used as a chopper, although its size and weight suggests such use. As ferrocrete sandstone was never employed in the manufacture of microlithic tools, this piece must be viewed as a tool rather than as an irregular core.

CORE TYPOLOGY

	No.	%	Restricted %
Halfa	164	33.0	43.1
Levallois	20	4.0	5.2
Single platform, unfaceted	45	9.0	11.8
Single platform, faceted	35	7.0	9.1

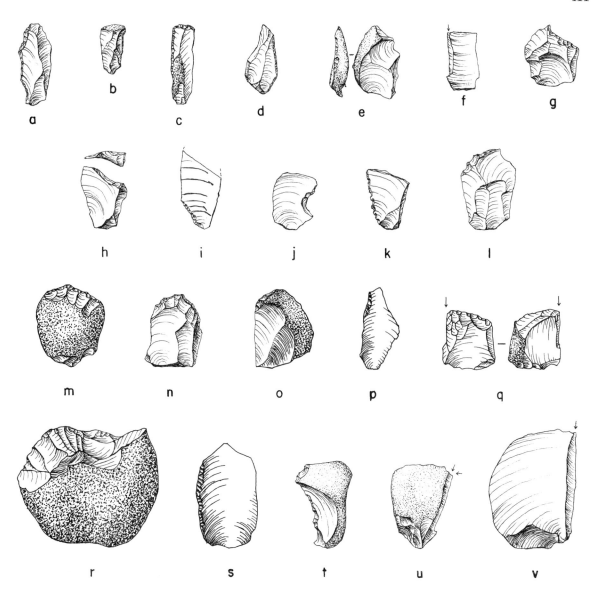

FIG. 13—Site 1020: Backed microblades (a-b, d, simple; c, truncated; e, partially backed); f, q, u-v, burins; g-h, truncated flakes; i, retouched flake; j, notched blade; k-l, t, denticulates; m-o, end-scrapers; p, retouched microblade; r, core scraper; s, inverse side-scraper. 4/5 natural size.

	No.	%	Restricted %
Opposed platform	54	10.8	13.9
Ninety degree	14	2.8	3.7
Opposite side	4	0.8	1.0
Bipolar	3	0.6	0.8
Discoidal	6	1.2	1.6
Wedge	2	0.4	0.5
Globular	1	0.2	0.3
Isolated flake	34	6.8	8.9
Unidentifiable	117	23.4	
	499	100.0	99.9

NOTES ON THE TYPOLOGY

A total of 1,018 cores and core fragments were found *in situ*. Of these 519 were small fragments, for the most part thermal fractured. Both their fragmentary condition and the thermal damage made it impossible to classify them in any way other than as core debris.

The remaining 499 cores were classifiable within general groups, including an "unclassifiable" group which included all of those which did not show any particular pattern of flaking.

The vast majority, 95.8 per cent, of the whole cores was made on Nile pebble. Agate was next with 2.6 per cent; then came Precambrian rock and fossil wood, each of which accounted for 0.6 per cent; and, finally, quartz was lowest with only 0.4 per cent.

Halfa (164). As at 1018, these are by far the most common identifiable cores. No pattern or variation is seen here that did not also occur at the former site. While the size range extends from 20 to 36 mm. for successfully utilized cores, 70 per cent fall between 24 and 29 mm. Of the 164 Halfa cores, 65 had been successfully struck (fig. 14, c-d). Seven had had the channel flake removed but had not been struck, while 25 had hinge fractured during an attempt to remove the Halfa flake (fig. 14, a-b). In addition, 28 examples were ruined while attempting to remove the channel flake, 14 were overpassed, while 25 were still in the early stages of production. It is apparent, therefore, that the biggest problem was the successful removal of both the channel and final Halfa flakes. They appear to have been equally difficult to remove successfully.

In spite of the numerous steps involved and the problems manifest in making such small cores, it is notable that almost 40 per cent of all Halfa cores were successfully completed.

Levallois (20). All are atypical and only one measures greater than 30 mm. in length. Very few have been struck, and many do not seem to have been fully prepared. As with all Levallois cores made on pebbles, there is a minimum of ventral preparation. They are in no way commensurate in quality with the Halfa cores.

Single platform, unfaceted (45). The vast majority has been little utilized (fig. 14, f-g). True microblade cores are missing, although some blades were produced from these cores. As a group, they are quite poor. Six examples have cortex platforms, while the rest have platforms formed by a single flake scar.

Single platform, faceted (35). These, too, show little utilization (fig. 14, e). In fact, aside from the faceting of the platforms, all comments made in the group above apply here.

Opposed platform (54). All are irregular. Many may have resulted from poor control during the early stages of Halfa core production.

The majority indicates removal of flakes, although a few microblade scars are visible.

Ninety degree (14). Again, these are not fully utilized and are quite poor.

Opposite side (4). Somewhat better than most core types, but quite rare.

Bipolar (3). Typical examples but not common in the Halfan.

Discoidal (6). Again, typical examples, all microlithic.

Wedge (2). Very poor examples, almost marginal in quality. These, however, are important as they gain in quality and popularity during Halfan development.

Globular (1). A typical example.

Isolated flake (34). Single flakes removed from Nile pebbles. For the most part, these pebbles are highly irregular in shape, which may account for their abandonment.

Unidentifiable (117). Nile pebbles which have been randomly flaked. Again, these were never extensively worked.

Summary

Site 1020 contains an assemblage which shows numerous diagnostic features. The Microlithic Index is high, 84.5, but the vast majority of tools is made on microflakes rather than on microblades as shown by the following: Blade Tool Index, 16.0; Flake Tool Index, 78.0; and Core Tool Index, 6.0.

Typologically, the dominant core type is the special Halfa core, which accounts for 43.1 per cent of all recognizable cores. Other significant types include opposed platform (13.9 per cent) and unfaceted single platform cores (11.8 per cent). There is also a small remnant of Levallois technology, seen in Levallois cores (5.2 per cent). It should be noted that wedge cores, a type later to become important, have already made their appearance, but only in small numbers.

The tool inventory heavily emphasizes Halfa flakes which account for just over half of all tools. Other tools of significance include scrapers, burins, and denticulates. None of these types, however, account for more than 7 per cent of all tools. Backed microblades and microflakes are rare, 4.5 per cent; but their appearance is significant in terms of later Halfan development.

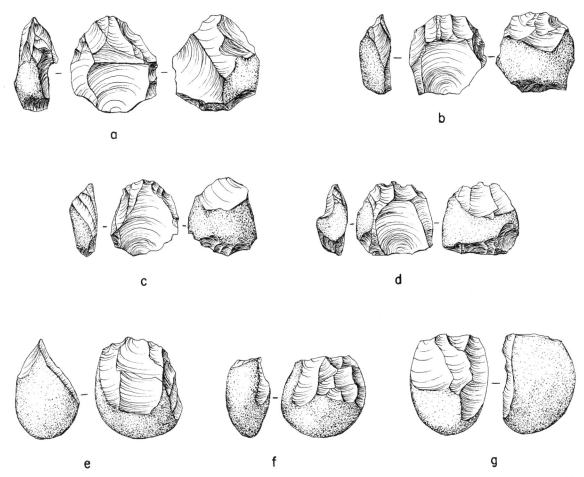

Fig. 14—Site 1020: a-d, Halfa cores; e, single platform, faceted core; f-g, single platform, unfaceted cores. 4/5 natural size.

The stage of development seen here is similar to that of Site 1018, but is somewhat earlier in time. At 1020 can be seen all the features which are to become important in Halfan lithic evolution, although none show much development at this point.

SITE 1018

Site 1018 lies on a branch of the Khor Musa, 3 km. due west of the Wadi Halfa airport building and 11 km. southwest of Wadi Halfa (map ref. 642.6/904.7). The site, 25 m. above present floodplain, is situated on a finger of a large sloping sand dune which descends evenly southward to the Khor bed. This slope reaches its highest elevations to the North, where it meets a remnant of the Dibeira-Jer formation at 30 m. above floodplain. The top of the finger and its upper slope cover an area of about 20 sq. m. The eastern side of the finger drops off steeply two meters to a wadi bed while the western side dips slightly to a very minor drainage depression. This western side, however, is merely part of a slope which extends horizontally for about 0.5 km. to the west, descending from remnants of the Dibeira-Jer formation and masses of Precambrian rock outcrops (fig. 15).

The finger and the upper part of the southern slope were covered by a surface concentration of chipped stone and weathered bone fragments. This concentration was less than 20 m. west of Site 443 and was separated from it only by a narrow wadi. The initial impression was that both concentrations were part of the same occu-

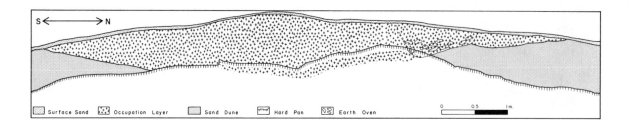

S ←――――→ N

⬚ Surface Sand   ⬚ Occupation Layer   ⬚ Sand Dune   ⬚ Hard Pan   ⬚ Earth Oven   0   0.5   1 m.

Fɪɢ. 15–Profile of Site 1018.

pation and that the formation of the wadi had cut the site in two.

Originally, excavation at this site was undertaken as a final part of the excavations at Site 443. It was intended that only a small test pit be placed on the finger to confirm the cultural uniformity with the main area of Site 443. When excavation began, it became apparent that a different assemblage was involved, so the work was expanded.

Once it was realized that a new site had been found, a one-meter square grid was placed across the area of surface concentration. A total of 17 sq. m. was excavated during the two weeks spent at the site in 1962, and an additional 4 sq. m. were excavated during the following field season. The surface concentration was found to be larger than the area remaining *in situ* which was little more than 16 sq. m. First, a series of one meter squares were excavated on an east-west line. This line was tied into the major east-west trench of Site 443 so that a complete stratigraphic profile of the two sites and the intervening wadi could be drawn. This line of squares was some 4 m. north of the crest of the finger, and stratigraphic observations there were disappointing. In this area of the site there was a thin surface layer of eolian sand mixed with some artifacts and weathered bone. Directly below, there was a layer of semiconsolidated sand, artifacts, and some burned clay. This rested on a hard calcareous cap which formed the core of the finger. The trench did, however, indicate that material existed *in situ* and that the northern edge of the site was along the trench line.

A series of squares was then excavated on a line down the slope to the south. Immediately south of the east-west trench, there was a true

occupation layer of loose dark sand, bone, chipped stone, and fire-stained sand under the surface layer. This occupation layer continued 4 m. to the south, where it finally tapered off into the thin surface concentration. At the crest of the finger the surface layer was from 1 to 2.5 cm. thick and the occupation layer up to 45 cm. thick, with the lower portion incorporated within the hard cap.

The vast majority of the excavated area consisted of the loose occupation layer. Within this, there were concentrations of bone and burned rock. It was only at a depth of about 20 cm., however, that observable evidence for specific hearths was seen. These, as those at other Halfan sites, were not true fire pits but appeared to be earth ovens. Two were found on the slope, close to the crest of the finger. Only the lower 10 cm. of each could be clearly seen in profile. There was, however, a definite concentration of burned bone in the 20 cm. of fill above each profiled earth oven.

Lithic Artifacts

A total of 7,895 artifacts were recovered. The vast majority was debitage and debris; 4,357 chips, 1,451 primary flakes, 892 unidentifiable core fragments, 255 cores, 481 flakes, and 243 blades. Only 216 finished tools were recovered, accounting for 2.7 per cent of all artifacts. Overall density of artifacts was 464.6 per square meter, but it was actually much higher in the southern section of the site.

The raw material predominantly used for tool production was chert from Nile pebbles. These were readily available in the immediate vicinity, on the deflated surface of the Dibeira-Jer formation. Chert, however, was not the only material utilized; agate, quartz, fossil wood, and Precambrian rock were also used. A study of the assemblage shows that while quartz occurs in significant amounts among the cores, very rarely were finished tools made from it. On the other hand, the occurrence of agate is consistent in both cores and tools. Only a single piece of fossil wood was found. This may be seen in Table 8.

TABLE 8
Utilization of Raw Materials at Site 1018

	Cores	Tools
Chert	88.2%	94.5%
Agate	3.6%	3.6%
Quartz	6.8%	0.9%
Fossil wood	0.0%	0.5%
Precambrian	0.4%	0.5%

TOOL TYPOLOGY

	No.	%
Halfa flakes, unretouched	99	45.8
Halfa flakes, retouched	22	10.2
End-scrapers	4	1.8
Core scrapers	7	3.2
Side-scrapers	3	1.4
Burins, dihedral déjeté	1	0.5
Burins, dihedral angle	1	0.5
Burins, angle on snapped pieces	1	0.5
Burins, "single blow"	1	0.5
Burins, on retouched truncations	3	1.4
Burins, on cores	6	2.8
Denticulates	10	4.7
Denticulate core scrapers	5	2.3
Notched pieces	10	4.7
Truncated flakes	5	2.3
Cortex backed knives	4	1.8
Partially backed flakes	2	0.9
Backed microblades	5	2.3
Backed microblades, broken	2	0.9
Partially backed microblades	3	1.4
Backed microblades, truncated	1	0.5
Backed microblades, retouched	4	1.8
Truncated microblades	2	0.9
Retouched microblades	7	3.2
Retouched flakes	6	2.8
Varia	2	0.9
	216	100.0

NOTES ON THE TYPOLOGY

Halfa flakes, unretouched (99). The form and technology of the Halfa flake has already been described in detail above. Of the 99 unretouched Halfa flakes, 57 are convexly faceted in *chapeau de gendarme* style, 32 are simple convex faceted, 4 are dihedral faceted, and 5 are unidentifiable. One is broken. They range in size from 15 to 33 mm., but most cluster between 19 to 25 mm. Halfa flakes vary in quality from excellent, having square or pointed tips (fig. 16, b-c, f-h, j-k), to ones which are barely recognizable (fig. 16, d). The majority, however, is well made.

Halfa flakes, retouched (22). On occasion Halfa flakes were retouched (fig. 16, a, i). This retouch is always in the form of backing which occurs on one or both lateral edges adjacent to the butt. It apparently serves the function of straightening the edges near the butt and, at the same time, blunting them. Only occasionally does the backing extend more than one-third of the way from the butt toward the tip (fig. 16, e).

Of the 22 retouched Halfa flakes, 11 have convexly faceted butts of the *chapeau de gendarme* type, 9 are simple convex, one is broken, and one is made on a very thin Halfa core. This last piece is highly atypical, but there is no question that the lateral edges of the core were backed. This was an unsuccessful Halfa core which had hinge fractured just at contact with the microblade scars. After this flake was removed, three more attempts were made to remove the true Halfa flake but each deeply hinge fractured close to the striking platform. It was at this point that the core was abandoned and the backing placed on the lateral edges. It is the only Halfa core which is thin, and it could easily have served as a large Halfa flake. The angle at the unfaceted platform is 47° and the core is only 7 mm. thick.

End-scrapers (4). All are quite atypical and poorly formed. Two are on primary flakes, one of which is very thick and approaches a core fragment. This retouched end is steep and only slightly convex. The other is on a thin flake with a scraping edge only partially retouched.

One example is on a microblade, 19 mm. in length. The working edge is only slightly convex, formed by semi-steep retouch. It approaches a truncation, except that the retouch continues a short way down both lateral edges. Another end-scraper is made on an irregular flake and has a slightly sinuous inversely retouched working end. It might well be considered a transverse side-scraper (fig. 17, i).

Core scrapers (7). Three are on unsuccessful Halfa cores (fig. 17, h). All have scraping edges formed by the addition of a fine retouch along the distal end of the core. Four have straight

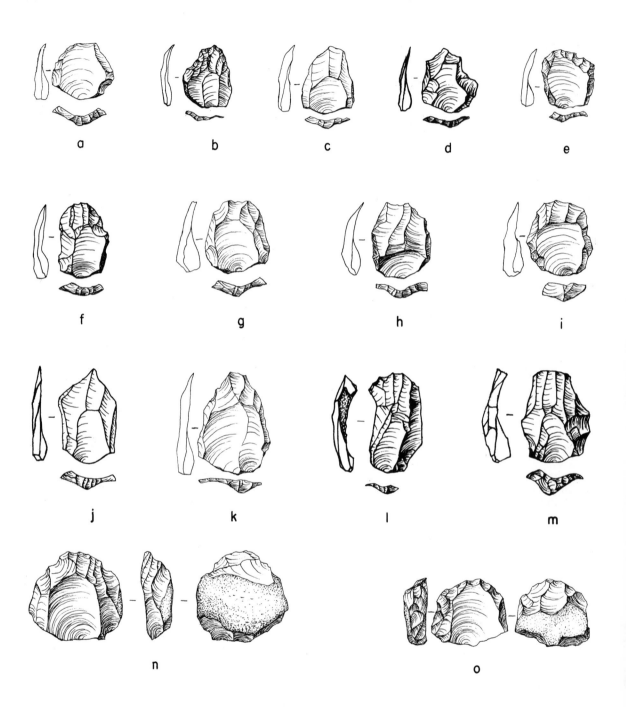

Fig. 16—Site 1018: a-k, unretouched and retouched Halfa flakes; l-m, overpassed Halfa flakes; n-o, Halfa cores. 4/5 natural size.

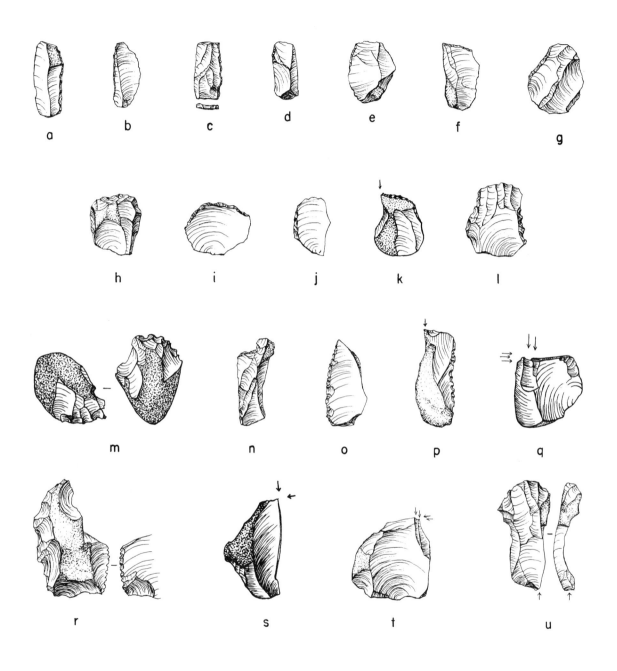

FIG. 17—Site 1018: Backed microblades (a-b, simple; c, basally truncated; d, partially backed); e, partially backed flake; f-g, truncated pieces; h-j, scrapers; k, q, s-u, burins; l, denticulate on an overpassed Halfa flake; m, denticulate core scraper; n, notched microblade; o, r, denticulates; p, burin-denticulate. 4/5 natural size.

scraping edges made on randomly flaked cores. In all cases the retouch is quite steep.

Side-scrapers (3). One is on a microflake with the scraping edge formed by a scaled retouch. Another is a corner scraper on a small flake, while the third is an inversely retouched, convex side-scraper on a microlithic flake fragment with semi-steep retouch (fig. 17, j). All are rather poor, as were the end-scrapers.

Burins, dihedral *déjeté* (1). A rather atypical example on an overpassed Halfan flake.

Burins, dihedral angle (1). A well made burin on an irregular flake (fig. 17, s).

Burins, angle on snapped pieces (1). A complex tool consisting of a burin made on a snapped microdenticulated primary blade (fig. 17, p).

Burins, "single blow" (1). A typical example, with the burin spall taken off one edge of a dihedral butt.

Burins, on retouched truncations (3). Two are well formed burins, one on a primary flake (fig. 17, k), and the other is on the truncated butt of an overpassed Halfa flake (fig. 17, u). The third piece is on a small flake, and the burin spall is somewhat irregular.

Burins, on cores (6). By far the most common type. There is one large dihedral burin, three "single blow" types, and two dihedral angle burins (fig. 17, q, t).

Denticulates (10). Denticulates form a unified and exceptionally well made group. Aside from the Halfa flakes, they must be considered the finest examples of lithic manufacture seen in this stage of the Halfan.

Three are made on blades measuring between 30 and 32 mm. in length. Serration is exceptionally fine and uniform with regular teeth, evenly spaced. One is made by inverse retouch and has a separate tooth every 1.3 mm. (fig. 17, o). Two others have been obversely retouched with teeth spaced every 2.2 mm. The length of the serrated edges ranges from 20 to 28 mm.

Two denticulates are made on elongated primary flakes. They measure 33 mm. and 35 mm. One is inversely retouched with a working edge of 20 mm. and small, uniform teeth every 1.5 mm. The other is obversely retouched with working edge of only 18 mm., with separate teeth every 2.2 mm.

The third group of denticulates occurs on un-

successful Halfa flakes. One, on an overpassed flake, has a short serrated edge of 12 mm. with a tooth every 3 mm. (fig. 17, l). The other three are on elongated sections of broken Halfa flakes. The breaks are such that the retouched fragments are blade shaped. One of these, measuring 39 mm., is inversely retouched with a working edge 18 mm. long and a tooth every 1.6 mm. Another has a convexly serrated edge of 21 mm. with extremely fine teeth, one every 1.6 mm.

A final denticulated flake is more complex. Although broken, it is possible to see exceedingly fine teeth along one edge, one every 1.9 mm. The opposite edge has a steep, rough retouch which is intermediate between a backing and a poorly formed denticulate (fig. 17, r). If the extremely fine serration which typifies this group as a whole is taken into account, the rough retouch should probably be considered a backing of some form. It must, however, be pointed out that all backing found in this assemblage is also exceedingly fine, making that typological element on this last piece highly atypical.

Denticulate core scrapers (5). None of these are true cores, as the angle of retouch is generally too steep to have resulted in flakes of any size. The serrations are heavier and more widely spaced than they are on denticulate tools made on flakes or blades (fig. 17, m).

Notched pieces (10). All notches are quite weak, and all measure less than 1 cm. across. Six are on microflakes and four on microblades. Three of the notches are at the distal ends of the microblades (fig. 17, n).

Truncated flakes (5). All are on microflakes. There is one straight truncation which cuts off a very small section of the tip of a pointed flake, one oblique truncation on a Precambrian flake, a concave truncation on a Halfa channel flake (fig. 17, g), and two concave truncations. The flakes range in length from 16 to 21 mm.

Cortex backed knives (4). These range in length from 37 to 47 mm. Two are large quartz flakes, and two are chert blades. Each shows use along its cutting edge.

Partially backed flakes (2). Both are microflakes which have a very fine, steep retouch along part of their left lateral edges (fig. 17, e).

Backed microblades (5). Backed microblades have backing similar to the partially backed flakes, i.e., the backing is exceedingly fine and steep, almost no more than a light retouch. This backing differs from that on Halfa flakes which tends to be heavier.

All backed microblades are complete, measuring between 17 and 19 mm. in length. The smaller two verge on being microflakes. Two have straight backing (fig. 17, b), while the remaining three are slightly convex (fig. 17, a).

Backed microblades, broken (2). Small fragments from backed microblades—too small for other observations.

Partially backed microblades (3). Two microblades have a partial backing of the type described for the partially backed flakes. In this group the backing barely cuts into the original blade edges (fig. 17, d).

An overpassed elongated Halfa flake has also been classified in this type as it has blade proportions. On this specimen, however, the backing is quite heavy, although it extends only half way along one lateral edge. The piece measures 28 mm. by 13 mm.

Backed microblades, truncated (1). A broken microblade has a continuous straight backing and a slightly concave basal truncation which removed only part of the bulb of percussion (fig. 17, c).

Backed microblades, retouched (4). One microblade with a somewhat irregular backing also has a continuous inverse retouch on the opposite edge. The others have an inverse retouch which is very flat and irregular, a form quite common at later Halfan sites.

Truncated microblades (2). Both have straight, oblique truncations (fig. 17, f).

Retouched microblades (7). Three have a small amount of inverse retouch, the rest have obverse retouch. In all cases, it is very light, approaching use retouch.

Retouched flakes (6). Two are inversely retouched. Both measure over 30 mm. in length. Four microflakes have flat, discontinuous retouch which is marginal.

Varia (2). These consist of two soft stone hammers, made from a light gray conglomerate. They are generally spheroid in shape, but one end of each has been flattened by use. They could almost be used either as hammers or as small anvils.

CORE TYPOLOGY

	No.	%	Restricted %
Halfa	86	33.6	45.3
Levallois	4	1.6	2.1
Single platform, unfaceted	30	11.8	15.9
Single platform, faceted	18	7.1	9.7
Opposed platform	25	9.8	13.2
Ninety degree	4	1.6	2.1
Wedge	6	2.3	3.2
Isolated flake	16	6.3	8.5
Unidentifiable	66	25.9	
	255	100.0	100.0

NOTES ON THE TYPOLOGY

While 1,147 cores and core fragments were recovered, 892 were either so small or so badly thermal fractured that they had to be classified as debris. The remaining 255 cores were classifiable, including 66 which had to be considered as randomly flaked.

Halfa (86). All stages of Halfa core production were found. Eighteen examples were in the early stages of preparation, prior to the removal of the channel flake. On seven pieces, the removal of the channel flake had been unsuccessful, while in 17 cases, the Halfa flake itself had hinge fractured or the platform had been crushed. Seven cores show the removal of the channel flake, but for unknown reasons, the platform had not been reshaped and the Halfa flake was unstruck. In addition, eight cores were struck, but an overpassed flake resulted. Finally, 29 Halfa cores had Halfa flakes successfully removed (fig. 16, n-o). That is, only about 34 per cent of all Halfa cores produced Halfa flakes.

Levallois (4). All are microlithic and only three had been struck. Two are poorly made, ovoid in shape, and in both cases, the main flake had hinge fractured. In every case, the under side of the core received some preparation, but the cortex was not completely removed.

Single platform, unfaceted (30). Five pebbles were split by single blows at one end, and unfaceted platforms were prepared at the opposite end so that the split surface formed the upper working face of the core. None have been intensively utilized.

Three cores have unfaceted platforms formed by old, weathered flake scars which, at the time of use, were patinated (fig. 18, b). These were used as platforms but were actually part of the

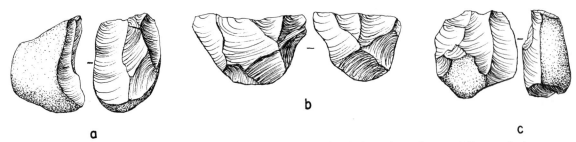

Fig. 18—Site 1018: a-b, single platform, unfaceted cores; c, single platform faceted core. 4/5 natural size.

pebble surface when utilized. One of these cores has three elongate flake scars which approach blade proportions (fig. 18, a). Another has short, wide flake scars, while the third has had a number of large flakes removed.

Twenty-two have platforms formed by single flake scars on whole pebbles. The great majority was abandoned after only a few flakes had been removed. In most cases, in fact, only primary flaking had taken place. Twelve were discarded because of structural faults in the pebbles which appeared during primary flaking and so precluded successful flake production. In six cases, the primary flakes deeply hinge fractured, making further work impossible. Two cores had been struck at angles such that the resulting flakes were minute and had a scaled appearance. After the second flake of this type, the core could not be further utilized from the same platform. Four are well made and appear to have no structural or manufactural imperfections. Only two of these, however, were extensively flaked—one as a microblade core.

Single platform, faceted (18). These cores are basically the same as the single platform, unfaceted type, except that the striking platforms have been given more preparation.

Four partially utilized cores have dihedral platforms (fig. 18, c). In each, flakes hinge fractured, and the cores were abandoned. Seven of these successfully received primary flaking but hinge fractured during the next flaking attempt. Seven were successful and show numerous flake scars, four of which, however, were finally abandoned on account of hinge fractures.

Opposed platform (25). The most common type has two unfaceted platforms oriented perpendicular to the long axis of the pebble. As is the case with the single unfaceted platform cores,

the majority has not been extensively utilized owing to hinge fracturing during primary flaking or shortly thereafter.

Ninety degree (4). All are poor flake cores which have two unopposed platforms. Again, none is extensively flaked.

Wedge (6). The wedge-shaped core derives its name from its profile, which is wedge-like due to the angle formed at the striking edge. These cores do not have prepared platforms but are bifacially struck from one edge, the platform being the very base of the flake scar on the side opposite the one from which the microblade is to be removed. The direction of the flake scars shows that the microblades were not removed along the long axis but at an angle to it. Normally, the two flaked surfaces are at opposed angles, one side with scars running to the left, and the others running to the right, while the core is in the same position.

The six wedge-shaped cores found here are not good examples. Only one shows any degree of skill. The unifying trait is the sharply acute angle at the flaked edge. This varies from 43° to 56°, all but one falling between 43° to 52°.

This type of core becomes much more important during subsequent development and is one of the prime sources for microblades at Site 443. This type is well illustrated in the site reports of both Sites 624 and 443.

Isolated flake (16). All these cores show the removal of a single flake from whole pebbles. Most could have been used as unfaceted striking platforms, but were not so utilized, either because of the irregular shape of the pebble or of too acute an angle of the flake scar.

It is interesting that a number of these are on materials other than Nile chert. Five are on quartz pebbles and two on agate. While agate is relatively common, quartz is not. It appears that quartz was not desired, and after a single flake, such pebbles were normally discarded.

Unidentifiable (66). These are mostly Nile pebbles which have been randomly flaked and show no recognizable pattern of intent.

Debitage

As the Halfan is an industry characterized by a very special flaking technique, particularly in its early periods, it is not surprising that the lithic debitage is also characteristic. Since this is a newly discovered industry, it is important that all phases of it be considered. Therefore, although debitage is usually not considered in detail in site reports, that material found in this assemblage will be described.

Debitage is considered here to be all flakes and blades not made into finished tools. This excludes small core fragments and chips which could not have been utilized further.

There are basically two types of flakes and blades: those which come from the various stages in the preparation of Halfa cores, and those derived from other core types.

A total of 724 pieces of debitage were excavated, of which 347 flakes and 131 blades were from cores other than Halfan. As a group, the flakes show no predominant shape, nor are they consistent as to thickness or size. The largest is 45 mm. long, but the vast majority are microlithic. These flakes come from cores with all types of platform preparation. The most common, 43.4 per cent, shows an unfaceted butt. Cortex butts account for 14.8 per cent; dihedral, 10.7 per cent; convex, only 5.1 per cent; unidentifiable, 20.4 per cent; and broken, 4.5 per cent. It must be remembered that these percentages do not include Halfa debitage, the vast majority of which has convexly faceted butts.

Again, blades show no particular pattern in shape or size. They range in length from 19 to 50 mm., but most fall between 20 and 35 mm. Recognizable butts are rare, most of them being unfaceted. Of the 79 complete blades, 46 are incurvate, indicating an indifferent control of the material. Twenty-five blades come from opposed platform cores, while the others either come from single platform cores or do not show their opposed platform origin.

The second class of debitage comes from the preparation of Halfa cores. There are a number of flaking processes which produce distinctive debitage. Primary flakes which were removed to form the opposed platform cannot, of course, be distinguished from primary flakes taken from other core types. Once the platforms are made, however, the debitage is easily recognizable.

The first process which produces distinctive debitage is the removal of the microblades from the distal end platform. They are normally under 10 mm. in length, quite thin and regular. Of 108 found, only 22 have recognizable butts—all unfaceted. Almost all are flat, although a few are slightly incurvate. Their extreme small size and thinness make them unadaptable for further utilization.

In addition to the type of blade already considered, there is another type associated with the Halfa flake. This type comes from poor flaking of the prepared core, which results in thin blades having finely convex faceted butts and showing flake scars coming from both directions. The extremely fine nature of the faceting indicates that these do not come from opposed platform cores as these are never finely faceted nor do opposed platform cores normally have convexly faceted platforms. Twenty blades of this type were recovered.

The next step which produces distinctive debitage is the removal of the channel flake. This flake has a convexly or dihedrally faceted butt and an upper surface which has superficial similarity with a Levallois flake. Close inspection of the thirty-one found, however, shows that the flake scars are basically oriented in only two directions. The distal end of the flakes shows tiny sections of the microblade scars, while the butt end has one or more flake scars normally oriented along the long axis of the flake. These never have butts of *chapeau de gendarme* type and are usually short and wide. The removal of the Halfa flake itself often resulted in debitage, as the Halfa flake was not always successfully removed. The final blow may either remove too much of the upper surface of the core so that an overpassed flake results, or the flake may come off before it reaches the microblade scars.

Forty-six flakes come from Halfa cores, but, while conforming to the normal configuration of the Halfa flake, they had gone too far and had taken off part of the distal platform (fig. 16, l-m). These are considered debitage as the sharp distal end of the Halfa flake had not been achieved. These overpassed flakes were, on occasion, retouched into tools, but in such cases the Halfa element is purely coincidental.

There is also a series of flakes which are the opposite of the overpassed flake—those which came off the core too short. There are 49 examples, which are short and wide, have only one flake scar on their upper surface, and normally have *chapeau de gendarme* butts. Only 13 of the total found had simple convex butts, and three were broken.

Summary

Site 1018 has a lithic assemblage which is microlithic. The Microlithic Index is 81.2 for all tools. The technology is heavily oriented toward flake production, and the vast majority of tools is made on flakes, the Flake Tool Index being 81.7. The Blade Tool Index is only 12.8, while the Core Tool Index stands at 5.5.

Typologically, the most diagnostic feature of the assemblage is the Halfa flake. Production of this tool type accounts for 45.3 per cent of all recognizable cores, 56.0 per cent of all tools, and about 34 per cent of all flake and blade debitage.

While 12.8 per cent of the finished tools were made on blades or microblades, there was only one true microblade core and six poorly formed wedge cores. Apparently, most blades either resulted from Halfa core preparation or came, fortuitously, from flake cores.

Prepared platforms are mainly restricted to Halfa flakes. These are carefully made and the *chapeau de gendarme* type predominates. Platform preparation, as indicated by flake debitage, shows a much less careful consideration of the striking surface. Only 15.8 per cent of the butts are faceted, 14.8 per cent are cortex, and 43.3 per cent are unfaceted. Only 16.8 per cent appear to have been struck off by a punch, showing only the point of percussion.

While tools other than Halfa flakes account for less than half of the assemblage, there are a number of well made types. Of particular interest are the denticulates and the burins. Both show a well developed technique of manufacture. Denti-

culates are finely serrated, with evenly placed teeth. There are a few less finely made, but these are not common. Denticulates were made on blades or on elongated, broken flakes. This is the only class of unbacked tool where blade proportions appear to have been desired. The backed microblades although present do not seem to be a developed aspect of the assemblage. To be so, there would have to be a reasonably developed microblade technology.

Without question, the lithic technology is based on flake production. The Halfa core, however, has the seeds of a blade technology in its preparation. The occurrence of a few wedge-shaped cores also points to a very incipient interest in blade production. It is almost as if the development of a blade technology was in the process of evolving out of the preparation technique needed for a Halfa core. This technology, however, has barely reached a conscious stage.

Backed pieces are few and are made on irregular microblades. Their backing is different from the normal Halfa flake backing, but the presence of one Halfa flake with such backing links the two groups. The tendency to back a microflake or microblade is just beginning; it accounts for no more than 7.8 per cent of all tools. This is not surprising if the backed microblade is viewed as part of a composite tool. If so, then the backed microblade was used as a barb on a spear or arrow shaft. The Halfa flake, however, also appears to be meant as a projectile point or arrow head. The Halfa flake is functionally only suitable for placement on the end of a shaft, while the backed microblade is functionally suited for use on the sides. If both were, in fact, hafted, it is not surprising that such a well developed Halfa flake technology should have so few backed microblades. The fact that such exist at all, points to the possible shift to the smaller and more easily hafted microblade and microflake. The loss of a Halfa flake from a shaft would render it useless, but the loss of one microblade or microflake from a shaft with a series of such would only slightly reduce its effectiveness.

Core technology is very poor. The only type which shows a high stage of development is the Halfa core. The basic orientation of the Halfa core to opposed platforms is reflected in the number of poor opposed platform flake cores. These, however, are never extensively utilized, and no real care has gone into their initial preparation. The Halfa core does, however, have a number of features which could lead to more generalized, yet effective, core types.

Levallois cores are present, but they are poorly made and have not received the careful attention that the Halfa cores have. In fact, the Levallois flake is merely a more generalized form of Halfa flake and as such could have been of no great value to an industry producing Halfa flakes.

SITE 624

Site 624 is located on the west bank of the Nile, 700 m. northeast of the Egyptian fort of Buhen and 450 m. west of the Nile (map ref. 644.8/913.5). The site is situated on a silt bench at about 147 m. absolute elevation, or 25 m. above floodplain.

The total site had been deflated and somewhat scattered by wind action. In spite of this, the surface concentration of artifacts was only 450 sq. m. in area (25 m. by 18 m.), and dense concentration covered no more than 140 sq. m. (fig. 19).

Artifacts were recovered from the surface and up to 5 cm. in a loose sand deposit. All artifacts were wind and sand abraded and none could be considered in exact original position. There was little question, however, that the movement of artifacts was minimal and that the site area had been only moderately expanded by shifting of artifacts.

The surface cover of eolian sand rested on silt. No artifacts were found in the silt, nor was there any indication of fire pits or earth ovens dug into the silt.

No bone, shell beads, or other non-lithic artifacts were found. A few fire-burned rocks were scattered on the surface, indicating the probable presence of earth ovens, but these must have been fully deflated.

The site was discovered by F. Wendorf during the 1963-1964 field season and 80 sq. m. of surface material was systematically collected and test pits placed in the silt in February, 1964, by W. McHugh.

Lithic Artifacts

A total of 9,632 artifacts were recovered. Of these, 5,764 were debris, 1,641 primary flakes, 941 cores and core fragments, 704 flakes, and 189 blades. Only 393 were classifiable as tools, which accounts for 4.1 per cent of the total collection. Artifacts were collected from both areas of dense concentration and those with less than average artifactual cover. Overall, however, the artifactual density of the site was 120.4 artifacts per square meter. This is appreciably lower than that at earlier Halfan sites.

As at all Halfan sites, chert from Nile pebble was the predominant raw material used for making tools. At this site there is very little difference between the proportions of raw materials used for cores and those used in final tool manufacture, as Table 9 shows.

TABLE 9
UTILIZATION OF RAW MATERIALS AT SITE 624

	Cores	Tools
Chert	96.2%	95.0%
Agate	0.6%	0.5%
Quartz	0.6%	1.2%
Fossil wood	1.0%	2.2%
Precambrian	1.6%	0.8%

TOOL TYPOLOGY

	No.	%
Halfa flakes, unretouched	22	5.6
Halfa flakes, retouched	11	2.8
Levallois flakes	4	1.0
End-scrapers	9	2.3
Nosed scrapers	3	0.8
Core scrapers	4	1.0
Side-scrapers	4	1.0
Burins, dihedral *déjeté*	1	0.3
Burins, "single blow"	1	0.3
Burins, angle on snapped pieces	2	0.5
Burins, on retouched truncations	4	1.0
Denticulates	5	1.3
Denticulate core scrapers	4	1.0
Notched pieces	19	4.8
Truncated flakes	17	4.3
Scaled pieces	4	1.0
Backed flakes	43	10.9
Partially backed flakes	22	5.6
Backed flakes, notched	1	0.3
Backed flakes, retouched	1	0.3
Backed blades	3	0.8
Backed microblades	59	15.0
Backed microblades, broken	44	11.2
Partially backed microblades	42	10.7
Backed microblades, retouched	11	2.8
Backed microblades, denticulate	1	0.3
Backed microblades, notched	10	2.5
Backed microblades, truncated	9	2.3

Fig. 19—Site 624, looking across site to the southwest.

	No.	%
Borers on backed microblades	1	0.3
Truncated microblades	2	0.5
Retouched microblades	15	3.8
Microburins	2	0.5
Retouched flakes	8	2.0
Double backed points	1	0.3
Varia	4	1.0
	393	100.1

NOTES ON THE TYPOLOGY

Halfa flakes, unretouched (22). As a group these are quite poor; four could be considered well made (fig. 20, aa), while the rest are indifferent at best (fig. 20, bb-cc). Only eight have *chapeau de gendarme* butts, six have simple convex butts, while the remainder are broken. The complete flakes measure between 20 and 35 mm., although all but one are under 30 mm. in length.

Halfa flakes, retouched (11). Again, these are generally poor (fig. 20, z). Retouch is the same as that found on Halfa flakes at Sites 1018 and 1020. One has a dihedral butt, the rest are *chapeau de gendarme*.

Levallois flakes (4). There is one typical example but the others are atypical. All are thick and somewhat incurvate.

End-scrapers (9). This is a mixed group, mostly atypical. Three are on primary flakes and are only partially retouched. One is really a microlithic transverse convex scraper formed by inverse retouch (fig. 20, ee). The others are on microblades (fig. 20, p), including one on a backed microblade fragment (fig. 20, o).

Nosed scrapers (3). All are poor examples on irregular flakes.

Core scrapers (4). Again, these are poor. There is one fairly nice end-like scraper on a core fragment (fig. 20, nn). One piece is rather curious. From the top it appears to be a well made Levallois flake core, but there has been no preparation of a flat cortex underside. Very fine retouch has been added to most of the periphery,

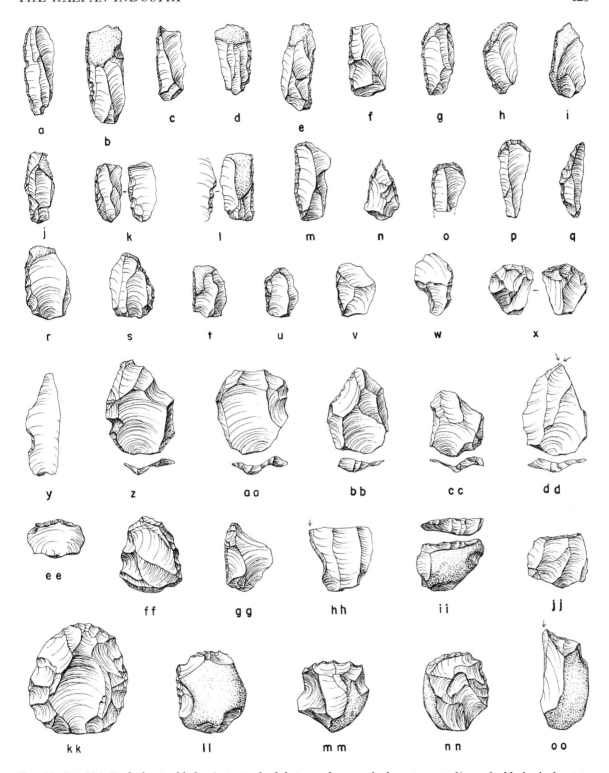

Fig. 20—Site 624: Backed microblades (a-i, simple; k-l, inversely retouched; m, truncated); n, double backed point; o-p, end-scrapers; q, lunate?; r-w, flakes (r-u, backed; v-w, partially backed); x, scaled piece; y, notched blade; z-cc, Halfa flakes; dd, hh, oo, burins; ee-gg, scrapers; ii-jj, truncated flakes; kk, nn, core scrapers; ll-mm, denticulates. 4/5 natural size.

making a somewhat circular core scraper which approaches a gouge (fig. 20, kk).

Side-scrapers (4). All are convex scrapers on irregular flakes. Retouch varies from semi-steep to almost flat and marginal (figs. 20, ff-gg).

Burins, dihedral *déjeté* (1). A good example on a questionable Halfa flake (fig. 20, dd).

Burins, "single blow" (1). A transverse burin spall has been struck from a naturally perpendicular lateral edge of an irregular flake.

Burins, angle on snapped pieces (2). Two typical examples (fig. 20, hh).

Burins, on retouched truncations (4). These are among the largest tools, ranging in length from 31 to 40 mm. All are typical and made on thick primary flakes (fig. 20, oo). Two have oblique straight and two oblique concave truncations.

Denticulates (5). These are all atypical for the Halfan. Unlike the denticulates from other sites, these are on irregular flakes and have poorly formed denticulated edges. All are microdenticulate and three of the five are worked at the distal ends (fig. 20, ll).

Denticulate core scrapers (4). As a group, these are better made than those on flakes but are still short of the quality seen at other Halfan sites (fig. 20, mm).

Notched pieces (19). All are micronotches. Eight are on microblades, three are formed by inverse (fig. 20, y) and five by obverse retouch. The remaining eleven notches are on irregular flakes, only four of which show inverse retouch.

Truncated flakes (17). There is some variation as to size and type of truncation. Five microflakes have obliquely concave truncations formed by inverse retouch. These verge on end notches but are somewhat too wide and shallow. There are four obliquely straight truncations on primary flakes (fig. 20, ii), and four straight truncations on irregular microflakes (fig. 20, jj). In addition, there are one basal truncation and three oblique truncations on very small flakes which gives them a pseudo-geometric look.

Scaled pieces (4). All are on microflakes but lack the regularity of treatment found in later examples (fig. 20, x).

Backed flakes (43). These comprise a unified group. All backing is light but very steep. Flakes are small, thin, and tend toward rectangular shapes, although a few are pointed. Normally, the backing does not greatly alter the original flake shape, but in a few cases it does somewhat modify one edge.

There are three types of backing: straight, convex, and concave. Straight backing, which does modify flake shape, is the most common, occurring on 23 flakes (fig. 20, t-u). Convex backing occurs on 16 (fig. 20, r-s), while concave backing is very rare, only three examples having been found.

The largest backed flake measures 28 mm. and the smallest 15 mm. with the others evenly scattered between these extremes. Of the 43 backed flakes, 74 per cent, or 30, are backed on the left side. This tendency is seen throughout the Halfan.

Partially backed flakes (22). These are similar to the backed flakes, except that the backing is only partial. Size range is the same as above, but half are backed on the left edge (fig. 20, v), and convex backing predominates with 12 pieces (fig. 20, w).

Backed flakes, notched (1). A flake convexly backed on its right side has a retouched micronotch near the butt on the backed edge.

Backed flakes, retouched (1). A flake with straight backing on its left edge also has some flat, inverse retouch along the right lateral edge.

Backed blades (3). Two measure 32 mm. in length, and one is 39 mm. long. This is the only criterion which separates them from the backed microblades. Cortex is present on all three, in two cases at the distal end. All are backed on the left side; two convexly (fig. 20, a-b), and one concavely. All are slightly incurvate.

Backed microblades (59). These represent the most common tool in the assemblage. Including broken and partially backed examples, they account for over 35 per cent of all tools.

Microblades of all types occur, and many are not well made. Twenty-seven have some cortex on their upper surface, which normally covers their distal ends (fig. 20, d, j). Forty-seven are generally parallel sided (fig. 20, c, f), nine are more or less pointed (fig. 20, m), and four are irregular.

Another common trait is for the microblades to be incurvate; 38 out of 59 are of that kind. This trait is particularly strong on those microblades with cortex, where 84 per cent are incurvate. On microblades without cortex only about 50 per cent are incurvate. This incurvate tendency comes not only from the curvature of the blades but also from their rather prominent bulbs of percussion.

Backing on microblades is predominately on the left side, accounting for 61 per cent or 35 examples, which is a somewhat lower frequency than for backed flakes.

Convex backing predominates with 33 pieces, while straight backing occurs on 23, and concave backing on only 3.

Microblades range in size from 16 to 30 mm., with 22 to 25 mm. being most common.

Backed microblades, broken (44). Fragmentary examples of the typical backed microblades. The only observation possible is on side preference for backing; 68.2 per cent, or 30 fragments, are backed on the left side.

Partially backed microblades (42). As on the backed microblades, left side backing is most common, occurring on 26 pieces, or 61.9 per cent of the time.

Twenty-three are generally parallel sided, but 10 are pointed and 9 are irregular. Cortex occurs on 23 examples of which 18, or 78.3 per cent, are incurvate. Those without cortex, 43.2 per cent, show only 10 incurvate pieces, while 9, or 47.3 per cent, are flat. These traits parallel those for fully backed microblades.

Half of this group has convex backing (fig. 20, g-h), 16 have straight backs (fig. 21, g), and 5 have concave backing (fig. 20, r). On the whole, these are more irregular in both microblade shape and control of the backed edge than are those which are fully backed.

Backed microblades, retouched (11). Typical backed microblades and microblade fragments which have retouch along the unbacked edge. Eight have inverse and three have obverse retouch. In all cases, the retouch is irregular and weak. Inverse retouch, as mentioned for other tools, is very flat (fig. 20, k-l). Five have straight and six convex backing. Seventy per cent, however, are backed on the left side.

Backed microblades, denticulate (1). A fragmentary example, convexly backed on the right edge, has an irregular inversely retouched denticulation on the opposite edge.

Backed microblades, notched (10). Typical backed microblades which have single micronotches on the edge opposite the backing. All but one are inverse, and all but two notches are about half way along the edge. The other two notches are near the butt ends. Eight are convexly backed on the left side.

Backed microblades, truncated (9). Four are obliquely truncated, two by inverse retouch. Another has a straight truncation (fig. 20, m), while four are basally truncated, three obliquely. Six of the microblades have backing on the left side, and six have straight backing.

Borers on backed microblades (1). A poor inverse example of a tool type found more frequently at Site 443.

Truncated microblades (2). Both are obliquely truncated.

Retouched microblades (15). All but five are obversely retouched. Most retouch is semi-steep and verges on backing; in many cases it may have been functionally the same.

Microburins (2). Because of their extreme rarity, as compared with the microblade technology, it must be assumed that these two examples are accidental.

Retouched flakes (8). Various irregular flakes and flake fragments which have partial, light retouch.

Double backed points (1). A single, small triangular point made by steep retouch on both edges (fig. 20, n).

Varia (4). There is one lunate-like tool with a denticulated backed edge (fig. 20, q), and there are three complexly retouched flakes which do not conform to any recognized tool type.

CORE TYPOLOGY			Restricted
	No.	%	%
Halfa	49	10.0	15.8
Levallois	17	3.5	5.5
Single platform, unfaceted	66	13.4	21.2
Single platform, faceted	63	12.8	20.2
Opposed platform	36	7.3	11.6
Ninety degree	19	3.9	6.1
Wedge	31	6.3	9.9
Bipolar	1	0.2	0.3
Opposite side	5	1.0	1.6
Discoidal	6	1.2	1.9
Globular	3	0.6	0.9
Isolated flake	15	3.1	4.8
Unidentifiable	179	36.7	–
	490	100.0	99.8

NOTES ON THE TYPOLOGY

A total of 941 cores and core fragments were collected. Of these, however, 451 were small fragments which could not be classified in any way. The remaining 490 are classified above.

Halfa (49). While Halfa cores are fairly common, they are not as well made as those at earlier Halfan sites. In fact, only thirteen (25 per cent) have been successfully completed (fig. 21, f). Eighteen are in the early stages of production, an equal number hinge fractured in the attempt to remove the channel flake, and only one shows the scar of an overpassed flake.

Levallois (17). All are atypical but do have fairly extensive preparation of the under surface.

Single platform, unfaceted (66). This type is one of the most common in the assemblage. They vary greatly as to quality but do show more overall intensive flaking per core than that at earlier Halfan sites. These cores indicate a greater control in the removal of microblades than was seen before. Just over 30 per cent, 20 examples, show successfully struck microblades (fig. 21, b).

Single platform, faceted (63). A very common core type which lacks the quality of the unfaceted examples. These too, however, are usually more fully utilized than was the case at earlier Halfan sites. Only 19, however, were true microblade cores (fig. 21, e); the vast majority produced only small flakes (fig. 21, d).

Opposed platform (36). For the most part, these are poor microblade cores (fig. 21, a). They rarely show extensive flaking.

Ninety degree (19). These are generally well formed microblade cores (fig. 21, c), although about one-third show little more than the removal of primary flakes.

Wedge (31). This type of core is fairly common and becomes even more so by Site 443. Here, flaking control is only fair, although some good examples occur (fig. 21, g).

Bipolar (1). A single, slightly battered example.

Opposite side (5). These are really no more than opposed platform cores which have been flaked on opposite sides of the core, rather than on the same side. All these are quite poor, and none can be called a successful microblade core.

Discoidal (6). All are atypical examples on Nile pebble.

Globular (3). Small chert core remnants.

Isolated flake (15). Pebbles which have had only one primary flake removed.

Unidentifiable (179). Slightly over one-third of all cores show no visible pattern of flaking. They are rarely utilized to any degree.

Summary

The overall picture presented by this assemblage is quite different from that of earlier Halfan sites. While artifact types are much the same, there has been a radical shift in proportions of types, in both the typology and the technology.

The assemblage is well on its way toward a true microblade technology with much better control of core flaking. This may be seen in the percentages of gross artifact types: 4.1 per cent tools, 3.6 per cent blades, 8.8 per cent flakes, 9.8 per cent cores, 17.0 per cent primary flakes, and 56.7 per cent debris. While blades are more common, they are not usually well formed as about 66 per cent are markedly incurvate and half have cortex on their upper surface.

Another aspect which shows great change from the earlier Halfan assemblages is a major decrease in the importance of the specific Halfan technology; Halfa cores account for no more than 15.8 per cent of all recognizable examples, and Halfa flakes make up only 8.4 per cent of the tool inventory.

Typologically, Site 624 is halfway between a flake tool and true microblade tool assemblage, as the following indicates: Blade Tool Index 54.4, Flake Tool Index 43.5, and Core Tool Index 2.1.

The assemblage is strongly microlithic, with a Microlithic Index of 91.7. The most common tool is the simple backed or partially backed microblade, which accounts for 36.9 per cent of all tools. When all backed microblades are included, both simple and complex forms, this percentage increases to 45.1, while all backed tools, blade and flake, account for 64.1 per cent.

Backed microblades and flakes show a number of specific traits. Most backing is on the left edge, which occurs 63.7 per cent of the time. All backing is extremely fine and steep, rarely cutting deeply into the original flake or blade shape. Backing may be straight, convex, or concave.

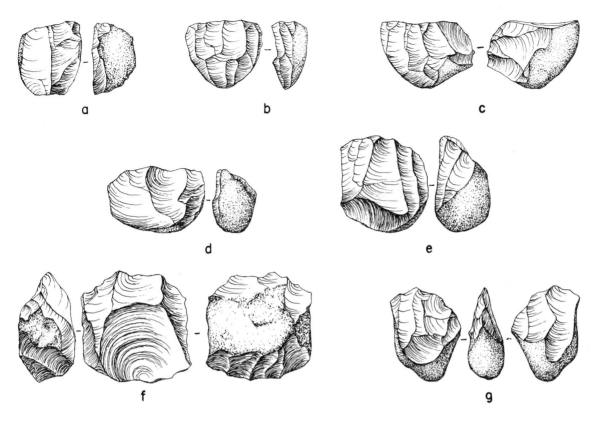

Fig. 21—Site 624: a, opposed platform; b, single platform, unfaceted core; c, ninety degree core; d-e, single platform, faceted cores; f, Halfa core; g, wedge core. 4/5 natural size.

Concave backing is exceedingly rare (6.2 per cent), straight backing more common (42.7 per cent), while convex backing accounts for just over one-half of all examples (51.1 per cent).

While convex backing is in the majority, the convexity is usually only very slight and in many cases grades into straight backing. Retouch added to backed pieces is normally inverse, 63.6 per cent, while simple retouched tools are made overwhelmingly by obverse retouch, 75.5 per cent.

Aside from the backed tools, perhaps only Halfa flakes could be considered diagnostic. Scrapers, burins, denticulates, truncations, notches, and scaled pieces all occur but only in small numbers and are probably more significant because of their very presence rather than because of their number.

SITE 443

Site 443 lies on a branch of the Khor Musa, 3

km. due west of the Wadi Halfa airport building and 11 km. southwest of Wadi Halfa (map ref. 642.6/904.7). The site, 25 m. above present floodplain, is situated on a sand dune remnant which slopes southward down to the Khor bed (fig. 22). The top of the dune and its slopes cover an oval area of about 250 sq. m. The western side of the dune is defined by a small wadi which cuts sharply to a depth of 2 m. below the dune crest. The eastern side of the dune slopes gradually to another small wadi. The dune itself is banked against an eroded bank of the Dibeira-Jer deposits to the north, the crest of the dune being 5 m. below the surface of the Dibeira-Jer formation (fig. 23).

The whole top of the dune, and its southern and eastern slopes, were covered by a surface concentration of flakes, cores, tools, and weathered bone fragments. During the 1962-1963 season, J. Guichard of the Combined Prehistoric Expedition, made an extensive surface collection

Fig. 22–Site 443, looking across site to the north.

and excavated a small test trench into the western side of the hill. The surface collection was not studied, and the excavation report, Site 443B, noted the presence of a large fire pit, while the excavated artifacts did not receive more than cursory inspection (Waechter, 1965, p. 138).

Early in the 1963-1964 season, it was decided that future excavation was warranted. Excavation took place during all of November under my direction, assisted by W. McHugh, and, at times, by M. B. Stokes and J. Marks. On November 1, work began with the clearing of windblown sand from the already excavated test trench. The profiles of the trench indicated that it had not encountered a fire pit but had entered into a dark deposit of occupation debris some 60 cm. thick. Careful inspection of the dune showed that this dark colored deposit was present over the whole top of the dune, under a thin covering of windblown sand. It was, therefore, decided that one trench, one meter wide, would

be placed across the whole dune, oriented east-west, and that another would be excavated perpendicular to it. In this way it was hoped that a clear picture of the extent and density of the occupation would emerge. Surface material was eliminated from study because most of it had already been collected as one unit the previous season, and an unknown portion of it was separated and sent to Europe.

A meter square grid was laid out over the whole of the dune, and a line of squares, running across the center of the hill in an east-west direction, was chosen for excavation. Each square was initially excavated as a unit, and the material from each was treated and catalogued separately. As the total picture of the occupation became clear, this system was modified so that fire pits were treated as separate units, although included in more than one square.

Vertical control was initially established by extending the old test pit so that it made contact

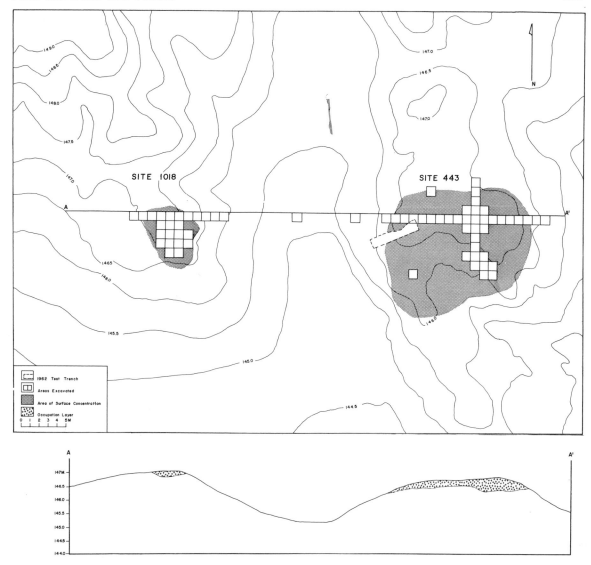

FIG. 23—Topographic map of Sites 443 and 1018.

with the projected trench. The profile thus established indicated a clear gross stratigraphy of three layers. The top layer consisted of loose windblown sand containing artifacts and bone. This layer undulated in thickness between 2 and 12 cm. It was clearly separated by its light tan color from the habitation layer below. The habitation layer at the trench line of 19 cm. consisted of fine, dark, and sand silt with burned rocks, bone, fresh artifacts, and small pockets of reddish burned clay. The habitation layer rested on an irregular surface of compact light tan eolian sand which formed the original shape of the dune.

This layer was sterile, although a few artifacts had been "walked" into it during the occupation (fig. 24).

Once this stratigraphy was clear, excavation began by the stripping of the top layer in the squares adjacent to the profile. This called for beginning the excavations in the western end of the east-west trench. In the westernmost square, only a small, thin layer of habitation debris was found. It tapered off at the edge of the slope, indicating some wind deflation. As excavation of the trench continued toward the center of the dune, it became clear that wind deflation had

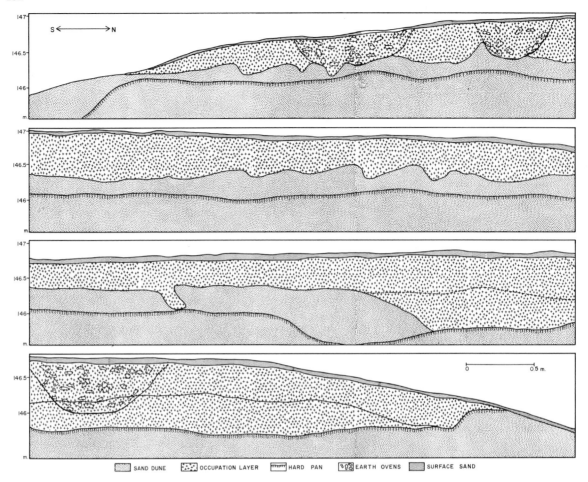

SAND DUNE   OCCUPATION LAYER   HARD PAN   EARTH OVENS   SURFACE SAND

Fig. 24—Profile of Site 443.

lowered much of the occupation layer. The occupation layer began to thicken, but by the crest it was no deeper than 25 cm.

After it was established that the relationship of the top layer to the occupation layer was consistent, excavation was begun at the extreme ends of the two trenches to ascertain the full extent of the occupation area. On the eastern and southern slopes, it was found that the occupation layer had been eroded by sheet wash and wind deflation, which transported artifacts down the slopes beyond the original limit of the occupation. On these two sides, there was a clear tapering off of the occupation layer with surface finds extending as much as 10 m. farther down slope.

The northernmost 3 m. of the north-south trench showed a different stratigraphic configuration. This section of the trench was on a rela-

tively flat surface, which had a small slope into a shallow saddle at the base of the incline to the 30 m. terrace. The northernmost square contained loose sterile eolian sand. The second square contained the same sand mixed with a little ash and a few artifacts. The third square showed a rather amorphous beginning of the occupation layer which was extremely powdery but dark in color.

Thus, the limits of the occupation layer were clearly seen, somewhat eroded on three sides but intact on the northern boundary. The total area covered by the extant occupation layer was about 150 sq. m. although the original site must have been somewhat larger.

As excavation progressed, it was seen that the eastern 6 m. of the east-west trench contained a thick occupation layer, comparable to that on the western side. It reached a thickness of 60 cm. and could be divided into two units. The upper half, from 20 to 40 cm. thick, was composed of a loose fill, while the lower portion was quite consolidated and rested on the calcarious hard cap. Five meters to the west from the end of the trench, this consolidated section tapered out at the same level as that where the consolidated sand met the occupation layer.

The evidence of a consolidated section of occupation debris indicates that the consolidation of the sand layer took place after the occupation while the hard cap apparently formed before the occupation, as in the eastern section of the trench the occupation debris rested on it.

Features

With the removal of the top layer a number of features became apparent. The whole surface of the occupation layer was criss-crossed by desiccation cracks filled with sand and artifacts from the top layer. The surface was also strewn with fire-cracked rocks. As no pattern was apparent in the distribution of the rocks in any one square, a 9 sq. m. area at the junction of the two trenches was stripped of the top layer. It was felt that a surface area of only 1 sq. m. perhaps did not give sufficient area for the understanding of their distribution. When this was completed, however, it was apparent that there was no concentration or series of concentrations and that the burned rocks were randomly scattered over the whole of the occupation surface. There was also a scattering of bone fragments over the entire area. The bone, however, did show areas of concentration. These areas also contained lumps of burned clay, and the fill below them was more compacted than it was over most of the area. Subsequent excavation revealed that these were probably earth ovens. They were, however, clearly visible only in profile, and then only their lower portions were sharply defined. A total of six earth ovens were excavated, also one true hearth.

Three earth ovens and one hearth were uncovered during the excavation of the western section of the east-west trench. The hearth only became clear 19 cm. below the surface of the occupation layer. Only half was excavated as the old test pit had cut into it. It was ovoid in

shape, and at a depth of 25 cm. below the top of the occupation layer there was a series of small burned stones which defined its outer limits. Within the stone line the fill was hard packed, containing small charcoal fragments, bone, and artifacts. The fill outside the stones was a loose dark sand mixed with occupation debris. Numerous bones and bone fragments were recovered, and a small charcoal sample was taken.

In the first 19 cm. of occupation debris over the hearth, there were numerous burned rocks and bones but no charcoal, and the fill was quite loose. This was the same for the earth ovens excavated; the upper portions had been disturbed and scattered.

Less than one meter to the northeast of the hearth, the only complete earth oven excavated was found. Its preservation was better than the others, and there was a clear indication of its position on the surface of the occupation layer (fig. 25). The earth oven, 30 cm. deep, was cut into the consolidated sterile sand below. There was no true ring of rocks, but the eastern side was somewhat lined. There were numerous burned stones in the area of the fire pit itself. Again, only the lower portion was truly distinct, in profile, from the surrounding occupation layer. The fill was consolidated, but at the edges this was purely relative. It had a rather amorphous form but covered an area of about 1 sq. m. The other five earth ovens followed the same pattern as those described above. Two more were found in the western area, one large one in the central area, and two on the southern slope. One of the southern earth ovens rested just at the top of the slope and had not been eroded. It covered an area of about 1 sq. m. and, as in the case of all the earth ovens, it cut into the sterile compacted sand. The other southern earth oven could not be clearly distinguished from the surrounding occupation layer except for a heavy concentration of burned stone, bone, and some charcoal.

The two fully excavated earth ovens were similar in size, depth, and amount of artifactual material recovered in each. One produced 58 finished tools, the other 52. These earth ovens were on opposite sides of the site, but there was no significant difference in the typology of the tools recovered, nor any in·the number and type of debitage found.

Fig. 25—Earth oven at Site 443.

Carbon samples were taken from two earth ovens. An additional carbon sample was taken from the consolidated occupation zone in the eastern part of the east-west trench. A combined sample from the earth ovens gave a date of 14,500 B.C. ± 500 years (WSU 201).

While most of the artifacts found were either microlithic stone tools or the debris from their manufacture, some other types of artifactual materials were also found.

Beads

Five ostrich shell beads in various stages of manufacture were found. Two beads were roughly shaped and holed, but still lacked final work. One finished bead, one semifinished fragment, and one finished fragment were also recovered.

The two unfinished beads permit an insight into their technique of manufacture (fig. 26, a-b). Both are roughly chipped into an ovoid shape, measuring 14 mm. by 12 mm. Both show chipping by a series of small flakes struck from the outer surface. Once the rough shape had been achieved, a hole was bored by rotary motion from the inside surface. The hole was taken most of the way through the shell, but the actual break to the outer surface was achieved by punching out the last, thin section of shell. The hole was then enlarged by a rocker motion, the result being an elongated hole. Neither of the unfinished beads had been taken beyond this point.

The semifinished fragment indicates the next steps in bead preparation. The hole had been

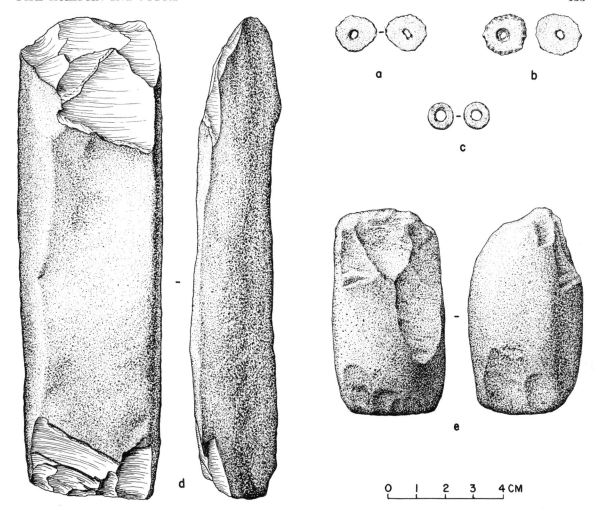

Fig. 26—Site 443: a-c, beads; d, chopper; e, hammerstone. 4–5 natural size.

treated with a rotary motion from the outer surface, enlarging but not completely rounding it. The rough shape had been modified to some degree by polishing. The polishing does not, however, extend across the whole of the chipped surface but only affects a small portion of it. This is done by positioning the edge at a steep angle so that only half the rim is in contact with the rubbing surface.

The whole bead and fragment complete the series and show that much additional work was needed before a bead was finished. The final form is circular with a large round hole and a flat edge. This outer edge is fully polished, and no trace is left of the chipping nor of the initial polishing. Although one bead is fragmentary, it is apparent that both are of the same size, 8 mm.

in diameter, with a hole 4 mm. in diameter (fig. 26, c).

It is interesting to note that these five ostrich shell beads were the only examples of ostrich shell found. Three came from the western section of the east-west trench, while the remainder came from the southern part of the site.

Varia

Six ferrocrete sandstone ventifacts from the jebels to the west were found in one earth oven. Two more were found in the occupation debris on the other side of the site. All had been burned and showed a red powdery substance over their surfaces. This was an iron oxide which made an excellent reddish stain, similar in color to hematite. None of the ventifacts showed flaking or grinding, but as the iron oxide readily rubs off the surface, only minimal contact is necessary to remove the coloring matter.

Twelve pieces of mica schist were also recovered. These were scattered through the occupation layer and showed no concentration. This material is not immediately available in the vicinity. Its source is probably to the south, in the Batn el-Hajar. Thus, it must have been purposefully brought to the site by its inhabitants. Its use is obscure, but it may have served as a coloring agent when mixed with animal fats.

Lithic Artifacts

During excavations 42 sq. m. were cleared to the sterile sand layer. Within this excavated area 43,265 artifacts were recovered. Most of these, 25,852 pieces, were small chips or heavily burned fragments. Other debitage included 6,695 primary flakes, 4,256 cores and core fragments, 3,165 flakes, and 1,333 blades and microblades. Only 1,964 finished tools, accounting for 4.5 per cent of the total collection, were found.

The most commonly utilized raw material was chert from Nile pebbles, although some other types of rock were also used. The dominance of chert, however, may be seen in Table 10.

TABLE 10

UTILIZATION OF RAW MATERIALS AT SITE 443

	Cores	Tools
Chert	95.3%	98.3%
Agate	3.4%	1.4%
Quartz	0.2%	0.0%
Fossil wood	0.9%	0.0%
Precambrian	0.2%	0.2%
Ferrocrete sandstone	0.0%	0.1%

TOOL TYPOLOGY

	No.	%
Halfa flakes, unretouched	14	0.7
Halfa flakes, retouched	13	0.7
Levallois flakes	10	0.5
End-scrapers	20	1.0
Ogival ends-scrapers	3	0.2
Nosed scrapers	2	0.1
Carinated scrapers	1	+
Core scrapers	23	1.2
Side-scrapers	5	0.3
Burins, dihedral straight	3	0.2
Burins, dihedral *déjeté*	1	+
Burins, dihedral angle	5	0.3
Burins, angle on snapped pieces	4	0.2
Burins, on retouched truncations	3	0.2
Burins, *plan*	2	0.1
Burins, transverse	2	0.1
Denticulates	13	0.7
Denticulate core scrapers	15	0.8
Notched pieces	43	2.2
Truncated flakes	18	0.9
Scaled pieces	16	0.8
Cortex backed knives	19	1.0
Backed flakes	209	10.6
Partially backed flakes	117	5.9
Backed flakes, truncated	4	0.2
Backed flakes, notched	4	0.2
Backed blades	39	2.0
Backed microblades	224	11.4
Partially backed microblades	295	15.0
Backed microblades, broken	569	28.9
Backed microblades, retouched	60	3.1
Backed microblades, denticulate	12	0.6
Backed microblades, notched	65	3.3
Backed microblades, end notched	5	0.3
Backed microblades, truncated	21	1.1
Borers on backed microblades	12	0.6
Alternately backed microblades	2	0.1
Double backed microblades	3	0.2
Microburins	1	+
Truncated microblades	11	0.6
Retouched microblades	42	2.1
Retouched flakes	21	1.0
Backed points	1	+
Backed truncated points	4	0.2
Varia	8	0.4
	1964	100.0

NOTES ON THE TYPOLOGY

Halfa flakes, unretouched (14). The Halfa flake is a newly recognized artifact type first described from the northern Sudan. The technological and typological description is to be found in detailed form in a preceding section of this report. All are more or less atypical (fig. 27, j), and all are microlithic.

Halfa flakes, retouched (13). The retouch on a Halfa flake is always limited to one or both lateral edges adjacent to the butt, extending no more than half the length of the edge. The retouch is in the form of a backing which normally has the effect of cutting the flake to make the lateral edges near the butt straight and at the same time dulling them. In the case where one lateral edge is naturally backed or is perpendicular to the flake surface, it is never retouched, while the opposite edge may be. There is one good example of this type found here.

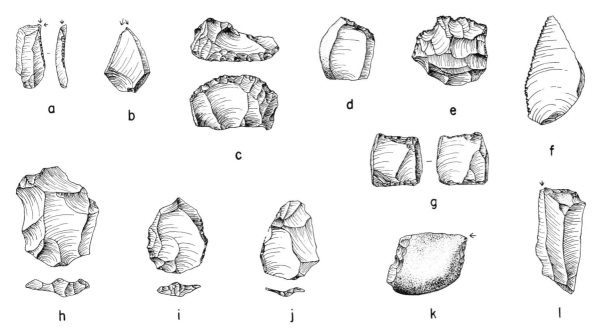

FIG. 27—Site 443: a-b, k-l, burins; c, core scraper; d, truncated flake; e, denticulate core scraper; f, denticulate; g, scaled piece; h, Levallois flake; i-j, Halfa flakes. 4/5 natural size.

Thirteen Halfa flakes were retouched. Four have been retouched only on the right hand side, while three have been retouched only on the left hand side. Six examples have bilateral retouch. Butts on these pieces reflect a lowering of technological standards; only two are *chapeau de gendarme*.

Levallois flakes (10). Levallois flakes are rare and indifferently made. Platform preparation shows four with cortex, one unfaceted, one plain, and two dihedral faceted. Two are unidentifiable. Of the 8 complete pieces, only three are microlithic, while the others measure between 30 and 40 mm. There are two prevalent shapes; five flakes are rectangular (fig. 27, h), longer than they are wide, and three are pointed but do not come from Levallois point cores.

End-scrapers (20). Six end-scrapers are made on backed microblades. Two are double convex (fig. 28, ff). The others are single convex, and all have been made by semi-steep retouch. They range in length from 11 to 29 mm. There is another on a backed blade 37 mm. long.

Four end-scrapers are made on blades showing cortex, only one of which is a true primary blade. All are broadly convex. None are as well made as those on backed microblades (fig. 28, hh).

Nine end-scrapers are made on flakes. They are all atypical, three approaching microlithic thumbnail shapes.

Ogival end-scrapers (3). Two are on backed microblades while the third is on a large cortex topped blade (fig. 28, gg).

Nosed scrapers (2). Two core fragments have been transformed into a nose scraper by fine, semi-steep retouch.

Carinated scrapers (1). It is on a core fragment but has received only light retouch so that the keeled shape is due to the natural shape of the fragment and not to the retouch.

Core scrapers (23). Eight are convex scrapers made on wedge shaped cores, the scraping edge being along the sharply acute angle of the striking platform. Each has been retouched along its whole length (fig. 27, c). Nine other convex scrapers approach a normal core angle of 75° at the scraping edge. One is convex with a small nose. Also, one concave scraper which approaches a notch is made on a pebble.

Side-scrapers (5). Side-scrapers form a poor group. There is one good concave side-scraper on a thick primary flake and two lightly retouched concave side-scrapers on thick flakes but, otherwise, they are poorly made convex scrapers on various shaped flakes. One is made on an agate flake by inverse retouch. All but one are microlithic.

Burins, dihedral straight (3). Three are on flake fragments. All are typical (fig. 27, b).

Burins, dihedral *déjeté* (1). A poor example on a flake.

Burins, dihedral angle (5). Three are formed on flakes, one is on a core fragment, and one is on the distal end of a notched and backed microblade (fig. 27, a).

Burins, angle on snapped pieces (4). Three of these are on reworked backed microblades, while the other is on a small flake. All are fairly typical, although no examples were found which could be considered really fine.

Burins, on retouched truncations (3). There is one good example on a reworked backed microblade with a straight oblique truncation. Another is on a thick blade fragment (fig. 27, 1), while the third is also on a broken blade.

Burins, *plan* (2). Both are on backed microblades which have been snapped.

Burins, transverse (2). Both are microlithic burins on lateral truncations (fig. 27, k).

Denticulates (13). All are microdenticulates, and all but three are made on the lateral edge of a flake or microblade. The most numerous group, four examples, is made on cortex backed flakes. The three largest, two with serrated edges of 25 mm., and one of 30 mm., are made by exceedingly fine retouch, two inverse and one normal (fig. 27, f). This retouch is uniform along the whole cutting edge, averaging a tooth every

12 mm. in length, with an average of one tooth every 1.25 mm.

Three denticulates are on wide blades; the serrations are formed by exceedingly fine retouch and average one tooth every 1.3 mm. These, however, are not as regularly serrated as the first group, nor are they inversely retouched.

Two denticulates are made on microblades, three by inverse retouch. While these have short working edges, none more than 14 mm. long, the serration is as fine as above, averaging a tooth every 1.3 mm.

Four denticulates are on small irregular flakes. Fine serration retouch covers the whole, or part, of one edge of each flake. Three of the four are slightly less fine than the above examples, each having a tooth every 1.6 mm. The fourth falls into a more typical denticulate class, made by four retouch notches, with a tooth every 3.2 mm.

Denticulate core scrapers (15). While this is not a generally recognized class of artifacts, it has been made such here as it forms half of the total core scrapers. These are similar to the normal core scrapers, but most have a scraping angle of about 75°. They are well made with relatively large teeth and show much retouch (fig. 27, e). One is made on a large quartz fragment.

Notched pieces (43). In this section all notches under 10 mm. in width are called micronotches, and all over 10 mm. in width macronotches.

All notches show evidence of use, i.e., minute flake scars are visible along the concavity of the notch. The macronotches are relatively small,

| | Normal | | | | Inverse | | | |
| | Macro | | Micro | | Macro | | Micro | |
	Perc.[1]	Ret.[2]	Perc.	Ret.	Perc.	Ret.	Perc.	Ret.
Flakes								
Lateral edge	3	4	1	1	2	1	1	2
Distal end	2	1	1	1	0	0	2	0
Microblades								
Lateral edge	0	0	0	4	2	5	1	6
Distal end	1	0	0	0	1	0	0	0
Fragments	1	0	0	0	0	0	0	0

[1] Percussion.
[2] Retouched.

1.2 mm., i.e., the denticulate with a cutting edge of 30 mm. has 27 distinct teeth. The remaining example has inversely serrated edges from 10 to

measuring between 1.3 and 1.6 mm. It is interesting to note that while the notches on flakes show no preference for either obverse or inverse retouch, notches on blades are predominantly made by inverse retouch. This reflects the pattern seen on backed microblades with lateral notches.

Truncated flakes (18). All are on microflakes, the smallest measuring 13 mm. in length. The most common type is a single oblique truncation which occurs on twelve examples (fig. 27, d). There are also two inverse, oblique truncations and four straight truncations.

Scaled pieces (16). Thirteen range in length from 14 to 22 mm. Four have opposed edges which are both bifacially chipped (fig. 27, g), while two have straight, unifacially retouched scaled edges. One of these is inversely scaled. The largest piece, 41 mm. long, is made on a split pebble and shows a rather battered edge, while two others are on exhausted cores. The remainder is on small flakes. None is the result of a bipolar core technique.

Cortex backed knives (19). As the bulk of this assemblage is made from pebbles, there is a huge number of flakes showing cortex on their upper surface. Surprisingly though, there are relatively few flakes or blades which are backed by cortex. When such a flake was produced, it was common for it to be used in the manufacture of a finished tool. Often these flakes or blades would be given additional retouch backing, although this backing was usually only partial. In the case of the cortex backed knives, there are two features which set them apart from the debitage—their large size and the evidence of use along their cutting edges.

There are two distinct groups: those which are on relatively large flakes or microblades, in size from 28 to 38 mm., one even attaining 60 mm. in length; and those made on microblades, measuring from 20 to 25 mm. This last group, comprising five examples, was perhaps functionally the same as simple, unretouched backed microblades.

The others are on thick blades, which are triangular in cross-section with the thickest part running along the right edge. All show use retouch.

Backed flakes (209). The utilization of flakes in the manufacture of backed tools shows a different pattern than does the utilization of microblades. Flakes were often backed, but rarely are

backed flakes made into more elaborate tools. All types of flakes were backed, even primary flakes which are completely covered by cortex on their upper surface (fig. 28, i). Twenty-eight such primary flakes were backed, 73 backed flakes show some cortex (fig. 28, j, l), while 180 are made on flakes with no cortex (fig. 28, k, m). The backed flakes are usually thin and tend toward rectangularity in shape, although no particular shape predominates. Ninety-eight backed flakes have straight backing, often cutting well into the flake to achieve the desired shape. Fifty-two are convexly backed and twenty are very slightly concave. There is no good example of a truly concave backing. Thirty-nine are fragmentary. The size range shows a clear grouping between 16 and 24 mm., with a peak at 19 mm. Only three measure more than 30 mm. in length.

Partially backed flakes (117). These show the same size range and shape pattern as the fully backed flakes have. All but two are microlithic.

Backed flakes, truncated (4). Two oblique truncations and two straight truncations were found. One of the oblique truncations is inversely retouched.

Backed flakes, notched (4). One flake has been bilaterally notched near the butt end by normal retouch. One is notched on the backed edge, and two are notched opposite the backed edge. All are short, wide flakes showing some cortex on their upper surface, and all the notches are close to, but do not cut into, the butts.

Backed blades (39). The same as backed microblades but these measure over 30 mm. in length (fig. 28, bb-cc). All but three are incurvate, and all but six have some cortex on their upper surface.

Backed microblades (224). The simple backed microblade and the partially backed microblade are by far the most common tools associated with this assemblage. The backing is achieved by a very fine, steep retouch. Four types of microblades were used, the most common being a generally parallel sided microblade with a square or broadly convex tip which is usually cortex covered (fig. 28, a-b, d-e). These account for 59.2 per cent. The next most common are microblades of a triangular shape, being narrow at the butt end and having a wide, cortex topped tip; they account for 23.9 per cent (fig. 28, c, g).

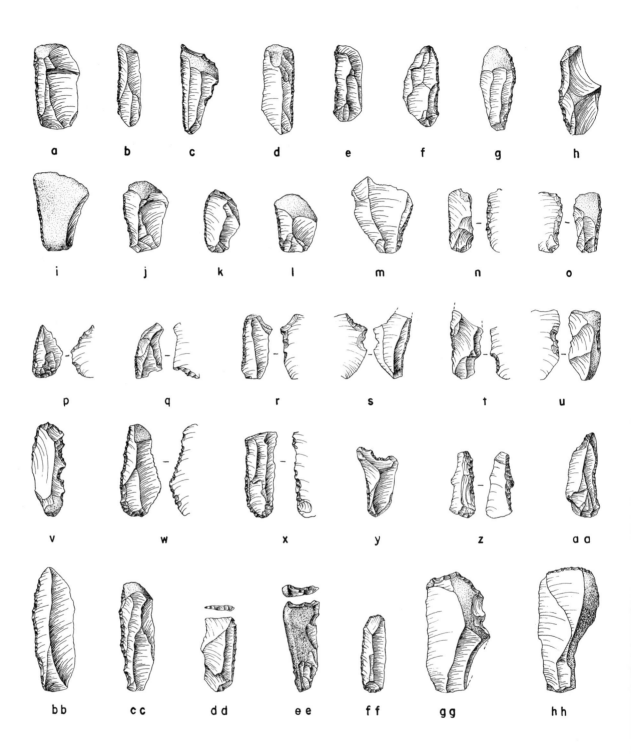

FIG. 28—Site 443: Backed microblades (a-h, simple; n-o, x, inversely retouched; q, dd, truncated; r-s, with inverse borers; t-u, y, notched; v-w, denticulated; z, alternately backed); i-m, backed flakes; p, aa, points?; bb-cc, backed blades; ee, truncated microblade; ff-hh, end-scrapers. 4/5 natural size.

A few are pointed, 9.8 per cent, but these are not uniform and none could be conceived of as points (fig. 28, f). There are an additional 7.7 per cent which are extremely irregular (fig. 28, h).

Microblades are either flat or incurvate. Flat microblades are few, accounting for only 33 per cent of the total, while the incurvate microblades account for 67 per cent. The backed edges of these microblades are for the most part straight. In many cases, the natural shape of the microblade was modified so as to achieve a straight edge. One hundred and fifty-one (67.4 per cent) have straight backs, sixty-three (28.2 per cent) are slightly convex, and only ten (4.4 per cent) are concave. The range in length is from only 15 to 30 mm., but over 99 per cent fall between 18 and 29 mm., with an apex between 23 and 25 mm.

Partially backed microblades (295). The partially backed microblades follow the same pattern as that described for the fully backed examples. One hundred and seventy-nine have straight backing; 92, convex; and 24, concave.

Backed microblades, broken (569). These are fragments of the normal types described above. None are complete enough for more detailed study.

Backed microblades, retouched (60). Nine of these backed microblades have obverse retouch, while 51 are inversely retouched. All obversely retouched pieces show a fine, discontinuous retouch. Inverse retouch is quite different from the obverse; it is generally flat and irregular, giving it a somewhat scaly appearance (fig. 28, n-o, x). Size range falls well into that of unretouched, backed microblades.

Backed microblades, denticulate (12). Five complete examples which range in length from 18 to 34 mm. were found. An additional seven are broken. Nine pieces were serrated by inverse retouch which is flat and generally irregular. One example made by inverse retouch has a convex denticulation of 16 teeth over a 23 mm. long edge (fig. 28, w). The remainder shows a more haphazard serration, individual teeth being anywhere from every 1.1 mm. to every 2.5 mm. Three denticulates are made by obverse retouch and follow the same variation as those made by inverse retouch (fig. 28, v).

Backed microblades, notched, (65). Thirty-nine backed microblades have retouched micro-notches along the central portion of the un-backed, lateral edge. Of these, twenty-nine are inverse notches (fig. 28, u) and ten are obverse. The length of the whole pieces ranges between 18 and 30 mm., but clusters around 21 mm. As a group, they are smaller than the average unretouched backed microblade, but no particular form of microblade was utilized, nor is there a clear preferential side for notching or backing. One has been notched on the backed edge.

Twenty-six are backed microblades which have been notched close to the butt. The most typical is notched by inverse retouch, very close to, but not actually encroaching on, the butt (fig. 28, t). Two other pieces have been notched on the backed edge. There is very little size range, the microblades clustering between 17 and 23 mm. in length. These notched microblades form a curious group, for while such a consistent notching near the butt end of microblades might imply hafting as a point, only four of the twenty-three complete examples are pointed, the remainder being convex or square at the tip. These notches are not part of a "microburin technology" as only one microburin was found, and it appears to have been accidental.

Backed microblades, end notched (5). Two types are apparent. Three examples are notched so that the end of the blades have a pseudo-shouldered appearance, one side of the notch extending out further than the other (fig. 28, y). Of these, all are micronotches, three achieved by percussion and two by retouch. All show evidence of use. The two remaining examples have shallow notches made by inverse retouch. Because of the incurvate form of the two blades, the notches cut only a small way into the end of the blades, when viewed from above, but they show the removal of numerous flakes on the inverse side. Both notches are made on the right hand corner of the distal end.

Backed microblades, truncated (21). The most common type is an oblique truncation. It accounts for sixteen examples. Seven are made by inverse retouch, the others by normal retouch. There are three straight truncations, two of which are made by inverse retouch (fig. 28, dd). There are also two concave inverse basal truncations (fig. 28, q). These fall into the size range for unretouched backed microblades.

Borers on backed microblades (12). Each is made on the unbacked lateral edge and is first formed by two inversely retouched notches and then is brought to a point by additional inverse retouch. This results in a small, sharply pointed, triangular borer (fig. 28, r-s). Eight were found on unbroken backed microblades which measure within the range for backed microblades.

Alternately backed microblades (2). These two pieces are backed on the right side by normal backing and backed inversely on the left hand side. One measures 21 mm., the other 16 mm. The larger piece has a small projection on the central section of the inversely backed edge, somewhat similar to a boring tip (fig. 28, z).

Double backed microblades (3). One fragment and two complete examples were found. The fragment approaches a point, but the tip is missing.

Microburins (1). It is on the distal end of a backed microblade and appears to be the result of accidental breaking during the process of backing.

Truncated microblades (11). Nine are oblique truncations, only two formed by inverse retouch. There is also one basal truncation and a concave truncation which approaches a notch (fig. 28, ee).

Retouched microblades (42). Four are obversely retouched, while 38 have inverse retouch. The obverse retouch is similar to the type used for backing, but the angle is not as steep. Only three examples show continuous retouch along the whole of one lateral edge.

Most of the inversely retouched microblades are fragmentary, only nine being intact. The retouch, in all cases, is fine and flat, rarely extending along the whole of any lateral edge.

Retouched flakes (21). Retouched flakes are those with a very light, partial retouch along one edge. Only one flake has continuous retouch, but this retouch is so light that it borders on "use retouch." Ten of these flakes are complete and roughly square in shape, while the others are fragments.

Backed points (1). This is the only backed piece which could be considered a point. It is 23 mm. long, has a straight backed edge with a small notch in it, and has an opposed tapering

convex edge which is unretouched. Its uniqueness may mean that its pointed form is accidental.

Backed truncated points (4). There are two backed microblades which have obverse, oblique, distal truncations which approach elongated points (fig. 28, aa). There are also two shorter blades which have inverse oblique truncation and also might be considered points (fig. 28, p).

Varia (8). There are two large choppers, one on a ventifact and one on a block of quartzite (fig. 26, d). There are also two cylindrical soft hammers (fig. 26, e), and five extensively retouched flakes which do not conform to the above types. These include one bilaterally notched microblade, a bec burin, and two pseudo-geometrics.

CORE TYPOLOGY

	No.	%	Restricted %
Halfa	24	4.0	4.4
Levallois	10	1.7	1.8
Single platform, unfaceted	218	36.5	39.7
Single platform, faceted	77	12.9	14.0
Opposed platform	43	7.1	7.8
Ninety degree	11	1.8	2.0
Wedge	89	14.9	16.2
Opposite side	7	1.2	1.3
Discoidal	13	2.2	2.4
Globular	5	0.8	0.9
Isolated flake	52	8.9	9.5
Unidentifiable	47	7.8	—
	596	99.8	100.0

NOTES ON THE TYPOLOGY

Four thousand two hundred and fifty-six cores were recovered from the excavations. Because of their vast number, it was decided to take a representative area and study those cores typologically. Thus, all cores found in the main occupation layer were studied. Cores from earth ovens, the subsurface layer, and the surface were excluded.

A total of 2,671 cores and core fragments were recovered from the occupation layer. Of these, 2,075 were either too burned or too fragmentary to be classified. The remaining 596 cores were typed.

Halfa (24). The technology and typology of the Halfa core has been discussed in detail at the beginning of this study. Of all the Halfa cores found here, 12 have been successfully struck (fig. 29, g). As a group, they are indifferently made and many are atypical.

Eight examples were abandoned because of hinge fracturing during the removal of the channel flake, while four are still in the early stages of preparation.

As with all Halfa cores, these are either microlithic or verge on it, ranging in length here from 22 to 35 mm.

Levallois (10). All are roughly oval in shape and eight are microlithic. Only two have received extensive preparation on the under surface (fig. 29, d); the rest show only minimal flaking. Six were struck, but all were hinge fractured. As a group, they are not typical.

Single platform, unfaceted (218). By far the most common core type, these account for 39.7 per cent of all recognizable cores. Normally, these cores show flaking on one face only, but occasionally, particularly in the microblade cores, the flaking extends around more than a single side. In these cases, however, only a single platform was utilized.

There are two distinct types of unfaceted platforms. Most are single flake scars which intersect the flaking surface at about 80°. There are a significant number, however, where the platform is at an acute angle to the flaking surface. These platforms are always less than 50° and often less than 40° to the flaking surface. This type is similar to the wedge core in this respect and may actually be the first stage in the production of the wedge core.

A majority of all these cores produced microblades (fig. 29, a-b). It is often difficult to be sure, however, as most were extensively utilized and were not abandoned until a number of hinge fractures or thick flakes made additional work unprofitable.

Single platform, faceted (77). These are similar to the unfaceted single platform core, except that a faceted platform was used. These are quite poor, however, compared with the unfaceted group. For the most part these are flake cores and are not extensively utilized (fig. 29, c).

Opposed platform (43). These form a poor group. The most typical shows only slight utilization, often no more than the removal of primary flakes. It is somewhat surprising that this type is so rare as it is important in many later Mesolithic industries.

Ninety degree (11). While rare in the Halfan, there are always some of these present. All of these are microblade but only a few are extensively or successfully utilized (fig. 29, i).

Wedge (89). At Site 443 this core type reaches the height of its popularity. Most are microlithic, but 20 per cent measure between 30 and 40 mm. (fig. 29, h). These too, however, are functionally microlithic as usually only half of the pebble is flaked. All show platforms with its angle below 50°, and in one example it is as low as 28°. Most are microblade cores and the vast majority is well utilized (fig. 29, j-k).

Opposite side (7). Generally a poor group. Most are microflake cores, and none has been extensively utilized. Only one is a microblade core (fig. 29, e).

Discoidal (13). While only a few were recovered, they are well made and seem to have been extensively flaked. All are microflake cores, and none has any platform preparation (fig. 29, f).

Globular (5). This type is atypical in the Halfan. All are small core remnants which show flake scars on all surfaces.

Isolated flake (52). These are merely pebbles which have had only one or two primary flakes removed. The majority shows that the first flake removed was taken from one end of the pebble, probably to prepare its platform.

Unidentifiable (47). Pebbles which have been randomly flaked and show no discernible pattern. Relatively few have been included here, but there were large numbers of such cores which were burned or fragmentary, so many that they were grouped with those not dealt with—some 2,075 examples.

Summary

At this site, we are dealing with a microlithic assemblage which is predominately of microblades. The Microlithic Index is very high, 96.2; and the Blade Tool Index shows 71.7. The Flake Tool Index is low, 25.7; while the Core Tool Index is barely significant, 2.6.

Technologically, this emphasis on microblade tools is not so clear. Within gross categories of

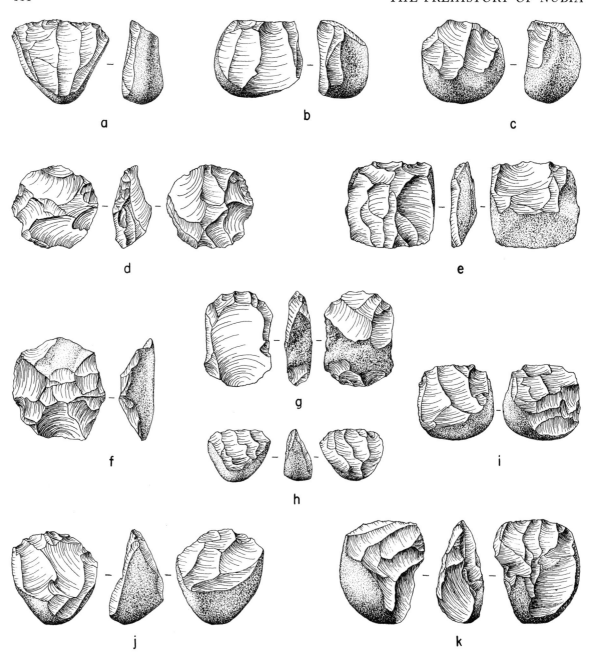

Fɪɢ. 29—Site 443: a-b, single platform, unfaceted cores; c, single platform, faceted core; d, Levallois core?; e, opposite side core; f, discoidal core; g, Halfa core; h, j-k, wedge cores; i, ninety degree core. 4/5 natural size.

artifact types, blades are still much in the minority. Tools total 4.5 per cent of all types; blades, 2.1 per cent; flakes, 7.4 per cent; cores, 9.8 per cent; primary flakes, 15.4 per cent; and debris, 59.8 per cent.

Another striking element, seen also at Site 624, is the poor quality of the microblades used in the manufacture of finished tools. A majority have some cortex on their upper surface, and 24.3 per cent are either highly irregular or are nothing more than elongated primary flakes. Another indication of the poor technical aspect of blade manufacture is that 82.9 per cent of all complete microblades are incurvate.

Blades appear to have been removed from cores by means of a punch as only 8.3 per cent show any platform remnant. Platform preparation of flakes, other than Halfa flakes, is undeveloped. About 20 per cent have thin unfaceted butts, and as many as 15 per cent have cortex butts.

Typologically, the overwhelming tool is the unretouched backed microblade. If all complete, broken, and partially backed examples are considered, they account for 55.3 per cent of all tools. All backed microblades, unretouched, and the more complex backed forms account for 64.6 per cent, while all backed tools, including flake forms, account for 82.5 per cent of all tools.

Backed flakes are common, at 16.9 per cent, but very few backed flakes have been made into more complex tools. This contrasts with the backed microblades, where numerous modifications have been added to the original form. End-scrapers, burins, denticulates, and various retouched, truncated, and notched forms occur. While these do not occur in large proportions, their variety is striking.

The backing on both microblades and flakes is exceedingly fine and steep. The most common backing is straight, often cutting into the original shape of the piece to achieve a truly straight edge. Of the unretouched backed microblades and flakes, straight backing accounts for 61.5 per cent of all pieces. Convex backing is usually only very slight and accounts, in backed microblades and flakes, for 27.6 per cent. Concave backing is rare (10.9 per cent) and, when present, is only very slight.

As it is at Site 624, the left side is preferred for backing. In all backed pieces, left side preference occurs 65 per cent of the time.

While numerous tool types have been recognized, there are relatively few "classic" types. Scrapers are rare, and the best are made on backed microblades. Burins, although seven types are present, show poor workmanship. There are only a few of each type, and many seem to have resulted as much from chance as from intent. At most, they are part of a declining burin technology. Burins account for only 1 per cent of all tools, while scrapers account for 2.8 per cent. Combined, they hardly form a significant percentage of all tools.

Denticulate tools on cores, on simple microblades and flakes, and on backed microblades appear to be typologically significant. While they account for only 2.1 per cent of all tools, they show a fine workmanship which is generally absent from other tools. As described in the detailed typology, the denticulates have a very fine and regular serration; so fine that most examples have distinct teeth at least every 1.5 mm.

There is a series of truncations, scaled pieces, and points which are more significant for their mere presence than for their proportion in the total tool assemblage.

The tools made on backed microblades represent a varied and typologically important element. These, including simple retouch, denticulates, notches, end notches, borers, and truncations, account for 9 per cent of all tools. Of particular note are the backed microblades with lateral notches. Sixty-five were found. They represent the single largest tool type with the exception of simple backed microblades and flakes. These notched pieces pose something of a problem. They would seem to represent a step toward the formation of microburins by snapping, but as only one microburin was found, this does not seem to be the case. There is no evidence that the microburin technique was used in the Halfan.

Retouch shows some variation, depending on where it is found. Obverse retouch is fine, regular, and semi-steep. Inverse retouch, on the other hand, is normally very flat, with short wide flake scars. Of all retouched tools, exclusive of backing, 44.2 per cent were obversely retouched and 55.8 per cent were inversely retouched. These figures are somewhat deceptive. Basically, there are two groups of retouched tools: those on simple flakes or microblades and those on backed microblades and backed flakes. Retouch on simple pieces is predominantly obverse (69.8 per cent), while it is rare on backed pieces (27.2 per cent). Thus, there appears to be a preferential combination of backing and inverse retouch, while retouch on simple pieces seems to be more commonly obverse.

The overall impression of the assemblage is one of typological monotony. Backed microblades and flakes overwhelm all other forms, although some variation occurs within the backed types.

The Halfa flake is still present but only in residual form, the transition to a truly microblade industry being almost complete.

SITE 2014

Site 2014 lies in a branch of the Khor Musa, 3 km. west of the Wadi Halfa airport building and 11 km. southwest of Wadi Halfa (map. ref. 642.6/904.6). It is situated on the eroded younger vertisol which fills the wadi. The site is directly across the wadi from Site 1018 (fig. 3).

The site was discovered during the end of the 1965 field season at a time when a number of important excavations were being carried out. As a result, only a very short time could be spent on the site, a fact which radically limited the size of the recovered sample. Additionally, shipping problems made it impossible to keep all debitage. Thus, many of the observations made for other Halfan sites cannot be made here. Only tools were kept, and a typology of the cores was done in the field on a very small sample. The collection of artifacts was made by J. Shiner in February, 1965.

The site was heavily deflated and covered no more than 15 sq. m. A small portion of this area contained, *in situ*, part of an earth oven. A charcoal sample from the earth oven gave a date of 17,200 B.C ± 375 years (WSU-332). This date is consistent with one from a similar assemblage at Ballana, Egypt, but is in conflict with a date of 14,550 B.C. ± 500 years (WSU-201) from Site 443.

LITHIC ARTIFACTS

A total of 99 cores and 187 tools were collected. As at all Halfan sites, chert was the predominant raw material as can be seen in Table 11.

TABLE 11
UTILIZATION OF RAW MATERIAL AT SITE 2014

	Cores	Tools
Chert	92.9%	96.8%
Agate	4.1%	3.2%
Quartz	0.0%	0.0%
Fossil wood	3.0%	0.0%

TOOL TYPOLOGY

	No.	%
Halfa flakes	1	0.5
Nosed scrapers	2	1.1
Core scrapers	1	0.5
Side-scrapers	2	1.1
Burins, "single blow"	1	0.5
Burins, angle on snapped pieces	1	0.5
Burins, on retouched truncations	1	0.5
Denticulates	2	1.1
Denticulate core scrapers	1	0.5
Notched pieces	4	2.1
Truncated flakes	1	0.5
Scaled pieces	4	2.1
Cortex backed knives	1	0.5
Backed flakes	17	9.1
Partially backed flakes	12	6.4
Backed flakes, retouched	1	0.5
Backed blades	1	0.5
Backed microblades	22	11.8
Partially backed microblades	20	10.7
Backed microblades, broken	55	29.4
Backed microblades, retouched	16	8.6
Backed microblades, denticulate	1	0.5
Backed microblades, notched	9	4.8
Backed microblades, truncated	1	0.5
Borers on backed microblades	1	0.5
Alternately backed microblades	1	0.5
Retouched microblades	6	3.2
Retouched flakes	1	0.5
Varia	1	0.5
	187	99.5

NOTES ON THE TYPOLOGY

Halfa flakes (1). A large example which was very slightly overpassed.

Nosed scrapers (2). Both are on irregular, thick primary flakes (fig. 30, q).

Core scrapers (1). A well formed convex scraper made on a thin core fragment. Retouch is continuous and semi-steep.

Side-scrapers (2). Both are on primary flakes. One, although well retouched, is slightly denticulated (fig. 30, p).

Burins, "single blow" (1). A poor example on a primary flake.

Burins, angle on snapped pieces (1). Again, a poor example on an elongated primary flake.

Burins, on retouched truncations (1). A well made burin on a thick flake fragment (fig. 30, t).

Denticulates (2). Both are on thick flakes, similar to core scrapers in shape (fig. 30, v). While rather well made, they do not compare in quality with those from Site 443.

Denticulate core scrapers (1). A well formed microdenticulate on the end of an irregular pebble.

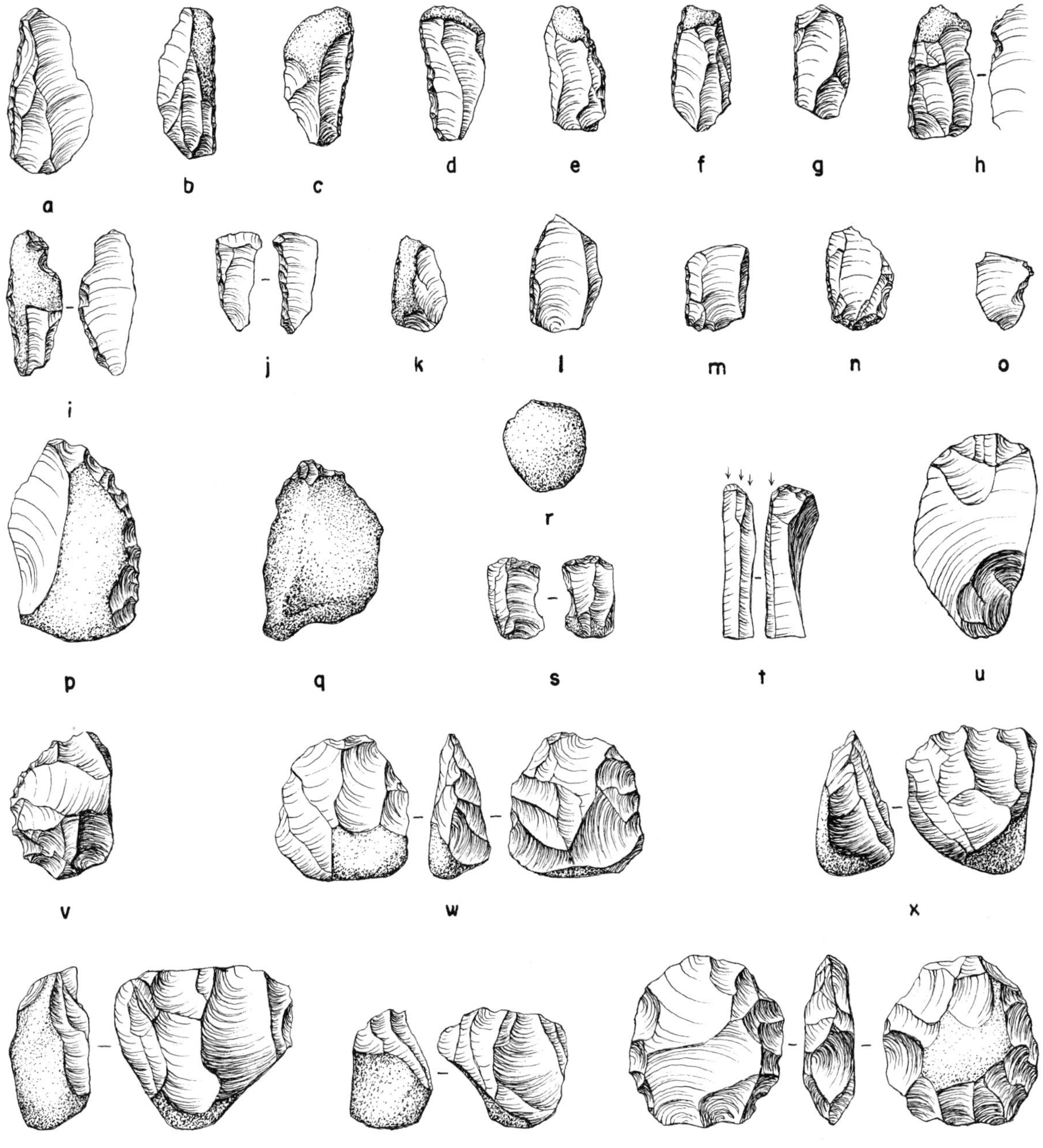

FIG. 30—Site 2014: Backed microblades (a-g, simple; h, notched; i, inversely retouched; j, alternately backed); k-o, backed flakes (m, simple; n, retouched; o, with inverse borer); p, side-scraper; q, nosed scraper; r, truncated flake; s, scaled piece; t, burin; u, varia; v, denticulate. Cores: w, wedge; x-y, single platform, unfaceted; z, single platform, faceted; aa, Levallois. 4/5 natural size.

Notched pieces (4). All are micronotches made on irregular flakes by percussion. One is inverse on a distal end.

Truncated flakes (1). A small oblique truncation on a primary flake (fig. 30, r).

Scaled pieces (4). Three are on core fragments but are too regular to have resulted from simple bipolar flaking (fig. 30, s). The other is on a primary flake and is scaled only on the inverse side of the distal end.

Cortex backed knives (1). A single example on a microblade, showing use retouch.

Backed flakes (17). All are microflakes with fine, steep backing along one lateral edge. Six are backed on the right side, eleven on the left. Seven examples have straight backing (fig. 30, m), and an equal number have convex backing (fig. 30, l). Only three have slightly concave backing.

Partially backed flakes (12). Similar to the above group but the backing does not extend along the whole length of one lateral edge. Here, however, eight pieces are backed on the right side. Of the twelve, seven have straight backing (fig. 30, k), one concave, and four convex.

Backed flakes, retouched (1). A microlithic flake, with straight backing on its left side, also has a semi-steep retouch along its right edge (fig. 30, n).

Backed blades (1). A single example measuring 34 mm. in length. It is highly incurvate, is partially covered by cortex, and has a straight backing on its left side.

Backed microblades (22). These show the same traits as those of all backed microblades found in the Halfan. Technologically, they are poor; sixteen are incurvate (72.7 per cent), and twelve have some cortex on their upper surface (54.5 per cent). They range in length from 17 to 26 mm.; however, all but two fall below 26 mm. Backing is predominantly on the left side, fifteen examples (68.1 per cent). Twelve have convex backing (fig. 30, a, c, f); seven have straight (fig. 30, b, g); while only three are concavely backed (fig. 30, d).

Partially backed microblades (20). These are similar to the above group in quality; 75 per cent are incurvate, and 70 per cent have some cortex on their upper surface. Left side backing again predominates (60 per cent). There are no concavely backed pieces, but 60 per cent are convexly backed (fig. 30, e), and the others are straight backed.

Backed microblades, broken (55). Fragmentary backed microblades whose size and condition prohibits almost all typological observation. Of the 50 where side preference can be seen, 62 per cent are backed on the left side.

Backed microblades, retouched (16). Eleven microblades backed on the left side and five

backed on the right side are also retouched on the unbacked lateral edge. All this retouch is inverse and very flat, while the backing is evenly divided between straight and convex. There is also an even division between microblades with and without cortex.

Backed microblades, denticulate (1). A broken microblade, with some cortex and left side backing, has a fine but irregular denticulation along the unbacked edge.

Backed microblades, notched (9). Typical backed microblades which have single, weak notches on the unbacked edge. All are micronotches, and all but two are inverse (fig. 30, h).

Backed microblades, truncated (1). A single example with left side backing and a straight retouched truncation.

Borers on backed microblades (1). A microblade fragment has a small borer formed by flat, inverse retouch on the lateral edge opposite the backing (fig. 30, o).

Alternately backed microblades (1). A fragmentary example (fig. 30, j).

Retouched microblades (6). All are incurvate, and half are inversely retouched. In all cases, retouch is light and discontinuous.

Retouched flakes (1). An irregular flake with discontinuous flat, inverse retouch.

Varia (1). A primary flake which has a number of flat, inverse flakes removed from the distal end. The resulting piece is quite atypical for the Halfan (fig. 30, u).

CORE TYPOLOGY

	No.	%	Restricted %
Halfa	3	3.0	3.2
Levallois	4	4.0	4.2
Single platform, unfaceted	56	56.5	59.4
Single platform, faceted	17	17.2	18.0
Opposed platform	3	3.0	3.2
Ninety degree	2	2.0	2.1
Wedge	5	5.0	5.3
Discoidal	1	1.0	1.1
Bipolar	3	3.0	3.2
Unidentifiable	5	5.0	—
	99	99.7	99.7

NOTES ON THE TYPOLOGY

The 99 cores collected do not represent the total cores available in the area collected. Only a subarea was chosen for core collection. Within this, however, the collection was systematic so that the sample represents a valid picture of the core technology.

Halfa (3). All are atypical, and none have been successfully struck.

Levallois (4). Again, these are mostly atypical. Only one was even partially successful (fig. 30, aa).

Single platform, unfaceted (56). All are microblade cores which have received extensive utilization. As at Site 443, there are examples of those with platforms almost perpendicular to the flaking surface (fig. 30, y) and of those with highly acute platforms (fig. 30, x).

Single platform, faceted (17). Generally poor examples, only a few of which were extensively utilized (fig. 30, z).

Opposed platform (3). Again, rather poorly utilized, although one seems to have had some microblades removed.

Ninety degree (2). One rather good example and one poor one.

Wedge (5). All are well formed with highly acute angles at the intersection of the microblade scars (fig. 30, w).

Discoidal (1). An atypical example.

Bipolar (3). All rather typical examples.

Unidentifiable (5). Pebbles which have been randomly flaked.

Summary

Although a relatively small sample was obtained from Site 2014, it was large enough to permit a detailed typological and technological study. The assemblage is highly microlithic with a Microlithic Index of 95.8. As would be expected in this stage of the Halfan, microblade tools predominate, as shown by the Blade Tool Index of 70.8. The Flake Tool Index of 25.6 is low, and the Core Tool Index of 2.6 is barely significant.

The poor quality of the microblades, seen at other sites, is also noticeable here where 78.3 per cent of all microblades are markedly incurvate.

Typologically, the backed microblade dominates the assemblage. If all simple forms of this tool type are considered, they total 52.4 per cent of all tools. All backed microblades, unretouched, and the more complex types account

for 67.8 per cent, while all backed tools, including flake forms, account for 83.8 per cent of all tools.

Of the tools, 16 per cent are backed flakes, but, unlike the backed microblades, there is only one example which has been made into a more complex tool. Scrapers, burins, denticulates, and scaled pieces occur but only in very small number, and, for the most part, they are poorly made. The lack of variety may be due in large part to the small sample available for study.

As at all Halfan sites, backing is exceedingly fine and steep. The most common backing is convex, 48.3 per cent, while straight backing is almost as common, 43.8 per cent. Concave backing is rare, occuring only 7.8 per cent of the time. Most of the backed pieces, 62.4 per cent, have been treated on the left edge, a trait consistent with other Halfan assemblages.

Tools made on backed microblades show some variation, but only those with simple retouch and with notches occur in any number.

Retouch varies according to whether it is obverse or inverse. Retouch on unbacked tools is predominantly obverse, occurring 80 per cent of the time, while inverse retouch dominates the complex backed tools, accounting for 77.5 per cent of that class. Thus, we see a pattern of backing combined with inverse retouch, while simple retouched tools are predominantly made by obverse retouch.

Again, the general impresssion of the assemblage is one of little variation, with only a very few types occurring in significant number.

SITE 1028

Site 1028 is located 200 m. east of the village of Nag el-Ikhtiariya, in Dibeira East (map ref. 930.1/655.2). The site is situated on a deflated silt bank at an absolute elevation of 142-143 m., or 21-22 m. above floodplain.[5]

The site, consisting of a surface concentration of artifacts and burned stone, was first found by Fairbridge in 1961. Excavations and close study, however, did not take place until 1963. During that year, J. Shiner mapped the site and carried out excavations and systematic surface collections.

The surface concentration covered an oval area

---

[5] This is somewhat high due to local tectonic action.

of 160 sq. m., with artifacts resting on and in a deflated silt remnant covered by a few centimeters of loose sand. The site area was divided into a series of grid squares, 2 m. by 2 m.; all surface artifacts were collected, and the loose sand was swept off the silt. Once the sand was removed, it was possible to see the remnants of four earth ovens which stood out as small fire-burned mounds. These mounds were then excavated as separate units, producing many lithic artifacts and much bone.

The earth ovens were clearly within the silt formation, indicating that the whole site had once been covered by silt.

Lithic Artifacts

The artifacts from Site 1028 presented something of a problem. The initial surface collection showed that there were two quite distinct technological traditions present: a developed Levallois technology and a microlithic blade technology. From experience gained at many other sites in Nubia, this combination seemed unlikely.

Site 1028 was only a short distance down slope from two Khormusan sites and only slightly above a site of the Qadan tradition. Therefore, there was a definite possibility that more than one component was present.

This problem was attacked from two directions. First, the artifactual content of each square was analyzed separately, and then the artifacts from *in situ* in the hearth mounds were also studied as discrete units. The results of these studies were then compared to see if there was any horizontal or vertical difference in artifact content. As was suspected, quite a difference was noticeable.

Surface material showed a differential distribution. The Levallois cores and flakes were heavily concentrated in a 20 sq. m. area on the extreme eastern edge of the site. In fact, well over half of all Levallois cores and flakes occurred in the easternmost 14 per cent of the squares. At the same time, there were relatively few microblades and associated debitage in the same squares. There were, however, both Levallois flakes and cores in other parts of the site. Therefore, while strong evidence was found that the surface material represented a mixture of components, it

was not possible to separate them fully on the basis of area. The possibility remained that at least some of the Levallois flakes and cores were truly associated with the Halfan assemblage.

The second step, that of analysis of the hearth mounds, showed that Levallois technology was exceedingly rare and not necessarily contemporary with the mounds. Only two Levallois flakes were found in the mounds and both were weathered, indicating that they either came from the very top of the mounds or that they were weathered prior to their inclusion in the mounds. Either way, however, there was little question that the Levallois technology was not a significant part of the Halfan assemblage.

While this seemed to be the case, there was no sure way of separating all mixed materials from the collections. That area containing so many Levallois flakes and cores was eliminated from the study altogether. Material from other squares, however, was studied and reported as found. Therefore, there are some pieces which may not belong to the Halfan component. These have been described, and their questionable association noted.

Within the 140 sq. m. which was systematically collected and studied, 11,072 artifacts were recovered. Of unretouched pieces, 7,825 were chips or other debris, 1,443 were primary flakes, 979 were cores and core fragments, 259 were flakes, and 277 were blades. Only 289 tools, 2.6 per cent of the total collection, were found.

As at all Halfan sites, the most common raw material utilized in tool manufacture was chert. On the other hand, because of an immediate availability of fossil wood, a fairly large number of fossil wood cores were found. This also applies to the debitage where thousands of fossil wood chips were present. Fossil wood, however, was rarely used for finished tools as can be seen in Table 12.

TABLE 12

UTILIZATION OF RAW MATERIALS AT SITE 1028

	Cores	Tools
Chert	80.9%	89.3%
Agate	1.2%	6.2%
Fossil wood	17.3%	3.8%
Precambrian	0.6%	0.7%

It is immediately apparent that much more

primary flaking of fossil wood than actual manufacturing of tools from fossil wood took place. This may be explained by the poor nature of most fossil wood for controlled flaking and the fact that the people who did the flaking wanted microblades which were very difficult to remove from fossil wood cores.

The relatively high percentage of agate tools reflects the greater utilization of agate microblade cores than was seen at earlier Halfan sites.

The large scale flaking of fossil wood has had another effect; the percentage of debris is much higher and primary flakes much lower than at other Halfan sites. This is fully understandable once one is familiar with trying to flake coarse-grained fossil wood.

TOOL TYPOLOGY

	No.	%
Halfa flakes	1	0.3
Levallois flakes	2	0.7
Ogival end-scrapers	1	0.3
Nosed scrapers	1	0.3
Side-scrapers	1	0.3
Core scrapers	2	0.7
Burins, dihedral angle	1	0.3
Burins, angle on snapped pieces	1	0.3
Burins, "single blow"	1	0.3
Burins, on retouched truncations	1	0.3
Burins, on cores	1	0.3
Denticulates	3	1.0
Denticulate core scrapers	3	1.0
Notched pieces	3	1.0
Scaled pieces	3	1.0
Cortex backed knives	3	1.0
Backed flakes	2	0.7
Backed blades	1	0.3
Backed microblades	37	12.8
Partially backed microblades	37	12.8
Backed microblades, broken	126	43.6
Backed micrbolades, retouched	22	7.6
Backed microblades, denticulate	4	1.4
Backed microblades, notched	6	2.1
Backed microblades, truncated	6	2.1
Borers on backed microblades	1	0.3
Alternately backed microblades	2	0.7
Double backed microblades	4	1.4
Truncated microblades	2	0.7
Retouched microblades	11	3.8
Retouched flakes	1	0.3
Varia	1	0.3
	289	99.7

NOTES ON THE TYPOLOGY

Halfa flakes (1). A fragmentary piece. Actually,

it is a distal end of an overpassed flake but is included here as it represents the sole direct typological continuation of the Halfa flake and core technology.

Levallois flakes (2). Fossil wood flakes with large convexly faceted butts. Probably belong with the Khormusan assemblage of 34 Upper.

Ogival end-scrapers (1). A good example on a large, rough blade (fig. 31, u).

Nosed scrapers (1). A well made thin nosed scraper on a broken microblade (fig. 31, o).

Side-scrapers (1). A fragment of a Levallois flake which has a light, bifacially retouched convex scraping edge. The obverse retouch is marginal, while the inverse retouch is extremely flat. This piece shows no evidence of wind or sand abrasion and appears certainly to be associated with the Halfan, although it is not a common type.

Core scrapers (2). One moderately utilized unfaceted single platform core has fine retouch along the platform. The other is a poor convex scraper on a core fragment.

Burins, dihedral angle (1). A rather large Levallois flake fragment with a massive convexly faceted butt. Certainly more typical of the Khormusan at 34 Upper than of the Halfan.

Burins, angle on snapped pieces (1). A good example on a small fossil wood blade fragment (fig. 31, v).

Burins, "single blow" (1). A poor burin on an elongated, microlithic primary flake.

Burins, on retouched truncations (1). Another good example on a broken blade. The truncation is straight oblique (fig. 31, p).

Burins, on cores (1). A questionable single blow burin on a battered chert core.

Denticulates (3). Mediocre examples on chert flakes.

Denticulate core scrapers (3). There is one good lateral denticulate on a core fragment, which is almost carinated. Another approaches a simple core scraper, but the working edge is slightly denticulated. The third is a microdenticulate on a split pebble (fig. 31, r). Not one of these is equal in quality to earlier Halfan examples.

Notched pieces (3). One large Levallois flake of fossil wood has a lateral macronotch. This piece, perhaps, belongs with the Khormusan. Its

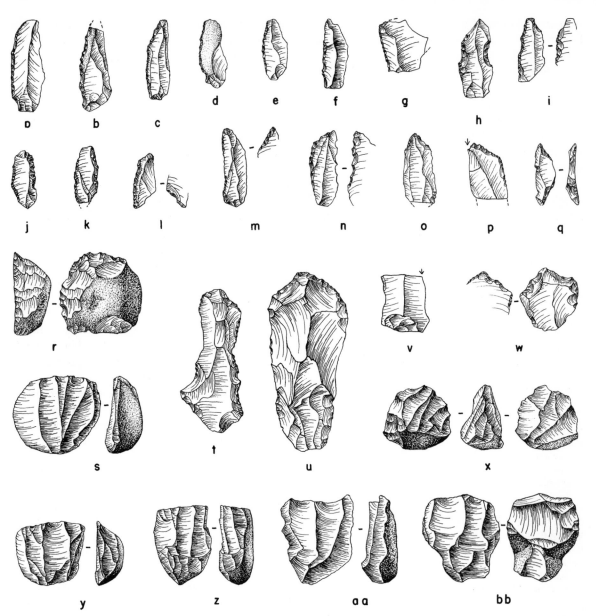

Fig. 31—Site 1028: Backed microblades (a-d, simple; e-f, partially backed; h, notched; i-j, retouched; k, double backed; l-m, truncated; n, denticulated); g, backed flake; o, nosed scraper; p, v, burins; q, lunates?; t, denticulate, r, core scraper; u, ogival end-scraper; w, scaled piece. Cores (x, wedge; s, single platform, faceted; y-aa, single platform, unfaceted; bb, ninety degree). 4/5 natural size.

size, 46 mm. in length, is well outside the normal range of Halfa flakes. Two small flakes have retouched micronotches, one of which is at a distal end.

Scaled pieces (3). One chert and two agate microflakes are scaled. All are typical (fig. 31, w).

Cortex backed knives (3). Two microblades with cortex backing show use retouch. The third example is a large broken blade fragment, measuring 38 mm. in length.

Backed flakes (2). Two microflakes have backing on the left edge. On one, the backing is straight (fig. 31, g); on the other, convex.

Backed blades (1). An irregular fossil wood blade, 32 mm. long, has convex backing along the left edge.

Backed microblades (37). All but three are backed along the left edge. The microblades show an improvement over earlier Halfan samples; only nine have any cortex on their upper surfaces, and only 21 are incurvate. Convex backing is overwhelmingly dominant, with 32 examples (fig. 31, a-d). At times, backing is somewhat irregular. They range in size from 10 to 30 mm., but most fall between 18 and 30 mm. in length.

Partially backed microblades (37). These fully parallel the completely backed type. The only difference is that the backing is not continuous along one edge (fig. 31, e-f).

Backed microblades, broken (126). Fragmentary pieces of backed microblades. Left side backing is dominant on those where the butt end is recognizable.

Backed microblades, retouched (22). Many of these are fragmentary. Here there is a slight reverse in the trend toward inverse retouch combined with backing, as only twelve fall in that class. Inverse retouch, as always, is flat and irregular (fig. 31, i), while obverse retouch is at a more normal angle (fig. 31, j). All are backed on the left edge and all but five have convex backing.

Backed microblades, denticulate (4). All are backed on the left edge, two convexly and two straight. Denticulation is formed by flat, inverse retouch, and the serrated edges are not as well made as those found at earlier Halfan sites (fig. 31, n).

Backed microblades, notched (6). All are convexly backed on the left edge, with four having inversely retouched micronotches. One example has an obversely retouched micronotch (fig. 31, h).

Backed microblades, truncated (6). All are backed along the left edge, two straight and three convex. Five have inverse, oblique truncations (fig. 31, m), two of which are at the butt end (fig. 31, l). The other has an obverse, oblique truncation at the distal end.

Borers on backed microblades (1). A fragmentary microblade with backing along one edge and a small borer formed by semi-steep retouch on the other.

Alternately backed microblades (2). Two fragmentary examples.

Double backed microblades (4). All are on small, flat microblades (fig. 31, k). These are fairly atypical in the Halfan but are typologically distinct from the *micropoincon* found in later industries.

Truncated microblades (2). Two microblades with oblique distal truncations.

Retouched microblades (11). All have partial light marginal retouch.

Retouched flakes (1). A single, fossil wood flake has a small amount of marginal, inverse retouch along one edge.

Varia (1). This is a poor lunate, shaped at the ends but unworked toward the center of the backed edge. It is highly atypical for the Halfan and may represent an intrusive element from a later period.

CORE TYPOLOGY

	No.	%	Restricted %	Adjusted %
Levallois	10	6.2	8.9	—
Single platform, unfaceted	62	38.2	55.3	60.7
Single platform, faceted	12	7.4	10.7	11.8
Opposed platform	15	9.2	13.4	14.7
Ninety degree	5	3.1	4.5	4.9
Wedge	1	0.6	0.9	1.0
Discoidal	1	0.6	0.9	1.0
Opposite side	4	2.5	3.6	3.9
Bipolar	2	1.2	1.8	2.0
Unidentifiable	50	30.6	—	—
	162	99.6	100.0	100.0

NOTES ON THE TYPOLOGY

This sample represents all cores collected in the studied squares. It is felt that certain cores do not belong in the Halfan assemblage, but it has been impossible to separate them other than by subjective means. Whenever these occur, they will be discussed. The typological list also has an additional column giving percentages for only those cores felt to be consistent with the apparent Halfan development.

Levallois (10). On the basis of the tool typology and technology, it seems that these cores may well belong with Khormusan Site 34 Upper, which is a short distance to the west. Unfortunately, there is no systematic way to separate these from the collection. Therefore, they are included, but an additional list of percentages is given without them for comparative purposes.

Eight are made on fossil wood and two on Precambrian rock. Their size, care taken in preparation, and shape are all typical of Khormusan. While they distort the sample, there are not so many as to mask the essential features of the Halfan core typology.

Single platform, unfaceted (62). The most common core type. All but three are on chert, one is on fossil wood, and two are on agate. The vast majority consists of well utilized microblade cores, with microblades struck from only one face of the core (fig. 31, y-aa).

Single platform, faceted (12). All are on pebble, and all are rather poor microblade cores worked on one face (fig. 31, s).

Opposed platform (15). These, again, are somewhat surprising considering the general trends throughout Halfan development. One cannot, however, exclude them as a Halfan type. Four are made on fossil wood, one on agate, while the rest are on pebble. Eight are flake cores, while seven are poor microblade cores.

Ninety degree (5). All are typical, all are microblade cores (fig. 31, bb).

Wedge (1). A single, good example (fig. 31, x).

Discoidal (1). A single, typical example.

Opposite side (4). All are rather poor microblade cores.

Bipolar (2). These are atypical in the Halfan and show no pattern of occurrence, although a few are present in every assemblage.

Unidentifiable (50). Various pebbles and pieces of fossil wood which have been flaked but show no discernible pattern.

Summary

As presented above, the assemblage from Site 1028 undoubtedly contains some artifacts which are not truly associated with the Halfan. These, however, are few and do not affect the basic Halfan traits as seen in the indices.

The assemblage has a high Microlithic Index of 96.3, the highest of all the Halfan. The vast majority of tools is on microblades or blades. The Blade Tool Index is 92.7; the Flake Tool Index, 5.2; and the Core Tool Index, 2.1.

A small improvement can be seen in micro-

blade production, as only 64.7 per cent of all microblades are incurvate.

Typologically, backed microblades have become the one important tool. If all simple forms are considered, they account for 69.2 per cent of all tools. When all forms of backed microblade and blade tools are counted, this percentage increases to 83.4. Backed flakes do not occur in significant number so that all backed tools, flake and blade, show an increase to only 84.1 per cent.

Unbacked tools occur: scrapers, burins, denticulates, scaled pieces, and notches; but all are exceedingly rare and poorly made. There is little question that typological emphasis was placed on backed microlithic blades.

There is a heightening of the Halfan tendency to back microblades and flakes along the left edge. At Site 2014, this occurred 62.4 per cent of the time, while here it occurs on 87.8 per cent of all backed pieces. At the same time, however, there is a radical shift to convex backing, which occurs on 80.6 per cent of all pieces. Concave backing has disappeared, and straight backing is relatively rare, 19.4 per cent.

The overall impression is a continuation of Halfan trends with certain erratic variations present. Most change, however, is in line with what might be expected. Perhaps the one surprising feature is the really low level of unbacked tools. It is true that this tendency runs throughout the Halfan, but it seems that here it has gone beyond a logical point. After all, it would seem that certain tools were necessary to make the shafts into which the many backed microblades were hafted.

SUGGESTED STAGES FOR THE HALFAN

A lithic industry, as one aspect of a continuous cultural tradition, does not readily lend itself to discrete stages. An industry will constantly develop, although change is often so slow as to be almost imperceptible over a short period of time. If the archaeologist were so fortunate as to recover a long series of assemblages from a single lithic tradition, representing an assemblage for every few years of the tradition's existence, each would be typologically transitional. This, however, has yet to happen.

In practice, the archaeologist is faced with

numerous problems and uncertainties. It is not always possible to judge the length of occupation of a site, while those long occupied produce assemblages which mask small scale changes. Often, assemblages in a series are not evenly spaced chronologically, so the major gaps in the lithic developmental sequence are apparent. Also, and perhaps most important, man does not always make his tools in a clearly predictable pattern. Minor variations in type frequencies may reflect evolutionary change or possibly no more than a slight difference in a group's activities from from site to site or season to season.

Thus, given a sound relative chronology based on stratigraphy, the archaeologist often finds that there are groups of assemblages which are more apparent than real: they represent artificial constructs on the part of the archaeologist to facilitate definitions and generalizations concerning cultural development.

Even with this in mind, there are occasionally specific indications of rapid change at a given point in the development of a lithic tradition. It is possible that certain tool types suddenly appear or that others are no longer made. A new technique may make an appearance and swiftly gain in popularity at the expense of older techniques. Thus, the tempo of change need not be uniform. This in itself also encourages the construction of stages within an industry. It would seem, however, that one stage may be distinguished from another only when a series of traits have shifted sufficiently so that the general aspect of the industry has changed, either typologically or technologically.

The Halfan industry lends itself to stage formulation because of the radical changes which take place. On the other hand, there remains a continuous typological thread which links all Halfan assemblages. One problem in the Halfan is that only six sites have been excavated, and these do not seem to cover the full span of Halfan development. On account of these limitations in the material evidence, some stages must be hypothetical, while others are represented by only a single assemblage.

Stages within the Halfan have been constructed on the basis of demonstrable typological and technological trends. These may be listed as follows:

1. A reduction of the specific Halfan technology of Halfa cores and flakes from a known high level to an almost total absence.

2. A marked increase in backed microblades from an insignificant number to a truly dominant role.

3. An increase and subsequent decrease in the importance of backed flakes as a typological element.

4. A shift from a microflake technology to a true microblade technology.

In addition, there are a number of other technological and typological traits which have chronological significance: percentage of microlithic tools, choice of raw materials, overall types of debitage, etc. These, however, do not normally lend themselves to stage designations as they seem to show either erratic or gradual change throughout.

The suggested stages within the Halfan must be considered tentative. The full range of variation within each stage is not known, and the lines dividing stages are still, as they must be, arbitrary (fig. 32).

STAGE I

This stage is purely hypothetical. It is based on the premise that the earliest known Halfan site, 1020, already dominated by a highly complex technological trait, must have developed out of another, more generalized stage.

This early stage should show indications of a development toward Halfa flake production which evolved from a basic Levallois technology. It would be expected that the industry was already microlithic and used Nile pebble as a chief source of raw material.

Microblade technology should be even less developed than it is at Site 1020, and there would be, perhaps, greater emphasis on burins, scrapers, and denticulates. These would not, however, dominate the industry at this stage.

In terms of absolute chronology, it must have occurred prior to 17,000 B.C., but maybe much earlier, and might typologically and technologically contain a number of definable substages of its own; particularly when Halfa technology reaches a parity with the assumed Levallois technological base.

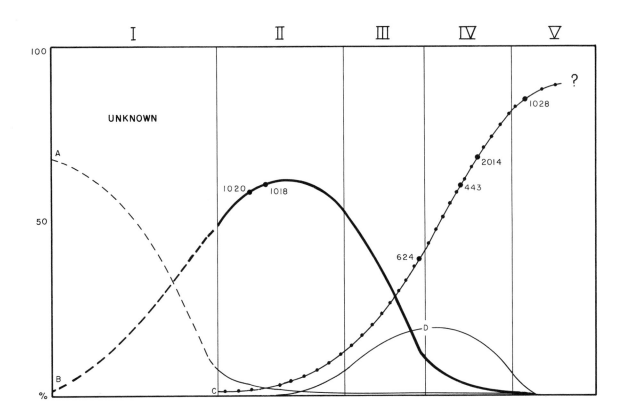

Fig. 32—Idealized graph of lithic change of major types during Halfan development. Key. A=Levallois flake production; B=Halfa flake production; C=backed microblade production; D=backed flake production.

Stage II

Stage II is represented by Sites 1020 and 1018. This stage is fully dominated by the Halfa flake and core, although there are now small numbers of backed microflakes and microblades. The industry is strongly microlithic, over 80 per cent of all tools measuring under 30 mm. in length. Tools are predominantly made on flakes, and blade production is still undeveloped. Scrapers, burins, denticulates, and other non-backed tools are present, but rarely does any one type account for more than, perhaps, 10 per cent of the total number of tools.

Stage III

This stage is represented by only one assemblage, 624. Therefore, it is to some extent hypothetical. It is basically a period of transition between two main Halfan stages. Halfa flakes are

still numerous but are no longer typologically dominant. The industry is still oriented toward flake production, although microblades are common. While the backed microblade is perhaps the most numerous tool, it still does not account for half of all tools, although when combined with backed flakes, backed tools do dominate the industry during the later part of this stage.

Scrapers, burins, denticulates, and other unbacked tools occur in relatively small numbers. Any one type rarely exceeds 5 per cent of the total tool inventory, half of that seen during Stage II. There is, however, a sudden appearance of scaled pieces, which occur in small numbers in each succeeding stage.

Tools are strongly microlithic, and only rarely are there examples which measure over 30 mm. in length.

During this stage, the wedge core begins to appear in significant numbers, although it is not nearly as common as the Halfa or the unfaceted, single platform cores.

STAGE IV

Stage IV is represented by two sites, 443 and 2014. It is seen as a logical evolution from Stage III and becomes definable when backed microblades finally dominate the tool inventory. It is a period of proliferation of retouched tools made on backed microblades. Although backed microblades now account for more than 50 per cent of all tools, backed flakes are still numerous, and flake production is still slightly more typical than microblade production. Halfa flakes are present but only in insignificant number—almost a fossil remnant from the earliest stages.

Scrapers, burins, and denticulates continue to be present but only in very small numbers, even less than during Stage III. Scaled pieces occur but do not increase in number over their first appearance in the previous stage.

Tools are almost fully microlithic with over 90 per cent measuring under 30 mm. in length. As it is in all other stages, chert is the dominant raw material.

The wedge core reaches its apex of popularity but is already in decline before the stage ends. There is, however, a major emphasis on unfaceted, single platform microblade cores, which account for about one-half of all recognizable forms.

STAGE V

Stage V represents the final known Halfan development. Only Site 1028 was found to fit within this period. The technology has finally become dominated by microblade production, although microflakes are still common. Wedge and Halfa cores are rarely present, and the core typology is mainly based on unfaceted, single platform and opposed platform microblade cores.

Typologically, the industry is almost totally made up of backed microblades. Backed flakes are exceedingly rare, as are Halfa flakes. Scrapers, burins, and denticulates still occur but in very small numbers—even less than in Stage IV. There is less elaboration of tools than in the preceding stage, and their quality has somewhat decreased.

The industry, as before, is highly microlithic, and chert remains the dominant raw material.

CONCLUSIONS

The Halfan industry represents a new and important discovery. Its importance rests on a number of factors: it is a newly discovered Late Pleistocene Nilotic industry which is totally unrelated to the Sebilian; it is fully microlithic at a very early date; it documents a transition from a microflake to true microblade industry; and, perhaps most important, it shows evidence for a microblade technology on the Nile much earlier than elsewhere in Africa.

While the Halfan shares certain traits with temporally similar Nubian industries, it is technologically and typologically distinct. In Nubia, the earliest known Halfan dates at least to 17,000 B.C., but may be older. This makes the Halfan perhaps partially synchronous with two other Nubian industries: late Khormusan and Gemaian (Wendorf, Shiner, and Marks, 1965).

It is possible that only Stage II of the Halfan is contemporary with the later Khormusan assemblages and with those of the Gemaian. Although all three industries occupied the area of the Second Cataract at about the same time, they are typologically and technologically unrelated. By the use of only a few characteristic traits, it is possible to see where the areas of greatest difference lie (table 13).

The relationship between Stage II of the Halfan and the late Khormusan is quite important as it has been suggested that they belong to the same industry. This was done when Sites 1020[6] and ANW-3 were grouped together in a preliminary report by J. Waechter (1965). At that time it was recognized that there were certain differences between these assemblages, but it was suggested that the differences were due to time (Waechter, 1965, p. 141). It is now believed that there is no significant time difference between the late Khormusan and Stage II of the Halfan.

A quick look at the comparative figures for these two groups will show that Stage II of the Halfan and the late Khormusan do not have any traits which are similar, much less any which overlap in frequency. Of specific importance,

---

[6] Referred to by Waechter as Site 443A.

TABLE 13

COMPARISON OF HALFAN, LATE KHORMUSAN, AND GEMAIAN TRAITS

Traits	Halfan Stage II	Late Khormusan	Gemaian
Raw Material	Chert	Mixed	Chert
Microlithic	81.2-84.5%	c.50-c.57%	36.0-47.4%
Blade Tool Index	12.8-16.0	2.7-8.7[1]	7.7-21.6
Typological Levallois Index	0.0-2.0	44.3-51.4	0.0-1.5
Halfa flakes	51.5-56.0%	0.0%	0.0%
Backed flakes	0.9-2.0%	0.0%	0.0-6.2%
Backed microblades	2.5-6.9%	0.0%	0.0-1.0%
Burins	6.2-6.5%	21.9-50.5%	1.3-4.8%
Denticulates	7.0-7.0%	8.1-15.1%	13.1-26.2%
Leaf shaped points	0.0%	0.0%	8.7-39.7%
Levallois cores	2.1-5.2%	40.3-46.9%	2.7-4.5%
Halfa cores	43.1-45.3%	0.0%	0.0%
Single platform, unfaceted	11.8-15.9%	4.2-6.6%	11.4-21.0%

[1] This includes Levallois blades which are not true blades.

beyond mere frequencies, is the total absence of the Halfa core and flake and the backed microblade from the Late Khormusan and the almost total absence of true Levallois flakes in Stage II of the Halfan. If Halfa flakes are considered no more than simple Levallois flakes, part of this difference disappears. This, however, is totally unjustified typologically. There is no question that Stage II of the Halfan and the Late Khormusan are part of discrete and separate lithic traditions.

The Gemaian and Stage II of the Halfan show certain traits in common. Both used chert as the main source of raw material, both have a relatively low Blade Tool Index, and both have a barely significant Levallois element. Typologically, many traits overlap in frequency, but of greatest importance is the exclusive nature of certain tool types. Again, the Halfa flake is totally missing from the Gemaian, and leaf shaped points, a characteristic Gemaian tool, are totally lacking in the Halfan. Denticulates are rare in the Halfan but common in the Gemaian. Although both use chert as a raw material, the Gemaian has a relatively small percentage of microlithic tools, while the Halfan is heavily microlithic. The similarities seen between the Gemaian and Stage II of the Halfan are, to a large extent, due to the common use of chert pebble and what must be considered a similar adaptation to the same environment. The extreme specialization of the Halfan, however, clearly indicates a separate lithic tradition. This is fully realized in

the subsequent development of both groups, where typological and technological divergence becomes marked.

Stage V of the Halfan dates to perhaps some part of the Sahaba formation. Although it is still questionable where the Sudanese Sebilian should be placed within the Sahaba formation, it is stratigraphically closest to the latest stage of the Halfan. Any comparison between them need not be very detailed. The differences are so great that there is little need to belabor the point. Table 14 gives some comparative figures which demonstrate this quite clearly.

TABLE 14

COMPARISON OF STAGE V OF THE HALFAN AND EARLY SEBILIAN

Traits	Halfan Stage V	Sebilian Early
Raw Material	Chert	Ferrocrete Sandstone
Levallois Index	1.0	14.3
Blade Tool Index	92.7	2.7
Microlithic Index	96.3	26.0
Truncations (all)	2.8%	78.3%
Backed microblades	83.4%	0.0%

The Halfan does not, by far, represent the earliest microlithic industry in the world. Even during the Mousterian, microlithic assemblages have been found both in Europe and the Near East. Often, as in the case of the Microdenticulate Mousterian from San Bernadino, Italy, the microlithic nature of the industry may be tied directly to the availability of only small river pebbles. On the other hand, the Micromousterian of Yabrud I, in Syria, cannot be explained in this way as there is an almost limitless supply of good flint in the immediate vicinity.

In Nubia, there are a number of raw materials available for tool manufacture: ferrocrete sandstone, fossil wood, quartz pebbles, Precambrian rocks, and Nile pebble of chert and agate. The overwhelming use of chert pebble in the Halfan can only be cultural as small amounts of all other raw materials were, on occasion, utilized. It is true that chert pebbles tend to be small and so limit the potential size of finished tools. On the other hand, the Gemaian industry also used chert pebbles almost exclusively and, yet, most of their tools were not microlithic.

There is, without doubt, a tendency toward microlithic tools in both the Gemaian and the late Khormusan. In neither industry, however, is the microlithic element nearly as developed as it is in the Halfan.

Farther north, in Egypt, there are no published reports of similar material. Recent work near Ballana has, however, recovered sites with a few typical Halfan cores and flakes and many backed microblades or microflakes.[7] This points to a contemporarity with Halfan Stage IV, or even perhaps to Stage V. Another unpublished site at Kom Ombo seems to be of the Stage II type.[8] Thus, it would seem that the early Halfan has a fairly wide distribution, in microlithic form, from Kom Ombo to the Second Cataract.

The important fact is that at least by the erosion of the Dibeira-Jer formation (c. 17,000 B.C. +) there was already a widespread Nilotic industry which was almost fully committed to microlithic tools. This commitment, combined with the use of chert pebble and the very special techniques used in preparing Halfa cores, may well account for the early development of a true microblade industry.

The early Halfan shows a preconditioning to a microblade industry. Halfa cores called for the removal of a series of microblades during initial stages of preparation. These, as has been noted, were overwhelmingly treated as debitage. Again, the specific Halfa technology had already

adopted the technique of blunting on the lower edges of Halfa flakes. Thus, Halfa technology contained all features necessary for a microblade technology and a backed microblade typology. All that was needed was a shift in emphasis, brought about, perhaps, by the greater efficiency of microlithic barbs on projectiles as compared with Halfa flakes. The transitional stage is seen at Site 624, and by the following stage the Halfan had a developed backed microblade typology.

It is quite difficult to find comparable material at such an early period. In North Africa, blade industries are quite old, but there is no evidence as yet, that they in any way affected the Halfan. As it is possible to trace the lithic evolution of the Halfan from a microflake into a microblade industry, the evidence seems to be against radical change brought about by direct culture contact. Of course, little is yet known of the Halfan to the north, the most likely area for contacts with the North African littoral. Microlithic backed blades play only a minor role in North Africa until the beginning of the Capsian and Oranian, at least 4,500 years later than Stage IV of the Halfan.

Therefore, at this time, there is no evidence that the microblade technology of the Halfan was in any way the result of contacts with North Africa but was a strictly local, Nilotic development.

South of Nubia, there are no blade industries of such early date, much less any characterized by backed microblades. Blade technology does not appear in Sub-Saharan Africa until the very end of the Middle Stone Age, and it is not until the Late Stone Age that microlithic backed blades play any significant role.

As almost nothing is known of the prehistory for a thousand miles south of Nubia, it is still too early to judge fully the southern limits of Halfan expansion. A short survey was carried out during 1965 south of Dongola, and, while numerous sites were found, there was no trace of any Halfan material. This might suggest that the Halfan never expanded beyond the Second Cataract, a view corroborated by the absence of Halfan sites between the Second and Third Cataracts. Therefore, on the basis of admittedly incomplete evidence, it would seem that the Halfan did not ex-

---

[7] Personal communication from F. Wendorf.
[8] Personal communication from P. Smith.

pand south of the Second Cataract and, thus, was not directly responsible for any diffusion of blade technology to East Africa.

The Halfan peoples left enough remains so that a general picture may be obtained of their life, at least in a very broad sense. All Halfan sites are small, and four of the six contained a number of disturbed earth ovens. This would seem to indicate that the Halfan peoples lived in small bands but remained at their sites for a relatively long period of time. This interpretation is reinforced by the thick occupation layer at Site 443 and the very dense concentrations of artifacts found at every site.

The Halfan peoples both hunted and fished for food. Fish remains were entirely cat fish, but with the exception of Site 1028 fish remains were rare. They hunted a variety of animals, including wild cattle, Hartebeest, gazelle, wild ass, and Hippo. Faunal remains indicate that both wild cattle and Hartebeest were either most preferred or most efficiently hunted. It is interesting to note that they hunted animals associated with both the Nilotic microenvironment and with the surrounding savanna. The small number of fish bones, however, indicate that the Nile itself did not play a major part in the economic life of the Halfan peoples.

They must have been effective hunters, because their settlements are relatively stable and the presence of beads and coloring materials at Halfan sites indicates that there was a sufficient surplus to permit occasional luxury pursuits.

In spite of the very good bone preservation at a number of Halfan sites, there is little evidence for a bone tool technology and none at all for a ground stone technology. This does not mean that the Halfan peoples collected no wild plants for food, merely that we do not have even indirect evidence that they did.

The major problem concerning the Halfan peoples is: where and when did they leave the area of the Second Cataract? At present there are no indications of any continuity with later lithic industries in the area. The limited number of Halfan sites suggests that, at best, the Halfan peoples were few around the Second Cataract. If such were the case, they might have been unable to resist the pressure of the new incoming groups of Qadan and perhaps Sebilian peoples.

In summary, the Halfan appears to be a Nilotic industry which evolved from a local tradition with a possible strong Levallois emphasis and extended from the Second Cataract in Nubia to at least as far north as Kom Ombo. Halfan development shows an early, yet isolated, transition from a highly specialized microflake technology to a true microblade technology. This development resulted in an industry which shows more in common with the North African cultures than with those in Sub-Saharan Africa. These similarities, however, must now be viewed as convergences rather than as the results of direct contact. The possibility of stimulous diffusion cannot be rejected, but at this time everything points to an indiginous development of a microblade technology out of the pre-existing specialized Halfa technology.

THE SEBILIAN INDUSTRY OF THE SECOND CATARACT

Anthony E. Marks

(SOUTHERN METHODIST UNIVERSITY)

INTRODUCTION

IN 1923, M. Vignard reported the discovery of a lithic industry on the Kom Ombo plain in Upper Egypt (Vignard, 1923). He named this industry the Sebilian after the town of Sebil, near the sites he discovered. Ever since that initial report the Sebilian has been a major problem in the archaeology of Egypt. The industry has been used to justify varying views of Egyptian cultural development: some workers have made it typologically meaningless by applying the industry name to a very wide and ill-defined range of lithic assemblages; the industry has been dated by guess, with little stratigraphic basis, to fit within whatever scheme of lithic development was being propounded; and, additional uncertainty was added because of unanswered questions concerning the extent of collection controls used by Vignard in his original work. All these factors have left the Sebilian both typologically and chronologically in almost total confusion.

Prior to the work carried out by the Combined Prehistoric Expedition and other groups during the last few years in Egypt and the Sudan, the prevailing view of the nature and place of the Sebilian in the Nilotic cultural development was based mainly on the reports of Vignard (1923, 1935, 1955) and the interpretations of this work made by Caton-Thompson (1946).

Vignard recognized three stages of Sebilian development, each found on the surface at descending elevations above the present Nile floodplain at Kom Ombo (Vignard, 1923, p. 14). These stages were characterized as follows (Vignard, 1923, p. 5; 1955, p. 439):

1. Sebilian I. Oldest stage, with Levallois debitage, found at the highest elevations.

2. Sebilian II. Intermediate stage, found at lower elevations on the surface of the alluvium.

3. Sebilian III. Microlithic stage, found at the lowest elevations on the surface of the alluvium.

These stages were also reported to be recognizable by specific typological and technological traits which showed change from stage to stage. Detailed review of these stages is given later in this paper. It need only be mentioned that the general pattern of change was from a basically flake industry with highly special tools toward a diminutization of flake size and the introduction in the last stage of true microlithic geometrics made on blades rather than flakes.

Once Vignard had described the Sebilian stages at Kom Ombo, other workers began to report Sebilian material from other areas in Egypt and in the northern Sudan. Sandford (1934) reported Sebilian material from along the Nile in Upper and Middle Egypt and in Nubia as far south as Kor Murshid in the Sudan (Sandford and Arkell, 1933).

In 1941, Huzayyin reported Sebilian material from beach lines in the Fayum found by him and Caton-Thompson (Huzayyin, 1941, pls. x-xi).

Thus, in the twenty years following Vignard's initial paper, Sebilian material had been reported along the Nile from Middle Egypt to south of the Second Cataract and in the north of Egypt in the Fayum. Only Vignard, however, had described what was actually found.

This problem was recognized by Caton-Thompson, and, on a detailed review of the limited evidence, she made a series of suggestions as to the typological and technological limits necessary before any material might be considered within the first two stages of the Sebilian (Caton-Thompson, 1946, pp. 100-112).

Using Vignard's descriptions as a base, Caton-Thompson decided that reasonable evidence for Sebilian I existed only along the Nile from Kom Ombo to the Second Cataract and that Sebilian II had a similar, if less clear, distribution (Caton-Thompson, 1946, pp. 105-112).

Thus, as of 1946, at least the first two stages of the Sebilian had been defined in terms of combinations of attributes and their distribution critically reviewed and limited to Upper Egypt and Nubia.

WORK OF THE COMBINED PREHISTORIC EXPEDITION

Considering the work of Sanford and Caton-Thompson, it was not surprising to find Sebilian material near the Second Cataract in Sudanese Nubia. The first Sebilian site was discovered during the 1961-1962 field season, and by the end of the 1965 field season, nine Sebilian sites, as well as a number of localities where isolated Sebilian tools were seen, had been found.

It would seem that the recently discovered Sebilian sites should be comparable with the typological and chronological structure presented by Vignard and Caton-Thompson. This, however, was not fully the case. Problems were encountered in the practical application of Vignard's typology, necessitating the adoption of a slightly different typological approach. Therefore, each Sudanese Sebilian site was studied separately, a typological list evolved, and a purely local chronological sequence based on typological, technological, and stratigraphic data was developed. Only after these studies were completed was any attempt made to fit the Sudanese Sebilian within the framework proposed by Vignard and Caton-Thompson.

There is no suggestion that the studies of the Sudanese Sebilian have solved all the problems relating to Sebilian development and its significance to Nilotic prehistory. It is hoped, however, that some insight may be obtained of the pattern of Sebilian life and of the history of the Sebilian peoples in Sudanese Nubia. Quantitative measurements of Sebilian technology and typology are given so that materials from Kom Ombo may be usefully compared with those from the Sudan. In addition, it is recognized that some of the suggestions concerning Sebilian origins and relations are tentative, but they are presented as possible guides toward further work.

TYPOLOGICAL AND TECHNOLOGICAL STUDIES

TYPOLOGY

To date, the typology of Sebilian tools has been very simple, particularly in regard to the Lower and Middle Sebilian stages. Vignard

(1923, 1955) recognized relatively few discrete tool types. For the most part, these were classified on the basis of their outline; that is, whether they seemed to be pointed, triangular, trapezoidal, or crescent shaped. The main types defined by Vignard (1955, pp. 443-446), may be summarized as follows:

1. Levallois flakes (*éclats levallois*). This is a well defined type and needs no comment.

2. End-scrapers (*grattoirs*). Again, this is a well defined general tool class, used in its normal sense.

3. Simple flakes-points (*éclats-pointes simples*). This seems to include a number of forms. All are flakes which have been basally truncated. Two main types are present. There is a true basal truncation where the butt has been snapped, removing the bulb of percussion prior to steep retouching; and then there are those where only steep retouch has been added to the butt of a flake, forming a retouched truncation which only partially cuts through the bulb of percussion (Vignard, 1955, p. 445, fig. 4, no. 3). Included within this type are flakes which are both pointed and rectangular. The latter are described as being somewhat similar to *tranchets*. The second type is represented by a few illustrated examples which show some lateral backing or truncation as well as basal truncation (Vignard, 1955, p. 445, fig. 4, nos. 7 and 9).

4. Retouched flakes-points (*éclats-pointes retouchés*). This type is defined as a basally truncated or basally retouched flake which also has the complete, or a portion of one, lateral edge blunted by steep retouch. This is sometimes at the extremity in the form of an oblique truncation or partial backing, sometimes along the whole length, sometimes on the right side, and sometimes on the left. There appears to be no standard orientation for viewing any piece.

5. Triangles (*triangles*). These are flakes similar to the above types, but they are blunted in such a way that they have the general appearance of triangles. From the illustrations, it would appear that no particular tool orientation is necessary, merely that in some orientation the piece has a triangular form (Vignard, 1955, p. 448, fig. 6, nos. 1-10).

6. Trapezes (*trapèzes*). These are flakes similar to the retouched flakes-points and the tri-

angles but, in outline, they appear to be closer to trapezes than to triangles or points (Vignard, 1955, p. 447, fig. 5, nos. 8-19).

7. Scalene triangles (*scalènes*). This type is defined as appearing in the Middle Sebilian. It is merely a flake with blunting which results in a scalene trianglar form. Some of these seem to have been made on blades (Vignard, 1955, p. 448, fig. 6, no. 18).

8. Lunates (*Segment de cercle, demi-lune*). These are made in the same manner as trapezes and triangles, but the blunting is convex. This definition does not include the usual attribute of having both extremities retouched to points as some pieces are illustrated where the retouch is only partial or where the tips are quite blunt (Vignard, 1955, p. 448, fig. 6, nos. 7-10).

9. Retouched blades (*Lames retouchées*). These are not illustrated but would seem to exclude all forms described above.

10. Microburins (*microburins*). These include both typical forms and what Vignard calls a prototype for a microburin (Vignard, 1955, p. 450, fig. f).

The only other specific tool type mentioned is burins. Vignard states that no burins have ever been found in association with Sebilian assemblages (Vignard, 1955, p. 446).

While this typology was perhaps acceptable for an initial definition of Sebilian I and II, it is now felt that the categories are too vague, too subjective, and too broad to permit a detailed definition and a comparison of Sebilian assemblages. The basic problem rests with the classification of specific Sebilian type tools: retouched flakes-points, triangles, trapezes, and lunates. All these types are formed by steep retouch, which either truncates or backs, or does both, on any given flake. Therefore, dealing with a Sebilian typology calls for special considerations.

Typical Sebilian tools are made by basal truncation, oblique truncation, backing, or by a combination of two or all of these. Often, the resulting tools do have, as Vignard recognized, certain similarities with geometric shapes. These tools, however, are not geometrics and should not be given geometric names. These are only confusing and do not truly describe most Sebilian tools. Terms such as trapeze, triangle, and lunate are used generally in a combined morphological

and functional sense. With the exception of Vignard, all authors, when referring to geometrics, refer either to microlithic or submicrolithic artifacts which are assumed to have been part of a composite tool, i.e., a series of geometrics were inserted into a wooden or bone shaft. While at times conforming to geometric shapes, Sebilian tools are, for the most part, unquestionably too large, and the backing or truncation is too thick to have been inserted in series into any shaft.

Typologically, it is extremely difficult to fit many Sebilian tools into geometric designations. It is very common for the same Sebilian artifact to have both a basal truncation and an oblique truncation. The form of the resulting piece depends on both the original shape of the flake and the extent and form of the truncations added. The basal truncation may be perpendicular to the long axis of the flake or may be somewhat off axis. The oblique truncation may be acute or quite oblique, straight, concave, or convex. If only a limited number of these possibilities occurred in the Sebilian, it might be possible to give geometric or pseudo-geometric designations. Unfortunately, this is not the case. Almost the total range of variations occurs within each Sebilian assemblage. One type grades into another, often with the majority of artifacts showing transitional forms. How close to a true trapeze must a tool be before it may be called a trapeze, particularly when it is not a blade tool formed by the classic methods of trapeze manufacture? What limits are to be set on what is called a triangle against what is merely a pointed retouched flake-point? Sebilian tools rarely present obvious answers.

Therefore, in order to avoid as much subjectivity as possible, these Sebilian assemblages will be typed according to specific attributes. The major attributes are considered to be basal truncation, oblique truncation, and backing. In addition, those artifacts which show a combination of these attributes will be grouped separately, depending on which two attributes are combined. When a Sebilian tool fits within the classic definition of a scalene triangle or lunate, these types will be used. For the most part, however, the final outline of the tool will not be of primary classificatory significance, but shape variation will be described within the typological comments.

These major typological attributes will be grouped under separate types, depending on whether they occur on flakes or blades. Blades are extremely rare, but their presence may be significant for comparisons with Sebilian material from other areas. In addition, a class of points will be recognized. These will be broken down into types by the major typological attributes but will be strictly defined as being symmetric.

The following types will be used in the basic type list of all Sebilian assemblages. The attributes associated with each type as well as the subdivisions found within each type are defined below. In all site reports the same criteria will be used, and only variation in quality, side preference, dominant shape patterns, and size will be discussed in the descriptive typology.

All tool types which conform to classic types (Levallois flakes, side-scrapers, denticulates, notches, microburins, end-scrapers, etc.) will be classified in accordance with accepted definitions and will be described. They will appear at the beginning of the type list in the following order:

1. Levallois flakes
2. Levallois blades
3. Levallois points
4. Side-scrapers
5. End-scrapers
6. Notched pieces
7. Denticulates
8. Bec burins
9. Burins
10. Borers
11. Cortex backed knives
12. Retouched flakes

Typical Sebilian tools will be classified in the manner, and with the typological definitions, presented below. All tools will be viewed with the original long axis of the flake directly along the line of vision, and the short axis perpendicular to it with the butt end down, regardless of the orientation of the retouched edges. The long axis is defined as that which is perpendicular to the butt of the flake and the short axis as that which is parallel to the butt (fig. 1, a-b).

13. Simple basal truncations. This includes all flakes and blades which show only basal truncations, with or without prior snapping of the butt.

The pieces may be pointed, rectangular, irregular, or any other shape. They correspond to Vignard's *éclats-pointes simples*.

a. Flakes
   1. Perpendicular basal truncations. Flakes with simple basal truncations which are perpendicular to the long axis (fig. 1, c).
   2. Oblique basal truncations. Flakes with simple basal truncations which are oblique to the long axis (fig. 1, d).
b. Blades
   1. Perpendicular basal truncations. As above, but on true blades.
   2. Oblique basal truncations. As above, but on true blades.

14. Basal and oblique truncations. These are pieces where there is both a basal and an oblique truncation present. The oblique truncation may take any form found under the simple oblique truncations, and the basal truncation may take any form under the simple basal truncations.

a. Flakes
   1. Basal and straight oblique truncations. These range in shape from what Vignard would call retouched flakes-points to trapezes. This depends on the obliqueness of the distal truncation, and all transitional forms are known (fig. 1, e).
   2. Basal and convex oblique truncations. Basally truncated flakes which also have a convex oblique truncation at their distal ends (fig. 1, f).
   3. Basal and concave oblique truncations. Basally truncated flakes which also have a concave oblique truncation at their distal ends (fig. 1, g).
b. Blades
   1. Basal and straight oblique truncations. As above, but on true blades.
   2. Basal and convex oblique truncations. As above, but on true blades.
   3. Basal and concave oblique truncations. As above, but on true blades.
c. Points. These almost always have straight oblique truncations; otherwise, they fit the definition of points, or of an equilateral or isosceles triangular form (fig. 1, h).

15. Simple oblique truncations. This includes all oblique truncations made on the distal ends of flakes and blades. No other typological at-

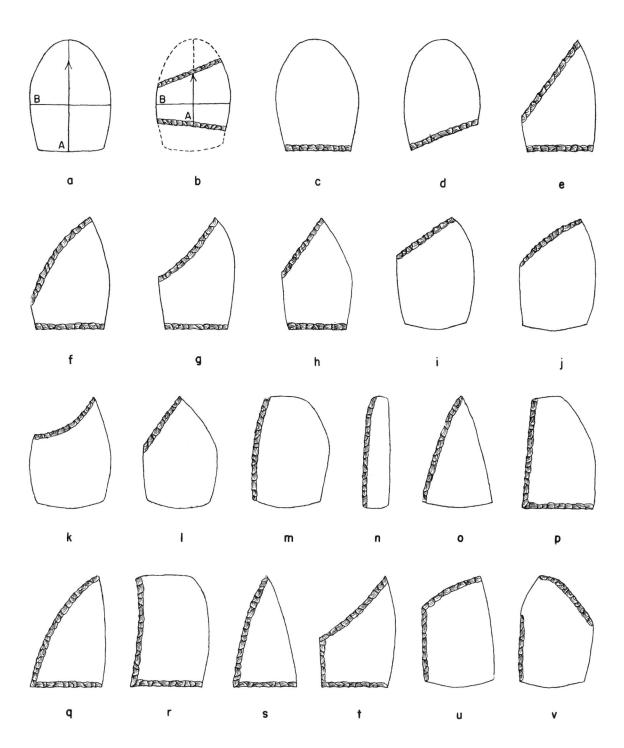

FIG. 1—Idealized Sebilian artifact forms: a-b, flake orientation; c-d, basal truncations; e-h, basal and oblique truncations; i-l, simple oblique truncations; m-o, simple backing; p-s, backing and basal truncations; t-v, other Sebilian types.

tribute is present. In all cases, the truncation appreciably alters the original shape of the flake or blade.

    a. Flakes

        1. Straight truncations. All flakes with only straight oblique truncations, regardless of the angle or side on which the truncation is formed (fig. 1, i).

        2. Convex truncations. As above, but the truncations are convex in form (fig. 1, j).

        3. Concave truncations. As above, but the truncations are concave in form (fig. 1, k).

    b. Blades

        1. Straight truncations. All blades with straight, oblique truncations, regardless of angle or side on which the truncation is formed.

        2. Convex truncations. As above, but the truncations are convex in form.

        3. Concave truncations. As above, but the truncations are concave in form.

    c. Points. Symmetric points formed by single oblique truncations (fig. 1, l).

16. Simple backed pieces.

    a. Backed flakes. All flakes where backing is the only typological attribute present. Backing is distinct from oblique truncation in that it does not appreciably alter the original shape of the flake. Full backing must extend to the butt, and the shape of the backed edge must not show a radical shift in angle, although convex backing and concave backing are present (fig. 1, m).

    b. Backed blades. All blades where backing is the only typological attribute. As above, but on true blades (fig. 1, n).

    c. Backed points. Flakes which are backed in such a way that the distal end of the flake forms a sharp point. The overall shape of the tool is either an equilateral triangle or an isosceles triangle (fig. 1, o). While oblique truncations often cause a generally pointed distal end, they never modify a flake so that it is either equilateral or isosceles in outline.

17. Backing and basal truncations. This includes all basally truncated pieces which are also backed. While the backing may not be perpendicular to the basal truncation, the backing al-ways meets the basal truncation at the edge of the butt, and there is never a sharp, radical change in angle along the backed edge.

    a. Flakes

        1. Basal and straight backing. Basally truncated flakes with straight backing (fig. 1, p).

        2. Basal and convex backing. Basally truncated flakes with convex backing (fig. 1, q).

        3. Basally truncated flakes with concave backing (fig. 1, r).

    b. Points. These are all basally truncated flakes with normally straight backing, which modifies the flake into an isosceles or equilateral triangle (fig. 1, s).

18. Other Sebilian types. Occasionally, there are Sebilian tools which do not conform to the above types. These may include basally truncated flakes which have both backing and oblique truncation, or those which have backing and oblique truncation without basal truncation. There are also a few flakes with distal truncations which are perpendicular to the long axis of the flake. All these types are rare and their number does not justify separate grouping. When these occur, they will be placed here and described in the typological comments (fig. 1, t-v).

19. Microburins. As defined and illustrated by Vignard. These include both prototypes and true microburins.

The specific ordering of these tools in the type list is governed solely by the effectiveness for graphing. Thus, those types which normally have numerous examples are separated from each other by those where examples are rare. This makes the cumulative graphs easier to read and minimizes confusion.

In the site reports there are two sets of percentages given for each type list. The first set includes percentages for all artifact groups on the list. The second set is restricted to retouched tools. That is, all unretouched Levallois flakes, blades, and points have been removed as well as microburins, which are really no more than a specialized form of debitage. It is felt that the restricted type list is the most significant for comparisons between Sudanese Sebilian assemblages and between Sudanese Sebilian and other industries.

TECHNOLOGY

Technological studies of the Sudanese Sebilian center on three primary quantitative observations: the amount of Levallois technology employed as seen through the proportions of Levallois pieces in the total flake and blade production; the percentage of flakes, blades, and points showing prepared or faceted butts; and the ratio of blade production to flake production. Each of these observations is expressed as an index, derived from the total number of flakes, blades, and points in each assemblage. The indices are computed in the following manner:

$$\text{Levallois Index (IL)} = \frac{\text{total number of Levallois flakes, blades, and points} \times 100}{\text{total number of flakes, blades, and points}}$$

$$\text{Faceting Index (IF)} = \frac{\text{total number of flakes, blades, and points with dihedral, convex, or straight faceted butts} \times 100}{\text{total number of flakes, blades, and points with recognizable butts}}$$

$$\text{Restricted Faceting Index (IFs)} = \frac{\text{total number of flakes, blades, and points with convex or straight faceted butts} \times 100}{\text{total number of flakes, blades, and points with recognizable butts}}$$

$$\text{Blade Index (Ib)} = \frac{\text{total number of Levallois and non-Levallois blades} \times 100}{\text{total number of flakes, blades, and points}}$$

In addition to these primary technological observations, a number of other technological features will be discussed. These include the following:

1. Types of raw material employed in tool and core manufacture.

2. The extent of basal snapping prior to truncation by retouch.

3. Side preference for backing and retouched oblique distal truncations as compared with occurrences on simple broken pieces.

4. Tool size.

DATING OF THE SEBILIAN

While Vignard and Caton-Thompson primarily concerned themselves with Sebilian typology and technology, they both suggested where the Sebilian at Kom Ombo fits chronologically in the Egyptian prehistoric culture sequence. Both Vignard and Caton-Thompson dated the Sebilian on generic relationships it was assumed to have with other poorly dated Egyptian industries. This pattern has remained the same for a number of years, with other workers either accepting the earlier suppositions or making guesses of their own. It is only within the last few years that there has been any sound stratigraphic information and radiocarbon dates which permit a re-evaluation of the whole problem of the absolute chronology of the Sebilian.

Vignard held that Sebilian I developed out of the Egyptian Mousterian and that the Sebilian III might be correlated with the "Tardenoisian" industries of Europe and the Near East (Vignard, 1923, pp. 72-74). Although Vignard gave no absolute dates, his position would place Sebilian I and II as spanning the whole of the time of the Upper Paleolithic in Europe and the Near East.

Caton-Thompson (1946, p. 100) agreed with Vignard in part, but derived the Sebilian out of the "last true Levalloisian phase." She, therefore, considered Sebilian I and II as being "approximate contemporaries of the earlier Wurmian industries of Europe—the Cave Mousterian and the Chatelperronian" (Caton-Thompson, 1946, p. 117). Thus, the earliest Sebilian would date well into the European Mousterian period, perhaps 45,000 B.C. or so, while the end of Sebilian II would have to be placed no later than, perhaps, 29,000 B.C.[1] Caton-Thompson did not deal directly with the problem of dating Sebilian III, but did say "the microlithic industries of Egypt, which appear to succeed epi-Levalloisian II . . . are fully glacial also in their European contemporaneity" (Caton-Thompson, 1946, p. 117). Thus, Caton-Thompson would place the Sebilian as being decidedly older than Vignard thought, mainly because of her initial dating of the "last true Levalloisian."

Alimen (1957, p. 97) does not concur with this view. She feels, with Vignard, that the Sebilian is post-Mousterian or Levalloiso-Mousterian, and so should be correlated in time with the begin-

[1] This date is based on equating the Chatelperronian with no later than Aurigancian II in the new terminology, which has been dated to 28,850 B.C. ± 250 years (GRN-1717) at Arcy sur Cure III (Oakley, 1964, p. 166a).

ning of the Upper Paleolithic. Therefore, Alimen would date the beginning of Sebilian I where Caton-Thompson would date the end of Sebilian II. Alimen also disagrees with Caton-Thompson in the dating of Sebilian III, which she would place as belonging to "the end of the Paleolithic and to the transition to the Neolithic" (Alimen, 1957, p. 100). Thus, in her thinking, the Sebilian spans a very long time, from perhaps 30,000 B.C. to 5,000 B.C.

Monod (1963, pp. 157-158) in review of Butzer's work presents dates for the Sebilian based on its association with Nile silts. The picture emerges of Sebilian I dating to the earliest and highest Nile aggradation at about 28,000 B.C. with Sebilian II also in the same silt formation. Sebilian III would appear to date during the incision of the Nile, with a minimum date of less than 8,000 B.C.

Thus, as of about ten years ago, workers, with the exception of Caton-Thompson, placed the beginning of the Sebilian as post Levalloiso-Mousterian dating to about 30,000 B.C. Sebilian II was placed relative to Sebilian I and III, but most would appear to date it as Upper Paleolithic, although Caton-Thompson again proposes an earlier date. Sebilian III seems to pose the greatest problem, being guess-dated from "fully glacial" by Caton-Thompson, about 8,000 B.C. by Butzer and Monod, and even into transitional Neolithic times by Alimen.

The justification for a beginning date for the Sebilian seems to have rested on the assumption that Sebilian I was directly descended from the Mousterian of Vignard (late Levalloisian of Caton-Thompson). This assumption meant that Sebilian I should have immediately followed the Middle Paleolithic industries and so, by analogy with Europe and the Near East, should have begun by 28,000 B.C. Quite apart from the questionable dating of the Middle Paleolithic in Egypt, it must be noted that up to that time Sebilian I had never been successfully dated by its position within a local stratigraphic sequence; Vignard only obtained a relative sequence based on absolute surface elevation at Kom Ombo.

The extremely early and extended dating of Sebilian development has changed radically during the past few years. Studies carried out by Butzer and Hansen (1965) in Egypt, and by de Heinzelin and Paepe (1965) in the Sudan and Egypt have finally clarified the complex sequence of Nile aggradation and erosion, and numerous radiocarbon dates from the Nile silts have finally given a sound basis for absolute dating.

The Sahaba and perhaps the Birbet formations are of importance because most Sebilian material can be dated to them both in Nubia and Kom Ombo (Butzer and Hansen, 1965, p. 81; Wendorf, Shiner, and Marks, 1965, pp. xvii-xviii).

The dating of the nine Sudanese Sebilian sites rests on two factors: radiocarbon dates from a hearth at one Sebilian site, and the geological position of the other sites within the dated stages of Nile aggradation and erosion just described.

Site 1024A was the only site where charcoal was found. Two dates were obtained: 9,050 B.C. ± 120 years (WSU-144), and 8,975 B.C. ± 140 years (WSU-188). This site was well up the Khor Musa, outside of direct contact with true Nile silts. On the basis of these dates, however, as compared with the dated silt formations, it is safe to place this site as being contemporary with the very end of the Sahaba formation or an early phase of the Birbet formation.

No other Sebilian site contained charcoal, but three geological positions were typical.[2]

1. Two sites were surface concentrations resting on the deflated surface of the Sahaba formation (83, and 1042). They were both fully deflated, but their position was such that they could not, in any way, have been contemporary with the Dibeira-Jer formation or the Ballana formation. The only possibility other than contemporaneity with the Sahaba formation is that these fully surface sites were later than the Sahaba formation and were never covered by Nile alluviation. This possibility is remote as other sites with the same typological attributes were found in a second geological context which can be directly dated to the end of the Sahaba formation.

2. Two sites, 81 and 2005, were found incorporated into *Unio* lines which represent beach formations of the late stage of the Sahaba formation. The artifacts were extremely fresh at Site 81, indicating that they were not transported for

---

[2] Specific site stratigraphy is given in the individual site reports. Site 2013 rested on a rock outcrop just above the highest alluviation of the Sahaba formation.

any distance but rested on the edge of the shore in the immediate area of the beach formation. They might have been covered by alluvium prior to their incorporation in the beach or might have come from an occupation along the water's edge just prior to their incorporation in the beach. These beaches, at 20 m., have been dated to about 10,000 B.C. but may be somewhat earlier. In either case, Site 81 could not have been occupied after the Sahaba formation nor even within the very early stages of it.

3. Two sites, 2010A and 2010B, rested on the deflated surface of the Dibeira-Jer formation. While these cannot be placed temporally within the Sahaba formation, there was no evidence that they had ever been subsurface, and technological and typological evidence shows them to be fully comparable with sites firmly placed within the Sahaba formation.

Thus, in Sudanese Nubia, all but two Sebilian sites must be correlated with the Sahaba formation or just post Sahaba formation; that is, from 15,000 B.C. to 9,000 B.C. (table 1). No Sebilian site can be safely attributed to any earlier formation and, therefore, there is no solid evidence for any Sebilian material dating prior to 15,000 B.C.

TABLE 1

RELATIVE STRATIGRAPHY OF SEBILIAN SITES NEAR THE SECOND CATARACT WITH SELECTED RADIOCARBON DATES

Geological Position	Sites	Dates
Early Birbet or terminal Sahaba	1024A	8,975 B.C. ± 140 years (WSU-188)
	1024C	9,050 B.C. ± 120 years (WSU-144)
Late Sahaba Formation: beach lines and silt edge	81 2005	
	2013 2010B	Typologically serriated
Sahaba Formation[1] (exact position unknown but pre-20 m. beach)	1042	Before 11,000 B.C. and after 15,000 B.C.
	83 2010A	Typologically serriated

[1] Sites 2010A and 2010B are not stratigraphically attributable to any formation.

In Kom Ombo recent work has also placed Sebilian sites within this time range, indicating a general contemporaneity between the Sebilian of Upper Egypt and that which is to be found in the Sudan.

The problem remains of where the Sebilian of Sudanese Nubia fits within Vignard's and Caton-Thompson's typological sequences. If any of the Sudanese material can be shown to be within Sebilian I, then there is no question but that the original dating of the beginning of the Sebilian is at least 15,000 years too old.

SEBILIAN SITE CHARACTERISTICS

DISTRIBUTION AND SIZE

Within the surveyed area from the Egyptian border to the Third Cataract at Firka, Sebilian sites occurred only in two small zones: on both banks of the Nile around the northern end of the Second Cataract, including the Khor Musa, and on the east bank of the Nile just south of Jebel el-Sahaba. In addition, a very few, scattered Sebilian tools were found a small distance south of the Khor Musa in the northern fringe of Batn el-Hajar and at the southern limit of the Second Cataract at Gemai North (fig. 2). No Sebilian material was found north of Jebel el-Sahaba nor was any found south of the Second Cataract.

The absence of Sebilian material north of the Jebel el-Sahaba in the Sudan might be accounted for by the scarcity of Sahaba formation silts. With the exception of a small area near Nag el-Ikhtiariya, both banks of the Nile north of Sahaba had only remnants of the Dibeira-Jer, Qadus, and Arkin formations. As most Sebilian sites were found in association with the Sahaba formation, it is not surprising that they were missing in that area where the sands and silts of this formation had been completely eroded.

South of the Second Cataract, in the Batn el-Hajar proper, the sequence of silt formations is not fully known. Therefore, it is impossible to tell which silts correspond to the Sahaba formation north of the Cataract. There are, however, numerous silt exposures and deflated remnants. In no case, however, were any Sebilian living or workshop sites found. Although it must remain hypothetical, it now appears that the Sebilian was not present in the Batn el-Hajar, and the two cases of finds of single Sebilian tools in the northern border of the Batn el-Hajar probably repre-

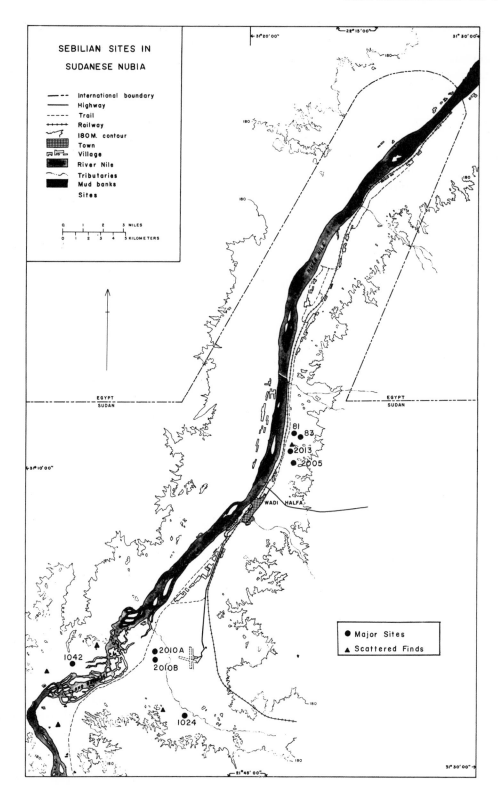

Fɪɢ. 2—Map of Sebilian sites north of the Second Cataract.

sents minor and temporary incursions into the area.

The overall distribution of Sebilian sites suggests a number of possibilities: (1) the general area between the Second Cataract and Jebel el-Sahaba is one isolated area of Sebilian occupation on the Nile; (2) the Second Cataract represents the southern limit of a generally continuous Sebilian occupation along the Nile; or (3) the hostile environment of the Batn el-Hajar resulted in a break of Sebilian occupation which is perhaps present south of the Batn el-Hajar.

This final possibility cannot be tested now, but a short reconnaissance survey south of the Batn el-Hajar in the neighborhood of Dongola failed to discover any Sebilian sites, although over one hundred sites were located.[3] This would tend to suggest that a southern limit of Sebilian occupation might be placed at the Second Cataract.

The presence of Sebilian sites at Ballana and near Luxor, Egypt, tends to suggest that Sebilian occupation was generally continuous along the Nile north of the Second Cataract, but much additional work will be necessary before this position can be demonstrated.

As most of the Sebilian sites were surface concentrations, deflated from the Sahaba formation alluvium, there was quite a variation in site size. Only three sites showed a minimum of deflation. They were Sites 1024A and 1024C away from the Nile alluvium in the Khor Musa, and Site 2013 which rested on a sandstone outcrop just above the highest level of the Sahaba silts. These three sites give a probable picture of the typical original size for all Sebilian sites, which is between 60 and 70 sq. m. The deflated sites ranged in area from 200 sq. m. to as much as 5,000 sq. m., but the artifactual density at these indicated that they were not originally so large. This problem will be discussed in greater detail below.

ARTIFACTUAL DENSITY, CONTENT, AND UTILIZATION OF RAW MATERIALS

The normal artifact sampling procedure was to make a systematic collection over an arbitrary area within the main concentration of a site. The size of the collection area depended upon the overall density of artifacts at the site being col-

---

[3] Unpublished data of the Northern Sudan Project.

lected and upon the number of retouched tools found in each square meter. In some cases, it was necessary to make systematic collections over most of a site in order to get a statistically valid tool sample for typological study. At others, because of greater artifactual density, only relatively small areas had to be collected. In the case of those sites which were found incorporated into Sahaba formation beach lines, Sites 81 and 2005, all artifacts were recovered by a screening of the gravels. As these sites obviously were disturbed by water action, it is probable that smaller artifacts were washed away. Therefore, no studies were made on artifactual density or content, although typological studies of retouched tools will be presented.

The density of artifacts per square meter at Sebilian sites varies greatly. This can be correlated directly with the apparent extent of surface deflation at each site. Those sites resting on heavily deflated surfaces of the Sahaba formation are those which have the least artifactual density, and are also those with the largest total site areas. On the other hand, those sites resting on silt or rock outcrops have the highest artifactual density per square meter; they are also those which have the smallest total site area. No Sebilian sites were found which had both a dense concentration of artifacts and covered a large area, nor were any small sites located where the density of artifacts was low (table 2).

TABLE 2

SITE AREA, COLLECTION AREA, DENSITY OF ARTIFACTS PER SQUARE METER, AND PERCENTAGE OF TOOLS TO TOTAL COLLECTIONS

Site	Total Area	Area Collected	Density Per Sq. M. Collected	Percentage of Tools in Collection
1024A	60 sq. m.	28 sq. m.	58.9	24.4
1024C	70 sq. m.	65 sq. m.	30.5	10.5
2013	60 sq. m.	21 sq. m.	55.2	18.9
83	200 sq. m.	180 sq. m.	12.4	21.2
2010A	300 sq. m.	136 sq. m.	5.2	29.4
2010B	400 sq. m.	136 sq. m.	3.6	43.5
1042	5,000 sq. m.	2,000 sq. m.	0.415	35.1

It is also worthy of note that those sites which are most deflated contained the highest percentages of tools. This is probably because of the loss of small chips and fragments during the process of deflation.

On the basis of the information given above, it is possible to suggest a generalization concerning Sebilian sites in Sudanese Nubia. Sebilian sites were small and contained a relatively high density of artifacts per square meter. The limited size of the undisturbed sites indicates that they were occupied by small groups of people, while the artifact density suggests that sites were occupied on more than a transitory basis. This view is reinforced by the relative high percentage of tools at each site, which suggests that intensive tool manufacture took place at each site.

The systematic collections of artifacts were broken down into five gross typological classes: tools (including Levallois flakes), flake and blade debitage, cores and core fragments, primary flakes, and debris. Each of these classes has different significance in the process of tool manufacture, and their relative proportions reflect the amount and type of flaking which took place at each site.

Tools obviously represent the finished product of the whole process of tool manufacture and Levallois flakes, considered "quasi-tools," might be classified with tools considering the amount of preparation necessary for their production. Flake and blade debitage represents those artifacts which could have been retouched into tools, falling within the minimal size range and quality of those flakes and blades which were actually made into finished tools. Cores have a totally different significance; they indicate the amount of flake production which took place at each site. Also, the ratio between cores and all flakes and blades indicates the extent of utilization of the cores. Primary flakes, those with over half of their dorsal surfaces covered by cortex or those which show unmodified, weathered dorsal surfaces, indicate the amount of primary core preparation which took place at each site. Debris, those chips and fragments which were too small and irregular to have been used in tool manufacture, also seem to be related to the process of flake production or to the actual manufacture of tools.

In Figure 3, two main patterns can be observed: that which is seen at Sites 1024A and 1024C, and that which typifies all other sites. At this time it seems difficult to explain the functional aspects of this difference, but it is brought about by a higher percentage of debris at Sites

1024A and 1024C than at other sites. It is worth noting that Site 2013, the only other site which was not deflated, also has a relatively high proportion of debris, although not reaching the level seen at Sites 1024A and 1024C. This tends to suggest that deflation and wind scattering played some part in this situation. It is also noteworthy that 1024A and 1024C represent the latest Sudanese Sebilian sites and that Site 2013 is typologically very similar to these later sites.

In spite of the rather marked difference in the proportions of debris between the earlier and later Sudanese Sebilian sites, there is a reasonable conformity in a number of the other classes.

Cores are very rare at Sebilian sites. They range from 1.4 to 12 per cent of the total collections. This spread is somewhat deceptive as only two sites contain more than 5.5 per cent, and both of these, Sites 2010A and 1042, are heavily deflated and are the earliest of the Sudanese Sebilian. This slightly higher core percentage may have temporal significance but the data are too incomplete to be conclusive. In any case, at no site are cores common, and it is quite apparent that much flake production took place outside the site areas. This is confirmed by the ratio of all flakes and blades to cores where it is indicated that, through time, less flakes were actually produced in the camp sites. At the earlier sites, 1042 and 2010A, the ratio of flakes and blades to cores is 5.5 to 1 and 7.8 to 1 respectively. The remaining sites show ratios from 13.9 to 1 to as high as 40.9 to 1 at Site 1024A.

As the earlier sites are also the most deflated, it is possible that the low ratio has something to do with the scattering of the artifacts and the possible loss of lighter flakes. On the other hand, those later sites which show little or no deflation have ratios which are so high that it must be concluded that many of the flakes found at the site were produced elsewhere.

This general picture is confirmed by the low occurrence of primary flakes at all Sudanese Sebilian sites. These range from 3.1 to 14.3 per cent of the total collections. As primary flakes are the initial waste material from core preparation, it is interesting to note that the ratio between primary flakes and cores at five sites is less than two primary flakes per core and at two others it is no more than four primary flakes per core. This

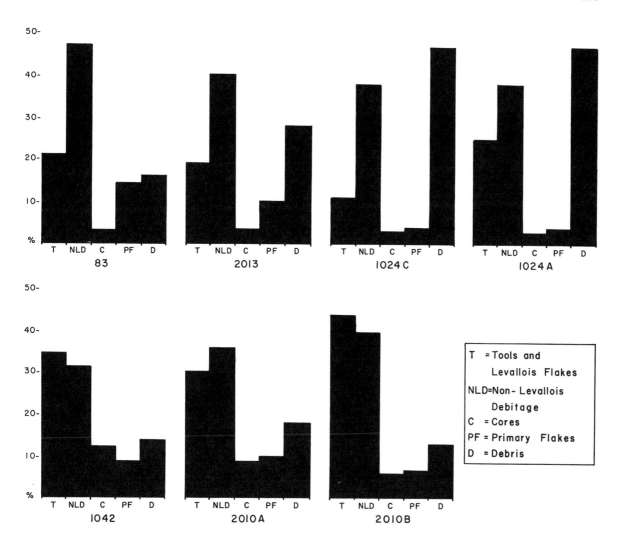

Fig. 3—Percentages of gross artifact types.

is hardly sufficient to produce usable "Mousterian" discoidal or Levallois cores from plaquettes which are cortex covered on two faces. This again indicates that even the cores which were found at the sites were prepared someplace outside the site areas, probably at flaking stations at the source of the raw material.

Another striking element of Sebilian sites is the high percentage of flakes and blades in proportion to all other classes of artifacts. If tools and flakes and blade debitage are considered one group, they account for between 42 and 75.6 per cent of the total collections, with all but two sites having between 49.6 and 67.8 per cent. This compares with less than 10 per cent for the

latest Halfan site (Marks, this volume), and less than 35 per cent for the most recent Khormusan site (Marks, this volume).

A striking feature of Sebilian technology is the raw materials chosen for use in tool manufacture. Three types are found at all Sudanese Sebilian sites: ferrocrete sandstone, a variety of Precambrian quartzites, and a devitrified dacite.[4] With the exception of a few pieces of quartz from Site 1042, these were the only raw materials utilized by the Sebilian peoples in Nubia. It is also inter-

_____

[4]This rock which was found at all Sebilian sites was identified by A. Richards, Department of Geology, Southern Methodist University, as "Devitrified Dacite Vitrophyre with the phonocrysts An_{30} plagioclase."

TABLE 3
UTILIZATION OF RAW MATERIALS AT SUDANESE SEBILIAN SITES

Dates	Sites Near the Khor Musa				Sites Near the Jebel el-Sahaba			
	Sites	*FSS*	*Prc'*	*Prc"*	*Sites*	*FSS[1]*	*Prc'[2]*	*Prc"[3]*
	2010A	50.6	40.5	8.9				
c. 15,000- 12,000 B.C.	1042	77.1	11.6	11.3				
c. 12,000- 9,000 B.C.	2010B	81.3	12.1	6.6	83	97.7	2.3	0.0
					81	94.4	4.7	0.9
					2005	94.6	3.4	2.0
					2013	96.5	2.2	1.3
c. 9,000 B.C.	1024C	84.8	6.6	8.6				
	1024A	92.8	4.3	2.9				

[1] FSS = Ferrocrete sandstone
[2] Prc' = Devitrified dacite vitrophyre
[3] Prc" = Precambrian quartzites. Also included are a few pieces of quartz at Site 1042.

esting to note that the dacite is found associated with only one other industry in Nubia. This site, 440, has an ill-defined industry, but it may be much earlier than the Sebilian and quite different typologically.

By far the most common material is ferrocrete sandstone, which is found in slabs on the edges of inselbergs in both the Eastern and Western Deserts. The dacite and the Precambrian quartzites are only found in the Batn el-Hajar, beginning on the southern side of the Khor Musa and continuing about 200 km. to the south.

The relative proportions of these rocks used in tool manufacture at any Sudanese Sebilian site is directly related to the immediate availability of the Precambrian rocks, tempered to some extent by small changes through time. Those sites farthest from the Khor Musa have the least number of tools made on Precambrian rock, although there are always a few even at those sites near the Jebel el-Sahaba. There appears to be a slight shift through time toward an increased use of ferrocrete sandstone. This may be seen by comparing the percentages of utilized raw materials at Sites 2010A and 2010B as shown in Table 3. These sites are close to one another on the southern edge of the Khor Musa. Site 2010A is early, while 2010B seems to be somewhat later. This is reflected in the higher percentage of ferrocrete sandstone at the latter site.

Those sites north of the Khor Musa in the area of Jebel el-Sahaba have the highest percentage of ferrocrete sandstone, although none are as late as Sites 1024A and 1024C (table 3).

A number of elements are quite apparent. With the exception of Sites 2010A and 1042, ferrocrete sandstone accounts for over 80 per cent of all tools at each site. Even at 2010A and 1042, ferrocrete sandstone accounts for over half of all tools. The total absence of fossil wood and chert should be considered as well as the rarity of quartz.

It is also seen that all Sudanese Sebilian sites in the area of Jebel el-Sahaba have proportionately less Precambrian rocks than those sites bordering on the Khor Musa. While this is to be expected, and obviously accounts for much of the variation in raw material utilization, it is somewhat surprising that any Precambrian rock should be found at those sites near Jebel el-Sahaba as they are more than 25 km. from the nearest outcrop of Precambrian rock.

While ferrocrete sandstone was the preferred raw material of the Nubian Middle Stone Age industries, by 21,000 B.C. it had already lost its popularity. By the late Khormusan (17,000 B.C.- 15,000 B.C.), ferrocrete sandstone tools were rare, and they do not occur at all in the Halfan and Gemaian—those industries which are generally contemporaneous with, or somewhat earlier than, the Sudanese Sebilian.

In short, the Sudanese Sebilian shows a strong preference for ferrocrete sandstone, although some Precambrian rock is always utilized. The degree of this utilization seems to depend on the immediate availability of the Precambrian rock with a greater interest in it shown at the earliest sites.

SUMMARY

On the basis of the varied data presented here, it is possible to posit a number of attributes and technological habits which appear to be consistent with the material evidence discussed above:

1. Sebilian peoples in the Sudan lived in small groups.

2. They occupied sites of very small size for relatively long periods—long enough to form heavy concentrations of tools and flake debitage.

3. Sebilian peoples normally chose ferrocrete sandstone for tool manufacture although numerous other raw materials were available.

4. The ferrocrete sandstone was quarried in the jebels and most of the primary flaking of cores took place there rather than at camp sites.

5. There is also evidence that much actual flake production also took place at the quarry sites, with flakes then transported to the camp sites for secondary retouching.

6. Some tools were carried from site to site, particularly those made on devitrified dacite.

7. The habits listed remained relatively constant throughout the Sebilian occupation of the Second Cataract.

Tools are made on flakes which vary in length from 15 to 70 mm., although the majority measure between 30 and 50 mm.

These general observations apply to all Sebilian assemblages found near the Second Cataract. In Nubia there is very little evidence for major technological change in basic flake or core production. Technological changes did take place, but these were mostly of a secondary nature; that is, they were techniques used in tool rather than flake production.

Levallois technology is not strongly developed, although there are some fine examples of both Levallois flakes and cores. The Levallois Indices from samples which were *in situ* vary from 9.8 (Site 1024C) to 15.4 (Site 1024A). Both of these sites are the same typologically, and both represent the latest known phase of the Sebilian in Nubia, dated by radiocarbon to about 9,000 B.C. Thus, even the small variation seen in the Levallois Indices does not represent any change through time but merely gives a range of variation for the late phase.[5] These Sebilian assemblages which predate Sites 1024A and 1024C show even less variation, from 10.9 to 14.3 (table 4).

TABLE 4

TECHNOLOGICAL INDICES OF SUDANESE SEBILIAN SITES

Index	1042	2010A	83	2013	2010B	2005	81	1024A	1024C
IL	13.8	10.9	14.3	10.9	13.6	22.2	11.1	15.1	9.8
IF	77.6	75.3	70.7	75.7	78.4	61.4	63.9	63.1	56.8
IFs	45.9	46.1	46.2	48.6	52.8	37.9	42.7	35.0	31.9
Ib	4.7	7.1	3.7	4.2	2.3	2.9	7.9	5.1	4.1

8. Minor variations are visible but do not alter the essential character of these Sebilian traits.

SEBILIAN TECHNOLOGY AND TYPOLOGY

This section will describe in detail the overall characteristics of the Sudanese Sebilian lithic industry and trace what changes are visible through time.

TECHNOLOGY

The Sebilian may be characterized technologically by an emphasis on faceted platform flakes, mainly produced from flat unifacial "Mousterian" discoidal cores. There are, however, a number of Levallois flakes and a few true blades, as well.

Faceting of core platforms, with the resulting faceted flakes, is strongly developed and, again, shows little variation from site to site. The earlier Sebilian assemblages have Faceting Indices from 70.7 to 78.4 and Restricted Faceting Indices from 45.9 to 48.6 (table 4). At Site 1024A and 1024C, is is possible to see a significant drop in faceting (IF, 56.8 and 63.1; IFs, 31.9 and 35.0). This is perhaps the most significant primary technological change noticeable in the development of the Sebilian in Nubia, although both assemblages from the beach lines have equally low indices. It is important to note that the number of faceted

---

[5] Site 2005 has an IL of 22.2, but the material was not *in situ* and the sample was small.

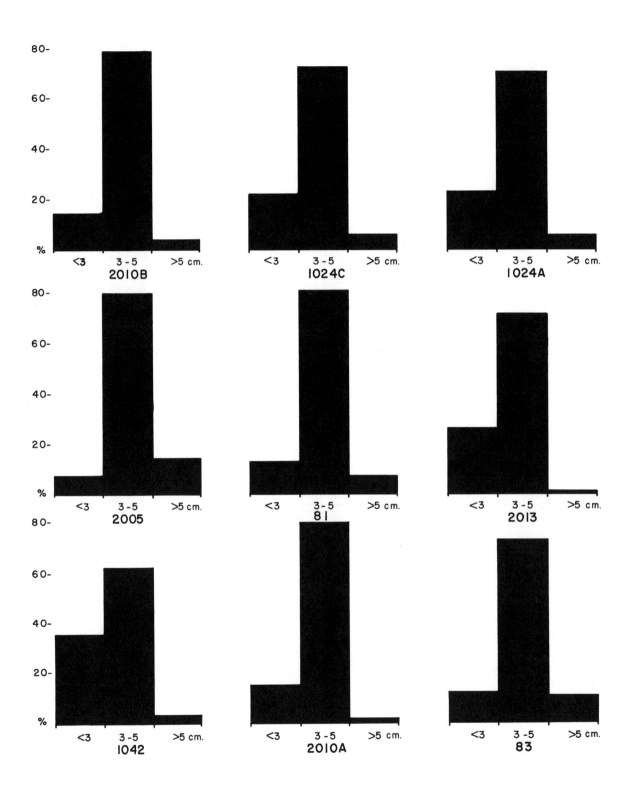

Fig. 4—Size of Sebilian tools.

flakes far exceeds the number of Levallois flakes, and, thus, there is no necessary correlation between faceted flakes and Levallois flakes.

There were relatively few blades found at Sebilian sites. Blade Indices range from 2.3 to 7.9 with no pattern of change visible from the earliest to the most recent sites (table 4).

In short, primary technological traits show little variation, and the only noticeable change during Sebilian development is manifest in a general lowering of the Faceting Indices.

Secondary technological traits are those which are associated with the actual production of retouched tools, after the production of cores, flakes, and blades had been completed. Secondary technological characteristics include size preference in the selection of flakes for tools, techniques used in initial treatment of raw flakes prior to final retouch, and the preferential placement of retouch on one edge of a flake as opposed to another edge or a random treatment.

Tool size was studied by measuring the lengths of all unbroken Levallois flakes and retouched tools. While there is still an overall similarity among most sites, definite variations are visible (fig. 4). The general pattern appears to be a gradual increase in the number of tools measuring between 2 and 5 cm., with the major increase in those between 2 and 3 cm. It must be admitted, however, that the change is not very great.

The earliest Sebilian site, 1042, has a relatively high proportion of tools under 3 cm. in length. This drops sharply, and a relatively stable pattern is then present throughout. It is of particular interest to note that there is no visible tendency toward a diminution in tool size. It might be said that the reverse is true, although it seems to be more a matter of small variations than of a significant pattern of change.

One of the definitions of the early Sebilian includes the observation that there are a large number of broken flakes "of uncertain purpose," plus the implication that the trait is even more prevalent in succeeding Sebilian stages (Caton-Thompson, 1946, p. 100). It does appear that there are relatively large numbers of broken flakes at Sebilian sites. If all flake tools and unretouched flakes and blades are considered from each site, between 27.5 and 45.7 per cent were either broken at the butt or tip end. This does not include those finished tools where retouch has been added to a broken or snapped edge. The actual range of variation here is somewhat misleading because only one site, 2005, had more than 38.6 per cent, and only one, 2010B, fell below 31.9 per cent. Again, the extreme homogeneity of Sebilian technology becomes apparent in this trait. In a study of these broken or snapped flakes it became apparent that there was a rather uniform pattern of breaking (fig. 5a). Breaks at the distal end occurred perpendicular to the long axis of the flakes on 42 to 54 per cent of all pieces at each site. Breaks which were oblique on the right edge occurred between 23 to 33 per cent at each site, while those on the left edge occurred between 18 and 26 per cent at each site.

This might be interpreted as nothing more than a random distribution of how flakes will naturally break, but there is strong evidence that this is not the case. First of all, there is the presence of microburins at every Sebilian site in Nubia. These quite clearly indicate that intentional snapping of flakes took place. Microburins, however, are rare until the most recent Sudanese Sebilian sites. It would be somewhat naive to think that intentional snapping of flakes and a developed microburin technique began simultaneously. The microburin technique is nothing but a way of controlling the angle and amount to be snapped. The tendency to snap flakes must have been present before the development of this special technique.

Another argument in favor of intentional snapping is that Sebilian tools are extremely uniform as to the side on which retouched backing or truncation occurs (fig. 5b). The vast majority of retouched tools which are either backed or obliquely truncated has this work on the left edge. A comparison between the simple broken or snapped pieces and backed and obliquely truncated pieces shows how different is the side occurrence. It is clear that perpendicular and right oblique edges were not desired, and when the snapping of a flake resulted in either of those types of breaks, the piece was not normally made into a retouched tool.

It is possible to see a small decline though in the tendency to retouch flakes along the left

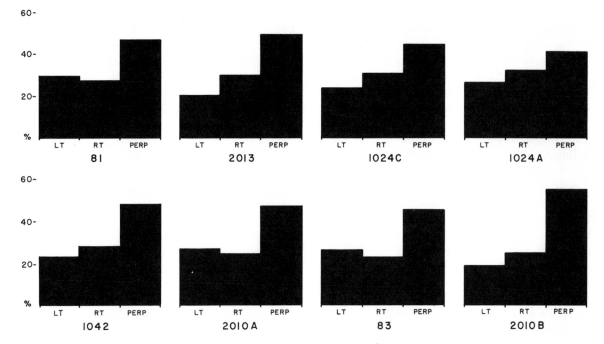

Fig. 5a—Side occurrence of snapped and broken edges on unretouched flakes. Key: LT=left side; RT=right side; PERP=perpendicular.

edge. At Sites 1024A and 1024C there is a slight increase of working on the right edge, although left edge retouch is still, by far, the most common. Perpendicular retouched truncations are always highly atypical.

A similar technological observation concerns the treatment of basally truncated flakes. Three types are found: those which have been snapped before retouch; those where the truncation is formed only by retouch; and those where the re-

the bulb and often much of the original platform are still present. Each of these types occurs at every Sebilian site. On the other hand, there is a decided change in the proportions of each type through time (table 5).

Basal truncation is one of the few technological attributes which shows any significant change during the relatively short period of Sebilian development in Sudanese Nubia. While the sites cannot be accurately seriated chronologically, the

TABLE 5
Types of Basal Truncations (Percentage)

Type	1042	2010A	83	2005	2013	81	2010B	1024C	1024A
Snapped and Retouched	36.8	36.4	40.9	42.1	54.8	55.3	55.3	52.1	65.9
Retouched Only	45.6	46.6	37.2	31.5	29.4	38.3	33.9	35.3	22.5
Poorly Retouched	17.6	17.0	21.9	26.4	15.8	6.4	10.8	12.6	11.6

touch is minimal, having no more than three irregular truncating flakes. In the first case, the snapping totally removes the bulb of percussion. In the second case, the retouch only partially removes the bulb, while in the third case most of

general chronological groupings shown here indicate a definite consistency. Although somewhat irregular, there is without doubt an increasing tendency through time to snap flakes before they were basally truncated by retouch. There is not,

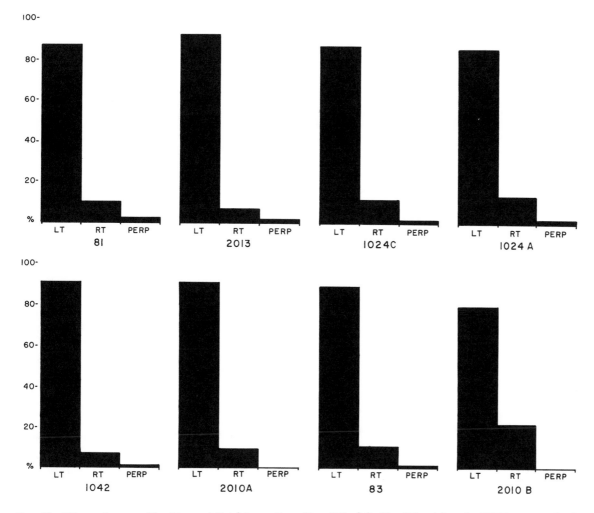

FIG. 5b—Side preference of backing and distal truncations. Key: LT=left side; RT=right side; PERP=perpendicular.

however, any noticeable shift to proportionately fewer poorly retouched examples beyond the effect of increased snapping.

The final technological process to be considered is the microburin technique. Microburins, including what Vignard refers to as a prototype for the microburin, occur at all sites. It is only at the most recent sites, 1024A and 1024C, that the microburin technique becomes important. All sites associated with the Sahaba formation have very few microburins and at most they account for no more than 2.9 per cent of all retouched tools. At Sites 1024A and 1024C, however, microburins are much more frequent and account for 17.8 per cent and 15.5 per cent respectively. This is perhaps the one major change seen in the Sebilian technology. It must be emphasized, how-

ever, that there is a weak microburin tradition throughout. This major shift is not paralleled by any significant typological change.

In short, the known Sebilian sites are extremely conservative technologically. From the earliest to the latest Sebilian sites there are few changes, and those which do take place are mainly associated with secondary technological processes. Significant changes are demonstrable only with respect to tool size, treatment of flake butts during basal truncation, and an increase of the microburin technique. Primary techniques of flake production, extent of faceting, amount of blade production, and choice of raw materials show little or no change during the few thousand years when Sebilian peoples inhabited the area of the Second Cataract.

Typology

Every Sudanese Sebilian site is characterized by an overwhelming proponderance of flake tools, each of which has one or two of the following typological attributes: (1) basal truncation, (2) oblique truncation, or (3) backing. Combinations of these attributes result in a series of retouched tools which vary in form from those which approach backed knives to those which look something like oversize geometrics. There are, however, no clear lines of demarcation between these types, with forms tending to merge into one another.

It is possible to classify these Sebilian tools by general form as well as by the type and placement of retouch. When this is done, there are three broadly recognizable shapes: those which are asymmetrically or symmetrically pointed at the distal end, those which are either rectangular or irregular in outline, and those which are longer than they are wide and often have the apearance of pseudo-geometrics. It must be emphasized, however, that this last group contains many examples which cannot be thought of as even pseudo-geometrics. When the Sebilian tools are classified in this way, it is possible to see a slight change through time in their relative proportions.

The pointed variety are normally the most common, erratically varying from site to site from 30 to 59.4 per cent of all recognizable pieces. Again, the rectangular forms vary from 21.3 to 52.2 per cent, without any coherent pattern of change throughout the sequence. On the other hand, those Sebilian types made on flakes which are wider along the original horizontal axis than they are along the original vertical axis do show a general increase in occurrence through time. At the earliest sites, 1042 and 2010A, they account for 15.6 per cent and 7.1 per cent of all Sebilian types. At Site 83, which is perhaps somewhat earlier than most of the other sites, they account for 12.8 per cent. At the most recent sites, 1024A and 1024C, they account for 28 per cent and 40.7 per cent, but at some sites which should be intermediate in the short sequence this type runs as high as 47 per cent. Therefore, while the increase of this form cannot be correlated exactly with the chronological ordering of the Sebilian

sites, there is a definite but erratic increase from early to late.

Non-Sebilian tools are not common. They include side-scrapers, end-scrapers, denticulates, notched pieces, borers, burins, cortex backed knives, and retouched flakes. By far the most typical are the notched pieces, but this is to be expected in an industry which has an incipient microburin technique. Unlike the Sebilian at Kom Ombo, there seems to be a slight decrease in the proportions of these types through time. They account for between 9.7 and 19.1 per cent of all retouched tools at all but the two most recent sites. At 1024A and 1024C, however, they drop to 7.7 per cent and 6.3 per cent respectively. While this perhaps indicates a slight change, it is too small and affects too few sites to be sure that it is due to anything more than chance.

It is significant that burins were found at a few sites. These have never been found associated with Sebilian material before, but there is little question that they form an erratic but definite part of the Sudanese Sebilian typology.

Another trait which shows some change is the percentage of retouched tools made on blades. Unlike the non-Sebilian tools, this change is only visible at the very beginning of the sequence. Sites 1042 and 2010A have three times as many tools on blades than have most of the other sites. It must be noted that in terms of absolute percentages, Sites 1042 and 2010A have very few blade tools, while the others have almost none.

Aside from these minor shifts in typological emphasis, the Sebilian shows a basic uniformity throughout its occupation of Sudanese Nubia. No tool types are introduced during the sequence and none totally disappear. The close typological similarity between all Sudanese sites is shown on the cumulative graph in Figure 6.

The core typology is extremely limited. Only the flat "Mousterian" discoidal cores and rather atypical Levallois cores occur consistently throughout the sequence. There are sporadic occurrences of rather thick discoidal, opposed platform, marginal, and isolated flake cores, but these are never important numerically. The most common core is the flat "Mousterian" discoidal and it might be considered the typical Sebilian core. It accounts for 27.7 to 54.6 per cent of all cores and core fragments at each site, although it ac-

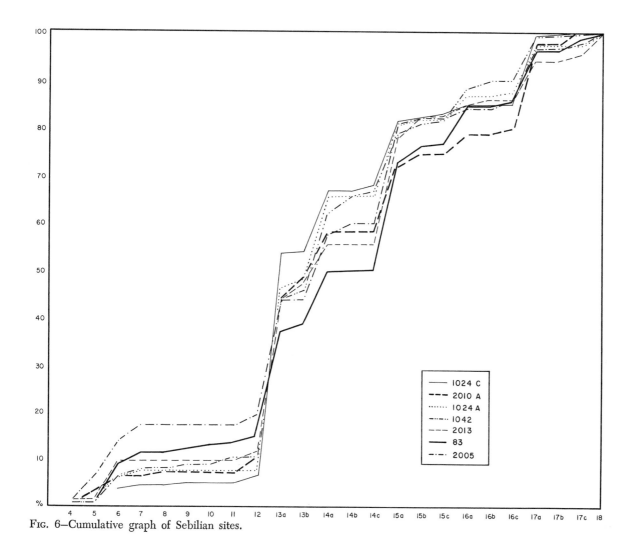

Fig. 6—Cumulative graph of Sebilian sites.

counts for about 40 per cent at most sites. The extremely small core samples make the significance of these percentages somewhat questionable. It is perhaps just as valid to characterize the Sudanese Sebilian core typology as basically oriented toward flat "Mousterian" discoidal cores made on plaquettes with a relatively small number of Levallois flake cores, again, mostly made on plaquettes.

SUMMARY

In order to summarize the technological and typological changes, we must view the Sebilian sites of Sudanese Nubia as belonging to three temporal groups. The first group consists of the earliest sites, 1042 and 2010A; the second group,

conceived of as being temporally next in order, consists of Sites 83, 2005, 81, 2013, and 2010B; while the third group, and most recent, is made up of Sites 1024A and 1024C. It must be emphasized that these groups are tentative, and no particular ordering of sites has been attempted within them. These divisions are based mainly on the weak stratigraphic evidence available, the two radiocarbon dates, and certain technological considerations. Typologically, all these sites form a very unified group and show no valid justification for any major subdivisions.

Technologically, the Sebilian of Sudanese Nubia may be characterized by a number of traits, only a few of which show change through time. These technological traits are the following:

1. Sebilian technology is overwhelmingly oriented toward flake production. Blade Indices, from 2.3 to 7.9, are low with little variation. No trend is visible.

2. Low Levallois Index, from 9.8 to 15.1, shows little variation. (An exception is 2005 with an IL of 22.2). No trend is visible.

3. High Faceting Indices at early sites and at most of the middle sites range from 70.7 to 78.4. Lower Faceting Indices at the latest sites and at two middle sites are from 56.8 to 63.9.

4. Restricted Faceting Indices are high at early and middle sites, 37.9 to 48.6, but somewhat lower at the latest sites, 31.9 to 35.0.

5. Microburin technique is present at all Sebilian sites. It is of minor importance at early and middle sites where it is from 0.3 to 4.8 per cent of all tools. At the latest sites, however, they have a major increase in importance. The range is from 12.5 to 15.1 per cent of all tools.

6. All Sebilian sites have a relatively high percentage of broken or snapped flakes. These vary between 22.3 and 45.7 per cent of all flakes and blades. No trend is visible.

7. The utilization of raw material varies from site to site depending on its location. Ferrocrete sandstone is always the dominant raw material used, but when quartzites and Precambrian rocks are available, they are utilized. Small amounts of Precambrian rock are found at all Sebilian sites regardless of location.

The typological traits are the following:

1. The Sebilian shows a very limited variety of retouched tools. The vast majority is made by basal truncation, oblique truncation, backing, or a combination of these. These tools account for between 80.9 and 95.7 per cent of all retouched tools at all sites.

2. Unretouched Levallois flakes, blades and points occur in moderate amounts at all Sebilian sites. With the exception of one site, they account for between 14.6 and 25 per cent of the tools. Site 2005 has 31.8 per cent. No trend is visible.

3. The most common non-Sebilian tool is the notched piece. It occurs at all sites, but this is not surprising due to the presence of the microburin technique. Again, there is no visible pattern of occurrence.

4. End-scrapers, side-scrapers, denticulates, and burins commonly occur at Sebilian sites in very small numbers. It should be noted that burins occur at four sites, both early and late in the Sebilian sequence.

5. The most common Sebilian tool is the simple basally truncated piece. It accounts for between 22.1 and 47.6 per cent of all retouched tools at all sites. There is a seeming tendencey for the later sites to have a somewhat higher percentage than the earlier sites have, but this is not consistent. All late sites have over 40 per cent, but so does one early site. The lowest occurrences, 22.1 per cent and 24.4 per cent, are from sites belonging to the middle group.

6. Simple oblique truncations occur about 15.5 per cent of the time at early sites, increase to about 25 per cent at the middle sites, and decrease to about 15.5 per cent at the later sites.

7. While numerous Sebilian tools are asymmetrically pointed, symmetric points are rare, never accounting for more than 4.1 per cent of all retouched tools and rarely for more than 2.8 per cent.

8. Simple backed tools are also uncommon. They vary from 2.1 to 9.8 per cent of all retouched tools, but no pattern of occurrence is noticeable.

9. Complex tools, those with basal truncation and either oblique truncation or backing, show little percentage variation from site to site. They range from 21.9 to 31.2 per cent of all retouched tools. If any pattern exists, the early and late sites have a slightly higher percentage than those at most of the middle sites.

10. There is a marked increase in the percentage of complex Sebilian tools which are wider than they are long. This increase is not consistent, but there are more in the later sites than in the early sites. These types bear a slight resemblance to pseudo-geometrics.

11. Only three artifacts were found which might be considered even similar to lunates. There are no true geometrics, nor is there any noticeable tendency toward diminutization of retouched tools.

12. The typical Sebilian core is an oval, flat discoidal core made on a ferrocrete sandstone plaquette. Levallois cores also occur at all sites but they are not numerous, nor are they normally good examples.

SITE REPORTS

The site reports are placed in a loose chronological order. Sites 1042 and 2010A, being the oldest, come first. Sites 1024A and 1024C are placed last as they appear to be the most recent. All other sites are generally in the same time range and no exact order is justified by the stratigraphic evidence, although perhaps Site 81 and 2005 are somewhat younger than the others. No special importance should be given to their order in this section.

SITE 1042

Site 1042 is located on the west bank of the Nile, 2 km. northeast of Mirgissa and some 200 m. west of the Nile (map ref. 903.7/635.5).[6] The site consists of a surface concentration of artifacts resting on deflated fluviatile sands of the Sahaba formation, 12 m. above present floodplain (fig. 2).

The concentration was extremely thin and covered an area of about 5,000 sq. m. The artifacts seemed to have been scattered during deflation as there was an area of some 200 sq. m. where there was a somewhat denser concentration. It is altogether possible that the artifacts had been lowered a few meters by deflation.

All artifacts showed signs of limited sand and wind abrasion, indicating that they had not been on the surface for a very extended period. The site situation, the looseness of the concentration, and the relatively fresh condition of the artifacts suggests that originally the site had been *in situ* in the middle part of the Sahaba formation; thus it might be datable to about 15,000 or 14,000 B.C. If this is the case, Site 1042 is perhaps one of the oldest Sebilian sites found near the Second Cataract.

A systematic collection was made over an area of 2,000 sq. m. A total of 831 artifacts were recovered, of which 292 were retouched tools or Levallois flakes, 261 were unretouched non-Levallois flakes and blades, 70 were primary flakes, 100 were cores and core fragments, while the remaining 108 were debris.

Because of the rather close proximity of the site to the Batn el-Hajar, a fairly high percentage of tools were made on Precambrian rocks (22.9 per cent). The remaining tools were made on

---

[6] All map references are to Egypt-New Series 1:25,000, printed by the Sudan Survey Department, April 1960.

ferrocrete sandstone (77.1 per cent). Most tools were of medium size, with less than 35 per cent measuring under 3 cm. in length. About one-third of all flakes and blades were broken.

The technological studies showed relatively little Levallois preparation (IL, 13.8) and very few true blades (Ib, 4.7). Faceting was well developed (IF, 77.6), with convex and straight faceted butts predominating (IFs, 45.7).

TOOL TYPOLOGY

	No.	%	Restricted %
1. Levallois flakes	55	18.9	
2. Levallois blades	8	2.7	
3. Levallois points	9	3.1	
4. Side-scrapers	2	0.7	0.9
6. Notched pieces	12	4.1	5.5
7. Denticulates	3	1.0	1.4
9. Burins	1	0.3	0.5
11. Cortex backed knives	3	1.0	1.4
13. Simple basal truncations			
a. Flakes			
1. Perpendicular	46	15.8	20.8
2. Oblique	28	9.6	12.6
b. Blades			
2. Oblique	5	1.7	2.3
14. Basal and oblique truncations			
a. Flakes			
1. Straight	12	4.2	5.5
2. Convex	15	5.1	6.7
3. Concave	8	2.7	3.6
b. Blades			
1. Straight	4	1.4	1.8
2. Convex	3	1.0	1.4
3. Concave	1	0.3	0.5
c. Points	2	0.7	0.9
15. Simple oblique truncations			
a. Flakes			
1. Straight	11	3.7	5.0
2. Convex	11	3.7	5.0
3. Concave	6	2.1	2.7
b. Blades			
1. Straight	1	0.3	0.5
2. Convex	1	0.3	0.5
3. Concave	2	0.7	0.9
c. Points	1	0.3	0.5
16. Simple backing			
a. Flakes	16	5.5	7.2
b. Blades	3	1.0	1.4
17. Backing and basal truncations			
a. Flakes			
1. Straight	7	2.4	3.2
2. Convex	8	2.7	3.6
3. Concave	4	1.4	1.8
c. Points	2	0.7	0.9
18. Other Sebilian types	1	0.3	0.5
19. Microburins	1	0.3	
	292	99.7	99.5

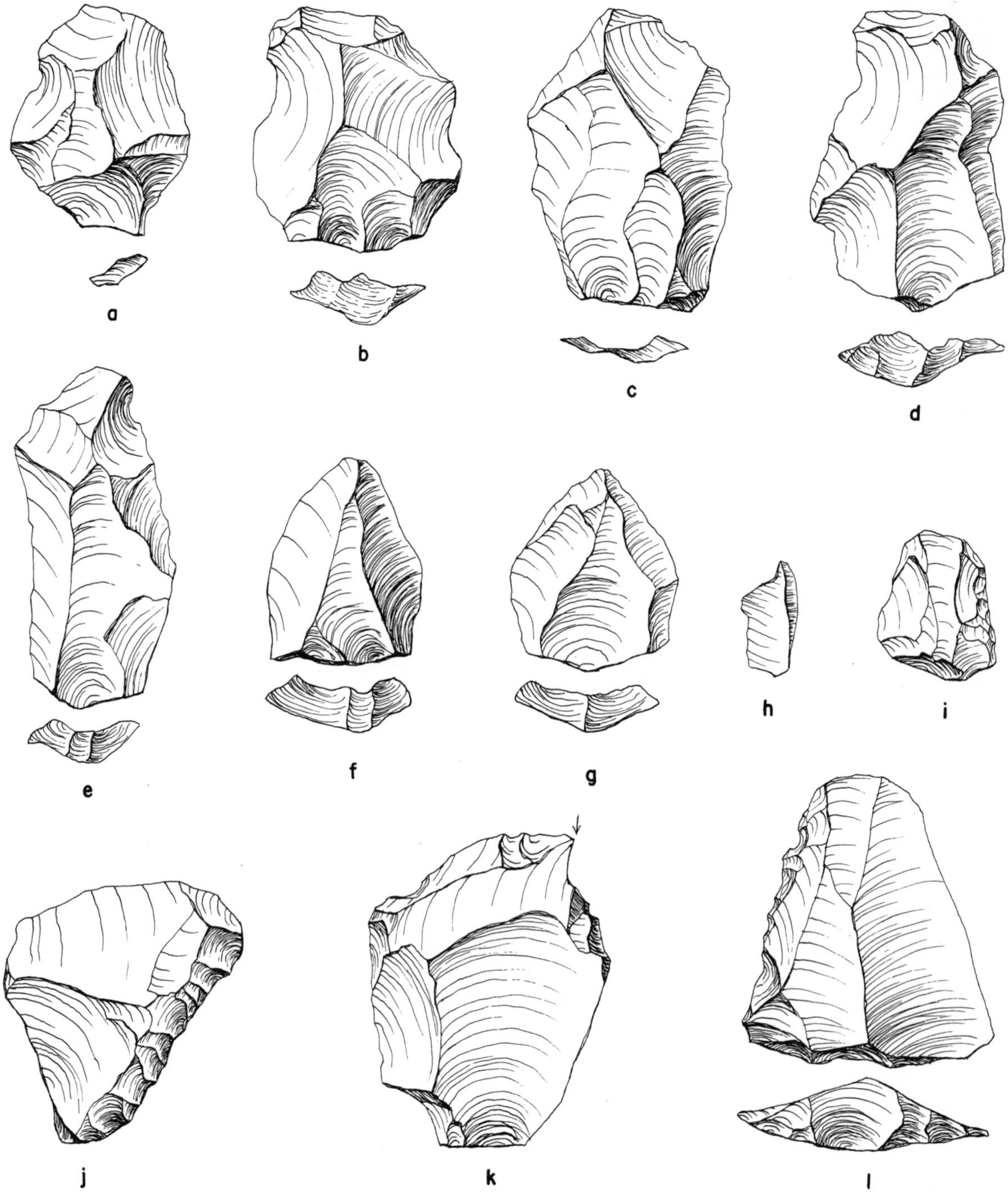

FIG. 7—Site 1042: a-d, Levallois flakes; e, Levallois blade; f-g, Levallois points; h, microburin; i-j, side-scrapers; k, burin; l, basally truncated flake with partial backing. 4/5 natural size.

NOTES ON THE TYPOLOGY

Levallois flakes (55). Forty-three are made on ferrocrete sandstone, nine are on Precambrian rock, and three are on quartz. As a group, they are roughly prepared, but when intact almost all have faceted butts. A few measure as much as 6.5 cm. in length, but most fall between 4 and 5 cm. They are more or less evenly divided between rough oval (fig. 7, a-b) and rectangular forms (fig. 7, c-d). Few are truly irregular.

Levallois blades (8). All but one are ferrocrete sandstone. The complete examples measure between 6 and 7 cm. in length (fig. 7, e), although one broken piece exceeds even that measurement.

Levallois points (9). These are all quite typical (fig. 7, f-g), although a few are very small.

Side-scrapers (2). There are two well made concave side-scrapers on Precambrian flakes (fig. 7, i-j).

Notched pieces (12). There are four distal end notches, six lateral notches, and two lateral notches near the butt end. All but two are obverse and all are quite small. Some may be considered associated with the poorly developed microburin technology.

Denticulates (3). There are two good macrodenticulates made by percussion on plaquettes and one oblique microdenticulate made by retouch on a Precambrian flake.

Burins (1). A single, poorly made burin on a truncation (fig. 7, k).

Cortex backed knives (3). These are more elongated flakes than true blades.

Simple basal truncations (79). Seventy-four simple basal truncations are on flakes. Of these, 46 truncations are perpendicular to the long axis of the flake, while 28 are oblique to the axis. All oblique truncations are on the right side of the flake (fig. 8, m). In addition, there are five blades which have oblique basal truncation. Two flake shapes dominate: rectangular (fig. 8, j-l) and pointed (fig. 8, n-p). Rectangular flakes are the most common (33), while roughly pointed flakes occur with less frequency (20). None of these could be considered intentional points. There are six examples which are wider across the truncated base than they are long (fig. 8, o, q). The rest are too fragmentary to classify. Almost all basally truncated flakes measure between 3 and 5 cm. in length. Only three measure between 2 and 3 cm., while two measure between 5 and 6 cm. Basally truncated blades measure between 3.6 and 4.6 cm. in length, and all are broken at the distal ends. In each case, the basal truncation is oblique on the right side of the blade.

Basal and oblique truncations (45). There are 35 flakes, eight blades, and two points which have been both basally and obliquely truncated. Oblique truncations are usually either slightly convex (19 examples) or straight (17 examples). Concave examples are rare, occurring on only eight flakes and one blade. It is important to note that those with convex oblique truncations do not even remotely approach the minimal morphological requirements of lunates. In spite of their unifying typological features, there are a number of visibly different subtypes. Two of them are points; that is, the oblique truncations have resulted in symmetrically pointed flakes (fig. 8, d). While it is true that many of these tools are pointed at the distal end, the points are rarely on the central axis of the flake or blade. Twenty-two examples have the point to the right of the central axis. These pieces tend to be elongated and decidedly asymmetric (fig. 8, e-i). Ten measure between 4 and 6 cm. in length. There is a group of ten examples which are either irregular in shape or on which the oblique truncation did not result in a true point (fig. 7, l). All these are longer than they are wide. In addition, there are eleven examples which are short and squat, forming what Vignard might call trapezes (fig. 8, a-c). It is recognized, however, that these merge with the asymmetrically pointed types and that no clear line can be drawn between them. In all examples their width is slightly greater than their length. They measure between 2.5 and 4.1 cm. in length and 2.7 and 4.6 cm. in width.

Simple oblique truncations (33). There are 28 flakes, four blades, and one point which fall into this category. Again, on the flakes and blades, convex and straight truncations occur in equal number, while concave truncations occur on only eight examples. The single point is irregular but still fits within the minimal definition (fig. 9, k). Most of the flakes are rather small and elongate forms are rare, except for the blades. The range in quality may be seen by comparing two concavely truncated flakes, one of which is short and irregular (fig. 9, c), and the other approaches a point (fig. 9, b). There are nine examples which are wider than they are long, while the remainder is asymmetrically pointed. All are small and are broadly comparable to pseudo-geometric forms, although it would be a mistake to consider them trapezes (fig. 9, a).

Simple backed pieces (19). Sixteen flakes and three blades fall into this category. These are

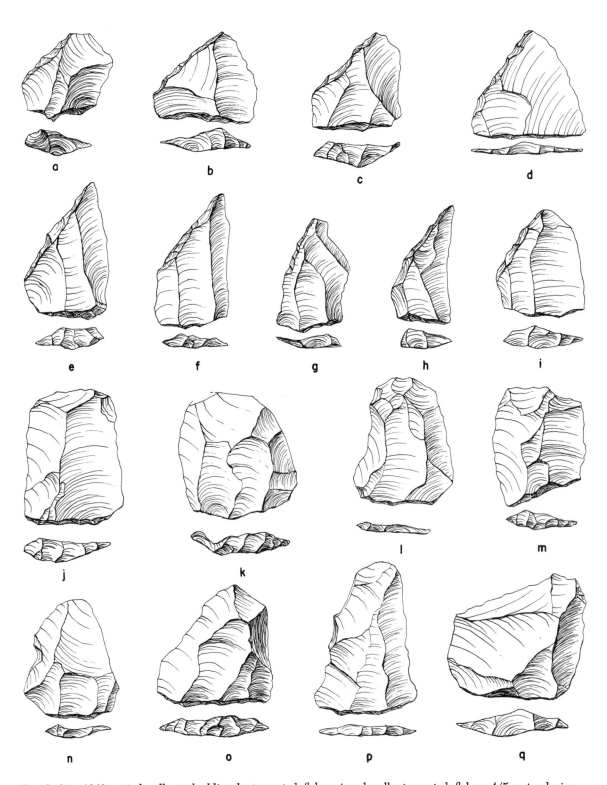

FIG. 8—Site 1042: a-i, basally and obliquely truncated flakes; j-q, basally truncated flakes. 4/5 natural size.

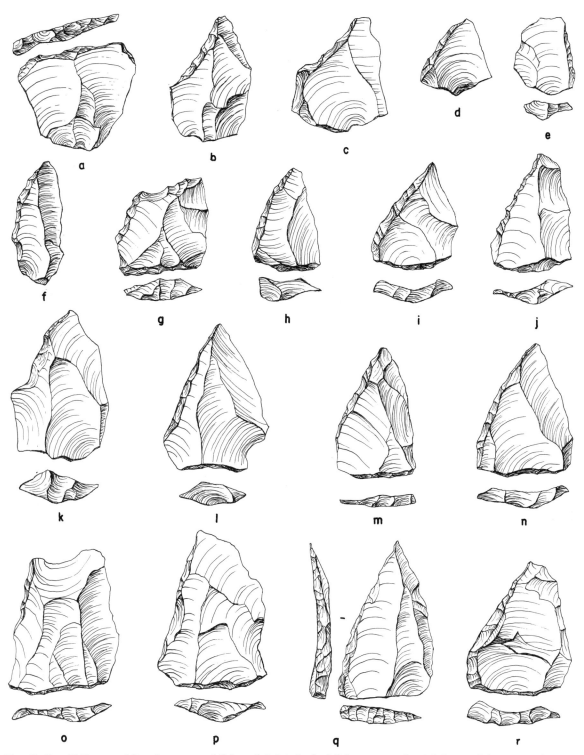

Fig. 9—Site 1042: a-c, obliquely truncated flakes; d-f, h-j, backed flakes; g, complex Sebilian tool; k, truncated point; l-n, backed and basally truncated points; o-r, backed and basally truncated flakes. 4/5 natural size.

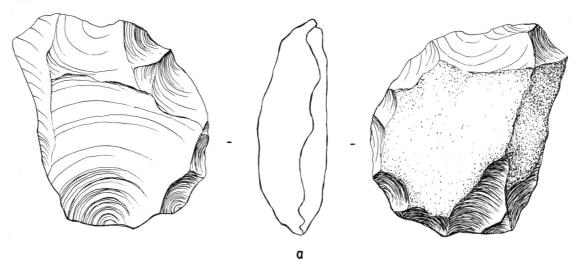

Fig. 10—Site 1042: a, Levallois core. 4/5 natural size.

mostly on irregular flakes (fig. 9, e). A few approach points (fig. 9, d), and one even approaches what Vignard might call a lunate (fig. 9, f). They range in size from 2.5 to 5.1 cm. in length, but most are small. Sixteen are convexly backed, two are straight backed, and only one has a concave backing. Twelve are asymmetrically pointed, four are rectangular, and three are too fragmentary to classify.

Backing and basal truncations (21). Nineteen flakes and two points have both backing and basal truncation. The important feature here is that the backing and the basal truncation meet. In the case of partially backed pieces, the significant factor is that the backing does not alter the direction of the edge (fig. 9, o). There is one convexly backed point, measuring 4.5 cm. in length (fig. 9, n) and one with a partial straight backing which approaches a truncation (fig. 9, m). Eleven pieces are pointed at the distal end. Again, as with the obliquely truncated flakes, the points are not on the central axis (fig. 9, i-j, l), or the shape is too irregular to be considered a true point (fig. 9, h). There is one particularly fine example which is transitional to a point and might be classified either way (fig. 9, q). There are seven which are not pointed, being either irregular or rectangular (fig. 9, o-p). There is another generally rectangular flake where the backing is intermediate between a true convex backing and a combination of a short backing and a convex oblique truncation (fig. 9, r).

Other Sebilian types (1). This piece has a basal truncation, a concave distal truncation, and a partial straight oblique truncation (fig. 9, g). It is wider than it is long.

Microburins (1). A single example snapped from the distal end of a flake (fig. 7, h).

CORE TYPOLOGY

	No.	%
Levallois flake	14	14.1
Discoidal, Type I	37	37.3
Discoidal, Type II	12	12.1
Opposed platform	10	10.1
Isolated flake	2	2.0
Single platform, unfaceted	3	3.0
Unidentifiable	21	21.2
	99	99.8

NOTES ON THE TYPOLOGY

Levallois flake (14). A number of raw materials were utilized, namely, ferrocrete sandstone, Precambrian rocks, and a devitrified dacite. These cores fall into two groups: those which are typical Levallois cores with tortoise backs, and those which are poor Levallois cores made on ferrocrete sandstone plaquettes (fig. 10, a). This latter group of seven examples ranges in thickness from 1.2 cm. to no more than 2.5 cm. They appear to be a compromise between a true Levallois core and a flat "Mousterian" discoidal core. The more typical Levallois cores are roughly shaped but range in thickness from 2.6 to 5.0 cm.

Discoidal, Type I (37). These are the typical Sebilian cores in Nubia. All but one are made on

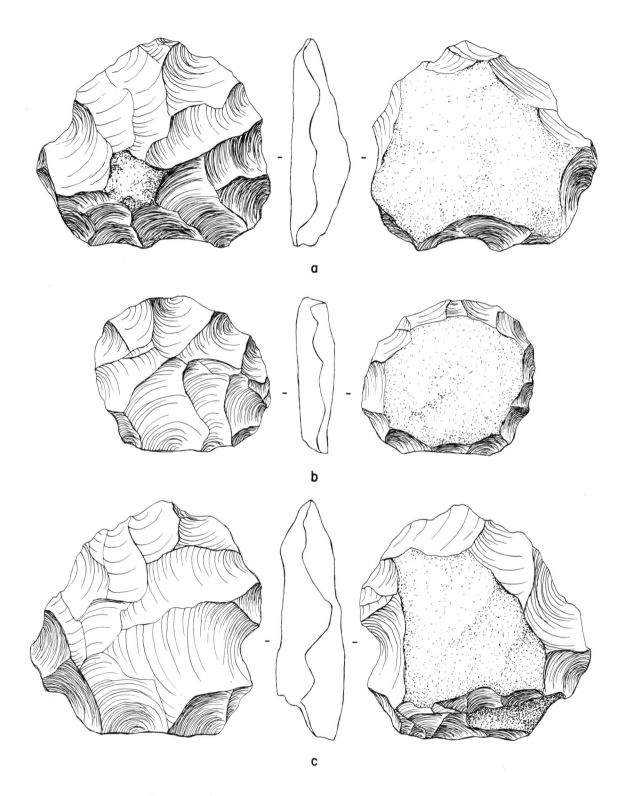

Fig. 11—Site 1042: a-c, flat discoidal cores. 4/5 natural size.

ferrocrete sandstone. They are extremely thin, from 1.2 to 2.5 cm., although they range in diameter from 5 to 9 cm. Most, however, fall between 5 and 7 cm. in diameter. All are made on plaquettes and most are of rough oval shape (fig. 11, a-c), although some tend toward rectangular forms. The under surface is always totally faceted around the circumference, while the remainder is cortex covered. The upper face is very flat, but there are some examples which are thicker at the center where the flake scars meet.

Discoidal, Type II (12). These are discoidal cores made on small cobbles of various materials. They are normally faceted, but not as regularly as those made on plaquettes. They range in length from 4 to 6 cm. and are usually about 3 cm. thick. The upper surfaces are flat or even concave. They are not typical of other Sebilian sites and seem to be related to a declining Levallois core technology.

Opposed platform (10). Seven of these are on ferrocrete sandstone and appear to be broken flat discoidal cores which have additional flaking along the broken edge. They tend to be rectangular which gives them the appearance of opposed platform cores. At best, they are highly atypical. None measures more than 6 cm. in length or 4.5 cm. in width. The other three are on devitrified dacite and are more typical. One of these shows the removal of a few long laminary flakes.

Isolated flake (2). Two flakes have been struck from small quartz pebbles.

Single platform, unfaceted (3). An atypical type made on small Precambrian and quartz pebbles.

Unidentifiable (21). All are small fragments which might have come from either flat discoidal cores or atypical Levallois cores.

Site 2010A

Site 2010A is located 2.5 km. due west of the Wadi Halfa airport tower in the area of the Khor Musa (map ref. 905.0/642.8). The site consists of a surface concentration of artifacts some 300 sq. m. in area. It rested on the deflated surface of the Dibeira-Jer formation, at an elevation of 28 m. above floodplain. Because of the elevation of the site, it was impossible to place it temporally

within the Sahaba formation. On the other hand, it was not associated with the aggradation of the Dibeira-Jer formation. No evidence was found that the artifacts had ever been *in situ*, although a few were in a thin surficial sand cover. The thin scattering of the artifacts suggests that there was some lowering of the site due to deflation.

A systematic surface collection was made from 136 sq. m. within the main site concentration. A total of 738 artifacts were recovered. Of these, 217 were retouched tools or Levallois flakes, 260 were unretouched non-Levallois flakes and blades, 68 were cores and core fragments, 62 were primary flakes, and the remaining 131 were debris.

Tools were made from a number of kinds of rocks, including ferrocrete sandstone, quartzites, and Precambrian rocks. Quartzites were least common (8.9 per cent), Precambrian rocks were numerous (40.5 per cent), and ferrocrete sandstone was the most common (50.6 per cent). One-third of all flakes and blades were broken.

Technological studies showed a small amount of Levallois preparation (IL, 10.9), few blades (Ib, 7.1), but a high Faceting Index (IF 75.3). Convexly faceted and straight faceted butts predominated (IFs, 46.1).

TOOL TYPOLOGY

	No.	%	Restricted %
1. Levallois flakes	28	12.9	
2. Levallois blades	1	0.5	
3. Levallois points	4	1.8	
4. Side-scrapers	3	1.4	1.7
5. End-scrapers	3	1.4	1.7
6. Notched pieces	6	2.9	3.3
8. Bec burins	1	0.5	0.6
12. Retouched flakes	5	2.3	2.8
13. Simple basal truncations			
a. Flakes			
1. Perpendicular	37	17.0	20.7
2. Oblique	26	11.9	14.5
b. Blades			
1. Perpendicular	3	1.4	1.7
2. Oblique	6	2.9	3.3
14. Basal and oblique truncations			
a. Flakes			
1. Straight	8	3.8	4.5
2. Convex	6	2.9	3.3
3. Concave	3	1.4	1.7
15. Simple oblique truncations			
a. Flakes			
1. Straight	11	5.1	6.1

	No.	%	Restricted %
2. Convex	7	3.2	3.9
3. Concave	7	3.2	3.9
b. Blades			
2. Convex	4	1.8	2.2
16. Simple backing			
a. Flakes	8	3.8	4.5
c. Points	2	0.9	1.1
17. Backing and basal truncations			
a. Flakes			
1. Straight	10	4.6	5.6
2. Convex	21	9.7	11.7
c. Points	2	0.9	1.1
19. Microburins	5	2.3	
	217	100.5	99.9

NOTES ON THE TYPOLOGY

Levallois flakes (28). For the most part, these are small and atypical. Almost half are broken, and complete examples show irregular outlines and careless preparation. Where present, butts are faceted. The largest flake measures 6.2 cm. in length, but most measure about 4 cm. in length (fig. 12, a). Just over one-half are on Precambrian rock.

Levallois blades (1). A broken example on Precambrian rock. It measures 4.8 cm. in length, indicating that originally it was quite long.

Levallois points (4). Small, atypical examples.

Side-scrapers (3). These are all atypical. Retouch is marginal and cannot be confused with the typical steep Sebilian retouch. One example approaches a raclette with a slightly convex scraping edge. The other two are larger, measuring between 3 and 4 cm. in length. These latter two have poorly formed convex scraping edges.

End-scrapers (3). Again, atypical examples. One is formed on the butt end of a small flake (fig. 12, c), while the others have poorly formed scraping edges. In all cases, the retouch is rather flat.

Notched pieces (6). There are four lateral and two distal notches on flakes. Two of the lateral notches are on broken flakes and appear to be examples of an unsuccessful microburin technology.

Bec burins (1). A mediocre example (fig. 12, b).

Retouched flakes (5). All show irregular inverse retouch on one lateral edge. None of the retouch is consistent enough to form a true scraping edge. It must be noted that inverse retouch is rare at Sebilian sites and is never used for making "typical" Sebilian tools.

Simple basal truncations (72). Sixty-three flakes and nine blades have simple basal truncations. A majority of flakes has perpendicular truncations (37), while oblique truncations are only somewhat less common (26). On the other hand, blades more commonly have oblique truncations (6) (fig. 12, d). Of the complete flakes, 23 are more or less rectangular (fig. 12, f), 13 generally pointed, five irregular in shape, and four are wider at the base than they are long (fig. 12, e). Eighteen examples are too fragmentary to classify as to shape, six of which have small notches at the left side of the broken edge. Although not fully conforming with the definition of a microburin, each of these might have been classified as a "microburin prototype." The basal truncations, however, are typologically diagnostic and so they have been placed with the simple basal truncations. If these pieces had been considered microburin "prototypes," the proportion of microburins would reach slightly over 5 per cent of the total tool inventory. Basally truncated flakes and blades measure between 3 and 5 cm. in length.

Basal and oblique truncations (17). This type is not too common. Of the 17 examples, eight have straight oblique distal truncations, six convex distal truncations, and three concave distal truncations. No blades have both basal and oblique truncations. Eight examples are more or less rectangular in shape, while nine are pointed at the distal end (fig. 12, g). As at Site 1042, the pointed pieces have the point to the right of the central axis (fig. 12, h). As a group, these are mostly poor, with no two examples conforming to the same shape. Again, none measures less than 3 cm. or greater than 5 cm. in length.

Simple oblique truncations (29). Twenty-five flakes and four blades fall into this category. Straight and convex truncations occur in equal number, while there are only seven concavely oblique examples. There is a large size range, from 2.5 to 5.5 cm. in length. Nine examples have asymmetric points at their distal ends (fig. 12, j), 13 are either irregular or have truncations which are extremely oblique, three are wider

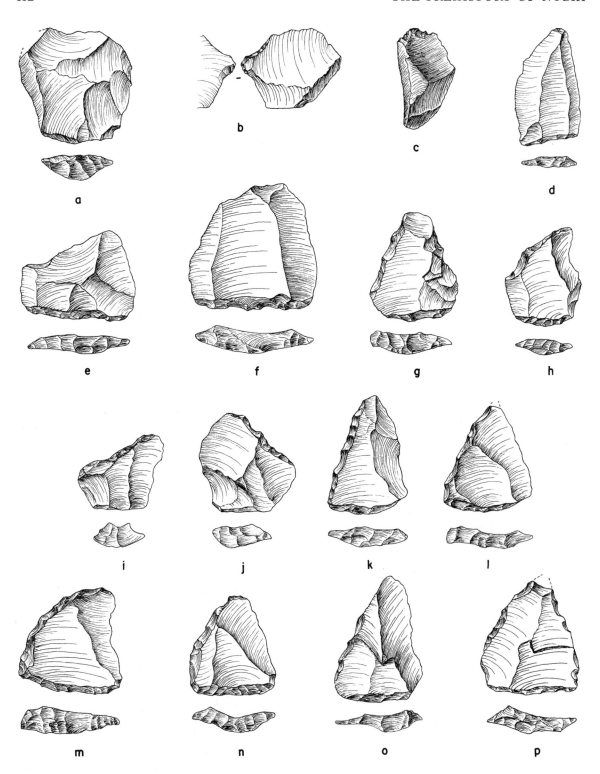

Fig. 12—Site 2010A: a, Levallois flake; b, bec burin; c, atypical end-scraper; d-f, basally truncated flakes; g-h, basal and obliquely truncated flakes; i-j, obliquely truncated flakes; k-l, backed and basally truncated points; m-p, backed and basally truncated flakes. 4/5 natural size.

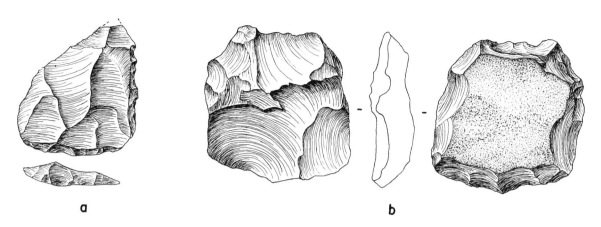

Fig. 13–Site 2010A: a, backed and basally truncated flake; b, flat discoidal core. 4/5 natural size.

than they are long (fig. 12, i), and four are too fragmentary to classify. On all examples the quality of retouch is mediocre, and the truncated edges tend to be irregular.

Simple backing (10). Eight flakes and two points have simple backing. The flakes are irregular in shape and mostly measure under 4 cm. in length, but there is one large, crude flake which measures 6.1 cm. in length. Five flakes have convex backing, two concave backing, and a single piece has a partial straight backing. Both points have straight backing and both measure under 3.5 cm. in length. Again, as a group, there is little consistency in shape or quality of retouch.

Backing and basal truncations (33). Thirty-one flakes and two points fall into this group (fig. 12, k-l). Twenty-one flakes have convex backing and ten have straight backing (fig. 13, a). No concave examples were found. Pointed and rectangular flakes were more or less evenly divided, while two examples were too fragmentary to classify. As with all pointed flakes, these points are also asymmetric (fig. 12, o-p). Some, however, come very close to true points. Others are only generally pointed (fig. 12, n). The rectangular examples are mostly squat, although only one is wider than it is long. A few have markedly convex backs and one even approaches a pseudo-geometric (fig. 12, m). As a group they are somewhat better made than the other types, and all measure between 3 and 4.5 cm. in length.

Microburins (5). Three distal end and two butt end examples.

CORE TYPOLOGY

	No.	%
Levallois flake	5	7.3
Discoidal, Type I	37	54.6
Discoidal, Type II	1	1.4
Unidentifiable	25	36.7
	68	100.0

NOTES ON THE TYPOLOGY

Levallois flake (5). As at 1042, these are very flat and have relatively little preparation on the under surface. All are made on plaquettes and are very similar to the typical Sebilian discoidal cores.

Discoidal, Type I (37). The typical Sebilian core. They range in diameter from 4.2 to 6.7 cm. Most are oval, but some tend toward rectangular forms (fig. 13, b).

Discoidal, Type II (1). A single example.

Unidentifiable (25). These include small fragments and those plaquettes which show no particular pattern of flaking.

SITE 83

Site 83 is located 2.6 km. south of Jebel el-Sahaba and .75 km. west of the Nile, behind the village of Nugu el-Sahaba (map ref. 921.1/652.6). The site consists of an oval surface concentration of artifacts, 200 sq. m. in area, resting on a sand layer above the silts of the Dibeira-Jer formation at an elevation of 19 m. above flood-plain.

Initially, it appeared that the site had rested

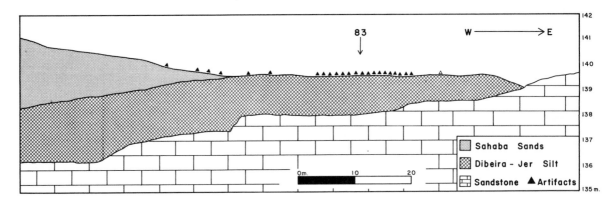

Fig. 14—West-east profile of Site 83.

on the surface of the Dibeira-Jer silts and had been covered by fluviatile sand of the Sahaba formation. It looked as if subsequent deflation had exposed the artifacts. Test excavations revealed, however, that there was no trace of artifacts at the contact between the Dibeira-Jer silts and the fluviatile sands of the Sahaba formation, and that some artifacts were present on a wedge of Sahaba sands which overlay the Dibeira-Jer silts (fig. 14). Thus, there is little question that the artifacts were originally in or on sands of the Sahaba formation and that they were uncovered by deflation during which they were lowered as much as one meter. Therefore, Site 83 must be dated as no earlier than the Sahaba formation. The deflation would account for the size of the site and the relatively low density of artifacts per square meter.

A systematic surface collection was made from 180 sq. m. in the center of the concentration. A total of 2,231 artifacts were recovered. Of these, 473 were retouched tools or Levallois flakes, 1044 were unretouched non-Levallois flakes and blades, 59 were cores or core fragments, 314 were primary flakes, and 341 were debris. Broken tools and flakes were numerous, accounting for 31.9 per cent of all flakes and blades.

Technological studies showed a low Levallois Index (IL, 14.3), very few blades (Ib, 3.7), and relatively high Faceting Indices (IF, 70.7; IFs, 46.2). These observations correspond well with other Sebilian sites, although the Faceting Indices are slightly lower than those at the earlier sites and slightly higher than those indices at the later sites. This should not be taken as an indica-

tion of a transitional stage, however, as these indices undoubtedly varied within a reasonable range without chronological significance.

TOOL TYPOLOGY

	No.	%	Restricted %
1. Levallois flakes	105	22.2	
2. Levallois blades	7	1.5	
3. Levallois points	6	1.3	
5. End-scrapers	3	0.6	0.9
6. Notched pieces	27	5.7	7.7
7. Denticulates	9	1.9	2.6
9. Burins	2	0.4	0.6
10. Borers	3	0.6	0.9
11. Cortex backed knives	1	0.2	0.3
12. Retouched flakes	5	1.0	1.4
13. Simple basal truncations			
a. Flakes			
1. Perpendicular	44	9.3	12.6
2. Oblique	33	6.9	9.5
b. Blades			
1. Perpendicular	2	0.4	0.6
2. Oblique	3	0.6	0.9
14. Basal and oblique truncations			
a. Flakes			
1. Straight	15	3.2	4.3
2. Convex	20	4.2	5.7
3. Concave	4	0.9	1.2
c. Points	1	0.2	0.3
15. Simple oblique truncations			
a. Flakes			
1. Straight	26	5.5	7.5
2. Convex	30	6.3	8.6
3. Concave	25	5.3	7.2
b. Blades			
1. Straight	4	0.9	1.2
2. Convex	3	0.6	0.9
3. Concave	4	0.9	1.2
c. Points	1	0.2	0.3
16. Simple backing			

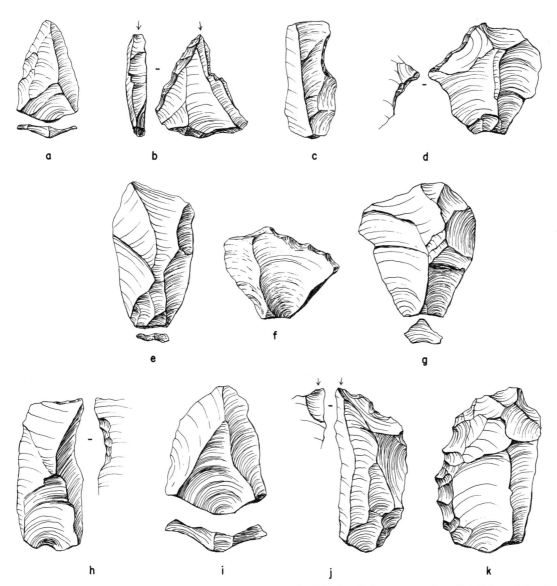

FIG. 15—Site 83: a, i, Levallois points; b, j, burins; c, notched blade; d, borer; e, g, Levallois flakes; f, k, denticulates; h, inversely retouched blade or shallow notch. 4/5 natural size.

	No.	%	Restricted %
a. Flakes	28	5.9	8.0
c. Points	4	0.9	1.2
17. Backing and basal truncations			
a. Flakes			
1. Straight	9	1.9	2.6
2. Convex	25	5.3	7.2
3. Concave	5	1.0	1.4
c. Points	8	1.7	2.3
18. Other Sebilian types	4	0.9	1.2
19. Microburins	7	1.5	
	473	99.9	100.3

NOTES ON THE TYPOLOGY

Levallois flakes (105). The vast majority are broken. All are made on ferrocrete sandstone, and only a few are really typical (fig. 15, g, e). All are fairly small, none measuring more than 5.2 cm. in length or less than 3 cm. They tend toward irregular rectangles, although a few are irregular ovoids.

Levallois blades (7). These are rare but typical. They range in length from 4.1 to 5.6 cm.

Levallois points (6). All are rather good examples, considering the effects of weathering of the edges (fig. 15, a, i). The largest is 5.3 cm. and the smallest is 3.7 cm. in length.

End-scrapers (3). All are atypical. There is one poor example on a broken flake. Another partially retouched end-scraper approaches a raclette, and an elongated flake has a poorly formed nosed scraper at its distal end.

Notched pieces (27). There are 24 notched flakes and three notched blades (fig. 15, c). There are nine lateral inverse notches and one inverse distal notch. Obverse notches are normally lateral, although there are two distal examples. All notches tend to be deep and are formed by no more than a very few blows.

Denticulates (9). Denticulates are generally poor (fig. 15, f) although there is one fine example with a convex lateral denticulation (fig. 15, k). It is similar to the best from other Sebilian sites. There is also one plaquette which is 1.5 cm. thick and has a coarse macrodenticulated edge. This piece is of particular interest as it was the only plaquette fragment found; thus, it furnished some indication of the probable thickness of the raw materials used in initial core preparation.

Burins (2). There is a fine burin on a basal and obliquely truncated flake (fig. 15, b), and a poor burin *plan* on an irregularly truncated blade (fig. 15, j).

Borers (3). These are atypical (fig. 15, d). They are also the only borers found in Sebilian context.

Cortex backed knives (1). A blade measuring 7.7 cm. in length.

Retouched flakes (5). Four flakes and one blade have small amounts of semi-steep inverse retouch. Inverse retouch is quite atypical in the Sebilian and is never used in backing or truncations. The retouch on the blade approaches a very shallow notch (fig. 15, h).

Simple basal truncations (82). Seventy-seven are on flakes and five are on blades. Forty-six are perpendicular to the central axis, while 36 are oblique to it. Broken flakes are in the majority, but of the 33 complete examples, 16 are generally pointed, 14 are irregular or rectangular (fig. 16, a-c), and three are wider than they are long. As a group, these simple basally truncated

flakes and blades are small, ranging in length from 3 to 4.5 cm.

Basal and oblique truncations (40). All but one are on flakes. The other is a point. Twenty-six are generally pointed in shape, four are rectangular, and three are wider than they are long. There are seven within the pointed group which have oblique truncations which verge on convex backing (fig. 16, p). These are elongate and might even be considered as backed and basally truncated knives. Five of these measure between 4.5 and 5 cm. in length, another is only 3.3 cm. long, while the last is broken. The remaining pointed flakes average about 1 cm. shorter. The three flakes which are wider than they are long do approach rough pseudo-geometrics in form. They vary in width from 2.2 to 4.1 cm. and in length from 1.6 to 2.6 cm. There is also a single symmetric point measuring 4.4 cm. in length. In addition, there are six flakes which were too fragmentary to classify.

Simple oblique truncations (93). There are 11 blades, one point, and 81 flakes which have simple oblique truncations. The blades are mostly broken (fig. 16, f), and all but two are asymmetrically pointed. The single symmetric point approaches a backed point and measures 3.7 cm. in length (fig. 16, q). Of the 81 flakes, 39 are asymmetrically pointed, including both large and small examples (fig. 16, e, g-i, k-m). There are two pieces which have a slightly different look than the others. They almost appear to be borers of some form (fig. 16, o). All measure between 3 and 5.4 cm. in length. There are also 14 obliquely truncated flakes where the truncation is almost perpendicular to the central axis (fig. 16, d, n). These are either rectangular or irregular in shape and are on the average about 1 cm. shorter than the pointed variety. Seventeen flakes are wider than they are long. Some approach pseudo-geometric shapes, but others could not be classified in this way (fig. 16, j). These range in width from 2.8 to 4.4 cm. and in length from 2.2 to 3.5 cm. In addition, there are eleven flakes too fragmentary to classify.

Simple backing (32). Twenty-eight flakes and four points fall into this class. The points vary from rough (fig. 16, r) to fine (fig. 17, a). Fourteen flakes are asymmetrically pointed, including one convexly backed piece which approaches a

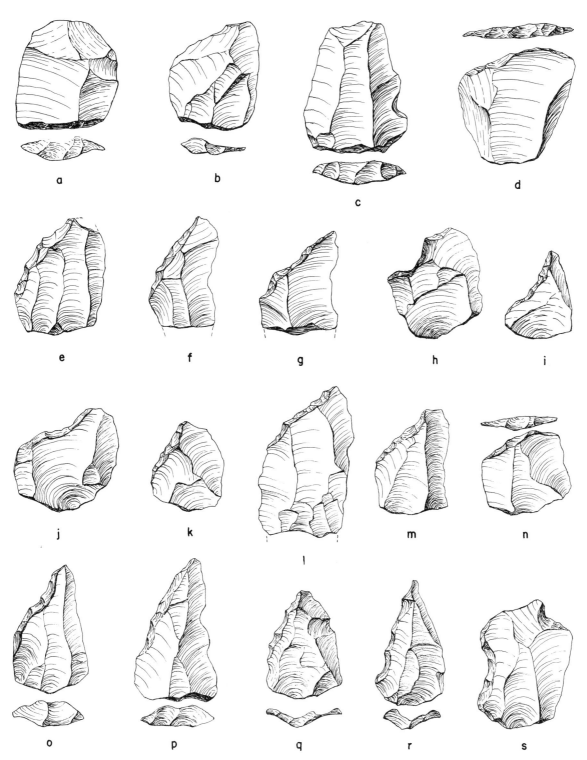

Fig. 16—Site 83: a-c, basally truncated flakes; d-o, obliquely truncated flakes; p, basal and obliquely truncated flake; q, truncated point; r, backed point; s, backed flake. 4/5 natural size.

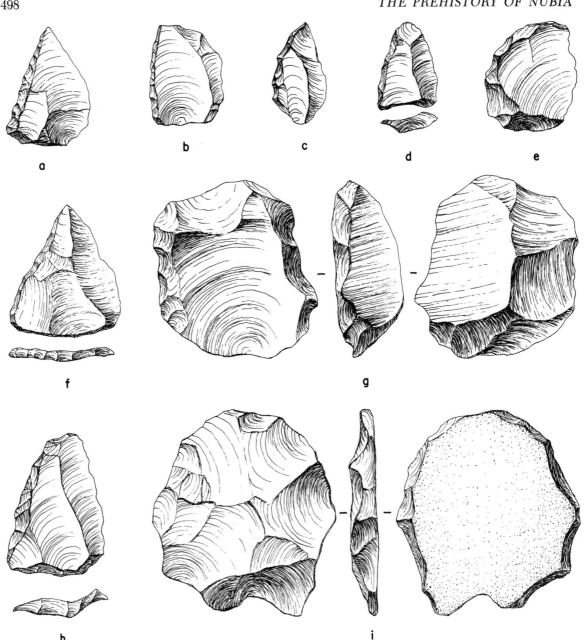

Fig. 17—Site 83: a, backed point; b-c, backed flakes; d, f, backed and basally truncated points; e, h, backed and basally truncated flakes; g, Levallois core; i, flat discoidal core. 4/5 natural size.

lunate (fig. 17, c). They range in size from 2.6 to 4.6 cm. in length. Eleven other flakes are either irregular or rectangular and fall within the same size range as the pointed flakes (fig. 17, b). Backing is convex on 20 flakes, concave on five (fig. 16, s), and straight on seven. There are also three backed flakes that were too fragmentary to classify by shape.

Backing and basal truncations (47). There are 39 flakes and eight points which are both backed and basally truncated. The points include both small examples with concave basal truncation (fig. 17, d), and large, almost equilateral triangles (fig. 17, f). Four points have slightly convex backing, while on three the backing is straight. There are also 19 flakes which are asymmetrically pointed, a few of which approach true symmetric points (fig. 17, h). These pointed examples vary in length from 2.5 to 4.7 cm. There are 11 flakes which are either irregular or rectangular in shape, including one which has a markedly convex back (fig. 17, e). These fall into the same size range as the pointed flakes. In addition, there are nine flakes which are too fragmentary to classify.

Other Sebilian types (4). These are flakes which have both backing and oblique truncation on the same edge. One is wider than it is long, while the others are somewhat rectangular in shape.

Microburins (7). In Vignard's terminology, all of these would be "prototypes."

CORE TYPOLOGY

	No.	%
Levallois flake	13	22.0
Discoidal, Type I	18	30.4
Discoidal, Type II	3	5.1
Marginal	8	13.5
Ninety degree	1	1.7
Unidentifiable	16	27.0
	59	99.7

NOTES ON THE TYPOLOGY

Levallois flake (13). Only four are on thin plaquettes. The rest are more typical, although preparation is generally rough (fig. 17, g).

Discoidal, Type I (18). These are the typical Sebilian cores made on plaquettes (fig. 17, i).

Discoidal, Type II (3). These are small discoidal cores made on wadi cobbles rather than on plaquettes.

Marginal (8). Plaquette fragments which have been flaked on one surface from opposite edges.

Ninety degree (1). A small wadi cobble which has been flaked on opposite faces so that the flake scars on one face are at right angles to the flake scars on the other.

Unidentifiable (16). Mostly fragments which show no clear pattern of flaking.

Site 2010B

Site 2010B is located 2.6 km. due west of the Wadi Halfa airport tower in the area of the Khor Musa (map. ref. 642.7/904.9). The site consisted of a loose surface concentration of artifacts some 400 sq. m. in area. This concentration rested on the deflated surface of the Dibeira-Jer formation at an elevation of about 28 m. above floodplain. Initially, it looked as if this site were merely a part of Site 2010A. Upon close inspection, however, it became clear that there were two discrete concentrations separated by about 50 m. of sterile surface. All artifacts were somewhat wind abraded, and there was no indication that any had even been incorporated within the Dibeira-Jer formation. A few were less weathered than others and were found in the thin surficial sand layer which covers the deflated Dibeira-Jer formation in this area.

A systematic surface collection was made from 136 sq. m. within the main site concentration. A total of 487 artifacts were collected, of which 207 were retouched tools or Levallois flakes, 161 were unretouched non-Levallois flakes and blades, 27 were cores and core fragments, 31 were primary flakes, and 61 were debris. Retouched tools and Levallois flakes accounted for 42.5 per cent of the total collection and 56.2 per cent of all potentially usable flakes and blades.

Although the site is in close proximity to the Batn el-Hajar, 81.3 per cent of all tools were made on ferrocrete sandstone; the remaining tools and Levallois flakes were made on Precambrian rocks. Broken flakes and blades were still numerous, but the proportion of these to the total number of flakes and blades dropped to 27.5 per cent.

Technological studies indicated a fairly low Levallois Index (IL, 13.6), almost no blades (Ib, 2.3), and the highest Faceting Indices of any Sebilian site in Nubia (IF, 78.4; IFs, 52.8).

TOOL TYPOLOGY

	No.	%	Restricted %
1. Levallois flakes	30	14.5	
2. Levallois blades	1	0.5	
3. Levallois points	3	1.4	
4. Side-scrapers	2	1.0	1.2
5. End-scrapers	4	1.9	2.5
6. Notched pieces	5	2.4	3.1
7. Denticulates	6	2.9	3.7
9. Burins	1	0.5	0.6
11. Cortex backed knives	1	0.5	0.6
12. Retouched flakes	3	1.4	1.8
13. Simple basal truncations			
a. Flakes			
1. Perpendicular	44	21.3	27.0
2. Oblique	30	14.5	18.4

	No.	%	Restricted %
14. Basal and oblique truncations			
a. Flakes			
1. Straight	9	4.3	5.5
2. Convex	8	3.9	4.9
3. Concave	10	4.8	6.1
b. Blades			
1. Straight	1	0.5	0.6
15. Simple oblique truncations			
a. Flakes			
1. Straight	7	3.4	4.3
2. Convex	7	3.4	4.3
3. Concave	5	2.4	3.1
b. Blades			
1. Straight	1	0.5	0.6
16. Simple backing			
a. Flakes	4	1.9	2.5
b. Blades	2	1.0	1.2
17. Backing and basal truncations			
a. Flakes			
1. Straight	2	1.0	1.2
2. Convex	9	4.3	5.5
18. Other Sebilian types	2	1.0	1.2
19. Microburins	10	4.8	
	207	100.0	99.9

NOTES ON THE TYPOLOGY

Levallois flakes (30). There is a major variation in size. The largest measures 7.3 cm. and the smallest only 2.2 cm. in length. Most, however, range between 3 and 5 cm. in length. Nineteen examples are fragmentary but all butts are faceted. All but four are on ferrocrete sandstone, and most are fairly well made (fig. 18, q).

Levallois blades (1). A broken example.

Levallois points (3). All are fragmentary and somewhat irregular.

Side-scrapers (2). One is a slightly convex scraper on a blade. The scraping edge is somewhat irregular and approaches a denticulate. There is also a small amount of retouch on the opposite edge (fig. 18, p). The other is a poor convex side-scraper.

End-scrapers (4). There are four atypical end-scrapers (fig. 18, b), one of which is on a broken blade (fig. 18, a).

Notched pieces (5). Four lateral notches and one end notch on irregular flakes.

Denticulates (6). These are well made. There is a convergent convex denticulate (fig. 18, n), and five lateral denticulates (fig. 18, o), all formed by percussion.

Burins (1). This is an atypical burin on a weak

oblique truncation. The flake also has been basally truncated (fig. 18, c).

Cortex backed knives (1). A ferrocrete sandstone example, measuring 7.3 cm. in length.

Retouched flakes (3). These are flakes with small amounts of semisteep obverse retouch. The angle of the retouch indicates that these were not intended to be typical Sebilian tools.

Simple basal truncations (74). All simple basal truncations are on flakes. Forty-four are perpendicular to the long axis and 30 are oblique to it (fig. 18, e). One striking element of these pieces is that a large number of them are wider than they are long. There are 38 examples of this kind and they account for over half of all pieces. Of this latter group just over half are pointed, while the others are asymmetrically trapezoidal (fig. 18, d) or rectangular. They range in width from 2.1 to 4.1 cm. and in length from 1.9 to 3.4 cm. Of those which are longer than they are wide, nine are rectangular, ten are asymmetrically pointed, and sixteen are broken. They range in length from 2.1 to 4.1 cm. It is possible that a few of the broken examples might have been wider than they were long.

Basal and oblique truncations (28). Twenty-seven are on flakes and one is on a blade. Ten are wider than they are long and approach pseudo-geometrics in form (fig. 18, f-g). They range in width from 2.3 to 4.5 cm. and in length from 2.1 to 3.6 cm. Of the others, thirteen are pointed (fig. 18, h), four are rectangular, and one is fragmentary. They range in size from 2.9 to 4 cm. in length.

Simple oblique truncations (20). Nineteen are on flakes and one is on a blade fragment. Six have oblique truncations which are almost perpendicular to the long axis of the flakes (fig. 18, k). Eight are asymmetrically pointed (fig. 18, j), and six are fragmentary. There is only one example which is wider than it is long. As a group, they range in length from 2.2 to 4.3 cm. Most, however, measure less than 3.5 cm. in length, which is somewhat smaller than that at most other Sebilian sites. Straight oblique truncations occur on eight pieces, convex on seven, and concave on five.

Simple backing (6). Four are on flakes and two are on blade fragments. Three are quite irregular, two are convex, and one is straight. All

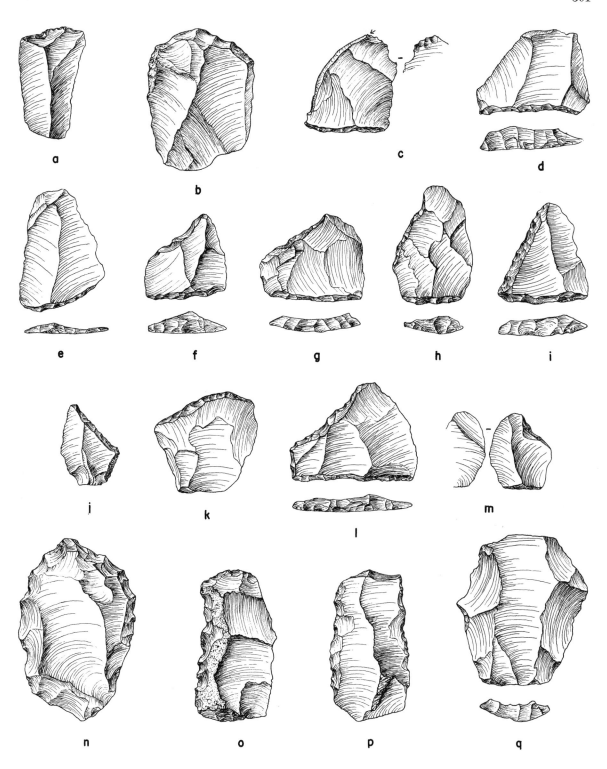

FIG. 18—Site 2010B: a-b, end-scrapers; c, burin; d-e, basally truncated flakes; f-h, basal and obliquely truncated flakes; i, backed and basally truncated flakes; j-k, obliquely truncated flakes; l, complex Sebilian tool; m, micro-burin; n-o, denticulates; p, side-scraper, slightly denticulated; q, Levallois flake. 4/5 natural size.

are rather mediocre in quality. They range in length from 4.5 to 3 cm. Two broken examples, however, were originally larger.

Backing and basal truncations (11). One approaches a true point (fig. 18, i). Of the others, three are generally pointed, one is rectangular, and six are pointed but are wider than they are long. Within this group, two have straight backing, while on the remainder it is convex.

Other Sebilian types (2). There is a wide flake with a basal truncation, a concave oblique truncation, and a short backing which joins the two truncations (fig. 18, 1). It is merely a variation of the backed and basally truncated flakes which are wider than they are long. The other piece has a backing on the left edge and an oblique truncation on the right edge. This is highly atypical in the Sebilian.

Microburins (10). All but three are from the proximal ends of flakes (fig. 18, m).

CORE TYPOLOGY

	No.	%
Levallois flake	2	7.8
Discoidal, Type I	13	48.0
Opposed platform	2	7.8
Unidentifiable	10	36.4
	27	100.0

NOTES ON THE TYPOLOGY

Levallois flake (2). Both are flat and similar to those described from other sites.

Discoidal, Type I (13). These are the most typical core type. They range in diameter from 5.2 to 7.9 cm. Most are oval but a few approach rectangular forms.

Opposed platform (2). Again, these seem to be no more than broken discoidal cores which have been reworked.

Unidentifiable (10). Mostly small fragments which show no clear pattern of flaking. At least half may be corners from flat discoidal cores.

SITE 2005

Site 2005 is located 3.6 km. south of Jebel el-Sahaba and 0.85 km. east of the Nile (map ref. 920.05/652.4). The site consists of a badly eroded beach line which partially cuts into a large wadi. This beach remnant is indicated by a cemented concentration of artifacts, gravel, and shell at an elevation of 20 m. above floodplain. Only the very bottom of the beach is still intact, but there is a scattering of shell and artifacts around the cemented remnants. The beach rests on sands of the Sahaba formation. Some artifacts were covered by a concretion which, when removed, showed them to be fresh. This suggests that the site is generally contemporary with the beach; that is, it might be dated to between 12,000 B.C. and 10,000 B.C.

A systematic surface collection was made from the site, and all artifacts were collected. As at Site 81, the artifacts cannot be considered *in situ*. The tool sample was not quite large enough to justify fully a detailed typological study. A total of 563 artifacts were collected. Of these 144 were either retouched tools or Levallois flakes, 206 were unretouched non-Levallois flakes and blades, 83 were cores and core fragments, 68 were primary flakes, and 62 were debris. Unfortunately, of the 144 pieces mentioned above, only 94 were retouched tools. The tools, however, will be described in detail, although the size of the sample must be taken into account.

Technological studies showed that this assemblage had the highest Levallois Index of any Sebilian site (IL, 22.2), that blades were rare (Ib, 2.9), and that the Faceting Indices fit within the range of the later Sebilian sites (IF, 61.4; IFs, 37.9).

TOOL TYPOLOGY

	No.	%	Restricted %
1. Levallois flakes	44	30.4	
2. Levallois blades	1	0.7	
3. Levallois points	1	0.7	
4. Side-scrapers	1	0.7	1.1
5. End-scrapers	5	3.5	5.3
6. Notched pieces	7	4.9	7.4
7. Denticulates	3	2.0	3.2
12. Retouched flakes	2	1.4	2.1
13. Simple basal truncations			
a. Flakes			
1. Perpendicular	13	9.0	13.8
2. Oblique	10	6.9	10.6
14. Basal and oblique truncations			
a. Flakes			
1. Straight	3	2.0	3.2
2. Convex	4	2.8	4.2
3. Concave	6	4.2	6.4
b. Blades			
2. Convex	1	0.7	1.1
3. Concave	1	0.7	1.1

	No.	%	Restricted %
15. Simple oblique truncations			
a. Flakes			
1. Straight	6	4.2	6.4
2. Convex	8	5.6	8.5
3. Concave	6	4.2	6.4
b. Blades			
1. Straight	1	0.7	1.1
16. Simple backing			
a. Flakes	2	1.4	2.1
c. Points	1	0.7	1.1
17. Backing and basal truncations			
a. Flakes			
1. Straight	1	0.7	1.1
2. Convex	8	5.6	8.5
3. Concave	2	1.4	2.1
c. Points	1	0.7	1.1
18. Other Sebilian types	2	1.4	2.1
19. Microburins	4	2.8	
	144	100.0	100.0

NOTES ON THE TYPOLOGY

Levallois flakes (44). Most are atypical, but some good examples were found (fig. 19, a). All are on ferrocrete sandstone, and the vast majority has faceted butts. They are all fairly large, with a number measuring over 5 cm. in length.

Levallois blades (1). A single, broken example.

Levallois points (1). A typical point, measuring 4.5 cm. in length.

Side-scrapers (1). This is a flake with a poor concave scraping edge made by marginal retouch.

End-scrapers (5). As a group, these are quite well made. Four are typical end-scrapers on broken flakes. The fifth example is somewhat atypical and is very slightly denticulated (fig. 19, i).

Notched pieces (7). There are six lateral notches on flakes and a single end notch on a broken blade.

Denticulates (3). These are not well made. They are thick, and one is made on a primary flake and approaches an end-scraper (fig. 19, b).

Retouched flakes (2). Two small flakes which show some marginal retouch.

Simple basal truncations (23). All are on ferrocrete sandstone flakes. Six are generally pointed, eight are rectangular or irregular in shape (fig. 19, h), one is wider than it is long, and eight are too fragmentary to classify. On thirteen flakes the basal truncation is perpendicular to the cen-

tral axis, and on ten it is oblique to it. As a group, they range in length from 3.2 to 5.3 cm.

Basal and oblique truncations (15). Thirteen are on flakes and two on blades. The blades are small, measuring between 3 and 4 cm. in length (fig. 19, e). There are five flakes which are wider than they are long. These vary in width from 2.9 to 4.2 cm. and in length from 2.4 to 3.8 cm. and do have the appearance of pseudo-geometrics (fig. 19, c-d). The remaining eight flakes are asymmetrically pointed (fig. 19, f-g) and range in length from 3.2 to 4.5 cm.

Simple oblique truncations (21). All but one are on flakes. Twelve are asymmetrically pointed (fig. 20, b), six are rectangular or irregular in shape, and three are wider than they are long (fig. 20, a). There is only a small size variation in the latter group, from 3.0 to 3.8 cm. in width and from 2.5 to 3.1 cm. in length. The largest pointed flake measures 5.5 cm. in length, and the smallest is only 3.2 cm. long.

Simple backing (3). Two flakes and a poor point have simple backing (fig. 20, d). One flake is asymmetrically pointed, while the other is rectangular. On both, the backing is slightly convex.

Backed and basal truncations (12). All are on flakes. Five are generally pointed (figs. 19, j; 20, g), two are rectangular (fig. 20, i), two are wider than they are long, one is a point (fig. 20, e), and two are too fragmentary to classify. They range in size from 2.8 to 5 cm. in length. Nine have convex backing, one has straight backing, and two have concave backing.

Other Sebilian types (2). These are flakes with basal truncations, oblique truncations, and short backed edges which connect the truncations. One is pointed (fig. 20, f), while the other approaches a pseudo-geometric shape and is wider than it is long (fig. 20, h).

Microburins (4). One distal end (fig. 20, c), and three flakes showing the results of a microburin technique.

CORE TYPOLOGY

	No.	%
Levallois flake	11	13.2
Discoidal, Type I	23	27.7
Marginal	3	3.6
Unidentifiable	46	55.4
	83	99.9

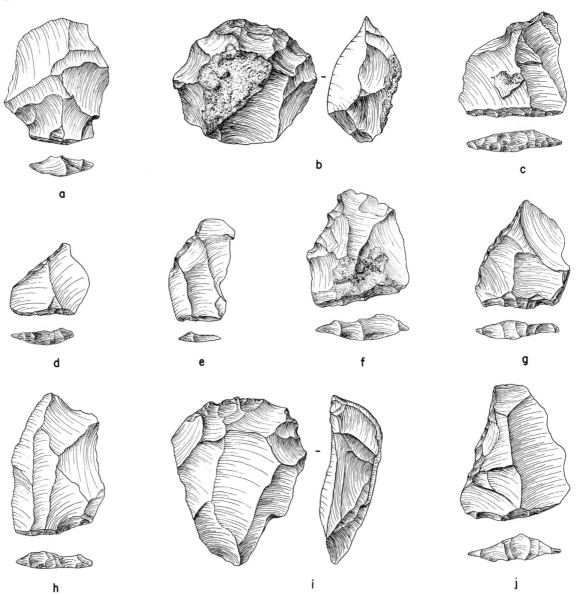

Fɪɢ. 19—Site 2005: a, Levallois flake; b, denticulate; c-g, basal and obliquely truncated flakes and blades; h, basally truncated flake; i, end-scraper; j, backed and basally truncated flake. 4/5 natural size.

NOTES ON THE TYPOLOGY

Levallois flake (11). These are all atypical. They are poorly prepared on both faces. Three are thick, but the rest are made from flat plaquettes. The smallest measures 5.2 cm. in length and the largest, 6.2 cm.

Discoidal, Type I (23). These are the typical Sebilian cores found at all Sebilian sites in Nubia. The larger examples are oval and measure be-tween 6 and 8 cm. in diameter (fig. 20, j). The smaller cores tend more toward rectangular shapes.

Marginal (3). These are fragments of small plaquettes which have been flaked on one face from opposite edges.

Unidentifiable (46). Four complete cores and forty-two fragments showed no obvious pattern of flaking. Many of the fragments may have come from flat discoidal cores.

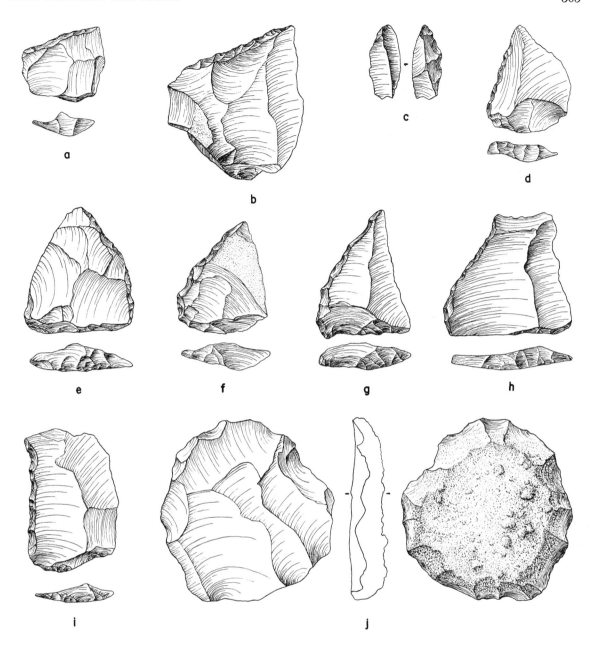

FIG. 20—Site 2005: a-b, obliquely truncated flakes; c, microburin; d, backed point; e, backed and basally truncated point; f, h, complex Sebilian tools; g, i, backed and basally truncated flakes; j, flat discoidal core. 4/5 natural size.

SITE 81

Site 81 is located 2.5 km. south of Jebel el-Sahaba and 0.6 km. east of the Nile, behind the village of Nugu el-Sahaba (map ref. 921.15/652.45). The site is a beach line that contains a 50 cm. thick deposit of shells, gravels, and artifacts, which rest on fluvial sands of the

Sahaba formation. The gravels and shells formed a compact matrix, leaving the beach line standing above the deflated sands of the Sahaba formation (fig. 21). The beach extends for 20 m. on a north-south line and is about 3 m. wide. It stands at an elevation of 20.5 m. above flood-plain and represents a final phase of the Sahaba

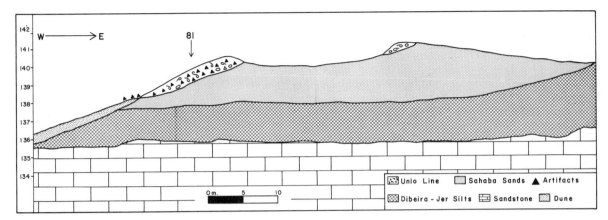

Fıɢ. 21—Profile of Site 81.

aggradation. Although a radiocarbon date was not obtained from shells at this site, dates were determined from shell taken from beach lines at the same elevation. These dates indicate that the beach was formed about 10,000 B.C., but the time may have been somewhat earlier.

Artifacts of two kinds had been incorporated into the beach line: very slightly weathered Sebilian tools and debitage made of ferrocrete sandstone and Precambrian rock, and fresh microlithic tools and debitage made on chert. From the condition of the artifacts, it was clear that neither component had been transported more than a few feet. The Sebilian tools appear to have been on the surface for a short time prior to their incorporation into the beach, but the chert microliths must have been deposited on the shore as the beach was forming. These chert artifacts are classifiable as Qadan and cannot be confused with the Sebilian in any way.[7]

Excavations were carried out over 22 sq. m. to an average depth of 50 cm. The excavated beach line was screened, and all artifacts were removed. Neither the Qadan nor the Sebilian material can be considered *in situ,* but as noted before, their displacement must have been minimal.

A total of 428 Sebilian artifacts were recovered. Of these, 103 were retouched tools or Levallois flakes, 199 were unretouched non-Levallois flakes and blades, 14 were cores and core fragments, 40 were primary flakes, and 72 were debris. It is realized that the tool sample is small, but the

---

[7] These are described under Site 81A (Shiner, this volume).

stratigraphic position of the site makes it important. Thus, a complete typological study was undertaken.

Technological studies show that the Levallois Index was typical of the Sebilian (IL, 11.1), the Blade Index in the higher range of other Sebilian assemblages (Ib, 7.9), while the Faceting Indices were fairly low, within the range of later Sebilian assemblages (IF, 63.9; IFs, 42.7).

TOOL TYPOLOGY

	No.	%	Restricted %
1. Levallois flakes	12	11.6	
2. Levallois blades	1	1.0	
3. Levallois points	2	2.0	
4. Side-scrapers	1	1.0	1.2
6. Notched pieces	7	6.0	8.2
7. Denticulates	2	2.0	2.3
12. Retouched flakes	2	2.0	2.3
13. Simple basal truncations			
a. Flakes			
1. Perpendicular	14	13.6	16.3
2. Oblique	13	12.6	15.3
b. Blades			
1. Perpendicular	2	2.0	2.3
2. Oblique	1	1.0	1.2
14. Basal and oblique truncations			
a. Flakes			
1. Straight	2	2.0	2.3
2. Convex	5	4.9	5.9
15. Simple oblique truncations			
a. Flakes			
1. Straight	5	4.9	5.9
2. Convex	10	9.7	11.8
3. Concave	5	4.9	5.9
b. Blades			
1. Straight	2	2.0	2.3
2. Convex	1	1.0	1.2

	No.	%	Restricted %
16. Simple backing			
a. Flakes	2	2.0	2.3
b. Blades	1	1.0	1.2
17. Backing and basal truncations			
a. Flakes			
1. Straight	1	1.0	1.2
2. Convex	2	2.0	2.3
3. Concave	4	3.9	4.7
c. Points	1	1.0	1.2
18. Other Sebilian tools	2	2.0	2.3
19. Microburins	3	2.9	
	103	100.0	99.6

NOTES ON THE TYPOLOGY

Levallois flakes (12). Most are fragmentary, but a few typical examples were still more or less intact (fig. 22, r).

Levallois blades (1). A broken example.

Levallois points (2). Both are very small, measuring under 3 cm. in length.

Side-scrapers (1). This is an inverse, convex raclette on a short flake.

Notched pieces (7). All are lateral notches on flakes. One even approaches a concave side-scraper (fig. 22, q).

Denticulates (2). Both are typical examples on flake fragments.

Retouched flakes (2). These are elongated flakes with light marginal retouch along part of one lateral edge.

Simple basal truncations (30). Twenty-seven flakes and three blades have simple basal truncations. Fourteen are generally pointed (fig. 22, m, o), five are either rectangular or irregular (fig. 22, n, p), three are wider than they are long, while eight were too fragmentary to classify by shape.

Basal and oblique truncations (7). All are on flakes. Six are asymmetrically pointed, and one is wider than it is long. Most are typical (fig. 22, s), but the oblique truncations on two examples approach convex backing (fig. 22, j-k). All measure under 4.5 cm. in length.

Simple oblique truncations (23). Twenty are on flakes and three are on blades. Convex truncation is most typical, occurring on 11 pieces. Straight truncations are on seven and concave on five. Seventeen examples are somewhat asymmetrically pointed (fig. 22, a-b, g), four are rectangular or irregular, and two are too fragmentary to classify by shape. As a group, they are small, all measuring under 4.5 cm. in length.

Simple backing (3). One blade and two pointed flakes (fig. 22, f) are backed. All have convex backing and all are rectangular in shape.

Backing and basal truncations (8). Seven flakes and one point are backed and basally truncated. Six flakes are generally pointed (fig. 22 c, h), and one is rectangular (fig. 22, i). The symmetric point is poor (fig. 22, l).

Other Sebilian tools (2). One is a broken flake which shows backing and oblique truncation on the same edge. The other has basal and oblique truncations as well as small amounts of backing which join the truncations.

Microburins (3). There is one "prototype" (fig. 22, e), and two are typical examples (fig. 22, d).

CORE TYPOLOGY

	No.	%
Levallois flake	2	14.3
Discoidal, Type I	6	42.8
Unidentifiable	6	42.8
	14	99.9

NOTES ON THE TYPOLOGY

Levallois flake (2). These include one nice example.

Discoidal, Type I (6). All are on ferrocrete sandstone, and are the typical Sebilian cores.

Unidentifiable (6). Small core fragments which may come from flat discoidal cores.

SITE 2013

Site 2013 is located 3.3 km. due south of Jebel el-Sahaba and 3.2 km. north-northwest of the beginning of the Cairo Road (map ref. 652.4/ 920.4). The site is situated on a rock outcrop 0.5 km. east of the Nile at an elevation of 21 m. above floodplain. This outcrop was cut off from the main desert by a narrow channel of Sahaba alluvium at 20 m. elevation, indicating that the site may have been occupied during a time when the water had dropped just below 20 m. above present floodplain (fig. 23). This would place the site during a late phase of the Sahaba formation, perhaps at about 10,000 B.C.

The site consisted of a dense oval surface concentration of artifacts covering an area of some 60 sq. m. Because of the density of the concen-

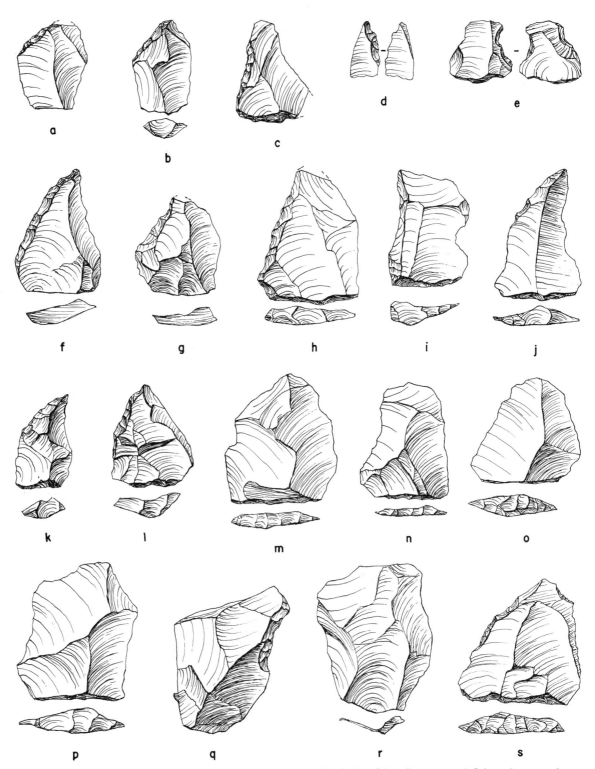

FIG. 22—Site 81: a-b, f, g, obliquely truncated flakes; c, h-i, backed and basally truncated flakes; d-e, microburins;
    f, simple backed flake; j-l, s, basal and obliquely truncated flakes; m-p, basally truncated flakes; q, notched flake;
    r, Levallois flake. 4/5 natural size.

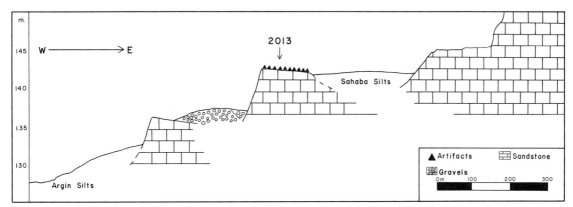

Fig. 23–Profile of Site 2013.

tration, only 21 sq. m. were systematically collected. Within this area 1,159 artifacts were recovered. Of these 218 were retouched tools or Levallois flakes, 465 were unretouched non-Levallois flakes and blades, 37 were cores, 116 were primary flakes, and 323 were debris.

The overwhelmingly dominant raw material employed was ferrocrete sandstone, which accounted for 96.5 per cent of all retouched tools and Levallois flakes. The remaining tools were made from quartzites and dacite. Tools and Levallois flakes ranged in length from 2 cm. to as much as 6 cm., but most measured between 3 and 4.2 cm. in length. Broken flakes accounted for 38.6 per cent of all flakes, whether they were made into tools or not.

Technological studies showed a low Levallois Index (IL, 10.9), very few blades (Ib, 4.2), and high Faceting Indices (IF, 75.7; IFs, 48.6).

TOOL TYPOLOGY

	No.	%	Restricted %
1. Levallois flakes	47	21.5	
2. Levallois blades	1	0.5	
3. Levallois points	6	2.7	
5. End-scrapers	1	0.5	0.6
6. Notched pieces	14	6.4	8.9
7. Denticulates	1	0.5	0.6
8. Bec burins	1	0.5	0.6
13. Simple basal truncations			
a. Flakes			
1. Perpendicular	37	16.9	23.3
2. Oblique	22	10.1	14.2
14. Basal and oblique truncations			
a. Flakes			
1. Straight	9	4.1	5.6
2. Convex	7	3.2	4.4

	No.	%	Restricted %
3. Concave	2	0.9	1.3
15. Simple oblique truncations			
a. Flakes			
1. Straight	12	5.5	7.6
2. Convex	19	8.7	11.9
3. Concave	6	2.7	3.8
b. Blades			
2. Convex	2	0.9	1.3
3. Concave	1	0.5	0.6
16. Simple backing			
a. Flakes	6	2.7	3.8
b. Blades	1	0.5	0.6
c. Points	1	0.5	0.6
17. Backing and basal truncations			
a. Flakes			
1. Straight	7	3.2	4.4
2. Convex	9	4.1	5.6
3. Concave	1	0.5	0.6
19. Microburins	5	2.3	
	218	99.9	100.3

NOTES ON THE TYPOLOGY

Levallois flakes (47). All but three are made on ferrocrete sandstone. As a group they are small, with most complete examples measuring between 3 and 4 cm. in length. All butts are faceted, and 39 flakes are broken at the distal end. For the most part, they are atypical, although a few good examples occur (fig. 24, d).

Levallois blades (1). A single, broken example.

Levallois points (6). All but two are fragmentary. One almost complete point is quite good (fig. 24, a).

End-scrapers (1). An atypical example made on a flake fragment.

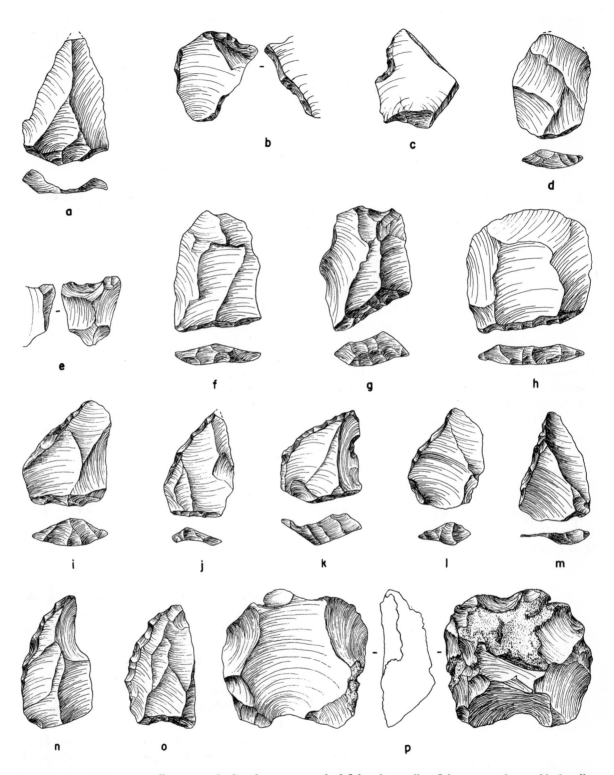

Fig. 24—Site 2013: a, Levallois point; b, bec burin; c, notched flake; d, Levallois flake; e, microburin; f-h, basally truncated flakes; i-j, basal and obliquely truncated flakes; k, n, obliquely truncated flakes; m, backed point; l, backed flake; o, backed and basally truncated flake; p, Levallois core. 4/5 natural size.

Notched pieces (14). There are three end notches, one of which is on a blade. There are also eleven lateral notches, again, one of which is on a blade. Five of these notches are inverse (fig. 24, c).

Denticulates (1). This is a very poor inverse lateral denticulate on a flake.

Bec burins (1). A rather atypical example (fig. 24, b).

Simple basal truncations (59). All simple basal truncations are on flakes. Thirty-seven are perpendicular to the long axis, and 22 are oblique to it on the right edge. Nine are wider than they are long (fig. 24, h), 37 are longer than they are wide, and 13 are too fragmentary to classify. Only four are pointed; the remaining 55 are either generally rectangular (fig. 24, f-g), or are broken at the distal end. The short, wide pieces range in width from 2.8 to 4.2 cm. and in length from 2.4 to 3.9 cm. The others vary in length from 2.9 to 4.4 cm. Three are made on dacite, but the rest are on ferrocrete sandstone.

Basal and oblique truncations (18). All are on flakes, and all but two are on ferrocrete sandstone. There are six which are wider than they are long and approach very rough pseudo-geometrics. These are not nearly as regular as those from most other sites. They range in width from 2.6 to 3.9 cm. and in length from 2.3 to 3.5 cm. All other examples are asymmetrically pointed and range in length from 2.3 to 4.2 cm. (fig. 24, i-j).

Simple oblique truncations (40). Thirty-seven flakes and three broken blades have simple oblique truncations. Half of these are asymmetrically pointed, with the truncations varying from almost perpendicular (fig. 24, k) to those which verge on backing (fig. 24, n). Again, there is a major size variation, from 2.9 to 4.5 cm. in length. There is another group of nine examples which are either irregular or rectangular in shape. These are somewhat smaller, measuring from 3 to 4 cm. in length. There are five other flakes which are wider than they are long. They range from 2.5 to 4.6 cm. in width and from 2.1 to 4 cm. in length. These, however, do not really have the appearance of even pseudo-geometrics. In addition there are six broken flakes which could not be classified.

Simple backing (8). There is one questionable blade which has a convex backing and approaches a crude lunate. There are two flakes which are wider than they are long, one of which is rectangular, while the other is somewhat pointed. In addition, there are two asymmetrically pointed pieces (fig. 24, 1), and two small fragments. There is also a well made backed point (fig. 24, m).

Backing and basal truncations (17). All are flakes. Eight are asymmetrically pointed. With the exception of an elongated flake with a concave basal truncation and a convex backing (fig. 24, o), all are quite small. The largest measures 3.6 cm. in length, but most fall between 3.0 and 3.4 cm. There is one rectangular flake and three which are wider than they are long. Again, they are not regular enough to be considered pseudo-geometrics. There is one large example of this kind which measures 5 cm. in width and 3.7 cm. in length, but the others do not exceed 3.5 cm. in width and 2.9 cm. in length. In addition, five flakes are fragmentary and could not be further classified.

Microburins (5). Three flakes with their distal ends snapped and two distal end microburins (fig. 24, e).

CORE TYPOLOGY

	No.	%
Levallois flake	4	10.8
Discoidal, Type I	15	40.5
Marginal	3	8.1
Unidentifiable	15	40.5
	37	99.9

NOTES ON THE TYPOLOGY

Levallois flake (4). One complete example and two fragments are flat and similar to the discoidal cores. The other is thicker and more typically Levallois (fig. 24, p).

Discoidal, Type I (15). All are typical, except for one which might be classified as a flat discoidal or a flat Levallois core (fig. 25, a).

Marginal (3). Three small plaquette fragments which have been flaked from only one edge.

Unidentifiable (15). These are mostly fragments which could not be classified. Most may well come from flat discoidal cores.

SITE 1024A

Site 1024A is actually part of a complex of sur-

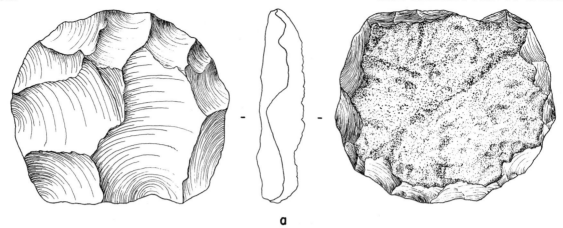

a

Fig. 25—Site 2013: a, flat discoidal core. 4/5 natural size.

face concentrations on the edge of the Khor Musa near the Wadi Halfa airport. This complex consisted of four discrete areas of surface artifacts. One of these was called 1024A, another 1024B, and a third 1024C, while the fourth was not named, but a large collection from it was given to the Joint Scandinavian Expedition. Site 1024B was systematically collected, but it contained too few tools to warrant study. Only 1024A and 1024C were studied.

The complex known as 1024 is located on the south side of the Khor Musa, 5.7 km. up the Khor and 3.8 km. north-northeast of the Wadi Halfa airport at an elevation of c. 32 m. above floodplain (map ref. 643.3/901.3). The complex of sites is situated on a wadi fan which joins the Khor Musa from the south, and all four concentrations occur in an area of about 2,000 sq. m. The location of the site is too far from the Nile to link it directly with Nile silts, but there is little question that the Khor Musa must have been active during the period of occupation.

In spite of the fact that the complex of sites was spread over a large area, Site 1024A was very small, covering no more than an oval area of 60 sq. m. It was noted by a dense concentration of artifacts, including fragments of weathered bone. Three-quarters of the concentration were systematically collected and mapped (fig. 26), while just outside the mapped area two amorphus fire pits were found with directly associated lithic artifacts and faunal remains. Charcoal from the pits gave two dates: 8,975 B.C. ±

140 years (WSU-188) and 9,050 B.C. ± 120 years (WSU-144). The dates indicate that Sites 1024A and 1024C are the most recent Sebilian assemblages found in Nubia. This is because all other Sebilian sites are in some way associated with the Sahaba formation and, at best, this formation was in its very final stage by 9,000 B.C.

In the systematic collection, a total of 1,650 artifacts was collected. This includes some 100 artifacts that came from *in situ*, immediately associated with the fire pits. Of the total lithic collection, 359 were retouched tools or Levallois flakes, 460 were unretouched non-Levallois flakes and blades, 23 were cores and core fragments, 64 were primary flakes, and 744 were debris. Three hundred and six flakes, blades, and tools were broken; they accounted for 34.9 per cent of all flakes and blades.

Technological studies show a somewhat high Levallois Index for a Sebilian assemblage (IL, 15.1), few blades (Ib, 5.1), and relatively low Faceting Indices (IF, 63.1; IFs, 35.0).

TOOL TYPOLOGY

	No.	%	Restricted %
1. Levallois flakes	52	14.5	
2. Levallois blades	3	0.8	
3. Levallois points	5	1.4	
5. End-scrapers	1	0.3	0.4
6. Notched pieces	14	3.9	5.7
7. Denticulates	4	1.1	1.6
13. Simple basal truncations a. Flakes 1. Perpendicular	50	13.9	20.4

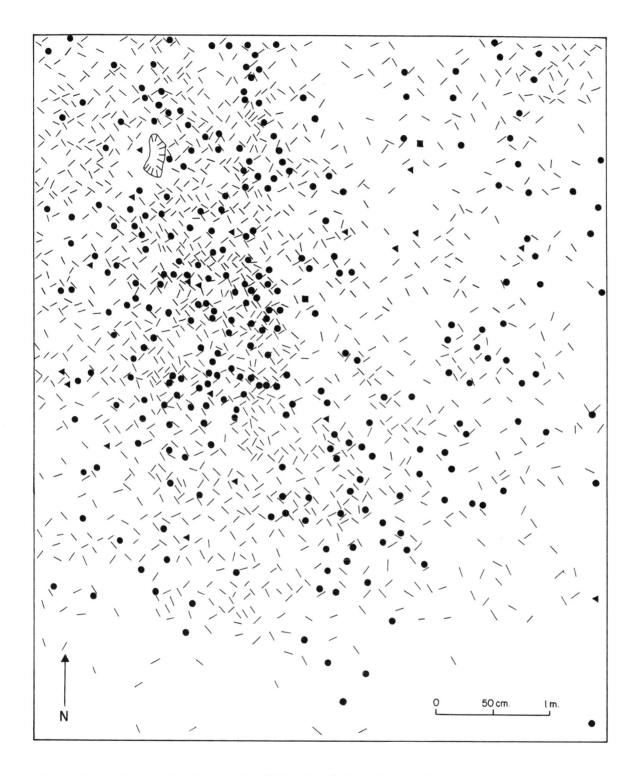

FIG. 26—Scatter diagram of artifacts at Site 1024A. Key: dash=debitage, circle=tool, triangle=core or core fragment.

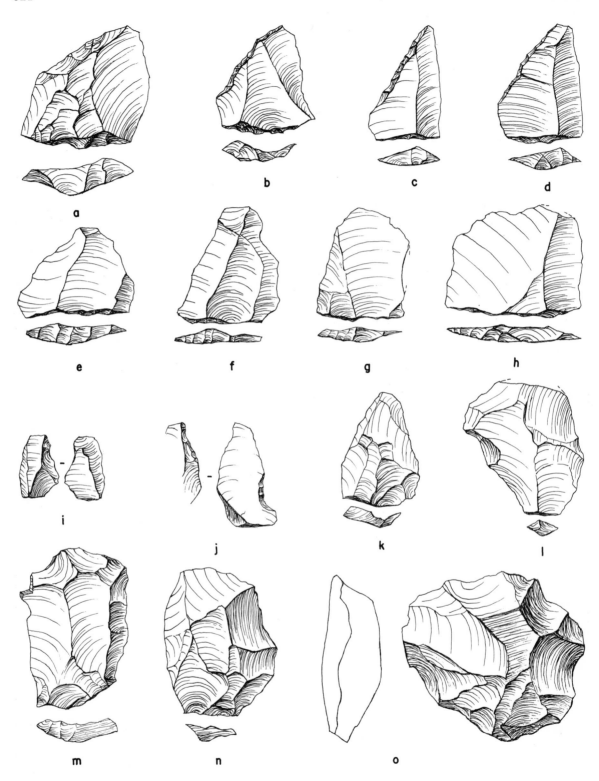

Fɪɢ. 27—Site 1024A: a-d, basal and obliquely truncated flakes; e-h, basally truncated flakes; i, microburin; j, notched flake; k, Levallois point; l-n, Levallois flakes; o, denticulate. 4/5 natural size.

	No.	%	Restricted %
2. Oblique	44	12.3	17.9
b. Blades			
1. Perpendicular	1	0.3	0.4
2. Oblique	4	1.1	1.6
14. Basal and oblique truncations			
a. Flakes			
1. Straight	18	5.0	7.3
2. Convex	19	5.3	7.7
3. Concave	5	1.4	2.0
c. Points	1	0.3	0.4
15. Simple oblique truncations			
a. Flakes			
1. Straight	13	3.6	5.3
2. Convex	12	3.3	4.9
3. Concave	13	3.6	5.3
b. Blades			
2. Convex	1	0.3	0.4
16. Simple backing			
a. Flakes	12	3.3	4.9
b. Blades	1	0.3	0.4
c. Points	2	0.6	0.8
17. Backing and basal truncations			
a. Flakes			
1. Straight	7	1.9	2.9
2. Convex	7	1.9	2.9
3. Concave	9	2.5	3.7
c. Points	1	0.3	0.4
18. Other Sebilian types	6	1.7	2.4
19. Microburins	54	15.1	
	359	100.0	99.7

NOTES ON THE TYPOLOGY

Levallois flakes (52). All but six are broken. There are a few typical examples (fig. 27, l-n), but most are atypical. There is one large flake which measures 10 cm. in length, but most fall between 4 and 6 cm. in length.

Levallois blades (3). All are fragmentary.

Levallois points (5). Four are typical and one is atypical (fig. 27, k).

End-scrapers (1). This is very atypical. It is a blade with a straight scraping edge at the distal end. It has the form of an oblique truncation, but the retouch is rather flat and quite different from that used in the formation of truncations.

Notched pieces (14). There are 11 lateral notches and three end notches. Four of the lateral notches are quite large—about 1.5 cm. across. All other flakes have small but fairly deep notches (fig. 27, j).

Denticulates (4). There is one *déjeté* macro-denticulate on a thick flake (fig. 27, o), a beautiful lateral and end denticulate on a flake, and

two large flakes with poorly formed lateral denticulations.

Simple basal truncations (99). Ninety-four simple basal truncations are on flakes and five are on blades. The blades are small, only one measuring over 3.5 cm. in length, and all are roughly rectangular in shape. The most common basally truncated flake is one which is somewhat pointed but which is wider than it is long. There are 39 examples of that kind (fig. 27, e). They range in width between 2.5 and 5 cm. and in length between 2.4 and 3.3 cm. There are also 13 flakes which are either rectangular or irregular in shape (fig. 27, g-h). These are also small, measuring between 2.8 and 4.5 cm. in length. Twenty-two flakes are generally pointed (fig. 27, f). They fall into the same size range as the rectangular variety. In addition, there are 25 flakes which were too fragmentary to classify as to original shape.

Basal and oblique truncations (43). All are on flakes. The most common type with 22 examples is an asymmetrically pointed flake. These are small and well made with even edges (fig. 27, c-d). The largest is only 4 cm. in length, and the smallest is 2.5 cm., and all but four measure under 3.5 cm. in length. There are only three flakes which are rectangular or irregular. On the other hand, there are 18 which are wider than they are long. A few do not conform very closely to geometric shapes (fig. 27, a), but most do (fig. 27, b). Again they are well made and small. The largest measures 4.1 cm. in width and 4 cm. in length, but all the rest are less than 3.5 cm. wide and 3.3 cm. long.

Simple oblique truncations (39). One blade and 38 flakes have simple oblique truncations. A majority, 21, is asymmetrically pointed (fig. 28, d). Three are irregular or rectangular (fig. 28, c), eight are wider than they are long (fig. 28, e), while seven are too fragmentary to classify. This is a rather mixed group, both in size and quality. The largest measures 5.8 cm. in length, and the smallest is only 1.7 cm. long. Most examples, however, are between 3 and 4.5 cm. long.

Simple backing (15). There are two points, one blade fragment and twelve flakes which have simple backing. There is one large point with a rather irregular backing (fig. 28, k), and another where the backing is slightly convex (fig. 28, b).

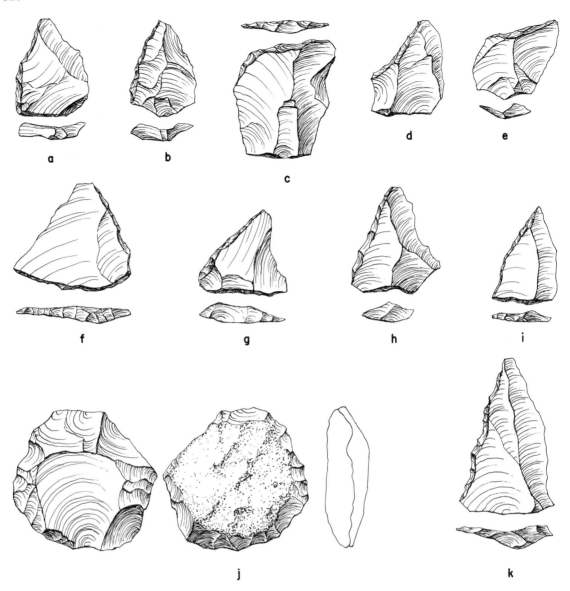

F<small>IG</small>. 28—Site 1024A: a-b, k, backed points; c-e, obliquely truncated points; f-g, i, backed and basally truncated flakes; h, backed and basally truncated point; j, Levallois core. 4/5 natural size.

Seven flakes and one blade have slightly convex backing, while three have concave and two have straight backing. Six are asymmetrically pointed, while the rest are broken at the distal end. Again, with the exception of one point, all are small and none measures over 4 cm. in length.

Backing and basal truncations (24). There are 23 flakes and one point which fall into this class. The point is poor but fits the minimal requirements (fig. 28, h). The flakes include seven which are wider than long (fig. 28, f-g), three which are rectangular or irregular, three which are broken, and ten which are asymmetrically pointed (fig. 29, a, c, e). There is a wide size range in the latter group, from 2.7 to 5.2 cm. in length. A few approach true points (fig. 28, i).

Other Sebilian types (6). Five flakes which are basally and obliquely truncated have a short backing which connects the truncations. All of these are wider than they are long and might be

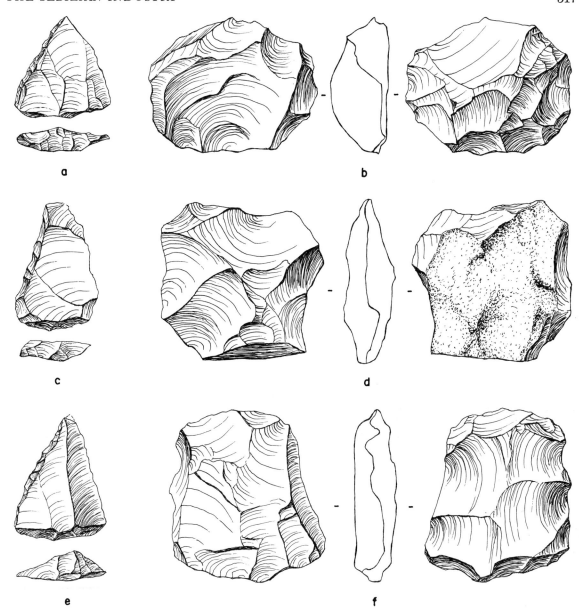

Fig. 29—Site 1024A: a, c, e, backed and basally truncated flakes; b, Levallois core; d, flat discoidal core; f, ninety degree core. 4/5 natural size.

considered pseudo-geometrics. The other piece has two concave oblique truncations on the same edge, one distal and the other basal.

Microburins (54). Ten are "prototypes," while the others are true microburins (fig. 27, i).

CORE TYPOLOGY

	No.	%
Levallois flake	7	30.4
Discoidal, Type I	8	34.8
Discoidal, Type II	2	8.7
Opposed platform	1	4.4
Ninety degree	1	4.4
Unidentifiable	4	17.3
	23	100.0

NOTES ON THE TYPOLOGY

Levallois flake (7). There are some fine examples (fig. 29, b; 30, a), for the most part

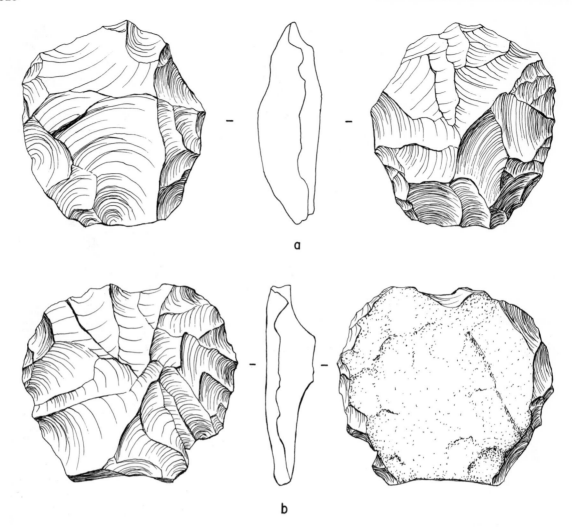

Fig. 30—Site 1024A: a, Levallois core; b, flat discoidal core. 4/5 natural size.

better than those seen at other Sebilian sites. Three are more typical of the Sebilian and are made on plaquettes (fig. 28, j).

Discoidal, Type I (8). Five are typical examples on plaquettes (figs. 29, d; 30, b), while three are made on large quartz pebbles.

Discoidal, Type II (2). Both are made on thick quartz pebbles.

Opposed platform (1). This appears to be a flat discoidal core fragment which has been reworked.

Ninety degree (1). A good example which has opposed platforms on opposite faces of the core. The flake scars on one face are at 90° to the flake scars on the other face (fig. 29, f).

Unidentifiable (4). All are fragments which show no clear pattern of flaking.

SITE 1024C

Site 1024C lay about 40 m. west of 1024A. It represented a fully delimited surface concentration of no more than 70 sq. m. in area. The clarity of the concentration and its small size made possible the collection of all artifacts. The concentration was also mapped to give a concept of the nature of a Sebilian camp (fig. 31).

This concentration contained 1,864 artifacts. Of these, 208 were retouched tools or Levallois flakes, 625 were unretouched non-Levallois flakes and blades, 50 were cores and core fragments,

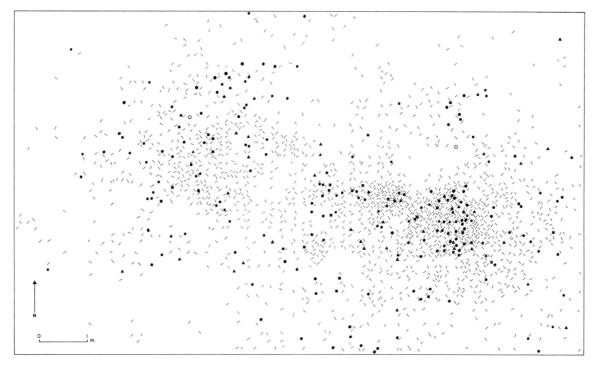

F<small>IG</small>. 31—Scatter diagram of artifacts at Site 1024C. Key: dash=debitage, circle=tool, square=core, triangle=core fragment.

61 were primary flakes, while 920 were debris. Broken flakes and tools accounted for 22.3 per cent of all flakes and blades.

TOOL TYPOLOGY

	No.	%	Restricted %
1. Levallois flakes	29	13.9	
2. Levallois blades	4	1.9	
3. Levallois points	4	1.9	
6. Notched pieces	5	2.4	3.5
7. Denticulates	1	0.5	0.7
9. Burins	1	0.5	0.7
12. Retouched flakes	2	1.0	1.4
13. Simple basal truncations			
a. Flakes			
1. Perpendicular	39	18.8	26.9
2. Oblique	29	13.9	20.0
b. Blades			
2. Oblique	1	0.5	0.7
14. Basal and oblique truncations			
a. Flakes			
1. Straight	5	2.4	3.5
2. Convex	8	3.8	5.5
3. Concave	5	2.4	3.5
c. Points	2	1.0	1.4
15. Simple oblique truncations			
a. Flakes			
1. Straight	6	2.9	4.0

	No.	%	Restricted %
2. Convex	8	3.8	5.5
3. Concave	6	2.9	4.0
b. Blades			
3. Concave	1	0.5	0.7
c. Points	1	0.5	0.7
16. Simple backing			
a. Flakes	3	1.4	2.1
17. Backing and basal truncations			
a. Flakes			
1. Straight	6	2.9	4.0
2. Convex	12	5.8	8.3
3. Concave	3	1.4	2.1
c. Points	1	0.5	0.7
19. Microburins	26	12.5	
	208	100.0	99.9

NOTES ON THE TYPOLOGY

Levallois flakes (29). Most are broken. Complete examples include some which measure between 5 and 6 cm. in length (fig. 32, r). One example is an elongated flake which approaches a highly atypical point (fig. 32, s).

Levallois blades (4). All are fragmentary.

Levallois points (4). Again, all are broken but appear to have been typical.

Notched pieces (5). There are five lateral

FIG. 32—Site 1024C: a, backed flake; b-d, obliquely truncated flakes; e, g-j, basal and obliquely truncated flakes; f, basal and obliquely truncated point; k-p, basally truncated flakes; q, denticulate; r-s, Levallois flakes. 4/5 natural size.

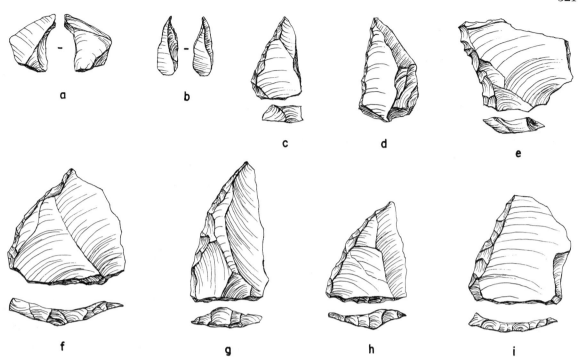

F<small>IG</small>. 33—Site 1024C: a-b, microburins; c, f-i, backed and basally truncated flakes; d, backed point; e, backed flake. 4/5 natural size.

notches on flakes, including an inverse notch on a partially backed flake.

Denticulates (1). A well made convex denticulate (fig. 32, q).

Burin (1). This is a poor angle burin on a snapped flake.

Retouched flakes (2). Two flakes have small amounts of flat retouch extending along one lateral edge.

Simple basal truncations (69). Sixty-eight flakes and one blade show simple oblique truncations. Of these flakes, 31 are too fragmentary to classify by shape, 15 are generally pointed (fig. 32, l), seven are rectangular (fig. 32, m-n), while 15 are wider than they are long (fig. 32, k, o-p). This latter group has some large examples measuring as much as 5.2 cm. in width and 3.5 cm. in length. The pointed and rectangular forms vary in length from 2.8 to 4.8 cm. in length.

Basal and oblique truncations (20). Eighteen flakes and two points fall into this category. The points are both small, and both have straight oblique truncations and minimal basal treatment (fig. 32, f). All but four of the flakes are asymmetrically pointed. There are a few rough ex-

amples (fig. 32, e), but most are well made (fig. 32, i-j), some verging on being wider than they are long (fig. 32, h). As a group, they range in length from 2.6 to 3.8 cm. There are also four flakes which are wider than they are long and might be considered pseudo-geometrics (fig. 32, g).

Simple oblique truncations (22). Twenty flakes, one blade, and one broken point have simple oblique truncations. The point is only a distal end so that originally it also might have been basally truncated. Of the flakes and blades, 13 are asymmetrically pointed (fig. 32, b-c), four are rectangular, four are wider than long (fig. 32, d), and one is too fragmentary to classify by shape. As a group, they range in length from 2.7 to 4.1 cm.

Simple backing (3). All are irregular flakes (fig. 32, a), one of which has a slightly denticulated backing (fig. 33, e).

Backing and basal truncations (22). Twenty-one flakes and one point are backed and basally truncated. The point measures 3 cm. in length and has straight backing (fig. 33, d). Nine flakes are asymmetrically pointed (fig. 33, c), including one which has a convex backing which approaches an oblique truncation (fig. 33, g). Five flakes are rectangular or irregular (fig. 33, i) and five are wider than they are long. These latter examples might be considered pseudo-geometrics (fig. 33, f). Two flakes were too fragmentary to classify by original shape.

Microburins (26). There are three "prototypes" (fig. 33, a) and 23 typical examples (fig. 33, b).

CORE TYPOLOGY

	No.	%
Levallois	5	10.0
Discoidal, Type I	20	40.0
Isolated flake	2	4.0
Unidentifiable	23	46.0
	50	100.0

NOTES ON THE TYPOLOGY

Levallois flake (5). These are relatively good examples on Precambrian rock.

Discoidal, Type I (20). These are the same as at all Sebilian sites.

Isolated flake (2). Two quartz pebbles have single flakes removed from one end.

Unidentifiable (23). This group includes ten quartz fragments and ten broken ferrocrete sandstone core fragments which might have come from flat discoidal cores. In addition, there are three thicker core fragments which might have come from Levallois cores.

THE SUDANESE AND KOM OMBO SEBILIAN

As the Sebilian from Sudanese Nubia does not represent a newly discovered industry, it is necessary to correlate it, as much as possible, with the already existing Sebilian sequence as known from Kom Ombo, Egypt.

As noted in the Introduction, the technological and typological characteristics of the Sebilian sequence at Kom Ombo were originally published by Vignard (1923) and later more fully defined by him (Vignard, 1955). After Vignard's original work Caton-Thompson (1946) also presented some ideas concerning Sebilian stages and distribution.

Vignard's sequence called for a three part division of the Sebilian, based on various sites' positions above the present Nile floodplain, com-

bined with recognizable changes in certain typological and technological attributes. In detail, the attributes which characterized the three Sebilian stages are the following:

Sebilian I

1. Raw material was mostly diorite, although ferrocrete sandstone and quartz were also used. Chert (*silex*) was rare, if present (Vignard, 1923, p. 5).

2. Cores. Technique was at first stated to be typically Mousterian and illustrations show both typical Levallois cores and "Mousterian" discoidal cores (Vignard, 1923, p. 6, pl. I and II bis). More recently, however, it is stated that the Levallois technique was the only one used at this stage at Burg el Makkazin (Vignard, 1955, p. 440).

3. Tools include numerous, rather small, unretouched Levallois flakes, a large number of basally truncated flakes (a trait which is important throughout Sebilian development), basally truncated flakes with some lateral or oblique truncation, and triangles and trapezes, some of which might be considered *tranchets* (Vignard, 1955, pp. 442-443). Both end-scrapers and side-scrapers were stated to be present at Sebil (Vignard, 1923, p. 11) but absent at Burg el Makkazin (Vignard, 1955, p. 443).

4. Blades are reported to be very rare at Sebil (Vignard, 1923, p. 11) and absent at Burg el Makkazin (Vignard, 1955, p. 443).

5. Anvils are rare but present (Vignard, 1923, p. 11; 1955, p. 443).

6. Microburins and microburin "prototypes" are not present.

Stage II

1. Diorite and ferrocrete sandstone have been almost completely replaced by flint or chert (*silex*) (Vignard, 1923, p. 14; 1955, p. 443).

2. Cores. There is a greater complexity of types than during Stage I. Levallois cores are present but there are also opposed platform blade and flake cores (Vignard, 1923, p. 15; 1955, p. 443), and some "Mousterian" discoidal cores (Vignard, 1923, p. 15) which were not mentioned in the 1955 report.

3. Tools include small Levallois flakes which are rather rare (Vignard, 1955, p. 443). End-scrapers gain in popularity, are fairly numerous and varied. Basal truncations are most characteristic and occur on both flakes and blades. Basally

truncated flakes with lateral or oblique truncations are common and merge into subgeometric forms such as triangles and trapezes. A very few scalene triangles are also present, as are lunates and retouched blades (Vignard, 1923, pp. 15-22; 1955, pp. 443-446).

4. Grinding stones were present at Sebil, but only a few fragments were found at other sites in the Kom Ombo plain (Vignard, 1955, p. 449).

5. This is the earliest stage where the microburin technique is present (Vignard, 1955, p. 449).

Stage III

1. Raw material is now restricted to either chert or flint (*silex*) (Vignard, 1923, p. 30).

2. The main core type is now an opposed platform core, which produced both flakes and blades. "Mousterian" discoidal cores are still present and ninety degree cores are fairly numerous (Vignard, 1923, pp. 31-32).

3. Levallois flakes are very rare. Simple basal truncations, while present, no longer dominate the industry, and those with lateral or oblique truncations are rare. This stage, however, has a large number of seemingly true triangles, trapezes, and particularly lunates made on small blades. End-scrapers, side-scrapers, borers, notched pieces, denticulates, etc., either occur for the first time, or for the first time in significant numbers (Vignard, 1923, pp. 32-56). In addition, there are a series of tools called unifacial points.

4. Although no mention is made of grinding stones in Vignard (1923), they are reported to be present in later writings (Alimen, 1957, p. 99).

Caton-Thompson (1946, pp. 100-112), defined the first two Sebilian stages by the following prime attributes:

Sebilian I

1. Deliberate shortening of the butt by basal truncation.

2. Steep retouch, wholly or partially along a lateral edge.

3. A high percentage of broken flakes.

4. Development of this industry directly out of the Late Levalloisian.

Sebilian II

1. Cores are still mainly Levallois or "Mousterian" discoidal, although a few opposed platform cores occur as well.

2. Very few, if any, blades.

3. Almost total disappearance of Levallois flakes.

4. Flakes are now steeply retouched into subgeometric forms.

5. Snapping prior to basal truncating is now common.

6. Lunates appear for the first time and are made on flakes rather than blades.

7. Although not mentioned in Caton-Thompson (1946), the presence of some microburins should be included here (Vignard, 1955).

Vignard's and Caton-Thompson's criteria for Sebilian I and II are basically in agreement. The only noticeable difference for Stage I is Caton-Thompson's insistence that Sebilian I is directly derived from the Late Levalloisian. The question of Sebilian origins will be discussed later and does not directly concern us now. Again, Stage II definitions are in agreement. The basic problem is that these definitions do not readily fit the Sebilian of Sudanese Nubia.

It is possible on a number of typological grounds to dismiss Sebilian III from consideration. The Sudanese material lacks grinding stones and true microlithic geometrics; also, opposed platform cores are rare, as are blades and non-Sebilian type tools.

This leaves Sebilian I and II. On the basis of the published definitions, it appears at first that the Sudanese Sebilian does not fully fit within either stage. Table 6 compares the basic traits of Sebilian I and II with the Sudanese Sebilian.

If primary technological attributes are considered first, the Sudanese sites seem to correlate well with Sebilian I. Raw materials, core types, and blade production are in good agreement. On the other hand, blade production is also low in Sebilian II, and the cores from the Sudanese sites seem to contain more "Mousterian" discoidal cores than is the case in Sebilian I at Kom Ombo.

Secondary technological traits, however, seem to correlate better with Sebilian II. The high frequency of broken flakes might correlate well with either Sebilian I or II, but the presence of a microburin technique and the strong tendency to snap flakes prior to basal retouch seem to be somewhat more indicative of Sebilian II than Sebilian I. It must be noted, however, that these traits are not quantified by either Vignard or

TABLE 6

COMPARISON OF SEBILIAN I AND II WITH SUDANESE SEBILIAN[1]

Traits	Sebilian I	Sebilian II	Sudanese Sebilian
Raw materials	Diorite and ferrocrete sandstone	Mostly *silex*, some diorite and ferrocrete sandstone	Mostly ferrocrete sandstone, some Precambrian rock (quartzite and dacite)
Cores	Levallois with some "Mousterian" discoidal cores	Levallois and "Mousterian" discoidal, plus opposed platform and blade cores	Mostly flat "Mousterian" discoidal, some Levallois. Very rare opposed platform.
Blades	Rare or absent	Rare	Blade Index: 2.3-7.9
Broken flakes	Numerous	Numerous?	22.3% to 45.7% of all flakes and blades
Anvils	Present but rare	Absent?	Absent
Typological Levallois Index	13.0-13.5	4.6-4.8	14.6-31.8
End-scrapers	0.0%-1.4%	9.2%-10.0%	0.0%-2.5%
Simple basal truncations (*éclats-points simples*)	36.2%-40.5%	21.6%-27.4%	15.9%-35.8%. Only two sites below 27.0%.
Technique of basal truncation	Some snapping prior to retouch	Snapping common prior to retouch	Often snapped prior to retouch: 36.4%-65.9% of all basal truncations
Scalene triangles	Absent	1.2%-4.8%	Absent
Lunates	0.0%-0.7%	3.2%-7.3%	Three doubtful examples for all sites
Retouched blades	Absent	2.1%-2.3%	Absent
Burins	Absent	Absent	Rare
Complex Sebilian Tools[2]	43.2%-50.0%	46.2%-50.3%	32.0%-44.2%.[3] One site falls to 29.0%.
Grinding stones	Absent	Present	Absent

[1] Percentages of Sebilian I and II were derived from the comparative table in Vignard (1955) by the removal of cores from the type lists.

[2] This includes Vignard's *éclats-pointes retouchés, triangles,* and *trapèzes.*

[3] This includes all basal and oblique truncations, backed and basal truncations, other Sebilian types, and simple oblique truncations. This last type is included because it appears that Vignard classified them under *éclats-pointes retouchés* (Vignard, 1955, p. 443).

Caton-Thompson for Sebilian I or II, and so accurate comparisons cannot be made.

Typologically, the Sudanese Sebilian fits well within Sebilian I. The presence of a relatively high Typological Levallois Index goes beyond either Sebilian I or II, but certainly is closer to Sebilian I than Sebilian II. The exceedingly few end-scrapers and the absence of lunates, scalene triangles, retouched blades, and grinding stones are all Sebilian I characteristics. Most Sudanese Sebilian sites have simple basal truncations in a proportion indicative of Sebilian I, while the number of complex Sebilian tools falls below both Sebilian I and II. This is probably the result of the relatively high number of unretouched Levallois flakes which force down all other percentages.

It would be too simple to say that the Sudanese Sebilian is transitional between Sebilian I and II, but tends toward Sebilian I. This would not be presenting a true picture. In all primary technological traits as well as in all typological considerations, the Sudanese Sebilian appears to be fully within Vignard's definition of Sebilian I. Those tool types recognized by Vignard fit well into the types proposed in this paper. There are, of course, some types which were not recognized by Vignard, or at least not placed on his tool lists: notched pieces, denticulates, cortex backed knives, side-scrapers, etc. It is expected, however, that these do occur in small numbers at Sebilian I sites, although such an expectation cannot now be tested.

The only real Sebilian II trait found in the Sudanese Sebilian is the presence of the microburin technique. It must be noted, however, that the original studies of the microburin technique at Kom Ombo were not complete, and Vignard even suggests that microburin prototypes must have occurred in Sebilian I (Vignard, 1955, p. 440). Therefore, not even the presence of microburins in the Sudanese Sebilian is fully outside the probable range of Sebilian I. Thus, it is concluded that the Sudanese Sebilian should be considered to correlate with Sebilian I from Kom Ombo.

The small technological changes which are visible within the Sudanese Sebilian do not now seem to be of an order which would justify a major subdivision. As more refined reports of the Kom Ombo Sebilian are published, perhaps it will then be necessary to consider Sites 1024A and 1024C as belonging to a recognizably later technological stage. Certainly the typology does not seem to warrant it.

Sebilian Connections and Origins

The Sebilian appeared in Nubia during the aggradation of the Sahaba formation; that is, no earlier than about 15,000 B.C. and perhaps as late as 13,000 B.C. It remained in Nubia until at least 9,000 B.C. At about 9,000 B.C. the Sebilian disappears from around the Second Cataract, perhaps moving northward into Sebilian occupied areas of Upper Egypt. While in Nubia, the Sebilian changed little. It forms a clearly unified and highly unique industry in the area. The Sebilian shows little typological and technological similarities with other Nilotic industries. The Khormusan (Marks, this volume), one of the common pre-Sebilian Nilotic industries, cannot have been its progenitor. A short comparison of significant traits of the latter Khormusan and the Sebilian show how little they have in common (table 7).

Perhaps even more important than a series of percentages is the general trend of Khormusan development. It is toward smaller tools with a

TABLE 7

Comparison of the Sudanese Sebilian with the Later Khormusan

Traits	Sebilian	Khormusan
Ferrocrete sandstone tools	50.6%-97.7%	22%-24%
Chert tools	0.0%	30%-35%
Precambrian tools	2.3%-49.4%	28%-32%
Levallois Index	9.8 to 15.1	23.2 to 30.1
Blade Index	2.3 to 7.9	9.0 to 14.1
Burins (restricted)	0.0%-0.7%	50.5%-53.6%
Scrapers (restricted)	0.0%-6.4%	9.3%-10.2%
Denticulates (restricted)	0.0%-2.6%	17.8%-22.1%
All truncations	71.1%-93.6%	0.8%-2.1%
Microburins	0.3%-17.7%	0.0%

greater utilization of chert, but with a continuing emphasis on burins and denticulates (Marks, this volume). By no stretch of the imagination could it have led directly into the Sebilian.

Two other industries occur in the Second Cataract area just before the Sebilian occupation: the Halfan and the Gemaian. Again, neither is typologically nor technologically related to the Sebilian. Comparative tables have already been provided in the study of the Halfan (Marks, this volume).

If the Sebilian is unrelated to the Nilotic industries of Nubia which are earlier and contemporary with it, where are its relations and its origins? At this time the known distribution of the early Sebilian is limited to the Nile Valley between Kom Ombo and the Second Cataract. It has not been found in the Oases of the Western Desert, nor is it known from the Eastern Desert. As such, it appears to be strictly Nilotic.

Two origins have been suggested for the Sebilian. Vignard believed that it was a direct development out of the Mousterian of Egypt, while Caton-Thompson defined Sebilian I as that industry which evolved directly out of the Late Levalloisian.

Vignard's suggestion is no longer tenable for a number of reasons. It would be difficult at best to derive the Sebilian directly from the Mousterian if for no other reason than that there is at least a 15,000 year gap between them. If one were to say that the Sebilian did develop secondarily out of the Mousterian, which is conceivable, it must be admitted that there are no known transitional industries which clearly document any such sequence.

Caton-Thompson's assertion that the Sebilian

is directly descended from the Late Levalloisian poses similar problems. Although the Upper Levalloisian of Kharga, which we assume to be the Late Levalloisian, has not been accurately dated, there is no reason to suppose that it is only slightly more than 15,000 years old. It may not be true Middle Paleolithic, but no date after 25,000 B.C. would seem to be justified. Its general similarities with the earliest Khormusan have already been noted (Marks, this volume), suggesting that a date of 25,000 B.C. may not be too incorrect.

If, however, the Upper Levalloisian is somewhat later than now thought, it might be chronologically possible for it to have been ancestral to the Sebilian. On the other hand, it is typologically unlikely. Caton-Thompson (1946, p. 100) notes that there are three major typological distinctions between the Upper Levalloisian and Sebilian I: basal shortening of flakes, steep retouch along lateral edges (truncations and backing), and many broken flakes. It is important to note that she considers each of these Sebilian attributes to be "innovations," not developments of traits already present in the Upper Levalloisian. As basal truncation, backing, and oblique truncation form the vast majority of Sebilian tools, what exactly are the typological continuities which might make the Upper Levalloisian the ancestor of the Sebilian? The only similarity which seems to be present is the common occurrence of a Levallois technique. The Upper Levalloisian has numerous side-scrapers and borers which do not occur in the Sebilian, and the flat "Mousterian" discoidal cores of the Sebilian appear to be lacking in the Upper Levalloisian. Objectively there appears to be no strong typological link between the two industries. The presence of a Levallois technology is obviously not sufficient cause, as Levallois technology is widespread in Africa among unrelated lithic traditions. It would seem that the Upper Levalloisian was judged to be the direct ancestor of the Sebilian to fulfil the demands of the concept of a long isolated Nilotic cultural development rather than being necessitated or even justified by the material evidence.

On the basis of the evidence, or lack of it, it is necessary to conclude that at this time there is no demonstrable ancestor for the Sebilian

within the known industries of Egypt or the Sudan.

The view that the Upper Levalloisian may be no older than 25,000 B.C. radically changes the dating of the "epi-Levalloisian" sequence at Kharga. While Caton-Thompson obtained no clear information concerning the relative sequence of Khargan and Aterian or their absolute dating, recent work at Dungul Oasis has produced evidence that the Khargan is datable to less than 21,000 B.C.[8] As such, the Khargan might be either somewhat earlier than, or even contemporary with, the Sebilian. There is little question that the Sebilian and the Khargan have a number of typological features in common. This is particularly true of the numerous simple basal and simple oblique truncations present in both industries. On the other hand, the Khargan shows a much greater variety in tool types and a much lower standard of tool manufacture. The exact relationship of these industries is at present difficult to determine, but Khargan assemblages from Dungul Oasis are now being studied, and these studies should shed some light on the problem. The initial impression is that, while they are similar in some typological respects, there are numerous important differences. This suggests that they may belong to the same broad industrial group without one being directly ancestral to the other. This, of course, is purely tentative.

With the exception of the Khargan, one must go far to find any industry which is typologically similar to the Sebilian. Having done so, we find, however, that there is at least one sub-Saharan industry which shows some amazing typological parallels with the Sebilian. This industry, the Tshitolian, has been well described for Angola (Clark, 1963) and also occurs to the north of the Congo and Gabon. There is also some evidence for the tradition in the Central African Republic, although a true Tshitolian has not been described for that area.[9]

In spite of the wide occurrence of the Tshitolian, it is still necessary to point out that no trace of it has been found within about 1,500

---

[8] Carried out by the Combined Prehistoric Expedition to Egypt.

[9] There is an excellent review of its distribution found in Clark's study of the Sangean/Lupemban/Tshitolian development in Angola (Clark, 1963, pp. 196-206.)

miles of the Second Cataract on the Nile. The well described Tshitolian material from Angola is even farther away from the known occurrences of the Sebilian, almost 2,500 miles. Therefore, the comparisons to be made below must be considered in that light. What will be described are typological similarities, which may show generic relationships, but may well illustrate nothing more than typological convergence.

The comparison of the Sebilian and the Tshitolian will rely on the published account of the Lower Tshitolian site at Cauma, Angola (Clark, 1963, pp. 156-167), and the Sebilian materials found in the Sudan and reported in this paper.

The Lower Tshitolian at Cauma is characterized as a predominantly flake industry with a small but significant proportion of bifacial core tools (Clark, 1963, p. 158). These core tools set the Lower Tshitolian apart from the Sebilian where bifacial tools are absent. It is within the flake tools and certain technological features that the Lower Tshitolian and the Sebilian show striking parallels.

Technologically, both the Sudanese Sebilian and the Lower Tshitolian have few blades: Sebilian Blade Index, 2.3 to 7.9, and Lower Tshitolian Blade Index, c. 2.6. While it is difficult to compare Levallois Indices, as the study of the Tshitolian does not recognize Levallois technology as such, 9 per cent of all flake debitage is reported to have come from "prepared cores." If this was broadly taken to signify the Levallois component, then it is comparable with the lowest Levallois Indices of the Sebilian. Another feature which both hold in common is a high percentage of broken flakes. At Cauma, they account for 30.8 per cent of all flake debitage, a figure quite in agreement with those from Sebilian sites.

There are, however, some major technological differences. At Cauma, flakes tend to be larger, with just over 20 per cent measuring more than 5 cm. in length. In the Sebilian, never more than 10 per cent of the tools measure in that size range. While the comparison is not exact, it does indicate an area of difference. The most important difference seems to rest in the types of cores used and the resulting amount of faceting found on flakes. In the early Sebilian the "Mousterian" discoidal core predominates, and the Faceting

Indices range from 61.4 to 78.4. At Cauma, the typical Lower Tshitolian cores are "biconical" which seem to be atypical forms of bifacial "Mousterian" discoids. In addition, there are a number of single platform and opposed platform cores. Prepared cores include some typical Levallois flake cores and many "high-backed" discoids, which from the illustrations appear to be atypical Levallois cores or "Mousterian" discoidal cores. In any case, the variety of types seen at Cauma is much greater than that in the Sebilian. In the case of faceting, which is to a large extent a function of the types of cores employed, the Lower Tshitolian has a Faceting Index of only 12.1. This is about one-sixth of the typical Faceting Index in the Sebilian.

Thus there are some major technological differences, while there are also a number of striking similarities.

Typologically, the Lower Tshitolian at Cauma produced 392 tools, including biface tools and such artifacts as anvils and grindstones. Retouched flake tools, however, number only 285. There are a limited number of types: scrapers, denticulates, notches, a few microliths, backed flakes, and *petits tranchets*. The *petit tranchet* is the dominant type, accounting for a large majority of all retouched tools. It is this tool type which must concern us most in any comparison with the Sebilian of Nubia.

Petits tranchets are described in the following manner: "long or short flakes . . . were snapped across the short axis probably by tapping on a conical anvil so as to remove the tip and butt ends. Selecting usually the centre section one or both snapped edges were steeply retouched thus giving the tool a rectangular, trapeze or triangular shape depending on the angle between the snapped edges. It seems probable that sometimes one edge was retouched before the butt or tip end was removed." (Clark, 1963, p. 159). This is an exact description of the probable process of making basal or obliquely truncated flakes, or simple oblique or basal truncations, all of which are typical in the Sebilian industry. Reference to the illustrated examples from Cauma (Clark, 1963, pp. 276-282) shows a long series of basally truncated flakes called *petits tranchets* with single edge retouch (Clark, 1963, pp. 276-277), which have been shown with the truncated edge toward the top of the page rather than toward the bottom as in this report. The *"petits tranchets with double edge retouch"* are typologically indistinguishable from the basal and obliquely truncated flakes of the Sebilian. Again, however, they have been oriented differently for illustration. As they were assumed to have been used as transverse points in many cases, the pieces have been oriented perpendicular to the original long axis of the flakes, rather than with the original butt end toward the bottom of the page. This tends to make them look quite different from those illustrated here, but they are morphologically exactly the same and seem to have been made in exactly the same way.

In addition, there is a small series of backed flakes and blades which are fully comparable to the simple backed flakes of the Sebilian.

These three types—*petits tranchets* with single edge retouch, *petits tranchets* with double edge retouch, and the backed flakes and blades—are morphologically the same as the vast majority of Sebilian tools. There are also a few other artifacts (Clark, 1963, pl. 29, nos. 6-8), which are no more than slight variations on the same theme and are also of Sebilian type.

The *petit tranchet* or the basal and obliquely truncated flake is a very special tool type. It is not a true *tranchet* in that the assumed working edge is not formed by a transverse blow, but is merely an unmodified section of one lateral edge. It is most comparable to the transverse arrow which, however, occurs normally only in Late Stone Age context. Also, the simple basal truncation is a rather special tool type. It does occur rarely in many industries but never assumes the importance seen in the Tshitolian and the Sebilian. In fact, in both industries these forms are the dominant tool types. Not only are they dominant in both, but their relative percentages are strikingly similar.

In the Lower Tshitolian at Cauma, those types which are morphologically the same as Sebilian tools account for 83.4 per cent of all retouched flake tools. In the Sudanese Sebilian these same types account for between 85.9 and 97.6 per cent of all retouched flake tools. Therefore, not only are the morphological features strikingly similar, but so are their proportional occurrences.

It must be admitted, of course, that the Tshito-

lian has other flake tools which are not comparable to Sebilian tools, although these are not common. Particularly, there is a small series of well made lunates at Cauma, while lunates are not found in the early Sudanese Sebilian. In addition, the Lower Tshitolian has some grindstone and anvils, both of which are missing in the Sudanese Sebilian, but are found in Sebilian I at Kom Ombo. It must be emphasized, however, that the Lower Tshitolian has a significant percentage of bifacial core tools, a feature totally lacking in the Sebilian. The Sebilian, on the other hand, contains microburins which are absent in the Lower Tshitolian. Considering their limited occurrence in the early Sebilian, it might be assumed that the microburin technique was a technological innovation new to the Sebilian, still only subsidiary to simple snapping.

While there is no question concerning the striking typological similarities between the Lower Tshitolian and the Early Sebilian, the significance of these is still obscure. There are three obvious possibilities: that these typological similarities are the result of direct or stimulus diffusion; that they represent no more than convergence, or that they document some generic relationship. Unfortunately, there is no conclusive evidence to demonstrate any of these alternatives. Each has certain points in its favor, but, also, there is evidence, or lack of it, which casts doubt on each.

The position that these typological similarities are due to diffusion seems to be untenable for a number of reasons. First, there is the large distance between the known distribution of the Lower Tshitolian and the Sebilian. This in itself is not an overwhelming argument, although it will be used again, because very little is known archaeologically of the intervening area. More important, these similarities are not just a matter of the presence of one or two similar tool types in geographically distant industries. Neither in the Sebilian, nor in the Tshitolian are these forms merely grafted on to already existing tool kits. They form a primary part of each tool kit, particularly in the case of the Sebilian.

The possibility that these typological and technological similarities are due to convergence seems somewhat plausible but not strongly so. Again, we are faced by the great distance between the Lower Tshitolian and the Sebilian, a fact which might lend support to the idea of convergence. On the other hand, to demonstrate convergence it is necessary to show separate development of like types from earlier, unconnected stages. This cannot be done for the Sebilian. It appears fully developed on the Nile and as of yet, no demonstrable progenitor has been found in Egypt or the Northern Sudan. While the occurrence of the Sebilian indicates a purely Nilotic distribution, technological and typological considerations indicate that it is foreign to the general pattern of Nilotic cultural development. It is merely the presence of a moderate Levallois technology which links it to the other, earlier Nilotic industries. As has been noted before, however, this alone proves nothing. The Levallois technique is also present in North Africa, East Africa, South Africa, and even in West Africa during this period.

The development of the Tshitolian is better documented. The core tools show an evolution from the Lupemban and the Lupembo-Tshitolian. This seems to indicate that the development of this tool form is native to the forest fringe of West Africa, and is fully within the Sangoan/Lupemban tradition. There is, however, a problem posed by the marked increase of the *petit tranchet* from the Lupembo/Tshitolian (2.9 per cent) to the Lower Tshitolian (56 per cent) (Clark, 1963, pp. 139, 159). It is assumed, however, that transitional sites exist.

Thus, it is possible to trace the development of the *petit tranchet* in Angola, but the morphologically identical tools in the Sebilian have as yet no clear line of development from an earlier Nilotic industry. Therefore, while convergence cannot be ruled out, it cannot be demonstrated. As the central Nile is relatively well known archaeologically, it seems unlikely that a Sebilian progenitor will be found there in the future. This tends to suggest that the position which favors a foreign origin for the Sebilian is correct.

The evidence favoring a generic connection between the Lower Tshitolian and the Sebilian is mostly circumstantial but is somewhat more convincing than the positive evidence for any other explanation of the typological similarities. One might first look at the negative evidence.

One main problem lies in the absolute dating

of the Lower Tshitolian and the Early Sebilian. They are more or less contemporary. The Lower Tshitolian has been radiocarbon dated to 12,970 B.P. $\pm$ 250 years (UCLA-172) at Calunda, Angola, and to 11,189 B.P. $\pm$ 490 years (C-580) at Mufo, Angola (Clark, 1963, p. 18 insert). This indicates a general date of 11,000 B.P. to 9,000 B.P. for the Lower Tshitolian. The earliest Sebilian, on the other hand, has not been dated directly by radiocarbon, but a site which may be the very end of the early Sebilian has been dated to 9,050 B.C. $\pm$ 120 years. Other Sudanese Sebilian sites are stratigraphically associated with the Sahaba formation and must date at the latest to between 13,000 B.C. and 10,000 B.C. Therefore, the early Sebilian and the Lower Tshitolian overlap in time, with the Sebilian at this point seeming to be somewhat older. On this basis, if there were generic connections between the two, it would be necessary either to posit a movement southwestward from the Nile, or a third area from which the highly specialized tools moved to both the Nile and West Africa. At the moment neither alternative seems to be very likely.

Another argument against generic connections is the total absence of bifacial core tools from even the earliest known Sebilian sites. While such tools account for only about 20 per cent of the tool inventory at Cauma (Clark, 1963, p. 159), they form a significant element of the industry as they are a direct link with the Lupembo/Tshitolian and the even earlier Upper Lupemban. If there were close generic connections between the Lower Tshitolian and the Sebilian it might be expected that the earliest Sebilian sites should contain a bifacial core tool element.

The question of distance between the industries again becomes relevant. Generic connections imply either geographical continuity or a major movement of people. The large area between the northern forest fringe and the Second Cataract on the Nile is unknown and so presents no positive evidence for cultural continuity or migration routes.

While the arguments against generic connections are strong, none is conclusive, nor when combined are they overwhelming. The most serious of the negative argument is that of absolute dating. It is important to note, however, that if generic connections exist between the Lower

Tshitolian and the early Sebilian, it does not necessarily mean that the Lower Tshitolian of Angola need be directly ancestral to the Sebilian nor the Sebilian to the Lower Tshitolian of Angola. Angola represents the southernmost area of the Lupemban/Tshitolian tradition. Because of the fine work of J. D. Clark, it seems as if Angola were the center of this tradition. This, however, is not necessarily the case, as both Lupemban and Tshitolian sites are known from the northern forest fringe in Gabon and the Central African Republic. Given such a large area for a single lithic tradition, and the very small amount of archaeological work which has been carried out within it, there is as yet no way of knowing where or when the earliest transition from the Upper Lupemban to the Tshitolian took place. It is altogether possible that the Lower Tshitolian of the Angola is relatively late as compared with that which is so far poorly known to the north of the Congo Basin. It seems that there is some evidence to this effect.

The extreme increase in the percentage of *petits tranchets* from the Angolan Lupembo/Tshitolian to the Angolan Lower Tshitolian, 2.9 per cent to 56 per cent, accompanied by an almost total loss of unifacial and bifacial lanceolate and tanged points in the Lower Tshitolian seems to indicate that a number of major typological changes took place outside of Angola between the Lupembo/Tshitolian and the Lower Tshitolian of Angola or that these transitional sites are as yet undiscovered. Therefore, it is possible that these changes took place north of the Congo Basin and spread southward, taking effect in Angola perhaps a few thousand years later than their inception to the north.

If this were the case, and it is admittedly hypothetical, then it is conceivable that dominance of the *petit tranchet* reached Angola about the same time peoples of the northern forest fringe reached the Nile.

It might be added that movements of Sangoan/Lupemban peoples from the West African forest fringe eastward to the Nile seem to be reasonably documented for the Sangoan/Lupemban or Lupemban stages at Kor Abu Anga (Arkell, 1949b) and near the Second Cataract in the Northern Sudan (Chmielewski, 1965, p. 158). If there is one documented movement eastward to

the Nile from West Africa, it is all the more conceivable that another, later movement might have taken place. This hypothesis does not negate the contemporaneity of the Nilotic Sebilian and the Lower Tshitolian of Angola but merely suggests that there are alternative explanations for it which do not rule out generic connections.

One argument against generic connections is the absence in the Sebilian of bifacial core tools which are so typical of the Sangoan/Lupemban/Tshitolian lithic tradition. There are two factors which bear on this problem. Even in Angola, there is a progressive decline in the importance of the bifacial tool element and by the Lower Tshitolian they account for only 23.3 per cent of the tool inventory, as opposed to 66.5 per cent during the Lupembo/Tshitolian (Clark, 1963, pp. 139, 159). This sharp decline took place within the forest fringe where it is assumed that the bifacial core tools were of optimum value for heavy woodworking. This last assumption bears directly on the second factor: the function of the bifacial core tools. If the assumption that they were meant for woodworking is correct (Clark, 1964, p. 173), then one would not expect to find them along the Nile. Even under the best of conditions, the area between the West African forest fringe and the Nile would never have been heavily forested. Perhaps the highland areas of the Bongo massif and Dafur would be forested, but there is a broad band from Kordofan in the south to the Western Desert on the north which would never have supported any more than a savanna vegetation. The fauna of such a savanna and the limited amount of surface water must have necessitated a more nomadic way of life than was necessary in the forest fringe itself. This would have discouraged heavy woodworking and reinforced the development of a light hunting kit which is the general trend seen even within the forest fringe. Thus, by the time the Nile was reached, the use of such bifacial core tools might already have been discarded in favor of a tool kit adapted to the hunting of fast-moving herbavors.

Again, it must be admitted that the evidence presented here is mostly hypothetical. On the other hand, the very little material evidence does support such a hypothesis.

The final argument against generic connections

between the Sangoan/Lupemban/Tshitolian tradition and the Sebilian is the absence of Lupembo/Tshitolian or Tshitolian and Sebilian sites between the Nile at the Second Cataract and the northern fringe in the Central African Republic—a distance of about 1,500 miles. This is a potent argument until it is realized that very little archaeological work has been carried out in this area. Virtually nothing is known of the prehistory of Bongo massif and Dafur, a likely migration route northeast for a forest oriented peoples. Again, nothing is known of the pre-history of Kordofan and the Western Desert, from south of Khartoum to north of Wadi Halfa, the area through which any peoples from the forest fringe of West Africa must have crossed to reach the Nile.

It is only within these areas that the problem of the typological similarities between the Lower Tshitolian and the Sebilian will ever be solved. Whether these similarities are due to generic connections, diffusion, or convergence, only material evidence from the interlaying areas is likely to provide a convincing answer.